Lecture Notes in Computer Science 2219

Edited by G. Goos, J. Hartmanis, and J. van Leeuwen

Springer-Verlag Berlin Heidelberg GmbH

S. Tucker Taft Robert A. Duff
Randall L. Brukardt Erhard Ploedereder (Eds.)

Consolidated
Ada Reference Manual

Language and Standard Libraries

International Standard ISO/IEC 8652/1995(E)
with Technical Corrigendum 1

 Springer

Volume Editors

S. Tucker Taft, Robert A. Duff
AverCom Corporation, 23 Fourth Avenue, Burlington, MA 01803-3303, USA
E-mail: stt/bob.duff@avercom.net

Randall L. Brukardt
AXE Consultants, 2318 Winnebago Street, Madison, WI 53704, USA
E-mail: randy@rrsoftware.com

Erhard Ploedereder
University of Stuttgart, Institute for Computer Science
Breitwiesenstr. 20-22, 70565 Stuttgart, Germany
E-mail: ploedere@informatik.uni-stuttgart.de

Cataloging-in-Publication Data applied for

Die Deutsche Bibliothek - CIP-Einheitsaufnahme
Consolidated Ada 95 reference manual : language and standard libraries ;
International standard ISO/IEC 8652:1995(E) with technical corrigendum 1 /
S. Tucker Taft ... (ed.).

(Lecture notes in computer science ; Vol. 2219)
ISBN   978-3-540-43038-4

CR Subject Classification (1998):D.1-3

ISSN 0302-9743
ISBN 978-3-540-43038-4   ISBN 978-3-540-45340-6 (eBook)
DOI 10.1007/978-3-540-45340-6
Ada Reference Manual - Language and Standard Libraries

Typesetting: Camera-ready by editors
Printed on acid-free paper   SPIN 10840907   06/3142   5 4 3 2 1 0

Ada Reference Manual

ISO/IEC 8652:1995(E)

with Technical Corrigendum 1

Language and Standard Libraries

Ada Reference Manual

ISO/IEC 8652:1995(E)

with Technical Corrigendum 1

Language and Standard Libraries

Table of Contents

Foreword to this version of the Ada Reference Manual

The International Standard for the programming language Ada is ISO/IEC 8652:1995(E). 0.1/1

The Ada Working Group ISO/IEC JTC1/SC 22/WG 9 is tasked by ISO with the work item to interpret and 0.2/1
maintain the International Standard and to produce Technical Corrigenda, as appropriate. The technical
work on the International Standard is performed by the Ada Rapporteur Group (ARG) of WG 9. In
September 2000, WG 9 approved and forwarded Technical Corrigendum 1 to SC 22 for ISO approval,
which was granted in February 2001.

The Technical Corrigendum lists the individual changes that need to be made to the text of the 0.3/1
International Standard to correct errors, omissions or inconsistencies. Once approved, the corrections
specified in Technical Corrigendum 1 will be part of the International Standard ISO/IEC 8652:1995(E).

When ISO publishes Technical Corrigendum 1, it is unlikely that ISO will also publish a document that 0.4/1
merges the Technical Corrigendum changes into the text of the International Standard. However, ISO rules
require that the project editor for the Technical Corrigendum be able to produce such a document on
demand.

This version of the Ada Reference Manual is what the project editor would provide to ISO in response to 0.5/1
such a request. It incorporates the changes specified in the Technical Corrigendum into the text of ISO/IEC
8652:1995(E). It should be understood that the publication of any ISO document involves changes in
general format, boilerplate, headers, etc., as well as a review by professional editors that may introduce
editorial changes to the text. This version of the Ada Reference Manual is therefore neither an official ISO
document, nor a version guaranteed to be identical to an official ISO document, should ISO decide to
reprint the International Standard incorporating an approved Technical Corrigendum. It is nevertheless a
best effort to be as close as possible to the technical content of such an updated document. In the case of a
conflict between this document and a Technical Corrigendum 1 approved by ISO (or between this
document and the original 8652:1995 in the case of paragraphs not changed by Technical Corrigendum 1),
the other documents contain the official text of the International Standard ISO/IEC 8652:1995(E).

As it is very inconvenient to have the Reference Manual for Ada specified in two documents, this 0.6/1
consolidated version of the Ada Reference Manual is made available to the public.

Using this version of the Ada Reference Manual

This document has been revised with the corrections specified in Technical Corrigendum 1 (ISO/IEC 0.7/1
8652:1995/COR1:2000). In addition, a variety of editorial errors have been corrected.

Changes to the original 8652:1995 can be identified by the version number /1 following the paragraph 0.8/1
number. Paragraphs not so marked are unchanged by Technical Corrigendum 1 or editorial corrections.
Paragraph numbers of unchanged paragraphs are the same as in the original Ada Reference Manual. In
addition, some versions of this document include revision bars near the paragraph numbers. Where
paragraphs are inserted, the paragraph numbers are of the form pp.nn, where pp is the number of the
preceding paragraph, and nn is an insertion number. For instance, the first paragraph inserted after
paragraph 8 is numbered 8.1, the second paragraph inserted is numbered 8.2, and so on. Deleted
paragraphs are indicated by the text *This paragraph was deleted*. Deleted paragraphs include empty
paragraphs that were numbered in the original Ada Reference Manual.

Acknowledgements for this version of the Ada Reference Manual

0.9/1 The editor [R. Brukardt (USA)] would like to thank the many people whose hard work and assistance has made this revision possible.

0.10/1 Thanks go out to all of the members of the ISO/IEC JTC 1/SC 22/WG 9 Ada Rapporteur Group, whose work on creating and editing the wording corrections was critical to the entire process. Especially valuable contributions came from the chairman of the ARG, E. Ploedereder (Germany), who kept the process moving; J. Barnes (UK) and K. Ishihata (Japan), whose extremely detailed reviews kept the editor on his toes; G. Dismukes (USA), M. Kamrad (USA), P. Leroy (France), S. Michell (Canada), T. Taft (USA), J. Tokar (USA), and other members too numerous to mention.

0.11/1 Special thanks go to R. Duff (USA) for his explanations of the previous system of formatting of these documents during the tedious conversion to more modern formats. Special thanks also go to the convener of ISO/IEC JTC 1/SC 22/WG 9, J. Moore (USA), without whose help and support the corrigendum and this consolidated reference manual would not have been possible.

Foreword

ISO (the International Organization for Standardization) and IEC (the International Electrotechnical Commission) form the specialized system for worldwide standardization. National bodies that are members of ISO or IEC participate in the development of International Standards through technical committees established by the respective organization to deal with particular fields of technical activity. ISO and IEC technical committees collaborate in fields of mutual interest. Other international organizations, governmental and non-governmental, in liaison with ISO and IEC, also take part in the work. 1

In the field of information technology, ISO and IEC have established a joint technical committee, ISO/IEC JTC 1. Draft International Standards adopted by the joint technical committee are circulated to national bodies for voting. Publication as an International Standard requires approval by at least 75 % of the national bodies casting a vote. 2

International Standard ISO/IEC 8652 was prepared by Joint Technical Committee ISO/IEC JTC 1, *Information Technology*. 3

This second edition cancels and replaces the first edition (ISO 8652:1987), of which it constitutes a technical revision. 4

Annexes A to J form an integral part of this International Standard. Annexes K to P are for information only. 5

Introduction

1   This is the Ada Reference Manual.

2   Other available Ada documents include:

3   • Rationale for the Ada Programming Language — 1995 edition, which gives an introduction to the new features of Ada, and explains the rationale behind them. Programmers should read this first.

4/1   • *This paragraph was deleted.*

5   • The Annotated Ada Reference Manual (AARM). The AARM contains all of the text in the RM95, plus various annotations. It is intended primarily for compiler writers, validation test writers, and others who wish to study the fine details. The annotations include detailed rationale for individual rules and explanations of some of the more arcane interactions among the rules.

Design Goals

6   Ada was originally designed with three overriding concerns: program reliability and maintenance, programming as a human activity, and efficiency. This revision to the language was designed to provide greater flexibility and extensibility, additional control over storage management and synchronization, and standardized packages oriented toward supporting important application areas, while at the same time retaining the original emphasis on reliability, maintainability, and efficiency.

7   The need for languages that promote reliability and simplify maintenance is well established. Hence emphasis was placed on program readability over ease of writing. For example, the rules of the language require that program variables be explicitly declared and that their type be specified. Since the type of a variable is invariant, compilers can ensure that operations on variables are compatible with the properties intended for objects of the type. Furthermore, error-prone notations have been avoided, and the syntax of the language avoids the use of encoded forms in favor of more English-like constructs. Finally, the language offers support for separate compilation of program units in a way that facilitates program development and maintenance, and which provides the same degree of checking between units as within a unit.

8   Concern for the human programmer was also stressed during the design. Above all, an attempt was made to keep to a relatively small number of underlying concepts integrated in a consistent and systematic way while continuing to avoid the pitfalls of excessive involution. The design especially aims to provide language constructs that correspond intuitively to the normal expectations of users.

9   Like many other human activities, the development of programs is becoming ever more decentralized and distributed. Consequently, the ability to assemble a program from independently produced software components continues to be a central idea in the design. The concepts of packages, of private types, and of generic units are directly related to this idea, which has ramifications in many other aspects of the language. An allied concern is the maintenance of programs to match changing requirements; type extension and the hierarchical library enable a program to be modified while minimizing disturbance to existing tested and trusted components.

10   No language can avoid the problem of efficiency. Languages that require over-elaborate compilers, or that lead to the inefficient use of storage or execution time, force these inefficiencies on all machines and on all programs. Every construct of the language was examined in the light of present implementation techniques. Any proposed construct whose implementation was unclear or that required excessive machine resources was rejected.

Language Summary

An Ada program is composed of one or more program units. Program units may be subprograms (which   11
define executable algorithms), packages (which define collections of entities), task units (which define
concurrent computations), protected units (which define operations for the coordinated sharing of data
between tasks), or generic units (which define parameterized forms of packages and subprograms). Each
program unit normally consists of two parts: a specification, containing the information that must be
visible to other units, and a body, containing the implementation details, which need not be visible to other
units. Most program units can be compiled separately.

This distinction of the specification and body, and the ability to compile units separately, allows a program   12
to be designed, written, and tested as a set of largely independent software components.

An Ada program will normally make use of a library of program units of general utility. The language   13
provides means whereby individual organizations can construct their own libraries. All libraries are
structured in a hierarchical manner; this enables the logical decomposition of a subsystem into individual
components. The text of a separately compiled program unit must name the library units it requires.

Program Units   14

A subprogram is the basic unit for expressing an algorithm. There are two kinds of subprograms: 15
procedures and functions. A procedure is the means of invoking a series of actions. For example, it may
read data, update variables, or produce some output. It may have parameters, to provide a controlled means
of passing information between the procedure and the point of call. A function is the means of invoking
the computation of a value. It is similar to a procedure, but in addition will return a result.

A package is the basic unit for defining a collection of logically related entities. For example, a package   16
can be used to define a set of type declarations and associated operations. Portions of a package can be
hidden from the user, thus allowing access only to the logical properties expressed by the package
specification.

Subprogram and package units may be compiled separately and arranged in hierarchies of parent and child   17
units giving fine control over visibility of the logical properties and their detailed implementation.

A task unit is the basic unit for defining a task whose sequence of actions may be executed concurrently   18
with those of other tasks. Such tasks may be implemented on multicomputers, multiprocessors, or with
interleaved execution on a single processor. A task unit may define either a single executing task or a task
type permitting the creation of any number of similar tasks.

A protected unit is the basic unit for defining protected operations for the coordinated use of data shared   19
between tasks. Simple mutual exclusion is provided automatically, and more elaborate sharing protocols
can be defined. A protected operation can either be a subprogram or an entry. A protected entry specifies a
Boolean expression (an entry barrier) that must be true before the body of the entry is executed. A
protected unit may define a single protected object or a protected type permitting the creation of several
similar objects.

Declarations and Statements   20

The body of a program unit generally contains two parts: a declarative part, which defines the logical   21
entities to be used in the program unit, and a sequence of statements, which defines the execution of the
program unit.

22   The declarative part associates names with declared entities. For example, a name may denote a type, a constant, a variable, or an exception. A declarative part also introduces the names and parameters of other nested subprograms, packages, task units, protected units, and generic units to be used in the program unit.

23   The sequence of statements describes a sequence of actions that are to be performed. The statements are executed in succession (unless a transfer of control causes execution to continue from another place).

24   An assignment statement changes the value of a variable. A procedure call invokes execution of a procedure after associating any actual parameters provided at the call with the corresponding formal parameters.

25   Case statements and if statements allow the selection of an enclosed sequence of statements based on the value of an expression or on the value of a condition.

26   The loop statement provides the basic iterative mechanism in the language. A loop statement specifies that a sequence of statements is to be executed repeatedly as directed by an iteration scheme, or until an exit statement is encountered.

27   A block statement comprises a sequence of statements preceded by the declaration of local entities used by the statements.

28   Certain statements are associated with concurrent execution. A delay statement delays the execution of a task for a specified duration or until a specified time. An entry call statement is written as a procedure call statement; it requests an operation on a task or on a protected object, blocking the caller until the operation can be performed. A called task may accept an entry call by executing a corresponding accept statement, which specifies the actions then to be performed as part of the rendezvous with the calling task. An entry call on a protected object is processed when the corresponding entry barrier evaluates to true, whereupon the body of the entry is executed. The requeue statement permits the provision of a service as a number of related activities with preference control. One form of the select statement allows a selective wait for one of several alternative rendezvous. Other forms of the select statement allow conditional or timed entry calls and the asynchronous transfer of control in response to some triggering event.

29   Execution of a program unit may encounter error situations in which normal program execution cannot continue. For example, an arithmetic computation may exceed the maximum allowed value of a number, or an attempt may be made to access an array component by using an incorrect index value. To deal with such error situations, the statements of a program unit can be textually followed by exception handlers that specify the actions to be taken when the error situation arises. Exceptions can be raised explicitly by a raise statement.

30   *Data Types*

31   Every object in the language has a type, which characterizes a set of values and a set of applicable operations. The main classes of types are elementary types (comprising enumeration, numeric, and access types) and composite types (including array and record types).

32   An enumeration type defines an ordered set of distinct enumeration literals, for example a list of states or an alphabet of characters. The enumeration types Boolean, Character, and Wide_Character are predefined.

33   Numeric types provide a means of performing exact or approximate numerical computations. Exact computations use integer types, which denote sets of consecutive integers. Approximate computations use either fixed point types, with absolute bounds on the error, or floating point types, with relative bounds on the error. The numeric types Integer, Float, and Duration are predefined.

Composite types allow definitions of structured objects with related components. The composite types in the language include arrays and records. An array is an object with indexed components of the same type. A record is an object with named components of possibly different types. Task and protected types are also forms of composite types. The array types String and Wide_String are predefined. 34

Record, task, and protected types may have special components called discriminants which parameterize the type. Variant record structures that depend on the values of discriminants can be defined within a record type. 35

Access types allow the construction of linked data structures. A value of an access type represents a reference to an object declared as aliased or to an object created by the evaluation of an allocator. Several variables of an access type may designate the same object, and components of one object may designate the same or other objects. Both the elements in such linked data structures and their relation to other elements can be altered during program execution. Access types also permit references to subprograms to be stored, passed as parameters, and ultimately dereferenced as part of an indirect call. 36

Private types permit restricted views of a type. A private type can be defined in a package so that only the logically necessary properties are made visible to the users of the type. The full structural details that are externally irrelevant are then only available within the package and any child units. 37

From any type a new type may be defined by derivation. A type, together with its derivatives (both direct and indirect) form a derivation class. Class-wide operations may be defined that accept as a parameter an operand of any type in a derivation class. For record and private types, the derivatives may be extensions of the parent type. Types that support these object-oriented capabilities of class-wide operations and type extension must be tagged, so that the specific type of an operand within a derivation class can be identified at run time. When an operation of a tagged type is applied to an operand whose specific type is not known until run time, implicit dispatching is performed based on the tag of the operand. 38

The concept of a type is further refined by the concept of a subtype, whereby a user can constrain the set of allowed values of a type. Subtypes can be used to define subranges of scalar types, arrays with a limited set of index values, and records and private types with particular discriminant values. 39

Other Facilities 40

Representation clauses can be used to specify the mapping between types and features of an underlying machine. For example, the user can specify that objects of a given type must be represented with a given number of bits, or that the components of a record are to be represented using a given storage layout. Other features allow the controlled use of low level, nonportable, or implementation-dependent aspects, including the direct insertion of machine code. 41

The predefined environment of the language provides for input-output and other capabilities (such as string manipulation and random number generation) by means of standard library packages. Input-output is supported for values of user-defined as well as of predefined types. Standard means of representing values in display form are also provided. Other standard library packages are defined in annexes of the standard to support systems with specialized requirements. 42

Finally, the language provides a powerful means of parameterization of program units, called generic program units. The generic parameters can be types and subprograms (as well as objects and packages) and so allow general algorithms and data structures to be defined that are applicable to all types of a given class. 43

Language Changes

44   This International Standard replaces the first edition of 1987. In this edition, the following major language changes have been incorporated:

45   • Support for standard 8-bit and 16-bit character sets. See Section 2, 3.5.2, 3.6.3, A.1, A.3, and A.4.

46   • Object-oriented programming with run-time polymorphism. See the discussions of classes, derived types, tagged types, record extensions, and private extensions in clauses 3.4, 3.9, and 7.3. See also the new forms of generic formal parameters that are allowed by 12.5.1, ''Formal Private and Derived Types'' and 12.7, ''Formal Packages''.

47   • Access types have been extended to allow an access value to designate a subprogram or an object declared by an object declaration (as opposed to just a heap-allocated object). See 3.10.

48   • Efficient data-oriented synchronization is provided via protected types. See Section 9.

49   • The library units of a library may be organized into a hierarchy of parent and child units. See Section 10.

50   • Additional support has been added for interfacing to other languages. See Annex B.

51   • The Specialized Needs Annexes have been added to provide specific support for certain application areas:

52   • Annex C, ''Systems Programming''

53   • Annex D, ''Real-Time Systems''

54   • Annex E, ''Distributed Systems''

55   • Annex F, ''Information Systems''

56   • Annex G, ''Numerics''

57   • Annex H, ''Safety and Security''

Instructions for Comment Submission

Informal comments on this International Standard may be sent via e-mail to **ada-comment@ada-auth.org**. If appropriate, the Project Editor will initiate the defect correction procedure. 58/1

Comments should use the following format: 59

> **!topic** *Title summarizing comment* 60
> **!reference** RM95-*ss.ss(pp)*
> **!from** *Author Name yy-mm-dd*
> **!keywords** *keywords related to topic*
> **!discussion**
>
> *text of discussion*

where *ss.ss* is the section, clause or subclause number, *pp* is the paragraph number where applicable, and *yy-mm-dd* is the date the comment was sent. The date is optional, as is the **!keywords** line. 61

Please use a descriptive "Subject" in your e-mail message, and limit each message to a single comment. 62/1

When correcting typographical errors or making minor wording suggestions, please put the correction directly as the topic of the comment; use square brackets [ ] to indicate text to be omitted and curly braces { } to indicate text to be added, and provide enough context to make the nature of the suggestion self-evident or put additional information in the body of the comment, for example: 63

> **!topic** [c]{C}haracter 64
> **!topic** it['] s meaning is not defined

Formal requests for interpretations and for reporting defects in this International Standard may be made in accordance with the ISO/IEC JTC1 Directives and the ISO/IEC JTC1/SC22 policy for interpretations. National Bodies may submit a Defect Report to ISO/IEC JTC1/SC22 for resolution under the JTC1 procedures. A response will be provided and, if appropriate, a Technical Corrigendum will be issued in accordance with the procedures. 65

Acknowledgements

66   This International Standard was prepared by the Ada 9X Mapping/Revision Team based at Intermetrics, Inc., which has included: W. Carlson, Program Manager; T. Taft, Technical Director; J. Barnes (consultant); B. Brosgol (consultant); R. Duff (Oak Tree Software); M. Edwards; C. Garrity; R. Hilliard; O. Pazy (consultant); D. Rosenfeld; L. Shafer; W. White; M. Woodger.

67   The following consultants to the Ada 9X Project contributed to the Specialized Needs Annexes: T. Baker (Real-Time/Systems Programming — SEI, FSU); K. Dritz (Numerics — Argonne National Laboratory); A. Gargaro (Distributed Systems — Computer Sciences); J. Goodenough (Real-Time/Systems Programming — SEI); J. McHugh (Secure Systems — consultant); B. Wichmann (Safety-Critical Systems — NPL: UK).

68   This work was regularly reviewed by the Ada 9X Distinguished Reviewers and the members of the Ada 9X Rapporteur Group (XRG): E. Ploedereder, Chairman of DRs and XRG (University of Stuttgart: Germany); B. Bardin (Hughes); J. Barnes (consultant: UK); B. Brett (DEC); B. Brosgol (consultant); R. Brukardt (RR Software); N. Cohen (IBM); R. Dewar (NYU); G. Dismukes (TeleSoft); A. Evans (consultant); A. Gargaro (Computer Sciences); M. Gerhardt (ESL); J. Goodenough (SEI); S. Heilbrunner (University of Salzburg: Austria); P. Hilfinger (UC/Berkeley); B. Källberg (CelsiusTech: Sweden); M. Kamrad II (Unisys); J. van Katwijk (Delft University of Technology: The Netherlands); V. Kaufman (Russia); P. Kruchten (Rational); R. Landwehr (CCI: Germany); C. Lester (Portsmouth Polytechnic: UK); L. Månsson (TELIA Research: Sweden); S. Michell (Multiprocessor Toolsmiths: Canada); M. Mills (US Air Force); D. Pogge (US Navy); K. Power (Boeing); O. Roubine (Verdix: France); A. Strohmeier (Swiss Fed Inst of Technology: Switzerland); W. Taylor (consultant: UK); J. Tokar (Tartan); E. Vasilescu (Grumman); J. Vladik (Prospeks s.r.o.: Czech Republic); S. Van Vlierberghe (OFFIS: Belgium).

69   Other valuable feedback influencing the revision process was provided by the Ada 9X Language Precision Team (Odyssey Research Associates), the Ada 9X User/Implementer Teams (AETECH, Tartan, TeleSoft), the Ada 9X Implementation Analysis Team (New York University) and the Ada community-at-large.

70   Special thanks go to R. Mathis, Convenor of ISO/IEC JTC1/SC22 Working Group 9.

71   The Ada 9X Project was sponsored by the Ada Joint Program Office. Christine M. Anderson at the Air Force Phillips Laboratory (Kirtland AFB, NM) was the project manager.

Changes

The International Standard is the same as this version of the Reference Manual, except: 72

- This list of Changes is not included in the International Standard. 73

- The ''Acknowledgements'' page is not included in the International Standard. 74

- The text in the running headers and footers on each page is slightly different in the International Standard. 75

- The title page(s) are different in the International Standard. 76

- This document is formatted for 8.5-by-11-inch paper, whereas the International Standard is formatted for A4 paper (210-by-297mm); thus, the page breaks are in different places. 77

- The ''Foreword to this version of the Ada Reference Manual'' clause is not included in the International Standard. 77.1/1

INTERNATIONAL STANDARD   ISO/IEC 8652:1995(E) with COR.1:2000

Information technology — Programming Languages — Ada

Section 1: General

Ada is a programming language designed to support the construction of long-lived, highly reliable software systems. The language includes facilities to define packages of related types, objects, and operations. The packages may be parameterized and the types may be extended to support the construction of libraries of reusable, adaptable software components. The operations may be implemented as subprograms using conventional sequential control structures, or as entries that include synchronization of concurrent threads of control as part of their invocation. The language treats modularity in the physical sense as well, with a facility to support separate compilation.   1

The language includes a complete facility for the support of real-time, concurrent programming. Errors can be signaled as exceptions and handled explicitly. The language also covers systems programming; this requires precise control over the representation of data and access to system-dependent properties. Finally, a predefined environment of standard packages is provided, including facilities for, among others, input-output, string manipulation, numeric elementary functions, and random number generation.   2

1.1 Scope

This International Standard specifies the form and meaning of programs written in Ada. Its purpose is to promote the portability of Ada programs to a variety of data processing systems.   1

1.1.1 Extent

This International Standard specifies: 1

- The form of a program written in Ada;   2
- The effect of translating and executing such a program;   3
- The manner in which program units may be combined to form Ada programs;   4
- The language-defined library units that a conforming implementation is required to supply;   5
- The permissible variations within the standard, and the manner in which they are to be documented;   6

S. Tucker Taft et al. (Eds.): Consolidated Ada Reference Manual, LNCS 2219, pp. 1–8, 2001.

7 • Those violations of the standard that a conforming implementation is required to detect, and the effect of attempting to translate or execute a program containing such violations;

8 • Those violations of the standard that a conforming implementation is not required to detect.

9 This International Standard does not specify:

10 • The means whereby a program written in Ada is transformed into object code executable by a processor;

11 • The means whereby translation or execution of programs is invoked and the executing units are controlled;

12 • The size or speed of the object code, or the relative execution speed of different language constructs;

13 • The form or contents of any listings produced by implementations; in particular, the form or contents of error or warning messages;

14 • The effect of unspecified execution.

15 • The size of a program or program unit that will exceed the capacity of a particular conforming implementation.

1.1.2 Structure

1 This International Standard contains thirteen sections, fourteen annexes, and an index.

2 The *core* of the Ada language consists of:

3 • Sections 1 through 13

4 • Annex A, ''Predefined Language Environment''

5 • Annex B, ''Interface to Other Languages''

6 • Annex J, ''Obsolescent Features''

7 The following *Specialized Needs Annexes* define features that are needed by certain application areas:

8 • Annex C, ''Systems Programming''

9 • Annex D, ''Real-Time Systems''

10 • Annex E, ''Distributed Systems''

11 • Annex F, ''Information Systems''

12 • Annex G, ''Numerics''

13 • Annex H, ''Safety and Security''

14 The core language and the Specialized Needs Annexes are normative, except that the material in each of the items listed below is informative:

15 • Text under a NOTES or Examples heading.

16 • Each clause or subclause whose title starts with the word ''Example'' or ''Examples''.

17 All implementations shall conform to the core language. In addition, an implementation may conform separately to one or more Specialized Needs Annexes.

The following Annexes are informative:

18

- Annex K, ''Language-Defined Attributes''

19

- Annex L, ''Language-Defined Pragmas''

20

- Annex M, ''Implementation-Defined Characteristics''

21

- Annex N, ''Glossary''

22

- Annex P, ''Syntax Summary''

23

Each section is divided into clauses and subclauses that have a common structure. Each section, clause, and subclause first introduces its subject. After the introductory text, text is labeled with the following headings:

24

Syntax

Syntax rules (indented).

25

Name Resolution Rules

Compile-time rules that are used in name resolution, including overload resolution.

26

Legality Rules

Rules that are enforced at compile time. A construct is *legal* if it obeys all of the Legality Rules.

27

Static Semantics

A definition of the compile-time effect of each construct.

28

Post-Compilation Rules

Rules that are enforced before running a partition. A partition is legal if its compilation units are legal and it obeys all of the Post-Compilation Rules.

29

Dynamic Semantics

A definition of the run-time effect of each construct.

30

Bounded (Run-Time) Errors

Situations that result in bounded (run-time) errors (see 1.1.5).

31

Erroneous Execution

Situations that result in erroneous execution (see 1.1.5).

32

Implementation Requirements

Additional requirements for conforming implementations.

33

Documentation Requirements

Documentation requirements for conforming implementations.

34

Metrics

Metrics that are specified for the time/space properties of the execution of certain language constructs.

35

Implementation Permissions

Additional permissions given to the implementer.

36

Implementation Advice

37   Optional advice given to the implementer. The word "should" is used to indicate that the advice is a recommendation, not a requirement. It is implementation defined whether or not a given recommendation is obeyed.

NOTES

38   1 Notes emphasize consequences of the rules described in the (sub)clause or elsewhere. This material is informative.

Examples

39   Examples illustrate the possible forms of the constructs described. This material is informative.

1.1.3 Conformity of an Implementation with the Standard

Implementation Requirements

1   A conforming implementation shall:

2   • Translate and correctly execute legal programs written in Ada, provided that they are not so large as to exceed the capacity of the implementation;

3   • Identify all programs or program units that are so large as to exceed the capacity of the implementation (or raise an appropriate exception at run time);

4   • Identify all programs or program units that contain errors whose detection is required by this International Standard;

5   • Supply all language-defined library units required by this International Standard;

6   • Contain no variations except those explicitly permitted by this International Standard, or those that are impossible or impractical to avoid given the implementation's execution environment;

7   • Specify all such variations in the manner prescribed by this International Standard.

8   The *external effect* of the execution of an Ada program is defined in terms of its interactions with its external environment. The following are defined as *external interactions*:

9   • Any interaction with an external file (see A.7);

10   • The execution of certain code_statements (see 13.8); which code_statements cause external interactions is implementation defined.

11   • Any call on an imported subprogram (see Annex B), including any parameters passed to it;

12   • Any result returned or exception propagated from a main subprogram (see 10.2) or an exported subprogram (see Annex B) to an external caller;

13   • Any read or update of an atomic or volatile object (see C.6);

14   • The values of imported and exported objects (see Annex B) at the time of any other interaction with the external environment.

15   A conforming implementation of this International Standard shall produce for the execution of a given Ada program a set of interactions with the external environment whose order and timing are consistent with the definitions and requirements of this International Standard for the semantics of the given program.

16   An implementation that conforms to this Standard shall support each capability required by the core language as specified. In addition, an implementation that conforms to this Standard may conform to one or more Specialized Needs Annexes (or to none). Conformance to a Specialized Needs Annex means that each capability required by the Annex is provided as specified.

An implementation conforming to this International Standard may provide additional attributes, library units, and pragmas. However, it shall not provide any attribute, library unit, or pragma having the same name as an attribute, library unit, or pragma (respectively) specified in a Specialized Needs Annex unless the provided construct is either as specified in the Specialized Needs Annex or is more limited in capability than that required by the Annex. A program that attempts to use an unsupported capability of an Annex shall either be identified by the implementation before run time or shall raise an exception at run time.   17

Documentation Requirements

Certain aspects of the semantics are defined to be either *implementation defined* or *unspecified*. In such cases, the set of possible effects is specified, and the implementation may choose any effect in the set. Implementations shall document their behavior in implementation-defined situations, but documentation is not required for unspecified situations. The implementation-defined characteristics are summarized in Annex M.   18

The implementation may choose to document implementation-defined behavior either by documenting what happens in general, or by providing some mechanism for the user to determine what happens in a particular case.   19

Implementation Advice

If an implementation detects the use of an unsupported Specialized Needs Annex feature at run time, it should raise Program_Error if feasible.   20

If an implementation wishes to provide implementation-defined extensions to the functionality of a language-defined library unit, it should normally do so by adding children to the library unit.   21

NOTES
2 The above requirements imply that an implementation conforming to this Standard may support some of the capabilities required by a Specialized Needs Annex without supporting all required capabilities.   22

1.1.4 Method of Description and Syntax Notation

The form of an Ada program is described by means of a context-free syntax together with context-dependent requirements expressed by narrative rules.   1

The meaning of Ada programs is described by means of narrative rules defining both the effects of each construct and the composition rules for constructs.   2

The context-free syntax of the language is described using a simple variant of Backus-Naur Form. In particular: 3

- Lower case words in a sans-serif font, some containing embedded underlines, are used to denote syntactic categories, for example: 4

      case_statement   5

- Boldface words are used to denote reserved words, for example: 6

      array   7

- Square brackets enclose optional items. Thus the two following rules are equivalent.   8

      return_statement ::= **return** [expression];   9
      return_statement ::= **return**; | **return** expression;

Conformity of an Implementation with the Standard   **1.1.3**

10 • Curly brackets enclose a repeated item. The item may appear zero or more times; the repetitions occur from left to right as with an equivalent left-recursive rule. Thus the two following rules are equivalent.

11
     term ::= factor {multiplying_operator factor}
     term ::= factor | term multiplying_operator factor

12 • A vertical line separates alternative items unless it occurs immediately after an opening curly bracket, in which case it stands for itself:

13
     constraint ::= scalar_constraint | composite_constraint
     discrete_choice_list ::= discrete_choice {| discrete_choice}

14 • If the name of any syntactic category starts with an italicized part, it is equivalent to the category name without the italicized part. The italicized part is intended to convey some semantic information. For example *subtype*_name and *task*_name are both equivalent to name alone.

15 A *syntactic category* is a nonterminal in the grammar defined in BNF under "Syntax." Names of syntactic categories are set in a different font, like_this.

16 A *construct* is a piece of text (explicit or implicit) that is an instance of a syntactic category defined under "Syntax."

17 A *constituent* of a construct is the construct itself, or any construct appearing within it.

18 Whenever the run-time semantics defines certain actions to happen in an *arbitrary order*, this means that the implementation shall arrange for these actions to occur in a way that is equivalent to some sequential order, following the rules that result from that sequential order. When evaluations are defined to happen in an arbitrary order, with conversion of the results to some subtypes, or with some run-time checks, the evaluations, conversions, and checks may be arbitrarily interspersed, so long as each expression is evaluated before converting or checking its value. Note that the effect of a program can depend on the order chosen by the implementation. This can happen, for example, if two actual parameters of a given call have side effects.

NOTES

19 3 The syntax rules describing structured constructs are presented in a form that corresponds to the recommended paragraphing. For example, an if_statement is defined as:

20
```
if_statement  : : =
    if condition then
        sequence_of_statements
    {elsif condition then
        sequence_of_statements}
    [else
        sequence_of_statements]
    end if;
```

21 4 The line breaks and indentation in the syntax rules indicate the recommended line breaks and indentation in the corresponding constructs. The preferred places for other line breaks are after semicolons.

1.1.5 Classification of Errors

Implementation Requirements

1 The language definition classifies errors into several different categories:

2 • Errors that are required to be detected prior to run time by every Ada implementation;

3 These errors correspond to any violation of a rule given in this International Standard, other than those listed below. In particular, violation of any rule that uses the terms shall, allowed,

permitted, legal, or illegal belongs to this category. Any program that contains such an error is not a legal Ada program; on the other hand, the fact that a program is legal does not mean, *per se*, that the program is free from other forms of error.

The rules are further classified as either compile time rules, or post compilation rules, depending on whether a violation has to be detected at the time a compilation unit is submitted to the compiler, or may be postponed until the time a compilation_unit is incorporated into a partition of a program. 4

- Errors that are required to be detected at run time by the execution of an Ada program; 5

  The corresponding error situations are associated with the names of the predefined exceptions. Every Ada compiler is required to generate code that raises the corresponding exception if such an error situation arises during program execution. If such an error situation is certain to arise in every execution of a construct, then an implementation is allowed (although not required) to report this fact at compilation time. 6

- Bounded errors; 7

  The language rules define certain kinds of errors that need not be detected either prior to or during run time, but if not detected, the range of possible effects shall be bounded. The errors of this category are called *bounded errors*. The possible effects of a given bounded error are specified for each such error, but in any case one possible effect of a bounded error is the raising of the exception Program_Error. 8

- Erroneous execution. 9

  In addition to bounded errors, the language rules define certain kinds of errors as leading to *erroneous execution*. Like bounded errors, the implementation need not detect such errors either prior to or during run time. Unlike bounded errors, there is no language-specified bound on the possible effect of erroneous execution; the effect is in general not predictable. 10

Implementation Permissions

An implementation may provide *nonstandard modes* of operation. Typically these modes would be selected by a pragma or by a command line switch when the compiler is invoked. When operating in a nonstandard mode, the implementation may reject compilation_units that do not conform to additional requirements associated with the mode, such as an excessive number of warnings or violation of coding style guidelines. Similarly, in a nonstandard mode, the implementation may apply special optimizations or alternative algorithms that are only meaningful for programs that satisfy certain criteria specified by the implementation. In any case, an implementation shall support a *standard* mode that conforms to the requirements of this International Standard; in particular, in the standard mode, all legal compilation_units shall be accepted. 11

Implementation Advice

If an implementation detects a bounded error or erroneous execution, it should raise Program_Error. 12

1.2 Normative References

The following standards contain provisions which, through reference in this text, constitute provisions of this International Standard. At the time of publication, the editions indicated were valid. All standards are subject to revision, and parties to agreements based on this International Standard are encouraged to investigate the possibility of applying the most recent editions of the standards indicated below. Members of IEC and ISO maintain registers of currently valid International Standards. 1

ISO/IEC 646:1991, *Information technology — ISO 7-bit coded character set for information interchange*. 2

3   ISO/IEC 1539:1991, *Information technology — Programming languages — FORTRAN*.

4   ISO 1989:1985, *Programming languages — COBOL*.

5   ISO/IEC 6429:1992, *Information technology — Control functions for coded graphic character sets*.

6   ISO/IEC 8859-1:1987, *Information processing — 8-bit single-byte coded character sets — Part 1: Latin alphabet No. 1*.

7   ISO/IEC 9899:1990, *Programming languages — C*.

8/1   ISO/IEC 10646-1:1993, *Information technology — Universal Multiple-Octet Coded Character Set (UCS) — Part 1: Architecture and Basic Multilingual Plane*, supplemented by Technical Corrigendum 1:1996.

1.3 Definitions

1   Terms are defined throughout this International Standard, indicated by *italic* type. Terms explicitly defined in this International Standard are not to be presumed to refer implicitly to similar terms defined elsewhere. Terms not defined in this International Standard are to be interpreted according to the *Webster's Third New International Dictionary of the English Language*. Informal descriptions of some terms are also given in Annex N, ''Glossary''.

Section 2: Lexical Elements

The text of a program consists of the texts of one or more compilations. The text of a compilation is a   1
sequence of lexical elements, each composed of characters; the rules of composition are given in this
section. Pragmas, which provide certain information for the compiler, are also described in this section.

2.1 Character Set

The only characters allowed outside of comments are the graphic_characters and format_effectors.   1

Syntax

character ::= graphic_character | format_effector | other_control_function   2

graphic_character ::= identifier_letter | digit | space_character | special_character   3

Static Semantics

The character repertoire for the text of an Ada program consists of the collection of characters called the   4
Basic Multilingual Plane (BMP) of the ISO 10646 Universal Multiple-Octet Coded Character Set, plus a
set of format_effectors and, in comments only, a set of other_control_functions; the coded representation
for these characters is implementation defined (it need not be a representation defined within ISO-10646-
1).

The description of the language definition in this International Standard uses the graphic symbols defined   5
for Row 00: Basic Latin and Row 00: Latin-1 Supplement of the ISO 10646 BMP; these correspond to the
graphic symbols of ISO 8859-1 (Latin-1); no graphic symbols are used in this International Standard for
characters outside of Row 00 of the BMP. The actual set of graphic symbols used by an implementation
for the visual representation of the text of an Ada program is not specified.

The categories of characters are defined as follows: 6

identifier_letter   7
> upper_case_identifier_letter | lower_case_identifier_letter

upper_case_identifier_letter   8
> Any character of Row 00 of ISO 10646 BMP whose name begins ''Latin Capital Letter''.

lower_case_identifier_letter   9
> Any character of Row 00 of ISO 10646 BMP whose name begins ''Latin Small Letter''.

digit   10
> One of the characters 0, 1, 2, 3, 4, 5, 6, 7, 8, or 9.

space_character   11
> The character of ISO 10646 BMP named ''Space''.

special_character   12
> Any character of the ISO 10646 BMP that is not reserved for a control function, and is not
> the space_character, an identifier_letter, or a digit.

format_effector   13
> The control functions of ISO 6429 called character tabulation (HT), line tabulation (VT),
> carriage return (CR), line feed (LF), and form feed (FF).

other_control_function   14
> Any control function, other than a format_effector, that is allowed in a comment; the set of
> other_control_functions allowed in comments is implementation defined.

S. Tucker Taft et al. (Eds.): Consolidated Ada Reference Manual, LNCS 2219, pp. 9–17, 2001.

15 The following names are used when referring to certain special_characters:

symbol	name	symbol	name
"	quotation mark	:	colon
#	number sign	;	semicolon
&	ampersand	<	less-than sign
'	apostrophe, tick	=	equals sign
(	left parenthesis	>	greater-than sign
)	right parenthesis	_	low line, underline
*	asterisk, multiply	|	vertical line
+	plus sign	[	left square bracket
,	comma	]	right square bracket
–	hyphen-minus, minus	{	left curly bracket
.	full stop, dot, point	}	right curly bracket
/	solidus, divide		

Implementation Permissions

16 In a nonstandard mode, the implementation may support a different character repertoire; in particular, the set of characters that are considered identifier_letters can be extended or changed to conform to local conventions.

NOTES

17 1 Every code position of ISO 10646 BMP that is not reserved for a control function is defined to be a graphic_character by this International Standard. This includes all code positions other than 0000 - 001F, 007F - 009F, and FFFE - FFFF.

18 2 The language does not specify the source representation of programs.

2.2 Lexical Elements, Separators, and Delimiters

Static Semantics

1 The text of a program consists of the texts of one or more compilations. The text of each compilation is a sequence of separate *lexical elements*. Each lexical element is formed from a sequence of characters, and is either a delimiter, an identifier, a reserved word, a numeric_literal, a character_literal, a string_literal, or a comment. The meaning of a program depends only on the particular sequences of lexical elements that form its compilations, excluding comments.

2 The text of a compilation is divided into *lines*. In general, the representation for an end of line is implementation defined. However, a sequence of one or more format_effectors other than character tabulation (HT) signifies at least one end of line.

3 In some cases an explicit *separator* is required to separate adjacent lexical elements. A separator is any of a space character, a format effector, or the end of a line, as follows:

4 • A space character is a separator except within a comment, a string_literal, or a character_literal.

5 • Character tabulation (HT) is a separator except within a comment.

6 • The end of a line is always a separator.

7 One or more separators are allowed between any two adjacent lexical elements, before the first of each compilation, or after the last. At least one separator is required between an identifier, a reserved word, or a numeric_literal and an adjacent identifier, reserved word, or numeric_literal.

A *delimiter* is either one of the following special characters   8

    & ' ( ) * + , - . / : ; < = > | 9

or one of the following *compound delimiters* each composed of two adjacent special characters   10

   => .. ** := /= >= <= << >> <>   11

Each of the special characters listed for single character delimiters is a single delimiter except if this   12
character is used as a character of a compound delimiter, or as a character of a comment, string_literal,
character_literal, or numeric_literal.

The following names are used when referring to compound delimiters: 13

delimiter	name
=>	arrow
..	double dot
**	double star, exponentiate
:=	assignment (pronounced: ''becomes'')
/=	inequality (pronounced: ''not equal'')
>=	greater than or equal
<=	less than or equal
<<	left label bracket
>>	right label bracket
<>	box

Implementation Requirements

An implementation shall support lines of at least 200 characters in length, not counting any characters used   14
to signify the end of a line. An implementation shall support lexical elements of at least 200 characters in
length. The maximum supported line length and lexical element length are implementation defined.

2.3 Identifiers

Identifiers are used as names.   1

Syntax

identifier ::=   2
  identifier_letter {[underline] letter_or_digit}

letter_or_digit ::= identifier_letter | digit   3

An identifier shall not be a reserved word.   4

Static Semantics

All characters of an identifier are significant, including any underline character. Identifiers differing only in   5
the use of corresponding upper and lower case letters are considered the same.

Implementation Permissions

In a nonstandard mode, an implementation may support other upper/lower case equivalence rules for   6
identifiers, to accommodate local conventions.

7   *Examples of identifiers:*

8   Count   X   Get_Symbol   Ethelyn   Marion

         Snobol_4   X1   Page_Count   Store_Next_Item

2.4 Numeric Literals

1   There are two kinds of numeric_literals, *real literals* and *integer literals*. A real literal is a numeric_literal that includes a point; an integer literal is a numeric_literal without a point.

2   numeric_literal ::= decimal_literal I based_literal

      NOTES

3   3 The type of an integer literal is *universal_integer*. The type of a real literal is *universal_real*.

2.4.1 Decimal Literals

1   A decimal_literal is a numeric_literal in the conventional decimal notation (that is, the base is ten).

2   decimal_literal ::= numeral [.numeral] [exponent]

3   numeral ::= digit {[underline] digit}

4   exponent ::= E [+] numeral I E – numeral

5   An exponent for an integer literal shall not have a minus sign.

6   An underline character in a numeric_literal does not affect its meaning. The letter E of an exponent can be written either in lower case or in upper case, with the same meaning.

7   An exponent indicates the power of ten by which the value of the decimal_literal without the exponent is to be multiplied to obtain the value of the decimal_literal with the exponent.

8   *Examples of decimal literals:*

9   12   0   1E6   123_456   -- *integer literals*

        12.0   0.0   0.456   3.14159_26   -- *real literals*

2.4.2 Based Literals

1   A based_literal is a numeric_literal expressed in a form that specifies the base explicitly.

2   based_literal ::=
       base # based_numeral [.based_numeral] # [exponent]

3   base ::= numeral

based_numeral ::=
    extended_digit {[underline] extended_digit}

4

extended_digit ::= digit | A | B | C | D | E | F

5

Legality Rules

The *base* (the numeric value of the decimal numeral preceding the first #) shall be at least two and at most sixteen. The extended_digits A through F represent the digits ten through fifteen, respectively. The value of each extended_digit of a based_literal shall be less than the base.

6

Static Semantics

The conventional meaning of based notation is assumed. An exponent indicates the power of the base by which the value of the based_literal without the exponent is to be multiplied to obtain the value of the based_literal with the exponent. The base and the exponent, if any, are in decimal notation.

7

The extended_digits A through F can be written either in lower case or in upper case, with the same meaning.

8

Examples

Examples of based literals:

9

```
2#1111_1111#   16#FF#    016#0ff#          -- integer literals of value 255          10
16#E#E1        2#1110_0000#                -- integer literals of value 224
16#F.FF#E+2    2#1.1111_1111_1110#E11      -- real literals of value 4095.0
```

2.5 Character Literals

A character_literal is formed by enclosing a graphic character between two apostrophe characters.

1

Syntax

character_literal ::= 'graphic_character'

2

NOTES
4 A character_literal is an enumeration literal of a character type. See 3.5.2.

3

Examples

Examples of character literals:

4

```
'A'   '*'   '''   ' '
```

5

2.6 String Literals

A string_literal is formed by a sequence of graphic characters (possibly none) enclosed between two quotation marks used as string brackets. They are used to represent operator_symbols (see 6.1), values of a string type (see 4.2), and array subaggregates (see 4.3.3).

1

Syntax

string_literal ::= "{string_element}"

2

string_element ::= "" | *non_quotation_mark*_graphic_character

3

A string_element is either a pair of quotation marks (""), or a single graphic_character other than a quotation mark.

4

Static Semantics

5 The *sequence of characters* of a string_literal is formed from the sequence of string_elements between the bracketing quotation marks, in the given order, with a string_element that is "" becoming a single quotation mark in the sequence of characters, and any other string_element being reproduced in the sequence.

6 A *null string literal* is a string_literal with no string_elements between the quotation marks.

NOTES
7 5 An end of line cannot appear in a string_literal.

Examples

8 *Examples of string literals:*

9   "Message of the day:"

        ""   -- *a null string literal*
        " " "A" """" -- *three string literals of length 1*

        "Characters such as $, %, and } are allowed in string literals"

2.7 Comments

1 A comment starts with two adjacent hyphens and extends up to the end of the line.

Syntax

2   comment ::= --{*non_end_of_line*_character}

3   A comment may appear on any line of a program.

Static Semantics

4 The presence or absence of comments has no influence on whether a program is legal or illegal. Furthermore, comments do not influence the meaning of a program; their sole purpose is the enlightenment of the human reader.

Examples

5 *Examples of comments:*

6   -- *the last sentence above echoes the Algol 68 report*

       end; -- *processing of Line is complete*

       -- *a long comment may be split onto*
       -- *two or more consecutive lines*

       --------------- *the first two hyphens start the comment*

2.8 Pragmas

1 A pragma is a compiler directive. There are language-defined pragmas that give instructions for optimization, listing control, etc. An implementation may support additional (implementation-defined) pragmas.

Syntax

pragma ::=   2
  pragma identifier [(pragma_argument_association {, pragma_argument_association})];

pragma_argument_association ::=   3
  [*pragma_argument_*identifier =>] name
  | [*pragma_argument_*identifier =>] expression

In a pragma, any pragma_argument_associations without a *pragma_argument_*identifier shall   4
precede any associations with a *pragma_argument_*identifier.

Pragmas are only allowed at the following places in a program: 5

- After a semicolon delimiter, but not within a formal_part or discriminant_part.   6

- At any place where the syntax rules allow a construct defined by a syntactic category whose   7
  name ends with "declaration", "statement", "clause", or "alternative", or one of the
  syntactic categories variant or exception_handler; but not in place of such a construct. Also
  at any place where a compilation_unit would be allowed.

Additional syntax rules and placement restrictions exist for specific pragmas.   8

The *name* of a pragma is the identifier following the reserved word **pragma**. The name or expression of a   9
pragma_argument_association is a *pragma argument*.

An *identifier specific to a pragma* is an identifier that is used in a pragma argument with special meaning   10
for that pragma.

Static Semantics

If an implementation does not recognize the name of a pragma, then it has no effect on the semantics of   11
the program. Inside such a pragma, the only rules that apply are the Syntax Rules.

Dynamic Semantics

Any pragma that appears at the place of an executable construct is executed. Unless otherwise specified   12
for a particular pragma, this execution consists of the evaluation of each evaluable pragma argument in an
arbitrary order.

Implementation Requirements

The implementation shall give a warning message for an unrecognized pragma name.   13

Implementation Permissions

An implementation may provide implementation-defined pragmas; the name of an implementation-defined   14
pragma shall differ from those of the language-defined pragmas.

An implementation may ignore an unrecognized pragma even if it violates some of the Syntax Rules, if   15
detecting the syntax error is too complex.

Implementation Advice

Normally, implementation-defined pragmas should have no semantic effect for error-free programs; that is,   16
if the implementation-defined pragmas are removed from a working program, the program should still be
legal, and should still have the same semantics.

Normally, an implementation should not define pragmas that can make an illegal program legal, except as   17
follows:

- A pragma used to complete a declaration, such as a pragma Import;   18

19   • A pragma used to configure the environment by adding, removing, or replacing library_items.

Syntax

20   The forms of List, Page, and Optimize pragmas are as follows:

21   **pragma** List(identifier);

22   **pragma** Page;

23   **pragma** Optimize(identifier);

24   Other pragmas are defined throughout this International Standard, and are summarized in Annex L.

Static Semantics

25   A pragma List takes one of the identifiers On or Off as the single argument. This pragma is allowed anywhere a pragma is allowed. It specifies that listing of the compilation is to be continued or suspended until a List pragma with the opposite argument is given within the same compilation. The pragma itself is always listed if the compiler is producing a listing.

26   A pragma Page is allowed anywhere a pragma is allowed. It specifies that the program text which follows the pragma should start on a new page (if the compiler is currently producing a listing).

27   A pragma Optimize takes one of the identifiers Time, Space, or Off as the single argument. This pragma is allowed anywhere a pragma is allowed, and it applies until the end of the immediately enclosing declarative region, or for a pragma at the place of a compilation_unit, to the end of the compilation. It gives advice to the implementation as to whether time or space is the primary optimization criterion, or that optional optimizations should be turned off. It is implementation defined how this advice is followed.

Examples

28   *Examples of pragmas:*

29
```
pragma List(Off);  -- turn off listing generation
pragma Optimize(Off);  -- turn off optional optimizations
pragma Inline(Set_Mask);  -- generate code for Set_Mask inline
pragma Suppress(Range_Check, On => Index);  -- turn off range checking on Index
```

2.9 Reserved Words

Syntax

This paragraph was deleted.   1/1

The following are the *reserved words* (ignoring upper/lower case distinctions):   2

abort	else	new	return
abs	elsif	not	reverse
abstract	end	null	
accept	entry		select
access	exception	of	separate
aliased	exit	or	subtype
all		others	
and	for	out	tagged
array	function		task
at		package	terminate
	generic	pragma	then
begin	goto	private	type
body		procedure	
	if	protected	until
case	in		use
constant	is	raise	
		range	when
declare	limited	record	while
delay	loop	rem	with
delta		renames	
digits	mod	requeue	xor
do			

NOTES

6 The reserved words appear in **lower case boldface** in this International Standard, except when used in the designator   3
of an attribute (see 4.1.4). Lower case boldface is also used for a reserved word in a string_literal used as an
operator_symbol. This is merely a convention — programs may be written in whatever typeface is desired and available.

Section 3: Declarations and Types

This section describes the types in the language and the rules for declaring constants, variables, and named numbers.

3.1 Declarations

The language defines several kinds of named *entities* that are declared by declarations. The entity's *name* is defined by the declaration, usually by a defining_identifier, but sometimes by a defining_character_literal or defining_operator_symbol.

There are several forms of declaration. A basic_declaration is a form of declaration defined as follows.

Syntax

```
basic_declaration ::=
      type_declaration           | subtype_declaration
    | object_declaration         | number_declaration
    | subprogram_declaration     | abstract_subprogram_declaration
    | package_declaration        | renaming_declaration
    | exception_declaration      | generic_declaration
    | generic_instantiation

defining_identifier ::= identifier
```

Static Semantics

A *declaration* is a language construct that associates a name with (a view of) an entity. A declaration may appear explicitly in the program text (an *explicit* declaration), or may be supposed to occur at a given place in the text as a consequence of the semantics of another construct (an *implicit* declaration).

Each of the following is defined to be a declaration: any basic_declaration; an enumeration_literal_-specification; a discriminant_specification; a component_declaration; a loop_parameter_specification; a parameter_specification; a subprogram_body; an entry_declaration; an entry_index_specification; a choice_parameter_specification; a generic_formal_parameter_declaration.

All declarations contain a *definition* for a *view* of an entity. A view consists of an identification of the entity (the entity *of* the view), plus view-specific characteristics that affect the use of the entity through that view (such as mode of access to an object, formal parameter names and defaults for a subprogram, or visibility to components of a type). In most cases, a declaration also contains the definition for the entity itself (a renaming_declaration is an example of a declaration that does not define a new entity, but instead defines a view of an existing entity (see 8.5)).

For each declaration, the language rules define a certain region of text called the *scope* of the declaration (see 8.2). Most declarations associate an identifier with a declared entity. Within its scope, and only there, there are places where it is possible to use the identifier to refer to the declaration, the view it defines, and the associated entity; these places are defined by the visibility rules (see 8.3). At such places the identifier is said to be a *name* of the entity (the direct_name or selector_name); the name is said to *denote* the declaration, the view, and the associated entity (see 8.6). The declaration is said to *declare* the name, the view, and in most cases, the entity itself.

As an alternative to an identifier, an enumeration literal can be declared with a character_literal as its name (see 3.5.1), and a function can be declared with an operator_symbol as its name (see 6.1).

S. Tucker Taft et al. (Eds.): Consolidated Ada Reference Manual, LNCS 2219, pp. 19–76, 2001.

10   The syntax rules use the terms defining_identifier, defining_character_literal, and defining_operator_-symbol for the defining occurrence of a name; these are collectively called *defining names*. The terms direct_name and selector_name are used for usage occurrences of identifiers, character_literals, and operator_symbols. These are collectively called *usage names*.

Dynamic Semantics

11   The process by which a construct achieves its run-time effect is called *execution*. This process is also called *elaboration* for declarations and *evaluation* for expressions. One of the terms execution, elaboration, or evaluation is defined by this International Standard for each construct that has a run-time effect.

NOTES
12   1 At compile time, the declaration of an entity *declares* the entity. At run time, the elaboration of the declaration *creates* the entity.

3.2 Types and Subtypes

Static Semantics

1   A *type* is characterized by a set of values, and a set of *primitive operations* which implement the fundamental aspects of its semantics. An *object* of a given type is a run-time entity that contains (has) a value of the type.

2   Types are grouped into *classes* of types, reflecting the similarity of their values and primitive operations. There exist several *language-defined classes* of types (see NOTES below). *Elementary* types are those whose values are logically indivisible; *composite* types are those whose values are composed of *component* values.

3   The elementary types are the *scalar* types (*discrete* and *real*) and the *access* types (whose values provide access to objects or subprograms). Discrete types are either *integer* types or are defined by enumeration of their values (*enumeration* types). Real types are either *floating point* types or *fixed point* types.

4   The composite types are the *record* types, *record extensions*, *array* types, *task* types, and *protected* types. A *private* type or *private extension* represents a partial view (see 7.3) of a type, providing support for data abstraction. A partial view is a composite type.

5   Certain composite types (and partial views thereof) have special components called *discriminants* whose values affect the presence, constraints, or initialization of other components. Discriminants can be thought of as parameters of the type.

6   The term *subcomponent* is used in this International Standard in place of the term component to indicate either a component, or a component of another subcomponent. Where other subcomponents are excluded, the term component is used instead. Similarly, a *part* of an object or value is used to mean the whole object or value, or any set of its subcomponents.

7   The set of possible values for an object of a given type can be subjected to a condition that is called a *constraint* (the case of a *null constraint* that specifies no restriction is also included); the rules for which values satisfy a given kind of constraint are given in 3.5 for range_constraints, 3.6.1 for index_constraints, and 3.7.1 for discriminant_constraints.

8   A *subtype* of a given type is a combination of the type, a constraint on values of the type, and certain attributes specific to the subtype. The given type is called the type *of* the subtype. Similarly, the associated

constraint is called the constraint *of* the subtype. The set of values of a subtype consists of the values of its type that satisfy its constraint. Such values *belong* to the subtype.

A subtype is called an *unconstrained* subtype if its type has unknown discriminants, or if its type allows range, index, or discriminant constraints, but the subtype does not impose such a constraint; otherwise, the subtype is called a *constrained* subtype (since it has no unconstrained characteristics).

NOTES

2 Any set of types that is closed under derivation (see 3.4) can be called a "class" of types. However, only certain classes are used in the description of the rules of the language — generally those that have their own particular set of primitive operations (see 3.2.3), or that correspond to a set of types that are matched by a given kind of generic formal type (see 12.5). The following are examples of "interesting" *language-defined classes*: elementary, scalar, discrete, enumeration, character, boolean, integer, signed integer, modular, real, floating point, fixed point, ordinary fixed point, decimal fixed point, numeric, access, access-to-object, access-to-subprogram, composite, array, string, (untagged) record, tagged, task, protected, nonlimited. Special syntax is provided to define types in each of these classes.

These language-defined classes are organized like this:

```
all types
        elementary
                scalar
                        discrete
                                enumeration
                                        character
                                        boolean
                                        other enumeration
                                integer
                                        signed integer
                                        modular integer
                        real
                                floating point
                                fixed point
                                        ordinary fixed point
                                        decimal fixed point
                access
                        access-to-object
                        access-to-subprogram
        composite
                array
                        string
                        other array
                untagged record
                tagged
                task
                protected
```

The classes "numeric" and "nonlimited" represent other classification dimensions and do not fit into the above strictly hierarchical picture.

3.2.1 Type Declarations

A type_declaration declares a type and its first subtype.

Syntax

type_declaration ::= full_type_declaration
    | incomplete_type_declaration
    | private_type_declaration
    | private_extension_declaration

3   full_type_declaration ::=
       type defining_identifier [known_discriminant_part] **is** type_definition;
      | task_type_declaration
      | protected_type_declaration

4   type_definition ::=
       enumeration_type_definition | integer_type_definition
      | real_type_definition | array_type_definition
      | record_type_definition | access_type_definition
      | derived_type_definition

Legality Rules

5   A given type shall not have a subcomponent whose type is the given type itself.

Static Semantics

6   The defining_identifier of a type_declaration denotes the *first subtype* of the type. The known_-discriminant_part, if any, defines the discriminants of the type (see 3.7, "Discriminants"). The remainder of the type_declaration defines the remaining characteristics of (the view of) the type.

7   A type defined by a type_declaration is a *named* type; such a type has one or more nameable subtypes. Certain other forms of declaration also include type definitions as part of the declaration for an object (including a parameter or a discriminant). The type defined by such a declaration is *anonymous* — it has no nameable subtypes. For explanatory purposes, this International Standard sometimes refers to an anonymous type by a pseudo-name, written in italics, and uses such pseudo-names at places where the syntax normally requires an identifier. For a named type whose first subtype is T, this International Standard sometimes refers to the type of T as simply "the type T."

8   A named type that is declared by a full_type_declaration, or an anonymous type that is defined as part of declaring an object of the type, is called a *full type*. The type_definition, task_definition, protected_-definition, or access_definition that defines a full type is called a *full type definition*. Types declared by other forms of type_declaration are not separate types; they are partial or incomplete views of some full type.

9   The definition of a type implicitly declares certain *predefined operators* that operate on the type, according to what classes the type belongs, as specified in 4.5, "Operators and Expression Evaluation".

10   The *predefined types* (for example the types Boolean, Wide_Character, Integer, *root_integer*, and *universal_integer*) are the types that are defined in a predefined library package called Standard; this package also includes the (implicit) declarations of their predefined operators. The package Standard is described in A.1.

Dynamic Semantics

11   The elaboration of a full_type_declaration consists of the elaboration of the full type definition. Each elaboration of a full type definition creates a distinct type and its first subtype.

Examples

12   *Examples of type definitions:*

13
```
(White, Red, Yellow, Green, Blue, Brown, Black)
range 1 .. 72
array(1 .. 10) of Integer
```

Examples of type declarations:

14

```
type Color  is (White, Red, Yellow, Green, Blue, Brown, Black);
type Column is range 1 .. 72;
type Table  is array(1 .. 10) of Integer;
```

15

NOTES

3 Each of the above examples declares a named type. The identifier given denotes the first subtype of the type. Other named subtypes of the type can be declared with subtype_declarations (see 3.2.2). Although names do not directly denote types, a phrase like "the type Column" is sometimes used in this International Standard to refer to the type of Column, where Column denotes the first subtype of the type. For an example of the definition of an anonymous type, see the declaration of the array Color_Table in 3.3.1; its type is anonymous — it has no nameable subtypes.

16

3.2.2 Subtype Declarations

A subtype_declaration declares a subtype of some previously declared type, as defined by a subtype_indication.

1

Syntax

subtype_declaration ::=
  subtype defining_identifier **is** subtype_indication;

2

subtype_indication ::= subtype_mark [constraint]

3

subtype_mark ::= *subtype_*name

4

constraint ::= scalar_constraint I composite_constraint

5

scalar_constraint ::=
  range_constraint I digits_constraint I delta_constraint

6

composite_constraint ::=
  index_constraint I discriminant_constraint

7

Name Resolution Rules

A subtype_mark shall resolve to denote a subtype. The type *determined by* a subtype_mark is the type of the subtype denoted by the subtype_mark.

8

Dynamic Semantics

The elaboration of a subtype_declaration consists of the elaboration of the subtype_indication. The elaboration of a subtype_indication creates a new subtype. If the subtype_indication does not include a constraint, the new subtype has the same (possibly null) constraint as that denoted by the subtype_mark. The elaboration of a subtype_indication that includes a constraint proceeds as follows:

9

- The constraint is first elaborated.

10

- A check is then made that the constraint is *compatible* with the subtype denoted by the subtype_mark.

11

The condition imposed by a constraint is the condition obtained after elaboration of the constraint. The rules defining compatibility are given for each form of constraint in the appropriate subclause. These rules are such that if a constraint is *compatible* with a subtype, then the condition imposed by the constraint cannot contradict any condition already imposed by the subtype on its values. The exception Constraint_Error is raised if any check of compatibility fails.

12

NOTES

4 A scalar_constraint may be applied to a subtype of an appropriate scalar type (see 3.5, 3.5.9, and J.3), even if the subtype is already constrained. On the other hand, a composite_constraint may be applied to a composite subtype (or an access-to-composite subtype) only if the composite subtype is unconstrained (see 3.6.1 and 3.7.1).

13

14 *Examples of subtype declarations:*

15
```
subtype Rainbow    is Color range Red .. Blue;    -- see 3.2.1
subtype Red_Blue   is Rainbow;
subtype Int        is Integer;
subtype Small_Int  is Integer range -10 .. 10;
subtype Up_To_K    is Column range 1 .. K;        -- see 3.2.1
subtype Square     is Matrix(1 .. 10, 1 .. 10);   -- see 3.6
subtype Male       is Person(Sex => M);           -- see 3.10.1
```

3.2.3 Classification of Operations

Static Semantics

1 An operation *operates on a type T* if it yields a value of type *T*, if it has an operand whose expected type (see 8.6) is *T*, or if it has an access parameter (see 6.1) designating *T*. A predefined operator, or other language-defined operation such as assignment or a membership test, that operates on a type, is called a *predefined operation* of the type. The *primitive operations* of a type are the predefined operations of the type, plus any user-defined primitive subprograms.

2 The *primitive subprograms* of a specific type are defined as follows:

3 • The predefined operators of the type (see 4.5);

4 • For a derived type, the inherited (see 3.4) user-defined subprograms;

5 • For an enumeration type, the enumeration literals (which are considered parameterless functions — see 3.5.1);

6 • For a specific type declared immediately within a package_specification, any subprograms (in addition to the enumeration literals) that are explicitly declared immediately within the same package_specification and that operate on the type;

7 • Any subprograms not covered above that are explicitly declared immediately within the same declarative region as the type and that override (see 8.3) other implicitly declared primitive subprograms of the type.

8 A primitive subprogram whose designator is an operator_symbol is called a *primitive operator*.

3.3 Objects and Named Numbers

1 Objects are created at run time and contain a value of a given type. An object can be created and initialized as part of elaborating a declaration, evaluating an allocator, aggregate, or function_call, or passing a parameter by copy. Prior to reclaiming the storage for an object, it is finalized if necessary (see 7.6.1).

Static Semantics

2 All of the following are objects:

3 • the entity declared by an object_declaration;

4 • a formal parameter of a subprogram, entry, or generic subprogram;

5 • a generic formal object;

6 • a loop parameter;

7 • a choice parameter of an exception_handler;

8 • an entry index of an entry_body;

- the result of dereferencing an access-to-object value (see 4.1); 9

- the result of evaluating a function_call (or the equivalent operator invocation — see 6.6); 10

- the result of evaluating an aggregate; 11

- a component, slice, or view conversion of another object. 12

An object is either a *constant* object or a *variable* object. The value of a constant object cannot be changed 13
between its initialization and its finalization, whereas the value of a variable object can be changed.
Similarly, a view of an object is either a *constant* or a *variable*. All views of a constant object are constant.
A constant view of a variable object cannot be used to modify the value of the variable. The terms constant
and variable by themselves refer to constant and variable views of objects.

The value of an object is *read* when the value of any part of the object is evaluated, or when the value of 14
an enclosing object is evaluated. The value of a variable is *updated* when an assignment is performed to
any part of the variable, or when an assignment is performed to an enclosing object.

Whether a view of an object is constant or variable is determined by the definition of the view. The 15
following (and no others) represent constants:

- an object declared by an object_declaration with the reserved word **constant**; 16

- a formal parameter or generic formal object of mode **in**; 17

- a discriminant; 18

- a loop parameter, choice parameter, or entry index; 19

- the dereference of an access-to-constant value; 20

- the result of evaluating a function_call or an aggregate; 21

- a selected_component, indexed_component, slice, or view conversion of a constant. 22

At the place where a view of an object is defined, a *nominal subtype* is associated with the view. The 23
object's *actual subtype* (that is, its subtype) can be more restrictive than the nominal subtype of the view; it
always is if the nominal subtype is an *indefinite subtype*. A subtype is an indefinite subtype if it is an
unconstrained array subtype, or if it has unknown discriminants or unconstrained discriminants without
defaults (see 3.7); otherwise the subtype is a *definite* subtype (all elementary subtypes are definite
subtypes). A class-wide subtype is defined to have unknown discriminants, and is therefore an indefinite
subtype. An indefinite subtype does not by itself provide enough information to create an object; an
additional constraint or explicit initialization expression is necessary (see 3.3.1). A component cannot
have an indefinite nominal subtype.

A *named number* provides a name for a numeric value known at compile time. It is declared by a 24
number_declaration.

NOTES
5 A constant cannot be the target of an assignment operation, nor be passed as an **in out** or **out** parameter, between its 25
initialization and finalization, if any.

6 The nominal and actual subtypes of an elementary object are always the same. For a discriminated or array object, if 26
the nominal subtype is constrained then so is the actual subtype.

3.3.1 Object Declarations

1   An object_declaration declares a *stand-alone* object with a given nominal subtype and, optionally, an explicit initial value given by an initialization expression. For an array, task, or protected object, the object_declaration may include the definition of the (anonymous) type of the object.

Syntax

2   object_declaration ::=
      defining_identifier_list : [**aliased**] [**constant**] subtype_indication [:= expression];
      | defining_identifier_list : [**aliased**] [**constant**] array_type_definition [:= expression];
      | single_task_declaration
      | single_protected_declaration

3   defining_identifier_list ::=
      defining_identifier {, defining_identifier}

Name Resolution Rules

4   For an object_declaration with an expression following the compound delimiter :=, the type expected for the expression is that of the object. This expression is called the *initialization expression*.

Legality Rules

5   An object_declaration without the reserved word **constant** declares a variable object. If it has a subtype_indication or an array_type_definition that defines an indefinite subtype, then there shall be an initialization expression. An initialization expression shall not be given if the object is of a limited type.

Static Semantics

6   An object_declaration with the reserved word **constant** declares a constant object. If it has an initialization expression, then it is called a *full constant declaration*. Otherwise it is called a *deferred constant declaration*. The rules for deferred constant declarations are given in clause 7.4. The rules for full constant declarations are given in this subclause.

7   Any declaration that includes a defining_identifier_list with more than one defining_identifier is equivalent to a series of declarations each containing one defining_identifier from the list, with the rest of the text of the declaration copied for each declaration in the series, in the same order as the list. The remainder of this International Standard relies on this equivalence; explanations are given for declarations with a single defining_identifier.

8   The subtype_indication or full type definition of an object_declaration defines the nominal subtype of the object. The object_declaration declares an object of the type of the nominal subtype.

Dynamic Semantics

9   If a composite object declared by an object_declaration has an unconstrained nominal subtype, then if this subtype is indefinite or the object is constant or aliased (see 3.10) the actual subtype of this object is constrained. The constraint is determined by the bounds or discriminants (if any) of its initial value; the object is said to be *constrained by its initial value*. In the case of an aliased object, this initial value may be either explicit or implicit; in the other cases, an explicit initial value is required. When not constrained by its initial value, the actual and nominal subtypes of the object are the same. If its actual subtype is constrained, the object is called a *constrained object*.

10   For an object_declaration without an initialization expression, any initial values for the object or its subcomponents are determined by the *implicit initial values* defined for its nominal subtype, as follows:

- The implicit initial value for an access subtype is the null value of the access type.   11

- The implicit initial (and only) value for each discriminant of a constrained discriminated subtype is defined by the subtype.   12

- For a (definite) composite subtype, the implicit initial value of each component with a default_expression is obtained by evaluation of this expression and conversion to the component's nominal subtype (which might raise Constraint_Error — see 4.6, ''Type Conversions''), unless the component is a discriminant of a constrained subtype (the previous case), or is in an excluded variant (see 3.8.1). For each component that does not have a default_expression, any implicit initial values are those determined by the component's nominal subtype.   13

- For a protected or task subtype, there is an implicit component (an entry queue) corresponding to each entry, with its implicit initial value being an empty queue.   14

The elaboration of an object_declaration proceeds in the following sequence of steps: 15

1. The subtype_indication, array_type_definition, single_task_declaration, or single_protected_declaration is first elaborated. This creates the nominal subtype (and the anonymous type in the latter three cases).   16

2. If the object_declaration includes an initialization expression, the (explicit) initial value is obtained by evaluating the expression and converting it to the nominal subtype (which might raise Constraint_Error — see 4.6).   17

3. The object is created, and, if there is not an initialization expression, any per-object expressions (see 3.8) are elaborated and any implicit initial values for the object or for its subcomponents are obtained as determined by the nominal subtype.   18/1

4. Any initial values (whether explicit or implicit) are assigned to the object or to the corresponding subcomponents. As described in 5.2 and 7.6, Initialize and Adjust procedures can be called.   19

For the third step above, the object creation and any elaborations and evaluations are performed in an arbitrary order, except that if the default_expression for a discriminant is evaluated to obtain its initial value, then this evaluation is performed before that of the default_expression for any component that depends on the discriminant, and also before that of any default_expression that includes the name of the discriminant. The evaluations of the third step and the assignments of the fourth step are performed in an arbitrary order, except that each evaluation is performed before the resulting value is assigned.   20

There is no implicit initial value defined for a scalar subtype. In the absence of an explicit initialization, a newly created scalar object might have a value that does not belong to its subtype (see 13.9.1 and H.1).   21

NOTES

7 Implicit initial values are not defined for an indefinite subtype, because if an object's nominal subtype is indefinite, an explicit initial value is required.   22

8 As indicated above, a stand-alone object is an object declared by an object_declaration. Similar definitions apply to ''stand-alone constant'' and ''stand-alone variable.'' A subcomponent of an object is not a stand-alone object, nor is an object that is created by an allocator. An object declared by a loop_parameter_specification, parameter_specification, entry_index_specification, choice_parameter_specification, or a formal_object_declaration is not called a stand-alone object.   23

9 The type of a stand-alone object cannot be abstract (see 3.9.3).   24

Examples

Example of a multiple object declaration: 25

```
-- the multiple object declaration
John, Paul : Person_Name := new Person(Sex => M);   -- see 3.10.1
```
   26
   27

28   -- *is equivalent to the two single object declarations in the order given*

29
```
John : Person_Name := new Person(Sex => M);
Paul : Person_Name := new Person(Sex => M);
```

30   *Examples of variable declarations:*

31
```
Count, Sum  : Integer;
Size        : Integer range 0 .. 10_000 := 0;
Sorted      : Boolean := False;
Color_Table : array(1 .. Max) of Color;
Option      : Bit_Vector(1 .. 10) := (others => True);
Hello       : constant String := "Hi, world.";
```

32   *Examples of constant declarations:*

33
```
Limit     : constant Integer := 10_000;
Low_Limit : constant Integer := Limit/10;
Tolerance : constant Real := Dispersion(1.15);
```

3.3.2 Number Declarations

1   A number_declaration declares a named number.

Syntax

2
```
number_declaration ::=
    defining_identifier_list : constant := static_expression;
```

Name Resolution Rules

3   The *static*_expression given for a number_declaration is expected to be of any numeric type.

Legality Rules

4   The *static*_expression given for a number declaration shall be a static expression, as defined by clause 4.9.

Static Semantics

5   The named number denotes a value of type *universal_integer* if the type of the *static*_expression is an integer type. The named number denotes a value of type *universal_real* if the type of the *static*_expression is a real type.

6   The value denoted by the named number is the value of the *static*_expression, converted to the corresponding universal type.

Dynamic Semantics

7   The elaboration of a number_declaration has no effect.

Examples

8   *Examples of number declarations:*

9
```
Two_Pi        : constant := 2.0*Ada.Numerics.Pi;   -- a real number (see A.5)
```

10
```
Max           : constant := 500;        -- an integer number
Max_Line_Size : constant := Max/6       -- the integer 83
Power_16      : constant := 2**16;       -- the integer 65_536
One, Un, Eins : constant := 1;           -- three different names for 1
```

3.4 Derived Types and Classes

A derived_type_definition defines a new type (and its first subtype) whose characteristics are *derived* from those of a *parent type*.   1

Syntax

derived_type_definition ::= [**abstract**] **new** *parent*_subtype_indication [record_extension_part]   2

Legality Rules

The *parent*_subtype_indication defines the *parent subtype*; its type is the parent type.   3

A type shall be completely defined (see 3.11.1) prior to being specified as the parent type in a derived_type_definition — the full_type_declarations for the parent type and any of its subcomponents have to precede the derived_type_definition.   4

If there is a record_extension_part, the derived type is called a *record extension* of the parent type. A record_extension_part shall be provided if and only if the parent type is a tagged type.   5

Static Semantics

The first subtype of the derived type is unconstrained if a known_discriminant_part is provided in the declaration of the derived type, or if the parent subtype is unconstrained. Otherwise, the constraint of the first subtype *corresponds* to that of the parent subtype in the following sense: it is the same as that of the parent subtype except that for a range constraint (implicit or explicit), the value of each bound of its range is replaced by the corresponding value of the derived type.   6

The characteristics of the derived type are defined as follows: 7

- Each class of types that includes the parent type also includes the derived type.   8

- If the parent type is an elementary type or an array type, then the set of possible values of the derived type is a copy of the set of possible values of the parent type. For a scalar type, the base range of the derived type is the same as that of the parent type.   9

- If the parent type is a composite type other than an array type, then the components, protected subprograms, and entries that are declared for the derived type are as follows: 10

  - The discriminants specified by a new known_discriminant_part, if there is one; otherwise, each discriminant of the parent type (implicitly declared in the same order with the same specifications) — in the latter case, the discriminants are said to be *inherited*, or if unknown in the parent, are also unknown in the derived type;   11

  - Each nondiscriminant component, entry, and protected subprogram of the parent type, implicitly declared in the same order with the same declarations; these components, entries, and protected subprograms are said to be *inherited*;   12

  - Each component declared in a record_extension_part, if any.   13

  Declarations of components, protected subprograms, and entries, whether implicit or explicit, occur immediately within the declarative region of the type, in the order indicated above, following the parent subtype_indication.   14

- The derived type is limited if and only if the parent type is limited.   15

- For each predefined operator of the parent type, there is a corresponding predefined operator of the derived type.   16

17 • For each user-defined primitive subprogram (other than a user-defined equality operator — see below) of the parent type that already exists at the place of the derived_type_definition, there exists a corresponding *inherited* primitive subprogram of the derived type with the same defining name. Primitive user-defined equality operators of the parent type are also inherited by the derived type, except when the derived type is a nonlimited record extension, and the inherited operator would have a profile that is type conformant with the profile of the corresponding predefined equality operator; in this case, the user-defined equality operator is not inherited, but is rather incorporated into the implementation of the predefined equality operator of the record extension (see 4.5.2).

18 The profile of an inherited subprogram (including an inherited enumeration literal) is obtained from the profile of the corresponding (user-defined) primitive subprogram of the parent type, after systematic replacement of each subtype of its profile (see 6.1) that is of the parent type with a *corresponding subtype* of the derived type. For a given subtype of the parent type, the corresponding subtype of the derived type is defined as follows:

19 • If the declaration of the derived type has neither a known_discriminant_part nor a record_extension_part, then the corresponding subtype has a constraint that corresponds (as defined above for the first subtype of the derived type) to that of the given subtype.

20 • If the derived type is a record extension, then the corresponding subtype is the first subtype of the derived type.

21 • If the derived type has a new known_discriminant_part but is not a record extension, then the corresponding subtype is constrained to those values that when converted to the parent type belong to the given subtype (see 4.6).

22 The same formal parameters have default_expressions in the profile of the inherited subprogram. Any type mismatch due to the systematic replacement of the parent type by the derived type is handled as part of the normal type conversion associated with parameter passing — see 6.4.1.

23 If a primitive subprogram of the parent type is visible at the place of the derived_type_definition, then the corresponding inherited subprogram is implicitly declared immediately after the derived_type_definition. Otherwise, the inherited subprogram is implicitly declared later or not at all, as explained in 7.3.1.

24 A derived type can also be defined by a private_extension_declaration (see 7.3) or a formal_derived_-type_definition (see 12.5.1). Such a derived type is a partial view of the corresponding full or actual type.

25 All numeric types are derived types, in that they are implicitly derived from a corresponding root numeric type (see 3.5.4 and 3.5.6).

Dynamic Semantics

26 The elaboration of a derived_type_definition creates the derived type and its first subtype, and consists of the elaboration of the subtype_indication and the record_extension_part, if any. If the subtype_indication depends on a discriminant, then only those expressions that do not depend on a discriminant are evaluated.

27 For the execution of a call on an inherited subprogram, a call on the corresponding primitive subprogram of the parent type is performed; the normal conversion of each actual parameter to the subtype of the corresponding formal parameter (see 6.4.1) performs any necessary type conversion as well. If the result type of the inherited subprogram is the derived type, the result of calling the parent's subprogram is converted to the derived type.

NOTES

28 10 Classes are closed under derivation — any class that contains a type also contains its derivatives. Operations available for a given class of types are available for the derived types in that class.

11 Evaluating an inherited enumeration literal is equivalent to evaluating the corresponding enumeration literal of the parent type, and then converting the result to the derived type. This follows from their equivalence to parameterless functions.   29

12 A generic subprogram is not a subprogram, and hence cannot be a primitive subprogram and cannot be inherited by a derived type. On the other hand, an instance of a generic subprogram can be a primitive subprogram, and hence can be inherited.   30

13 If the parent type is an access type, then the parent and the derived type share the same storage pool; there is a **null** access value for the derived type and it is the implicit initial value for the type. See 3.10.   31

14 If the parent type is a boolean type, the predefined relational operators of the derived type deliver a result of the predefined type Boolean (see 4.5.2). If the parent type is an integer type, the right operand of the predefined exponentiation operator is of the predefined type Integer (see 4.5.6).   32

15 Any discriminants of the parent type are either all inherited, or completely replaced with a new set of discriminants.   33

16 For an inherited subprogram, the subtype of a formal parameter of the derived type need not have any value in common with the first subtype of the derived type.   34

17 If the reserved word **abstract** is given in the declaration of a type, the type is abstract (see 3.9.3).   35

Examples

Examples of derived type declarations: 36

```
type Local_Coordinate is new Coordinate;      -- two different types       37
type Midweek is new Day range Tue .. Thu;     -- see 3.5.1
type Counter is new Positive;                 -- same range as Positive

type Special_Key is new Key_Manager.Key;      -- see 7.3.1                  38
     -- the inherited subprograms have the following specifications:
--        procedure Get_Key(K : out Special_Key);
--        function "<"(X,Y : Special_Key) return Boolean;
```

3.4.1 Derivation Classes

In addition to the various language-defined classes of types, types can be grouped into *derivation classes*.   1

Static Semantics

A derived type is *derived from* its parent type *directly*; it is derived *indirectly* from any type from which its parent type is derived. The derivation class of types for a type T (also called the class *rooted* at T) is the set consisting of T (the *root type* of the class) and all types derived from T (directly or indirectly) plus any associated universal or class-wide types (defined below).   2

Every type is either a *specific* type, a *class-wide* type, or a *universal* type. A specific type is one defined by a type_declaration, a formal_type_declaration, or a full type definition embedded in a declaration for an object. Class-wide and universal types are implicitly defined, to act as representatives for an entire class of types, as follows: 3

Class-wide types   4

Class-wide types are defined for (and belong to) each derivation class rooted at a tagged type (see 3.9). Given a subtype S of a tagged type T, S'Class is the subtype_mark for a corresponding subtype of the tagged class-wide type T'Class. Such types are called "class-wide" because when a formal parameter is defined to be of a class-wide type T'Class, an actual parameter of any type in the derivation class rooted at T is acceptable (see 8.6).

The set of values for a class-wide type T'Class is the discriminated union of the set of values of each specific type in the derivation class rooted at T (the tag acts as the implicit discriminant — see 3.9). Class-wide types have no primitive subprograms of their own. However, as explained in 3.9.2, operands of a class-wide type T'Class can be used as part of a dispatching call on a primitive subprogram of the type T. The only components (including   5 discriminants) of T'Class that are visible are those of *T*. If S is a first subtype, then S'Class is a first subtype.

6   Universal types

Universal types are defined for (and belong to) the integer, real, and fixed point classes, and are referred to in this standard as respectively, *universal_integer*, *universal_real*, and *universal_fixed*. These are analogous to class-wide types for these language-defined numeric classes. As with class-wide types, if a formal parameter is of a universal type, then an actual parameter of any type in the corresponding class is acceptable. In addition, a value of a universal type (including an integer or real numeric_literal) is ''universal'' in that it is acceptable where some particular type in the class is expected (see 8.6).

7   The set of values of a universal type is the undiscriminated union of the set of values possible for any definable type in the associated class. Like class-wide types, universal types have no primitive subprograms of their own. However, their ''universality'' allows them to be used as operands with the primitive subprograms of any type in the corresponding class.

8   The integer and real numeric classes each have a specific root type in addition to their universal type, named respectively *root_integer* and *root_real*.

9   A class-wide or universal type is said to *cover* all of the types in its class. A specific type covers only itself.

10   A specific type *T2* is defined to be a *descendant* of a type *T1* if *T2* is the same as *T1*, or if *T2* is derived (directly or indirectly) from *T1*. A class-wide type *T2*'Class is defined to be a descendant of type *T1* if *T2* is a descendant of *T1*. Similarly, the universal types are defined to be descendants of the root types of their classes. If a type *T2* is a descendant of a type *T1*, then *T1* is called an *ancestor* of *T2*. The *ultimate ancestor* of a type is the ancestor of the type that is not a descendant of any other type.

11   An inherited component (including an inherited discriminant) of a derived type is inherited *from* a given ancestor of the type if the corresponding component was inherited by each derived type in the chain of derivations going back to the given ancestor.

NOTES

12   18 Because operands of a universal type are acceptable to the predefined operators of any type in their class, ambiguity can result. For *universal_integer* and *universal_real*, this potential ambiguity is resolved by giving a preference (see 8.6) to the predefined operators of the corresponding root types (*root_integer* and *root_real*, respectively). Hence, in an apparently ambiguous expression like

13       $1 + 4 < 7$

14   where each of the literals is of type *universal_integer*, the predefined operators of *root_integer* will be preferred over those of other specific integer types, thereby resolving the ambiguity.

3.5 Scalar Types

1   *Scalar* types comprise enumeration types, integer types, and real types. Enumeration types and integer types are called *discrete* types; each value of a discrete type has a *position number* which is an integer value. Integer types and real types are called *numeric* types. All scalar types are ordered, that is, all relational operators are predefined for their values.

Syntax

2   range_constraint ::= **range** range

3   range ::= range_attribute_reference
        | simple_expression .. simple_expression

A *range* has a *lower bound* and an *upper bound* and specifies a subset of the values of some scalar type (the *type of the range*). A range with lower bound L and upper bound R is described by ''L .. R''. If R is less than L, then the range is a *null range*, and specifies an empty set of values. Otherwise, the range specifies the values of the type from the lower bound to the upper bound, inclusive. A value *belongs* to a range if it is of the type of the range, and is in the subset of values specified by the range. A value *satisfies* a range constraint if it belongs to the associated range. One range is *included* in another if all values that belong to the first range also belong to the second.   4

Name Resolution Rules

For a subtype_indication containing a range_constraint, either directly or as part of some other scalar_constraint, the type of the range shall resolve to that of the type determined by the subtype_mark of the subtype_indication. For a range of a given type, the simple_expressions of the range (likewise, the simple_expressions of the equivalent range for a range_attribute_reference) are expected to be of the type of the range.   5

Static Semantics

The *base range* of a scalar type is the range of finite values of the type that can be represented in every unconstrained object of the type; it is also the range supported at a minimum for intermediate values during the evaluation of expressions involving predefined operators of the type.   6

A constrained scalar subtype is one to which a range constraint applies. The *range* of a constrained scalar subtype is the range associated with the range constraint of the subtype. The *range* of an unconstrained scalar subtype is the base range of its type.   7

Dynamic Semantics

A range is *compatible* with a scalar subtype if and only if it is either a null range or each bound of the range belongs to the range of the subtype. A range_constraint is *compatible* with a scalar subtype if and only if its range is compatible with the subtype.   8

The elaboration of a range_constraint consists of the evaluation of the range. The evaluation of a range determines a lower bound and an upper bound. If simple_expressions are given to specify bounds, the evaluation of the range evaluates these simple_expressions in an arbitrary order, and converts them to the type of the range. If a range_attribute_reference is given, the evaluation of the range consists of the evaluation of the range_attribute_reference.   9

Attributes   10

For every scalar subtype S, the following attributes are defined: 11

S'First   S'First denotes the lower bound of the range of S. The value of this attribute is of the type of S.   12

S'Last   S'Last denotes the upper bound of the range of S. The value of this attribute is of the type of S.   13

S'Range   S'Range is equivalent to the range S'First .. S'Last.   14

S'Base   S'Base denotes an unconstrained subtype of the type of S. This unconstrained subtype is called the *base subtype* of the type.   15

S'Min   S'Min denotes a function with the following specification: 16

```
function S'Min(Left, Right : S'Base)
    return S'Base
```
17

The function returns the lesser of the values of the two parameters.   18

19 S'Max   S'Max denotes a function with the following specification:

20
```
function S'Max(Left, Right : S'Base)
   return S'Base
```

21   The function returns the greater of the values of the two parameters.

22 S'Succ   S'Succ denotes a function with the following specification:

23
```
function S'Succ(Arg : S'Base)
   return S'Base
```

24   For an enumeration type, the function returns the value whose position number is one more
            than that of the value of *Arg*; Constraint_Error is raised if there is no such value of the type.
            For an integer type, the function returns the result of adding one to the value of *Arg*. For a
            fixed point type, the function returns the result of adding *small* to the value of *Arg*. For a
            floating point type, the function returns the machine number (as defined in 3.5.7)
            immediately above the value of *Arg*; Constraint_Error is raised if there is no such machine
            number.

25 S'Pred   S'Pred denotes a function with the following specification:

26
```
function S'Pred(Arg : S'Base)
   return S'Base
```

27   For an enumeration type, the function returns the value whose position number is one less
            than that of the value of *Arg*; Constraint_Error is raised if there is no such value of the type.
            For an integer type, the function returns the result of subtracting one from the value of *Arg*.
            For a fixed point type, the function returns the result of subtracting *small* from the value of
            Arg. For a floating point type, the function returns the machine number (as defined in 3.5.7)
            immediately below the value of *Arg*; Constraint_Error is raised if there is no such machine
            number.

28 S'Wide_Image S'Wide_Image denotes a function with the following specification:

29
```
function S'Wide_Image(Arg : S'Base)
   return Wide_String
```

30   The function returns an *image* of the value of *Arg*, that is, a sequence of characters
            representing the value in display form. The lower bound of the result is one.

31   The image of an integer value is the corresponding decimal literal, without underlines,
            leading zeros, exponent, or trailing spaces, but with a single leading character that is either
            a minus sign or a space.

32   The image of an enumeration value is either the corresponding identifier in upper case or
            the corresponding character literal (including the two apostrophes); neither leading nor
            trailing spaces are included. For a *nongraphic character* (a value of a character type that
            has no enumeration literal associated with it), the result is a corresponding language-defined
            or implementation-defined name in upper case (for example, the image of the nongraphic
            character identified as *nul* is ''NUL'' — the quotes are not part of the image).

33   The image of a floating point value is a decimal real literal best approximating the value
            (rounded away from zero if halfway between) with a single leading character that is either a
            minus sign or a space, a single digit (that is nonzero unless the value is zero), a decimal
            point, S'Digits−1 (see 3.5.8) digits after the decimal point (but one if S'Digits is one), an
            upper case E, the sign of the exponent (either + or −), and two or more digits (with leading
            zeros if necessary) representing the exponent. If S'Signed_Zeros is True, then the leading
            character is a minus sign for a negatively signed zero.

34   The image of a fixed point value is a decimal real literal best approximating the value
            (rounded away from zero if halfway between) with a single leading character that is either a
            minus sign or a space, one or more digits before the decimal point (with no redundant
            leading zeros), a decimal point, and S'Aft (see 3.5.10) digits after the decimal point.

S'Image S'Image denotes a function with the following specification: 35

```
function S'Image(Arg : S'Base)                                          36
   return String
```

The function returns an image of the value of *Arg* as a String. The lower bound of the result 37
is one. The image has the same sequence of graphic characters as that defined for
S'Wide_Image if all the graphic characters are defined in Character; otherwise the sequence
of characters is implementation defined (but no shorter than that of S'Wide_Image for the
same value of *Arg*).

S'Wide_Width   38
S'Wide_Width denotes the maximum length of a Wide_String returned by S'Wide_Image
over all values of the subtype S. It denotes zero for a subtype that has a null range. Its type
is *universal_integer*.

S'Width S'Width denotes the maximum length of a String returned by S'Image over all values of the 39
subtype S. It denotes zero for a subtype that has a null range. Its type is *universal_integer*.

S'Wide_Value   40
S'Wide_Value denotes a function with the following specification:

```
function S'Wide_Value(Arg : Wide_String)                               41
   return S'Base
```

This function returns a value given an image of the value as a Wide_String, ignoring any 42
leading or trailing spaces.

For the evaluation of a call on S'Wide_Value for an enumeration subtype S, if the sequence 43
of characters of the parameter (ignoring leading and trailing spaces) has the syntax of an
enumeration literal and if it corresponds to a literal of the type of S (or corresponds to the
result of S'Wide_Image for a nongraphic character of the type), the result is the
corresponding enumeration value; otherwise Constraint_Error is raised.

For the evaluation of a call on S'Wide_Value (or S'Value) for an integer subtype S, if the 44
sequence of characters of the parameter (ignoring leading and trailing spaces) has the syntax
of an integer literal, with an optional leading sign character (plus or minus for a signed type;
only plus for a modular type), and the corresponding numeric value belongs to the base
range of the type of S, then that value is the result; otherwise Constraint_Error is raised.

For the evaluation of a call on S'Wide_Value (or S'Value) for a real subtype S, if the 45
sequence of characters of the parameter (ignoring leading and trailing spaces) has the syntax
of one of the following:

- numeric_literal   46

- numeral.[exponent]   47

- .numeral[exponent]   48

- base#based_numeral.#[exponent]   49

- base#.based_numeral#[exponent]   50

with an optional leading sign character (plus or minus), and if the corresponding numeric 51
value belongs to the base range of the type of S, then that value is the result; otherwise
Constraint_Error is raised. The sign of a zero value is preserved (positive if none has been
specified) if S'Signed_Zeros is True.

S'Value S'Value denotes a function with the following specification: 52

```
function S'Value(Arg : String)                                         53
   return S'Base
```

54 This function returns a value given an image of the value as a String, ignoring any leading or trailing spaces.

55 For the evaluation of a call on S'Value for an enumeration subtype S, if the sequence of characters of the parameter (ignoring leading and trailing spaces) has the syntax of an enumeration literal and if it corresponds to a literal of the type of S (or corresponds to the result of S'Image for a value of the type), the result is the corresponding enumeration value; otherwise Constraint_Error is raised. For a numeric subtype S, the evaluation of a call on S'Value with *Arg* of type String is equivalent to a call on S'Wide_Value for a corresponding *Arg* of type Wide_String.

Implementation Permissions

56 An implementation may extend the Wide_Value, Value, Wide_Image, and Image attributes of a floating point type to support special values such as infinities and NaNs.

NOTES

57 19 The evaluation of S'First or S'Last never raises an exception. If a scalar subtype S has a nonnull range, S'First and S'Last belong to this range. These values can, for example, always be assigned to a variable of subtype S.

58 20 For a subtype of a scalar type, the result delivered by the attributes Succ, Pred, and Value might not belong to the subtype; similarly, the actual parameters of the attributes Succ, Pred, and Image need not belong to the subtype.

59 21 For any value V (including any nongraphic character) of an enumeration subtype S, S'Value(S'Image(V)) equals V, as does S'Wide_Value(S'Wide_Image(V)). Neither expression ever raises Constraint_Error.

Examples

60 *Examples of ranges:*

61
```
-10 .. 10
X .. X + 1
0.0 .. 2.0*Pi
Red .. Green      -- see 3.5.1
1 .. 0            -- a null range
Table'Range       -- a range attribute reference (see 3.6)
```

62 *Examples of range constraints:*

63
```
range -999.0 .. +999.0
range S'First+1 .. S'Last-1
```

3.5.1 Enumeration Types

1 An enumeration_type_definition defines an enumeration type.

Syntax

2 enumeration_type_definition ::=
      (enumeration_literal_specification {, enumeration_literal_specification})

3 enumeration_literal_specification ::= defining_identifier I defining_character_literal

4 defining_character_literal ::= character_literal

Legality Rules

5 The defining_identifiers and defining_character_literals listed in an enumeration_type_definition shall be distinct.

Static Semantics

Each enumeration_literal_specification is the explicit declaration of the corresponding *enumeration* 6
literal: it declares a parameterless function, whose defining name is the defining_identifier or defining_-
character_literal, and whose result type is the enumeration type.

Each enumeration literal corresponds to a distinct value of the enumeration type, and to a distinct position 7
number. The position number of the value of the first listed enumeration literal is zero; the position
number of the value of each subsequent enumeration literal is one more than that of its predecessor in the
list.

The predefined order relations between values of the enumeration type follow the order of corresponding 8
position numbers.

If the same defining_identifier or defining_character_literal is specified in more than one enumeration_- 9
type_definition, the corresponding enumeration literals are said to be *overloaded*. At any place where an
overloaded enumeration literal occurs in the text of a program, the type of the enumeration literal has to be
determinable from the context (see 8.6).

Dynamic Semantics

The elaboration of an enumeration_type_definition creates the enumeration type and its first subtype, 10
which is constrained to the base range of the type.

When called, the parameterless function associated with an enumeration literal returns the corresponding 11
value of the enumeration type.

NOTES
22 If an enumeration literal occurs in a context that does not otherwise suffice to determine the type of the literal, then 12
qualification by the name of the enumeration type is one way to resolve the ambiguity (see 4.7).

Examples

Examples of enumeration types and subtypes: 13

```
type Day    is (Mon, Tue, Wed, Thu, Fri, Sat, Sun);        14
type Suit   is (Clubs, Diamonds, Hearts, Spades);
type Gender is (M, F);
type Level  is (Low, Medium, Urgent);
type Color  is (White, Red, Yellow, Green, Blue, Brown, Black);
type Light  is (Red, Amber, Green);  -- Red and Green are overloaded

type Hexa   is ('A', 'B', 'C', 'D', 'E', 'F');             15
type Mixed  is ('A', 'B', '*', B, None, '?', '%');

subtype Weekday is Day   range Mon .. Fri;                 16
subtype Major   is Suit  range Hearts .. Spades;
subtype Rainbow is Color range Red .. Blue;  -- the Color Red, not the Light
```

3.5.2 Character Types

Static Semantics

An enumeration type is said to be a *character type* if at least one of its enumeration literals is a 1
character_literal.

The predefined type Character is a character type whose values correspond to the 256 code positions of 2
Row 00 (also known as Latin-1) of the ISO 10646 Basic Multilingual Plane (BMP). Each of the graphic
characters of Row 00 of the BMP has a corresponding character_literal in Character. Each of the
nongraphic positions of Row 00 (0000-001F and 007F-009F) has a corresponding language-defined name,

which is not usable as an enumeration literal, but which is usable with the attributes (Wide_)Image and (Wide_)Value; these names are given in the definition of type Character in A.1, "The Package Standard", but are set in *italics*.

3   The predefined type Wide_Character is a character type whose values correspond to the 65536 code positions of the ISO 10646 Basic Multilingual Plane (BMP). Each of the graphic characters of the BMP has a corresponding character_literal in Wide_Character. The first 256 values of Wide_Character have the same character_literal or language-defined name as defined for Character. The last 2 values of Wide_Character correspond to the nongraphic positions FFFE and FFFF of the BMP, and are assigned the language-defined names *FFFE* and *FFFF*. As with the other language-defined names for nongraphic characters, the names *FFFE* and *FFFF* are usable only with the attributes (Wide_)Image and (Wide_)Value; they are not usable as enumeration literals. All other values of Wide_Character are considered graphic characters, and have a corresponding character_literal.

Implementation Permissions

4   In a nonstandard mode, an implementation may provide other interpretations for the predefined types Character and Wide_Character, to conform to local conventions.

Implementation Advice

5   If an implementation supports a mode with alternative interpretations for Character and Wide_Character, the set of graphic characters of Character should nevertheless remain a proper subset of the set of graphic characters of Wide_Character. Any character set "localizations" should be reflected in the results of the subprograms defined in the language-defined package Characters.Handling (see A.3) available in such a mode. In a mode with an alternative interpretation of Character, the implementation should also support a corresponding change in what is a legal identifier_letter.

NOTES

6   23 The language-defined library package Characters.Latin_1 (see A.3.3) includes the declaration of constants denoting control characters, lower case characters, and special characters of the predefined type Character.

7   24 A conventional character set such as *EBCDIC* can be declared as a character type; the internal codes of the characters can be specified by an enumeration_representation_clause as explained in clause 13.4.

Examples

8   *Example of a character type:*

9
```
type Roman_Digit is ('I', 'V', 'X', 'L', 'C', 'D', 'M');
```

3.5.3 Boolean Types

Static Semantics

1   There is a predefined enumeration type named Boolean, declared in the visible part of package Standard. It has the two enumeration literals False and True ordered with the relation False < True. Any descendant of the predefined type Boolean is called a *boolean* type.

3.5.4 Integer Types

1   An integer_type_definition defines an integer type; it defines either a *signed* integer type, or a *modular* integer type. The base range of a signed integer type includes at least the values of the specified range. A modular type is an integer type with all arithmetic modulo a specified positive *modulus*; such a type corresponds to an unsigned type with wrap-around semantics.

Syntax

integer_type_definition ::= signed_integer_type_definition I modular_type_definition   2

signed_integer_type_definition ::= **range** *static*_simple_expression .. *static*_simple_expression   3

modular_type_definition ::= **mod** *static*_expression   4

Name Resolution Rules

Each simple_expression in a signed_integer_type_definition is expected to be of any integer type; they   5
need not be of the same type. The expression in a modular_type_definition is likewise expected to be of
any integer type.

Legality Rules

The simple_expressions of a signed_integer_type_definition shall be static, and their values shall be in   6
the range System.Min_Int .. System.Max_Int.

The expression of a modular_type_definition shall be static, and its value (the *modulus*) shall be positive,   7
and shall be no greater than System.Max_Binary_Modulus if a power of 2, or no greater than
System.Max_Nonbinary_Modulus if not.

Static Semantics

The set of values for a signed integer type is the (infinite) set of mathematical integers, though only values   8
of the base range of the type are fully supported for run-time operations. The set of values for a modular
integer type are the values from 0 to one less than the modulus, inclusive.

A signed_integer_type_definition defines an integer type whose base range includes at least the values of   9
the simple_expressions and is symmetric about zero, excepting possibly an extra negative value. A
signed_integer_type_definition also defines a constrained first subtype of the type, with a range whose
bounds are given by the values of the simple_expressions, converted to the type being defined.

A modular_type_definition defines a modular type whose base range is from zero to one less than the   10
given modulus. A modular_type_definition also defines a constrained first subtype of the type with a range
that is the same as the base range of the type.

There is a predefined signed integer subtype named Integer, declared in the visible part of package   11
Standard. It is constrained to the base range of its type.

Integer has two predefined subtypes, declared in the visible part of package Standard: 12

```
    subtype Natural  is Integer range 0 .. Integer'Last;
    subtype Positive is Integer range 1 .. Integer'Last;
```
     13

A type defined by an integer_type_definition is implicitly derived from *root_integer*, an anonymous   14
predefined (specific) integer type, whose base range is System.Min_Int .. System.Max_Int. However, the
base range of the new type is not inherited from *root_integer*, but is instead determined by the range or
modulus specified by the integer_type_definition. Integer literals are all of the type *universal_integer*, the
universal type (see 3.4.1) for the class rooted at *root_integer*, allowing their use with the operations of any
integer type.

The *position number* of an integer value is equal to the value.   15

For every modular subtype S, the following attribute is defined: 16

S'Modulus   S'Modulus yields the modulus of the type of S, as a value of the type *universal_integer*.   17

Dynamic Semantics

18 The elaboration of an integer_type_definition creates the integer type and its first subtype.

19 For a modular type, if the result of the execution of a predefined operator (see 4.5) is outside the base range of the type, the result is reduced modulo the modulus of the type to a value that is within the base range of the type.

20 For a signed integer type, the exception Constraint_Error is raised by the execution of an operation that cannot deliver the correct result because it is outside the base range of the type. For any integer type, Constraint_Error is raised by the operators "/", "**rem**", and "**mod**" if the right operand is zero.

Implementation Requirements

21 In an implementation, the range of Integer shall include the range $-2**15+1 .. +2**15-1$.

22 If Long_Integer is predefined for an implementation, then its range shall include the range $-2**31+1 .. +2**31-1$.

23 System.Max_Binary_Modulus shall be at least $2**16$.

Implementation Permissions

24 For the execution of a predefined operation of a signed integer type, the implementation need not raise Constraint_Error if the result is outside the base range of the type, so long as the correct result is produced.

25 An implementation may provide additional predefined signed integer types, declared in the visible part of Standard, whose first subtypes have names of the form Short_Integer, Long_Integer, Short_Short_Integer, Long_Long_Integer, etc. Different predefined integer types are allowed to have the same base range. However, the range of Integer should be no wider than that of Long_Integer. Similarly, the range of Short_Integer (if provided) should be no wider than Integer. Corresponding recommendations apply to any other predefined integer types. There need not be a named integer type corresponding to each distinct base range supported by an implementation. The range of each first subtype should be the base range of its type.

26 An implementation may provide *nonstandard integer types*, descendants of *root_integer* that are declared outside of the specification of package Standard, which need not have all the standard characteristics of a type defined by an integer_type_definition. For example, a nonstandard integer type might have an asymmetric base range or it might not be allowed as an array or loop index (a very long integer). Any type descended from a nonstandard integer type is also nonstandard. An implementation may place arbitrary restrictions on the use of such types; it is implementation defined whether operators that are predefined for "any integer type" are defined for a particular nonstandard integer type. In any case, such types are not permitted as explicit_generic_actual_parameters for formal scalar types — see 12.5.2.

27 For a one's complement machine, the high bound of the base range of a modular type whose modulus is one less than a power of 2 may be equal to the modulus, rather than one less than the modulus. It is implementation defined for which powers of 2, if any, this permission is exercised.

27.1/1 For a one's complement machine, implementations may support non-binary modulus values greater than System.Max_Nonbinary_Modulus. It is implementation defined which specific values greater than System.Max_Nonbinary_Modulus, if any, are supported.

Implementation Advice

28 An implementation should support Long_Integer in addition to Integer if the target machine supports 32-bit (or longer) arithmetic. No other named integer subtypes are recommended for package Standard. Instead, appropriate named integer subtypes should be provided in the library package Interfaces (see B.2).

3.5.4 Integer Types

An implementation for a two's complement machine should support modular types with a binary modulus up to System.Max_Int*2+2. An implementation should support a nonbinary modulus up to Integer'Last.

29

NOTES

25 Integer literals are of the anonymous predefined integer type *universal_integer*. Other integer types have no literals. However, the overload resolution rules (see 8.6, ''The Context of Overload Resolution'') allow expressions of the type *universal_integer* whenever an integer type is expected.

30

26 The same arithmetic operators are predefined for all signed integer types defined by a signed_integer_type_definition (see 4.5, ''Operators and Expression Evaluation''). For modular types, these same operators are predefined, plus bit-wise logical operators (**and**, **or**, **xor**, and **not**). In addition, for the unsigned types declared in the language-defined package Interfaces (see B.2), functions are defined that provide bit-wise shifting and rotating.

31

27 Modular types match a generic_formal_parameter_declaration of the form "**type** T **is mod** <>;"; signed integer types match "**type** T **is range** <>;" (see 12.5.2).

32

Examples

Examples of integer types and subtypes:

33

```
type Page_Num  is range 1 .. 2_000;
type Line_Size is range 1 .. Max_Line_Size;
```

34

```
subtype Small_Int   is Integer   range -10 .. 10;
subtype Column_Ptr  is Line_Size range 1 .. 10;
subtype Buffer_Size is Integer   range 0 .. Max;
```

35

```
type Byte       is mod 256;  -- an unsigned byte
type Hash_Index is mod 97;   -- modulus is prime
```

36

3.5.5 Operations of Discrete Types

Static Semantics

For every discrete subtype S, the following attributes are defined:

1

S'Pos   S'Pos denotes a function with the following specification:

2

```
function S'Pos(Arg : S'Base)
   return universal_integer
```

3

This function returns the position number of the value of *Arg*, as a value of type *universal_integer*.

4

S'Val   S'Val denotes a function with the following specification:

5

```
function S'Val(Arg : universal_integer)
   return S'Base
```

6

This function returns a value of the type of S whose position number equals the value of *Arg*. For the evaluation of a call on S'Val, if there is no value in the base range of its type with the given position number, Constraint_Error is raised.

7

Implementation Advice

For the evaluation of a call on S'Pos for an enumeration subtype, if the value of the operand does not correspond to the internal code for any enumeration literal of its type (perhaps due to an uninitialized variable), then the implementation should raise Program_Error. This is particularly important for enumeration types with noncontiguous internal codes specified by an enumeration_representation_clause.

8

NOTES

28 Indexing and loop iteration use values of discrete types.

9

29 The predefined operations of a discrete type include the assignment operation, qualification, the membership tests, and the relational operators; for a boolean type they include the short-circuit control forms and the logical operators; for

10

an integer type they include type conversion to and from other numeric types, as well as the binary and unary adding operators – and +, the multiplying operators, the unary operator **abs**, and the exponentiation operator. The assignment operation is described in 5.2. The other predefined operations are described in Section 4.

11   30 As for all types, objects of a discrete type have Size and Address attributes (see 13.3).

12   31 For a subtype of a discrete type, the result delivered by the attribute Val might not belong to the subtype; similarly, the actual parameter of the attribute Pos need not belong to the subtype. The following relations are satisfied (in the absence of an exception) by these attributes:

13
```
S'Val(S'Pos(X)) = X
S'Pos(S'Val(N)) = N
```

Examples

14   *Examples of attributes of discrete subtypes:*

15   *-- For the types and subtypes declared in subclause 3.5.1 the following hold:*

16
```
--   Color'First   = White,    Color'Last   = Black
--   Rainbow'First = Red,      Rainbow'Last = Blue
```

17
```
--   Color'Succ(Blue) = Rainbow'Succ(Blue) = Brown
--   Color'Pos(Blue)  = Rainbow'Pos(Blue)  = 4
--   Color'Val(0)     = Rainbow'Val(0)     = White
```

3.5.6 Real Types

1   Real types provide approximations to the real numbers, with relative bounds on errors for floating point types, and with absolute bounds for fixed point types.

Syntax

2   real_type_definition ::=
        floating_point_definition | fixed_point_definition

Static Semantics

3   A type defined by a real_type_definition is implicitly derived from *root_real*, an anonymous predefined (specific) real type. Hence, all real types, whether floating point or fixed point, are in the derivation class rooted at *root_real*.

4   Real literals are all of the type *universal_real*, the universal type (see 3.4.1) for the class rooted at *root_real*, allowing their use with the operations of any real type. Certain multiplying operators have a result type of *universal_fixed* (see 4.5.5), the universal type for the class of fixed point types, allowing the result of the multiplication or division to be used where any specific fixed point type is expected.

Dynamic Semantics

5   The elaboration of a real_type_definition consists of the elaboration of the floating_point_definition or the fixed_point_definition.

Implementation Requirements

6   An implementation shall perform the run-time evaluation of a use of a predefined operator of *root_real* with an accuracy at least as great as that of any floating point type definable by a floating_point_definition.

Implementation Permissions

7   For the execution of a predefined operation of a real type, the implementation need not raise Constraint_Error if the result is outside the base range of the type, so long as the correct result is produced, or the Machine_Overflows attribute of the type is false (see G.2).

An implementation may provide *nonstandard real types*, descendants of *root_real* that are declared 8
outside of the specification of package Standard, which need not have all the standard characteristics of a
type defined by a real_type_definition. For example, a nonstandard real type might have an asymmetric or
unsigned base range, or its predefined operations might wrap around or "saturate" rather than overflow
(modular or saturating arithmetic), or it might not conform to the accuracy model (see G.2). Any type
descended from a nonstandard real type is also nonstandard. An implementation may place arbitrary
restrictions on the use of such types; it is implementation defined whether operators that are predefined for
"any real type" are defined for a particular nonstandard real type. In any case, such types are not
permitted as explicit_generic_actual_parameters for formal scalar types — see 12.5.2.

NOTES
32 As stated, real literals are of the anonymous predefined real type *universal_real*. Other real types have no literals.   9
However, the overload resolution rules (see 8.6) allow expressions of the type *universal_real* whenever a real type is
expected.

3.5.7 Floating Point Types

For floating point types, the error bound is specified as a relative precision by giving the required   1
minimum number of significant decimal digits.

Syntax

floating_point_definition ::=   2
  digits *static*_expression [real_range_specification]

real_range_specification ::=   3
  range *static*_simple_expression .. *static*_simple_expression

Name Resolution Rules

The *requested decimal precision*, which is the minimum number of significant decimal digits required for   4
the floating point type, is specified by the value of the expression given after the reserved word **digits**.
This expression is expected to be of any integer type.

Each simple_expression of a real_range_specification is expected to be of any real type; the types need   5
not be the same.

Legality Rules

The requested decimal precision shall be specified by a static expression whose value is positive and no   6
greater than System.Max_Base_Digits. Each simple_expression of a real_range_specification shall also
be static. If the real_range_specification is omitted, the requested decimal precision shall be no greater
than System.Max_Digits.

A floating_point_definition is illegal if the implementation does not support a floating point type that   7
satisfies the requested decimal precision and range.

Static Semantics

The set of values for a floating point type is the (infinite) set of rational numbers. The *machine numbers* of   8
a floating point type are the values of the type that can be represented exactly in every unconstrained
variable of the type. The base range (see 3.5) of a floating point type is symmetric around zero, except that
it can include some extra negative values in some implementations.

9   The *base decimal precision* of a floating point type is the number of decimal digits of precision representable in objects of the type. The *safe range* of a floating point type is that part of its base range for which the accuracy corresponding to the base decimal precision is preserved by all predefined operations.

10 A floating_point_definition defines a floating point type whose base decimal precision is no less than the requested decimal precision. If a real_range_specification is given, the safe range of the floating point type (and hence, also its base range) includes at least the values of the simple expressions given in the real_range_specification. If a real_range_specification is not given, the safe (and base) range of the type includes at least the values of the range $-10.0**(4*D)$ .. $+10.0**(4*D)$ where D is the requested decimal precision. The safe range might include other values as well. The attributes Safe_First and Safe_Last give the actual bounds of the safe range.

11 A floating_point_definition also defines a first subtype of the type. If a real_range_specification is given, then the subtype is constrained to a range whose bounds are given by a conversion of the values of the simple_expressions of the real_range_specification to the type being defined. Otherwise, the subtype is unconstrained.

12 There is a predefined, unconstrained, floating point subtype named Float, declared in the visible part of package Standard.

Dynamic Semantics

13 The elaboration of a floating_point_definition creates the floating point type and its first subtype.

Implementation Requirements

14 In an implementation that supports floating point types with 6 or more digits of precision, the requested decimal precision for Float shall be at least 6.

15 If Long_Float is predefined for an implementation, then its requested decimal precision shall be at least 11.

Implementation Permissions

16 An implementation is allowed to provide additional predefined floating point types, declared in the visible part of Standard, whose (unconstrained) first subtypes have names of the form Short_Float, Long_Float, Short_Short_Float, Long_Long_Float, etc. Different predefined floating point types are allowed to have the same base decimal precision. However, the precision of Float should be no greater than that of Long_Float. Similarly, the precision of Short_Float (if provided) should be no greater than Float. Corresponding recommendations apply to any other predefined floating point types. There need not be a named floating point type corresponding to each distinct base decimal precision supported by an implementation.

Implementation Advice

17 An implementation should support Long_Float in addition to Float if the target machine supports 11 or more digits of precision. No other named floating point subtypes are recommended for package Standard. Instead, appropriate named floating point subtypes should be provided in the library package Interfaces (see B.2).

NOTES
18   33 If a floating point subtype is unconstrained, then assignments to variables of the subtype involve only Overflow_Checks, never Range_Checks.

Examples of floating point types and subtypes: 19

```
type Coefficient is digits 10 range -1.0 .. 1.0;
```
20

```
type Real is digits 8;
type Mass is digits 7 range 0.0 .. 1.0E35;
```
21

```
subtype Probability is Real range 0.0 .. 1.0;    -- a subtype with a smaller range
```
22

3.5.8 Operations of Floating Point Types

Static Semantics

The following attribute is defined for every floating point subtype S: 1

S'Digits   S'Digits denotes the requested decimal precision for the subtype S. The value of this   2/1
attribute is of the type *universal_integer*. The requested decimal precision of the base
subtype of a floating point type *T* is defined to be the largest value of *d* for which
ceiling(d * log(10) / log(T'Machine_Radix)) + g <= T'Model_Mantissa
where g is 0 if Machine_Radix is a positive power of 10 and 1 otherwise.

NOTES
34 The predefined operations of a floating point type include the assignment operation, qualification, the membership   3
tests, and explicit conversion to and from other numeric types. They also include the relational operators and the
following predefined arithmetic operators: the binary and unary adding operators – and +, certain multiplying operators,
the unary operator **abs**, and the exponentiation operator.

35 As for all types, objects of a floating point type have Size and Address attributes (see 13.3). Other attributes of   4
floating point types are defined in A.5.3.

3.5.9 Fixed Point Types

A fixed point type is either an ordinary fixed point type, or a decimal fixed point type. The error bound of   1
a fixed point type is specified as an absolute value, called the *delta* of the fixed point type.

Syntax

fixed_point_definition ::= ordinary_fixed_point_definition | decimal_fixed_point_definition   2

ordinary_fixed_point_definition ::=   3
   delta *static_*expression real_range_specification

decimal_fixed_point_definition ::=   4
   delta *static_*expression **digits** *static_*expression [real_range_specification]

digits_constraint ::=   5
   digits *static_*expression [range_constraint]

Name Resolution Rules

For a type defined by a fixed_point_definition, the *delta* of the type is specified by the value of the   6
expression given after the reserved word **delta**; this expression is expected to be of any real type. For a
type defined by a decimal_fixed_point_definition (a *decimal* fixed point type), the number of significant
decimal digits for its first subtype (the *digits* of the first subtype) is specified by the expression given after
the reserved word **digits**; this expression is expected to be of any integer type.

Legality Rules

In a fixed_point_definition or digits_constraint, the expressions given after the reserved words **delta** and   7
digits shall be static; their values shall be positive.

8 The set of values of a fixed point type comprise the integral multiples of a number called the *small* of the type. For a type defined by an ordinary_fixed_point_definition (an *ordinary* fixed point type), the *small* may be specified by an attribute_definition_clause (see 13.3); if so specified, it shall be no greater than the *delta* of the type. If not specified, the *small* of an ordinary fixed point type is an implementation-defined power of two less than or equal to the *delta*.

9 For a decimal fixed point type, the *small* equals the *delta*; the *delta* shall be a power of 10. If a real_range_specification is given, both bounds of the range shall be in the range $-(10**digits-1)*delta$ .. $+(10**digits-1)*delta$.

10 A fixed_point_definition is illegal if the implementation does not support a fixed point type with the given *small* and specified range or *digits*.

11 For a subtype_indication with a digits_constraint, the subtype_mark shall denote a decimal fixed point subtype.

Static Semantics

12 The base range (see 3.5) of a fixed point type is symmetric around zero, except possibly for an extra negative value in some implementations.

13 An ordinary_fixed_point_definition defines an ordinary fixed point type whose base range includes at least all multiples of *small* that are between the bounds specified in the real_range_specification. The base range of the type does not necessarily include the specified bounds themselves. An ordinary_fixed_point_- definition also defines a constrained first subtype of the type, with each bound of its range given by the closer to zero of:

14 • the value of the conversion to the fixed point type of the corresponding expression of the real_range_specification;

15 • the corresponding bound of the base range.

16 A decimal_fixed_point_definition defines a decimal fixed point type whose base range includes at least the range $-(10**digits-1)*delta$ .. $+(10**digits-1)*delta$. A decimal_fixed_point_definition also defines a constrained first subtype of the type. If a real_range_specification is given, the bounds of the first subtype are given by a conversion of the values of the expressions of the real_range_specification. Otherwise, the range of the first subtype is $-(10**digits-1)*delta$ .. $+(10**digits-1)*delta$.

Dynamic Semantics

17 The elaboration of a fixed_point_definition creates the fixed point type and its first subtype.

18 For a digits_constraint on a decimal fixed point subtype with a given *delta*, if it does not have a range_constraint, then it specifies an implicit range $-(10**D-1)*delta$ .. $+(10**D-1)*delta$, where D is the value of the expression. A digits_constraint is *compatible* with a decimal fixed point subtype if the value of the expression is no greater than the *digits* of the subtype, and if it specifies (explicitly or implicitly) a range that is compatible with the subtype.

19 The elaboration of a digits_constraint consists of the elaboration of the range_constraint, if any. If a range_constraint is given, a check is made that the bounds of the range are both in the range $-(10**D-1)*delta$ .. $+(10**D-1)*delta$, where D is the value of the (static) expression given after the reserved word **digits**. If this check fails, Constraint_Error is raised.

Implementation Requirements

20 The implementation shall support at least 24 bits of precision (including the sign bit) for fixed point types.

Implementation Permissions

Implementations are permitted to support only *small*s that are a power of two. In particular, all decimal fixed point type declarations can be disallowed. Note however that conformance with the Information Systems Annex requires support for decimal *small*s, and decimal fixed point type declarations with *digits* up to at least 18.

NOTES
36 The base range of an ordinary fixed point type need not include the specified bounds themselves so that the range specification can be given in a natural way, such as:

```
type Fraction is delta 2.0**(-15) range -1.0 .. 1.0;
```

With 2's complement hardware, such a type could have a signed 16-bit representation, using 1 bit for the sign and 15 bits for fraction, resulting in a base range of $-1.0 .. 1.0-2.0**(-15)$.

Examples

Examples of fixed point types and subtypes:

```
type Volt is delta 0.125 range 0.0 .. 255.0;
   -- A pure fraction which requires all the available
   -- space in a word can be declared as the type Fraction:
type Fraction is delta System.Fine_Delta range -1.0 .. 1.0;
   -- Fraction'Last = 1.0 - System.Fine_Delta

type Money is delta 0.01 digits 15;   -- decimal fixed point
subtype Salary is Money digits 10;
   -- Money'Last = 10.0**13 - 0.01, Salary'Last = 10.0**8 - 0.01
```

3.5.10 Operations of Fixed Point Types

Static Semantics

The following attributes are defined for every fixed point subtype S:

S'Small   S'Small denotes the *small* of the type of S. The value of this attribute is of the type *universal_real*. Small may be specified for nonderived ordinary fixed point types via an attribute_definition_clause (see 13.3); the expression of such a clause shall be static.

S'Delta   S'Delta denotes the *delta* of the fixed point subtype S. The value of this attribute is of the type *universal_real*.

S'Fore   S'Fore yields the minimum number of characters needed before the decimal point for the decimal representation of any value of the subtype S, assuming that the representation does not include an exponent, but includes a one-character prefix that is either a minus sign or a space. (This minimum number does not include superfluous zeros or underlines, and is at least 2.) The value of this attribute is of the type *universal_integer*.

S'Aft   S'Aft yields the number of decimal digits needed after the decimal point to accommodate the *delta* of the subtype S, unless the *delta* of the subtype S is greater than 0.1, in which case the attribute yields the value one. (S'Aft is the smallest positive integer N for which $(10**N)*S'Delta$ is greater than or equal to one.) The value of this attribute is of the type *universal_integer*.

The following additional attributes are defined for every decimal fixed point subtype S:

S'Digits   S'Digits denotes the *digits* of the decimal fixed point subtype S, which corresponds to the number of decimal digits that are representable in objects of the subtype. The value of this attribute is of the type *universal_integer*. Its value is determined as follows:

8   • For a first subtype or a subtype defined by a subtype_indication with a digits_constraint, the digits is the value of the expression given after the reserved word **digits**;

9   • For a subtype defined by a subtype_indication without a digits_constraint, the digits of the subtype is the same as that of the subtype denoted by the subtype_mark in the subtype_indication.

10   • The digits of a base subtype is the largest integer D such that the range $-(10**D-1)*delta$ .. $+(10**D-1)*delta$ is included in the base range of the type.

11   S'Scale   S'Scale denotes the *scale* of the subtype S, defined as the value N such that S'Delta = $10.0**(-N)$. The scale indicates the position of the point relative to the rightmost significant digits of values of subtype S. The value of this attribute is of the type *universal_integer*.

12   S'Round   S'Round denotes a function with the following specification:

13
```
function S'Round(X : universal_real)
    return S'Base
```

14   The function returns the value obtained by rounding X (away from 0, if X is midway between two values of the type of S).

NOTES

15   37 All subtypes of a fixed point type will have the same value for the Delta attribute, in the absence of delta_constraints (see J.3).

16   38 S'Scale is not always the same as S'Aft for a decimal subtype; for example, if S'Delta = 1.0 then S'Aft is 1 while S'Scale is 0.

17   39 The predefined operations of a fixed point type include the assignment operation, qualification, the membership tests, and explicit conversion to and from other numeric types. They also include the relational operators and the following predefined arithmetic operators: the binary and unary adding operators – and +, multiplying operators, and the unary operator **abs**.

18   40 As for all types, objects of a fixed point type have Size and Address attributes (see 13.3). Other attributes of fixed point types are defined in A.5.4.

3.6 Array Types

1   An *array* object is a composite object consisting of components which all have the same subtype. The name for a component of an array uses one or more index values belonging to specified discrete types. The value of an array object is a composite value consisting of the values of the components.

Syntax

2   array_type_definition ::=
     unconstrained_array_definition | constrained_array_definition

3   unconstrained_array_definition ::=
     array(index_subtype_definition {, index_subtype_definition}) **of** component_definition

4   index_subtype_definition ::= subtype_mark **range** <>

5   constrained_array_definition ::=
     array (discrete_subtype_definition {, discrete_subtype_definition}) **of** component_definition

6   discrete_subtype_definition ::= *discrete_*subtype_indication | range

7   component_definition ::= [**aliased**] subtype_indication

Name Resolution Rules

For a discrete_subtype_definition that is a range, the range shall resolve to be of some specific discrete   8
type; which discrete type shall be determined without using any context other than the bounds of the range
itself (plus the preference for *root_integer* — see 8.6).

Legality Rules

Each index_subtype_definition or discrete_subtype_definition in an array_type_definition defines an   9
index subtype; its type (the *index type*) shall be discrete.

The subtype defined by the subtype_indication of a component_definition (the *component subtype*) shall   10
be a definite subtype.

Within the definition of a nonlimited composite type (or a limited composite type that later in its   11
immediate scope becomes nonlimited — see 7.3.1 and 7.5), if a component_definition contains the
reserved word **aliased** and the type of the component is discriminated, then the nominal subtype of the
component shall be constrained.

Static Semantics

An array is characterized by the number of indices (the *dimensionality* of the array), the type and position   12
of each index, the lower and upper bounds for each index, and the subtype of the components. The order of
the indices is significant.

A one-dimensional array has a distinct component for each possible index value. A multidimensional array   13
has a distinct component for each possible sequence of index values that can be formed by selecting one
value for each index position (in the given order). The possible values for a given index are all the values
between the lower and upper bounds, inclusive; this range of values is called the *index range*. The *bounds*
of an array are the bounds of its index ranges. The *length* of a dimension of an array is the number of
values of the index range of the dimension (zero for a null range). The *length* of a one-dimensional array is
the length of its only dimension.

An array_type_definition defines an array type and its first subtype. For each object of this array type, the   14
number of indices, the type and position of each index, and the subtype of the components are as in the
type definition; the values of the lower and upper bounds for each index belong to the corresponding index
subtype of its type, except for null arrays (see 3.6.1).

An unconstrained_array_definition defines an array type with an unconstrained first subtype. Each   15
index_subtype_definition defines the corresponding index subtype to be the subtype denoted by the
subtype_mark. The compound delimiter <> (called a *box*) of an index_subtype_definition stands for an
undefined range (different objects of the type need not have the same bounds).

A constrained_array_definition defines an array type with a constrained first subtype. Each discrete_-   16
subtype_definition defines the corresponding index subtype, as well as the corresponding index range for
the constrained first subtype. The *constraint* of the first subtype consists of the bounds of the index ranges.

The discrete subtype defined by a discrete_subtype_definition is either that defined by the subtype_-   17
indication, or a subtype determined by the range as follows:

- If the type of the range resolves to *root_integer*, then the discrete_subtype_definition defines a   18
  subtype of the predefined type Integer with bounds given by a conversion to Integer of the
  bounds of the range;

- Otherwise, the discrete_subtype_definition defines a subtype of the type of the range, with the   19
  bounds given by the range.

20   The component_definition of an array_type_definition defines the nominal subtype of the components. If the reserved word **aliased** appears in the component_definition, then each component of the array is aliased (see 3.10).

Dynamic Semantics

21   The elaboration of an array_type_definition creates the array type and its first subtype, and consists of the elaboration of any discrete_subtype_definitions and the component_definition.

22/1   The elaboration of a discrete_subtype_definition that does not contain any per-object expressions creates the discrete subtype, and consists of the elaboration of the subtype_indication or the evaluation of the range. The elaboration of a discrete_subtype_definition that contains one or more per-object expressions is defined in 3.8. The elaboration of a component_definition in an array_type_definition consists of the elaboration of the subtype_indication. The elaboration of any discrete_subtype_definitions and the elaboration of the component_definition are performed in an arbitrary order.

NOTES

23   41 All components of an array have the same subtype. In particular, for an array of components that are one-dimensional arrays, this means that all components have the same bounds and hence the same length.

24   42 Each elaboration of an array_type_definition creates a distinct array type. A consequence of this is that each object whose object_declaration contains an array_type_definition is of its own unique type.

Examples

25   *Examples of type declarations with unconstrained array definitions:*

26
```
type Vector     is array(Integer  range <>) of Real;
type Matrix     is array(Integer  range <>, Integer range <>) of Real;
type Bit_Vector is array(Integer  range <>) of Boolean;
type Roman      is array(Positive range <>) of Roman_Digit;  -- see 3.5.2
```

27   *Examples of type declarations with constrained array definitions:*

28
```
type Table    is array(1 .. 10) of Integer;
type Schedule is array(Day) of Boolean;
type Line     is array(1 .. Max_Line_Size) of Character;
```

29   *Examples of object declarations with array type definitions:*

30
```
Grid : array(1 .. 80, 1 .. 100) of Boolean;
Mix  : array(Color range Red .. Green) of Boolean;
Page : array(Positive range <>) of Line :=  -- an array of arrays
  (1 | 50  => Line'(1 | Line'Last => '+', others => '-'),  -- see 4.3.3
   2 .. 49 => Line'(1 | Line'Last => '|', others => ' '));
  -- Page is constrained by its initial value to (1..50)
```

3.6.1 Index Constraints and Discrete Ranges

1   An index_constraint determines the range of possible values for every index of an array subtype, and thereby the corresponding array bounds.

Syntax

2   index_constraint ::= (discrete_range {, discrete_range})

3   discrete_range ::= *discrete*_subtype_indication | range

The type of a discrete_range is the type of the subtype defined by the subtype_indication, or the type of   4
the range. For an index_constraint, each discrete_range shall resolve to be of the type of the
corresponding index.

An index_constraint shall appear only in a subtype_indication whose subtype_mark denotes either an   5
unconstrained array subtype, or an unconstrained access subtype whose designated subtype is an
unconstrained array subtype; in either case, the index_constraint shall provide a discrete_range for each
index of the array type.

A discrete_range defines a range whose bounds are given by the range, or by the range of the subtype   6
defined by the subtype_indication.

An index_constraint is *compatible* with an unconstrained array subtype if and only if the index range   7
defined by each discrete_range is compatible (see 3.5) with the corresponding index subtype. If any of the
discrete_ranges defines a null range, any array thus constrained is a *null array*, having no components. An
array value *satisfies* an index_constraint if at each index position the array value and the index_constraint
have the same index bounds.

The elaboration of an index_constraint consists of the evaluation of the discrete_range(s), in an arbitrary   8
order. The evaluation of a discrete_range consists of the elaboration of the subtype_indication or the
evaluation of the range.

NOTES
43 The elaboration of a subtype_indication consisting of a subtype_mark followed by an index_constraint checks the   9
compatibility of the index_constraint with the subtype_mark (see 3.2.2).

44 Even if an array value does not satisfy the index constraint of an array subtype, Constraint_Error is not raised on   10
conversion to the array subtype, so long as the length of each dimension of the array value and the array subtype match.
See 4.6.

Examples of array declarations including an index constraint: 11

```
Board     : Matrix(1 .. 8,  1 .. 8);   -- see 3.6            12
Rectangle : Matrix(1 .. 20, 1 .. 30);
Inverse   : Matrix(1 .. N,  1 .. N);   -- N need not be static

Filter    : Bit_Vector(0 .. 31);                            13
```

Example of array declaration with a constrained array subtype: 14

```
My_Schedule : Schedule;   -- all arrays of type Schedule have the same bounds     15
```

Example of record type with a component that is an array: 16

```
type Var_Line(Length : Natural) is                          17
   record
      Image : String(1 .. Length);
   end record;
Null_Line : Var_Line(0);   -- Null_Line.Image is a null array                     18
```

3.6.2 Operations of Array Types

Legality Rules

1   The argument N used in the attribute_designators for the N-th dimension of an array shall be a static expression of some integer type. The value of N shall be positive (nonzero) and no greater than the dimensionality of the array.

Static Semantics

2/1   The following attributes are defined for a prefix A that is of an array type (after any implicit dereference), or denotes a constrained array subtype:

3   A'First   A'First denotes the lower bound of the first index range; its type is the corresponding index type.

4   A'First(N)   A'First(N) denotes the lower bound of the N-th index range; its type is the corresponding index type.

5   A'Last   A'Last denotes the upper bound of the first index range; its type is the corresponding index type.

6   A'Last(N)   A'Last(N) denotes the upper bound of the N-th index range; its type is the corresponding index type.

7   A'Range   A'Range is equivalent to the range A'First .. A'Last, except that the prefix A is only evaluated once.

8   A'Range(N)   A'Range(N) is equivalent to the range A'First(N) .. A'Last(N), except that the prefix A is only evaluated once.

9   A'Length   A'Length denotes the number of values of the first index range (zero for a null range); its type is *universal_integer*.

10   A'Length(N)   A'Length(N) denotes the number of values of the N-th index range (zero for a null range); its type is *universal_integer*.

Implementation Advice

11   An implementation should normally represent multidimensional arrays in row-major order, consistent with the notation used for multidimensional array aggregates (see 4.3.3). However, if a **pragma** Convention(Fortran, ...) applies to a multidimensional array type, then column-major order should be used instead (see B.5, "Interfacing with Fortran").

NOTES

12   45 The attribute_references A'First and A'First(1) denote the same value. A similar relation exists for the attribute_references A'Last, A'Range, and A'Length. The following relation is satisfied (except for a null array) by the above attributes if the index type is an integer type:

13
```
A'Length(N) = A'Last(N) - A'First(N) + 1
```

14   46 An array type is limited if its component type is limited (see 7.5).

15   47 The predefined operations of an array type include the membership tests, qualification, and explicit conversion. If the array type is not limited, they also include assignment and the predefined equality operators. For a one-dimensional array type, they include the predefined concatenation operators (if nonlimited) and, if the component type is discrete, the predefined relational operators; if the component type is boolean, the predefined logical operators are also included.

16   48 A component of an array can be named with an indexed_component. A value of an array type can be specified with an array_aggregate, unless the array type is limited. For a one-dimensional array type, a slice of the array can be named; also, string literals are defined if the component type is a character type.

Examples (using arrays declared in the examples of subclause 3.6.1):   17

```
--  Filter'First      =   0   Filter'Last      =  31   Filter'Length =  32     18
--  Rectangle'Last(1) =  20   Rectangle'Last(2) =  30
```

3.6.3 String Types

A one-dimensional array type whose component type is a character type is called a *string* type.   1

There are two predefined string types, String and Wide_String, each indexed by values of the predefined   2
subtype Positive; these are declared in the visible part of package Standard:

```
subtype Positive is Integer range 1 .. Integer'Last;                  3

type String is array(Positive range <>) of Character;                 4
type Wide_String is array(Positive range <>) of Wide_Character;
```

NOTES
49 String literals (see 2.6 and 4.2) are defined for all string types. The concatenation operator & is predefined for string   5
types, as for all nonlimited one-dimensional array types. The ordering operators <, <=, >, and >= are predefined for
string types, as for all one-dimensional discrete array types; these ordering operators correspond to lexicographic order
(see 4.5.2).

Examples of string objects: 6

```
Stars      : String(1 .. 120) := (1 .. 120 => '*' );                          7
Question   : constant String  := "How many characters?";
                                 -- Question'First = 1, Question'Last = 20
                                 -- Question'Length = 20 (the number of characters)

Ask_Twice  : String  := Question & Question;       -- constrained to (1..40)    8
Ninety_Six : constant Roman  := "XCVI";  -- see 3.5.2 and 3.6
```

3.7 Discriminants

A composite type (other than an array type) can have discriminants, which parameterize the type. A   1
known_discriminant_part specifies the discriminants of a composite type. A discriminant of an object is a
component of the object, and is either of a discrete type or an access type. An unknown_discriminant_part
in the declaration of a partial view of a type specifies that the discriminants of the type are unknown for the
given view; all subtypes of such a partial view are indefinite subtypes.

discriminant_part ::= unknown_discriminant_part | known_discriminant_part   2

unknown_discriminant_part ::= (<>)   3

known_discriminant_part ::=   4
    (discriminant_specification {; discriminant_specification})

discriminant_specification ::=   5
    defining_identifier_list : subtype_mark [:= default_expression]
    | defining_identifier_list : access_definition [:= default_expression]

default_expression ::= expression   6

7   The expected type for the default_expression of a discriminant_specification is that of the corresponding discriminant.

8/1   A discriminant_part is only permitted in a declaration for a composite type that is not an array type (this includes generic formal types). A type declared with a known_discriminant_part is called a *discriminated* type, as is a type that inherits (known) discriminants.

9   The subtype of a discriminant may be defined by a subtype_mark, in which case the subtype_mark shall denote a discrete or access subtype, or it may be defined by an access_definition (in which case the subtype_mark of the access_definition may denote any kind of subtype). A discriminant that is defined by an access_definition is called an *access discriminant* and is of an anonymous general access-to-variable type whose designated subtype is denoted by the subtype_mark of the access_definition.

10   A discriminant_specification for an access discriminant shall appear only in the declaration for a task or protected type, or for a type with the reserved word **limited** in its (full) definition or in that of one of its ancestors. In addition to the places where Legality Rules normally apply (see 12.3), this rule applies also in the private part of an instance of a generic unit.

11   Default_expressions shall be provided either for all or for none of the discriminants of a known_- discriminant_part. No default_expressions are permitted in a known_discriminant_part in a declaration of a tagged type or a generic formal type.

12   For a type defined by a derived_type_definition, if a known_discriminant_part is provided in its declaration, then:

13   • The parent subtype shall be constrained;

14   • If the parent type is not a tagged type, then each discriminant of the derived type shall be used in the constraint defining the parent subtype;

15   • If a discriminant is used in the constraint defining the parent subtype, the subtype of the discriminant shall be statically compatible (see 4.9.1) with the subtype of the corresponding parent discriminant.

16   The type of the default_expression, if any, for an access discriminant shall be convertible to the anonymous access type of the discriminant (see 4.6).

17   A discriminant_specification declares a discriminant; the subtype_mark denotes its subtype unless it is an access discriminant, in which case the discriminant's subtype is the anonymous access-to-variable subtype defined by the access_definition.

18   For a type defined by a derived_type_definition, each discriminant of the parent type is either inherited, constrained to equal some new discriminant of the derived type, or constrained to the value of an expression. When inherited or constrained to equal some new discriminant, the parent discriminant and the discriminant of the derived type are said to *correspond*. Two discriminants also correspond if there is some common discriminant to which they both correspond. A discriminant corresponds to itself as well. If a discriminant of a parent type is constrained to a specific value by a derived_type_definition, then that discriminant is said to be *specified* by that derived_type_definition.

A constraint that appears within the definition of a discriminated type *depends on a discriminant* of the type if it names the discriminant as a bound or discriminant value. A component_definition depends on a discriminant if its constraint depends on the discriminant, or on a discriminant that corresponds to it. 19

A component *depends on a discriminant* if: 20

- Its component_definition depends on the discriminant; or 21

- It is declared in a variant_part that is governed by the discriminant; or 22

- It is a component inherited as part of a derived_type_definition, and the constraint of the parent_subtype_indication depends on the discriminant; or 23

- It is a subcomponent of a component that depends on the discriminant. 24

Each value of a discriminated type includes a value for each component of the type that does not depend on a discriminant; this includes the discriminants themselves. The values of discriminants determine which other component values are present in the value of the discriminated type. 25

A type declared with a known_discriminant_part is said to have *known discriminants*; its first subtype is unconstrained. A type declared with an unknown_discriminant_part is said to have *unknown discriminants*. A type declared without a discriminant_part has no discriminants, unless it is a derived type; if derived, such a type has the same sort of discriminants (known, unknown, or none) as its parent (or ancestor) type. A tagged class-wide type also has unknown discriminants. Any subtype of a type with unknown discriminants is an unconstrained and indefinite subtype (see 3.2 and 3.3). 26

Dynamic Semantics

An access_definition is elaborated when the value of a corresponding access discriminant is defined, either by evaluation of its default_expression or by elaboration of a discriminant_constraint. The elaboration of an access_definition creates the anonymous access type. When the expression defining the access discriminant is evaluated, it is converted to this anonymous access type (see 4.6). 27

NOTES

50 If a discriminated type has default_expressions for its discriminants, then unconstrained variables of the type are permitted, and the values of the discriminants can be changed by an assignment to such a variable. If defaults are not provided for the discriminants, then all variables of the type are constrained, either by explicit constraint or by their initial value; the values of the discriminants of such a variable cannot be changed after initialization. 28

51 The default_expression for a discriminant of a type is evaluated when an object of an unconstrained subtype of the type is created. 29

52 Assignment to a discriminant of an object (after its initialization) is not allowed, since the name of a discriminant is a constant; neither assignment_statements nor assignments inherent in passing as an **in out** or **out** parameter are allowed. Note however that the value of a discriminant can be changed by assigning to the enclosing object, presuming it is an unconstrained variable. 30

53 A discriminant that is of a named access type is not called an access discriminant; that term is used only for discriminants defined by an access_definition. 31

Examples

Examples of discriminated types: 32

```
type Buffer(Size : Buffer_Size := 100)  is      -- see 3.5.4
   record
      Pos   : Buffer_Size := 0;
      Value : String(1 .. Size);
   end record;
```
33

34
```
type Matrix_Rec(Rows, Columns : Integer) is
   record
      Mat : Matrix(1 .. Rows, 1 .. Columns);        -- see 3.6
   end record;
```

35
```
type Square(Side : Integer) is new
   Matrix_Rec(Rows => Side, Columns => Side);
```

36
```
type Double_Square(Number : Integer) is
   record
      Left  : Square(Number);
      Right : Square(Number);
   end record;
```

37
```
type Item(Number : Positive) is
   record
      Content : Integer;
      -- no component depends on the discriminant
   end record;
```

3.7.1 Discriminant Constraints

1   A discriminant_constraint specifies the values of the discriminants for a given discriminated type.

Syntax

2   discriminant_constraint ::=
      (discriminant_association {, discriminant_association})

3   discriminant_association ::=
      [*discriminant*_selector_name {| *discriminant*_selector_name} =>] expression

4   A discriminant_association is said to be *named* if it has one or more *discriminant*_selector_names;
it is otherwise said to be *positional*. In a discriminant_constraint, any positional associations shall
precede any named associations.

Name Resolution Rules

5   Each selector_name of a named discriminant_association shall resolve to denote a discriminant of the
subtype being constrained; the discriminants so named are the *associated discriminants* of the named
association. For a positional association, the *associated discriminant* is the one whose discriminant_-
specification occurred in the corresponding position in the known_discriminant_part that defined the
discriminants of the subtype being constrained.

6   The expected type for the expression in a discriminant_association is that of the associated
discriminant(s).

Legality Rules

7/1   A discriminant_constraint is only allowed in a subtype_indication whose subtype_mark denotes either an
unconstrained discriminated subtype, or an unconstrained access subtype whose designated subtype is an
unconstrained discriminated subtype. However, in the case of a general access subtype, a discriminant_-
constraint is illegal if there is a place within the immediate scope of the designated subtype where the
designated subtype's view is constrained.

8   A named discriminant_association with more than one selector_name is allowed only if the named
discriminants are all of the same type. A discriminant_constraint shall provide exactly one value for each
discriminant of the subtype being constrained.

9   The expression associated with an access discriminant shall be of a type convertible to the anonymous
access type.

Dynamic Semantics

A discriminant_constraint is *compatible* with an unconstrained discriminated subtype if each discriminant value belongs to the subtype of the corresponding discriminant. 10

A composite value *satisfies* a discriminant constraint if and only if each discriminant of the composite value has the value imposed by the discriminant constraint. 11

For the elaboration of a discriminant_constraint, the expressions in the discriminant_associations are evaluated in an arbitrary order and converted to the type of the associated discriminant (which might raise Constraint_Error — see 4.6); the expression of a named association is evaluated (and converted) once for each associated discriminant. The result of each evaluation and conversion is the value imposed by the constraint for the associated discriminant. 12

NOTES
54 The rules of the language ensure that a discriminant of an object always has a value, either from explicit or implicit initialization. 13

Examples

Examples (using types declared above in clause 3.7): 14

```
Large    : Buffer(200);    -- constrained, always 200 characters    15
                           --  (explicit discriminant value)
Message  : Buffer;         -- unconstrained, initially 100 characters
                           --  (default discriminant value)
Basis    : Square(5);      -- constrained, always 5 by 5
Illegal  : Square;         -- illegal, a Square has to be constrained
```

3.7.2 Operations of Discriminated Types

If a discriminated type has default_expressions for its discriminants, then unconstrained variables of the type are permitted, and the discriminants of such a variable can be changed by assignment to the variable. For a formal parameter of such a type, an attribute is provided to determine whether the corresponding actual parameter is constrained or unconstrained. 1

Static Semantics

For a prefix A that is of a discriminated type (after any implicit dereference), the following attribute is defined: 2

A'Constrained 3
> Yields the value True if A denotes a constant, a value, or a constrained variable, and False otherwise.

Erroneous Execution

The execution of a construct is erroneous if the construct has a constituent that is a name denoting a subcomponent that depends on discriminants, and the value of any of these discriminants is changed by this execution between evaluating the name and the last use (within this execution) of the subcomponent denoted by the name. 4

3.8 Record Types

A record object is a composite object consisting of named components. The value of a record object is a composite value consisting of the values of the components. 1

Syntax

2   record_type_definition ::= [[**abstract**] **tagged**] [**limited**] record_definition

3   record_definition ::=
      record
       component_list
      end record
      | **null record**

4   component_list ::=
      component_item {component_item}
      | {component_item} variant_part
      | **null**;

5/1   component_item ::= component_declaration | aspect_clause

6   component_declaration ::=
      defining_identifier_list : component_definition [:= default_expression];

Name Resolution Rules

7   The expected type for the default_expression, if any, in a component_declaration is the type of the component.

Legality Rules

8   A default_expression is not permitted if the component is of a limited type.

9   Each component_declaration declares a *component* of the record type. Besides components declared by component_declarations, the components of a record type include any components declared by discriminant_specifications of the record type declaration. The identifiers of all components of a record type shall be distinct.

10   Within a type_declaration, a name that denotes a component, protected subprogram, or entry of the type is allowed only in the following cases:

11   • A name that denotes any component, protected subprogram, or entry is allowed within a representation item that occurs within the declaration of the composite type.

12   • A name that denotes a noninherited discriminant is allowed within the declaration of the type, but not within the discriminant_part. If the discriminant is used to define the constraint of a component, the bounds of an entry family, or the constraint of the parent subtype in a derived_type_definition then its name shall appear alone as a direct_name (not as part of a larger expression or expanded name). A discriminant shall not be used to define the constraint of a scalar component.

13   If the name of the current instance of a type (see 8.6) is used to define the constraint of a component, then it shall appear as a direct_name that is the prefix of an attribute_reference whose result is of an access type, and the attribute_reference shall appear alone.

Static Semantics

14   The component_definition of a component_declaration defines the (nominal) subtype of the component. If the reserved word **aliased** appears in the component_definition, then the component is aliased (see 3.10).

15   If the component_list of a record type is defined by the reserved word **null** and there are no discriminants, then the record type has no components and all records of the type are *null records*. A record_definition of **null record** is equivalent to **record null; end record**.

The elaboration of a record_type_definition creates the record type and its first subtype, and consists of the   16
elaboration of the record_definition. The elaboration of a record_definition consists of the elaboration of
its component_list, if any.

The elaboration of a component_list consists of the elaboration of the component_items and variant_part,   17
if any, in the order in which they appear. The elaboration of a component_declaration consists of the
elaboration of the component_definition.

Within the definition of a composite type, if a component_definition or discrete_subtype_definition (see   18/1
9.5.2) includes a name that denotes a discriminant of the type, or that is an attribute_reference whose
prefix denotes the current instance of the type, the expression containing the name is called a *per-object
expression*, and the constraint or range being defined is called a *per-object constraint*. For the elaboration
of a component_definition of a component_declaration or the discrete_subtype_definition of an entry_-
declaration for an entry family (see 9.5.2), if the constraint or range of the subtype_indication or
discrete_subtype_definition is not a per-object constraint, then the subtype_indication or discrete_-
subtype_definition is elaborated. On the other hand, if the constraint or range is a per-object constraint,
then the elaboration consists of the evaluation of any included expression that is not part of a per-object
expression. Each such expression is evaluated once unless it is part of a named association in a
discriminant constraint, in which case it is evaluated once for each associated discriminant.

When a per-object constraint is elaborated (as part of creating an object), each per-object expression of the   18.1/1
constraint is evaluated. For other expressions, the values determined during the elaboration of the
component_definition or entry_declaration are used. Any checks associated with the enclosing
subtype_indication or discrete_subtype_definition are performed, including the subtype compatibility
check (see 3.2.2), and the associated subtype is created.

NOTES
55 A component_declaration with several identifiers is equivalent to a sequence of single component_declarations, as   19
explained in 3.3.1.

56 The default_expression of a record component is only evaluated upon the creation of a default-initialized object of   20
the record type (presuming the object has the component, if it is in a variant_part — see 3.3.1).

57 The subtype defined by a component_definition (see 3.6) has to be a definite subtype.   21

58 If a record type does not have a variant_part, then the same components are present in all values of the type.   22

59 A record type is limited if it has the reserved word **limited** in its definition, or if any of its components are limited   23
(see 7.5).

60 The predefined operations of a record type include membership tests, qualification, and explicit conversion. If the   24
record type is nonlimited, they also include assignment and the predefined equality operators.

61 A component of a record can be named with a selected_component. A value of a record can be specified with a   25
record_aggregate, unless the record type is limited.

Examples

Examples of record type declarations: 26

```
type Date is
   record
      Day    : Integer range 1 .. 31;
      Month  : Month_Name;
      Year   : Integer range 0 .. 4000;
   end record;
```
    27

28
```
type Complex is
   record
       Re : Real := 0.0;
       Im : Real := 0.0;
   end record;
```

29   *Examples of record variables:*

30
```
Tomorrow, Yesterday : Date;
A, B, C : Complex;
```

31   *-- both components of A, B, and C are implicitly initialized to zero*

3.8.1 Variant Parts and Discrete Choices

1   A record type with a variant_part specifies alternative lists of components. Each variant defines the components for the value or values of the discriminant covered by its discrete_choice_list.

2   variant_part ::=
   case *discriminant*_direct_name **is**
      variant
      {variant}
   end case;

3   variant ::=
   when discrete_choice_list =>
      component_list

4   discrete_choice_list ::= discrete_choice {| discrete_choice}

5   discrete_choice ::= expression | discrete_range | **others**

6   The *discriminant*_direct_name shall resolve to denote a discriminant (called the *discriminant of the* variant_part) specified in the known_discriminant_part of the full_type_declaration that contains the variant_part. The expected type for each discrete_choice in a variant is the type of the discriminant of the variant_part.

7   The discriminant of the variant_part shall be of a discrete type.

8   The expressions and discrete_ranges given as discrete_choices in a variant_part shall be static. The discrete_choice **others** shall appear alone in a discrete_choice_list, and such a discrete_choice_list, if it appears, shall be the last one in the enclosing construct.

9   A discrete_choice is defined to *cover a value* in the following cases:

10   • A discrete_choice that is an expression covers a value if the value equals the value of the expression converted to the expected type.

11   • A discrete_choice that is a discrete_range covers all values (possibly none) that belong to the range.

12   • The discrete_choice **others** covers all values of its expected type that are not covered by previous discrete_choice_lists of the same construct.

13   A discrete_choice_list covers a value if one of its discrete_choices covers the value.

The possible values of the discriminant of a variant_part shall be covered as follows: 14

- If the discriminant is of a static constrained scalar subtype, then each non-**others** discrete_-   15
  choice shall cover only values in that subtype, and each value of that subtype shall be covered by
  some discrete_choice (either explicitly or by **others**);

- If the type of the discriminant is a descendant of a generic formal scalar type then the   16
  variant_part shall have an **others** discrete_choice;

- Otherwise, each value of the base range of the type of the discriminant shall be covered (either   17
  explicitly or by **others**).

Two distinct discrete_choices of a variant_part shall not cover the same value.   18

Static Semantics

If the component_list of a variant is specified by **null**, the variant has no components.   19

The discriminant of a variant_part is said to *govern* the variant_part and its variants. In addition, the   20
discriminant of a derived type governs a variant_part and its variants if it corresponds (see 3.7) to the
discriminant of the variant_part.

Dynamic Semantics

A record value contains the values of the components of a particular variant only if the value of the   21
discriminant governing the variant is covered by the discrete_choice_list of the variant. This rule applies
in turn to any further variant that is, itself, included in the component_list of the given variant.

The elaboration of a variant_part consists of the elaboration of the component_list of each variant in the   22
order in which they appear.

Examples

Example of record type with a variant part: 23

```
type Device is (Printer, Disk, Drum);                                                                  24
type State  is (Open, Closed);
type Peripheral(Unit : Device := Disk) is                                                              25
   record
       Status : State;
       case Unit is
          when Printer =>
              Line_Count : Integer range 1 .. Page_Size;
          when others =>
              Cylinder   : Cylinder_Index;
              Track      : Track_Number;
          end case;
   end record;
```

Examples of record subtypes: 26

```
subtype Drum_Unit is Peripheral(Drum);                                                                 27
subtype Disk_Unit is Peripheral(Disk);
```

Examples of constrained record variables: 28

```
Writer  : Peripheral(Unit => Printer);                                                                  29
Archive : Disk_Unit;
```

3.9 Tagged Types and Type Extensions

1 Tagged types and type extensions support object-oriented programming, based on inheritance with extension and run-time polymorphism via *dispatching operations*.

Static Semantics

2 A record type or private type that has the reserved word **tagged** in its declaration is called a *tagged* type. When deriving from a tagged type, additional components may be defined. As for any derived type, additional primitive subprograms may be defined, and inherited primitive subprograms may be overridden. The derived type is called an *extension* of the ancestor type, or simply a *type extension*. Every type extension is also a tagged type, and is either a *record extension* or a *private extension* of some other tagged type. A record extension is defined by a derived_type_definition with a record_extension_part. A private extension, which is a partial view of a record extension, can be declared in the visible part of a package (see 7.3) or in a generic formal part (see 12.5.1).

3 An object of a tagged type has an associated (run-time) *tag* that identifies the specific tagged type used to create the object originally. The tag of an operand of a class-wide tagged type *T*'Class controls which subprogram body is to be executed when a primitive subprogram of type *T* is applied to the operand (see 3.9.2); using a tag to control which body to execute is called *dispatching*.

4 The tag of a specific tagged type identifies the full_type_declaration of the type. If a declaration for a tagged type occurs within a generic_package_declaration, then the corresponding type declarations in distinct instances of the generic package are associated with distinct tags. For a tagged type that is local to a generic package body, the language does not specify whether repeated instantiations of the generic body result in distinct tags.

5 The following language-defined library package exists:

6
```
package Ada.Tags is
    type Tag is private;
```

7
```
    function Expanded_Name(T : Tag) return String;
    function External_Tag(T : Tag) return String;
    function Internal_Tag(External : String) return Tag;
```

8
```
    Tag_Error : exception;
```

9
```
private
    ... -- not specified by the language
end Ada.Tags;
```

10 The function Expanded_Name returns the full expanded name of the first subtype of the specific type identified by the tag, in upper case, starting with a root library unit. The result is implementation defined if the type is declared within an unnamed block_statement.

11 The function External_Tag returns a string to be used in an external representation for the given tag. The call External_Tag(S'Tag) is equivalent to the attribute_reference S'External_Tag (see 13.3).

12 The function Internal_Tag returns the tag that corresponds to the given external tag, or raises Tag_Error if the given string is not the external tag for any specific type of the partition.

13 For every subtype S of a tagged type *T* (specific or class-wide), the following attributes are defined:

14 S'Class   S'Class denotes a subtype of the class-wide type (called *T*'Class in this International Standard) for the class rooted at *T* (or if S already denotes a class-wide subtype, then S'Class is the same as S).

S'Class is unconstrained. However, if S is constrained, then the values of S'Class are only 15
those that when converted to the type *T* belong to S.

S'Tag   S'Tag denotes the tag of the type *T* (or if *T* is class-wide, the tag of the root type of the 16
corresponding class). The value of this attribute is of type Tag.

Given a prefix X that is of a class-wide tagged type (after any implicit dereference), the following attribute 17
is defined:

X'Tag   X'Tag denotes the tag of X. The value of this attribute is of type Tag. 18

Dynamic Semantics

The tag associated with an object of a tagged type is determined as follows: 19

- The tag of a stand-alone object, a component, or an **aggregate** of a specific tagged type *T* 20
  identifies *T*.

- The tag of an object created by an allocator for an access type with a specific designated tagged 21
  type *T*, identifies *T*.

- The tag of an object of a class-wide tagged type is that of its initialization expression. 22

- The tag of the result returned by a function whose result type is a specific tagged type *T* 23
  identifies *T*.

- The tag of the result returned by a function with a class-wide result type is that of the return 24
  expression.

The tag is preserved by type conversion and by parameter passing. The tag of a value is the tag of the 25
associated object (see 6.2).

Implementation Permissions

The implementation of the functions in Ada.Tags may raise Tag_Error if no specific type corresponding to 26
the tag passed as a parameter exists in the partition at the time the function is called.

NOTES
62 A type declared with the reserved word **tagged** should normally be declared in a package_specification, so that new 27
primitive subprograms can be declared for it.

63 Once an object has been created, its tag never changes. 28

64 Class-wide types are defined to have unknown discriminants (see 3.7). This means that objects of a class-wide type 29
have to be explicitly initialized (whether created by an object_declaration or an allocator), and that aggregates have to be
explicitly qualified with a specific type when their expected type is class-wide.

65 If S denotes an untagged private type whose full type is tagged, then S'Class is also allowed before the full type 30
definition, but only in the private part of the package in which the type is declared (see 7.3.1). Similarly, the Class
attribute is defined for incomplete types whose full type is tagged, but only within the library unit in which the
incomplete type is declared (see 3.10.1).

Examples

Examples of tagged record types: 31

```
type Point is tagged                                                    32
  record
    X, Y : Real := 0.0;
  end record;

type Expression is tagged null record;                                  33
  -- Components will be added by each extension
```

3.9.1 Type Extensions

1   Every type extension is a tagged type, and is either a *record extension* or a *private extension* of some other tagged type.

Syntax

2   record_extension_part ::= **with** record_definition

Legality Rules

3   The parent type of a record extension shall not be a class-wide type. If the parent type is nonlimited, then each of the components of the record_extension_part shall be nonlimited. The accessibility level (see 3.10.2) of a record extension shall not be statically deeper than that of its parent type. In addition to the places where Legality Rules normally apply (see 12.3), these rules apply also in the private part of an instance of a generic unit.

4   A type extension shall not be declared in a generic body if the parent type is declared outside that body.

Dynamic Semantics

5   The elaboration of a record_extension_part consists of the elaboration of the record_definition.

NOTES

6   66 The term ''type extension'' refers to a type as a whole. The term ''extension part'' refers to the piece of text that defines the additional components (if any) the type extension has relative to its specified ancestor type.

7   67 The accessibility rules imply that a tagged type declared in a library package_specification can be extended only at library level or as a generic formal. When the extension is declared immediately within a package_body, primitive subprograms are inherited and are overridable, but new primitive subprograms cannot be added.

8   68 A name that denotes a component (including a discriminant) of the parent type is not allowed within the record_extension_part. Similarly, a name that denotes a component defined within the record_extension_part is not allowed within the record_extension_part. It is permissible to use a name that denotes a discriminant of the record extension, providing there is a new known_discriminant_part in the enclosing type declaration. (The full rule is given in 3.8.)

9   69 Each visible component of a record extension has to have a unique name, whether the component is (visibly) inherited from the parent type or declared in the record_extension_part (see 8.3).

Examples

10 *Examples of record extensions (of types defined above in 3.9):*

11 ```
    type Painted_Point is new Point with
       record
          Paint : Color := White;
       end record;
          -- Components X and Y are inherited
    ```

12  ```
    Origin : constant Painted_Point := (X | Y => 0.0, Paint => Black);
    ```

13 ```
    type Literal is new Expression with
       record   -- a leaf in an Expression tree
          Value : Real;
       end record;
    ```

14  ```
    type Expr_Ptr is access all Expression'Class;
                            -- see 3.10
    ```

15 ```
    type Binary_Operation is new Expression with
       record   -- an internal node in an Expression tree
          Left, Right : Expr_Ptr;
       end record;
    ```
    ```

```
type Addition is new Binary_Operation with null record;                  16
type Subtraction is new Binary_Operation with null record;
   -- No additional components needed for these extensions

Tree : Expr_Ptr :=            -- A tree representation of "5.0 + (13.0-7.0)"  17
   new Addition'(
      Left  => new Literal'(Value => 5.0),
      Right => new Subtraction'(
         Left  => new Literal'(Value => 13.0),
         Right => new Literal'(Value => 7.0)));
```

3.9.2 Dispatching Operations of Tagged Types

The primitive subprograms of a tagged type are called *dispatching operations*. A dispatching operation can   1
be called using a statically determined *controlling* tag, in which case the body to be executed is determined
at compile time. Alternatively, the controlling tag can be dynamically determined, in which case the call
dispatches to a body that is determined at run time; such a call is termed a *dispatching call*. As explained
below, the properties of the operands and the context of a particular call on a dispatching operation
determine how the controlling tag is determined, and hence whether or not the call is a dispatching call.
Run-time polymorphism is achieved when a dispatching operation is called by a dispatching call.

Static Semantics

A *call on a dispatching operation* is a call whose name or prefix denotes the declaration of a primitive   2
subprogram of a tagged type, that is, a dispatching operation. A *controlling operand* in a call on a
dispatching operation of a tagged type *T* is one whose corresponding formal parameter is of type *T* or is of
an anonymous access type with designated type *T*; the corresponding formal parameter is called a
controlling formal parameter. If the controlling formal parameter is an access parameter, the controlling
operand is the object designated by the actual parameter, rather than the actual parameter itself. If the call
is to a (primitive) function with result type *T*, then the call has a *controlling result* — the context of the call
can control the dispatching.

A name or expression of a tagged type is either *statically* tagged, *dynamically* tagged, or *tag*   3
indeterminate, according to whether, when used as a controlling operand, the tag that controls dispatching
is determined statically by the operand's (specific) type, dynamically by its tag at run time, or from context.
A qualified_expression or parenthesized expression is statically, dynamically, or indeterminately tagged
according to its operand. For other kinds of names and expressions, this is determined as follows:

- The name or expression is *statically tagged* if it is of a specific tagged type and, if it is a call   4
  with a controlling result, it has at least one statically tagged controlling operand;

- The name or expression is *dynamically tagged* if it is of a class-wide type, or it is a call with a   5
  controlling result and at least one dynamically tagged controlling operand;

- The name or expression is *tag indeterminate* if it is a call with a controlling result, all of whose   6
  controlling operands (if any) are tag indeterminate.

A type_conversion is statically or dynamically tagged according to whether the type determined by the   7/1
subtype_mark is specific or class-wide, respectively. For an object that is designated by an expression
whose expected type is an anonymous access-to-specific tagged type, the object is dynamically tagged if
the expression, ignoring enclosing parentheses, is of the form X'Access, where X is of a class-wide type, or
is of the form **new** T'(...), where T denotes a class-wide subtype. Otherwise, the object is statically or
dynamically tagged according to whether the designated type of the type of the expression is specific or
class-wide, respectively.

Legality Rules

8 A call on a dispatching operation shall not have both dynamically tagged and statically tagged controlling operands.

9/1 If the expected type for an expression or name is some specific tagged type, then the expression or name shall not be dynamically tagged unless it is a controlling operand in a call on a dispatching operation. Similarly, if the expected type for an expression is an anonymous access-to-specific tagged type, then the object designated by the expression shall not be dynamically tagged unless it is a controlling operand in a call on a dispatching operation.

10/1 In the declaration of a dispatching operation of a tagged type, everywhere a subtype of the tagged type appears as a subtype of the profile (see 6.1), it shall statically match the first subtype of the tagged type. If the dispatching operation overrides an inherited subprogram, it shall be subtype conformant with the inherited subprogram. The convention of an inherited or overriding dispatching operation is the convention of the corresponding primitive operation of the parent type. An explicitly declared dispatching operation shall not be of convention Intrinsic.

11 The default_expression for a controlling formal parameter of a dispatching operation shall be tag indeterminate. A controlling formal parameter that is an access parameter shall not have a default_expression.

12 A given subprogram shall not be a dispatching operation of two or more distinct tagged types.

13 The explicit declaration of a primitive subprogram of a tagged type shall occur before the type is frozen (see 13.14). For example, new dispatching operations cannot be added after objects or values of the type exist, nor after deriving a record extension from it, nor after a body.

Dynamic Semantics

14 For the execution of a call on a dispatching operation of a type *T*, the *controlling tag value* determines which subprogram body is executed. The controlling tag value is defined as follows:

15 • If one or more controlling operands are statically tagged, then the controlling tag value is *statically determined* to be the tag of *T*.

16 • If one or more controlling operands are dynamically tagged, then the controlling tag value is not statically determined, but is rather determined by the tags of the controlling operands. If there is more than one dynamically tagged controlling operand, a check is made that they all have the same tag. If this check fails, Constraint_Error is raised unless the call is a function_call whose name denotes the declaration of an equality operator (predefined or user defined) that returns Boolean, in which case the result of the call is defined to indicate inequality, and no subprogram_body is executed. This check is performed prior to evaluating any tag-indeterminate controlling operands.

17 • If all of the controlling operands are tag-indeterminate, then:

18 • If the call has a controlling result and is itself a (possibly parenthesized or qualified) controlling operand of an enclosing call on a dispatching operation of type *T*, then its controlling tag value is determined by the controlling tag value of this enclosing call;

19 • Otherwise, the controlling tag value is statically determined to be the tag of type *T*.

20 For the execution of a call on a dispatching operation, the body executed is the one for the corresponding primitive subprogram of the specific type identified by the controlling tag value. The body for an explicitly declared dispatching operation is the corresponding explicit body for the subprogram. The body for an implicitly declared dispatching operation that is overridden is the body for the overriding subprogram, even if the overriding occurs in a private part. The body for an inherited dispatching operation that is not overridden is the body of the corresponding subprogram of the parent or ancestor type.

NOTES

70 The body to be executed for a call on a dispatching operation is determined by the tag; it does not matter whether   21
that tag is determined statically or dynamically, and it does not matter whether the subprogram's declaration is visible at
the place of the call.

71 This subclause covers calls on primitive subprograms of a tagged type. Rules for tagged type membership tests are   22
described in 4.5.2. Controlling tag determination for an assignment_statement is described in 5.2.

72 A dispatching call can dispatch to a body whose declaration is not visible at the place of the call.   23

73 A call through an access-to-subprogram value is never a dispatching call, even if the access value designates a   24
dispatching operation. Similarly a call whose prefix denotes a subprogram_renaming_declaration cannot be a
dispatching call unless the renaming itself is the declaration of a primitive subprogram.

3.9.3 Abstract Types and Subprograms

An *abstract type* is a tagged type intended for use as a parent type for type extensions, but which is not   1
allowed to have objects of its own. An *abstract subprogram* is a subprogram that has no body, but is
intended to be overridden at some point when inherited. Because objects of an abstract type cannot be
created, a dispatching call to an abstract subprogram always dispatches to some overriding body.

Legality Rules

An *abstract type* is a specific type that has the reserved word **abstract** in its declaration. Only a tagged   2
type is allowed to be declared abstract.

A subprogram declared by an abstract_subprogram_declaration (see 6.1) is an *abstract subprogram*. If it   3
is a primitive subprogram of a tagged type, then the tagged type shall be abstract.

For a derived type, if the parent or ancestor type has an abstract primitive subprogram, or a primitive   4
function with a controlling result, then:

- If the derived type is abstract or untagged, the inherited subprogram is *abstract*.   5

- Otherwise, the subprogram shall be overridden with a nonabstract subprogram; for a type   6
  declared in the visible part of a package, the overriding may be either in the visible or the private
  part. However, if the type is a generic formal type, the subprogram need not be overridden for
  the formal type itself; a nonabstract version will necessarily be provided by the actual type.

A call on an abstract subprogram shall be a dispatching call; nondispatching calls to an abstract   7
subprogram are not allowed.

The type of an aggregate, or of an object created by an object_declaration or an allocator, or a generic   8
formal object of mode **in**, shall not be abstract. The type of the target of an assignment operation (see 5.2)
shall not be abstract. The type of a component shall not be abstract. If the result type of a function is
abstract, then the function shall be abstract.

If a partial view is not abstract, the corresponding full view shall not be abstract. If a generic formal type is   9
abstract, then for each primitive subprogram of the formal that is not abstract, the corresponding primitive
subprogram of the actual shall not be abstract.

For an abstract type declared in a visible part, an abstract primitive subprogram shall not be declared in the   10
private part, unless it is overriding an abstract subprogram implicitly declared in the visible part. For a
tagged type declared in a visible part, a primitive function with a controlling result shall not be declared in
the private part, unless it is overriding a function implicitly declared in the visible part.

A generic actual subprogram shall not be an abstract subprogram. The prefix of an attribute_reference for   11
the Access, Unchecked_Access, or Address attributes shall not denote an abstract subprogram.

NOTES

12 74 Abstractness is not inherited; to declare an abstract type, the reserved word **abstract** has to be used in the declaration of the type extension.

13 75 A class-wide type is never abstract. Even if a class is rooted at an abstract type, the class-wide type for the class is not abstract, and an object of the class-wide type can be created; the tag of such an object will identify some nonabstract type in the class.

Examples

14 *Example of an abstract type representing a set of natural numbers:*

15
```
package Sets is
    subtype Element_Type is Natural;
    type Set is abstract tagged null record;
    function Empty return Set is abstract;
    function Union(Left, Right : Set) return Set is abstract;
    function Intersection(Left, Right : Set) return Set is abstract;
    function Unit_Set(Element : Element_Type) return Set is abstract;
    procedure Take(Element : out Element_Type;
                   From : in out Set) is abstract;
end Sets;
```

NOTES

16 76 *Notes on the example:* Given the above abstract type, one could then derive various (nonabstract) extensions of the type, representing alternative implementations of a set. One might use a bit vector, but impose an upper bound on the largest element representable, while another might use a hash table, trading off space for flexibility.

3.10 Access Types

1 A value of an access type (an *access value*) provides indirect access to the object or subprogram it *designates*. Depending on its type, an access value can designate either subprograms, objects created by allocators (see 4.8), or more generally *aliased* objects of an appropriate type.

Syntax

2 access_type_definition ::=
    access_to_object_definition
    | access_to_subprogram_definition

3 access_to_object_definition ::=
    access [general_access_modifier] subtype_indication

4 general_access_modifier ::= **all** | **constant**

5 access_to_subprogram_definition ::=
    access [**protected**] **procedure** parameter_profile
    | **access** [**protected**] **function** parameter_and_result_profile

6 access_definition ::= **access** subtype_mark

Static Semantics

7/1 There are two kinds of access types, *access-to-object* types, whose values designate objects, and *access-to-subprogram* types, whose values designate subprograms. Associated with an access-to-object type is a *storage pool*; several access types may share the same storage pool. All descendants of an access type share the same storage pool. A storage pool is an area of storage used to hold dynamically allocated objects (called *pool elements*) created by allocators; storage pools are described further in 13.11, ''Storage Management''.

8 Access-to-object types are further subdivided into *pool-specific* access types, whose values can designate only the elements of their associated storage pool, and *general* access types, whose values can designate

the elements of any storage pool, as well as aliased objects created by declarations rather than allocators, and aliased subcomponents of other objects.

A view of an object is defined to be *aliased* if it is defined by an object_declaration or component_- 9 definition with the reserved word **aliased**, or by a renaming of an aliased view. In addition, the dereference of an access-to-object value denotes an aliased view, as does a view conversion (see 4.6) of an aliased view. Finally, the current instance of a limited type, and a formal parameter or generic formal object of a tagged type are defined to be aliased. Aliased views are the ones that can be designated by an access value. If the view defined by an object_declaration is aliased, and the type of the object has discriminants, then the object is constrained; if its nominal subtype is unconstrained, then the object is constrained by its initial value. Similarly, if the object created by an allocator has discriminants, the object is constrained, either by the designated subtype, or by its initial value.

An access_to_object_definition defines an access-to-object type and its first subtype; the subtype_- 10 indication defines the *designated subtype* of the access type. If a general_access_modifier appears, then the access type is a general access type. If the modifier is the reserved word **constant**, then the type is an *access-to-constant type*; a designated object cannot be updated through a value of such a type. If the modifier is the reserved word **all**, then the type is an *access-to-variable type*; a designated object can be both read and updated through a value of such a type. If no general_access_modifier appears in the access_to_object_definition, the access type is a pool-specific access-to-variable type.

An access_to_subprogram_definition defines an access-to-subprogram type and its first subtype; the 11 parameter_profile or parameter_and_result_profile defines the *designated profile* of the access type. There is a *calling convention* associated with the designated profile; only subprograms with this calling convention can be designated by values of the access type. By default, the calling convention is "*protected*" if the reserved word **protected** appears, and "Ada" otherwise. See Annex B for how to override this default.

An access_definition defines an anonymous general access-to-variable type; the subtype_mark denotes its 12 *designated subtype*. An access_definition is used in the specification of an access discriminant (see 3.7) or an access parameter (see 6.1).

For each (named) access type, there is a literal **null** which has a null access value designating no entity at 13 all. The null value of a named access type is the default initial value of the type. Other values of an access type are obtained by evaluating an attribute_reference for the Access or Unchecked_Access attribute of an aliased view of an object or non-intrinsic subprogram, or, in the case of a named access-to-object type, an allocator, which returns an access value designating a newly created object (see 3.10.2).

All subtypes of an access-to-subprogram type are constrained. The first subtype of a type defined by an 14/1 access_definition or an access_to_object_definition is unconstrained if the designated subtype is an unconstrained array or discriminated subtype; otherwise it is constrained.

Dynamic Semantics

A composite_constraint is *compatible* with an unconstrained access subtype if it is compatible with the 15 designated subtype. An access value *satisfies* a composite_constraint of an access subtype if it equals the null value of its type or if it designates an object whose value satisfies the constraint.

The elaboration of an access_type_definition creates the access type and its first subtype. For an access- 16 to-object type, this elaboration includes the elaboration of the subtype_indication, which creates the designated subtype.

17 The elaboration of an access_definition creates an anonymous general access-to-variable type (this happens as part of the initialization of an access parameter or access discriminant).

NOTES

18 77 Access values are called "pointers" or "references" in some other languages.

19 78 Each access-to-object type has an associated storage pool; several access types can share the same pool. An object can be created in the storage pool of an access type by an allocator (see 4.8) for the access type. A storage pool (roughly) corresponds to what some other languages call a "heap." See 13.11 for a discussion of pools.

20 79 Only index_constraints and discriminant_constraints can be applied to access types (see 3.6.1 and 3.7.1).

Examples

21 *Examples of access-to-object types:*

22
```
type Peripheral_Ref is access Peripheral;   -- see 3.8.1
type Binop_Ptr is access all Binary_Operation'Class;
                                             -- general access-to-class-wide, see 3.9.1
```

23 *Example of an access subtype:*

24
```
subtype Drum_Ref is Peripheral_Ref(Drum);   -- see 3.8.1
```

25 *Example of an access-to-subprogram type:*

26
```
type Message_Procedure is access procedure (M : in String := "Error!");
procedure Default_Message_Procedure(M : in String);
Give_Message : Message_Procedure := Default_Message_Procedure'Access;
...
procedure Other_Procedure(M : in String);
...
Give_Message := Other_Procedure'Access;
...
Give_Message("File not found.");   -- call with parameter (.all is optional)
Give_Message.all;                  -- call with no parameters
```

3.10.1 Incomplete Type Declarations

1 There are no particular limitations on the designated type of an access type. In particular, the type of a component of the designated type can be another access type, or even the same access type. This permits mutually dependent and recursive access types. An incomplete_type_declaration can be used to introduce a type to be used as a designated type, while deferring its full definition to a subsequent full_type_declaration.

Syntax

2 incomplete_type_declaration ::= **type** defining_identifier [discriminant_part];

Legality Rules

3 An incomplete_type_declaration requires a completion, which shall be a full_type_declaration. If the incomplete_type_declaration occurs immediately within either the visible part of a package_specification or a declarative_part, then the full_type_declaration shall occur later and immediately within this visible part or declarative_part. If the incomplete_type_declaration occurs immediately within the private part of a given package_specification, then the full_type_declaration shall occur later and immediately within either the private part itself, or the declarative_part of the corresponding package_body.

4 If an incomplete_type_declaration has a known_discriminant_part, then a full_type_declaration that completes it shall have a fully conforming (explicit) known_discriminant_part (see 6.3.1). If an incomplete_type_declaration has no discriminant_part (or an unknown_discriminant_part), then a

corresponding full_type_declaration is nevertheless allowed to have discriminants, either explicitly, or inherited via derivation.

The only allowed uses of a name that denotes an incomplete_type_declaration are as follows: 5

- as the subtype_mark in the subtype_indication of an access_to_object_definition; the only   6
  form of constraint allowed in this subtype_indication is a discriminant_constraint;

- as the subtype_mark defining the subtype of a parameter or result of an access_to_-   7
  subprogram_definition;

- as the subtype_mark in an access_definition;   8

- as the prefix of an attribute_reference whose attribute_designator is Class; such an attribute_-   9
  reference is similarly restricted to the uses allowed here; when used in this way, the
  corresponding full_type_declaration shall declare a tagged type, and the attribute_reference
  shall occur in the same library unit as the incomplete_type_declaration.

A dereference (whether implicit or explicit — see 4.1) shall not be of an incomplete type.   10

Static Semantics

An incomplete_type_declaration declares an incomplete type and its first subtype; the first subtype is   11
unconstrained if a known_discriminant_part appears.

Dynamic Semantics

The elaboration of an incomplete_type_declaration has no effect.   12

NOTES
80 Within a declarative_part, an incomplete_type_declaration and a corresponding full_type_declaration cannot be   13
separated by an intervening body. This is because a type has to be completely defined before it is frozen, and a body
freezes all types declared prior to it in the same declarative_part (see 13.14).

Examples

Example of a recursive type: 14

```
type Cell;   -- incomplete type declaration     15
type Link is access Cell;

type Cell is     16
   record
        Value  : Integer;
        Succ   : Link;
        Pred   : Link;
   end record;
Head   : Link  := new Cell'(0, null, null);     17
Next   : Link  := Head.Succ;
```

Examples of mutually dependent access types: 18

```
type Person(<>);     -- incomplete type declaration     19
type Car;            -- incomplete type declaration

type Person_Name is access Person;     20
type Car_Name    is access all Car;

type Car is     21
   record
        Number  : Integer;
        Owner   : Person_Name;
   end record;
```

22
```
type Person(Sex : Gender) is
    record
        Name      : String(1 .. 20);
        Birth     : Date;
        Age       : Integer range 0 .. 130;
        Vehicle   : Car_Name;
        case Sex is
            when M => Wife            : Person_Name(Sex => F);
            when F => Husband         : Person_Name(Sex => M);
        end case;
    end record;
```

23
```
My_Car, Your_Car, Next_Car : Car_Name := new Car;    -- see 4.8
George : Person_Name := new Person(M);
    ...
George.Vehicle := Your_Car;
```

3.10.2 Operations of Access Types

1 The attribute Access is used to create access values designating aliased objects and non-intrinsic subprograms. The "accessibility" rules prevent dangling references (in the absence of uses of certain unchecked features — see Section 13).

Name Resolution Rules

2 For an attribute_reference with attribute_designator Access (or Unchecked_Access — see 13.10), the expected type shall be a single access type; the prefix of such an attribute_reference is never interpreted as an implicit_dereference. If the expected type is an access-to-subprogram type, then the expected profile of the prefix is the designated profile of the access type.

Static Semantics

3 The accessibility rules, which prevent dangling references, are written in terms of *accessibility levels*, which reflect the run-time nesting of *masters*. As explained in 7.6.1, a master is the execution of a task_body, a block_statement, a subprogram_body, an entry_body, or an accept_statement. An accessibility level is *deeper than* another if it is more deeply nested at run time. For example, an object declared local to a called subprogram has a deeper accessibility level than an object declared local to the calling subprogram. The accessibility rules for access types require that the accessibility level of an object designated by an access value be no deeper than that of the access type. This ensures that the object will live at least as long as the access type, which in turn ensures that the access value cannot later designate an object that no longer exists. The Unchecked_Access attribute may be used to circumvent the accessibility rules.

4 A given accessibility level is said to be *statically deeper* than another if the given level is known at compile time (as defined below) to be deeper than the other for all possible executions. In most cases, accessibility is enforced at compile time by Legality Rules. Run-time accessibility checks are also used, since the Legality Rules do not cover certain cases involving access parameters and generic packages.

5 Each master, and each entity and view created by it, has an accessibility level:

6 • The accessibility level of a given master is deeper than that of each dynamically enclosing master, and deeper than that of each master upon which the task executing the given master directly depends (see 9.3).

7 • An entity or view created by a declaration has the same accessibility level as the innermost enclosing master, except in the cases of renaming and derived access types described below. A parameter of a master has the same accessibility level as the master.

- The accessibility level of a view of an object or subprogram defined by a renaming_declaration is the same as that of the renamed view. 8

- The accessibility level of a view conversion is the same as that of the operand. 9

- For a function whose result type is a return-by-reference type, the accessibility level of the result object is the same as that of the master that elaborated the function body. For any other function, the accessibility level of the result object is that of the execution of the called function. 10

- The accessibility level of a derived access type is the same as that of its ultimate ancestor. 11

- The accessibility level of the anonymous access type of an access discriminant is the same as that of the containing object or associated constrained subtype. 12

- The accessibility level of the anonymous access type of an access parameter is the same as that of the view designated by the actual. If the actual is an allocator, this is the accessibility level of the execution of the called subprogram. 13

- The accessibility level of an object created by an allocator is the same as that of the access type. 14

- The accessibility level of a view of an object or subprogram denoted by a dereference of an access value is the same as that of the access type. 15

- The accessibility level of a component, protected subprogram, or entry of (a view of) a composite object is the same as that of (the view of) the composite object. 16

One accessibility level is defined to be *statically deeper* than another in the following cases: 17

- For a master that is statically nested within another master, the accessibility level of the inner master is statically deeper than that of the outer master. 18

- The statically deeper relationship does not apply to the accessibility level of the anonymous type of an access parameter; that is, such an accessibility level is not considered to be statically deeper, nor statically shallower, than any other. 19

- For determining whether one level is statically deeper than another when within a generic package body, the generic package is presumed to be instantiated at the same level as where it was declared; run-time checks are needed in the case of more deeply nested instantiations. 20

- For determining whether one level is statically deeper than another when within the declarative region of a type_declaration, the current instance of the type is presumed to be an object created at a deeper level than that of the type. 21

The accessibility level of all library units is called the *library level*; a library-level declaration or entity is one whose accessibility level is the library level. 22

The following attribute is defined for a prefix X that denotes an aliased view of an object: 23

X'Access   X'Access yields an access value that designates the object denoted by X. The type of X'Access is an access-to-object type, as determined by the expected type. The expected type shall be a general access type. X shall denote an aliased view of an object, including possibly the current instance (see 8.6) of a limited type within its definition, or a formal parameter or generic formal object of a tagged type. The view denoted by the prefix X shall satisfy the following additional requirements, presuming the expected type for X'Access is the general access type *A* with designated type *D*: 24/1

   - If *A* is an access-to-variable type, then the view shall be a variable; on the other hand, if *A* is an access-to-constant type, the view may be either a constant or a variable. 25

26   • The view shall not be a subcomponent that depends on discriminants of a variable whose nominal subtype is unconstrained, unless this subtype is indefinite, or the variable is aliased.

27/1   • If *A* is a named access type and *D* is a tagged type, then the type of the view shall be covered by *D*; if *A* is anonymous and *D* is tagged, then the type of the view shall be either *D*'Class or a type covered by D; if *D* is untagged, then the type of the view shall be *D*, and *A*'s designated subtype shall either statically match the nominal subtype of the view or be discriminated and unconstrained;

28   • The accessibility level of the view shall not be statically deeper than that of the access type *A*. In addition to the places where Legality Rules normally apply (see 12.3), this rule applies also in the private part of an instance of a generic unit.

29   A check is made that the accessibility level of X is not deeper than that of the access type *A*. If this check fails, Program_Error is raised.

30   If the nominal subtype of X does not statically match the designated subtype of *A*, a view conversion of X to the designated subtype is evaluated (which might raise Constraint_Error — see 4.6) and the value of X'Access designates that view.

31   The following attribute is defined for a prefix P that denotes a subprogram:

32   P'Access   P'Access yields an access value that designates the subprogram denoted by P. The type of P'Access is an access-to-subprogram type (*S*), as determined by the expected type. The accessibility level of P shall not be statically deeper than that of *S*. In addition to the places where Legality Rules normally apply (see 12.3), this rule applies also in the private part of an instance of a generic unit. The profile of P shall be subtype-conformant with the designated profile of *S*, and shall not be Intrinsic. If the subprogram denoted by P is declared within a generic body, *S* shall be declared within the generic body.

      NOTES

33   81 The Unchecked_Access attribute yields the same result as the Access attribute for objects, but has fewer restrictions (see 13.10). There are other predefined operations that yield access values: an allocator can be used to create an object, and return an access value that designates it (see 4.8); evaluating the literal **null** yields a null access value that designates no entity at all (see 4.2).

34   82 The predefined operations of an access type also include the assignment operation, qualification, and membership tests. Explicit conversion is allowed between general access types with matching designated subtypes; explicit conversion is allowed between access-to-subprogram types with subtype conformant profiles (see 4.6). Named access types have predefined equality operators; anonymous access types do not (see 4.5.2).

35   83 The object or subprogram designated by an access value can be named with a dereference, either an explicit_dereference or an implicit_dereference. See 4.1.

36   84 A call through the dereference of an access-to-subprogram value is never a dispatching call.

37   85 The accessibility rules imply that it is not possible to use the Access attribute to implement "downward closures" — that is, to pass a more-nested subprogram as a parameter to a less-nested subprogram, as might be desired for example for an iterator abstraction. Instead, downward closures can be implemented using generic formal subprograms (see 12.6). Note that Unchecked_Access is not allowed for subprograms.

38   86 Note that using an access-to-class-wide tagged type with a dispatching operation is a potentially more structured alternative to using an access-to-subprogram type.

39   87 An implementation may consider two access-to-subprogram values to be unequal, even though they designate the same subprogram. This might be because one points directly to the subprogram, while the other points to a special prologue that performs an Elaboration_Check and then jumps to the subprogram. See 4.5.2.

Example of use of the Access attribute: 40

```
Martha : Person_Name := new Person(F);    -- see 3.10.1    41
Cars   : array (1..2) of aliased Car;
   ...
Martha.Vehicle := Cars(1)'Access;
George.Vehicle := Cars(2)'Access;
```

3.11 Declarative Parts

A declarative_part contains declarative_items (possibly none).   1

Syntax

declarative_part ::= {declarative_item}   2

declarative_item ::=   3
   basic_declarative_item | body

basic_declarative_item ::=   4/1
   basic_declaration | aspect_clause | use_clause

body ::= proper_body | body_stub   5

proper_body ::=   6
   subprogram_body | package_body | task_body | protected_body

Dynamic Semantics

The elaboration of a declarative_part consists of the elaboration of the declarative_items, if any, in the   7
order in which they are given in the declarative_part.

An elaborable construct is in the *elaborated* state after the normal completion of its elaboration. Prior to   8
that, it is *not yet elaborated*.

For a construct that attempts to use a body, a check (Elaboration_Check) is performed, as follows: 9

- For a call to a (non-protected) subprogram that has an explicit body, a check is made that the   10/1
  body is already elaborated. This check and the evaluations of any actual parameters of the call
  are done in an arbitrary order.

- For a call to a protected operation of a protected type (that has a body — no check is performed   11
  if a pragma Import applies to the protected type), a check is made that the protected_body is
  already elaborated. This check and the evaluations of any actual parameters of the call are done
  in an arbitrary order.

- For the activation of a task, a check is made by the activator that the task_body is already   12
  elaborated. If two or more tasks are being activated together (see 9.2), as the result of the
  elaboration of a declarative_part or the initialization for the object created by an allocator, this
  check is done for all of them before activating any of them.

- For the instantiation of a generic unit that has a body, a check is made that this body is already   13
  elaborated. This check and the evaluation of any explicit_generic_actual_parameters of the
  instantiation are done in an arbitrary order.

The exception Program_Error is raised if any of these checks fails.   14

3.11.1 Completions of Declarations

1/1 Declarations sometimes come in two parts. A declaration that requires a second part is said to *require completion*. The second part is called the *completion* of the declaration (and of the entity declared), and is either another declaration, a body, or a pragma. A *body* is a body, an entry_body, or a renaming-as-body (see 8.5.4).

2 A construct that can be a completion is interpreted as the completion of a prior declaration only if:

3 • The declaration and the completion occur immediately within the same declarative region;

4 • The defining name or defining_program_unit_name in the completion is the same as in the declaration, or in the case of a pragma, the pragma applies to the declaration;

5 • If the declaration is overloadable, then the completion either has a type-conformant profile, or is a pragma.

6 An implicit declaration shall not have a completion. For any explicit declaration that is specified to *require completion*, there shall be a corresponding explicit completion.

7 At most one completion is allowed for a given declaration. Additional requirements on completions appear where each kind of completion is defined.

8 A type is *completely defined* at a place that is after its full type definition (if it has one) and after all of its subcomponent types are completely defined. A type shall be completely defined before it is frozen (see 13.14 and 7.3).

NOTES
9 88 Completions are in principle allowed for any kind of explicit declaration. However, for some kinds of declaration, the only allowed completion is a pragma Import, and implementations are not required to support pragma Import for every kind of entity.

10 89 There are rules that prevent premature uses of declarations that have a corresponding completion. The Elaboration_Checks of 3.11 prevent such uses at run time for subprograms, protected operations, tasks, and generic units. The rules of 13.14, "Freezing Rules" prevent, at compile time, premature uses of other entities such as private types and deferred constants.

Section 4: Names and Expressions

The rules applicable to the different forms of name and expression, and to their evaluation, are given in this section. 1

4.1 Names

Names can denote declared entities, whether declared explicitly or implicitly (see 3.1). Names can also denote objects or subprograms designated by access values; the results of type_conversions or function_calls; subcomponents and slices of objects and values; protected subprograms, single entries, entry families, and entries in families of entries. Finally, names can denote attributes of any of the foregoing. 1

Syntax

```
name ::=
    direct_name          | explicit_dereference
    | indexed_component  | slice
    | selected_component | attribute_reference
    | type_conversion    | function_call
    | character_literal
```
2

direct_name ::= identifier | operator_symbol 3

prefix ::= name | implicit_dereference 4

explicit_dereference ::= name.**all** 5

implicit_dereference ::= name 6

Certain forms of name (indexed_components, selected_components, slices, and attributes) include a prefix that is either itself a name that denotes some related entity, or an implicit_dereference of an access value that designates some related entity. 7

Name Resolution Rules

The name in a *dereference* (either an implicit_dereference or an explicit_dereference) is expected to be of any access type. 8

Static Semantics

If the type of the name in a dereference is some access-to-object type T, then the dereference denotes a view of an object, the *nominal subtype* of the view being the designated subtype of T. 9

If the type of the name in a dereference is some access-to-subprogram type S, then the dereference denotes a view of a subprogram, the *profile* of the view being the designated profile of S. 10

Dynamic Semantics

The evaluation of a name determines the entity denoted by the name. This evaluation has no other effect for a name that is a direct_name or a character_literal. 11

The evaluation of a name that has a prefix includes the evaluation of the prefix. The evaluation of a prefix consists of the evaluation of the name or the implicit_dereference. The prefix denotes the entity denoted by the name or the implicit_dereference. 12

S. Tucker Taft et al. (Eds.): Consolidated Ada Reference Manual, LNCS 2219, pp. 77–109, 2001.

13 The evaluation of a dereference consists of the evaluation of the name and the determination of the object or subprogram that is designated by the value of the name. A check is made that the value of the name is not the null access value. Constraint_Error is raised if this check fails. The dereference denotes the object or subprogram designated by the value of the name.

Examples

14 *Examples of direct names:*

15
```
Pi       -- the direct name of a number          (see 3.3.2)
Limit    -- the direct name of a constant         (see 3.3.1)
Count    -- the direct name of a scalar variable  (see 3.3.1)
Board    -- the direct name of an array variable  (see 3.6.1)
Matrix   -- the direct name of a type             (see 3.6)
Random   -- the direct name of a function         (see 6.1)
Error    -- the direct name of an exception       (see 11.1)
```

16 *Examples of dereferences:*

17
```
Next_Car.all      -- explicit dereference denoting the object designated by
                  -- the access variable Next_Car (see 3.10.1)
Next_Car.Owner    -- selected component with implicit dereference;
                  -- same as Next_Car.all.Owner
```

4.1.1 Indexed Components

1 An indexed_component denotes either a component of an array or an entry in a family of entries.

Syntax

2 indexed_component ::= prefix(expression {, expression})

Name Resolution Rules

3 The prefix of an indexed_component with a given number of expressions shall resolve to denote an array (after any implicit dereference) with the corresponding number of index positions, or shall resolve to denote an entry family of a task or protected object (in which case there shall be only one expression).

4 The expected type for each expression is the corresponding index type.

Static Semantics

5 When the prefix denotes an array, the indexed_component denotes the component of the array with the specified index value(s). The nominal subtype of the indexed_component is the component subtype of the array type.

6 When the prefix denotes an entry family, the indexed_component denotes the individual entry of the entry family with the specified index value.

Dynamic Semantics

7 For the evaluation of an indexed_component, the prefix and the expressions are evaluated in an arbitrary order. The value of each expression is converted to the corresponding index type. A check is made that each index value belongs to the corresponding index range of the array or entry family denoted by the prefix. Constraint_Error is raised if this check fails.

Examples of indexed components: 8

```
My_Schedule(Sat)      -- a component of a one-dimensional array   (see 3.6.1)
Page(10)              -- a component of a one-dimensional array   (see 3.6)
Board(M, J + 1)       -- a component of a two-dimensional array   (see 3.6.1)
Page(10)(20)          -- a component of a component               (see 3.6)
Request(Medium)       -- an entry in a family of entries          (see 9.1)
Next_Frame(L)(M, N)   -- a component of a function call           (see 6.1)
```

9

NOTES

1 *Notes on the examples:* Distinct notations are used for components of multidimensional arrays (such as Board) and   10
arrays of arrays (such as Page). The components of an array of arrays are arrays and can therefore be indexed. Thus
Page(10)(20) denotes the 20th component of Page(10). In the last example Next_Frame(L) is a function call returning an
access value that designates a two-dimensional array.

4.1.2 Slices

A slice denotes a one-dimensional array formed by a sequence of consecutive components of a one-   1
dimensional array. A slice of a variable is a variable; a slice of a constant is a constant; a slice of a value is
a value.

slice ::= prefix(discrete_range)   2

The prefix of a slice shall resolve to denote a one-dimensional array (after any implicit dereference).   3

The expected type for the discrete_range of a slice is the index type of the array type.   4

A slice denotes a one-dimensional array formed by the sequence of consecutive components of the array   5
denoted by the prefix, corresponding to the range of values of the index given by the discrete_range.

The type of the slice is that of the prefix. Its bounds are those defined by the discrete_range.   6

For the evaluation of a slice, the prefix and the discrete_range are evaluated in an arbitrary order. If the   7
slice is not a *null slice* (a slice where the discrete_range is a null range), then a check is made that the
bounds of the discrete_range belong to the index range of the array denoted by the prefix.
Constraint_Error is raised if this check fails.

NOTES

2 A slice is not permitted as the prefix of an Access attribute_reference, even if the components or the array as a whole   8
are aliased. See 3.10.2.

3 For a one-dimensional array A, the slice A(N .. N) denotes an array that has only one component; its type is the type of   9
A. On the other hand, A(N) denotes a component of the array A and has the corresponding component type.

10 *Examples of slices:*

11
```
Stars(1 .. 15)          -- a slice of 15 characters       (see 3.6.3)
Page(10 .. 10 + Size)   -- a slice of 1 + Size components (see 3.6)
Page(L)(A .. B)         -- a slice of the array Page(L)    (see 3.6)
Stars(1 .. 0)           -- a null slice                    (see 3.6.3)
My_Schedule(Weekday)    -- bounds given by subtype         (see 3.6.1 and 3.5.1)
Stars(5 .. 15)(K)       -- same as Stars(K)                (see 3.6.3)
                        -- provided that K is in 5 .. 15
```

4.1.3 Selected Components

1 Selected_components are used to denote components (including discriminants), entries, entry families, and protected subprograms; they are also used as expanded names as described below.

Syntax

2 selected_component ::= prefix . selector_name

3 selector_name ::= identifier | character_literal | operator_symbol

Name Resolution Rules

4 A selected_component is called an *expanded name* if, according to the visibility rules, at least one possible interpretation of its prefix denotes a package or an enclosing named construct (directly, not through a subprogram_renaming_declaration or generic_renaming_declaration).

5 A selected_component that is not an expanded name shall resolve to denote one of the following:

6 • A component (including a discriminant):

7 The prefix shall resolve to denote an object or value of some non-array composite type (after any implicit dereference). The selector_name shall resolve to denote a discriminant_specification of the type, or, unless the type is a protected type, a component_declaration of the type. The selected_component denotes the corresponding component of the object or value.

8 • A single entry, an entry family, or a protected subprogram:

9 The prefix shall resolve to denote an object or value of some task or protected type (after any implicit dereference). The selector_name shall resolve to denote an entry_declaration or subprogram_declaration occurring (implicitly or explicitly) within the visible part of that type. The selected_component denotes the corresponding entry, entry family, or protected subprogram.

10 An expanded name shall resolve to denote a declaration that occurs immediately within a named declarative region, as follows:

11 • The prefix shall resolve to denote either a package (including the current instance of a generic package, or a rename of a package), or an enclosing named construct.

12 • The selector_name shall resolve to denote a declaration that occurs immediately within the declarative region of the package or enclosing construct (the declaration shall be visible at the place of the expanded name — see 8.3). The expanded name denotes that declaration.

13 • If the prefix does not denote a package, then it shall be a direct_name or an expanded name, and it shall resolve to denote a program unit (other than a package), the current instance of a type, a block_statement, a loop_statement, or an accept_statement (in the case of an accept_statement or entry_body, no family index is allowed); the expanded name shall occur within the declarative region of this construct. Further, if this construct is a callable construct and the prefix

denotes more than one such enclosing callable construct, then the expanded name is ambiguous, independently of the selector_name.

Dynamic Semantics

The evaluation of a selected_component includes the evaluation of the prefix.   14

For a selected_component that denotes a component of a variant, a check is made that the values of the   15
discriminants are such that the value or object denoted by the prefix has this component. The exception
Constraint_Error is raised if this check fails.

Examples

Examples of selected components: 16

```
Tomorrow.Month        -- a record component          (see 3.8)          17
Next_Car.Owner        -- a record component          (see 3.10.1)
Next_Car.Owner.Age    -- a record component          (see 3.10.1)
                      -- the previous two lines involve implicit dereferences
Writer.Unit           -- a record component (a discriminant)   (see 3.8.1)
Min_Cell(H).Value     -- a record component of the result   (see 6.1)
                      -- of the function call Min_Cell(H)
Control.Seize         -- an entry of a protected object   (see 9.4)
Pool(K).Write         -- an entry of the task Pool(K)   (see 9.4)
```

Examples of expanded names: 18

```
Key_Manager."<"       -- an operator of the visible part of a package (see 7.3.1)          19
Dot_Product.Sum       -- a variable declared in a function body   (see 6.1)
Buffer.Pool           -- a variable declared in a protected unit   (see 9.11)
Buffer.Read           -- an entry of a protected unit   (see 9.11)
Swap.Temp             -- a variable declared in a block statement   (see 5.6)
Standard.Boolean      -- the name of a predefined type   (see A.1)
```

4.1.4 Attributes

An *attribute* is a characteristic of an entity that can be queried via an attribute_reference or a range_-   1
attribute_reference.

Syntax

attribute_reference ::= prefix'attribute_designator   2

attribute_designator ::=   3
    identifier[(*static_*expression)]
    | Access | Delta | Digits

range_attribute_reference ::= prefix'range_attribute_designator   4

range_attribute_designator ::= Range[(*static_*expression)]   5

Name Resolution Rules

In an attribute_reference, if the attribute_designator is for an attribute defined for (at least some) objects   6
of an access type, then the prefix is never interpreted as an implicit_dereference; otherwise (and for all
range_attribute_references), if the type of the name within the prefix is of an access type, the prefix is
interpreted as an implicit_dereference. Similarly, if the attribute_designator is for an attribute defined for
(at least some) functions, then the prefix is never interpreted as a parameterless function_call; otherwise
(and for all range_attribute_references), if the prefix consists of a name that denotes a function, it is
interpreted as a parameterless function_call.

7 The expression, if any, in an attribute_designator or range_attribute_designator is expected to be of any integer type.

8 The expression, if any, in an attribute_designator or range_attribute_designator shall be static.

9 An attribute_reference denotes a value, an object, a subprogram, or some other kind of program entity.

10 A range_attribute_reference X'Range(N) is equivalent to the range X'First(N) .. X'Last(N), except that the prefix is only evaluated once. Similarly, X'Range is equivalent to X'First .. X'Last, except that the prefix is only evaluated once.

11 The evaluation of an attribute_reference (or range_attribute_reference) consists of the evaluation of the prefix.

12/1 An implementation may provide implementation-defined attributes; the identifier for an implementation-defined attribute shall differ from those of the language-defined attributes unless supplied for compatibility with a previous edition of this International Standard.

NOTES

13 4 Attributes are defined throughout this International Standard, and are summarized in Annex K.

14/1 5 In general, the name in a prefix of an attribute_reference (or a range_attribute_reference) has to be resolved without using any context. However, in the case of the Access attribute, the expected type for the prefix has to be a single access type, and if it is an access-to-subprogram type (see 3.10.2) then the resolution of the name can use the fact that the profile of the callable entity denoted by the prefix has to be type conformant with the designated profile of the access type.

15 *Examples of attributes:*

16
```
Color'First          -- minimum value of the enumeration type Color   (see 3.5.1)
Rainbow'Base'First   -- same as Color'First                           (see 3.5.1)
Real'Digits          -- precision of the type Real                    (see 3.5.7)
Board'Last(2)        -- upper bound of the second dimension of Board  (see 3.6.1)
Board'Range(1)       -- index range of the first dimension of Board   (see 3.6.1)
Pool(K)'Terminated   -- True if task Pool(K) is terminated            (see 9.1)
Date'Size            -- number of bits for records of type Date       (see 3.8)
Message'Address      -- address of the record variable Message        (see 3.7.1)
```

4.2 Literals

1 A *literal* represents a value literally, that is, by means of notation suited to its kind. A literal is either a numeric_literal, a character_literal, the literal **null**, or a string_literal.

2 The expected type for a literal **null** shall be a single access type.

3 For a name that consists of a character_literal, either its expected type shall be a single character type, in which case it is interpreted as a parameterless function_call that yields the corresponding value of the character type, or its expected profile shall correspond to a parameterless function with a character result

type, in which case it is interpreted as the name of the corresponding parameterless function declared as part of the character type's definition (see 3.5.1). In either case, the character_literal denotes the enumeration_literal_specification.

The expected type for a primary that is a string_literal shall be a single string type. 4

A character_literal that is a name shall correspond to a defining_character_literal of the expected type, or of the result type of the expected profile. 5

For each character of a string_literal with a given expected string type, there shall be a corresponding defining_character_literal of the component type of the expected string type. 6

A literal null shall not be of an anonymous access type, since such types do not have a null value (see 3.10). 7

Static Semantics

An integer literal is of type *universal_integer*. A real literal is of type *universal_real*. 8

Dynamic Semantics

The evaluation of a numeric literal, or the literal **null**, yields the represented value. 9

The evaluation of a string_literal that is a primary yields an array value containing the value of each 10 character of the sequence of characters of the string_literal, as defined in 2.6. The bounds of this array value are determined according to the rules for positional_array_aggregates (see 4.3.3), except that for a null string literal, the upper bound is the predecessor of the lower bound.

For the evaluation of a string_literal of type *T*, a check is made that the value of each character of the 11 string_literal belongs to the component subtype of *T*. For the evaluation of a null string literal, a check is made that its lower bound is greater than the lower bound of the base range of the index type. The exception Constraint_Error is raised if either of these checks fails.

NOTES
6 Enumeration literals that are identifiers rather than character_literals follow the normal rules for identifiers when used 12 in a name (see 4.1 and 4.1.3). Character_literals used as selector_names follow the normal rules for expanded names (see 4.1.3).

Examples

Examples of literals: 13

```
3.14159_26536    -- a real literal          14
1_345            -- an integer literal
'A'              -- a character literal
"Some Text"      -- a string literal
```

4.3 Aggregates

An *aggregate* combines component values into a composite value of an array type, record type, or record 1 extension.

Syntax

aggregate ::= record_aggregate | extension_aggregate | array_aggregate 2

Name Resolution Rules

3   The expected type for an aggregate shall be a single nonlimited array type, record type, or record extension.

Legality Rules

4   An aggregate shall not be of a class-wide type.

Dynamic Semantics

5   For the evaluation of an aggregate, an anonymous object is created and values for the components or ancestor part are obtained (as described in the subsequent subclause for each kind of the aggregate) and assigned into the corresponding components or ancestor part of the anonymous object. Obtaining the values and the assignments occur in an arbitrary order. The value of the aggregate is the value of this object.

6   If an aggregate is of a tagged type, a check is made that its value belongs to the first subtype of the type. Constraint_Error is raised if this check fails.

4.3.1 Record Aggregates

1   In a record_aggregate, a value is specified for each component of the record or record extension value, using either a named or a positional association.

Syntax

2   record_aggregate ::= (record_component_association_list)

3   record_component_association_list ::=
       record_component_association {, record_component_association}
      | **null record**

4   record_component_association ::=
       [component_choice_list =>] expression

5   component_choice_list ::=
       *component*_selector_name {| *component*_selector_name}
      | **others**

6   A record_component_association is a *named component association* if it has a component_choice_list; otherwise, it is a *positional component association*. Any positional component associations shall precede any named component associations. If there is a named association with a component_choice_list of **others**, it shall come last.

7   In the record_component_association_list for a record_aggregate, if there is only one association, it shall be a named association.

Name Resolution Rules

8   The expected type for a record_aggregate shall be a single nonlimited record type or record extension.

9   For the record_component_association_list of a record_aggregate, all components of the composite value defined by the aggregate are *needed*; for the association list of an extension_aggregate, only those components not determined by the ancestor expression or subtype are needed (see 4.3.2). Each selector_-name in a record_component_association shall denote a needed component (including possibly a discriminant).

The expected type for the expression of a record_component_association is the type of the *associated* component(s); the associated component(s) are as follows:

- For a positional association, the component (including possibly a discriminant) in the corresponding relative position (in the declarative region of the type), counting only the needed components;

- For a named association with one or more *component*_selector_names, the named component(s);

- For a named association with the reserved word **others**, all needed components that are not associated with some previous association.

Legality Rules

If the type of a record_aggregate is a record extension, then it shall be a descendant of a record type, through one or more record extensions (and no private extensions).

If there are no components needed in a given record_component_association_list, then the reserved words **null record** shall appear rather than a list of record_component_associations.

Each record_component_association shall have at least one associated component, and each needed component shall be associated with exactly one record_component_association. If a record_-component_association has two or more associated components, all of them shall be of the same type.

If the components of a variant_part are needed, then the value of a discriminant that governs the variant_part shall be given by a static expression.

Dynamic Semantics

The evaluation of a record_aggregate consists of the evaluation of the record_component_association_-list.

For the evaluation of a record_component_association_list, any per-object constraints (see 3.8) for components specified in the association list are elaborated and any expressions are evaluated and converted to the subtype of the associated component. Any constraint elaborations and expression evaluations (and conversions) occur in an arbitrary order, except that the expression for a discriminant is evaluated (and converted) prior to the elaboration of any per-object constraint that depends on it, which in turn occurs prior to the evaluation and conversion of the expression for the component with the per-object constraint.

The expression of a record_component_association is evaluated (and converted) once for each associated component.

NOTES
7 For a record_aggregate with positional associations, expressions specifying discriminant values appear first since the known_discriminant_part is given first in the declaration of the type; they have to be in the same order as in the known_discriminant_part.

Examples

Example of a record aggregate with positional associations:

```
(4, July, 1776)                              -- see 3.8
```

Examples of record aggregates with named associations:

```
(Day => 4, Month => July, Year => 1776)
(Month => July, Day => 4, Year => 1776)
```

10
11
12
13
14
15
16
17
18
19
20
21
22
23
24
25

26
```
(Disk, Closed, Track => 5, Cylinder => 12)          -- see 3.8.1
(Unit => Disk, Status => Closed, Cylinder => 9, Track => 1)
```

27 *Example of component association with several choices:*

28
```
(Value => 0, Succ|Pred => new Cell'(0, null, null))     -- see 3.10.1
```

29 `-- The allocator is evaluated twice: Succ and Pred designate different cells`

30 *Examples of record aggregates for tagged types (see 3.9 and 3.9.1):*

31
```
Expression'(null record)
Literal'(Value => 0.0)
Painted_Point'(0.0, Pi/2.0, Paint => Red)
```

4.3.2 Extension Aggregates

1   An extension_aggregate specifies a value for a type that is a record extension by specifying a value or subtype for an ancestor of the type, followed by associations for any components not determined by the ancestor_part.

Syntax

2   extension_aggregate ::=
      (ancestor_part **with** record_component_association_list)

3   ancestor_part ::= expression | subtype_mark

Name Resolution Rules

4   The expected type for an extension_aggregate shall be a single nonlimited type that is a record extension. If the ancestor_part is an expression, it is expected to be of any nonlimited tagged type.

Legality Rules

5   If the ancestor_part is a subtype_mark, it shall denote a specific tagged subtype. The type of the extension_aggregate shall be derived from the type of the ancestor_part, through one or more record extensions (and no private extensions).

Static Semantics

6   For the record_component_association_list of an extension_aggregate, the only components *needed* are those of the composite value defined by the aggregate that are not inherited from the type of the ancestor_part, plus any inherited discriminants if the ancestor_part is a subtype_mark that denotes an unconstrained subtype.

Dynamic Semantics

7   For the evaluation of an extension_aggregate, the record_component_association_list is evaluated. If the ancestor_part is an expression, it is also evaluated; if the ancestor_part is a subtype_mark, the components of the value of the aggregate not given by the record_component_association_list are initialized by default as for an object of the ancestor type. Any implicit initializations or evaluations are performed in an arbitrary order, except that the expression for a discriminant is evaluated prior to any other evaluation or initialization that depends on it.

8   If the type of the ancestor_part has discriminants that are not inherited by the type of the extension_aggregate, then, unless the ancestor_part is a subtype_mark that denotes an unconstrained subtype, a check is made that each discriminant of the ancestor has the value specified for a corresponding

discriminant, either in the record_component_association_list, or in the derived_type_definition for some ancestor of the type of the extension_aggregate. Constraint_Error is raised if this check fails.

NOTES

8 If all components of the value of the extension_aggregate are determined by the ancestor_part, then the record_-
component_association_list is required to be simply **null record**.   9

9 If the ancestor_part is a subtype_mark, then its type can be abstract. If its type is controlled, then as the last step of evaluating the aggregate, the Initialize procedure of the ancestor type is called, unless the Initialize procedure is abstract (see 7.6).   10

Examples

Examples of extension aggregates (for types defined in 3.9.1):   11

```
Painted_Point'(Point with Red)
(Point'(P) with Paint => Black)
```
  12

```
(Expression with Left => 1.2, Right => 3.4)
Addition'(Binop with null record)
          -- presuming Binop is of type Binary_Operation
```
  13

4.3.3 Array Aggregates

In an array_aggregate, a value is specified for each component of an array, either positionally or by its index. For a positional_array_aggregate, the components are given in increasing-index order, with a final **others**, if any, representing any remaining components. For a named_array_aggregate, the components are identified by the values covered by the discrete_choices.   1

Syntax

array_aggregate ::=   2
  positional_array_aggregate | named_array_aggregate

positional_array_aggregate ::=   3
  (expression, expression {, expression})
  | (expression {, expression}, **others** => expression)

named_array_aggregate ::=   4
  (array_component_association {, array_component_association})

array_component_association ::=   5
  discrete_choice_list => expression

An *n-dimensional* array_aggregate is one that is written as n levels of nested array_aggregates (or at the bottom level, equivalent string_literals). For the multidimensional case (n >= 2) the array_aggregates (or equivalent string_literals) at the n–1 lower levels are called *subaggregate*s of the enclosing n-dimensional array_aggregate. The expressions of the bottom level subaggregates (or of the array_aggregate itself if one-dimensional) are called the *array component expressions* of the enclosing n-dimensional array_aggregate.   6

Name Resolution Rules

The expected type for an array_aggregate (that is not a subaggregate) shall be a single nonlimited array type. The component type of this array type is the expected type for each array component expression of the array_aggregate.   7

The expected type for each discrete_choice in any discrete_choice_list of a named_array_aggregate is the type of the *corresponding index*; the corresponding index for an array_aggregate that is not a   8 subaggregate is the first index of its type; for an (n–m)-dimensional subaggregate within an array_aggregate of an n-dimensional type, the corresponding index is the index in position m+1.

Legality Rules

9   An array_aggregate of an n-dimensional array type shall be written as an n-dimensional array_aggregate.

10   An **others** choice is allowed for an array_aggregate only if an *applicable index constraint* applies to the array_aggregate. An applicable index constraint is a constraint provided by certain contexts where an array_aggregate is permitted that can be used to determine the bounds of the array value specified by the aggregate. Each of the following contexts (and none other) defines an applicable index constraint:

11   • For an explicit_actual_parameter, an explicit_generic_actual_parameter, the expression of a return_statement, the initialization expression in an object_declaration, or a default_-expression (for a parameter or a component), when the nominal subtype of the corresponding formal parameter, generic formal parameter, function result, object, or component is a constrained array subtype, the applicable index constraint is the constraint of the subtype;

12   • For the expression of an assignment_statement where the name denotes an array variable, the applicable index constraint is the constraint of the array variable;

13   • For the operand of a qualified_expression whose subtype_mark denotes a constrained array subtype, the applicable index constraint is the constraint of the subtype;

14   • For a component expression in an aggregate, if the component's nominal subtype is a constrained array subtype, the applicable index constraint is the constraint of the subtype;

15   • For a parenthesized expression, the applicable index constraint is that, if any, defined for the expression.

16   The applicable index constraint *applies* to an array_aggregate that appears in such a context, as well as to any subaggregates thereof. In the case of an explicit_actual_parameter (or default_expression) for a call on a generic formal subprogram, no applicable index constraint is defined.

17   The discrete_choice_list of an array_component_association is allowed to have a discrete_choice that is a nonstatic expression or that is a discrete_range that defines a nonstatic or null range, only if it is the single discrete_choice of its discrete_choice_list, and there is only one array_component_association in the array_aggregate.

18   In a named_array_aggregate with more than one discrete_choice, no two discrete_choices are allowed to cover the same value (see 3.8.1); if there is no **others** choice, the discrete_choices taken together shall exactly cover a contiguous sequence of values of the corresponding index type.

19   A bottom level subaggregate of a multidimensional array_aggregate of a given array type is allowed to be a string_literal only if the component type of the array type is a character type; each character of such a string_literal shall correspond to a defining_character_literal of the component type.

Static Semantics

20   A subaggregate that is a string_literal is equivalent to one that is a positional_array_aggregate of the same length, with each expression being the character_literal for the corresponding character of the string_literal.

Dynamic Semantics

21   The evaluation of an array_aggregate of a given array type proceeds in two steps:

22   1. Any discrete_choices of this aggregate and of its subaggregates are evaluated in an arbitrary order, and converted to the corresponding index type;

2. The array component expressions of the aggregate are evaluated in an arbitrary order and their values are converted to the component subtype of the array type; an array component expression is evaluated once for each associated component.   23

The bounds of the index range of an array_aggregate (including a subaggregate) are determined as follows: 24

- For an array_aggregate with an **others** choice, the bounds are those of the corresponding index range from the applicable index constraint;   25

- For a positional_array_aggregate (or equivalent string_literal) without an **others** choice, the lower bound is that of the corresponding index range in the applicable index constraint, if defined, or that of the corresponding index subtype, if not; in either case, the upper bound is determined from the lower bound and the number of expressions (or the length of the string_literal);   26

- For a named_array_aggregate without an **others** choice, the bounds are determined by the smallest and largest index values covered by any discrete_choice_list.   27

For an array_aggregate, a check is made that the index range defined by its bounds is compatible with the corresponding index subtype.   28

For an array_aggregate with an **others** choice, a check is made that no expression is specified for an index value outside the bounds determined by the applicable index constraint.   29

For a multidimensional array_aggregate, a check is made that all subaggregates that correspond to the same index have the same bounds.   30

The exception Constraint_Error is raised if any of the above checks fail.   31

NOTES
10 In an array_aggregate, positional notation may only be used with two or more expressions; a single expression in parentheses is interpreted as a parenthesized_expression. A named_array_aggregate, such as (1 => X), may be used to specify an array with a single component.   32

Examples

Examples of array aggregates with positional associations: 33

```
(7, 9, 5, 1, 3, 2, 4, 8, 6, 0)
Table'(5, 8, 4, 1, others => 0)    -- see 3.6
```
34

Examples of array aggregates with named associations: 35

```
(1 .. 5 => (1 .. 8 => 0.0))       -- two-dimensional
(1 .. N => new Cell)              -- N new cells, in particular for N = 0
```
36

```
Table'(2 | 4 | 10 => 1, others => 0)
Schedule'(Mon .. Fri => True,  others => False)   -- see 3.6
Schedule'(Wed | Sun  => False, others => True)
Vector'(1 => 2.5)                           -- single-component vector
```
37

Examples of two-dimensional array aggregates: 38

```
-- Three aggregates for the same value of subtype Matrix(1..2,1..3) (see 3.6):
```
39

```
((1.1, 1.2, 1.3), (2.1, 2.2, 2.3))
(1 => (1.1, 1.2, 1.3), 2 => (2.1, 2.2, 2.3))
(1 => (1 => 1.1, 2 => 1.2, 3 => 1.3), 2 => (1 => 2.1, 2 => 2.2, 3 => 2.3))
```
40

Examples of aggregates as initial values:

41
42

```
A : Table := (7, 9, 5, 1, 3, 2, 4, 8, 6, 0);          -- A(1)=7, A(10)=0
B : Table := (2 | 4 | 10 => 1, others => 0);          -- B(1)=0, B(10)=1
C : constant Matrix := (1 .. 5 => (1 .. 8 => 0.0));   -- C'Last(1)=5, C'Last(2)=8
```

43

```
D : Bit_Vector(M .. N) := (M .. N => True);           -- see 3.6
E : Bit_Vector(M .. N) := (others => True);
F : String(1 .. 1) := (1 => 'F');     -- a one component aggregate: same as "F"
```

4.4 Expressions

1   An *expression* is a formula that defines the computation or retrieval of a value. In this International Standard, the term ''expression'' refers to a construct of the syntactic category expression or of any of the other five syntactic categories defined below.

Syntax

2   expression ::=
       relation {**and** relation} | relation {**and then** relation}
       | relation {**or** relation} | relation {**or else** relation}
       | relation {**xor** relation}

3   relation ::=
       simple_expression [relational_operator simple_expression]
       | simple_expression [**not**] **in** range
       | simple_expression [**not**] **in** subtype_mark

4   simple_expression ::= [unary_adding_operator] term {binary_adding_operator term}

5   term ::= factor {multiplying_operator factor}

6   factor ::= primary [** primary] | **abs** primary | **not** primary

7   primary ::=
       numeric_literal | **null** | string_literal | aggregate
       | name | qualified_expression | allocator | (expression)

Name Resolution Rules

8   A name used as a primary shall resolve to denote an object or a value.

Static Semantics

9   Each expression has a type; it specifies the computation or retrieval of a value of that type.

Dynamic Semantics

10   The value of a primary that is a name denoting an object is the value of the object.

Implementation Permissions

11   For the evaluation of a primary that is a name denoting an object of an unconstrained numeric subtype, if the value of the object is outside the base range of its type, the implementation may either raise Constraint_Error or return the value of the object.

Examples of primaries: 12

```
4.0                         -- real literal                              13
Pi                          -- named number
(1 .. 10 => 0)              -- array aggregate
Sum                         -- variable
Integer'Last                -- attribute
Sine(X)                     -- function call
Color'(Blue)                -- qualified expression
Real(M*N)                   -- conversion
(Line_Count + 10)           -- parenthesized expression
```

Examples of expressions: 14

```
Volume                            -- primary                            15
not Destroyed                     -- factor
2*Line_Count                      -- term
-4.0                              -- simple expression
-4.0 + A                          -- simple expression
B**2 - 4.0*A*C                    -- simple expression
Password(1 .. 3) = "Bwv"          -- relation
Count in Small_Int                -- relation
Count not in Small_Int            -- relation
Index = 0 or Item_Hit             -- expression
(Cold and Sunny) or Warm          -- expression (parentheses are required)
A**(B**C)                         -- expression (parentheses are required)
```

4.5 Operators and Expression Evaluation

The language defines the following six categories of operators (given in order of increasing precedence). 1
The corresponding operator_symbols, and only those, can be used as designators in declarations of
functions for user-defined operators. See 6.6, "Overloading of Operators".

logical_operator ::=	**and** | **or** | **xor**	2
relational_operator ::=	= | /= | < | <= | > | >=	3
binary_adding_operator ::=	+ | − | &	4
unary_adding_operator ::=	+ | −	5
multiplying_operator ::=	* | / | **mod** | **rem**	6
highest_precedence_operator ::=	** | **abs** | **not**	7

For a sequence of operators of the same precedence level, the operators are associated with their operands 8
in textual order from left to right. Parentheses can be used to impose specific associations.

For each form of type definition, certain of the above operators are *predefined*; that is, they are implicitly 9
declared immediately after the type definition. For each such implicit operator declaration, the parameters
are called Left and Right for *binary* operators; the single parameter is called Right for *unary* operators. An
expression of the form X op Y, where op is a binary operator, is equivalent to a function_call of the form
"op"(X, Y). An expression of the form op Y, where op is a unary operator, is equivalent to a function_call
of the form "op"(Y). The predefined operators and their effects are described in subclauses 4.5.1 through
4.5.6.

Dynamic Semantics

10   The predefined operations on integer types either yield the mathematically correct result or raise the exception Constraint_Error. For implementations that support the Numerics Annex, the predefined operations on real types yield results whose accuracy is defined in Annex G, or raise the exception Constraint_Error.

Implementation Requirements

11   The implementation of a predefined operator that delivers a result of an integer or fixed point type may raise Constraint_Error only if the result is outside the base range of the result type.

12   The implementation of a predefined operator that delivers a result of a floating point type may raise Constraint_Error only if the result is outside the safe range of the result type.

Implementation Permissions

13   For a sequence of predefined operators of the same precedence level (and in the absence of parentheses imposing a specific association), an implementation may impose any association of the operators with operands so long as the result produced is an allowed result for the left-to-right association, but ignoring the potential for failure of language-defined checks in either the left-to-right or chosen order of association.

> NOTES
>
> 14   11 The two operands of an expression of the form X op Y, where op is a binary operator, are evaluated in an arbitrary order, as for any function_call (see 6.4).

Examples

15   *Examples of precedence:*

16
```
not Sunny or Warm       -- same as (not Sunny) or Warm
X > 4.0 and Y > 0.0     -- same as (X > 4.0) and (Y > 0.0)
```

17
```
-4.0*A**2               -- same as -(4.0 * (A**2))
abs(1 + A) + B          -- same as (abs (1 + A)) + B
Y**(-3)                 -- parentheses are necessary
A / B * C               -- same as (A/B)*C
A + (B + C)             -- evaluate B + C before adding it to A
```

4.5.1 Logical Operators and Short-circuit Control Forms

Name Resolution Rules

1   An expression consisting of two relations connected by **and then** or **or else** (a *short-circuit control form*) shall resolve to be of some boolean type; the expected type for both relations is that same boolean type.

Static Semantics

2   The following logical operators are predefined for every boolean type *T*, for every modular type *T*, and for every one-dimensional array type *T* whose component type is a boolean type:

3
```
function "and"(Left, Right : T) return T
function "or" (Left, Right : T) return T
function "xor"(Left, Right : T) return T
```

4   For boolean types, the predefined logical operators **and**, **or**, and **xor** perform the conventional operations of conjunction, inclusive disjunction, and exclusive disjunction, respectively.

5   For modular types, the predefined logical operators are defined on a bit-by-bit basis, using the binary representation of the value of the operands to yield a binary representation for the result, where zero

represents False and one represents True. If this result is outside the base range of the type, a final subtraction by the modulus is performed to bring the result into the base range of the type.

The logical operators on arrays are performed on a component-by-component basis on matching components (as for equality — see 4.5.2), using the predefined logical operator for the component type. The bounds of the resulting array are those of the left operand.   6

Dynamic Semantics

The short-circuit control forms **and then** and **or else** deliver the same result as the corresponding predefined **and** and **or** operators for boolean types, except that the left operand is always evaluated first, and the right operand is not evaluated if the value of the left operand determines the result.   7

For the logical operators on arrays, a check is made that for each component of the left operand there is a matching component of the right operand, and vice versa. Also, a check is made that each component of the result belongs to the component subtype. The exception Constraint_Error is raised if either of the above checks fails.   8

NOTES
12 The conventional meaning of the logical operators is given by the following truth table: 9

| A | B | (A **and** B) | (A **or** B) | (A **xor** B) | 10
|---|---|---|---|---|
| True | True | True | True | False |
| True | False | False | True | True |
| False | True | False | True | True |
| False | False | False | False | False |

Examples

Examples of logical operators: 11

```
Sunny or Warm                                                        12
Filter(1 .. 10) and Filter(15 .. 24)    -- see 3.6.1
```

Examples of short-circuit control forms: 13

```
Next_Car.Owner /= null and then Next_Car.Owner.Age > 25   -- see 3.10.1   14
N = 0 or else A(N) = Hit_Value
```

4.5.2 Relational Operators and Membership Tests

The *equality operators* = (equals) and /= (not equals) are predefined for nonlimited types. The other relational_operators are the *ordering operators* < (less than), <= (less than or equal), > (greater than), and >= (greater than or equal). The ordering operators are predefined for scalar types, and for *discrete array types*, that is, one-dimensional array types whose components are of a discrete type.   1

A *membership test*, using **in** or **not in**, determines whether or not a value belongs to a given subtype or range, or has a tag that identifies a type that is covered by a given type. Membership tests are allowed for all types.   2

Name Resolution Rules

The *tested type* of a membership test is the type of the range or the type determined by the subtype_mark. If the tested type is tagged, then the simple_expression shall resolve to be of a type that covers or is covered by the tested type; if untagged, the expected type for the simple_expression is the tested type.   3

4   For a membership test, if the simple_expression is of a tagged class-wide type, then the tested type shall be (visibly) tagged.

5   The result type of a membership test is the predefined type Boolean.

6   The equality operators are predefined for every specific type *T* that is not limited, and not an anonymous access type, with the following specifications:

7
```
function "=" (Left, Right : T) return Boolean
function "/="(Left, Right : T) return Boolean
```

8   The ordering operators are predefined for every specific scalar type *T*, and for every discrete array type *T*, with the following specifications:

9
```
function "<" (Left, Right : T) return Boolean
function "<="(Left, Right : T) return Boolean
function ">" (Left, Right : T) return Boolean
function ">="(Left, Right : T) return Boolean
```

10   For discrete types, the predefined relational operators are defined in terms of corresponding mathematical operations on the position numbers of the values of the operands.

11   For real types, the predefined relational operators are defined in terms of the corresponding mathematical operations on the values of the operands, subject to the accuracy of the type.

12   Two access-to-object values are equal if they designate the same object, or if both are equal to the null value of the access type.

13   Two access-to-subprogram values are equal if they are the result of the same evaluation of an Access attribute_reference, or if both are equal to the null value of the access type. Two access-to-subprogram values are unequal if they designate different subprograms. It is unspecified whether two access values that designate the same subprogram but are the result of distinct evaluations of Access attribute_references are equal or unequal.

14   For a type extension, predefined equality is defined in terms of the primitive (possibly user-defined) equals operator of the parent type and of any tagged components of the extension part, and predefined equality for any other components not inherited from the parent type.

15   For a private type, if its full type is tagged, predefined equality is defined in terms of the primitive equals operator of the full type; if the full type is untagged, predefined equality for the private type is that of its full type.

16   For other composite types, the predefined equality operators (and certain other predefined operations on composite types — see 4.5.1 and 4.6) are defined in terms of the corresponding operation on *matching components*, defined as follows:

17   • For two composite objects or values of the same non-array type, matching components are those that correspond to the same component_declaration or discriminant_specification;

18   • For two one-dimensional arrays of the same type, matching components are those (if any) whose index values match in the following sense: the lower bounds of the index ranges are defined to match, and the successors of matching indices are defined to match;

19   • For two multidimensional arrays of the same type, matching components are those whose index values match in successive index positions.

The analogous definitions apply if the types of the two objects or values are convertible, rather than being the same. 20

Given the above definition of matching components, the result of the predefined equals operator for composite types (other than for those composite types covered earlier) is defined as follows: 21

- If there are no components, the result is defined to be True; 22

- If there are unmatched components, the result is defined to be False; 23

- Otherwise, the result is defined in terms of the primitive equals operator for any matching tagged components, and the predefined equals for any matching untagged components. 24

For any composite type, the order in which "=" is called for components is unspecified. Furthermore, if the result can be determined before calling "=" on some components, it is unspecified whether "=" is called on those components. 24.1/1

The predefined "/=" operator gives the complementary result to the predefined "=" operator. 25

For a discrete array type, the predefined ordering operators correspond to *lexicographic order* using the predefined order relation of the component type: A null array is lexicographically less than any array having at least one component. In the case of nonnull arrays, the left operand is lexicographically less than the right operand if the first component of the left operand is less than that of the right; otherwise the left operand is lexicographically less than the right operand only if their first components are equal and the tail of the left operand is lexicographically less than that of the right (the *tail* consists of the remaining components beyond the first and can be null). 26

For the evaluation of a membership test, the simple_expression and the range (if any) are evaluated in an arbitrary order. 27

A membership test using **in** yields the result True if: 28

- The tested type is scalar, and the value of the simple_expression belongs to the given range, or the range of the named subtype; or 29

- The tested type is not scalar, and the value of the simple_expression satisfies any constraints of the named subtype, and, if the type of the simple_expression is class-wide, the value has a tag that identifies a type covered by the tested type. 30

Otherwise the test yields the result False. 31

A membership test using **not in** gives the complementary result to the corresponding membership test using **in**. 32

Implementation Requirements

For all nonlimited types declared in language-defined packages, the "=" and "/=" operators of the type shall behave as if they were the predefined equality operators for the purposes of the equality of composite types and generic formal types. 32.1/1

NOTES
13 No exception is ever raised by a membership test, by a predefined ordering operator, or by a predefined equality operator for an elementary type, but an exception can be raised by the evaluation of the operands. A predefined equality operator for a composite type can only raise an exception if the type has a tagged part whose primitive equals operator propagates an exception. 33

14 If a composite type has components that depend on discriminants, two values of this type have matching components if and only if their discriminants are equal. Two nonnull arrays have matching components if and only if the length of each dimension is the same for both. 34

Relational Operators and Membership Tests **4.5.2**

35 *Examples of expressions involving relational operators and membership tests:*

36
```
X /= Y
```

37
```
"" < "A" and "A" < "Aa"      -- True
"Aa" < "B" and "A" < "A  "   -- True
```

38
```
My_Car = null               -- true if My_Car has been set to null (see 3.10.1)
My_Car = Your_Car           -- true if we both share the same car
My_Car.all = Your_Car.all   -- true if the two cars are identical
```

39
```
N not in 1 .. 10            -- range membership test
Today in Mon .. Fri        -- range membership test
Today in Weekday           -- subtype membership test (see 3.5.1)
Archive in Disk_Unit       -- subtype membership test (see 3.8.1)
Tree.all in Addition'Class -- class membership test (see 3.9.1)
```

4.5.3 Binary Adding Operators

Static Semantics

1 The binary adding operators + (addition) and − (subtraction) are predefined for every specific numeric type *T* with their conventional meaning. They have the following specifications:

2
```
function "+"(Left, Right : T) return T
function "-"(Left, Right : T) return T
```

3 The concatenation operators & are predefined for every nonlimited, one-dimensional array type *T* with component type *C*. They have the following specifications:

4
```
function "&"(Left : T; Right : T) return T
function "&"(Left : T; Right : C) return T
function "&"(Left : C; Right : T) return T
function "&"(Left : C; Right : C) return T
```

Dynamic Semantics

5 For the evaluation of a concatenation with result type *T*, if both operands are of type *T*, the result of the concatenation is a one-dimensional array whose length is the sum of the lengths of its operands, and whose components comprise the components of the left operand followed by the components of the right operand. If the left operand is a null array, the result of the concatenation is the right operand. Otherwise, the lower bound of the result is determined as follows:

6 • If the ultimate ancestor of the array type was defined by a constrained_array_definition, then the lower bound of the result is that of the index subtype;

7 • If the ultimate ancestor of the array type was defined by an unconstrained_array_definition, then the lower bound of the result is that of the left operand.

8 The upper bound is determined by the lower bound and the length. A check is made that the upper bound of the result of the concatenation belongs to the range of the index subtype, unless the result is a null array. Constraint_Error is raised if this check fails.

9 If either operand is of the component type *C*, the result of the concatenation is given by the above rules, using in place of such an operand an array having this operand as its only component (converted to the component subtype) and having the lower bound of the index subtype of the array type as its lower bound.

10 The result of a concatenation is defined in terms of an assignment to an anonymous object, as for any function call (see 6.5).

NOTES

15 As for all predefined operators on modular types, the binary adding operators + and − on modular types include a final reduction modulo the modulus if the result is outside the base range of the type.   11

Examples

Examples of expressions involving binary adding operators: 12

```
Z + 0.1          -- Z has to be of a real type
```
13

```
"A" & "BCD"      -- concatenation of two string literals
'A' & "BCD"      -- concatenation of a character literal and a string literal
'A' & 'A'        -- concatenation of two character literals
```
14

4.5.4 Unary Adding Operators

Static Semantics

The unary adding operators + (identity) and − (negation) are predefined for every specific numeric type T with their conventional meaning. They have the following specifications: 1

```
function "+"(Right : T) return T
function "-"(Right : T) return T
```
2

NOTES

16 For modular integer types, the unary adding operator −, when given a nonzero operand, returns the result of subtracting the value of the operand from the modulus; for a zero operand, the result is zero.   3

4.5.5 Multiplying Operators

Static Semantics

The multiplying operators * (multiplication), / (division), **mod** (modulus), and **rem** (remainder) are predefined for every specific integer type T: 1

```
function "*"  (Left, Right : T) return T
function "/"  (Left, Right : T) return T
function "mod"(Left, Right : T) return T
function "rem"(Left, Right : T) return T
```
2

Signed integer multiplication has its conventional meaning.   3

Signed integer division and remainder are defined by the relation: 4

```
A = (A/B)*B + (A rem B)
```
5

where (A **rem** B) has the sign of A and an absolute value less than the absolute value of B. Signed integer division satisfies the identity: 6

```
(-A)/B = -(A/B) = A/(-B)
```
7

The signed integer modulus operator is defined such that the result of A **mod** B has the sign of B and an absolute value less than the absolute value of B; in addition, for some signed integer value N, this result satisfies the relation: 8

```
A = B*N + (A mod B)
```
9

The multiplying operators on modular types are defined in terms of the corresponding signed integer operators, followed by a reduction modulo the modulus if the result is outside the base range of the type (which is only possible for the "*" operator).   10

Multiplication and division operators are predefined for every specific floating point type T: 11

12

```
function "*"(Left, Right : T) return T
function "/"(Left, Right : T) return T
```

13 The following multiplication and division operators, with an operand of the predefined type Integer, are predefined for every specific fixed point type *T*:

14

```
function "*"(Left : T; Right : Integer) return T
function "*"(Left : Integer; Right : T) return T
function "/"(Left : T; Right : Integer) return T
```

15 All of the above multiplying operators are usable with an operand of an appropriate universal numeric type. The following additional multiplying operators for *root_real* are predefined, and are usable when both operands are of an appropriate universal or root numeric type, and the result is allowed to be of type *root_real*, as in a number_declaration:

16

```
function "*"(Left, Right : root_real) return root_real
function "/"(Left, Right : root_real) return root_real
```

17

```
function "*"(Left : root_real; Right : root_integer) return root_real
function "*"(Left : root_integer; Right : root_real) return root_real
function "/"(Left : root_real; Right : root_integer) return root_real
```

18 Multiplication and division between any two fixed point types are provided by the following two predefined operators:

19

```
function "*"(Left, Right : universal_fixed) return universal_fixed
function "/"(Left, Right : universal_fixed) return universal_fixed
```

Legality Rules

20 The above two fixed-fixed multiplying operators shall not be used in a context where the expected type for the result is itself *universal_fixed* — the context has to identify some other numeric type to which the result is to be converted, either explicitly or implicitly.

Dynamic Semantics

21 The multiplication and division operators for real types have their conventional meaning. For floating point types, the accuracy of the result is determined by the precision of the result type. For decimal fixed point types, the result is truncated toward zero if the mathematical result is between two multiples of the *small* of the specific result type (possibly determined by context); for ordinary fixed point types, if the mathematical result is between two multiples of the *small*, it is unspecified which of the two is the result.

22 The exception Constraint_Error is raised by integer division, **rem**, and **mod** if the right operand is zero. Similarly, for a real type *T* with *T*'Machine_Overflows True, division by zero raises Constraint_Error.

NOTES

23 17 For positive A and B, A/B is the quotient and A **rem** B is the remainder when A is divided by B. The following relations are satisfied by the rem operator:

24

```
    A  rem (-B)  =   A rem B
  (-A)  rem    B  = -(A rem B)
```

25 18 For any signed integer K, the following identity holds:

26

```
  A mod B   =   (A + K*B) mod B
```

The relations between signed integer division, remainder, and modulus are illustrated by the following table: 27

A	B	A/B	A **rem** B	A **mod** B	A	B	A/B	A **rem** B	A **mod** B	28
10	5	2	0	0	-10	5	-2	0	0	29
11	5	2	1	1	-11	5	-2	-1	4	
12	5	2	2	2	-12	5	-2	-2	3	
13	5	2	3	3	-13	5	-2	-3	2	
14	5	2	4	4	-14	5	-2	-4	1	

A	B	A/B	A **rem** B	A **mod** B	A	B	A/B	A **rem** B	A **mod** B	30
10	-5	-2	0	0	-10	-5	2	0	0	
11	-5	-2	1	-4	-11	-5	2	-1	-1	
12	-5	-2	2	-3	-12	-5	2	-2	-2	
13	-5	-2	3	-2	-13	-5	2	-3	-3	
14	-5	-2	4	-1	-14	-5	2	-4	-4	

Examples

Examples of expressions involving multiplying operators: 31

```
I : Integer := 1;                                                    32
J : Integer := 2;
K : Integer := 3;

X : Real := 1.0;             --   see 3.5.7                           33
Y : Real := 2.0;

F : Fraction := 0.25;        --   see 3.5.9                           34
G : Fraction := 0.5;
```

Expression	Value	Result Type	35
I*J	2	same as I and J, that is, Integer	
K/J	1	same as K and J, that is, Integer	
K **mod** J	1	same as K and J, that is, Integer	
X/Y	0.5	same as X and Y, that is, Real	
F/2	0.125	same as F, that is, Fraction	
3*F	0.75	same as F, that is, Fraction	
0.75*G	0.375	universal_fixed, implicitly convertible to any fixed point type	
Fraction(F*G)	0.125	Fraction, as stated by the conversion	
Real(J)*Y	4.0	Real, the type of both operands after conversion of J	

4.5.6 Highest Precedence Operators

Static Semantics

The highest precedence unary operator **abs** (absolute value) is predefined for every specific numeric type   1
T, with the following specification:

```
function "abs"(Right : T) return T                                   2
```

The highest precedence unary operator **not** (logical negation) is predefined for every boolean type T, every   3
modular type T, and for every one-dimensional array type T whose components are of a boolean type, with
the following specification:

```
function "not"(Right : T) return T                                   4
```

The result of the operator **not** for a modular type is defined as the difference between the high bound of the   5
base range of the type and the value of the operand. For a binary modulus, this corresponds to a bit-wise
complement of the binary representation of the value of the operand.

6   The operator **not** that applies to a one-dimensional array of boolean components yields a one-dimensional boolean array with the same bounds; each component of the result is obtained by logical negation of the corresponding component of the operand (that is, the component that has the same index value). A check is made that each component of the result belongs to the component subtype; the exception Constraint_Error is raised if this check fails.

7   The highest precedence *exponentiation* operator ** is predefined for every specific integer type *T* with the following specification:

8   **function** "**"(Left : *T*; Right : Natural) **return** *T*

9   Exponentiation is also predefined for every specific floating point type as well as *root_real*, with the following specification (where *T* is *root_real* or the floating point type):

10   **function** "**"(Left : *T*; Right : Integer'Base) **return** *T*

11   The right operand of an exponentiation is the *exponent*. The expression X**N with the value of the exponent N positive is equivalent to the expression X*X*...X (with N–1 multiplications) except that the multiplications are associated in an arbitrary order. With N equal to zero, the result is one. With the value of N negative (only defined for a floating point operand), the result is the reciprocal of the result using the absolute value of N as the exponent.

Implementation Permissions

12   The implementation of exponentiation for the case of a negative exponent is allowed to raise Constraint_Error if the intermediate result of the repeated multiplications is outside the safe range of the type, even though the final result (after taking the reciprocal) would not be. (The best machine approximation to the final result in this case would generally be 0.0.)

NOTES
13   19 As implied by the specification given above for exponentiation of an integer type, a check is made that the exponent is not negative. Constraint_Error is raised if this check fails.

4.6 Type Conversions

1   Explicit type conversions, both value conversions and view conversions, are allowed between closely related types as defined below. This clause also defines rules for value and view conversions to a particular subtype of a type, both explicit ones and those implicit in other constructs.

Syntax

2   type_conversion ::=
           subtype_mark(expression)
          | subtype_mark(name)

3   The *target subtype* of a type_conversion is the subtype denoted by the subtype_mark. The *operand* of a type_conversion is the expression or name within the parentheses; its type is the *operand type*.

4   One type is *convertible* to a second type if a type_conversion with the first type as operand type and the second type as target type is legal according to the rules of this clause. Two types are convertible if each is convertible to the other.

5/1 A type_conversion whose operand is the name of an object is called a *view conversion* if both its target type and operand type are tagged, or if it appears as an actual parameter of mode **out** or **in out**; other type_conversions are called *value conversions*.

Name Resolution Rules

The operand of a type_conversion is expected to be of any type. 6

The operand of a view conversion is interpreted only as a name; the operand of a value conversion is interpreted as an expression. 7

Legality Rules

If the target type is a numeric type, then the operand type shall be a numeric type. 8

If the target type is an array type, then the operand type shall be an array type. Further: 9

- The types shall have the same dimensionality; 10

- Corresponding index types shall be convertible; 11/1

- The component subtypes shall statically match; and 12/1

- In a view conversion, the target type and the operand type shall both or neither have aliased components. 12.1/1

If the target type is a general access type, then the operand type shall be an access-to-object type. Further: 13

- If the target type is an access-to-variable type, then the operand type shall be an access-to-variable type; 14

- If the target designated type is tagged, then the operand designated type shall be convertible to the target designated type; 15

- If the target designated type is not tagged, then the designated types shall be the same, and either the designated subtypes shall statically match or the target designated subtype shall be discriminated and unconstrained; and 16

- The accessibility level of the operand type shall not be statically deeper than that of the target type. In addition to the places where Legality Rules normally apply (see 12.3), this rule applies also in the private part of an instance of a generic unit. 17

If the target type is an access-to-subprogram type, then the operand type shall be an access-to-subprogram type. Further: 18

- The designated profiles shall be subtype-conformant. 19

- The accessibility level of the operand type shall not be statically deeper than that of the target type. In addition to the places where Legality Rules normally apply (see 12.3), this rule applies also in the private part of an instance of a generic unit. If the operand type is declared within a generic body, the target type shall be declared within the generic body. 20

If the target type is not included in any of the above four cases, there shall be a type that is an ancestor of both the target type and the operand type. Further, if the target type is tagged, then either: 21

- The operand type shall be covered by or descended from the target type; or 22

- The operand type shall be a class-wide type that covers the target type. 23

In a view conversion for an untagged type, the target type shall be convertible (back) to the operand type. 24

Static Semantics

A type_conversion that is a value conversion denotes the value that is the result of converting the value of the operand to the target subtype. 25

26   A type_conversion that is a view conversion denotes a view of the object denoted by the operand. This view is a variable of the target type if the operand denotes a variable; otherwise it is a constant of the target type.

27   The nominal subtype of a type_conversion is its target subtype.

Dynamic Semantics

28   For the evaluation of a type_conversion that is a value conversion, the operand is evaluated, and then the value of the operand is *converted* to a *corresponding* value of the target type, if any. If there is no value of the target type that corresponds to the operand value, Constraint_Error is raised; this can only happen on conversion to a modular type, and only when the operand value is outside the base range of the modular type. Additional rules follow:

29   • Numeric Type Conversion

30   • If the target and the operand types are both integer types, then the result is the value of the target type that corresponds to the same mathematical integer as the operand.

31   • If the target type is a decimal fixed point type, then the result is truncated (toward 0) if the value of the operand is not a multiple of the *small* of the target type.

32   • If the target type is some other real type, then the result is within the accuracy of the target type (see G.2, ''Numeric Performance Requirements'', for implementations that support the Numerics Annex).

33   • If the target type is an integer type and the operand type is real, the result is rounded to the nearest integer (away from zero if exactly halfway between two integers).

34   • Enumeration Type Conversion

35   • The result is the value of the target type with the same position number as that of the operand value.

36   • Array Type Conversion

37   • If the target subtype is a constrained array subtype, then a check is made that the length of each dimension of the value of the operand equals the length of the corresponding dimension of the target subtype. The bounds of the result are those of the target subtype.

38   • If the target subtype is an unconstrained array subtype, then the bounds of the result are obtained by converting each bound of the value of the operand to the corresponding index type of the target type. For each nonnull index range, a check is made that the bounds of the range belong to the corresponding index subtype.

39   • In either array case, the value of each component of the result is that of the matching component of the operand value (see 4.5.2).

40   • Composite (Non-Array) Type Conversion

41   • The value of each nondiscriminant component of the result is that of the matching component of the operand value.

42   • The tag of the result is that of the operand. If the operand type is class-wide, a check is made that the tag of the operand identifies a (specific) type that is covered by or descended from the target type.

43   • For each discriminant of the target type that corresponds to a discriminant of the operand type, its value is that of the corresponding discriminant of the operand value; if it corresponds to more than one discriminant of the operand type, a check is made that all these discriminants are equal in the operand value.

- For each discriminant of the target type that corresponds to a discriminant that is specified   44
  by the derived_type_definition for some ancestor of the operand type (or if class-wide,
  some ancestor of the specific type identified by the tag of the operand), its value in the
  result is that specified by the derived_type_definition.

- For each discriminant of the operand type that corresponds to a discriminant that is   45
  specified by the derived_type_definition for some ancestor of the target type, a check is
  made that in the operand value it equals the value specified for it.

- For each discriminant of the result, a check is made that its value belongs to its subtype.   46

- Access Type Conversion   47

  - For an access-to-object type, a check is made that the accessibility level of the operand type   48
    is not deeper than that of the target type.

  - If the target type is an anonymous access type, a check is made that the value of the operand   49
    is not null; if the target is not an anonymous access type, then the result is null if the
    operand value is null.

  - If the operand value is not null, then the result designates the same object (or subprogram)   50
    as is designated by the operand value, but viewed as being of the target designated subtype
    (or profile); any checks associated with evaluating a conversion to the target designated
    subtype are performed.

After conversion of the value to the target type, if the target subtype is constrained, a check is performed   51
that the value satisfies this constraint.

For the evaluation of a view conversion, the operand name is evaluated, and a new view of the object   52
denoted by the operand is created, whose type is the target type; if the target type is composite, checks are
performed as above for a value conversion.

The properties of this new view are as follows: 53

- If the target type is composite, the bounds or discriminants (if any) of the view are as defined   54/1
  above for a value conversion; each nondiscriminant component of the view denotes the matching
  component of the operand object; the subtype of the view is constrained if either the target
  subtype or the operand object is constrained, or if the target subtype is indefinite, or if the
  operand type is a descendant of the target type, and has discriminants that were not inherited
  from the target type;

- If the target type is tagged, then an assignment to the view assigns to the corresponding part of   55
  the object denoted by the operand; otherwise, an assignment to the view assigns to the object,
  after converting the assigned value to the subtype of the object (which might raise
  Constraint_Error);

- Reading the value of the view yields the result of converting the value of the operand object to   56
  the target subtype (which might raise Constraint_Error), except if the object is of an access type
  and the view conversion is passed as an **out** parameter; in this latter case, the value of the
  operand object is used to initialize the formal parameter without checking against any constraint
  of the target subtype (see 6.4.1).

If an Accessibility_Check fails, Program_Error is raised. Any other check associated with a conversion   57
raises Constraint_Error if it fails.

Conversion to a type is the same as conversion to an unconstrained subtype of the type.   58

NOTES   59
20 In addition to explicit type_conversions, type conversions are performed implicitly in situations where the expected
type and the actual type of a construct differ, as is permitted by the type resolution rules (see 8.6). For example, an

integer literal is of the type *universal_integer*, and is implicitly converted when assigned to a target of some specific integer type. Similarly, an actual parameter of a specific tagged type is implicitly converted when the corresponding formal parameter is of a class-wide type.

60 21 Even when the expected and actual types are the same, implicit subtype conversions are performed to adjust the array bounds (if any) of an operand to match the desired target subtype, or to raise Constraint_Error if the (possibly adjusted) value does not satisfy the constraints of the target subtype.

61 A ramification of the overload resolution rules is that the operand of an (explicit) type_conversion cannot be the literal **null**, an allocator, an aggregate, a string_literal, a character_literal, or an attribute_reference for an Access or Unchecked_Access attribute. Similarly, such an expression enclosed by parentheses is not allowed. A qualified_expression (see 4.7) can be used instead of such a type_conversion.

62 22 The constraint of the target subtype has no effect for a type_conversion of an elementary type passed as an **out** parameter. Hence, it is recommended that the first subtype be specified as the target to minimize confusion (a similar recommendation applies to renaming and generic formal **in out** objects).

Examples

63 *Examples of numeric type conversion:*

64
```
Real(2*J)        -- value is converted to floating point
Integer(1.6)     -- value is 2
Integer(-0.4)    -- value is 0
```

65 *Example of conversion between derived types:*

66
```
type A_Form is new B_Form;
```

67
```
X : A_Form;
Y : B_Form;
```

68
```
X := A_Form(Y);
Y := B_Form(X);    -- the reverse conversion
```

69 *Examples of conversions between array types:*

70
```
type Sequence is array (Integer range <>) of Integer;
subtype Dozen is Sequence(1 .. 12);
Ledger : array(1 .. 100) of Integer;
```

71
```
Sequence(Ledger)            -- bounds are those of Ledger
Sequence(Ledger(31 .. 42))  -- bounds are 31 and 42
Dozen(Ledger(31 .. 42))     -- bounds are those of Dozen
```

4.7 Qualified Expressions

1 A qualified_expression is used to state explicitly the type, and to verify the subtype, of an operand that is either an expression or an aggregate.

Syntax

2 qualified_expression ::=
      subtype_mark'(expression) | subtype_mark'aggregate

Name Resolution Rules

3 The *operand* (the expression or aggregate) shall resolve to be of the type determined by the subtype_-mark, or a universal type that covers it.

Dynamic Semantics

4 The evaluation of a qualified_expression evaluates the operand (and if of a universal type, converts it to the type determined by the subtype_mark) and checks that its value belongs to the subtype denoted by the subtype_mark. The exception Constraint_Error is raised if this check fails.

NOTES

23 When a given context does not uniquely identify an expected type, a qualified_expression can be used to do so. In 5
particular, if an overloaded name or aggregate is passed to an overloaded subprogram, it might be necessary to qualify
the operand to resolve its type.

Examples

Examples of disambiguating expressions using qualification: 6

```
type Mask is (Fix, Dec, Exp, Signif);        7
type Code is (Fix, Cla, Dec, Tnz, Sub);

Print (Mask'(Dec));   -- Dec is of type Mask    8
Print (Code'(Dec));   -- Dec is of type Code

for J in Code'(Fix) .. Code'(Dec) loop ... -- qualification needed for either Fix or Dec    9
for J in Code range Fix .. Dec loop ...     -- qualification unnecessary
for J in Code'(Fix) .. Dec loop ...         -- qualification unnecessary for Dec
Dozen'(1 | 3 | 5 | 7 => 2, others => 0) -- see 4.6        10
```

4.8 Allocators

The evaluation of an allocator creates an object and yields an access value that designates the object. 1

Syntax

allocator ::= 2
    new subtype_indication | **new** qualified_expression

Name Resolution Rules

The expected type for an allocator shall be a single access-to-object type with designated type D such that 3/1
either D covers the type determined by the subtype_mark of the subtype_indication or
qualified_expression, or the expected type is anonymous and the determined type is D'Class.

Legality Rules

An *initialized* allocator is an allocator with a qualified_expression. An *uninitialized* allocator is one with a 4
subtype_indication. In the subtype_indication of an uninitialized allocator, a constraint is permitted only
if the subtype_mark denotes an unconstrained composite subtype; if there is no constraint, then the
subtype_mark shall denote a definite subtype.

If the type of the allocator is an access-to-constant type, the allocator shall be an initialized allocator. If the 5
designated type is limited, the allocator shall be an uninitialized allocator.

Static Semantics

If the designated type of the type of the allocator is elementary, then the subtype of the created object is the 6
designated subtype. If the designated type is composite, then the created object is always constrained; if
the designated subtype is constrained, then it provides the constraint of the created object; otherwise, the
object is constrained by its initial value (even if the designated subtype is unconstrained with defaults).

Dynamic Semantics

For the evaluation of an allocator, the elaboration of the subtype_indication or the evaluation of the 7
qualified_expression is performed first. For the evaluation of an initialized allocator, an object of the
designated type is created and the value of the qualified_expression is converted to the designated subtype
and assigned to the object.

For the evaluation of an uninitialized allocator: 8

9   • If the designated type is elementary, an object of the designated subtype is created and any implicit initial value is assigned;

10/1   • If the designated type is composite, an object of the designated type is created with tag, if any, determined by the subtype_mark of the subtype_indication; any per-object constraints on subcomponents are elaborated (see 3.8) and any implicit initial values for the subcomponents of the object are obtained as determined by the subtype_indication and assigned to the corresponding subcomponents. A check is made that the value of the object belongs to the designated subtype. Constraint_Error is raised if this check fails. This check and the initialization of the object are performed in an arbitrary order.

11   If the created object contains any tasks, they are activated (see 9.2). Finally, an access value that designates the created object is returned.

NOTES

12   24 Allocators cannot create objects of an abstract type. See 3.9.3.

13   25 If any part of the created object is controlled, the initialization includes calls on corresponding Initialize or Adjust procedures. See 7.6.

14   26 As explained in 13.11, "Storage Management", the storage for an object allocated by an allocator comes from a storage pool (possibly user defined). The exception Storage_Error is raised by an allocator if there is not enough storage. Instances of Unchecked_Deallocation may be used to explicitly reclaim storage.

15   27 Implementations are permitted, but not required, to provide garbage collection (see 13.11.3).

Examples

16   *Examples of allocators:*

17
```
new Cell'(0, null, null)                        -- initialized explicitly, see 3.10.1
new Cell'(Value => 0, Succ => null, Pred => null) -- initialized explicitly
new Cell                                        -- not initialized
```

18
```
new Matrix(1 .. 10, 1 .. 20)                    -- the bounds only are given
new Matrix'(1 .. 10 => (1 .. 20 => 0.0))        -- initialized explicitly
```

19
```
new Buffer(100)                                 -- the discriminant only is given
new Buffer'(Size => 80, Pos => 0, Value => (1 .. 80 => 'A')) -- initialized explicitly
```

20
```
Expr_Ptr'(new Literal)                          -- allocator for access-to-class-wide type, see 3.9.1
Expr_Ptr'(new Literal'(Expression with 3.5))    -- initialized explicitly
```

4.9 Static Expressions and Static Subtypes

1   Certain expressions of a scalar or string type are defined to be static. Similarly, certain discrete ranges are defined to be static, and certain scalar and string subtypes are defined to be static subtypes. *Static* means determinable at compile time, using the declared properties or values of the program entities.

2   A static expression is a scalar or string expression that is one of the following:

3   • a numeric_literal;

4   • a string_literal of a static string subtype;

5   • a name that denotes the declaration of a named number or a static constant;

6   • a function_call whose *function_*name or *function_*prefix statically denotes a static function, and whose actual parameters, if any (whether given explicitly or by default), are all static expressions;

7   • an attribute_reference that denotes a scalar value, and whose prefix denotes a static scalar subtype;

- an attribute_reference whose prefix statically denotes a statically constrained array object or array subtype, and whose attribute_designator is First, Last, or Length, with an optional dimension; 8

- a type_conversion whose subtype_mark denotes a static scalar subtype, and whose operand is a static expression; 9

- a qualified_expression whose subtype_mark denotes a static (scalar or string) subtype, and whose operand is a static expression; 10

- a membership test whose simple_expression is a static expression, and whose range is a static range or whose subtype_mark denotes a static (scalar or string) subtype; 11

- a short-circuit control form both of whose relations are static expressions; 12

- a static expression enclosed in parentheses. 13

A name *statically denotes* an entity if it denotes the entity and: 14

- It is a direct_name, expanded name, or character_literal, and it denotes a declaration other than a renaming_declaration; or 15

- It is an attribute_reference whose prefix statically denotes some entity; or 16

- It denotes a renaming_declaration with a name that statically denotes the renamed entity. 17

A *static function* is one of the following: 18

- a predefined operator whose parameter and result types are all scalar types none of which are descendants of formal scalar types; 19

- a predefined concatenation operator whose result type is a string type; 20

- an enumeration literal; 21

- a language-defined attribute that is a function, if the prefix denotes a static scalar subtype, and if the parameter and result types are scalar. 22

In any case, a generic formal subprogram is not a static function. 23

A *static constant* is a constant view declared by a full constant declaration or an object_renaming_-declaration with a static nominal subtype, having a value defined by a static scalar expression or by a static string expression whose value has a length not exceeding the maximum length of a string_literal in the implementation. 24

A *static range* is a range whose bounds are static expressions, or a range_attribute_reference that is equivalent to such a range. A *static* discrete_range is one that is a static range or is a subtype_indication that defines a static scalar subtype. The base range of a scalar type is a static range, unless the type is a descendant of a formal scalar type. 25

A *static subtype* is either a *static scalar subtype* or a *static string subtype*. A static scalar subtype is an unconstrained scalar subtype whose type is not a descendant of a formal scalar type, or a constrained scalar subtype formed by imposing a compatible static constraint on a static scalar subtype. A static string subtype is an unconstrained string subtype whose index subtype and component subtype are static (and whose type is not a descendant of a formal array type), or a constrained string subtype formed by imposing a compatible static constraint on a static string subtype. In any case, the subtype of a generic formal object of mode **in out**, and the result subtype of a generic formal function, are not static. 26

The different kinds of *static constraint* are defined as follows: 27

- A null constraint is always static; 28

Static Expressions and Static Subtypes   **4.9**

29 • A scalar constraint is static if it has no range_constraint, or one with a static range;

30 • An index constraint is static if each discrete_range is static, and each index subtype of the corresponding array type is static;

31 • A discriminant constraint is static if each expression of the constraint is static, and the subtype of each discriminant is static.

32 A subtype is *statically constrained* if it is constrained, and its constraint is static. An object is *statically constrained* if its nominal subtype is statically constrained, or if it is a static string constant.

Legality Rules

33 A static expression is evaluated at compile time except when it is part of the right operand of a static short-circuit control form whose value is determined by its left operand. This evaluation is performed exactly, without performing Overflow_Checks. For a static expression that is evaluated:

34 • The expression is illegal if its evaluation fails a language-defined check other than Overflow_-Check.

35 • If the expression is not part of a larger static expression, then its value shall be within the base range of its expected type. Otherwise, the value may be arbitrarily large or small.

36 • If the expression is of type *universal_real* and its expected type is a decimal fixed point type, then its value shall be a multiple of the *small* of the decimal type.

37 The last two restrictions above do not apply if the expected type is a descendant of a formal scalar type (or a corresponding actual type in an instance).

Implementation Requirements

38 For a real static expression that is not part of a larger static expression, and whose expected type is not a descendant of a formal scalar type, the implementation shall round or truncate the value (according to the Machine_Rounds attribute of the expected type) to the nearest machine number of the expected type; if the value is exactly half-way between two machine numbers, any rounding shall be performed away from zero. If the expected type is a descendant of a formal scalar type, no special rounding or truncating is required — normal accuracy rules apply (see Annex G).

NOTES

39 28 An expression can be static even if it occurs in a context where staticness is not required.

40 29 A static (or run-time) type_conversion from a real type to an integer type performs rounding. If the operand value is exactly half-way between two integers, the rounding is performed away from zero.

Examples

41 *Examples of static expressions:*

42
```
1 + 1        -- 2
abs(-10)*3   -- 30
```

43
```
Kilo : constant := 1000;
Mega : constant := Kilo*Kilo;    -- 1_000_000
Long : constant := Float'Digits*2;
```

44
```
Half_Pi    : constant := Pi/2;               -- see 3.3.2
Deg_To_Rad : constant := Half_Pi/90;
Rad_To_Deg : constant := 1.0/Deg_To_Rad;  -- equivalent to 1.0/((3.14159_26536/2)/90)
```

4.9.1 Statically Matching Constraints and Subtypes

Static Semantics

A constraint *statically matches* another constraint if both are null constraints, both are static and have equal corresponding bounds or discriminant values, or both are nonstatic and result from the same elaboration of a constraint of a subtype_indication or the same evaluation of a range of a discrete_-subtype_definition.   1

A subtype *statically matches* another subtype of the same type if they have statically matching constraints. Two anonymous access subtypes statically match if their designated subtypes statically match.   2

Two ranges of the same type *statically match* if both result from the same evaluation of a range, or if both are static and have equal corresponding bounds.   3

A constraint is *statically compatible* with a scalar subtype if it statically matches the constraint of the subtype, or if both are static and the constraint is compatible with the subtype. A constraint is *statically compatible* with an access or composite subtype if it statically matches the constraint of the subtype, or if the subtype is unconstrained. One subtype is *statically compatible* with a second subtype if the constraint of the first is statically compatible with the second subtype.   4

Section 5: Statements

A statement defines an action to be performed upon its execution.   1

This section describes the general rules applicable to all statements. Some statements are discussed in   2
later sections: Procedure_call_statements and return_statements are described in 6, "Subprograms".
Entry_call_statements, requeue_statements, delay_statements, accept_statements, select_statements,
and abort_statements are described in 9, "Tasks and Synchronization". Raise_statements are described
in 11, "Exceptions", and code_statements in 13. The remaining forms of statements are presented in
this section.

5.1 Simple and Compound Statements - Sequences of Statements

A statement is either simple or compound. A simple_statement encloses no other statement. A   1
compound_statement can enclose simple_statements and other compound_statements.

Syntax

sequence_of_statements ::= statement {statement}   2

statement ::=   3
  {label} simple_statement | {label} compound_statement

simple_statement ::= null_statement   4
  | assignment_statement | exit_statement
  | goto_statement | procedure_call_statement
  | return_statement | entry_call_statement
  | requeue_statement | delay_statement
  | abort_statement | raise_statement
  | code_statement

compound_statement ::=   5
    if_statement | case_statement
  | loop_statement | block_statement
  | accept_statement | select_statement

null_statement ::= **null**;   6

label ::= <<*label*_statement_identifier>>   7

statement_identifier ::= direct_name   8

The direct_name of a statement_identifier shall be an identifier (not an operator_symbol).   9

Name Resolution Rules

The direct_name of a statement_identifier shall resolve to denote its corresponding implicit declaration   10
(see below).

Legality Rules

Distinct identifiers shall be used for all statement_identifiers that appear in the same body, including inner   11
block_statements but excluding inner program units.

Static Semantics

For each statement_identifier, there is an implicit declaration (with the specified identifier) at the end of   12
the declarative_part of the innermost block_statement or body that encloses the statement_identifier. The

S. Tucker Taft et al. (Eds.): Consolidated Ada Reference Manual, LNCS 2219, pp. 111–120, 2001.

implicit declarations occur in the same order as the statement_identifiers occur in the source text. If a usage name denotes such an implicit declaration, the entity it denotes is the label, loop_statement, or block_statement with the given statement_identifier.

Dynamic Semantics

13 The execution of a null_statement has no effect.

14 A *transfer of control* is the run-time action of an exit_statement, return_statement, goto_statement, or requeue_statement, selection of a terminate_alternative, raising of an exception, or an abort, which causes the next action performed to be one other than what would normally be expected from the other rules of the language. As explained in 7.6.1, a transfer of control can cause the execution of constructs to be completed and then left, which may trigger finalization.

15 The execution of a sequence_of_statements consists of the execution of the individual statements in succession until the sequence_ is completed.

NOTES

16 1 A statement_identifier that appears immediately within the declarative region of a named loop_statement or an accept_statement is nevertheless implicitly declared immediately within the declarative region of the innermost enclosing body or block_statement; in other words, the expanded name for a named statement is not affected by whether the statement occurs inside or outside a named loop or an accept_statement — only nesting within block_statements is relevant to the form of its expanded name.

Examples

17 *Examples of labeled statements:*

18   <<Here>> <<Ici>> <<Aqui>> <<Hier>> **null**;

19   <<After>> X := 1;

5.2 Assignment Statements

1 An assignment_statement replaces the current value of a variable with the result of evaluating an expression.

Syntax

2   assignment_statement ::=
      *variable_*name := expression;

3 The execution of an assignment_statement includes the evaluation of the expression and the *assignment* of the value of the expression into the *target*. An assignment operation (as opposed to an assignment_-statement) is performed in other contexts as well, including object initialization and by-copy parameter passing. The *target* of an assignment operation is the view of the object to which a value is being assigned; the target of an assignment_statement is the variable denoted by the *variable_*name.

Name Resolution Rules

4 The *variable_*name of an assignment_statement is expected to be of any nonlimited type. The expected type for the expression is the type of the target.

Legality Rules

5 The target denoted by the *variable_*name shall be a variable.

6 If the target is of a tagged class-wide type *T*'Class, then the expression shall either be dynamically tagged, or of type *T* and tag-indeterminate (see 3.9.2).

Dynamic Semantics

For the execution of an assignment_statement, the *variable*_name and the expression are first evaluated in an arbitrary order. 7

When the type of the target is class-wide: 8

- If the expression is tag-indeterminate (see 3.9.2), then the controlling tag value for the expression is the tag of the target; 9

- Otherwise (the expression is dynamically tagged), a check is made that the tag of the value of the expression is the same as that of the target; if this check fails, Constraint_Error is raised. 10

The value of the expression is converted to the subtype of the target. The conversion might raise an exception (see 4.6). 11

In cases involving controlled types, the target is finalized, and an anonymous object might be used as an intermediate in the assignment, as described in 7.6.1, "Completion and Finalization". In any case, the converted value of the expression is then *assigned* to the target, which consists of the following two steps: 12

- The value of the target becomes the converted value. 13

- If any part of the target is controlled, its value is adjusted as explained in clause 7.6. 14

NOTES
2 The tag of an object never changes; in particular, an assignment_statement does not change the tag of the target. 15

3 The values of the discriminants of an object designated by an access value cannot be changed (not even by assigning a complete value to the object itself) since such objects are always constrained; however, subcomponents of such objects may be unconstrained. 16

Examples

Examples of assignment statements: 17

```
Value := Max_Value - 1;                                                    18
Shade := Blue;

Next_Frame(F)(M, N) := 2.5;         -- see 4.1.1                          19
U := Dot_Product(V, W);             -- see 6.3

Writer := (Status => Open, Unit => Printer, Line_Count => 60);   -- see 3.8.1   20
Next_Car.all := (72074, null);      -- see 3.10.1
```

Examples involving scalar subtype conversions: 21

```
I, J : Integer range 1 .. 10 := 5;                                        22
K    : Integer range 1 .. 20 := 15;
   ...

I := J;   -- identical ranges                                             23
K := J;   -- compatible ranges
J := K;   -- will raise Constraint_Error if K > 10
```

Examples involving array subtype conversions: 24

```
A : String(1 .. 31);                                                      25
B : String(3 .. 33);
   ...

A := B;   -- same number of components                                    26
A(1 .. 9)  := "tar sauce";                                                27
A(4 .. 12) := A(1 .. 9);   -- A(1 .. 12) = "tartar sauce"
```

NOTES

28   4 *Notes on the examples:* Assignment_statements are allowed even in the case of overlapping slices of the same array, because the *variable_*name and expression are both evaluated before copying the value into the variable. In the above example, an implementation yielding A(1 .. 12) = "tartartartar" would be incorrect.

5.3 If Statements

1   An if_statement selects for execution at most one of the enclosed sequences_of_statements, depending on the (truth) value of one or more corresponding conditions.

Syntax

2   if_statement ::=
        if condition **then**
          sequence_of_statements
        {**elsif** condition **then**
          sequence_of_statements}
        [**else**
          sequence_of_statements]
        end if;

3   condition ::= *boolean_*expression

Name Resolution Rules

4   A condition is expected to be of any boolean type.

Dynamic Semantics

5   For the execution of an if_statement, the condition specified after **if**, and any conditions specified after **elsif**, are evaluated in succession (treating a final **else** as **elsif** True **then**), until one evaluates to True or all conditions are evaluated and yield False. If a condition evaluates to True, then the corresponding sequence_of_statements is executed; otherwise none of them is executed.

Examples

6   *Examples of if statements:*

7
```
if Month = December and Day = 31 then
   Month := January;
   Day   := 1;
   Year  := Year + 1;
end if;
```

8
```
if Line_Too_Short then
   raise Layout_Error;
elsif Line_Full then
   New_Line;
   Put(Item);
else
   Put(Item);
end if;
```

9
```
if My_Car.Owner.Vehicle /= My_Car then        -- see 3.10.1
   Report ("Incorrect data");
end if;
```

5.4 Case Statements

A case_statement selects for execution one of a number of alternative sequences_of_statements; the chosen alternative is defined by the value of an expression.   1

Syntax

```
case_statement ::=
  case expression is
    case_statement_alternative
    {case_statement_alternative}
  end case;
```
   2

```
case_statement_alternative ::=
  when discrete_choice_list =>
    sequence_of_statements
```
   3

Name Resolution Rules

The expression is expected to be of any discrete type. The expected type for each discrete_choice is the type of the expression.   4

Legality Rules

The expressions and discrete_ranges given as discrete_choices of a case_statement shall be static. A discrete_choice **others**, if present, shall appear alone and in the last discrete_choice_list.   5

The possible values of the expression shall be covered as follows: 6

- If the expression is a name (including a type_conversion or a function_call) having a static and constrained nominal subtype, or is a qualified_expression whose subtype_mark denotes a static and constrained scalar subtype, then each non-**others** discrete_choice shall cover only values in that subtype, and each value of that subtype shall be covered by some discrete_choice (either explicitly or by **others**).   7

- If the type of the expression is *root_integer*, *universal_integer*, or a descendant of a formal scalar type, then the case_statement shall have an **others** discrete_choice.   8

- Otherwise, each value of the base range of the type of the expression shall be covered (either explicitly or by **others**).   9

Two distinct discrete_choices of a case_statement shall not cover the same value.   10

Dynamic Semantics

For the execution of a case_statement the expression is first evaluated.   11

If the value of the expression is covered by the discrete_choice_list of some case_statement_alternative, then the sequence_of_statements of the _alternative is executed.   12

Otherwise (the value is not covered by any discrete_choice_list, perhaps due to being outside the base range), Constraint_Error is raised.   13

NOTES
5 The execution of a case_statement chooses one and only one alternative. Qualification of the expression of a case_statement by a static subtype can often be used to limit the number of choices that need be given explicitly.   14

15 *Examples of case statements:*

16
```
case Sensor is
    when Elevation => Record_Elevation(Sensor_Value);
    when Azimuth   => Record_Azimuth  (Sensor_Value);
    when Distance  => Record_Distance (Sensor_Value);
    when others    => null;
end case;
```

17
```
case Today is
    when Mon          => Compute_Initial_Balance;
    when Fri          => Compute_Closing_Balance;
    when Tue .. Thu => Generate_Report(Today);
    when Sat .. Sun => null;
end case;
```

18
```
case Bin_Number(Count) is
    when 1       => Update_Bin(1);
    when 2       => Update_Bin(2);
    when 3 | 4 =>
        Empty_Bin(1);
        Empty_Bin(2);
    when others       => raise Error;
end case;
```

5.5 Loop Statements

1   A loop_statement includes a sequence_of_statements that is to be executed repeatedly, zero or more times.

2   loop_statement ::=
    [*loop*_statement_identifier:]
    [iteration_scheme] **loop**
      sequence_of_statements
    end loop [*loop*_identifier];

3   iteration_scheme ::= **while** condition
    | **for** loop_parameter_specification

4   loop_parameter_specification ::=
    defining_identifier **in** [**reverse**] discrete_subtype_definition

5   If a loop_statement has a *loop*_statement_identifier, then the identifier shall be repeated after the **end loop**; otherwise, there shall not be an identifier after the **end loop**.

6   A loop_parameter_specification declares a *loop parameter*, which is an object whose subtype is that defined by the discrete_subtype_definition.

7   For the execution of a loop_statement, the sequence_of_statements is executed repeatedly, zero or more times, until the loop_statement is complete. The loop_statement is complete when a transfer of control occurs that transfers control out of the loop, or, in the case of an iteration_scheme, as specified below.

8   For the execution of a loop_statement with a **while** iteration_scheme, the condition is evaluated before each execution of the sequence_of_statements; if the value of the condition is True, the sequence_of_-statements is executed; if False, the execution of the loop_statement is complete.

For the execution of a loop_statement with a **for** iteration_scheme, the loop_parameter_specification is 9
first elaborated. This elaboration creates the loop parameter and elaborates the discrete_subtype_-
definition. If the discrete_subtype_definition defines a subtype with a null range, the execution of the
loop_statement is complete. Otherwise, the sequence_of_statements is executed once for each value of
the discrete subtype defined by the discrete_subtype_definition (or until the loop is left as a consequence
of a transfer of control). Prior to each such iteration, the corresponding value of the discrete subtype is
assigned to the loop parameter. These values are assigned in increasing order unless the reserved word
reverse is present, in which case the values are assigned in decreasing order.

NOTES
6 A loop parameter is a constant; it cannot be updated within the sequence_of_statements of the loop (see 3.3). 10

7 An object_declaration should not be given for a loop parameter, since the loop parameter is automatically declared by 11
the loop_parameter_specification. The scope of a loop parameter extends from the loop_parameter_specification to the
end of the loop_statement, and the visibility rules are such that a loop parameter is only visible within the
sequence_of_statements of the loop.

8 The discrete_subtype_definition of a for loop is elaborated just once. Use of the reserved word **reverse** does not alter 12
the discrete subtype defined, so that the following iteration_schemes are not equivalent; the first has a null range.

```
for J in reverse 1 .. 0
for J in 0 .. 1
```
13

Examples

Example of a loop statement without an iteration scheme: 14

```
loop
   Get(Current_Character);
   exit when Current_Character = '*';
end loop;
```
15

*Example of a loop statement with a **while** iteration scheme:* 16

```
while Bid(N).Price < Cut_Off.Price loop
   Record_Bid(Bid(N).Price);
   N := N + 1;
end loop;
```
17

*Example of a loop statement with a **for** iteration scheme:* 18

```
for J in Buffer'Range loop       -- works even with a null range
   if Buffer(J) /= Space then
      Put(Buffer(J));
   end if;
end loop;
```
19

Example of a loop statement with a name: 20

```
Summation:
   while Next /= Head loop       -- see 3.10.1
      Sum  := Sum + Next.Value;
      Next := Next.Succ;
   end loop Summation;
```
21

5.6 Block Statements

A block_statement encloses a handled_sequence_of_statements optionally preceded by a 1
declarative_part.

Syntax

2   block_statement ::=
         [*block*_statement_identifier:]
            [**declare**
               declarative_part]
            begin
               handled_sequence_of_statements
            end [*block*_identifier];

3   If a block_statement has a *block*_statement_identifier, then the identifier shall be repeated after the
      end; otherwise, there shall not be an identifier after the **end**.

Static Semantics

4   A block_statement that has no explicit declarative_part has an implicit empty declarative_part.

Dynamic Semantics

5   The execution of a block_statement consists of the elaboration of its declarative_part followed by the
      execution of its handled_sequence_of_statements.

Examples

6   *Example of a block statement with a local variable:*

7   ```
      Swap:
         declare
            Temp : Integer;
         begin
            Temp := V; V := U; U := Temp;
         end Swap;
      ```

## 5.7 Exit Statements

1     An exit_statement is used to complete the execution of an enclosing loop_statement; the completion is
      conditional if the exit_statement includes a condition.

*Syntax*

2     exit_statement ::=
         **exit** [*loop*_name] [**when** condition];

*Name Resolution Rules*

3     The *loop*_name, if any, in an exit_statement shall resolve to denote a loop_statement.

*Legality Rules*

4     Each exit_statement *applies to* a loop_statement; this is the loop_statement being exited. An exit_-
      statement with a name is only allowed within the loop_statement denoted by the name, and applies to
      that loop_statement. An exit_statement without a name is only allowed within a loop_statement, and
      applies to the innermost enclosing one. An exit_statement that applies to a given loop_statement shall not
      appear within a body or accept_statement, if this construct is itself enclosed by the given
      loop_statement.
      ```

Dynamic Semantics

For the execution of an exit_statement, the condition, if present, is first evaluated. If the value of the   5
condition is True, or if there is no condition, a transfer of control is done to complete the loop_statement.
If the value of the condition is False, no transfer of control takes place.

NOTES

9 Several nested loops can be exited by an exit_statement that names the outer loop.   6

Examples

Examples of loops with exit statements: 7

```
for N in 1 .. Max_Num_Items loop
   Get_New_Item(New_Item);
   Merge_Item(New_Item, Storage_File);
   exit when New_Item = Terminal_Item;
end loop;
```
8

```
Main_Cycle:
   loop
      -- initial statements
      exit Main_Cycle when Found;
      -- final statements
   end loop Main_Cycle;
```
9

5.8 Goto Statements

A goto_statement specifies an explicit transfer of control from this statement to a target statement with a   1
given label.

Syntax

goto_statement ::= **goto** *label*_name;   2

Name Resolution Rules

The *label*_name shall resolve to denote a label; the statement with that label is the *target statement*.   3

Legality Rules

The innermost sequence_of_statements that encloses the target statement shall also enclose the   4
goto_statement. Furthermore, if a goto_statement is enclosed by an accept_statement or a body, then
the target statement shall not be outside this enclosing construct.

Dynamic Semantics

The execution of a goto_statement transfers control to the target statement, completing the execution of   5
any compound_statement that encloses the goto_statement but does not enclose the target.

NOTES

10 The above rules allow transfer of control to a statement of an enclosing sequence_of_statements but not the reverse.   6
Similarly, they prohibit transfers of control such as between alternatives of a case_statement, if_statement, or
select_statement; between exception_handlers; or from an exception_handler of a handled_sequence_of_statements
back to its sequence_of_statements.

Examples

7   *Example of a loop containing a goto statement:*

8
```
<<Sort>>
for I in 1 .. N-1 loop
   if A(I) > A(I+1) then
      Exchange(A(I), A(I+1));
      goto Sort;
   end if;
end loop;
```

Section 6: Subprograms

A subprogram is a program unit or intrinsic operation whose execution is invoked by a subprogram call. There are two forms of subprogram: procedures and functions. A procedure call is a statement; a function call is an expression and returns a value. The definition of a subprogram can be given in two parts: a subprogram declaration defining its interface, and a subprogram_body defining its execution. Operators and enumeration literals are functions.   1

A *callable entity* is a subprogram or entry (see Section 9). A callable entity is invoked by a *call*; that is, a subprogram call or entry call. A *callable construct* is a construct that defines the action of a call upon a callable entity: a subprogram_body, entry_body, or accept_statement.   2

6.1 Subprogram Declarations

A subprogram_declaration declares a procedure or function.   1

Syntax

subprogram_declaration ::= subprogram_specification;   2

abstract_subprogram_declaration ::= subprogram_specification **is abstract**;   3

subprogram_specification ::=   4
    procedure defining_program_unit_name parameter_profile
  | **function** defining_designator parameter_and_result_profile

designator ::= [parent_unit_name .]identifier I operator_symbol   5

defining_designator ::= defining_program_unit_name I defining_operator_symbol   6

defining_program_unit_name ::= [parent_unit_name .]defining_identifier   7

The optional parent_unit_name is only allowed for library units (see 10.1.1).   8

operator_symbol ::= string_literal   9

The sequence of characters in an operator_symbol shall correspond to an operator belonging to one of the six classes of operators defined in clause 4.5 (spaces are not allowed and the case of letters is not significant).   10

defining_operator_symbol ::= operator_symbol   11

parameter_profile ::= [formal_part]   12

parameter_and_result_profile ::= [formal_part] **return** subtype_mark   13

formal_part ::=   14
    (parameter_specification {; parameter_specification})

parameter_specification ::=   15
    defining_identifier_list : mode subtype_mark [:= default_expression]
  | defining_identifier_list : access_definition [:= default_expression]

mode ::= [**in**] I **in out** I **out**   16

Name Resolution Rules

A *formal parameter* is an object directly visible within a subprogram_body that represents the actual parameter passed to the subprogram in a call; it is declared by a parameter_specification. For a formal parameter, the expected type for its default_expression, if any, is that of the formal parameter.   17

S. Tucker Taft et al. (Eds.): Consolidated Ada Reference Manual, LNCS 2219, pp. 121–132, 2001.

Legality Rules

18   The *parameter mode* of a formal parameter conveys the direction of information transfer with the actual parameter: **in**, **in out**, or **out**. Mode **in** is the default, and is the mode of a parameter defined by an access_definition. The formal parameters of a function, if any, shall have the mode **in**.

19   A default_expression is only allowed in a parameter_specification for a formal parameter of mode **in**.

20   A subprogram_declaration or a generic_subprogram_declaration requires a completion: a body, a renaming_declaration (see 8.5), or a **pragma** Import (see B.1). A completion is not allowed for an abstract_subprogram_declaration.

21   A name that denotes a formal parameter is not allowed within the formal_part in which it is declared, nor within the formal_part of a corresponding body or accept_statement.

Static Semantics

22   The *profile* of (a view of) a callable entity is either a parameter_profile or parameter_and_result_profile; it embodies information about the interface to that entity — for example, the profile includes information about parameters passed to the callable entity. All callable entities have a profile — enumeration literals, other subprograms, and entries. An access-to-subprogram type has a designated profile. Associated with a profile is a calling convention. A subprogram_declaration declares a procedure or a function, as indicated by the initial reserved word, with name and profile as given by its specification.

23   The nominal subtype of a formal parameter is the subtype denoted by the subtype_mark, or defined by the access_definition, in the parameter_specification.

24   An *access parameter* is a formal **in** parameter specified by an access_definition. An access parameter is of an anonymous general access-to-variable type (see 3.10). Access parameters allow dispatching calls to be controlled by access values.

25   The *subtypes of a profile* are:

26   • For any non-access parameters, the nominal subtype of the parameter.

27   • For any access parameters, the designated subtype of the parameter type.

28   • For any result, the result subtype.

29   The *types of a profile* are the types of those subtypes.

30   A subprogram declared by an abstract_subprogram_declaration is abstract; a subprogram declared by a subprogram_declaration is not. See 3.9.3, ''Abstract Types and Subprograms''.

Dynamic Semantics

31   The elaboration of a subprogram_declaration or an abstract_subprogram_declaration has no effect.

     NOTES

32   1 A parameter_specification with several identifiers is equivalent to a sequence of single parameter_specifications, as explained in 3.3.

33   2 Abstract subprograms do not have bodies, and cannot be used in a nondispatching call (see 3.9.3, ''Abstract Types and Subprograms'').

34   3 The evaluation of default_expressions is caused by certain calls, as described in 6.4.1. They are not evaluated during the elaboration of the subprogram declaration.

35   4 Subprograms can be called recursively and can be called concurrently from multiple tasks.

Examples of subprogram declarations: 36

```
procedure Traverse_Tree;                                                        37
procedure Increment(X : in out Integer);
procedure Right_Indent(Margin : out Line_Size);        -- see 3.5.4
procedure Switch(From, To : in out Link);              -- see 3.10.1

function Random return Probability;                    -- see 3.5.7      38

function Min_Cell(X : Link) return Cell;               -- see 3.10.1     39
function Next_Frame(K : Positive) return Frame;        -- see 3.10
function Dot_Product(Left, Right : Vector) return Real; -- see 3.6

function "*"(Left, Right : Matrix) return Matrix;      -- see 3.6       40
```

*Examples of **in** parameters with default expressions:* 41

```
procedure Print_Header(Pages  : in Natural;                              42
            Header : in Line    :=  (1 .. Line'Last => ' ');  -- see 3.6
            Center : in Boolean := True);
```

6.2 Formal Parameter Modes

A parameter_specification declares a formal parameter of mode **in**, **in out**, or **out**. 1

A parameter is passed either *by copy* or *by reference*. When a parameter is passed by copy, the formal 2
parameter denotes a separate object from the actual parameter, and any information transfer between the
two occurs only before and after executing the subprogram. When a parameter is passed by reference, the
formal parameter denotes (a view of) the object denoted by the actual parameter; reads and updates of the
formal parameter directly reference the actual parameter object.

A type is a *by-copy type* if it is an elementary type, or if it is a descendant of a private type whose full type 3
is a by-copy type. A parameter of a by-copy type is passed by copy.

A type is a *by-reference type* if it is a descendant of one of the following: 4

- a tagged type; 5

- a task or protected type; 6

- a nonprivate type with the reserved word **limited** in its declaration; 7

- a composite type with a subcomponent of a by-reference type; 8

- a private type whose full type is a by-reference type. 9

A parameter of a by-reference type is passed by reference. Each value of a by-reference type has an 10
associated object. For a parenthesized expression, qualified_expression, or type_conversion, this object is
the one associated with the operand.

For parameters of other types, it is unspecified whether the parameter is passed by copy or by reference. 11

If one name denotes a part of a formal parameter, and a second name denotes a part of a distinct formal 12
parameter or an object that is not part of a formal parameter, then the two names are considered *distinct
access paths*. If an object is of a type for which the parameter passing mechanism is not specified, then it is
a bounded error to assign to the object via one access path, and then read the value of the object via a
distinct access path, unless the first access path denotes a part of a formal parameter that no longer exists at

the point of the second access (due to leaving the corresponding callable construct). The possible consequences are that Program_Error is raised, or the newly assigned value is read, or some old value of the object is read.

NOTES

13   5 A formal parameter of mode **in** is a constant view (see 3.3); it cannot be updated within the subprogram_body.

6.3 Subprogram Bodies

1   A subprogram_body specifies the execution of a subprogram.

Syntax

2   subprogram_body ::=
       subprogram_specification **is**
         declarative_part
       begin
         handled_sequence_of_statements
       end [designator];

3   If a designator appears at the end of a subprogram_body, it shall repeat the defining_designator of the subprogram_specification.

Legality Rules

4   In contrast to other bodies, a subprogram_body need not be the completion of a previous declaration, in which case the body declares the subprogram. If the body is a completion, it shall be the completion of a subprogram_declaration or generic_subprogram_declaration. The profile of a subprogram_body that completes a declaration shall conform fully to that of the declaration.

Static Semantics

5   A subprogram_body is considered a declaration. It can either complete a previous declaration, or itself be the initial declaration of the subprogram.

Dynamic Semantics

6   The elaboration of a non-generic subprogram_body has no other effect than to establish that the subprogram can from then on be called without failing the Elaboration_Check.

7   The execution of a subprogram_body is invoked by a subprogram call. For this execution the declarative_part is elaborated, and the handled_sequence_of_statements is then executed.

Examples

8   *Example of procedure body:*

9
```
    procedure Push(E : in Element_Type; S : in out Stack) is
    begin
       if S.Index = S.Size then
          raise Stack_Overflow;
       else
          S.Index := S.Index + 1;
          S.Space(S.Index) := E;
       end if;
    end Push;
```

Example of a function body:

```
function Dot_Product(Left, Right : Vector) return Real is
   Sum : Real := 0.0;
begin
   Check(Left'First = Right'First and Left'Last = Right'Last);
   for J in Left'Range loop
      Sum := Sum + Left(J)*Right(J);
   end loop;
   return Sum;
end Dot_Product;
```

10
11

6.3.1 Conformance Rules

When subprogram profiles are given in more than one place, they are required to conform in one of four   1
ways: type conformance, mode conformance, subtype conformance, or full conformance.

Static Semantics

As explained in B.1, ''Interfacing Pragmas'', a *convention* can be specified for an entity. Unless this   2/1
International Standard states otherwise, the default convention of an entity is Ada. For a callable entity or
access-to-subprogram type, the convention is called the *calling convention*. The following conventions are
defined by the language:

- The default calling convention for any subprogram not listed below is *Ada*. A pragma   3
  Convention, Import, or Export may be used to override the default calling convention (see B.1).

- The *Intrinsic* calling convention represents subprograms that are ''built in'' to the compiler. The   4
  default calling convention is Intrinsic for the following:

  - an enumeration literal;   5

  - a "/=" operator declared implicitly due to the declaration of "=" (see 6.6);   6

  - any other implicitly declared subprogram unless it is a dispatching operation of a tagged   7
    type;

  - an inherited subprogram of a generic formal tagged type with unknown discriminants;   8

  - an attribute that is a subprogram;   9

  - a subprogram declared immediately within a protected_body.   10

  The Access attribute is not allowed for Intrinsic subprograms.   11

- The default calling convention is *protected* for a protected subprogram, and for an access-to-   12
  subprogram type with the reserved word **protected** in its definition.

- The default calling convention is *entry* for an entry.   13

- If not specified above as Intrinsic, the calling convention for any inherited or overriding   13.1/1
  dispatching operation of a tagged type is that of the corresponding subprogram of the parent
  type. The default calling convention for a new dispatching operation of a tagged type is the
  convention of the type.

Of these four conventions, only Ada and Intrinsic are allowed as a *convention*_identifier in a pragma   14
Convention, Import, or Export.

Two profiles are *type conformant* if they have the same number of parameters, and both have a result if   15
either does, and corresponding parameter and result types are the same, or, for access parameters,
corresponding designated types are the same.

16   Two profiles are *mode conformant* if they are type-conformant, and corresponding parameters have identical modes, and, for access parameters, the designated subtypes statically match.

17   Two profiles are *subtype conformant* if they are mode-conformant, corresponding subtypes of the profile statically match, and the associated calling conventions are the same. The profile of a generic formal subprogram is not subtype-conformant with any other profile.

18   Two profiles are *fully conformant* if they are subtype-conformant, and corresponding parameters have the same names and have default_expressions that are fully conformant with one another.

19   Two expressions are *fully conformant* if, after replacing each use of an operator with the equivalent function_call:

20   • each constituent construct of one corresponds to an instance of the same syntactic category in the other, except that an expanded name may correspond to a direct_name (or character_literal) or to a different expanded name in the other; and

21   • each direct_name, character_literal, and selector_name that is not part of the prefix of an expanded name in one denotes the same declaration as the corresponding direct_name, character_literal, or selector_name in the other; and

21.1/1   • each attribute_designator in one must be the same as the corresponding attribute_designator in the other; and

22   • each primary that is a literal in one has the same value as the corresponding literal in the other.

23   Two known_discriminant_parts are *fully conformant* if they have the same number of discriminants, and discriminants in the same positions have the same names, statically matching subtypes, and default_expressions that are fully conformant with one another.

24   Two discrete_subtype_definitions are *fully conformant* if they are both subtype_indications or are both ranges, the subtype_marks (if any) denote the same subtype, and the corresponding simple_expressions of the ranges (if any) fully conform.

Implementation Permissions

25   An implementation may declare an operator declared in a language-defined library unit to be intrinsic.

6.3.2 Inline Expansion of Subprograms

1   Subprograms may be expanded in line at the call site.

Syntax

2   The form of a pragma Inline, which is a program unit pragma (see 10.1.5), is as follows:

3   **pragma** Inline(name {, name});

Legality Rules

4   The pragma shall apply to one or more callable entities or generic subprograms.

Static Semantics

5   If a pragma Inline applies to a callable entity, this indicates that inline expansion is desired for all calls to that entity. If a pragma Inline applies to a generic subprogram, this indicates that inline expansion is desired for all calls to all instances of that generic subprogram.

Implementation Permissions

For each call, an implementation is free to follow or to ignore the recommendation expressed by the pragma. 6

NOTES

6 The name in a pragma Inline can denote more than one entity in the case of overloading. Such a pragma applies to all of the denoted entities. 7

6.4 Subprogram Calls

A *subprogram call* is either a procedure_call_statement or a function_call; it invokes the execution of the subprogram_body. The call specifies the association of the actual parameters, if any, with formal parameters of the subprogram. 1

Syntax

procedure_call_statement ::= 2
   *procedure_*name;
  | *procedure_*prefix actual_parameter_part;

function_call ::= 3
   *function_*name
  | *function_*prefix actual_parameter_part

actual_parameter_part ::= 4
   (parameter_association {, parameter_association})

parameter_association ::= 5
   [*formal_parameter_*selector_name =>] explicit_actual_parameter

explicit_actual_parameter ::= expression | *variable_*name 6

A parameter_association is *named* or *positional* according to whether or not the *formal_-parameter_*selector_name is specified. Any positional associations shall precede any named associations. Named associations are not allowed if the prefix in a subprogram call is an attribute_-reference. 7

Name Resolution Rules

The name or prefix given in a procedure_call_statement shall resolve to denote a callable entity that is a procedure, or an entry renamed as (viewed as) a procedure. The name or prefix given in a function_call shall resolve to denote a callable entity that is a function. When there is an actual_parameter_part, the prefix can be an implicit_dereference of an access-to-subprogram value. 8

A subprogram call shall contain at most one association for each formal parameter. Each formal parameter without an association shall have a default_expression (in the profile of the view denoted by the name or prefix). This rule is an overloading rule (see 8.6). 9

Dynamic Semantics

For the execution of a subprogram call, the name or prefix of the call is evaluated, and each parameter_-association is evaluated (see 6.4.1). If a default_expression is used, an implicit parameter_association is assumed for this rule. These evaluations are done in an arbitrary order. The subprogram_body is then executed. Finally, if the subprogram completes normally, then after it is left, any necessary assigning back of formal to actual parameters occurs (see 6.4.1). 10

The exception Program_Error is raised at the point of a function_call if the function completes normally without executing a return_statement. 11

          Inline Expansion of Subprograms **6.3.2**

12 A function_call denotes a constant, as defined in 6.5; the nominal subtype of the constant is given by the result subtype of the function.

Examples

13 *Examples of procedure calls:*

14
```
Traverse_Tree;                                        -- see 6.1
Print_Header(128, Title, True);                       -- see 6.1
```

15
```
Switch(From => X, To => Next);                        -- see 6.1
Print_Header(128, Header => Title, Center => True);   -- see 6.1
Print_Header(Header => Title, Center => True, Pages => 128); -- see 6.1
```

16 *Examples of function calls:*

17
```
Dot_Product(U, V)      -- see 6.1 and 6.3
Clock                  -- see 9.6
F.all                  -- presuming F is of an access-to-subprogram type — see 3.10
```

18 *Examples of procedures with default expressions:*

19
```
procedure Activate(Process : in Process_Name;
                   After   : in Process_Name := No_Process;
                   Wait    : in Duration := 0.0;
                   Prior   : in Boolean := False);
```

20
```
procedure Pair(Left, Right : in Person_Name := new Person);    -- see 3.10.1
```

21 *Examples of their calls:*

22
```
Activate(X);
Activate(X, After => Y);
Activate(X, Wait => 60.0, Prior => True);
Activate(X, Y, 10.0, False);
```

23
```
Pair;
Pair(Left => new Person, Right => new Person);
```

NOTES

24 7 If a default_expression is used for two or more parameters in a multiple parameter_specification, the default_-expression is evaluated once for each omitted parameter. Hence in the above examples, the two calls of Pair are equivalent.

Examples

25 *Examples of overloaded subprograms:*

26
```
procedure Put(X : in Integer);
procedure Put(X : in String);
```

27
```
procedure Set(Tint   : in Color);
procedure Set(Signal : in Light);
```

28 *Examples of their calls:*

29
```
Put(28);
Put("no possible ambiguity here");
```

30
```
Set(Tint   => Red);
Set(Signal => Red);
Set(Color'(Red));
```

31
```
-- Set(Red) would be ambiguous since Red may
-- denote a value either of type Color or of type Light
```

6.4.1 Parameter Associations

A parameter association defines the association between an actual parameter and a formal parameter. 1

Name Resolution Rules

The *formal_parameter*_selector_name of a parameter_association shall resolve to denote a parameter_- 2
specification of the view being called.

The *actual parameter* is either the explicit_actual_parameter given in a parameter_association for a 3
given formal parameter, or the corresponding default_expression if no parameter_association is given
for the formal parameter. The expected type for an actual parameter is the type of the corresponding formal
parameter.

If the mode is **in**, the actual is interpreted as an expression; otherwise, the actual is interpreted only as a 4
name, if possible.

Legality Rules

If the mode is **in out** or **out**, the actual shall be a name that denotes a variable. 5

The type of the actual parameter associated with an access parameter shall be convertible (see 4.6) to its 6
anonymous access type.

Dynamic Semantics

For the evaluation of a parameter_association: 7

- The actual parameter is first evaluated. 8

- For an access parameter, the access_definition is elaborated, which creates the anonymous 9
  access type.

- For a parameter (of any mode) that is passed by reference (see 6.2), a view conversion of the 10
  actual parameter to the nominal subtype of the formal parameter is evaluated, and the formal
  parameter denotes that conversion.

- For an **in** or **in out** parameter that is passed by copy (see 6.2), the formal parameter object is 11
  created, and the value of the actual parameter is converted to the nominal subtype of the formal
  parameter and assigned to the formal.

- For an **out** parameter that is passed by copy, the formal parameter object is created, and: 12

  - For an access type, the formal parameter is initialized from the value of the actual, 13
    without a constraint check;

  - For a composite type with discriminants or that has implicit initial values for any 14
    subcomponents (see 3.3.1), the behavior is as for an **in out** parameter passed by copy.

  - For any other type, the formal parameter is uninitialized. If composite, a view 15
    conversion of the actual parameter to the nominal subtype of the formal is evaluated
    (which might raise Constraint_Error), and the actual subtype of the formal is that of
    the view conversion. If elementary, the actual subtype of the formal is given by its
    nominal subtype.

A formal parameter of mode **in out** or **out** with discriminants is constrained if either its nominal subtype or 16
the actual parameter is constrained.

17   After normal completion and leaving of a subprogram, for each **in out** or **out** parameter that is passed by copy, the value of the formal parameter is converted to the subtype of the variable given as the actual parameter and assigned to it. These conversions and assignments occur in an arbitrary order.

6.5 Return Statements

1   A return_statement is used to complete the execution of the innermost enclosing subprogram_body, entry_body, or accept_statement.

Syntax

2   return_statement ::= **return** [expression];

Name Resolution Rules

3   The expression, if any, of a return_statement is called the *return expression*. The *result subtype* of a function is the subtype denoted by the subtype_mark after the reserved word **return** in the profile of the function. The expected type for a return expression is the result type of the corresponding function.

Legality Rules

4   A return_statement shall be within a callable construct, and it *applies to* the innermost one. A return_-statement shall not be within a body that is within the construct to which the return_statement applies.

5   A function body shall contain at least one return_statement that applies to the function body, unless the function contains code_statements. A return_statement shall include a return expression if and only if it applies to a function body.

Dynamic Semantics

6   For the execution of a return_statement, the expression (if any) is first evaluated and converted to the result subtype.

7   If the result type is class-wide, then the tag of the result is the tag of the value of the expression.

8   If the result type is a specific tagged type:

9   • If it is limited, then a check is made that the tag of the value of the return expression identifies the result type. Constraint_Error is raised if this check fails.

10   • If it is nonlimited, then the tag of the result is that of the result type.

11   A type is a *return-by-reference* type if it is a descendant of one of the following:

12   • a tagged limited type;

13   • a task or protected type;

14   • a nonprivate type with the reserved word **limited** in its declaration;

15   • a composite type with a subcomponent of a return-by-reference type;

16   • a private type whose full type is a return-by-reference type.

17   If the result type is a return-by-reference type, then a check is made that the return expression is one of the following:

18   • a name that denotes an object view whose accessibility level is not deeper than that of the master that elaborated the function body; or

- a parenthesized expression or qualified_expression whose operand is one of these kinds of expressions. | 19

The exception Program_Error is raised if this check fails. | 20

For a function with a return-by-reference result type the result is returned by reference; that is, the function call denotes a constant view of the object associated with the value of the return expression. For any other function, the result is returned by copy; that is, the converted value is assigned into an anonymous constant created at the point of the return_statement, and the function call denotes that object. | 21

Finally, a transfer of control is performed which completes the execution of the callable construct to which the return_statement applies, and returns to the caller. | 22

Examples

Examples of return statements: | 23

```
return;                        -- in a procedure body, entry_body, or accept_statement
return Key_Value(Last_Index);  -- in a function body
```
| 24

6.6 Overloading of Operators

An *operator* is a function whose designator is an operator_symbol. Operators, like other functions, may be overloaded. | 1

Name Resolution Rules

Each use of a unary or binary operator is equivalent to a function_call with *function*_prefix being the corresponding operator_symbol, and with (respectively) one or two positional actual parameters being the operand(s) of the operator (in order). | 2

Legality Rules

The subprogram_specification of a unary or binary operator shall have one or two parameters, respectively. A generic function instantiation whose designator is an operator_symbol is only allowed if the specification of the generic function has the corresponding number of parameters. | 3

Default_expressions are not allowed for the parameters of an operator (whether the operator is declared with an explicit subprogram_specification or by a generic_instantiation). | 4

An explicit declaration of "/=" shall not have a result type of the predefined type Boolean. | 5

Static Semantics

A declaration of "=" whose result type is Boolean implicitly declares a declaration of "/=" that gives the complementary result. | 6

NOTES
8 The operators "+" and "−" are both unary and binary operators, and hence may be overloaded with both one- and two-parameter functions. | 7

8   *Examples of user-defined operators:*

9
```
function "+" (Left, Right : Matrix) return Matrix;
function "+" (Left, Right : Vector) return Vector;
```

```
-- assuming that A, B, and C are of the type Vector
-- the following two statements are equivalent:
```

```
A := B + C;
A := "+"(B, C);
```

Section 7: Packages

Packages are program units that allow the specification of groups of logically related entities. Typically, a 1
package contains the declaration of a type (often a private type or private extension) along with the
declarations of primitive subprograms of the type, which can be called from outside the package, while
their inner workings remain hidden from outside users.

7.1 Package Specifications and Declarations

A package is generally provided in two parts: a package_specification and a package_body. Every 1
package has a package_specification, but not all packages have a package_body.

Syntax

package_declaration ::= package_specification; 2

package_specification ::= 3
   package defining_program_unit_name **is**
    {basic_declarative_item}
  [**private**
    {basic_declarative_item}]
   end [[parent_unit_name.]identifier]

If an identifier or parent_unit_name.identifier appears at the end of a package_specification, then 4
this sequence of lexical elements shall repeat the defining_program_unit_name.

Legality Rules

A package_declaration or generic_package_declaration requires a completion (a body) if it contains any 5
declarative_item that requires a completion, but whose completion is not in its package_specification.

Static Semantics

The first list of declarative_items of a package_specification of a package other than a generic formal 6
package is called the *visible part* of the package. The optional list of declarative_items after the reserved
word **private** (of any package_specification) is called the *private part* of the package. If the reserved
word **private** does not appear, the package has an implicit empty private part.

An entity declared in the private part of a package is visible only within the declarative region of the 7
package itself (including any child units — see 10.1.1). In contrast, expanded names denoting entities
declared in the visible part can be used even outside the package; furthermore, direct visibility of such
entities can be achieved by means of use_clauses (see 4.1.3 and 8.4).

Dynamic Semantics

The elaboration of a package_declaration consists of the elaboration of its basic_declarative_items in the 8
given order.

NOTES
1 The visible part of a package contains all the information that another program unit is able to know about the package. 9

2 If a declaration occurs immediately within the specification of a package, and the declaration has a corresponding 10
completion that is a body, then that body has to occur immediately within the body of the package.

S. Tucker Taft et al. (Eds.): Consolidated Ada Reference Manual, LNCS 2219, pp. 133–145, 2001.

Examples

11   *Example of a package declaration:*

12
```
package Rational_Numbers is
```

13
```
    type Rational is
        record
            Numerator   : Integer;
            Denominator : Positive;
        end record;
```

14
```
    function "="(X,Y : Rational) return Boolean;
```

15
```
    function "/"  (X,Y : Integer)  return Rational;   -- to construct a rational number
```

16
```
    function "+"  (X,Y : Rational)  return Rational;
    function "-"  (X,Y : Rational)  return Rational;
    function "*"  (X,Y : Rational)  return Rational;
    function "/"  (X,Y : Rational)  return Rational;
end Rational_Numbers;
```

17   There are also many examples of package declarations in the predefined language environment (see Annex A).

7.2 Package Bodies

1   In contrast to the entities declared in the visible part of a package, the entities declared in the package_body are visible only within the package_body itself. As a consequence, a package with a package_body can be used for the construction of a group of related subprograms in which the logical operations available to clients are clearly isolated from the internal entities.

Syntax

2   package_body ::=
   package body defining_program_unit_name **is**
      declarative_part
   [**begin**
      handled_sequence_of_statements]
   end [[parent_unit_name.]identifier];

3   If an identifier or parent_unit_name.identifier appears at the end of a package_body, then this sequence of lexical elements shall repeat the defining_program_unit_name.

Legality Rules

4   A package_body shall be the completion of a previous package_declaration or generic_package_-declaration. A library package_declaration or library generic_package_declaration shall not have a body unless it requires a body; **pragma** Elaborate_Body can be used to require a library_unit_declaration to have a body (see 10.2.1) if it would not otherwise require one.

Static Semantics

5   In any package_body without statements there is an implicit null_statement. For any package_-declaration without an explicit completion, there is an implicit package_body containing a single null_statement. For a noninstance, nonlibrary package, this body occurs at the end of the declarative_part of the innermost enclosing program unit or block_statement; if there are several such packages, the order of the implicit package_bodies is unspecified. (For an instance, the implicit package_body occurs at the place of the instantiation (see 12.3). For a library package, the place is partially determined by the elaboration dependences (see Section 10).)

Dynamic Semantics

For the elaboration of a nongeneric package_body, its declarative_part is first elaborated, and its handled_sequence_of_statements is then executed. 6

NOTES

3 A variable declared in the body of a package is only visible within this body and, consequently, its value can only be changed within the package_body. In the absence of local tasks, the value of such a variable remains unchanged between calls issued from outside the package to subprograms declared in the visible part. The properties of such a variable are similar to those of a "static" variable of C. 7

4 The elaboration of the body of a subprogram explicitly declared in the visible part of a package is caused by the elaboration of the body of the package. Hence a call of such a subprogram by an outside program unit raises the exception Program_Error if the call takes place before the elaboration of the package_body (see 3.11). 8

Examples

Example of a package body (see 7.1): 9

```
package body Rational_Numbers is                                        10

   procedure Same_Denominator (X,Y : in out Rational) is                11
   begin
      -- reduces X and Y to the same denominator:
      ...
   end Same_Denominator;

   function "="(X,Y : Rational) return Boolean is                       12
      U : Rational := X;
      V : Rational := Y;
   begin
      Same_Denominator (U,V);
      return U.Numerator = V.Numerator;
   end "=";

   function "/" (X,Y : Integer) return Rational is                      13
   begin
      if Y > 0 then
         return (Numerator => X,  Denominator => Y);
      else
         return (Numerator => -X, Denominator => -Y);
      end if;
   end "/";

   function "+" (X,Y : Rational) return Rational is ... end "+";        14
   function "-" (X,Y : Rational) return Rational is ... end "-";
   function "*" (X,Y : Rational) return Rational is ... end "*";
   function "/" (X,Y : Rational) return Rational is ... end "/";

end Rational_Numbers;                                                   15
```

7.3 Private Types and Private Extensions

The declaration (in the visible part of a package) of a type as a private type or private extension serves to separate the characteristics that can be used directly by outside program units (that is, the logical properties) from other characteristics whose direct use is confined to the package (the details of the definition of the type itself). See 3.9.1 for an overview of type extensions. 1

Syntax

private_type_declaration ::= 2
    type defining_identifier [discriminant_part] **is** [[**abstract**] **tagged**] [**limited**] **private**;

private_extension_declaration ::= 3
    type defining_identifier [discriminant_part] **is**
    [**abstract**] **new** *ancestor*_subtype_indication **with private**;

Legality Rules

4   A private_type_declaration or private_extension_declaration declares a *partial view* of the type; such a declaration is allowed only as a declarative_item of the visible part of a package, and it requires a completion, which shall be a full_type_declaration that occurs as a declarative_item of the private part of the package. The view of the type declared by the full_type_declaration is called the *full view*. A generic formal private type or a generic formal private extension is also a partial view.

5   A type shall be completely defined before it is frozen (see 3.11.1 and 13.14). Thus, neither the declaration of a variable of a partial view of a type, nor the creation by an allocator of an object of the partial view are allowed before the full declaration of the type. Similarly, before the full declaration, the name of the partial view cannot be used in a generic_instantiation or in a representation item.

6   A private type is limited if its declaration includes the reserved word **limited**; a private extension is limited if its ancestor type is limited. If the partial view is nonlimited, then the full view shall be nonlimited. If a tagged partial view is limited, then the full view shall be limited. On the other hand, if an untagged partial view is limited, the full view may be limited or nonlimited.

7   If the partial view is tagged, then the full view shall be tagged. On the other hand, if the partial view is untagged, then the full view may be tagged or untagged. In the case where the partial view is untagged and the full view is tagged, no derivatives of the partial view are allowed within the immediate scope of the partial view; derivatives of the full view are allowed.

8   The *ancestor subtype* of a private_extension_declaration is the subtype defined by the *ancestor_-subtype_indication*; the ancestor type shall be a specific tagged type. The full view of a private extension shall be derived (directly or indirectly) from the ancestor type. In addition to the places where Legality Rules normally apply (see 12.3), the requirement that the ancestor be specific applies also in the private part of an instance of a generic unit.

9   If the declaration of a partial view includes a known_discriminant_part, then the full_type_declaration shall have a fully conforming (explicit) known_discriminant_part (see 6.3.1, ''Conformance Rules''). The ancestor subtype may be unconstrained; the parent subtype of the full view is required to be constrained (see 3.7).

10   If a private extension inherits known discriminants from the ancestor subtype, then the full view shall also inherit its discriminants from the ancestor subtype, and the parent subtype of the full view shall be constrained if and only if the ancestor subtype is constrained.

11   If a partial view has unknown discriminants, then the full_type_declaration may define a definite or an indefinite subtype, with or without discriminants.

12   If a partial view has neither known nor unknown discriminants, then the full_type_declaration shall define a definite subtype.

13   If the ancestor subtype of a private extension has constrained discriminants, then the parent subtype of the full view shall impose a statically matching constraint on those discriminants.

Static Semantics

14   A private_type_declaration declares a private type and its first subtype. Similarly, a private_extension_-declaration declares a private extension and its first subtype.

15   A declaration of a partial view and the corresponding full_type_declaration define two views of a single type. The declaration of a partial view together with the visible part define the operations that are available to outside program units; the declaration of the full view together with the private part define other

operations whose direct use is possible only within the declarative region of the package itself. Moreover, within the scope of the declaration of the full view, the *characteristics* of the type are determined by the full view; in particular, within its scope, the full view determines the classes that include the type, which components, entries, and protected subprograms are visible, what attributes and other predefined operations are allowed, and whether the first subtype is static. See 7.3.1.

A private extension inherits components (including discriminants unless there is a new discriminant_part specified) and user-defined primitive subprograms from its ancestor type, in the same way that a record extension inherits components and user-defined primitive subprograms from its parent type (see 3.4).   16

Dynamic Semantics

The elaboration of a private_type_declaration creates a partial view of a type. The elaboration of a private_extension_declaration elaborates the *ancestor*_subtype_indication, and creates a partial view of a type.   17

NOTES
5 The partial view of a type as declared by a private_type_declaration is defined to be a composite view (in 3.2). The full view of the type might or might not be composite. A private extension is also composite, as is its full view.   18

6 Declaring a private type with an unknown_discriminant_part is a way of preventing clients from creating uninitialized objects of the type; they are then forced to initialize each object by calling some operation declared in the visible part of the package. If such a type is also limited, then no objects of the type can be declared outside the scope of the full_type_declaration, restricting all object creation to the package defining the type. This allows complete control over all storage allocation for the type. Objects of such a type can still be passed as parameters, however.   19

7 The ancestor type specified in a private_extension_declaration and the parent type specified in the corresponding declaration of a record extension given in the private part need not be the same — the parent type of the full view can be any descendant of the ancestor type. In this case, for a primitive subprogram that is inherited from the ancestor type and not overridden, the formal parameter names and default expressions (if any) come from the corresponding primitive subprogram of the specified ancestor type, while the body comes from the corresponding primitive subprogram of the parent type of the full view. See 3.9.2.   20

Examples

Examples of private type declarations: 21

```
type Key is private;
type File_Name is limited private;
```
22

Example of a private extension declaration: 23

```
type List is new Ada.Finalization.Controlled with private;
```
24

7.3.1 Private Operations

For a type declared in the visible part of a package or generic package, certain operations on the type do not become visible until later in the package — either in the private part or the body. Such *private operations* are available only inside the declarative region of the package or generic package.   1

Static Semantics

The predefined operators that exist for a given type are determined by the classes to which the type belongs. For example, an integer type has a predefined "+" operator. In most cases, the predefined operators of a type are declared immediately after the definition of the type; the exceptions are explained below. Inherited subprograms are also implicitly declared immediately after the definition of the type, except as stated below.   2

3/1 For a composite type, the characteristics (see 7.3) of the type are determined in part by the characteristics of its component types. At the place where the composite type is declared, the only characteristics of component types used are those characteristics visible at that place. If later immediately within the declarative region in which the composite type is declared additional characteristics become visible for a component type, then any corresponding characteristics become visible for the composite type. Any additional predefined operators are implicitly declared at that place.

4/1 The corresponding rule applies to a type defined by a derived_type_definition, if there is a place immediately within the declarative region in which the type is declared where additional characteristics of its parent type become visible.

5/1 For example, an array type whose component type is limited private becomes nonlimited if the full view of the component type is nonlimited and visible at some later place immediately within the declarative region in which the array type is declared. In such a case, the predefined "=" operator is implicitly declared at that place, and assignment is allowed after that place.

6/1 Inherited primitive subprograms follow a different rule. For a derived_type_definition, each inherited primitive subprogram is implicitly declared at the earliest place, if any, immediately within the declarative region in which the type_declaration occurs, but after the type_declaration, where the corresponding declaration from the parent is visible. If there is no such place, then the inherited subprogram is not declared at all. An inherited subprogram that is not declared at all cannot be named in a call and cannot be overridden, but for a tagged type, it is possible to dispatch to it.

7 For a private_extension_declaration, each inherited subprogram is declared immediately after the private_extension_declaration if the corresponding declaration from the ancestor is visible at that place. Otherwise, the inherited subprogram is not declared for the private extension, though it might be for the full type.

8 The Class attribute is defined for tagged subtypes in 3.9. In addition, for every subtype S of an untagged private type whose full view is tagged, the following attribute is defined:

9 S'Class   Denotes the class-wide subtype corresponding to the full view of S. This attribute is allowed only from the beginning of the private part in which the full view is declared, until the declaration of the full view. After the full view, the Class attribute of the full view can be used.

NOTES

10 8 Because a partial view and a full view are two different views of one and the same type, outside of the defining package the characteristics of the type are those defined by the visible part. Within these outside program units the type is just a private type or private extension, and any language rule that applies only to another class of types does not apply. The fact that the full declaration might implement a private type with a type of a particular class (for example, as an array type) is relevant only within the declarative region of the package itself including any child units.

11 The consequences of this actual implementation are, however, valid everywhere. For example: any default initialization of components takes place; the attribute Size provides the size of the full view; finalization is still done for controlled components of the full view; task dependence rules still apply to components that are task objects.

12 9 Partial views provide assignment (unless the view is limited), membership tests, selected components for the selection of discriminants and inherited components, qualification, and explicit conversion.

13 10 For a subtype S of a partial view, S'Size is defined (see 13.3). For an object A of a partial view, the attributes A'Size and A'Address are defined (see 13.3). The Position, First_Bit, and Last_Bit attributes are also defined for discriminants and inherited components.

Example of a type with private operations: 14

```
package Key_Manager is                                        15
   type Key is private;
   Null_Key : constant Key;  -- a deferred constant declaration (see 7.4)
   procedure Get_Key(K : out Key);
   function "<" (X, Y : Key) return Boolean;
private
   type Key is new Natural;
   Null_Key : constant Key := Key'First;
end Key_Manager;
```

```
package body Key_Manager is                                   16
   Last_Key : Key := Null_Key;
   procedure Get_Key(K : out Key) is
   begin
      Last_Key := Last_Key + 1;
      K := Last_Key;
   end Get_Key;
```

```
   function "<" (X, Y : Key) return Boolean is                17
   begin
      return Natural(X) < Natural(Y);
   end "<";
end Key_Manager;
```

NOTES

11 *Notes on the example:* Outside of the package Key_Manager, the operations available for objects of type Key include   18
assignment, the comparison for equality or inequality, the procedure Get_Key and the operator "<"; they do not include
other relational operators such as ">=", or arithmetic operators.

The explicitly declared operator "<" hides the predefined operator "<" implicitly declared by the full_type_declaration.   19
Within the body of the function, an explicit conversion of X and Y to the subtype Natural is necessary to invoke the "<"
operator of the parent type. Alternatively, the result of the function could be written as not (X >= Y), since the operator
">=" is not redefined.

The value of the variable Last_Key, declared in the package body, remains unchanged between calls of the procedure   20
Get_Key. (See also the NOTES of 7.2.)

7.4 Deferred Constants

Deferred constant declarations may be used to declare constants in the visible part of a package, but with   1
the value of the constant given in the private part. They may also be used to declare constants imported
from other languages (see Annex B).

A *deferred constant declaration* is an object_declaration with the reserved word **constant** but no   2
initialization expression. The constant declared by a deferred constant declaration is called a *deferred
constant*. A deferred constant declaration requires a completion, which shall be a full constant declaration
(called the *full declaration* of the deferred constant), or a pragma Import (see Annex B).

A deferred constant declaration that is completed by a full constant declaration shall occur immediately   3
within the visible part of a package_specification. For this case, the following additional rules apply to the
corresponding full declaration:

- The full declaration shall occur immediately within the private part of the same package;   4

- The deferred and full constants shall have the same type;   5

- If the subtype defined by the subtype_indication in the deferred declaration is constrained, then   6
  the subtype defined by the subtype_indication in the full declaration shall match it statically. On

the other hand, if the subtype of the deferred constant is unconstrained, then the full declaration is still allowed to impose a constraint. The constant itself will be constrained, like all constants;

7   • If the deferred constant declaration includes the reserved word **aliased**, then the full declaration shall also.

8   A deferred constant declaration that is completed by a pragma Import need not appear in the visible part of a package_specification, and has no full constant declaration.

9   The completion of a deferred constant declaration shall occur before the constant is frozen (see 7.4).

Dynamic Semantics

10   The elaboration of a deferred constant declaration elaborates the subtype_indication or (only allowed in the case of an imported constant) the array_type_definition.

NOTES

11   12 The full constant declaration for a deferred constant that is of a given private type or private extension is not allowed before the corresponding full_type_declaration. This is a consequence of the freezing rules for types (see 13.14).

Examples

12   *Examples of deferred constant declarations:*

13   ```
Null_Key : constant Key;   -- see 7.3.1
```

14   ```
CPU_Identifier : constant String(1..8);
pragma Import(Assembler, CPU_Identifier, Link_Name => "CPU_ID");
                                 -- see B.1
```

7.5 Limited Types

1   A limited type is (a view of) a type for which the assignment operation is not allowed. A nonlimited type is a (view of a) type for which the assignment operation is allowed.

Legality Rules

2   If a tagged record type has any limited components, then the reserved word **limited** shall appear in its record_type_definition.

Static Semantics

3   A type is *limited* if it is a descendant of one of the following:

4   • a type with the reserved word **limited** in its definition;

5   • a task or protected type;

6   • a composite type with a limited component.

7   Otherwise, the type is nonlimited.

8   There are no predefined equality operators for a limited type.

NOTES

9   13 The following are consequences of the rules for limited types:

10   • An initialization expression is not allowed in an object_declaration if the type of the object is limited.

11   • A default expression is not allowed in a component_declaration if the type of the record component is limited.

12   • An initialized allocator is not allowed if the designated type is limited.

13   • A generic formal parameter of mode **in** must not be of a limited type.

14 Aggregates are not available for a limited composite type. Concatenation is not available for a limited array type.   14

15 The rules do not exclude a default_expression for a formal parameter of a limited type; they do not exclude a   15
deferred constant of a limited type if the full declaration of the constant is of a nonlimited type.

16 As illustrated in 7.3.1, an untagged limited type can become nonlimited under certain circumstances.   16

Examples

Example of a package with a limited type: 17

```
package IO_Package is                                                  18
    type File_Name is limited private;

    procedure Open (F : in out File_Name);                            19
    procedure Close(F : in out File_Name);
    procedure Read (F : in File_Name; Item : out Integer);
    procedure Write(F : in File_Name; Item : in  Integer);
private
    type File_Name is
        limited record
            Internal_Name : Integer := 0;
        end record;
end IO_Package;

package body IO_Package is                                            20
    Limit : constant := 200;
    type File_Descriptor is record  ... end record;
    Directory : array (1 .. Limit) of File_Descriptor;
    ...
    procedure Open (F : in out File_Name) is  ...  end;
    procedure Close(F : in out File_Name) is  ...  end;
    procedure Read (F : in File_Name; Item : out Integer) is ... end;
    procedure Write(F : in File_Name; Item : in  Integer) is ... end;
begin
    ...
end IO_Package;
```

NOTES

17 *Notes on the example:* In the example above, an outside subprogram making use of IO_Package may obtain a file   21
name by calling Open and later use it in calls to Read and Write. Thus, outside the package, a file name obtained from
Open acts as a kind of password; its internal properties (such as containing a numeric value) are not known and no other
operations (such as addition or comparison of internal names) can be performed on a file name. Most importantly, clients
of the package cannot make copies of objects of type File_Name.

This example is characteristic of any case where complete control over the operations of a type is desired. Such packages   22
serve a dual purpose. They prevent a user from making use of the internal structure of the type. They also implement the
notion of an encapsulated data type where the only operations on the type are those given in the package specification.

The fact that the full view of File_Name is explicitly declared **limited** means that parameter passing and function return   23
will always be by reference (see 6.2 and 6.5).

7.6 User-Defined Assignment and Finalization

Three kinds of actions are fundamental to the manipulation of objects: initialization, finalization, and   1
assignment. Every object is initialized, either explicitly or by default, after being created (for example, by
an object_declaration or allocator). Every object is finalized before being destroyed (for example, by
leaving a subprogram_body containing an object_declaration, or by a call to an instance of
Unchecked_Deallocation). An assignment operation is used as part of assignment_statements, explicit
initialization, parameter passing, and other operations.

Default definitions for these three fundamental operations are provided by the language, but a *controlled*   2
type gives the user additional control over parts of these operations. In particular, the user can define, for a
controlled type, an Initialize procedure which is invoked immediately after the normal default initialization

of a controlled object, a Finalize procedure which is invoked immediately before finalization of any of the components of a controlled object, and an Adjust procedure which is invoked as the last step of an assignment to a (nonlimited) controlled object.

Static Semantics

3　The following language-defined library package exists:

4/1
```
package Ada.Finalization is
    pragma Preelaborate(Finalization);
    pragma Remote_Types(Finalization);
```

5
```
    type Controlled is abstract tagged private;
```

6
```
    procedure Initialize  (Object : in out Controlled);
    procedure Adjust      (Object : in out Controlled);
    procedure Finalize    (Object : in out Controlled);
```

7
```
    type Limited_Controlled is abstract tagged limited private;
```

8
```
    procedure Initialize  (Object : in out Limited_Controlled);
    procedure Finalize    (Object : in out Limited_Controlled);
private
    ...  -- not specified by the language
end Ada.Finalization;
```

9　A controlled type is a descendant of Controlled or Limited_Controlled. The (default) implementations of Initialize, Adjust, and Finalize have no effect. The predefined "=" operator of type Controlled always returns True, since this operator is incorporated into the implementation of the predefined equality operator of types derived from Controlled, as explained in 4.5.2. The type Limited_Controlled is like Controlled, except that it is limited and it lacks the primitive subprogram Adjust.

Dynamic Semantics

10　During the elaboration of an object_declaration, for every controlled subcomponent of the object that is not assigned an initial value (as defined in 3.3.1), Initialize is called on that subcomponent. Similarly, if the object as a whole is controlled and is not assigned an initial value, Initialize is called on the object. The same applies to the evaluation of an allocator, as explained in 4.8.

11/1　For an extension_aggregate whose ancestor_part is a subtype_mark, for each controlled subcomponent of the ancestor part, either Initialize is called, or its initial value is assigned, as appropriate; if the type of the ancestor part is itself controlled, the Initialize procedure of the ancestor type is called, unless that Initialize procedure is abstract.

12　Initialize and other initialization operations are done in an arbitrary order, except as follows. Initialize is applied to an object after initialization of its subcomponents, if any (including both implicit initialization and Initialize calls). If an object has a component with an access discriminant constrained by a per-object expression, Initialize is applied to this component after any components that do not have such discriminants. For an object with several components with such a discriminant, Initialize is applied to them in order of their component_declarations. For an allocator, any task activations follow all calls on Initialize.

13　When a target object with any controlled parts is assigned a value, either when created or in a subsequent assignment_statement, the *assignment operation* proceeds as follows:

14　　• The value of the target becomes the assigned value.

15　　• The value of the target is *adjusted.*

16　To adjust the value of a (nonlimited) composite object, the values of the components of the object are first adjusted in an arbitrary order, and then, if the object is controlled, Adjust is called. Adjusting the value of an elementary object has no effect, nor does adjusting the value of a composite object with no controlled parts.

For an assignment_statement, after the name and expression have been evaluated, and any conversion (including constraint checking) has been done, an anonymous object is created, and the value is assigned into it; that is, the assignment operation is applied. (Assignment includes value adjustment.) The target of the assignment_statement is then finalized. The value of the anonymous object is then assigned into the target of the assignment_statement. Finally, the anonymous object is finalized. As explained below, the implementation may eliminate the intermediate anonymous object, so this description subsumes the one given in 5.2, "Assignment Statements". 17

Implementation Requirements

For an aggregate of a controlled type whose value is assigned, other than by an assignment_statement or a return_statement, the implementation shall not create a separate anonymous object for the aggregate. The aggregate value shall be constructed directly in the target of the assignment operation and Adjust is not called on the target object. 17.1/1

Implementation Permissions

An implementation is allowed to relax the above rules (for nonlimited controlled types) in the following ways: 18

- For an assignment_statement that assigns to an object the value of that same object, the implementation need not do anything. 19

- For an assignment_statement for a noncontrolled type, the implementation may finalize and assign each component of the variable separately (rather than finalizing the entire variable and assigning the entire new value) unless a discriminant of the variable is changed by the assignment. 20

- For an aggregate or function call whose value is assigned into a target object, the implementation need not create a separate anonymous object if it can safely create the value of the aggregate or function call directly in the target object. Similarly, for an assignment_-statement, the implementation need not create an anonymous object if the value being assigned is the result of evaluating a name denoting an object (the source object) whose storage cannot overlap with the target. If the source object might overlap with the target object, then the implementation can avoid the need for an intermediary anonymous object by exercising one of the above permissions and perform the assignment one component at a time (for an overlapping array assignment), or not at all (for an assignment where the target and the source of the assignment are the same object). Even if an anonymous object is created, the implementation may move its value to the target object as part of the assignment without re-adjusting so long as the anonymous object has no aliased subcomponents. 21

7.6.1 Completion and Finalization

This subclause defines *completion* and *leaving* of the execution of constructs and entities. A *master* is the execution of a construct that includes finalization of local objects after it is complete (and after waiting for any local tasks — see 9.3), but before leaving. Other constructs and entities are left immediately upon completion. 1

Dynamic Semantics

The execution of a construct or entity is *complete* when the end of that execution has been reached, or when a transfer of control (see 5.1) causes it to be abandoned. Completion due to reaching the end of 2 execution, or due to the transfer of control of an exit_, return_, goto_, or requeue_statement or of the selection of a terminate_alternative is *normal completion*. Completion is *abnormal* otherwise — when control is transferred out of a construct due to abort or the raising of an exception.

3   After execution of a construct or entity is complete, it is *left*, meaning that execution continues with the next action, as defined for the execution that is taking place. Leaving an execution happens immediately after its completion, except in the case of a *master*: the execution of a task_body, a block_statement, a subprogram_body, an entry_body, or an accept_statement. A master is finalized after it is complete, and before it is left.

4   For the *finalization* of a master, dependent tasks are first awaited, as explained in 9.3. Then each object whose accessibility level is the same as that of the master is finalized if the object was successfully initialized and still exists. These actions are performed whether the master is left by reaching the last statement or via a transfer of control. When a transfer of control causes completion of an execution, each included master is finalized in order, from innermost outward.

5   For the *finalization* of an object:

6   • If the object is of an elementary type, finalization has no effect;

7   • If the object is of a controlled type, the Finalize procedure is called;

8   • If the object is of a protected type, the actions defined in 9.4 are performed;

9   • If the object is of a composite type, then after performing the above actions, if any, every component of the object is finalized in an arbitrary order, except as follows: if the object has a component with an access discriminant constrained by a per-object expression, this component is finalized before any components that do not have such discriminants; for an object with several components with such a discriminant, they are finalized in the reverse of the order of their component_declarations.

10   Immediately before an instance of Unchecked_Deallocation reclaims the storage of an object, the object is finalized. If an instance of Unchecked_Deallocation is never applied to an object created by an allocator, the object will still exist when the corresponding master completes, and it will be finalized then.

11   The order in which the finalization of a master performs finalization of objects is as follows: Objects created by declarations in the master are finalized in the reverse order of their creation. For objects that were created by allocators for an access type whose ultimate ancestor is declared in the master, this rule is applied as though each such object that still exists had been created in an arbitrary order at the first freezing point (see 13.14) of the ultimate ancestor type.

12   The target of an assignment statement is finalized before copying in the new value, as explained in 7.6.

13/1 If the object_name in an object_renaming_declaration, or the actual parameter for a generic formal **in out** parameter in a generic_instantiation, denotes any part of an anonymous object created by a function call, the anonymous object is not finalized until after it is no longer accessible via any name. Otherwise, an anonymous object created by a function call or by an aggregate is finalized no later than the end of the innermost enclosing declarative_item or statement; if that is a compound_statement, the object is finalized before starting the execution of any statement within the compound_statement.

13.1/1 If a transfer of control or raising of an exception occurs prior to performing a finalization of an anonymous object, the anonymous object is finalized as part of the finalizations due to be performed for the object's innermost enclosing master.

Bounded (Run-Time) Errors

It is a bounded error for a call on Finalize or Adjust that occurs as part of object finalization or assignment to propagate an exception. The possible consequences depend on what action invoked the Finalize or Adjust operation: 14/1

- For a Finalize invoked as part of an assignment_statement, Program_Error is raised at that point.   15

- For an Adjust invoked as part of the initialization of a controlled object, other adjustments due to be performed might or might not be performed, and then Program_Error is raised. During its propagation, finalization might or might not be applied to objects whose Adjust failed. For an Adjust invoked as part of an assignment statement, any other adjustments due to be performed are performed, and then Program_Error is raised.   16/1

- For a Finalize invoked as part of a call on an instance of Unchecked_Deallocation, any other finalizations due to be performed are performed, and then Program_Error is raised.   17

- For a Finalize invoked as part of the finalization of the anonymous object created by a function call or aggregate, any other finalizations due to be performed are performed, and then Program_Error is raised.   17.1/1

- For a Finalize invoked due to reaching the end of the execution of a master, any other finalizations associated with the master are performed, and Program_Error is raised immediately after leaving the master.   17.2/1

- For a Finalize invoked by the transfer of control of an exit_, return_, goto_, or requeue_-statement, Program_Error is raised no earlier than after the finalization of the master being finalized when the exception occurred, and no later than the point where normal execution would have continued. Any other finalizations due to be performed up to that point are performed before raising Program_Error.   18

- For a Finalize invoked by a transfer of control that is due to raising an exception, any other finalizations due to be performed for the same master are performed; Program_Error is raised immediately after leaving the master.   19

- For a Finalize invoked by a transfer of control due to an abort or selection of a terminate alternative, the exception is ignored; any other finalizations due to be performed are performed.   20

NOTES

18 The rules of Section 10 imply that immediately prior to partition termination, Finalize operations are applied to library-level controlled objects (including those created by allocators of library-level access types, except those already finalized). This occurs after waiting for library-level tasks to terminate.   21

19 A constant is only constant between its initialization and finalization. Both initialization and finalization are allowed to change the value of a constant.   22

20 Abort is deferred during certain operations related to controlled types, as explained in 9.8. Those rules prevent an abort from causing a controlled object to be left in an ill-defined state.   23

21 The Finalize procedure is called upon finalization of a controlled object, even if Finalize was called earlier, either explicitly or as part of an assignment; hence, if a controlled type is visibly controlled (implying that its Finalize primitive is directly callable), or is nonlimited (implying that assignment is allowed), its Finalize procedure should be designed to have no ill effect if it is applied a second time to the same object.   24

Section 8: Visibility Rules

The rules defining the scope of declarations and the rules defining which identifiers, character_literals, and operator_symbols are visible at (or from) various places in the text of the program are described in this section. The formulation of these rules uses the notion of a declarative region.   1

As explained in Section 3, a declaration declares a view of an entity and associates a defining name with that view. The view comprises an identification of the viewed entity, and possibly additional properties. A usage name denotes a declaration. It also denotes the view declared by that declaration, and denotes the entity of that view. Thus, two different usage names might denote two different views of the same entity; in this case they denote the same entity.   2

8.1 Declarative Region

Static Semantics

For each of the following constructs, there is a portion of the program text called its *declarative region*, within which nested declarations can occur: 1

- any declaration, other than that of an enumeration type, that is not a completion of a previous declaration;   2
- a block_statement;   3
- a loop_statement;   4
- an accept_statement;   5
- an exception_handler.   6

The declarative region includes the text of the construct together with additional text determined (recursively), as follows: 7

- If a declaration is included, so is its completion, if any.   8
- If the declaration of a library unit (including Standard — see 10.1.1) is included, so are the declarations of any child units (and their completions, by the previous rule). The child declarations occur after the declaration.   9
- If a body_stub is included, so is the corresponding subunit.   10
- If a type_declaration is included, then so is a corresponding record_representation_clause, if any.   11

The declarative region of a declaration is also called the *declarative region* of any view or entity declared by the declaration.   12

A declaration occurs *immediately within* a declarative region if this region is the innermost declarative region that encloses the declaration (the *immediately enclosing* declarative region), not counting the declarative region (if any) associated with the declaration itself.   13

A declaration is *local* to a declarative region if the declaration occurs immediately within the declarative region. An entity is *local* to a declarative region if the entity is declared by a declaration that is local to the declarative region.   14

S. Tucker Taft et al. (Eds.): Consolidated Ada Reference Manual, LNCS 2219, pp. 147–158, 2001.

15   A declaration is *global* to a declarative region if the declaration occurs immediately within another declarative region that encloses the declarative region. An entity is *global* to a declarative region if the entity is declared by a declaration that is global to the declarative region.

NOTES

16   1 The children of a parent library unit are inside the parent's declarative region, even though they do not occur inside the parent's declaration or body. This implies that one can use (for example) "P.Q" to refer to a child of P whose defining name is Q, and that after "**use** P;" Q can refer (directly) to that child.

17   2 As explained above and in 10.1.1, "Compilation Units - Library Units", all library units are descendants of Standard, and so are contained in the declarative region of Standard. They are *not* inside the declaration or body of Standard, but they *are* inside its declarative region.

18   3 For a declarative region that comes in multiple parts, the text of the declarative region does not contain any text that might appear between the parts. Thus, when a portion of a declarative region is said to extend from one place to another in the declarative region, the portion does not contain any text that might appear between the parts of the declarative region.

8.2 Scope of Declarations

1   For each declaration, the language rules define a certain portion of the program text called the *scope* of the declaration. The scope of a declaration is also called the scope of any view or entity declared by the declaration. Within the scope of an entity, and only there, there are places where it is legal to refer to the declared entity. These places are defined by the rules of visibility and overloading.

Static Semantics

2   The *immediate scope* of a declaration is a portion of the declarative region immediately enclosing the declaration. The immediate scope starts at the beginning of the declaration, except in the case of an overloadable declaration, in which case the immediate scope starts just after the place where the profile of the callable entity is determined (which is at the end of the _specification for the callable entity, or at the end of the generic_instantiation if an instance). The immediate scope extends to the end of the declarative region, with the following exceptions:

3   • The immediate scope of a library_item includes only its semantic dependents.

4   • The immediate scope of a declaration in the private part of a library unit does not include the visible part of any public descendant of that library unit.

5   The *visible part* of (a view of) an entity is a portion of the text of its declaration containing declarations that are visible from outside. The *private part* of (a view of) an entity that has a visible part contains all declarations within the declaration of (the view of) the entity, except those in the visible part; these are not visible from outside. Visible and private parts are defined only for these kinds of entities: callable entities, other program units, and composite types.

6   • The visible part of a view of a callable entity is its profile.

7   • The visible part of a composite type other than a task or protected type consists of the declarations of all components declared (explicitly or implicitly) within the type_declaration.

8   • The visible part of a generic unit includes the generic_formal_part. For a generic package, it also includes the first list of basic_declarative_items of the package_specification. For a generic subprogram, it also includes the profile.

9   • The visible part of a package, task unit, or protected unit consists of declarations in the program unit's declaration other than those following the reserved word **private**, if any; see 7.1 and 12.7 for packages, 9.1 for task units, and 9.4 for protected units.

The scope of a declaration always contains the immediate scope of the declaration. In addition, for a given declaration that occurs immediately within the visible part of an outer declaration, or is a public child of an outer declaration, the scope of the given declaration extends to the end of the scope of the outer declaration, except that the scope of a library_item includes only its semantic dependents.   10

The immediate scope of a declaration is also the immediate scope of the entity or view declared by the declaration. Similarly, the scope of a declaration is also the scope of the entity or view declared by the declaration.   11

NOTES
4 There are notations for denoting visible declarations that are not directly visible. For example, parameter_-   12
specifications are in the visible part of a subprogram_declaration so that they can be used in named-notation calls
appearing outside the called subprogram. For another example, declarations of the visible part of a package can be
denoted by expanded names appearing outside the package, and can be made directly visible by a use_clause.

8.3 Visibility

The *visibility rules*, given below, determine which declarations are visible and directly visible at each place within a program. The visibility rules apply to both explicit and implicit declarations.   1

Static Semantics

A declaration is defined to be *directly visible* at places where a name consisting of only an identifier or operator_symbol is sufficient to denote the declaration; that is, no selected_component notation or special context (such as preceding => in a named association) is necessary to denote the declaration. A declaration is defined to be *visible* wherever it is directly visible, as well as at other places where some name (such as a selected_component) can denote the declaration.   2

The syntactic category direct_name is used to indicate contexts where direct visibility is required. The syntactic category selector_name is used to indicate contexts where visibility, but not direct visibility, is required.   3

There are two kinds of direct visibility: *immediate visibility* and *use-visibility*. A declaration is immediately visible at a place if it is directly visible because the place is within its immediate scope. A declaration is use-visible if it is directly visible because of a use_clause (see 8.4). Both conditions can apply.   4

A declaration can be *hidden*, either from direct visibility, or from all visibility, within certain parts of its scope. Where *hidden from all visibility*, it is not visible at all (neither using a direct_name nor a selector_name). Where *hidden from direct visibility*, only direct visibility is lost; visibility using a selector_name is still possible.   5

Two or more declarations are *overloaded* if they all have the same defining name and there is a place where they are all directly visible.   6

The declarations of callable entities (including enumeration literals) are *overloadable*, meaning that overloading is allowed for them.   7

Two declarations are *homographs* if they have the same defining name, and, if both are overloadable, their profiles are type conformant. An inner declaration hides any outer homograph from direct visibility.   8

Two homographs are not generally allowed immediately within the same declarative region unless one *overrides* the other (see Legality Rules below). The only declarations that are *overridable* are the implicit declarations for predefined operators and inherited primitive subprograms. A declaration overrides another homograph that occurs immediately within the same declarative region in the following cases: 9/1

10/1 • A declaration that is not overridable overrides one that is overridable, regardless of which declaration occurs first;

11 • The implicit declaration of an inherited operator overrides that of a predefined operator;

12 • An implicit declaration of an inherited subprogram overrides a previous implicit declaration of an inherited subprogram.

13 • For an implicit declaration of a primitive subprogram in a generic unit, there is a copy of this declaration in an instance. However, a whole new set of primitive subprograms is implicitly declared for each type declared within the visible part of the instance. These new declarations occur immediately after the type declaration, and override the copied ones. The copied ones can be called only from within the instance; the new ones can be called only from outside the instance, although for tagged types, the body of a new one can be executed by a call to an old one.

14 A declaration is visible within its scope, except where hidden from all visibility, as follows:

15 • An overridden declaration is hidden from all visibility within the scope of the overriding declaration.

16 • A declaration is hidden from all visibility until the end of the declaration, except:

17 • For a record type or record extension, the declaration is hidden from all visibility only until the reserved word **record**;

18 • For a package_declaration, task declaration, protected declaration, generic_package_-declaration, or subprogram_body, the declaration is hidden from all visibility only until the reserved word **is** of the declaration.

19 • If the completion of a declaration is a declaration, then within the scope of the completion, the first declaration is hidden from all visibility. Similarly, a discriminant_specification or parameter_specification is hidden within the scope of a corresponding discriminant_-specification or parameter_specification of a corresponding completion, or of a corresponding accept_statement.

20 • The declaration of a library unit (including a library_unit_renaming_declaration) is hidden from all visibility except at places that are within its declarative region or within the scope of a with_clause that mentions it. For each declaration or renaming of a generic unit as a child of some parent generic package, there is a corresponding declaration nested immediately within each instance of the parent. Such a nested declaration is hidden from all visibility except at places that are within the scope of a with_clause that mentions the child.

21 A declaration with a defining_identifier or defining_operator_symbol is immediately visible (and hence directly visible) within its immediate scope except where hidden from direct visibility, as follows:

22 • A declaration is hidden from direct visibility within the immediate scope of a homograph of the declaration, if the homograph occurs within an inner declarative region;

23 • A declaration is also hidden from direct visibility where hidden from all visibility.

Name Resolution Rules

24 A direct_name shall resolve to denote a directly visible declaration whose defining name is the same as the direct_name. A selector_name shall resolve to denote a visible declaration whose defining name is the same as the selector_name.

25 These rules on visibility and direct visibility do not apply in a context_clause, a parent_unit_name, or a pragma that appears at the place of a compilation_unit. For those contexts, see the rules in 10.1.6, ''Environment-Level Visibility Rules''.

Legality Rules

A non-overridable declaration is illegal if there is a homograph occurring immediately within the same declarative region that is visible at the place of the declaration, and is not hidden from all visibility by the non-overridable declaration. In addition, a type extension is illegal if somewhere within its immediate scope it has two visible components with the same name. Similarly, the context_clause for a subunit is illegal if it mentions (in a with_clause) some library unit, and there is a homograph of the library unit that is visible at the place of the corresponding stub, and the homograph and the mentioned library unit are both declared immediately within the same declarative region. These rules also apply to dispatching operations declared in the visible part of an instance of a generic unit. However, they do not apply to other overloadable declarations in an instance; such declarations may have type conformant profiles in the instance, so long as the corresponding declarations in the generic were not type conformant. 26/1

NOTES

5 Visibility for compilation units follows from the definition of the environment in 10.1.4, except that it is necessary to apply a with_clause to obtain visibility to a library_unit_declaration or library_unit_renaming_declaration. 27

6 In addition to the visibility rules given above, the meaning of the occurrence of a direct_name or selector_name at a given place in the text can depend on the overloading rules (see 8.6). 28

7 Not all contexts where an identifier, character_literal, or operator_symbol are allowed require visibility of a corresponding declaration. Contexts where visibility is not required are identified by using one of these three syntactic categories directly in a syntax rule, rather than using direct_name or selector_name. 29

8.4 Use Clauses

A use_package_clause achieves direct visibility of declarations that appear in the visible part of a package; a use_type_clause achieves direct visibility of the primitive operators of a type. 1

Syntax

use_clause ::= use_package_clause | use_type_clause 2

use_package_clause ::= **use** *package_*name {, *package_*name}; 3

use_type_clause ::= **use type** subtype_mark {, subtype_mark}; 4

Legality Rules

A *package_*name of a use_package_clause shall denote a package. 5

Static Semantics

For each use_clause, there is a certain region of text called the *scope* of the use_clause. For a use_clause within a context_clause of a library_unit_declaration or library_unit_renaming_declaration, the scope is the entire declarative region of the declaration. For a use_clause within a context_clause of a body, the scope is the entire body and any subunits (including multiply nested subunits). The scope does not include context_clauses themselves. 6

For a use_clause immediately within a declarative region, the scope is the portion of the declarative region starting just after the use_clause and extending to the end of the declarative region. However, the scope of a use_clause in the private part of a library unit does not include the visible part of any public descendant of that library unit. 7

For each package denoted by a *package_*name of a use_package_clause whose scope encloses a place, each declaration that occurs immediately within the declarative region of the package is *potentially use-visible* at this place if the declaration is visible at this place. For each type *T* or *T*Class determined by a 8 subtype_mark of a use_type_clause whose scope encloses a place, the declaration of each primitive operator of type *T* is potentially use-visible at this place if its declaration is visible at this place.

9   A declaration is *use-visible* if it is potentially use-visible, except in these naming-conflict cases:

10 • A potentially use-visible declaration is not use-visible if the place considered is within the immediate scope of a homograph of the declaration.

11 • Potentially use-visible declarations that have the same identifier are not use-visible unless each of them is an overloadable declaration.

Dynamic Semantics

12 The elaboration of a use_clause has no effect.

Examples

13 *Example of a use clause in a context clause:*

14   **with** Ada.Calendar; **use** Ada;

15 *Example of a use type clause:*

16   **use type** Rational_Numbers.Rational; *-- see 7.1*
    Two_Thirds: Rational_Numbers.Rational := 2/3;

8.5 Renaming Declarations

1   A renaming_declaration declares another name for an entity, such as an object, exception, package, subprogram, entry, or generic unit. Alternatively, a subprogram_renaming_declaration can be the completion of a previous subprogram_declaration.

Syntax

2   renaming_declaration ::=
       object_renaming_declaration
      | exception_renaming_declaration
      | package_renaming_declaration
      | subprogram_renaming_declaration
      | generic_renaming_declaration

Dynamic Semantics

3   The elaboration of a renaming_declaration evaluates the name that follows the reserved word **renames** and thereby determines the view and entity denoted by this name (the *renamed view* and *renamed entity*). A name that denotes the renaming_declaration denotes (a new view of) the renamed entity.

NOTES

4   8 Renaming may be used to resolve name conflicts and to act as a shorthand. Renaming with a different identifier or operator_symbol does not hide the old name; the new name and the old name need not be visible at the same places.

5   9 A task or protected object that is declared by an explicit object_declaration can be renamed as an object. However, a single task or protected object cannot be renamed since the corresponding type is anonymous (meaning it has no nameable subtypes). For similar reasons, an object of an anonymous array or access type cannot be renamed.

6   10 A subtype defined without any additional constraint can be used to achieve the effect of renaming another subtype (including a task or protected subtype) as in

7   **subtype** Mode **is** Ada.Text_IO.File_Mode;

8.5.1 Object Renaming Declarations

An object_renaming_declaration is used to rename an object.   1

Syntax

object_renaming_declaration ::= defining_identifier : subtype_mark **renames** *object*_name;   2

Name Resolution Rules

The type of the *object*_name shall resolve to the type determined by the subtype_mark.   3

Legality Rules

The renamed entity shall be an object.   4

The renamed entity shall not be a subcomponent that depends on discriminants of a variable whose   5/1
nominal subtype is unconstrained, unless this subtype is indefinite, or the variable is aliased. A slice of an
array shall not be renamed if this restriction disallows renaming of the array. In addition to the places
where Legality Rules normally apply, these rules apply also in the private part of an instance of a generic
unit. These rules also apply for a renaming that appears in the body of a generic unit, with the additional
requirement that even if the nominal subtype of the variable is indefinite, its type shall not be a descendant
of an untagged generic formal derived type.

Static Semantics

An object_renaming_declaration declares a new view of the renamed object whose properties are   6
identical to those of the renamed view. Thus, the properties of the renamed object are not affected by the
renaming_declaration. In particular, its value and whether or not it is a constant are unaffected; similarly,
the constraints that apply to an object are not affected by renaming (any constraint implied by the
subtype_mark of the object_renaming_declaration is ignored).

Examples

Example of renaming an object: 7

```
declare
    L : Person renames Leftmost_Person;  -- see 3.10.1
begin
    L.Age := L.Age + 1;
end;
```
   8

8.5.2 Exception Renaming Declarations

An exception_renaming_declaration is used to rename an exception.   1

Syntax

exception_renaming_declaration ::= defining_identifier : **exception renames** *exception*_name;   2

Legality Rules

The renamed entity shall be an exception.   3

Static Semantics

An exception_renaming_declaration declares a new view of the renamed exception.   4

Examples

5   *Example of renaming an exception:*

6   EOF : **exception renames** Ada.IO_Exceptions.End_Error; *-- see A.13*

8.5.3 Package Renaming Declarations

1   A package_renaming_declaration is used to rename a package.

Syntax

2   package_renaming_declaration ::=
    package defining_program_unit_name **renames** *package*_name;

Legality Rules

3   The renamed entity shall be a package.

Static Semantics

4   A package_renaming_declaration declares a new view of the renamed package.

Examples

5   *Example of renaming a package:*

6   **package** TM **renames** Table_Manager;

8.5.4 Subprogram Renaming Declarations

1   A subprogram_renaming_declaration can serve as the completion of a subprogram_declaration; such a renaming_declaration is called a *renaming-as-body*. A subprogram_renaming_declaration that is not a completion is called a *renaming-as-declaration*, and is used to rename a subprogram (possibly an enumeration literal) or an entry.

Syntax

2   subprogram_renaming_declaration ::= subprogram_specification **renames** *callable_entity*_name;

Name Resolution Rules

3   The expected profile for the *callable_entity*_name is the profile given in the subprogram_specification.

Legality Rules

4   The profile of a renaming-as-declaration shall be mode-conformant with that of the renamed callable entity.

5/1   The profile of a renaming-as-body shall conform fully to that of the declaration it completes. If the renaming-as-body completes that declaration before the subprogram it declares is frozen, the profile shall be mode-conformant with that of the renamed callable entity and the subprogram it declares takes its convention from the renamed subprogram; otherwise, the profile shall be subtype-conformant with that of the renamed callable entity and the convention of the renamed subprogram shall not be Intrinsic. A renaming-as-body is illegal if the declaration occurs before the subprogram whose declaration it completes is frozen, and the renaming renames the subprogram itself, through one or more subprogram renaming declarations, none of whose subprograms has been frozen.

6   A name that denotes a formal parameter of the subprogram_specification is not allowed within the *callable_entity*_name.

Static Semantics

A renaming-as-declaration declares a new view of the renamed entity. The profile of this new view takes its subtypes, parameter modes, and calling convention from the original profile of the callable entity, while taking the formal parameter names and default_expressions from the profile given in the subprogram_renaming_declaration. The new view is a function or procedure, never an entry.   7

Dynamic Semantics

For a call to a subprogram whose body is given as a renaming-as-body, the execution of the renaming-as-body is equivalent to the execution of a subprogram_body that simply calls the renamed subprogram with its formal parameters as the actual parameters and, if it is a function, returns the value of the call.   7.1/1

For a call on a renaming of a dispatching subprogram that is overridden, if the overriding occurred before the renaming, then the body executed is that of the overriding declaration, even if the overriding declaration is not visible at the place of the renaming; otherwise, the inherited or predefined subprogram is called.   8

Bounded (Run-Time) Errors

If a subprogram directly or indirectly renames itself, then it is a bounded error to call that subprogram. Possible consequences are that Program_Error or Storage_Error is raised, or that the call results in infinite recursion.   8.1/1

NOTES

11 A procedure can only be renamed as a procedure. A function whose defining_designator is either an identifier or an operator_symbol can be renamed with either an identifier or an operator_symbol; for renaming as an operator, the subprogram specification given in the renaming_declaration is subject to the rules given in 6.6 for operator declarations. Enumeration literals can be renamed as functions; similarly, attribute_references that denote functions (such as references to Succ and Pred) can be renamed as functions. An entry can only be renamed as a procedure; the new name is only allowed to appear in contexts that allow a procedure name. An entry of a family can be renamed, but an entry family cannot be renamed as a whole.   9

12 The operators of the root numeric types cannot be renamed because the types in the profile are anonymous, so the corresponding specifications cannot be written; the same holds for certain attributes, such as Pos.   10

13 Calls with the new name of a renamed entry are procedure_call_statements and are not allowed at places where the syntax requires an entry_call_statement in conditional_ and timed_entry_calls, nor in an asynchronous_select; similarly, the Count attribute is not available for the new name.   11

14 The primitiveness of a renaming-as-declaration is determined by its profile, and by where it occurs, as for any declaration of (a view of) a subprogram; primitiveness is not determined by the renamed view. In order to perform a dispatching call, the subprogram name has to denote a primitive subprogram, not a non-primitive renaming of a primitive subprogram.   12

Examples

Examples of subprogram renaming declarations: 13

```
procedure My_Write(C : in Character) renames Pool(K).Write;  -- see 4.1.3
```
   14
```
function Real_Plus(Left, Right : Real   ) return Real    renames "+";
function Int_Plus (Left, Right : Integer) return Integer renames "+";
```
   15
```
function Rouge return Color renames Red;   -- see 3.5.1
function Rot   return Color renames Red;
function Rosso return Color renames Rouge;
```
   16
```
function Next(X : Color) return Color renames Color'Succ;  -- see 3.5.1
```
   17

Example of a subprogram renaming declaration with new parameter names: 18

```
function "*" (X,Y : Vector) return Real renames Dot_Product;  -- see 6.1
```
   19

20
21

Example of a subprogram renaming declaration with a new default expression:

```
function Minimum(L : Link := Head) return Cell renames Min_Cell;  -- see 6.1
```

8.5.5 Generic Renaming Declarations

1   A generic_renaming_declaration is used to rename a generic unit.

Syntax

2   generic_renaming_declaration ::=
    generic package   defining_program_unit_name **renames** *generic_package_*name;
    | **generic procedure**   defining_program_unit_name **renames** *generic_procedure_*name;
    | **generic function**   defining_program_unit_name **renames** *generic_function_*name;

Legality Rules

3   The renamed entity shall be a generic unit of the corresponding kind.

Static Semantics

4   A generic_renaming_declaration declares a new view of the renamed generic unit.

NOTES

5   15 Although the properties of the new view are the same as those of the renamed view, the place where the generic_renaming_declaration occurs may affect the legality of subsequent renamings and instantiations that denote the generic_renaming_declaration, in particular if the renamed generic unit is a library unit (see 10.1.1).

Examples

6   *Example of renaming a generic unit:*

7   ```
generic package Enum_IO renames Ada.Text_IO.Enumeration_IO; -- see A.10.10
```

## 8.6 The Context of Overload Resolution

1    Because declarations can be overloaded, it is possible for an occurrence of a usage name to have more than one possible interpretation; in most cases, ambiguity is disallowed. This clause describes how the possible interpretations resolve to the actual interpretation.

2    Certain rules of the language (the Name Resolution Rules) are considered ''overloading rules''. If a possible interpretation violates an overloading rule, it is assumed not to be the intended interpretation; some other possible interpretation is assumed to be the actual interpretation. On the other hand, violations of non-overloading rules do not affect which interpretation is chosen; instead, they cause the construct to be illegal. To be legal, there usually has to be exactly one acceptable interpretation of a construct that is a ''complete context'', not counting any nested complete contexts.

3    The syntax rules of the language and the visibility rules given in 8.3 determine the possible interpretations. Most type checking rules (rules that require a particular type, or a particular class of types, for example) are overloading rules. Various rules for the matching of formal and actual parameters are overloading rules.

*Name Resolution Rules*

4    Overload resolution is applied separately to each *complete context*, not counting inner complete contexts. Each of the following constructs is a *complete context*:

5    • A context_item.
```

- A declarative_item or declaration.   6

- A statement.   7

- A pragma_argument_association.   8

- The expression of a case_statement.   9

An (overall) *interpretation* of a complete context embodies its meaning, and includes the following   10
information about the constituents of the complete context, not including constituents of inner complete
contexts:

- for each constituent of the complete context, to which syntactic categories it belongs, and by   11
  which syntax rules; and

- for each usage name, which declaration it denotes (and, therefore, which view and which entity it   12
  denotes); and

- for a complete context that is a declarative_item, whether or not it is a completion of a   13
  declaration, and (if so) which declaration it completes.

A *possible interpretation* is one that obeys the syntax rules and the visibility rules. An *acceptable*   14
interpretation is a possible interpretation that obeys the *overloading rules*, that is, those rules that specify
an expected type or expected profile, or specify how a construct shall *resolve* or be *interpreted*.

The *interpretation* of a constituent of a complete context is determined from the overall interpretation of   15
the complete context as a whole. Thus, for example, "interpreted as a function_call," means that the
construct's interpretation says that it belongs to the syntactic category function_call.

Each occurrence of a usage name *denotes* the declaration determined by its interpretation. It also denotes   16
the view declared by its denoted declaration, except in the following cases:

- If a usage name appears within the declarative region of a type_declaration and denotes that   17
  same type_declaration, then it denotes the *current instance* of the type (rather than the type
  itself). The current instance of a type is the object or value of the type that is associated with the
  execution that evaluates the usage name.

- If a usage name appears within the declarative region of a generic_declaration (but not within its   18
  generic_formal_part) and it denotes that same generic_declaration, then it denotes the *current*
  instance of the generic unit (rather than the generic unit itself). See also 12.3.

A usage name that denotes a view also denotes the entity of that view.   19

The *expected type* for a given expression, name, or other construct determines, according to the *type*   20
resolution rules given below, the types considered for the construct during overload resolution. The type
resolution rules provide support for class-wide programming, universal numeric literals, dispatching
operations, and anonymous access types:

- If a construct is expected to be of any type in a class of types, or of the universal or class-wide   21
  type for a class, then the type of the construct shall resolve to a type in that class or to a universal
  type that covers the class.

- If the expected type for a construct is a specific type T, then the type of the construct shall   22
  resolve either to T, or:

    - to T'Class; or   23

    - to a universal type that covers T; or   24

    - when T is an anonymous access type (see 3.10) with designated type D, to an access-   25
      to-variable type whose designated type is D'Class or is covered by D.

The Context of Overload Resolution   **8.6**

26   In certain contexts, such as in a subprogram_renaming_declaration, the Name Resolution Rules define an *expected profile* for a given name; in such cases, the name shall resolve to the name of a callable entity whose profile is type conformant with the expected profile.

Legality Rules

27   When the expected type for a construct is required to be a *single* type in a given class, the type expected for the construct shall be determinable solely from the context in which the construct appears, excluding the construct itself, but using the requirement that it be in the given class; the type of the construct is then this single expected type. Furthermore, the context shall not be one that expects any type in some class that contains types of the given class; in particular, the construct shall not be the operand of a type_conversion.

28   A complete context shall have at least one acceptable interpretation; if there is exactly one, then that one is chosen.

29   There is a *preference* for the primitive operators (and ranges) of the root numeric types *root_integer* and *root_real*. In particular, if two acceptable interpretations of a constituent of a complete context differ only in that one is for a primitive operator (or range) of the type *root_integer* or *root_real*, and the other is not, the interpretation using the primitive operator (or range) of the root numeric type is *preferred*.

30   For a complete context, if there is exactly one overall acceptable interpretation where each constituent's interpretation is the same as or preferred (in the above sense) over those in all other overall acceptable interpretations, then that one overall acceptable interpretation is chosen. Otherwise, the complete context is *ambiguous*.

31   A complete context other than a pragma_argument_association shall not be ambiguous.

32   A complete context that is a pragma_argument_association is allowed to be ambiguous (unless otherwise specified for the particular pragma), but only if every acceptable interpretation of the pragma argument is as a name that statically denotes a callable entity. Such a name denotes all of the declarations determined by its interpretations, and all of the views declared by these declarations.

NOTES

33   16 If a usage name has only one acceptable interpretation, then it denotes the corresponding entity. However, this does not mean that the usage name is necessarily legal since other requirements exist which are not considered for overload resolution; for example, the fact that an expression is static, whether an object is constant, mode and subtype conformance rules, freezing rules, order of elaboration, and so on.

34   Similarly, subtypes are not considered for overload resolution (the violation of a constraint does not make a program illegal but raises an exception during program execution).

Section 9: Tasks and Synchronization

The execution of an Ada program consists of the execution of one or more *tasks*. Each task represents a separate thread of control that proceeds independently and concurrently between the points where it *interacts* with other tasks. The various forms of task interaction are described in this section, and include: 1

- the activation and termination of a task; 2

- a call on a protected subprogram of a *protected object*, providing exclusive read-write access, or concurrent read-only access to shared data; 3

- a call on an entry, either of another task, allowing for synchronous communication with that task, or of a protected object, allowing for asynchronous communication with one or more other tasks using that same protected object; 4

- a timed operation, including a simple delay statement, a timed entry call or accept, or a timed asynchronous select statement (see next item); 5

- an asynchronous transfer of control as part of an asynchronous select statement, where a task stops what it is doing and begins execution at a different point in response to the completion of an entry call or the expiration of a delay; 6

- an abort statement, allowing one task to cause the termination of another task. 7

In addition, tasks can communicate indirectly by reading and updating (unprotected) shared variables, presuming the access is properly synchronized through some other kind of task interaction. 8

Static Semantics

The properties of a task are defined by a corresponding task declaration and task_body, which together define a program unit called a *task unit*. 9

Dynamic Semantics

Over time, tasks proceed through various *states*. A task is initially *inactive*; upon activation, and prior to its *termination* it is either *blocked* (as part of some task interaction) or *ready* to run. While ready, a task competes for the available *execution resources* that it requires to run. 10

NOTES
1 Concurrent task execution may be implemented on multicomputers, multiprocessors, or with interleaved execution on a single physical processor. On the other hand, whenever an implementation can determine that the required semantic effects can be achieved when parts of the execution of a given task are performed by different physical processors acting in parallel, it may choose to perform them in this way. 11

9.1 Task Units and Task Objects

A task unit is declared by a *task declaration*, which has a corresponding task_body. A task declaration may be a task_type_declaration, in which case it declares a named task type; alternatively, it may be a single_task_declaration, in which case it defines an anonymous task type, as well as declaring a named task object of that type. 1

Syntax

```
task_type_declaration ::=
    task type defining_identifier [known_discriminant_part] [is task_definition];
```
2

```
single_task_declaration ::=
    task defining_identifier [is task_definition];
```
3

S. Tucker Taft et al. (Eds.): Consolidated Ada Reference Manual, LNCS 2219, pp. 159–186, 2001.

4   task_definition ::=
          {task_item}
        [**private**
          {task_item}]
        end [*task*_identifier]

5/1   task_item ::= entry_declaration I aspect_clause

6   task_body ::=
        task body defining_identifier **is**
          declarative_part
        begin
          handled_sequence_of_statements
        end [*task*_identifier];

7   If a *task*_identifier appears at the end of a task_definition or task_body, it shall repeat the
       defining_identifier.

Legality Rules

8   A task declaration requires a completion, which shall be a task_body, and every task_body shall be the
       completion of some task declaration.

Static Semantics

9   A task_definition defines a task type and its first subtype. The first list of task_items of a task_definition,
       together with the known_discriminant_part, if any, is called the visible part of the task unit. The optional
       list of task_items after the reserved word **private** is called the private part of the task unit.

9.1/1 For a task declaration without a task_definition, a task_definition without task_items is assumed.

Dynamic Semantics

10   The elaboration of a task declaration elaborates the task_definition. The elaboration of a single_task_-
       declaration also creates an object of an (anonymous) task type.

11   The elaboration of a task_definition creates the task type and its first subtype; it also includes the
       elaboration of the entry_declarations in the given order.

12/1   As part of the initialization of a task object, any aspect_clauses and any per-object constraints associated
       with entry_declarations of the corresponding task_definition are elaborated in the given order.

13   The elaboration of a task_body has no effect other than to establish that tasks of the type can from then on
       be activated without failing the Elaboration_Check.

14   The execution of a task_body is invoked by the activation of a task of the corresponding type (see 9.2).

15   The content of a task object of a given task type includes:

16   • The values of the discriminants of the task object, if any;

17   • An entry queue for each entry of the task object;

18   • A representation of the state of the associated task.

       NOTES
19   2 Within the declaration or body of a task unit, the name of the task unit denotes the current instance of the unit (see
       8.6), rather than the first subtype of the corresponding task type (and thus the name cannot be used as a subtype_mark).

20   3 The notation of a selected_component can be used to denote a discriminant of a task (see 4.1.3). Within a task unit,
       the name of a discriminant of the task type denotes the corresponding discriminant of the current instance of the unit.

4 A task type is a limited type (see 7.5), and hence has neither an assignment operation nor predefined equality 21 operators. If an application needs to store and exchange task identities, it can do so by defining an access type designating the corresponding task objects and by using access values for identification purposes. Assignment is available for such an access type as for any access type. Alternatively, if the implementation supports the Systems Programming Annex, the Identity attribute can be used for task identification (see C.7).

Examples

Examples of declarations of task types: 22

```
task type Server is                                              23
   entry Next_Work_Item(WI : in Work_Item);
   entry Shut_Down;
end Server;

task type Keyboard_Driver(ID : Keyboard_ID := New_ID) is         24
   entry Read (C : out Character);
   entry Write(C : in  Character);
end Keyboard_Driver;
```

Examples of declarations of single tasks: 25

```
task Controller is                                               26
   entry Request(Level)(D : Item);   -- a family of entries
end Controller;

task Parser is                                                   27
   entry Next_Lexeme(L : in  Lexical_Element);
   entry Next_Action(A : out Parser_Action);
end;

task User;   -- has no entries                                   28
```

Examples of task objects: 29

```
Agent      : Server;                                             30
Teletype : Keyboard_Driver(TTY_ID);
Pool     : array(1 .. 10) of Keyboard_Driver;
```

Example of access type designating task objects: 31

```
type Keyboard is access Keyboard_Driver;                         32
Terminal : Keyboard := new Keyboard_Driver(Term_ID);
```

9.2 Task Execution - Task Activation

Dynamic Semantics

The execution of a task of a given task type consists of the execution of the corresponding task_body. The 1 initial part of this execution is called the *activation* of the task; it consists of the elaboration of the declarative_part of the task_body. Should an exception be propagated by the elaboration of its declarative_part, the activation of the task is defined to have *failed*, and it becomes a completed task.

A task object (which represents one task) can be created either as part of the elaboration of an object_- 2 declaration occurring immediately within some declarative region, or as part of the evaluation of an allocator. All tasks created by the elaboration of object_declarations of a single declarative region (including subcomponents of the declared objects) are activated together. Similarly, all tasks created by the evaluation of a single allocator are activated together. The activation of a task is associated with the innermost allocator or object_declaration that is responsible for its creation.

For tasks created by the elaboration of object_declarations of a given declarative region, the activations 3 are initiated within the context of the handled_sequence_of_statements (and its associated exception_-

handlers if any — see 11.2), just prior to executing the statements of the _sequence. For a package without an explicit body or an explicit handled_sequence_of_statements, an implicit body or an implicit null_statement is assumed, as defined in 7.2.

4   For tasks created by the evaluation of an allocator, the activations are initiated as the last step of evaluating the allocator, after completing any initialization for the object created by the allocator, and prior to returning the new access value.

5   The task that created the new tasks and initiated their activations (the *activator*) is blocked until all of these activations complete (successfully or not). Once all of these activations are complete, if the activation of any of the tasks has failed (due to the propagation of an exception), Tasking_Error is raised in the activator, at the place at which it initiated the activations. Otherwise, the activator proceeds with its execution normally. Any tasks that are aborted prior to completing their activation are ignored when determining whether to raise Tasking_Error.

6   Should the task that created the new tasks never reach the point where it would initiate the activations (due to an abort or the raising of an exception), the newly created tasks become terminated and are never activated.

NOTES

7   5 An entry of a task can be called before the task has been activated.

8   6 If several tasks are activated together, the execution of any of these tasks need not await the end of the activation of the other tasks.

9   7 A task can become completed during its activation either because of an exception or because it is aborted (see 9.8).

Examples

10   *Example of task activation:*

11
```
procedure P is
   A, B : Server;      -- elaborate the task objects A, B
   C    : Server;      -- elaborate the task object C
begin
   -- the tasks A, B, C are activated together before the first statement
   ...
end;
```

9.3 Task Dependence - Termination of Tasks

Dynamic Semantics

1   Each task (other than an environment task — see 10.2) *depends* on one or more masters (see 7.6.1), as follows:

2   • If the task is created by the evaluation of an allocator for a given access type, it depends on each master that includes the elaboration of the declaration of the ultimate ancestor of the given access type.

3   • If the task is created by the elaboration of an object_declaration, it depends on each master that includes this elaboration.

4   Furthermore, if a task depends on a given master, it is defined to depend on the task that executes the master, and (recursively) on any master of that task.

5   A task is said to be *completed* when the execution of its corresponding task_body is completed. A task is said to be *terminated* when any finalization of the task_body has been performed (see 7.6.1). The first step of finalizing a master (including a task_body) is to wait for the termination of any tasks dependent on the

master. The task executing the master is blocked until all the dependents have terminated. Any remaining finalization is then performed and the master is left.

Completion of a task (and the corresponding task_body) can occur when the task is blocked at a select_statement with an open terminate_alternative (see 9.7.1); the open terminate_alternative is selected if and only if the following conditions are satisfied: 6/1

- The task depends on some completed master;   7

- Each task that depends on the master considered is either already terminated or similarly blocked at a select_statement with an open terminate_alternative.   8

When both conditions are satisfied, the task considered becomes completed, together with all tasks that depend on the master considered that are not yet completed.   9

NOTES
8 The full view of a limited private type can be a task type, or can have subcomponents of a task type. Creation of an object of such a type creates dependences according to the full type.   10

9 An object_renaming_declaration defines a new view of an existing entity and hence creates no further dependence.   11

10 The rules given for the collective completion of a group of tasks all blocked on select_statements with open terminate_alternatives ensure that the collective completion can occur only when there are no remaining active tasks that could call one of the tasks being collectively completed.   12

11 If two or more tasks are blocked on select_statements with open terminate_alternatives, and become completed collectively, their finalization actions proceed concurrently.   13

12 The completion of a task can occur due to any of the following: 14

- the raising of an exception during the elaboration of the declarative_part of the corresponding task_body;   15
- the completion of the handled_sequence_of_statements of the corresponding task_body;   16
- the selection of an open terminate_alternative of a select_statement in the corresponding task_body;   17
- the abort of the task.   18

Examples

Example of task dependence: 19

```
declare                                                            20
    type Global is access Server;           -- see 9.1
    A, B : Server;
    G    : Global;
begin
    -- activation of A and B
    declare
        type Local is access Server;
        X : Global := new Server;     -- activation of X.all
        L : Local  := new Server;     -- activation of L.all
        C : Server;
    begin
        -- activation of C
        G := X;    -- both G and X designate the same task object
        . . .
    end;    -- await termination of C and L.all (but not X.all)
    . . .
end;    -- await termination of A, B, and G.all
```

9.4 Protected Units and Protected Objects

A *protected object* provides coordinated access to shared data, through calls on its visible *protected operations*, which can be *protected subprograms* or *protected entries*. A *protected unit* is declared by a *protected declaration*, which has a corresponding protected_body. A protected declaration may be a   1 protected_type_declaration, in which case it declares a named protected type; alternatively, it may be a single_protected_declaration, in which case it defines an anonymous protected type, as well as declaring a named protected object of that type.

2   protected_type_declaration ::=
    protected type defining_identifier [known_discriminant_part] **is** protected_definition;

3   single_protected_declaration ::=
    protected defining_identifier **is** protected_definition;

4   protected_definition ::=
    { protected_operation_declaration }
    [**private**
      { protected_element_declaration }]
    end [*protected*_identifier]

5/1   protected_operation_declaration ::= subprogram_declaration
    | entry_declaration
    | aspect_clause

6   protected_element_declaration ::= protected_operation_declaration
    | component_declaration

7   protected_body ::=
    protected body defining_identifier **is**
      { protected_operation_item }
    end [*protected*_identifier];

8/1   protected_operation_item ::= subprogram_declaration
    | subprogram_body
    | entry_body
    | aspect_clause

9   If a *protected*_identifier appears at the end of a protected_definition or protected_body, it shall repeat the defining_identifier.

10   A protected declaration requires a completion, which shall be a protected_body, and every protected_-body shall be the completion of some protected declaration.

11   A protected_definition defines a protected type and its first subtype. The list of protected_operation_-declarations of a protected_definition, together with the known_discriminant_part, if any, is called the visible part of the protected unit. The optional list of protected_element_declarations after the reserved word **private** is called the private part of the protected unit.

12   The elaboration of a protected declaration elaborates the protected_definition. The elaboration of a single_protected_declaration also creates an object of an (anonymous) protected type.

13   The elaboration of a protected_definition creates the protected type and its first subtype; it also includes the elaboration of the component_declarations and protected_operation_declarations in the given order.

14   As part of the initialization of a protected object, any per-object constraints (see 3.8) are elaborated.

The elaboration of a protected_body has no other effect than to establish that protected operations of the type can from then on be called without failing the Elaboration_Check.

15

The content of an object of a given protected type includes:

16

- The values of the components of the protected object, including (implicitly) an entry queue for each entry declared for the protected object;

17

- A representation of the state of the execution resource *associated* with the protected object (one such resource is associated with each protected object).

18

The execution resource associated with a protected object has to be acquired to read or update any components of the protected object; it can be acquired (as part of a protected action — see 9.5.1) either for concurrent read-only access, or for exclusive read-write access.

19

As the first step of the *finalization* of a protected object, each call remaining on any entry queue of the object is removed from its queue and Program_Error is raised at the place of the corresponding entry_-call_statement.

20

NOTES

13 Within the declaration or body of a protected unit, the name of the protected unit denotes the current instance of the unit (see 8.6), rather than the first subtype of the corresponding protected type (and thus the name cannot be used as a subtype_mark).

21

14 A selected_component can be used to denote a discriminant of a protected object (see 4.1.3). Within a protected unit, the name of a discriminant of the protected type denotes the corresponding discriminant of the current instance of the unit.

22

15 A protected type is a limited type (see 7.5), and hence has neither an assignment operation nor predefined equality operators.

23

16 The bodies of the protected operations given in the protected_body define the actions that take place upon calls to the protected operations.

24

17 The declarations in the private part are only visible within the private part and the body of the protected unit.

25

Examples

Example of declaration of protected type and corresponding body:

26

```
protected type Resource is
   entry Seize;
   procedure Release;
private
   Busy : Boolean := False;
end Resource;
```

27

```
protected body Resource is
   entry Seize when not Busy is
   begin
      Busy := True;
   end Seize;
```

28

```
   procedure Release is
   begin
      Busy := False;
   end Release;
end Resource;
```

29

₃₀ *Example of a single protected declaration and corresponding body:*

₃₁
```
protected Shared_Array is
    -- Index, Item, and Item_Array are global types
    function  Component     (N : in Index) return Item;
    procedure Set_Component(N : in Index; E : in  Item);
private
    Table : Item_Array(Index) := (others => Null_Item);
end Shared_Array;
```

₃₂
```
protected body Shared_Array is
    function Component(N : in Index) return Item is
    begin
        return Table(N);
    end Component;
```

₃₃
```
    procedure Set_Component(N : in Index; E : in Item) is
    begin
        Table(N) := E;
    end Set_Component;
end Shared_Array;
```

₃₄ *Examples of protected objects:*

₃₅
```
Control  : Resource;
Flags    : array(1 .. 100) of Resource;
```

9.5 Intertask Communication

₁ The primary means for intertask communication is provided by calls on entries and protected subprograms. Calls on protected subprograms allow coordinated access to shared data objects. Entry calls allow for blocking the caller until a given condition is satisfied (namely, that the corresponding entry is open — see 9.5.3), and then communicating data or control information directly with another task or indirectly via a shared protected object.

Static Semantics

₂ Any call on an entry or on a protected subprogram identifies a *target object* for the operation, which is either a task (for an entry call) or a protected object (for an entry call or a protected subprogram call). The target object is considered an implicit parameter to the operation, and is determined by the operation name (or prefix) used in the call on the operation, as follows:

₃ • If it is a direct_name or expanded name that denotes the declaration (or body) of the operation, then the target object is implicitly specified to be the current instance of the task or protected unit immediately enclosing the operation; such a call is defined to be an *internal call*;

₄ • If it is a selected_component that is not an expanded name, then the target object is explicitly specified to be the task or protected object denoted by the prefix of the name; such a call is defined to be an *external call*;

₅ • If the name or prefix is a dereference (implicit or explicit) of an access-to-protected-subprogram value, then the target object is determined by the prefix of the Access attribute_reference that produced the access value originally, and the call is defined to be an *external call*;

₆ • If the name or prefix denotes a subprogram_renaming_declaration, then the target object is as determined by the name of the renamed entity.

₇ A corresponding definition of target object applies to a requeue_statement (see 9.5.4), with a corresponding distinction between an *internal requeue* and an *external requeue*.

Dynamic Semantics

Within the body of a protected operation, the current instance (see 8.6) of the immediately enclosing protected unit is determined by the target object specified (implicitly or explicitly) in the call (or requeue) on the protected operation.

8

Any call on a protected procedure or entry of a target protected object is defined to be an update to the object, as is a requeue on such an entry.

9

9.5.1 Protected Subprograms and Protected Actions

A *protected subprogram* is a subprogram declared immediately within a protected_definition. Protected procedures provide exclusive read-write access to the data of a protected object; protected functions provide concurrent read-only access to the data.

1

Static Semantics

Within the body of a protected function (or a function declared immediately within a protected_body), the current instance of the enclosing protected unit is defined to be a constant (that is, its subcomponents may be read but not updated). Within the body of a protected procedure (or a procedure declared immediately within a protected_body), and within an entry_body, the current instance is defined to be a variable (updating is permitted).

2

Dynamic Semantics

For the execution of a call on a protected subprogram, the evaluation of the name or prefix and of the parameter associations, and any assigning back of **in out** or **out** parameters, proceeds as for a normal subprogram call (see 6.4). If the call is an internal call (see 9.5), the body of the subprogram is executed as for a normal subprogram call. If the call is an external call, then the body of the subprogram is executed as part of a new *protected action* on the target protected object; the protected action completes after the body of the subprogram is executed. A protected action can also be started by an entry call (see 9.5.3).

3

A new protected action is not started on a protected object while another protected action on the same protected object is underway, unless both actions are the result of a call on a protected function. This rule is expressible in terms of the execution resource associated with the protected object:

4

- *Starting* a protected action on a protected object corresponds to *acquiring* the execution resource associated with the protected object, either for concurrent read-only access if the protected action is for a call on a protected function, or for exclusive read-write access otherwise;

5

- *Completing* the protected action corresponds to *releasing* the associated execution resource.

6

After performing an operation on a protected object other than a call on a protected function, but prior to completing the associated protected action, the entry queues (if any) of the protected object are serviced (see 9.5.3).

7

Bounded (Run-Time) Errors

During a protected action, it is a bounded error to invoke an operation that is *potentially blocking*. The following are defined to be potentially blocking operations:

8

- a select_statement;

9

- an accept_statement;

10

- an entry_call_statement;

11

- a delay_statement;

12

13 • an abort_statement;

14 • task creation or activation;

15 • an external call on a protected subprogram (or an external requeue) with the same target object as that of the protected action;

16 • a call on a subprogram whose body contains a potentially blocking operation.

17 If the bounded error is detected, Program_Error is raised. If not detected, the bounded error might result in deadlock or a (nested) protected action on the same target object.

18 Certain language-defined subprograms are potentially blocking. In particular, the subprograms of the language-defined input-output packages that manipulate files (implicitly or explicitly) are potentially blocking. Other potentially blocking subprograms are identified where they are defined. When not specified as potentially blocking, a language-defined subprogram is nonblocking.

NOTES

19 18 If two tasks both try to start a protected action on a protected object, and at most one is calling a protected function, then only one of the tasks can proceed. Although the other task cannot proceed, it is not considered blocked, and it might be consuming processing resources while it awaits its turn. There is no language-defined ordering or queuing presumed for tasks competing to start a protected action — on a multiprocessor such tasks might use busy-waiting; for monoprocessor considerations, see D.3, ''Priority Ceiling Locking''.

20 19 The body of a protected unit may contain declarations and bodies for local subprograms. These are not visible outside the protected unit.

21 20 The body of a protected function can contain internal calls on other protected functions, but not protected procedures, because the current instance is a constant. On the other hand, the body of a protected procedure can contain internal calls on both protected functions and procedures.

22 21 From within a protected action, an internal call on a protected subprogram, or an external call on a protected subprogram with a different target object is not considered a potentially blocking operation.

Examples

23 *Examples of protected subprogram calls (see 9.4):*

24
```
Shared_Array.Set_Component(N, E);
E := Shared_Array.Component(M);
Control.Release;
```

9.5.2 Entries and Accept Statements

1 Entry_declarations, with the corresponding entry_bodies or accept_statements, are used to define potentially queued operations on tasks and protected objects.

Syntax

2 entry_declaration ::=
    entry defining_identifier [(discrete_subtype_definition)] parameter_profile;

3 accept_statement ::=
    accept *entry*_direct_name [(entry_index)] parameter_profile [**do**
        handled_sequence_of_statements
    end [*entry*_identifier]];

4 entry_index ::= expression

```
entry_body ::=
  entry defining_identifier entry_body_formal_part entry_barrier is
    declarative_part
  begin
    handled_sequence_of_statements
  end [entry_identifier];
```
5

entry_body_formal_part ::= [(entry_index_specification)] parameter_profile   6

entry_barrier ::= when condition   7

entry_index_specification ::= for defining_identifier in discrete_subtype_definition   8

If an *entry*_identifier appears at the end of an accept_statement, it shall repeat the *entry*_direct_-   9
name. If an *entry*_identifier appears at the end of an entry_body, it shall repeat the defining_-
identifier.

An entry_declaration is allowed only in a protected or task declaration.   10

Name Resolution Rules

In an accept_statement, the expected profile for the *entry*_direct_name is that of the entry_declaration;   11
the expected type for an entry_index is that of the subtype defined by the discrete_subtype_definition of
the corresponding entry_declaration.

Within the handled_sequence_of_statements of an accept_statement, if a selected_component has a   12
prefix that denotes the corresponding entry_declaration, then the entity denoted by the prefix is the
accept_statement, and the selected_component is interpreted as an expanded name (see 4.1.3); the
selector_name of the selected_component has to be the identifier for some formal parameter of the
accept_statement.

Legality Rules

An entry_declaration in a task declaration shall not contain a specification for an access parameter (see   13
3.10).

For an accept_statement, the innermost enclosing body shall be a task_body, and the *entry*_direct_name   14
shall denote an entry_declaration in the corresponding task declaration; the profile of the accept_-
statement shall conform fully to that of the corresponding entry_declaration. An accept_statement shall
have a parenthesized entry_index if and only if the corresponding entry_declaration has a discrete_-
subtype_definition.

An accept_statement shall not be within another accept_statement that corresponds to the same entry_-   15
declaration, nor within an asynchronous_select inner to the enclosing task_body.

An entry_declaration of a protected unit requires a completion, which shall be an entry_body, and every   16
entry_body shall be the completion of an entry_declaration of a protected unit. The profile of the entry_-
body shall conform fully to that of the corresponding declaration.

An entry_body_formal_part shall have an entry_index_specification if and only if the corresponding   17
entry_declaration has a discrete_subtype_definition. In this case, the discrete_subtype_definitions of the
entry_declaration and the entry_index_specification shall fully conform to one another (see 6.3.1).

A name that denotes a formal parameter of an entry_body is not allowed within the entry_barrier of the   18
entry_body.

Entries and Accept Statements **9.5.2**

Static Semantics

19   The parameter modes defined for parameters in the parameter_profile of an entry_declaration are the same as for a subprogram_declaration and have the same meaning (see 6.2).

20   An entry_declaration with a discrete_subtype_definition (see 3.6) declares a *family* of distinct entries having the same profile, with one such entry for each value of the *entry index subtype* defined by the discrete_subtype_definition. A name for an entry of a family takes the form of an indexed_component, where the prefix denotes the entry_declaration for the family, and the index value identifies the entry within the family. The term *single entry* is used to refer to any entry other than an entry of an entry family.

21   In the entry_body for an entry family, the entry_index_specification declares a named constant whose subtype is the entry index subtype defined by the corresponding entry_declaration; the value of the *named entry index* identifies which entry of the family was called.

Dynamic Semantics

22/1   The elaboration of an entry_declaration for an entry family consists of the elaboration of the discrete_-subtype_definition, as described in 3.8. The elaboration of an entry_declaration for a single entry has no effect.

23   The actions to be performed when an entry is called are specified by the corresponding accept_statements (if any) for an entry of a task unit, and by the corresponding entry_body for an entry of a protected unit.

24   For the execution of an accept_statement, the entry_index, if any, is first evaluated and converted to the entry index subtype; this index value identifies which entry of the family is to be accepted. Further execution of the accept_statement is then blocked until a caller of the corresponding entry is selected (see 9.5.3), whereupon the handled_sequence_of_statements, if any, of the accept_statement is executed, with the formal parameters associated with the corresponding actual parameters of the selected entry call. Upon completion of the handled_sequence_of_statements, the accept_statement completes and is left. When an exception is propagated from the handled_sequence_of_statements of an accept_statement, the same exception is also raised by the execution of the corresponding entry_call_statement.

25   The above interaction between a calling task and an accepting task is called a *rendezvous*. After a rendezvous, the two tasks continue their execution independently.

26   An entry_body is executed when the condition of the entry_barrier evaluates to True and a caller of the corresponding single entry, or entry of the corresponding entry family, has been selected (see 9.5.3). For the execution of the entry_body, the declarative_part of the entry_body is elaborated, and the handled_-sequence_of_statements of the body is executed, as for the execution of a subprogram_body. The value of the named entry index, if any, is determined by the value of the entry index specified in the *entry*_name of the selected entry call (or intermediate requeue_statement — see 9.5.4).

NOTES

27   22 A task entry has corresponding accept_statements (zero or more), whereas a protected entry has a corresponding entry_body (exactly one).

28   23 A consequence of the rule regarding the allowed placements of accept_statements is that a task can execute accept_statements only for its own entries.

29   24 A return_statement (see 6.5) or a requeue_statement (see 9.5.4) may be used to complete the execution of an accept_statement or an entry_body.

30   25 The condition in the entry_barrier may reference anything visible except the formal parameters of the entry. This includes the entry index (if any), the components (including discriminants) of the protected object, the Count attribute of an entry of that protected object, and data global to the protected unit.

The restriction against referencing the formal parameters within an entry_barrier ensures that all calls of the same entry see the same barrier value. If it is necessary to look at the parameters of an entry call before deciding whether to handle it, the entry_barrier can be "**when** True" and the caller can be requeued (on some private entry) when its parameters indicate that it cannot be handled immediately.   31

Examples

Examples of entry declarations: 32

```
entry Read(V : out Item);
entry Seize;
entry Request(Level)(D : Item);   -- a family of entries
```
33

Examples of accept statements: 34

```
accept Shut_Down;
```
35

```
accept Read(V : out Item) do
   V := Local_Item;
end Read;
```
36

```
accept Request(Low)(D : Item) do
   ...
end Request;
```
37

9.5.3 Entry Calls

An entry_call_statement (an *entry call*) can appear in various contexts. A *simple* entry call is a stand-alone statement that represents an unconditional call on an entry of a target task or a protected object. Entry calls can also appear as part of select_statements (see 9.7).   1

Syntax

entry_call_statement ::= *entry*_name [actual_parameter_part];   2

Name Resolution Rules

The *entry*_name given in an entry_call_statement shall resolve to denote an entry. The rules for parameter associations are the same as for subprogram calls (see 6.4 and 6.4.1).   3

Static Semantics

The *entry*_name of an entry_call_statement specifies (explicitly or implicitly) the target object of the call, the entry or entry family, and the entry index, if any (see 9.5).   4

Dynamic Semantics

Under certain circumstances (detailed below), an entry of a task or protected object is checked to see whether it is *open* or *closed*:   5

- An entry of a task is open if the task is blocked on an accept_statement that corresponds to the entry (see 9.5.2), or on a selective_accept (see 9.7.1) with an open accept_alternative that corresponds to the entry; otherwise it is closed.   6

- An entry of a protected object is open if the condition of the entry_barrier of the corresponding entry_body evaluates to True; otherwise it is closed. If the evaluation of the condition propagates an exception, the exception Program_Error is propagated to all current callers of all entries of the protected object.   7

For the execution of an entry_call_statement, evaluation of the name and of the parameter associations is as for a subprogram call (see 6.4). The entry call is then *issued*: For a call on an entry of a protected object,   8 a new protected action is started on the object (see 9.5.1). The named entry is checked to see if it is open; if open, the entry call is said to be *selected immediately*, and the execution of the call proceeds as follows:

9   • For a call on an open entry of a task, the accepting task becomes ready and continues the execution of the corresponding accept_statement (see 9.5.2).

10   • For a call on an open entry of a protected object, the corresponding entry_body is executed (see 9.5.2) as part of the protected action.

11   If the accept_statement or entry_body completes other than by a requeue (see 9.5.4), return is made to the caller (after servicing the entry queues — see below); any necessary assigning back of formal to actual parameters occurs, as for a subprogram call (see 6.4.1); such assignments take place outside of any protected action.

12   If the named entry is closed, the entry call is added to an *entry queue* (as part of the protected action, for a call on a protected entry), and the call remains queued until it is selected or cancelled; there is a separate (logical) entry queue for each entry of a given task or protected object (including each entry of an entry family).

13   When a queued call is *selected*, it is removed from its entry queue. Selecting a queued call from a particular entry queue is called *servicing* the entry queue. An entry with queued calls can be serviced under the following circumstances:

14   • When the associated task reaches a corresponding accept_statement, or a selective_accept with a corresponding open accept_alternative;

15   • If after performing, as part of a protected action on the associated protected object, an operation on the object other than a call on a protected function, the entry is checked and found to be open.

16   If there is at least one call on a queue corresponding to an open entry, then one such call is selected according to the *entry queuing policy* in effect (see below), and the corresponding accept_statement or entry_body is executed as above for an entry call that is selected immediately.

17   The entry queuing policy controls selection among queued calls both for task and protected entry queues. The default entry queuing policy is to select calls on a given entry queue in order of arrival. If calls from two or more queues are simultaneously eligible for selection, the default entry queuing policy does not specify which queue is serviced first. Other entry queuing policies can be specified by pragmas (see D.4).

18   For a protected object, the above servicing of entry queues continues until there are no open entries with queued calls, at which point the protected action completes.

19   For an entry call that is added to a queue, and that is not the triggering_statement of an asynchronous_-select (see 9.7.4), the calling task is blocked until the call is cancelled, or the call is selected and a corresponding accept_statement or entry_body completes without requeuing. In addition, the calling task is blocked during a rendezvous.

20   An attempt can be made to cancel an entry call upon an abort (see 9.8) and as part of certain forms of select_statement (see 9.7.2, 9.7.3, and 9.7.4). The cancellation does not take place until a point (if any) when the call is on some entry queue, and not protected from cancellation as part of a requeue (see 9.5.4); at such a point, the call is removed from the entry queue and the call completes due to the cancellation. The cancellation of a call on an entry of a protected object is a protected action, and as such cannot take place while any other protected action is occurring on the protected object. Like any protected action, it includes servicing of the entry queues (in case some entry barrier depends on a Count attribute).

21   A call on an entry of a task that has already completed its execution raises the exception Tasking_Error at the point of the call; similarly, this exception is raised at the point of the call if the called task completes its

execution or becomes abnormal before accepting the call or completing the rendezvous (see 9.8). This applies equally to a simple entry call and to an entry call as part of a select_statement.

Implementation Permissions

An implementation may perform the sequence of steps of a protected action using any thread of control; it need not be that of the task that started the protected action. If an entry_body completes without requeuing, then the corresponding calling task may be made ready without waiting for the entire protected action to complete. 22

When the entry of a protected object is checked to see whether it is open, the implementation need not reevaluate the condition of the corresponding entry_barrier if no variable or attribute referenced by the condition (directly or indirectly) has been altered by the execution (or cancellation) of a protected procedure or entry call on the object since the condition was last evaluated. 23

An implementation may evaluate the conditions of all entry_barriers of a given protected object any time any entry of the object is checked to see if it is open. 24

When an attempt is made to cancel an entry call, the implementation need not make the attempt using the thread of control of the task (or interrupt) that initiated the cancellation; in particular, it may use the thread of control of the caller itself to attempt the cancellation, even if this might allow the entry call to be selected in the interim. 25

NOTES
26 If an exception is raised during the execution of an entry_body, it is propagated to the corresponding caller (see 11.4). 26

27 For a call on a protected entry, the entry is checked to see if it is open prior to queuing the call, and again thereafter if its Count attribute (see 9.9) is referenced in some entry barrier. 27

28 In addition to simple entry calls, the language permits timed, conditional, and asynchronous entry calls (see 9.7.2, 9.7.3, and see 9.7.4). 28

29 The condition of an entry_barrier is allowed to be evaluated by an implementation more often than strictly necessary, even if the evaluation might have side effects. On the other hand, an implementation need not reevaluate the condition if nothing it references was updated by an intervening protected action on the protected object, even if the condition references some global variable that might have been updated by an action performed from outside of a protected action. 29

Examples

Examples of entry calls: 30

```
Agent.Shut_Down;                        -- see 9.1
Parser.Next_Lexeme(E);                  -- see 9.1
Pool(5).Read(Next_Char);                -- see 9.1
Controller.Request(Low)(Some_Item);     -- see 9.1
Flags(3).Seize;                         -- see 9.4
```
  31

9.5.4 Requeue Statements

A requeue_statement can be used to complete an accept_statement or entry_body, while redirecting the corresponding entry call to a new (or the same) entry queue. Such a *requeue* can be performed with or without allowing an intermediate cancellation of the call, due to an abort or the expiration of a delay. 1

Syntax

requeue_statement ::= **requeue** *entry_*name [**with abort**]; 2

Name Resolution Rules

3   The *entry*_name of a requeue_statement shall resolve to denote an entry (the *target entry*) that either has no parameters, or that has a profile that is type conformant (see 6.3.1) with the profile of the innermost enclosing entry_body or accept_statement.

Legality Rules

4   A requeue_statement shall be within a callable construct that is either an entry_body or an accept_statement, and this construct shall be the innermost enclosing body or callable construct.

5   If the target entry has parameters, then its profile shall be subtype conformant with the profile of the innermost enclosing callable construct.

6   In a requeue_statement of an accept_statement of some task unit, either the target object shall be a part of a formal parameter of the accept_statement, or the accessibility level of the target object shall not be equal to or statically deeper than any enclosing accept_statement of the task unit. In a requeue_-statement of an entry_body of some protected unit, either the target object shall be a part of a formal parameter of the entry_body, or the accessibility level of the target object shall not be statically deeper than that of the entry_declaration.

Dynamic Semantics

7   The execution of a requeue_statement proceeds by first evaluating the *entry*_name, including the prefix identifying the target task or protected object and the expression identifying the entry within an entry family, if any. The entry_body or accept_statement enclosing the requeue_statement is then completed, finalized, and left (see 7.6.1).

8   For the execution of a requeue on an entry of a target task, after leaving the enclosing callable construct, the named entry is checked to see if it is open and the requeued call is either selected immediately or queued, as for a normal entry call (see 9.5.3).

9   For the execution of a requeue on an entry of a target protected object, after leaving the enclosing callable construct:

10   • if the requeue is an internal requeue (that is, the requeue is back on an entry of the same protected object — see 9.5), the call is added to the queue of the named entry and the ongoing protected action continues (see 9.5.1);

11   • if the requeue is an external requeue (that is, the target protected object is not implicitly the same as the current object — see 9.5), a protected action is started on the target object and proceeds as for a normal entry call (see 9.5.3).

12   If the new entry named in the requeue_statement has formal parameters, then during the execution of the accept_statement or entry_body corresponding to the new entry, the formal parameters denote the same objects as did the corresponding formal parameters of the callable construct completed by the requeue. In any case, no parameters are specified in a requeue_statement; any parameter passing is implicit.

13   If the requeue_statement includes the reserved words **with abort** (it is a *requeue-with-abort*), then:

14   • if the original entry call has been aborted (see 9.8), then the requeue acts as an abort completion point for the call, and the call is cancelled and no requeue is performed;

15   • if the original entry call was timed (or conditional), then the original expiration time is the expiration time for the requeued call.

16   If the reserved words **with abort** do not appear, then the call remains protected against cancellation while queued as the result of the requeue_statement.

NOTES

30 A requeue is permitted from a single entry to an entry of an entry family, or vice-versa. The entry index, if any, plays   17
no part in the subtype conformance check between the profiles of the two entries; an entry index is part of the
*entry*_name for an entry of a family.

Examples

Examples of requeue statements: 18

```
requeue Request(Medium) with abort;
            -- requeue on a member of an entry family of the current task, see 9.1
```
    19

```
requeue Flags(I).Seize;
            -- requeue on an entry of an array component, see 9.4
```
    20

9.6 Delay Statements, Duration, and Time

A delay_statement is used to block further execution until a specified *expiration time* is reached. The   1
expiration time can be specified either as a particular point in time (in a delay_until_statement), or in
seconds from the current time (in a delay_relative_statement). The language-defined package Calendar
provides definitions for a type Time and associated operations, including a function Clock that returns the
current time.

Syntax

delay_statement ::= delay_until_statement I delay_relative_statement   2

delay_until_statement ::= **delay until** *delay*_expression;   3

delay_relative_statement ::= **delay** *delay*_expression;   4

Name Resolution Rules

The expected type for the *delay*_expression in a delay_relative_statement is the predefined type   5
Duration. The *delay*_expression in a delay_until_statement is expected to be of any nonlimited type.

Legality Rules

There can be multiple time bases, each with a corresponding clock, and a corresponding *time type*. The   6
type of the *delay*_expression in a delay_until_statement shall be a time type — either the type Time
defined in the language-defined package Calendar (see below), or some other implementation-defined time
type (see D.8).

Static Semantics

There is a predefined fixed point type named Duration, declared in the visible part of package Standard; a   7
value of type Duration is used to represent the length of an interval of time, expressed in seconds. The type
Duration is not specific to a particular time base, but can be used with any time base.

A value of the type Time in package Calendar, or of some other implementation-defined time type,   8
represents a time as reported by a corresponding clock.

The following language-defined library package exists: 9

    10

```
package Ada.Calendar is
    type Time is private;
    subtype Year_Number  is Integer range 1901 .. 2099;
    subtype Month_Number is Integer range 1 .. 12;
    subtype Day_Number   is Integer range 1 .. 31;
    subtype Day_Duration is Duration range 0.0 .. 86_400.0;
```
    11

```
12      function Clock return Time;

13      function Year    (Date : Time) return Year_Number;
        function Month   (Date : Time) return Month_Number;
        function Day     (Date : Time) return Day_Number;
        function Seconds (Date : Time) return Day_Duration;

14      procedure Split (Date   : in Time;
                         Year    : out Year_Number;
                         Month   : out Month_Number;
                         Day     : out Day_Number;
                         Seconds : out Day_Duration);

15      function Time_Of(Year   : Year_Number;
                         Month  : Month_Number;
                         Day    : Day_Number;
                         Seconds : Day_Duration := 0.0)
          return Time;

16      function "+" (Left : Time;     Right : Duration) return Time;
        function "+" (Left : Duration; Right : Time) return Time;
        function "-" (Left : Time;     Right : Duration) return Time;
        function "-" (Left : Time;     Right : Time) return Duration;

17      function "<" (Left, Right : Time) return Boolean;
        function "<="(Left, Right : Time) return Boolean;
        function ">" (Left, Right : Time) return Boolean;
        function ">="(Left, Right : Time) return Boolean;

18      Time_Error : exception;

19    private
        ... -- not specified by the language
      end Ada.Calendar;
```

Dynamic Semantics

20 For the execution of a delay_statement, the *delay*_expression is first evaluated. For a delay_until_statement, the expiration time for the delay is the value of the *delay*_expression, in the time base associated with the type of the expression. For a delay_relative_statement, the expiration time is defined as the current time, in the time base associated with relative delays, plus the value of the *delay*_expression converted to the type Duration, and then rounded up to the next clock tick. The time base associated with relative delays is as defined in D.9, "Delay Accuracy" or is implementation defined.

21 The task executing a delay_statement is blocked until the expiration time is reached, at which point it becomes ready again. If the expiration time has already passed, the task is not blocked.

22 If an attempt is made to *cancel* the delay_statement (as part of an asynchronous_select or abort — see 9.7.4 and 9.8), the _statement is cancelled if the expiration time has not yet passed, thereby completing the delay_statement.

23 The time base associated with the type Time of package Calendar is implementation defined. The function Clock of package Calendar returns a value representing the current time for this time base. The implementation-defined value of the named number System.Tick (see 13.7) is an approximation of the length of the real-time interval during which the value of Calendar.Clock remains constant.

24 The functions Year, Month, Day, and Seconds return the corresponding values for a given value of the type Time, as appropriate to an implementation-defined timezone; the procedure Split returns all four corresponding values. Conversely, the function Time_Of combines a year number, a month number, a day number, and a duration, into a value of type Time. The operators "+" and "−" for addition and subtraction of times and durations, and the relational operators for times, have the conventional meaning.

If Time_Of is called with a seconds value of 86_400.0, the value returned is equal to the value of Time_Of for the next day with a seconds value of 0.0. The value returned by the function Seconds or through the Seconds parameter of the procedure Split is always less than 86_400.0.   25

The exception Time_Error is raised by the function Time_Of if the actual parameters do not form a proper date. This exception is also raised by the operators "+" and "−" if the result is not representable in the type Time or Duration, as appropriate. This exception is also raised by the functions Year, Month, Day, and Seconds and the procedure Split if the year number of the given date is outside of the range of the subtype Year_Number.   26/1

Implementation Requirements

The implementation of the type Duration shall allow representation of time intervals (both positive and negative) up to at least 86400 seconds (one day); Duration'Small shall not be greater than twenty milliseconds. The implementation of the type Time shall allow representation of all dates with year numbers in the range of Year_Number; it may allow representation of other dates as well (both earlier and later).   27

Implementation Permissions

An implementation may define additional time types (see D.8).   28

An implementation may raise Time_Error if the value of a *delay*_expression in a delay_until_statement of a select_statement represents a time more than 90 days past the current time. The actual limit, if any, is implementation-defined.   29

Implementation Advice

Whenever possible in an implementation, the value of Duration'Small should be no greater than 100 microseconds.   30

The time base for delay_relative_statements should be monotonic; it need not be the same time base as used for Calendar.Clock.   31

NOTES
31 A delay_relative_statement with a negative value of the *delay*_expression is equivalent to one with a zero value.   32

32 A delay_statement may be executed by the environment task; consequently delay_statements may be executed as part of the elaboration of a library_item or the execution of the main subprogram. Such statements delay the environment task (see 10.2).   33

33 A delay_statement is an abort completion point and a potentially blocking operation, even if the task is not actually blocked.   34

34 There is no necessary relationship between System.Tick (the resolution of the clock of package Calendar) and Duration'Small (the *small* of type Duration).   35

35 Additional requirements associated with delay_statements are given in D.9, ''Delay Accuracy''.   36

Examples

Example of a relative delay statement: 37

```
delay 3.0;   -- delay 3.0 seconds
```
    38

Example of a periodic task:

39
40

```
declare
    use Ada.Calendar;
    Next_Time : Time := Clock + Period;
                        -- Period is a global constant of type Duration
begin
    loop                    -- repeated every Period seconds
        delay until Next_Time;
        ... -- perform some actions
        Next_Time := Next_Time + Period;
    end loop;
end;
```

9.7 Select Statements

1 There are four forms of the select_statement. One form provides a selective wait for one or more select_alternatives. Two provide timed and conditional entry calls. The fourth provides asynchronous transfer of control.

Syntax

2 select_statement ::=
     selective_accept
   | timed_entry_call
   | conditional_entry_call
   | asynchronous_select

Examples

3 *Example of a select statement:*

4
```
select
    accept Driver_Awake_Signal;
or
    delay 30.0*Seconds;
    Stop_The_Train;
end select;
```

9.7.1 Selective Accept

1 This form of the select_statement allows a combination of waiting for, and selecting from, one or more alternatives. The selection may depend on conditions associated with each alternative of the selective_accept.

Syntax

2 selective_accept ::=
     select
      [guard]
        select_alternative
   { **or**
      [guard]
        select_alternative }
   [**else**
      sequence_of_statements]
     end select;

3 guard ::= **when** condition =>

```
select_alternative ::=
  accept_alternative
| delay_alternative
| terminate_alternative
```
4

```
accept_alternative ::=
  accept_statement [sequence_of_statements]
```
5

```
delay_alternative ::=
  delay_statement [sequence_of_statements]
```
6

terminate_alternative ::= **terminate**;
7

A selective_accept shall contain at least one accept_alternative. In addition, it can contain:
8

- a terminate_alternative (only one); or
9

- one or more delay_alternatives; or
10

- an *else part* (the reserved word **else** followed by a sequence_of_statements).
11

These three possibilities are mutually exclusive.
12

Legality Rules

If a selective_accept contains more than one delay_alternative, then all shall be delay_relative_-
statements, or all shall be delay_until_statements for the same time type.
13

Dynamic Semantics

A select_alternative is said to be *open* if it is not immediately preceded by a guard, or if the condition of
its guard evaluates to True. It is said to be *closed* otherwise.
14

For the execution of a selective_accept, any guard conditions are evaluated; open alternatives are thus
determined. For an open delay_alternative, the *delay*_expression is also evaluated. Similarly, for an open
accept_alternative for an entry of a family, the entry_index is also evaluated. These evaluations are
performed in an arbitrary order, except that a *delay*_expression or entry_index is not evaluated until after
evaluating the corresponding condition, if any. Selection and execution of one open alternative, or of the
else part, then completes the execution of the selective_accept; the rules for this selection are described
below.
15

Open accept_alternatives are first considered. Selection of one such alternative takes place immediately if
the corresponding entry already has queued calls. If several alternatives can thus be selected, one of them
is selected according to the entry queuing policy in effect (see 9.5.3 and D.4). When such an alternative is
selected, the selected call is removed from its entry queue and the handled_sequence_of_statements (if
any) of the corresponding accept_statement is executed; after the rendezvous completes any subsequent
sequence_of_statements of the alternative is executed. If no selection is immediately possible (in the
above sense) and there is no else part, the task blocks until an open alternative can be selected.
16

Selection of the other forms of alternative or of an else part is performed as follows:
17

- An open delay_alternative is selected when its expiration time is reached if no accept_-
  alternative or other delay_alternative can be selected prior to the expiration time. If several
  delay_alternatives have this same expiration time, one of them is selected according to the
  queuing policy in effect (see D.4); the default queuing policy chooses arbitrarily among the
  delay_alternatives whose expiration time has passed.
18

- The else part is selected and its sequence_of_statements is executed if no accept_alternative
  can immediately be selected; in particular, if all alternatives are closed.
19

20   • An open terminate_alternative is selected if the conditions stated at the end of clause 9.3 are satisfied.

21   The exception Program_Error is raised if all alternatives are closed and there is no else part.

NOTES

22   36 A selective_accept is allowed to have several open delay_alternatives. A selective_accept is allowed to have several open accept_alternatives for the same entry.

Examples

23   *Example of a task body with a selective accept:*

24
```
task body Server is
    Current_Work_Item : Work_Item;
begin
    loop
        select
            accept Next_Work_Item(WI : in Work_Item) do
                Current_Work_Item := WI;
            end;
            Process_Work_Item(Current_Work_Item);
        or
            accept Shut_Down;
            exit;           -- Premature shut down requested
        or
            terminate;      -- Normal shutdown at end of scope
        end select;
    end loop;
end Server;
```

9.7.2 Timed Entry Calls

1   A timed_entry_call issues an entry call that is cancelled if the call (or a requeue-with-abort of the call) is not selected before the expiration time is reached.

Syntax

2   timed_entry_call ::=
     select
      entry_call_alternative
     or
      delay_alternative
     end select;

3   entry_call_alternative ::=
     entry_call_statement [sequence_of_statements]

Dynamic Semantics

4   For the execution of a timed_entry_call, the *entry*_name and the actual parameters are evaluated, as for a simple entry call (see 9.5.3). The expiration time (see 9.6) for the call is determined by evaluating the *delay*_expression of the delay_alternative; the entry call is then issued.

5   If the call is queued (including due to a requeue-with-abort), and not selected before the expiration time is reached, an attempt to cancel the call is made. If the call completes due to the cancellation, the optional sequence_of_statements of the delay_alternative is executed; if the entry call completes normally, the optional sequence_of_statements of the entry_call_alternative is executed.

Example of a timed entry call: 6

```
select
    Controller.Request(Medium)(Some_Item);
or
    delay 45.0;
    -- controller too busy, try something else
end select;
```
7

9.7.3 Conditional Entry Calls

A conditional_entry_call issues an entry call that is then cancelled if it is not selected immediately (or if a   1
requeue-with-abort of the call is not selected immediately).

Syntax

```
conditional_entry_call ::=
  select
   entry_call_alternative
  else
   sequence_of_statements
  end select;
```
2

Dynamic Semantics

The execution of a conditional_entry_call is defined to be equivalent to the execution of a timed_entry_-   3
call with a delay_alternative specifying an immediate expiration time and the same sequence_of_-
statements as given after the reserved word **else**.

NOTES
37 A conditional_entry_call may briefly increase the Count attribute of the entry, even if the conditional call is not   4
selected.

Examples

Example of a conditional entry call: 5

```
procedure Spin(R : in Resource) is
begin
   loop
      select
         R.Seize;
         return;
      else
         null;   -- busy waiting
      end select;
   end loop;
end;
```
6

9.7.4 Asynchronous Transfer of Control

An asynchronous select_statement provides asynchronous transfer of control upon completion of an entry   1
call or the expiration of a delay.

Syntax

2
```
asynchronous_select ::=
  select
   triggering_alternative
  then abort
   abortable_part
  end select;
```

3   triggering_alternative ::= triggering_statement [sequence_of_statements]

4   triggering_statement ::= entry_call_statement | delay_statement

5   abortable_part ::= sequence_of_statements

Dynamic Semantics

6   For the execution of an asynchronous_select whose triggering_statement is an entry_call_statement, the *entry*_name and actual parameters are evaluated as for a simple entry call (see 9.5.3), and the entry call is issued. If the entry call is queued (or requeued-with-abort), then the abortable_part is executed. If the entry call is selected immediately, and never requeued-with-abort, then the abortable_part is never started.

7   For the execution of an asynchronous_select whose triggering_statement is a delay_statement, the *delay*_expression is evaluated and the expiration time is determined, as for a normal delay_statement. If the expiration time has not already passed, the abortable_part is executed.

8   If the abortable_part completes and is left prior to completion of the triggering_statement, an attempt to cancel the triggering_statement is made. If the attempt to cancel succeeds (see 9.5.3 and 9.6), the asynchronous_select is complete.

9   If the triggering_statement completes other than due to cancellation, the abortable_part is aborted (if started but not yet completed — see 9.8). If the triggering_statement completes normally, the optional sequence_of_statements of the triggering_alternative is executed after the abortable_part is left.

Examples

10   *Example of a main command loop for a command interpreter:*

11
```
loop
    select
        Terminal.Wait_For_Interrupt;
        Put_Line("Interrupted");
    then abort
        -- This will be abandoned upon terminal interrupt
        Put_Line("-> ");
        Get_Line(Command, Last);
        Process_Command(Command(1..Last));
    end select;
end loop;
```

12   *Example of a time-limited calculation:*

13
```
select
    delay 5.0;
    Put_Line("Calculation does not converge");
then abort
    -- This calculation should finish in 5.0 seconds;
    -- if not, it is assumed to diverge.
    Horribly_Complicated_Recursive_Function(X, Y);
end select;
```

9.8 Abort of a Task - Abort of a Sequence of Statements

An abort_statement causes one or more tasks to become abnormal, thus preventing any further interaction with such tasks. The completion of the triggering_statement of an asynchronous_select causes a sequence_of_statements to be aborted. 1

Syntax

abort_statement ::= **abort** *task*_name { , *task*_name }; 2

Name Resolution Rules

Each *task*_name is expected to be of any task type; they need not all be of the same task type. 3

Dynamic Semantics

For the execution of an abort_statement, the given *task*_names are evaluated in an arbitrary order. Each named task is then *aborted*, which consists of making the task *abnormal* and aborting the execution of the corresponding task_body, unless it is already completed. 4

When the execution of a construct is *aborted* (including that of a task_body or of a sequence_of_-statements), the execution of every construct included within the aborted execution is also aborted, except for executions included within the execution of an *abort-deferred* operation; the execution of an abort-deferred operation continues to completion without being affected by the abort; the following are the abort-deferred operations: 5

- a protected action; 6

- waiting for an entry call to complete (after having initiated the attempt to cancel it — see below); 7

- waiting for the termination of dependent tasks; 8

- the execution of an Initialize procedure as the last step of the default initialization of a controlled object; 9

- the execution of a Finalize procedure as part of the finalization of a controlled object; 10

- an assignment operation to an object with a controlled part. 11

The last three of these are discussed further in 7.6. 12

When a master is aborted, all tasks that depend on that master are aborted. 13

The order in which tasks become abnormal as the result of an abort_statement or the abort of a sequence_of_statements is not specified by the language. 14

If the execution of an entry call is aborted, an immediate attempt is made to cancel the entry call (see 9.5.3). If the execution of a construct is aborted at a time when the execution is blocked, other than for an entry call, at a point that is outside the execution of an abort-deferred operation, then the execution of the construct completes immediately. For an abort due to an abort_statement, these immediate effects occur before the execution of the abort_statement completes. Other than for these immediate cases, the execution of a construct that is aborted does not necessarily complete before the abort_statement completes. However, the execution of the aborted construct completes no later than its next *abort completion point* (if any) that occurs outside of an abort-deferred operation; the following are abort completion points for an execution: 15

- the point where the execution initiates the activation of another task; 16

17 • the end of the activation of a task;

18 • the start or end of the execution of an entry call, accept_statement, delay_statement, or abort_statement;

19 • the start of the execution of a select_statement, or of the sequence_of_statements of an exception_handler.

Bounded (Run-Time) Errors

20 An attempt to execute an asynchronous_select as part of the execution of an abort-deferred operation is a bounded error. Similarly, an attempt to create a task that depends on a master that is included entirely within the execution of an abort-deferred operation is a bounded error. In both cases, Program_Error is raised if the error is detected by the implementation; otherwise the operations proceed as they would outside an abort-deferred operation, except that an abort of the abortable_part or the created task might or might not have an effect.

Erroneous Execution

21 If an assignment operation completes prematurely due to an abort, the assignment is said to be *disrupted*; the target of the assignment or its parts can become abnormal, and certain subsequent uses of the object can be erroneous, as explained in 13.9.1.

NOTES

22 38 An abort_statement should be used only in situations requiring unconditional termination.

23 39 A task is allowed to abort any task it can name, including itself.

24 40 Additional requirements associated with abort are given in D.6, ''Preemptive Abort''.

9.9 Task and Entry Attributes

Dynamic Semantics

1 For a prefix T that is of a task type (after any implicit dereference), the following attributes are defined:

2 T'Callable   Yields the value True when the task denoted by T is *callable*, and False otherwise; a task is callable unless it is completed or abnormal. The value of this attribute is of the predefined type Boolean.

3 T'Terminated Yields the value True if the task denoted by T is terminated, and False otherwise. The value of this attribute is of the predefined type Boolean.

4 For a prefix E that denotes an entry of a task or protected unit, the following attribute is defined. This attribute is only allowed within the body of the task or protected unit, but excluding, in the case of an entry of a task unit, within any program unit that is, itself, inner to the body of the task unit.

5 E'Count   Yields the number of calls presently queued on the entry E of the current instance of the unit. The value of this attribute is of the type *universal_integer*.

NOTES

6 41 For the Count attribute, the entry can be either a single entry or an entry of a family. The name of the entry or entry family can be either a direct_name or an expanded name.

7 42 Within task units, algorithms interrogating the attribute E'Count should take precautions to allow for the increase of the value of this attribute for incoming entry calls, and its decrease, for example with timed_entry_calls. Also, a conditional_entry_call may briefly increase this value, even if the conditional call is not accepted.

8 43 Within protected units, algorithms interrogating the attribute E'Count in the entry_barrier for the entry E should take precautions to allow for the evaluation of the condition of the barrier both before and after queuing a given caller.

9.10 Shared Variables

Static Semantics

If two different objects, including nonoverlapping parts of the same object, are *independently addressable*, they can be manipulated concurrently by two different tasks without synchronization. Normally, any two nonoverlapping objects are independently addressable. However, if packing, record layout, or Component_Size is specified for a given composite object, then it is implementation defined whether or not two nonoverlapping parts of that composite object are independently addressable.   1

Dynamic Semantics

Separate tasks normally proceed independently and concurrently with one another. However, task interactions can be used to synchronize the actions of two or more tasks to allow, for example, meaningful communication by the direct updating and reading of variables shared between the tasks. The actions of two different tasks are synchronized in this sense when an action of one task *signals* an action of the other task; an action A1 is defined to signal an action A2 under the following circumstances: 2

- If A1 and A2 are part of the execution of the same task, and the language rules require A1 to be performed before A2;   3

- If A1 is the action of an activator that initiates the activation of a task, and A2 is part of the execution of the task that is activated;   4

- If A1 is part of the activation of a task, and A2 is the action of waiting for completion of the activation;   5

- If A1 is part of the execution of a task, and A2 is the action of waiting for the termination of the task;   6

- If A1 is the termination of a task T, and A2 is either the evaluation of the expression T'Terminated or a call to Ada.Task_Identification.Is_Terminated with an actual parameter that identifies T (see C.7.1);   6.1/1

- If A1 is the action of issuing an entry call, and A2 is part of the corresponding execution of the appropriate entry_body or accept_statement.   7

- If A1 is part of the execution of an accept_statement or entry_body, and A2 is the action of returning from the corresponding entry call;   8

- If A1 is part of the execution of a protected procedure body or entry_body for a given protected object, and A2 is part of a later execution of an entry_body for the same protected object;   9

- If A1 signals some action that in turn signals A2.   10

Erroneous Execution

Given an action of assigning to an object, and an action of reading or updating a part of the same object (or of a neighboring object if the two are not independently addressable), then the execution of the actions is erroneous unless the actions are *sequential*. Two actions are sequential if one of the following is true: 11

- One action signals the other;   12

- Both actions occur as part of the execution of the same task;   13

- Both actions occur as part of protected actions on the same protected object, and at most one of the actions is part of a call on a protected function of the protected object.   14

A pragma Atomic or Atomic_Components may also be used to ensure that certain reads and updates are sequential — see C.6.   15

9.11 Example of Tasking and Synchronization

Examples

1 The following example defines a buffer protected object to smooth variations between the speed of output of a producing task and the speed of input of some consuming task. For instance, the producing task might have the following structure:

2
```
task Producer;
```

3
```
task body Producer is
   Char : Character;
begin
   loop
      ... -- produce the next character Char
      Buffer.Write(Char);
      exit when Char = ASCII.EOT;
   end loop;
end Producer;
```

4 and the consuming task might have the following structure:

5
```
task Consumer;
```

6
```
task body Consumer is
   Char : Character;
begin
   loop
      Buffer.Read(Char);
      exit when Char = ASCII.EOT;
      ... -- consume the character Char
   end loop;
end Consumer;
```

7 The buffer object contains an internal pool of characters managed in a round-robin fashion. The pool has two indices, an In_Index denoting the space for the next input character and an Out_Index denoting the space for the next output character.

8
```
protected Buffer is
   entry Read (C : out Character);
   entry Write(C : in  Character);
private
   Pool       : String(1 .. 100);
   Count      : Natural := 0;
   In_Index, Out_Index : Positive := 1;
end Buffer;
```

9
```
protected body Buffer is
   entry Write(C : in Character)
      when Count < Pool'Length is
   begin
      Pool(In_Index) := C;
      In_Index := (In_Index mod Pool'Length) + 1;
      Count    := Count + 1;
   end Write;
```

10
```
   entry Read(C : out Character)
      when Count > 0 is
   begin
      C := Pool(Out_Index);
      Out_Index := (Out_Index mod Pool'Length) + 1;
      Count     := Count - 1;
   end Read;
end Buffer;
```

Section 10: Program Structure and Compilation Issues

The overall structure of programs and the facilities for separate compilation are described in this section. A   1
program is a set of *partitions*, each of which may execute in a separate address space, possibly on a
separate computer.

As explained below, a partition is constructed from *library units*. Syntactically, the declaration of a library   2
unit is a library_item, as is the body of a library unit. An implementation may support a concept of a
program library (or simply, a ''library''), which contains library_items and their subunits. Library units
may be organized into a hierarchy of children, grandchildren, and so on.

This section has two clauses: 10.1, ''Separate Compilation'' discusses compile-time issues related to   3
separate compilation. 10.2, ''Program Execution'' discusses issues related to what is traditionally known
as ''link time'' and ''run time'' — building and executing partitions.

10.1 Separate Compilation

A *program unit* is either a package, a task unit, a protected unit, a protected entry, a generic unit, or an   1
explicitly declared subprogram other than an enumeration literal. Certain kinds of program units can be
separately compiled. Alternatively, they can appear physically nested within other program units.

The text of a program can be submitted to the compiler in one or more compilations. Each compilation is a   2
succession of compilation_units. A compilation_unit contains either the declaration, the body, or a
renaming of a program unit. The representation for a compilation is implementation-defined.

A library unit is a separately compiled program unit, and is always a package, subprogram, or generic unit.   3
Library units may have other (logically nested) library units as children, and may have other program units
physically nested within them. A root library unit, together with its children and grandchildren and so on,
form a *subsystem*.

Implementation Permissions

An implementation may impose implementation-defined restrictions on compilations that contain multiple   4
compilation_units.

10.1.1 Compilation Units - Library Units

A library_item is a compilation unit that is the declaration, body, or renaming of a library unit. Each library   1
unit (except Standard) has a *parent unit*, which is a library package or generic library package. A library
unit is a *child* of its parent unit. The *root* library units are the children of the predefined library package
Standard.

Syntax

```
compilation ::= {compilation_unit}                                          2

compilation_unit ::=                                                        3
   context_clause library_item
 | context_clause subunit

library_item ::= [private] library_unit_declaration                         4
 | library_unit_body
 | [private] library_unit_renaming_declaration
```

S. Tucker Taft et al. (Eds.): Consolidated Ada Reference Manual, LNCS 2219, pp. 187–198, 2001.

5   library_unit_declaration ::=
           subprogram_declaration | package_declaration
           | generic_declaration | generic_instantiation

6   library_unit_renaming_declaration ::=
           package_renaming_declaration
           | generic_renaming_declaration
           | subprogram_renaming_declaration

7   library_unit_body ::= subprogram_body | package_body

8   parent_unit_name ::= name

9   A *library unit* is a program unit that is declared by a library_item. When a program unit is a library unit, the prefix "library" is used to refer to it (or "generic library" if generic), as well as to its declaration and body, as in "library procedure", "library package_body", or "generic library package". The term *compilation unit* is used to refer to a compilation_unit. When the meaning is clear from context, the term is also used to refer to the library_item of a compilation_unit or to the proper_body of a subunit (that is, the compilation_unit without the context_clause and the **separate** (parent_unit_name)).

10   The *parent declaration* of a library_item (and of the library unit) is the declaration denoted by the parent_-unit_name, if any, of the defining_program_unit_name of the library_item. If there is no parent_-unit_name, the parent declaration is the declaration of Standard, the library_item is a *root* library_item, and the library unit (renaming) is a *root* library unit (renaming). The declaration and body of Standard itself have no parent declaration. The *parent unit* of a library_item or library unit is the library unit declared by its parent declaration.

11   The children of a library unit occur immediately within the declarative region of the declaration of the library unit. The *ancestors* of a library unit are itself, its parent, its parent's parent, and so on. (Standard is an ancestor of every library unit.) The *descendant* relation is the inverse of the ancestor relation.

12   A library_unit_declaration or a library_unit_renaming_declaration is *private* if the declaration is immediately preceded by the reserved word **private**; it is otherwise *public*. A library unit is private or public according to its declaration. The *public descendants* of a library unit are the library unit itself, and the public descendants of its public children. Its other descendants are *private descendants*.

Legality Rules

13   The parent unit of a library_item shall be a library package or generic library package.

14   If a defining_program_unit_name of a given declaration or body has a parent_unit_name, then the given declaration or body shall be a library_item. The body of a program unit shall be a library_item if and only if the declaration of the program unit is a library_item. In a library_unit_renaming_declaration, the (old) name shall denote a library_item.

15   A parent_unit_name (which can be used within a defining_program_unit_name of a library_item and in the **separate** clause of a subunit), and each of its prefixes, shall not denote a renaming_declaration. On the other hand, a name that denotes a library_unit_renaming_declaration is allowed in a with_clause and other places where the name of a library unit is allowed.

16   If a library package is an instance of a generic package, then every child of the library package shall either be itself an instance or be a renaming of a library unit.

17   A child of a generic library package shall either be itself a generic unit or be a renaming of some other child of the same generic unit. The renaming of a child of a generic package shall occur only within the declarative region of the generic package.

A child of a parent generic package shall be instantiated or renamed only within the declarative region of the parent generic. 18

For each declaration or renaming of a generic unit as a child of some parent generic package, there is a corresponding declaration nested immediately within each instance of the parent. This declaration is visible only within the scope of a with_clause that mentions the child generic unit. 19

A library subprogram shall not override a primitive subprogram. 20

The defining name of a function that is a compilation unit shall not be an operator_symbol. 21

Static Semantics

A subprogram_renaming_declaration that is a library_unit_renaming_declaration is a renaming-as-declaration, not a renaming-as-body. 22

There are two kinds of dependences among compilation units: 23

- The *semantic dependences* (see below) are the ones needed to check the compile-time rules across compilation unit boundaries; a compilation unit depends semantically on the other compilation units needed to determine its legality. The visibility rules are based on the semantic dependences. 24

- The *elaboration dependences* (see 10.2) determine the order of elaboration of library_items. 25

A library_item depends semantically upon its parent declaration. A subunit depends semantically upon its parent body. A library_unit_body depends semantically upon the corresponding library_unit_declaration, if any. A compilation unit depends semantically upon each library_item mentioned in a with_clause of the compilation unit. In addition, if a given compilation unit contains an attribute_reference of a type defined in another compilation unit, then the given compilation unit depends semantically upon the other compilation unit. The semantic dependence relationship is transitive. 26

NOTES
1 A simple program may consist of a single compilation unit. A compilation need not have any compilation units; for example, its text can consist of pragmas. 27

2 The designator of a library function cannot be an operator_symbol, but a nonlibrary renaming_declaration is allowed to rename a library function as an operator. Within a partition, two library subprograms are required to have distinct names and hence cannot overload each other. However, renaming_declarations are allowed to define overloaded names for such subprograms, and a locally declared subprogram is allowed to overload a library subprogram. The expanded name Standard.L can be used to denote a root library unit L (unless the declaration of Standard is hidden) since root library unit declarations occur immediately within the declarative region of package Standard. 28

Examples

Examples of library units: 29

```
package Rational_Numbers.IO is   -- public child of Rational_Numbers, see 7.1
   procedure Put(R : in  Rational);
   procedure Get(R : out Rational);
end Rational_Numbers.IO;
```
30

```
private procedure Rational_Numbers.Reduce(R : in out Rational);
                              -- private child of Rational_Numbers
```
31

```
with Rational_Numbers.Reduce;    -- refer to a private child
package body Rational_Numbers is
   ...
end Rational_Numbers;
```
32

33
```
with Rational_Numbers.IO; use Rational_Numbers;
with Ada.Text_io;              -- see A.10
procedure Main is              -- a root library procedure
   R : Rational;
begin
   R := 5/3;                   -- construct a rational number, see 7.1
   Ada.Text_IO.Put("The answer is: ");
   IO.Put(R);
   Ada.Text_IO.New_Line;
end Main;
```

34
```
with Rational_Numbers.IO;
package Rational_IO renames Rational_Numbers.IO;
                               -- a library unit renaming declaration
```

35   Each of the above library_items can be submitted to the compiler separately.

10.1.2 Context Clauses - With Clauses

1   A context_clause is used to specify the library_items whose names are needed within a compilation unit.

Syntax

2   context_clause ::= {context_item}

3   context_item ::= with_clause | use_clause

4   with_clause ::= **with** *library_unit_*name {, *library_unit_*name};

Name Resolution Rules

5   The *scope* of a with_clause that appears on a library_unit_declaration or library_unit_renaming_declaration consists of the entire declarative region of the declaration, which includes all children and subunits. The scope of a with_clause that appears on a body consists of the body, which includes all subunits.

6   A library_item is *mentioned* in a with_clause if it is denoted by a *library_unit_*name or a prefix in the with_clause.

7   Outside its own declarative region, the declaration or renaming of a library unit can be visible only within the scope of a with_clause that mentions it. The visibility of the declaration or renaming of a library unit otherwise follows from its placement in the environment.

Legality Rules

8   If a with_clause of a given compilation_unit mentions a private child of some library unit, then the given compilation_unit shall be either the declaration of a private descendant of that library unit or the body or subunit of a (public or private) descendant of that library unit.

NOTES

9   3 A library_item mentioned in a with_clause of a compilation unit is visible within the compilation unit and hence acts just like an ordinary declaration. Thus, within a compilation unit that mentions its declaration, the name of a library package can be given in use_clauses and can be used to form expanded names, a library subprogram can be called, and instances of a generic library unit can be declared. If a child of a parent generic package is mentioned in a with_clause, then the corresponding declaration nested within each visible instance is visible within the compilation unit.

10.1.3 Subunits of Compilation Units

Subunits are like child units, with these (important) differences: subunits support the separate compilation   1
of bodies only (not declarations); the parent contains a body_stub to indicate the existence and place of
each of its subunits; declarations appearing in the parent's body can be visible within the subunits.

Syntax

body_stub ::=   2
subprogram_body_stub | package_body_stub | task_body_stub | protected_body_stub

subprogram_body_stub ::= subprogram_specification **is separate**;   3

package_body_stub ::= **package body** defining_identifier **is separate**;   4

task_body_stub ::= **task body** defining_identifier **is separate**;   5

protected_body_stub ::= **protected body** defining_identifier **is separate**;   6

subunit ::= **separate** (parent_unit_name) proper_body   7

Legality Rules

The *parent body* of a subunit is the body of the program unit denoted by its parent_unit_name. The term   8
subunit is used to refer to a subunit and also to the proper_body of a subunit.

The parent body of a subunit shall be present in the current environment, and shall contain a corresponding   9
body_stub with the same defining_identifier as the subunit.

A package_body_stub shall be the completion of a package_declaration or generic_package_-   10
declaration; a task_body_stub shall be the completion of a task_declaration; a protected_body_stub
shall be the completion of a protected_declaration.

In contrast, a subprogram_body_stub need not be the completion of a previous declaration, in which case   11
the _stub declares the subprogram. If the _stub is a completion, it shall be the completion of a
subprogram_declaration or generic_subprogram_declaration. The profile of a subprogram_body_stub
that completes a declaration shall conform fully to that of the declaration.

A subunit that corresponds to a body_stub shall be of the same kind (package_, subprogram_, task_, or   12
protected_) as the body_stub. The profile of a subprogram_body subunit shall be fully conformant to that
of the corresponding body_stub.

A body_stub shall appear immediately within the declarative_part of a compilation unit body. This rule   13
does not apply within an instance of a generic unit.

The defining_identifiers of all body_stubs that appear immediately within a particular declarative_part   14
shall be distinct.

Post-Compilation Rules

For each body_stub, there shall be a subunit containing the corresponding proper_body.   15

NOTES
4 The rules in 10.1.4, ''The Compilation Process'' say that a body_stub is equivalent to the corresponding proper_body.   16
This implies:

- Visibility within a subunit is the visibility that would be obtained at the place of the corresponding   17
  body_stub (within the parent body) if the context_clause of the subunit were appended to that of the parent
  body.
- The effect of the elaboration of a body_stub is to elaborate the subunit.   18

Examples

19   The package Parent is first written without subunits:

20
```
package Parent is
    procedure Inner;
end Parent;
```

21
```
with Ada.Text_IO;
package body Parent is
    Variable : String := "Hello, there.";
    procedure Inner is
    begin
        Ada.Text_IO.Put_Line(Variable);
    end Inner;
end Parent;
```

22   The body of procedure Inner may be turned into a subunit by rewriting the package body as follows (with the declaration of Parent remaining the same):

23
```
package body Parent is
    Variable : String := "Hello, there.";
    procedure Inner is separate;
end Parent;
```

24
```
with Ada.Text_IO;
separate(Parent)
procedure Inner is
begin
    Ada.Text_IO.Put_Line(Variable);
end Inner;
```

10.1.4 The Compilation Process

1   Each compilation unit submitted to the compiler is compiled in the context of an *environment* declarative_part (or simply, an *environment*), which is a conceptual declarative_part that forms the outermost declarative region of the context of any compilation. At run time, an environment forms the declarative_part of the body of the environment task of a partition (see 10.2, ''Program Execution'').

2   The declarative_items of the environment are library_items appearing in an order such that there are no forward semantic dependences. Each included subunit occurs in place of the corresponding stub. The visibility rules apply as if the environment were the outermost declarative region, except that with_clauses are needed to make declarations of library units visible (see 10.1.2).

3   The mechanisms for creating an environment and for adding and replacing compilation units within an environment are implementation defined.

Name Resolution Rules

4/1   If a library_unit_body that is a subprogram_body is submitted to the compiler, it is interpreted only as a completion if a library_unit_declaration with the same defining_program_unit_name already exists in the environment for a subprogram other than an instance of a generic subprogram or for a generic subprogram (even if the profile of the body is not type conformant with that of the declaration); otherwise the subprogram_body is interpreted as both the declaration and body of a library subprogram.

Legality Rules

5   When a compilation unit is compiled, all compilation units upon which it depends semantically shall already exist in the environment; the set of these compilation units shall be *consistent* in the sense that the new compilation unit shall not semantically depend (directly or indirectly) on two different versions of the same compilation unit, nor on an earlier version of itself.

Implementation Permissions

The implementation may require that a compilation unit be legal before inserting it into the environment.   6

When a compilation unit that declares or renames a library unit is added to the environment, the   7
implementation may remove from the environment any preexisting library_item with the same defining_-
program_unit_name. When a compilation unit that is a subunit or the body of a library unit is added to the
environment, the implementation may remove from the environment any preexisting version of the same
compilation unit. When a given compilation unit is removed from the environment, the implementation
may also remove any compilation unit that depends semantically upon the given one. If the given
compilation unit contains the body of a subprogram to which a pragma Inline applies, the implementation
may also remove any compilation unit containing a call to that subprogram.

NOTES
5 The rules of the language are enforced across compilation and compilation unit boundaries, just as they are enforced   8
within a single compilation unit.

6 An implementation may support a concept of a *library*, which contains library_items. If multiple libraries are   9
supported, the implementation has to define how a single environment is constructed when a compilation unit is
submitted to the compiler. Naming conflicts between different libraries might be resolved by treating each library as the
root of a hierarchy of child library units.

7 A compilation unit containing an instantiation of a separately compiled generic unit does not semantically depend on   10
the body of the generic unit. Therefore, replacing the generic body in the environment does not result in the removal of
the compilation unit containing the instantiation.

10.1.5 Pragmas and Program Units

This subclause discusses pragmas related to program units, library units, and compilations.   1

Name Resolution Rules

Certain pragmas are defined to be *program unit pragmas*. A name given as the argument of a program   2
unit pragma shall resolve to denote the declarations or renamings of one or more program units that occur
immediately within the declarative region or compilation in which the pragma immediately occurs, or it
shall resolve to denote the declaration of the immediately enclosing program unit (if any); the pragma
applies to the denoted program unit(s). If there are no names given as arguments, the pragma applies to
the immediately enclosing program unit.

Legality Rules

A program unit pragma shall appear in one of these places: 3

- At the place of a compilation_unit, in which case the pragma shall immediately follow in the   4
  same compilation (except for other pragmas) a library_unit_declaration that is a subprogram_-
  declaration, generic_subprogram_declaration, or generic_instantiation, and the pragma shall
  have an argument that is a name denoting that declaration.

- Immediately within the declaration of a program unit and before any nested declaration (but not   5/1
  within a generic formal part), in which case the argument, if any, shall be a direct_name that
  denotes the immediately enclosing program unit declaration.

- At the place of a declaration other than the first, of a declarative_part or program unit   6
  declaration, in which case the pragma shall have an argument, which shall be a direct_name that
  denotes one or more of the following (and nothing else): a subprogram_declaration, a generic_-
  subprogram_declaration, or a generic_instantiation, of the same declarative_part or program
  unit declaration.

7 Certain program unit pragmas are defined to be *library unit pragmas*. The name, if any, in a library unit pragma shall denote the declaration of a library unit.

Static Semantics

7.1/1 A library unit pragma that applies to a generic unit does not apply to its instances, unless a specific rule for the pragma specifies the contrary.

Implementation Advice

7.2/1 When applied to a generic unit, a program unit pragma that is not a library unit pragma should apply to each instance of the generic unit for which there is not an overriding pragma applied directly to the instance.

Post-Compilation Rules

8 Certain pragmas are defined to be *configuration pragmas*; they shall appear before the first compilation_unit of a compilation. They are generally used to select a partition-wide or system-wide option. The pragma applies to all compilation_units appearing in the compilation, unless there are none, in which case it applies to all future compilation_units compiled into the same environment.

Implementation Permissions

9 An implementation may place restrictions on configuration pragmas, so long as it allows them when the environment contains no library_items other than those of the predefined environment.

10.1.6 Environment-Level Visibility Rules

1 The normal visibility rules do not apply within a parent_unit_name or a context_clause, nor within a pragma that appears at the place of a compilation unit. The special visibility rules for those contexts are given here.

Static Semantics

2 Within the parent_unit_name at the beginning of a library_item, and within a with_clause, the only declarations that are visible are those that are library_items of the environment, and the only declarations that are directly visible are those that are root library_items of the environment. Notwithstanding the rules of 4.1.3, an expanded name in a with_clause may consist of a prefix that denotes a generic package and a selector_name that denotes a child of that generic package. (The child is necessarily a generic unit; see 10.1.1.)

3 Within a use_clause or pragma that is within a context_clause, each library_item mentioned in a previous with_clause of the same context_clause is visible, and each root library_item so mentioned is directly visible. In addition, within such a use_clause, if a given declaration is visible or directly visible, each declaration that occurs immediately within the given declaration's visible part is also visible. No other declarations are visible or directly visible.

4 Within the parent_unit_name of a subunit, library_items are visible as they are in the parent_unit_name of a library_item; in addition, the declaration corresponding to each body_stub in the environment is also visible.

5 Within a pragma that appears at the place of a compilation unit, the immediately preceding library_item and each of its ancestors is visible. The ancestor root library_item is directly visible.

10.2 Program Execution

An Ada *program* consists of a set of *partitions*, which can execute in parallel with one another, possibly in   1
a separate address space, and possibly on a separate computer.

Post-Compilation Rules

A partition is a program or part of a program that can be invoked from outside the Ada implementation.   2
For example, on many systems, a partition might be an executable file generated by the system linker. The
user can *explicitly assign* library units to a partition. The assignment is done in an implementation-defined
manner. The compilation units included in a partition are those of the explicitly assigned library units, as
well as other compilation units *needed by* those library units. The compilation units needed by a given
compilation unit are determined as follows (unless specified otherwise via an implementation-defined
pragma, or by some other implementation-defined means):

- A compilation unit needs itself;   3

- If a compilation unit is needed, then so are any compilation units upon which it depends   4
  semantically;

- If a library_unit_declaration is needed, then so is any corresponding library_unit_body;   5

- If a compilation unit with stubs is needed, then so are any corresponding subunits.   6

The user can optionally designate (in an implementation-defined manner) one subprogram as the *main*   7
subprogram for the partition. A main subprogram, if specified, shall be a subprogram.

Each partition has an anonymous *environment task*, which is an implicit outermost task whose execution   8
elaborates the library_items of the environment declarative_part, and then calls the main subprogram, if
there is one. A partition's execution is that of its tasks.

The order of elaboration of library units is determined primarily by the *elaboration dependences*. There is   9
an elaboration dependence of a given library_item upon another if the given library_item or any of its
subunits depends semantically on the other library_item. In addition, if a given library_item or any of its
subunits has a pragma Elaborate or Elaborate_All that mentions another library unit, then there is an
elaboration dependence of the given library_item upon the body of the other library unit, and, for
Elaborate_All only, upon each library_item needed by the declaration of the other library unit.

The environment task for a partition has the following structure: 10

```
    task Environment_Task;                                                                          11

    task body Environment_Task is                                                                   12
        ... (1)  -- The environment declarative_part
                 -- (that is, the sequence of library_items) goes here.
    begin
        ... (2)  -- Call the main subprogram, if there is one.
    end Environment_Task;
```

The environment declarative_part at (1) is a sequence of declarative_items consisting of copies of the   13
library_items included in the partition. The order of elaboration of library_items is the order in which they
appear in the environment declarative_part:

- The order of all included library_items is such that there are no forward elaboration   14
  dependences.

- Any included library_unit_declaration to which a pragma Elaborate_Body applies is   15
  immediately followed by its library_unit_body, if included.

Program Execution   **10.2**

16   • All library_items declared pure occur before any that are not declared pure.

17   • All preelaborated library_items occur before any that are not preelaborated.

18   There shall be a total order of the library_items that obeys the above rules. The order is otherwise implementation defined.

19   The full expanded names of the library units and subunits included in a given partition shall be distinct.

20   The sequence_of_statements of the environment task (see (2) above) consists of either:

21   • A call to the main subprogram, if the partition has one. If the main subprogram has parameters, they are passed; where the actuals come from is implementation defined. What happens to the result of a main function is also implementation defined.

22   or:

23   • A null_statement, if there is no main subprogram.

24   The mechanisms for building and running partitions are implementation defined. These might be combined into one operation, as, for example, in dynamic linking, or ''load-and-go'' systems.

Dynamic Semantics

25   The execution of a program consists of the execution of a set of partitions. Further details are implementation defined. The execution of a partition starts with the execution of its environment task, ends when the environment task terminates, and includes the executions of all tasks of the partition. The execution of the (implicit) task_body of the environment task acts as a master for all other tasks created as part of the execution of the partition. When the environment task completes (normally or abnormally), it waits for the termination of all such tasks, and then finalizes any remaining objects of the partition.

Bounded (Run-Time) Errors

26   Once the environment task has awaited the termination of all other tasks of the partition, any further attempt to create a task (during finalization) is a bounded error, and may result in the raising of Program_Error either upon creation or activation of the task. If such a task is activated, it is not specified whether the task is awaited prior to termination of the environment task.

Implementation Requirements

27   The implementation shall ensure that all compilation units included in a partition are consistent with one another, and are legal according to the rules of the language.

Implementation Permissions

28   The kind of partition described in this clause is known as an *active* partition. An implementation is allowed to support other kinds of partitions, with implementation-defined semantics.

29   An implementation may restrict the kinds of subprograms it supports as main subprograms. However, an implementation is required to support all main subprograms that are public parameterless library procedures.

30   If the environment task completes abnormally, the implementation may abort any dependent tasks.

NOTES

31   8 An implementation may provide inter-partition communication mechanism(s) via special packages and pragmas. Standard pragmas for distribution and methods for specifying inter-partition communication are defined in Annex E, ''Distributed Systems''. If no such mechanisms are provided, then each partition is isolated from all others, and behaves as a program in and of itself.

9 Partitions are not required to run in separate address spaces. For example, an implementation might support dynamic linking via the partition concept.   32

10 An order of elaboration of library_items that is consistent with the partial ordering defined above does not always ensure that each library_unit_body is elaborated before any other compilation unit whose elaboration necessitates that the library_unit_body be already elaborated. (In particular, there is no requirement that the body of a library unit be elaborated as soon as possible after the library_unit_declaration is elaborated, unless the pragmas in subclause 10.2.1 are used.)   33

11 A partition (active or otherwise) need not have a main subprogram. In such a case, all the work done by the partition would be done by elaboration of various library_items, and by tasks created by that elaboration. Passive partitions, which cannot have main subprograms, are defined in Annex E, ''Distributed Systems''.   34

10.2.1 Elaboration Control

This subclause defines pragmas that help control the elaboration order of library_items.   1

Syntax

The form of a pragma Preelaborate is as follows: 2

pragma Preelaborate[(*library_unit_*name)];   3

A pragma Preelaborate is a library unit pragma.   4

Legality Rules

An elaborable construct is preelaborable unless its elaboration performs any of the following actions: 5

- The execution of a statement other than a null_statement.   6

- A call to a subprogram other than a static function.   7

- The evaluation of a primary that is a name of an object, unless the name is a static expression, or statically denotes a discriminant of an enclosing type.   8

- The creation of a default-initialized object (including a component) of a descendant of a private type, private extension, controlled type, task type, or protected type with entry_declarations; similarly the evaluation of an extension_aggregate with an ancestor subtype_mark denoting a subtype of such a type.   9

A generic body is preelaborable only if elaboration of a corresponding instance body would not perform any such actions, presuming that the actual for each formal private type (or extension) is a private type (or extension), and the actual for each formal subprogram is a user-defined subprogram.   10

If a pragma Preelaborate (or pragma Pure — see below) applies to a library unit, then it is *preelaborated*.   11/1
If a library unit is preelaborated, then its declaration, if any, and body, if any, are elaborated prior to all non-preelaborated library_items of the partition. The declaration and body of a preelaborated library unit, and all subunits that are elaborated as part of elaborating the library unit, shall be preelaborable. In addition to the places where Legality Rules normally apply (see 12.3), this rule applies also in the private part of an instance of a generic unit. In addition, all compilation units of a preelaborated library unit shall depend semantically only on compilation units of other preelaborated library units.

Implementation Advice

In an implementation, a type declared in a preelaborated package should have the same representation in every elaboration of a given version of the package, whether the elaborations occur in distinct executions of the same program, or in executions of distinct programs or partitions that include the given version.   12

Syntax

13   The form of a pragma Pure is as follows:

14   **pragma** Pure[(*library_unit_*name)];

15   A pragma Pure is a library unit pragma.

Legality Rules

16   A *pure* library_item is a preelaborable library_item that does not contain the declaration of any variable or named access type, except within a subprogram, generic subprogram, task unit, or protected unit.

17   A pragma Pure is used to declare that a library unit is pure. If a pragma Pure applies to a library unit, then its compilation units shall be pure, and they shall depend semantically only on compilation units of other library units that are declared pure.

Implementation Permissions

18   If a library unit is declared pure, then the implementation is permitted to omit a call on a library-level subprogram of the library unit if the results are not needed after the call. Similarly, it may omit such a call and simply reuse the results produced by an earlier call on the same subprogram, provided that none of the parameters are of a limited type, and the addresses and values of all by-reference actual parameters, and the values of all by-copy-in actual parameters, are the same as they were at the earlier call. This permission applies even if the subprogram produces other side effects when called.

Syntax

19   The form of a pragma Elaborate, Elaborate_All, or Elaborate_Body is as follows:

20   **pragma** Elaborate(*library_unit_*name{, *library_unit_*name});

21   **pragma** Elaborate_All(*library_unit_*name{, *library_unit_*name});

22   **pragma** Elaborate_Body[(*library_unit_*name)];

23   A pragma Elaborate or Elaborate_All is only allowed within a context_clause.

24   A pragma Elaborate_Body is a library unit pragma.

Legality Rules

25   If a pragma Elaborate_Body applies to a declaration, then the declaration requires a completion (a body).

Static Semantics

26   A pragma Elaborate specifies that the body of the named library unit is elaborated before the current library_item. A pragma Elaborate_All specifies that each library_item that is needed by the named library unit declaration is elaborated before the current library_item. A pragma Elaborate_Body specifies that the body of the library unit is elaborated immediately after its declaration.

NOTES

27   12 A preelaborated library unit is allowed to have non-preelaborable children.

28   13 A library unit that is declared pure is allowed to have impure children.

Section 11: Exceptions

This section defines the facilities for dealing with errors or other exceptional situations that arise during program execution. An *exception* represents a kind of exceptional situation; an occurrence of such a situation (at run time) is called an *exception occurrence*. To *raise* an exception is to abandon normal program execution so as to draw attention to the fact that the corresponding situation has arisen. Performing some actions in response to the arising of an exception is called *handling* the exception.

1

An exception_declaration declares a name for an exception. An exception is raised initially either by a raise_statement or by the failure of a language-defined check. When an exception arises, control can be transferred to a user-provided exception_handler at the end of a handled_sequence_of_statements, or it can be propagated to a dynamically enclosing execution.

2

11.1 Exception Declarations

An exception_declaration declares a name for an exception.

1

Syntax

exception_declaration ::= defining_identifier_list : **exception**;

2

Static Semantics

Each single exception_declaration declares a name for a different exception. If a generic unit includes an exception_declaration, the exception_declarations implicitly generated by different instantiations of the generic unit refer to distinct exceptions (but all have the same defining_identifier). The particular exception denoted by an exception name is determined at compilation time and is the same regardless of how many times the exception_declaration is elaborated.

3

The *predefined* exceptions are the ones declared in the declaration of package Standard: Constraint_Error, Program_Error, Storage_Error, and Tasking_Error; one of them is raised when a language-defined check fails.

4

Dynamic Semantics

The elaboration of an exception_declaration has no effect.

5

The execution of any construct raises Storage_Error if there is insufficient storage for that execution. The amount of storage needed for the execution of constructs is unspecified.

6

Examples

Examples of user-defined exception declarations:

7

```
Singular : exception;
Error    : exception;
Overflow, Underflow : exception;
```

8

11.2 Exception Handlers

The response to one or more exceptions is specified by an exception_handler.

1

S. Tucker Taft et al. (Eds.): Consolidated Ada Reference Manual, LNCS 2219, pp. 199–207, 2001.

Syntax

2   handled_sequence_of_statements ::=
         sequence_of_statements
      [**exception**
         exception_handler
         {exception_handler}]

3   exception_handler ::=
      when [choice_parameter_specification:] exception_choice {| exception_choice} =>
         sequence_of_statements

4   choice_parameter_specification ::= defining_identifier

5   exception_choice ::= *exception*_name | **others**

Legality Rules

6   A choice with an *exception*_name *covers* the named exception. A choice with **others** covers all exceptions
     not named by previous choices of the same handled_sequence_of_statements. Two choices in different
     exception_handlers of the same handled_sequence_of_statements shall not cover the same exception.

7   A choice with **others** is allowed only for the last handler of a handled_sequence_of_statements and as
     the only choice of that handler.

8   An *exception*_name of a choice shall not denote an exception declared in a generic formal package.

Static Semantics

9   A choice_parameter_specification declares a *choice parameter*, which is a constant object of type
     Exception_Occurrence (see 11.4.1). During the handling of an exception occurrence, the choice parameter,
     if any, of the handler represents the exception occurrence that is being handled.

Dynamic Semantics

10   The execution of a handled_sequence_of_statements consists of the execution of the sequence_of_-
     statements. The optional handlers are used to handle any exceptions that are propagated by the
     sequence_of_statements.

Examples

11   *Example of an exception handler:*

12
```
begin
    Open(File, In_File, "input.txt");    -- see A.8.2
exception
    when E : Name_Error =>
        Put("Cannot open input file : ");
        Put_Line(Exception_Message(E));   -- see 11.4.1
        raise;
end;
```

11.3 Raise Statements

1   A raise_statement raises an exception.

Syntax

2   raise_statement ::= **raise** [*exception*_name];

Legality Rules

The name, if any, in a raise_statement shall denote an exception. A raise_statement with no   3
*exception*_name (that is, a *re-raise statement*) shall be within a handler, but not within a body enclosed by
that handler.

Dynamic Semantics

To *raise an exception* is to raise a new occurrence of that exception, as explained in 11.4. For the   4
execution of a raise_statement with an *exception*_name, the named exception is raised. For the execution
of a re-raise statement, the exception occurrence that caused transfer of control to the innermost enclosing
handler is raised again.

Examples

Examples of raise statements: 5

```
raise Ada.IO_Exceptions.Name_Error;    -- see A.13    6
raise;                                  -- re-raise the current exception    7
```

11.4 Exception Handling

When an exception occurrence is raised, normal program execution is abandoned and control is transferred   1
to an applicable exception_handler, if any. To *handle* an exception occurrence is to respond to the
exceptional event. To *propagate* an exception occurrence is to raise it again in another context; that is, to
fail to respond to the exceptional event in the present context.

Dynamic Semantics

Within a given task, if the execution of construct *a* is defined by this International Standard to consist (in   2
part) of the execution of construct *b*, then while *b* is executing, the execution of *a* is said to *dynamically
enclose* the execution of *b*. The *innermost dynamically enclosing* execution of a given execution is the
dynamically enclosing execution that started most recently.

When an exception occurrence is raised by the execution of a given construct, the rest of the execution of   3
that construct is *abandoned*; that is, any portions of the execution that have not yet taken place are not
performed. The construct is first completed, and then left, as explained in 7.6.1. Then:

- If the construct is a task_body, the exception does not propagate further;   4
- If the construct is the sequence_of_statements of a handled_sequence_of_statements that   5
  has a handler with a choice covering the exception, the occurrence is handled by that handler;
- Otherwise, the occurrence is *propagated* to the innermost dynamically enclosing execution,   6
  which means that the occurrence is raised again in that context.

When an occurrence is *handled* by a given handler, the choice_parameter_specification, if any, is first   7
elaborated, which creates the choice parameter and initializes it to the occurrence. Then, the
sequence_of_statements of the handler is executed; this execution replaces the abandoned portion of the
execution of the sequence_of_statements.

NOTES
1 Note that exceptions raised in a declarative_part of a body are not handled by the handlers of the handled_-   8
sequence_of_statements of that body.

11.4.1 The Package Exceptions

Static Semantics

1 The following language-defined library package exists:

2
```
package Ada.Exceptions is
    type Exception_Id is private;
    Null_Id : constant Exception_Id;
    function Exception_Name(Id : Exception_Id) return String;
```
3
```
    type Exception_Occurrence is limited private;
    type Exception_Occurrence_Access is access all Exception_Occurrence;
    Null_Occurrence : constant Exception_Occurrence;
```
4
```
    procedure Raise_Exception(E : in Exception_Id;
                              Message : in String := "");
    function Exception_Message(X : Exception_Occurrence) return String;
    procedure Reraise_Occurrence(X : in Exception_Occurrence);
```
5
```
    function Exception_Identity(X : Exception_Occurrence)
                               return Exception_Id;
    function Exception_Name(X : Exception_Occurrence) return String;
        -- Same as Exception_Name(Exception_Identity(X)).
    function Exception_Information(X : Exception_Occurrence) return String;
```
6
```
    procedure Save_Occurrence(Target : out Exception_Occurrence;
                              Source : in Exception_Occurrence);
    function Save_Occurrence(Source : Exception_Occurrence)
                             return Exception_Occurrence_Access;
private
    ... -- not specified by the language
end Ada.Exceptions;
```

7 Each distinct exception is represented by a distinct value of type Exception_Id. Null_Id does not represent any exception, and is the default initial value of type Exception_Id. Each occurrence of an exception is represented by a value of type Exception_Occurrence. Null_Occurrence does not represent any exception occurrence, and is the default initial value of type Exception_Occurrence.

8/1 For a prefix E that denotes an exception, the following attribute is defined:

9 E'Identity   E'Identity returns the unique identity of the exception. The type of this attribute is Exception_Id.

10 Raise_Exception raises a new occurrence of the identified exception. In this case, Exception_Message returns the Message parameter of Raise_Exception. For a raise_statement with an *exception*_name, Exception_Message returns implementation-defined information about the exception occurrence. Reraise_Occurrence reraises the specified exception occurrence.

11 Exception_Identity returns the identity of the exception of the occurrence.

12 The Exception_Name functions return the full expanded name of the exception, in upper case, starting with a root library unit. For an exception declared immediately within package Standard, the defining_-identifier is returned. The result is implementation defined if the exception is declared within an unnamed block_statement.

13 Exception_Information returns implementation-defined information about the exception occurrence.

14 Raise_Exception and Reraise_Occurrence have no effect in the case of Null_Id or Null_Occurrence. Exception_Message, Exception_Identity, Exception_Name, and Exception_Information raise Constraint_Error for a Null_Id or Null_Occurrence.

The Save_Occurrence procedure copies the Source to the Target. The Save_Occurrence function uses an allocator of type Exception_Occurrence_Access to create a new object, copies the Source to this new object, and returns an access value designating this new object; the result may be deallocated using an instance of Unchecked_Deallocation. 15

Implementation Requirements

The implementation of the Write attribute (see 13.13.2) of Exception_Occurrence shall support writing a representation of an exception occurrence to a stream; the implementation of the Read attribute of Exception_Occurrence shall support reconstructing an exception occurrence from a stream (including one written in a different partition). 16

Implementation Permissions

An implementation of Exception_Name in a space-constrained environment may return the defining_-identifier instead of the full expanded name. 17

The string returned by Exception_Message may be truncated (to no less than 200 characters) by the Save_Occurrence procedure (not the function), the Reraise_Occurrence procedure, and the re-raise statement. 18

Implementation Advice

Exception_Message (by default) and Exception_Information should produce information useful for debugging. Exception_Message should be short (about one line), whereas Exception_Information can be long. Exception_Message should not include the Exception_Name. Exception_Information should include both the Exception_Name and the Exception_Message. 19

11.4.2 Example of Exception Handling

Examples

Exception handling may be used to separate the detection of an error from the response to that error: 1

```
with Ada.Exceptions;                                                    2
use Ada;
package File_System is
    type File_Handle is limited private;

    File_Not_Found : exception;                                         3
    procedure Open(F : in out File_Handle; Name : String);
        -- raises File_Not_Found if named file does not exist

    End_Of_File : exception;                                            4
    procedure Read(F : in out File_Handle; Data : out Data_Type);
        -- raises End_Of_File if the file is not open

    ...                                                                 5
end File_System;

package body File_System is                                             6
    procedure Open(F : in out File_Handle; Name : String) is
    begin
        if File_Exists(Name) then
            ...
        else
            Exceptions.Raise_Exception(File_Not_Found'Identity,
                            "File not found: " & Name & ".");
        end if;
    end Open;
```

7
```
procedure Read(F : in out File_Handle; Data : out Data_Type) is
begin
    if F.Current_Position <= F.Last_Position then
        ...
    else
        raise End_Of_File;
    end if;
end Read;
```

8   ...

9   `end File_System;`

10
```
with Ada.Text_IO;
with Ada.Exceptions;
with File_System; use File_System;
use Ada;
procedure Main is
begin
    ... -- call operations in File_System
exception
    when End_Of_File =>
        Close(Some_File);
    when Not_Found_Error : File_Not_Found =>
        Text_IO.Put_Line(Exceptions.Exception_Message(Not_Found_Error));
    when The_Error : others =>
        Text_IO.Put_Line("Unknown error:");
        if Verbosity_Desired then
            Text_IO.Put_Line(Exceptions.Exception_Information(The_Error));
        else
            Text_IO.Put_Line(Exceptions.Exception_Name(The_Error));
            Text_IO.Put_Line(Exceptions.Exception_Message(The_Error));
        end if;
        raise;
end Main;
```

11   In the above example, the File_System package contains information about detecting certain exceptional situations, but it does not specify how to handle those situations. Procedure Main specifies how to handle them; other clients of File_System might have different handlers, even though the exceptional situations arise from the same basic causes.

11.5 Suppressing Checks

1   A pragma Suppress gives permission to an implementation to omit certain language-defined checks.

2   A *language-defined check* (or simply, a "check") is one of the situations defined by this International Standard that requires a check to be made at run time to determine whether some condition is true. A check *fails* when the condition being checked is false, causing an exception to be raised.

Syntax

3   The form of a pragma Suppress is as follows:

4   **pragma** Suppress(identifier [, [On =>] name]);

5   A pragma Suppress is allowed only immediately within a declarative_part, immediately within a package_specification, or as a configuration pragma.

Legality Rules

6   The identifier shall be the name of a check. The name (if present) shall statically denote some entity.

For a pragma Suppress that is immediately within a package_specification and includes a name, the name shall denote an entity (or several overloaded subprograms) declared immediately within the package_specification.   7

A pragma Suppress gives permission to an implementation to omit the named check from the place of the   8
pragma to the end of the innermost enclosing declarative region, or, if the pragma is given in a package_-
specification and includes a name, to the end of the scope of the named entity. If the pragma includes a
name, the permission applies only to checks performed on the named entity, or, for a subtype, on objects
and values of its type. Otherwise, the permission applies to all entities. If permission has been given to
suppress a given check, the check is said to be *suppressed*.

The following are the language-defined checks: 9

- The following checks correspond to situations in which the exception Constraint_Error is raised   10
  upon failure.

  Access_Check   11/1
  When evaluating a dereference (explicit or implicit), check that the value of the name
  is not **null**. When passing an actual parameter to a formal access parameter, check that
  the value of the actual parameter is not **null**. When evaluating a
  discriminant_association for an access discriminant, check that the value of the
  discriminant is not **null**.

  Discriminant_Check   12
  Check that the discriminants of a composite value have the values imposed by a
  discriminant constraint. Also, when accessing a record component, check that it exists
  for the current discriminant values.

  Division_Check   13
  Check that the second operand is not zero for the operations /, rem and mod.

  Index_Check   14
  Check that the bounds of an array value are equal to the corresponding bounds of an
  index constraint. Also, when accessing a component of an array object, check for each
  dimension that the given index value belongs to the range defined by the bounds of the
  array object. Also, when accessing a slice of an array object, check that the given
  discrete range is compatible with the range defined by the bounds of the array object.

  Length_Check   15
  Check that two arrays have matching components, in the case of array subtype
  conversions, and logical operators for arrays of boolean components.

  Overflow_Check   16
  Check that a scalar value is within the base range of its type, in cases where the
  implementation chooses to raise an exception instead of returning the correct
  mathematical result.

  Range_Check   17
  Check that a scalar value satisfies a range constraint. Also, for the elaboration of a
  subtype_indication, check that the constraint (if present) is compatible with the
  subtype denoted by the subtype_mark. Also, for an aggregate, check that an index or
  discriminant value belongs to the corresponding subtype. Also, check that when the
  result of an operation yields an array, the value of each component belongs to the
  component subtype.

18   Tag_Check
            Check that operand tags in a dispatching call are all equal. Check for the correct tag on
            tagged type conversions, for an assignment_statement, and when returning a tagged
            limited object from a function.

19   • The following checks correspond to situations in which the exception Program_Error is raised
      upon failure.

20   Elaboration_Check
            When a subprogram or protected entry is called, a task activation is accomplished, or a
            generic instantiation is elaborated, check that the body of the corresponding unit has
            already been elaborated.

21   Accessibility_Check
            Check the accessibility level of an entity or view.

22   • The following check corresponds to situations in which the exception Storage_Error is raised
      upon failure.

23   Storage_Check
            Check that evaluation of an allocator does not require more space than is available for
            a storage pool. Check that the space available for a task or subprogram has not been
            exceeded.

24   • The following check corresponds to all situations in which any predefined exception is raised.

25   All_Checks
            Represents the union of all checks; suppressing All_Checks suppresses all checks.

Erroneous Execution

26   If a given check has been suppressed, and the corresponding error situation occurs, the execution of the
      program is erroneous.

Implementation Permissions

27   An implementation is allowed to place restrictions on Suppress pragmas. An implementation is allowed to
      add additional check names, with implementation-defined semantics. When Overflow_Check has been
      suppressed, an implementation may also suppress an unspecified subset of the Range_Checks.

Implementation Advice

28   The implementation should minimize the code executed for checks that have been suppressed.

      NOTES
29   2 There is no guarantee that a suppressed check is actually removed; hence a pragma Suppress should be used only for
      efficiency reasons.

Examples

30   *Examples of suppressing checks:*

31   ```
      pragma Suppress(Range_Check);
      pragma Suppress(Index_Check, On => Table);
      ```

# 11.6 Exceptions and Optimization

1     This clause gives permission to the implementation to perform certain ''optimizations'' that do not
      necessarily preserve the canonical semantics.
      ```

Dynamic Semantics

The rest of this International Standard (outside this clause) defines the *canonical semantics* of the language. The canonical semantics of a given (legal) program determines a set of possible external effects that can result from the execution of the program with given inputs.   2

As explained in 1.1.3, "Conformity of an Implementation with the Standard", the external effect of a program is defined in terms of its interactions with its external environment. Hence, the implementation can perform any internal actions whatsoever, in any order or in parallel, so long as the external effect of the execution of the program is one that is allowed by the canonical semantics, or by the rules of this clause.   3

Implementation Permissions

The following additional permissions are granted to the implementation: 4

- An implementation need not always raise an exception when a language-defined check fails. Instead, the operation that failed the check can simply yield an *undefined result*. The exception need be raised by the implementation only if, in the absence of raising it, the value of this undefined result would have some effect on the external interactions of the program. In determining this, the implementation shall not presume that an undefined result has a value that belongs to its subtype, nor even to the base range of its type, if scalar. Having removed the raise of the exception, the canonical semantics will in general allow the implementation to omit the code for the check, and some or all of the operation itself.   5

- If an exception is raised due to the failure of a language-defined check, then upon reaching the corresponding exception_handler (or the termination of the task, if none), the external interactions that have occurred need reflect only that the exception was raised somewhere within the execution of the sequence_of_statements with the handler (or the task_body), possibly earlier (or later if the interactions are independent of the result of the checked operation) than that defined by the canonical semantics, but not within the execution of some abort-deferred operation or *independent* subprogram that does not dynamically enclose the execution of the construct whose check failed. An independent subprogram is one that is defined outside the library unit containing the construct whose check failed, and has no Inline pragma applied to it. Any assignment that occurred outside of such abort-deferred operations or independent subprograms can be disrupted by the raising of the exception, causing the object or its parts to become abnormal, and certain subsequent uses of the object to be erroneous, as explained in 13.9.1.   6

NOTES

3 The permissions granted by this clause can have an effect on the semantics of a program only if the program fails a language-defined check.   7

Section 12: Generic Units

A *generic unit* is a program unit that is either a generic subprogram or a generic package. A generic unit is a *template*, which can be parameterized, and from which corresponding (nongeneric) subprograms or packages can be obtained. The resulting program units are said to be *instances* of the original generic unit. 1

A generic unit is declared by a generic_declaration. This form of declaration has a generic_formal_part declaring any generic formal parameters. An instance of a generic unit is obtained as the result of a generic_instantiation with appropriate generic actual parameters for the generic formal parameters. An instance of a generic subprogram is a subprogram. An instance of a generic package is a package. 2

Generic units are templates. As templates they do not have the properties that are specific to their nongeneric counterparts. For example, a generic subprogram can be instantiated but it cannot be called. In contrast, an instance of a generic subprogram is a (nongeneric) subprogram; hence, this instance can be called but it cannot be used to produce further instances. 3

12.1 Generic Declarations

A generic_declaration declares a generic unit, which is either a generic subprogram or a generic package. A generic_declaration includes a generic_formal_part declaring any generic formal parameters. A generic formal parameter can be an object; alternatively (unlike a parameter of a subprogram), it can be a type, a subprogram, or a package. 1

Syntax

generic_declaration ::= generic_subprogram_declaration I generic_package_declaration 2

generic_subprogram_declaration ::= 3
    generic_formal_part subprogram_specification;

generic_package_declaration ::= 4
    generic_formal_part package_specification;

generic_formal_part ::= **generic** {generic_formal_parameter_declaration I use_clause} 5

generic_formal_parameter_declaration ::= 6
    formal_object_declaration
    I formal_type_declaration
    I formal_subprogram_declaration
    I formal_package_declaration

The only form of subtype_indication allowed within a generic_formal_part is a subtype_mark (that is, the subtype_indication shall not include an explicit constraint). The defining name of a generic subprogram shall be an identifier (not an operator_symbol). 7

Static Semantics

A generic_declaration declares a generic unit — a generic package, generic procedure or generic function, as appropriate. 8

An entity is a *generic formal* entity if it is declared by a generic_formal_parameter_declaration. "Generic formal," or simply "formal," is used as a prefix in referring to objects, subtypes (and types), functions, procedures and packages, that are generic formal entities, as well as to their respective declarations. Examples: "generic formal procedure" or a "formal integer type declaration." 9

S. Tucker Taft et al. (Eds.): Consolidated Ada Reference Manual, LNCS 2219, pp. 209–223, 2001.

Dynamic Semantics

10   The elaboration of a generic_declaration has no effect.

NOTES

11   1 Outside a generic unit a name that denotes the generic_declaration denotes the generic unit. In contrast, within the declarative region of the generic unit, a name that denotes the generic_declaration denotes the current instance.

12   2 Within a generic subprogram_body, the name of this program unit acts as the name of a subprogram. Hence this name can be overloaded, and it can appear in a recursive call of the current instance. For the same reason, this name cannot appear after the reserved word **new** in a (recursive) generic_instantiation.

13   3 A default_expression or default_name appearing in a generic_formal_part is not evaluated during elaboration of the generic_formal_part; instead, it is evaluated when used. (The usual visibility rules apply to any name used in a default: the denoted declaration therefore has to be visible at the place of the expression.)

Examples

14   *Examples of generic formal parts:*

15
```
generic        -- parameterless
```

16
```
generic
    Size : Natural;   -- formal object
```

17
```
generic
    Length : Integer := 200;              -- formal object with a default expression
```

18
```
    Area   : Integer := Length*Length; -- formal object with a default expression
```

19
```
generic
    type Item  is private;                      -- formal type
    type Index is (<>);                         -- formal type
    type Row   is array(Index range <>) of Item; -- formal type
    with function "<"(X, Y : Item) return Boolean;      -- formal subprogram
```

20   *Examples of generic declarations declaring generic subprograms Exchange and Squaring:*

21
```
generic
    type Elem is private;
procedure Exchange(U, V : in out Elem);
```

22
```
generic
    type Item is private;
    with function "*"(U, V : Item) return Item is <>;
function Squaring(X : Item) return Item;
```

23   *Example of a generic declaration declaring a generic package:*

24
```
generic
    type Item   is private;
    type Vector is array (Positive range <>) of Item;
    with function Sum(X, Y : Item) return Item;
package On_Vectors is
    function Sum  (A, B : Vector) return Vector;
    function Sigma(A    : Vector) return Item;
    Length_Error : exception;
end On_Vectors;
```

12.2 Generic Bodies

The body of a generic unit (a *generic body*) is a template for the instance bodies. The syntax of a generic   1
body is identical to that of a nongeneric body.

Dynamic Semantics

The elaboration of a generic body has no other effect than to establish that the generic unit can from then   2
on be instantiated without failing the Elaboration_Check. If the generic body is a child of a generic
package, then its elaboration establishes that each corresponding declaration nested in an instance of the
parent (see 10.1.1) can from then on be instantiated without failing the Elaboration_Check.

NOTES
4 The syntax of generic subprograms implies that a generic subprogram body is always the completion of a declaration.   3

Examples

Example of a generic procedure body: 4

```
procedure Exchange(U, V : in out Elem) is   -- see 12.1
   T : Elem;   -- the generic formal type
begin
   T := U;
   U := V;
   V := T;
end Exchange;
```
    5

Example of a generic function body: 6

```
function Squaring(X : Item) return Item is   -- see 12.1
begin
   return X*X;   -- the formal operator "*"
end Squaring;
```
    7

Example of a generic package body: 8

```
package body On_Vectors is   -- see 12.1
```
    9

```
   function Sum(A, B : Vector) return Vector is
      Result : Vector(A'Range);   -- the formal type Vector
      Bias   : constant Integer := B'First - A'First;
   begin
      if A'Length /= B'Length then
         raise Length_Error;
      end if;
```
    10

```
      for N in A'Range loop
         Result(N) := Sum(A(N), B(N + Bias));   -- the formal function Sum
      end loop;
      return Result;
   end Sum;
```
    11

```
   function Sigma(A : Vector) return Item is
      Total : Item := A(A'First);   -- the formal type Item
   begin
      for N in A'First + 1 .. A'Last loop
         Total := Sum(Total, A(N));   -- the formal function Sum
      end loop;
      return Total;
   end Sigma;
end On_Vectors;
```
    12

12.3 Generic Instantiation

1 An instance of a generic unit is declared by a generic_instantiation.

Syntax

2   generic_instantiation ::=
         package defining_program_unit_name **is**
             new *generic_package_*name [generic_actual_part];
         | **procedure** defining_program_unit_name **is**
             new *generic_procedure_*name [generic_actual_part];
         | **function** defining_designator **is**
             new *generic_function_*name [generic_actual_part];

3   generic_actual_part ::=
         (generic_association {, generic_association})

4   generic_association ::=
         [*generic_formal_parameter_*selector_name =>] explicit_generic_actual_parameter

5   explicit_generic_actual_parameter ::= expression | *variable_*name
         | *subprogram_*name | *entry_*name | subtype_mark
         | *package_instance_*name

6 A generic_association is *named* or *positional* according to whether or not the *generic_formal_-parameter_*selector_name is specified. Any positional associations shall precede any named associations.

7 The *generic actual parameter* is either the explicit_generic_actual_parameter given in a generic_-parameter_association for each formal, or the corresponding default_expression or default_name if no generic_parameter_association is given for the formal. When the meaning is clear from context, the term ''generic actual,'' or simply ''actual,'' is used as a synonym for ''generic actual parameter'' and also for the view denoted by one, or the value of one.

Legality Rules

8 In a generic_instantiation for a particular kind of program unit (package, procedure, or function), the name shall denote a generic unit of the corresponding kind (generic package, generic procedure, or generic function, respectively).

9 The *generic_formal_parameter_*selector_name of a generic_association shall denote a generic_formal_parameter_declaration of the generic unit being instantiated. If two or more formal subprograms have the same defining name, then named associations are not allowed for the corresponding actuals.

10 A generic_instantiation shall contain at most one generic_association for each formal. Each formal without an association shall have a default_expression or subprogram_default.

11 In a generic unit Legality Rules are enforced at compile time of the generic_declaration and generic body, given the properties of the formals. In the visible part and formal part of an instance, Legality Rules are enforced at compile time of the generic_instantiation, given the properties of the actuals. In other parts of an instance, Legality Rules are not enforced; this rule does not apply when a given rule explicitly specifies otherwise.

Static Semantics

A generic_instantiation declares an instance; it is equivalent to the instance declaration (a package_- 12
declaration or subprogram_declaration) immediately followed by the instance body, both at the place of
the instantiation.

The instance is a copy of the text of the template. Each use of a formal parameter becomes (in the copy) a 13
use of the actual, as explained below. An instance of a generic package is a package, that of a generic
procedure is a procedure, and that of a generic function is a function.

The interpretation of each construct within a generic declaration or body is determined using the 14
overloading rules when that generic declaration or body is compiled. In an instance, the interpretation of
each (copied) construct is the same, except in the case of a name that denotes the generic_declaration or
some declaration within the generic unit; the corresponding name in the instance then denotes the
corresponding copy of the denoted declaration. The overloading rules do not apply in the instance.

In an instance, a generic_formal_parameter_declaration declares a view whose properties are identical to 15
those of the actual, except as specified in 12.4, ''Formal Objects'' and 12.6, ''Formal Subprograms''.
Similarly, for a declaration within a generic_formal_parameter_declaration, the corresponding
declaration in an instance declares a view whose properties are identical to the corresponding declaration
within the declaration of the actual.

Implicit declarations are also copied, and a name that denotes an implicit declaration in the generic denotes 16
the corresponding copy in the instance. However, for a type declared within the visible part of the generic,
a whole new set of primitive subprograms is implicitly declared for use outside the instance, and may differ
from the copied set if the properties of the type in some way depend on the properties of some actual type
specified in the instantiation. For example, if the type in the generic is derived from a formal private type,
then in the instance the type will inherit subprograms from the corresponding actual type.

These new implicit declarations occur immediately after the type declaration in the instance, and override 17
the copied ones. The copied ones can be called only from within the instance; the new ones can be called
only from outside the instance, although for tagged types, the body of a new one can be executed by a call
to an old one.

In the visible part of an instance, an explicit declaration overrides an implicit declaration if they are 18
homographs, as described in 8.3. On the other hand, an explicit declaration in the private part of an
instance overrides an implicit declaration in the instance, only if the corresponding explicit declaration in
the generic overrides a corresponding implicit declaration in the generic. Corresponding rules apply to the
other kinds of overriding described in 8.3.

Post-Compilation Rules

Recursive generic instantiation is not allowed in the following sense: if a given generic unit includes an 19
instantiation of a second generic unit, then the instance generated by this instantiation shall not include an
instance of the first generic unit (whether this instance is generated directly, or indirectly by intermediate
instantiations).

Dynamic Semantics

For the elaboration of a generic_instantiation, each generic_association is first evaluated. If a default is 20
used, an implicit generic_association is assumed for this rule. These evaluations are done in an arbitrary
order, except that the evaluation for a default actual takes place after the evaluation for another actual if the
default includes a name that denotes the other one. Finally, the instance declaration and body are
elaborated.

21 For the evaluation of a generic_association the generic actual parameter is evaluated. Additional actions are performed in the case of a formal object of mode **in** (see 12.4).

NOTES

22 5 If a formal type is not tagged, then the type is treated as an untagged type within the generic body. Deriving from such a type in a generic body is permitted; the new type does not get a new tag value, even if the actual is tagged. Overriding operations for such a derived type cannot be dispatched to from outside the instance.

Examples

23 *Examples of generic instantiations (see 12.1):*

24
```
procedure Swap is new Exchange(Elem => Integer);
procedure Swap is new Exchange(Character);        -- Swap is overloaded
function Square is new Squaring(Integer);         -- "*" of Integer used by default
function Square is new Squaring(Item => Matrix, "*" => Matrix_Product);
function Square is new Squaring(Matrix, Matrix_Product);  -- same as previous
```

25
```
package Int_Vectors is new On_Vectors(Integer, Table, "+");
```

26 *Examples of uses of instantiated units:*

27
```
Swap(A, B);
A := Square(A);
```

28
```
T : Table(1 .. 5) := (10, 20, 30, 40, 50);
N : Integer := Int_Vectors.Sigma(T);   -- 150 (see 12.2, "Generic Bodies" for the body of
Sigma)
```

29
```
use Int_Vectors;
M : Integer := Sigma(T);   -- 150
```

12.4 Formal Objects

1 A generic formal object can be used to pass a value or variable to a generic unit.

Syntax

2 formal_object_declaration ::=
    defining_identifier_list : mode subtype_mark [:= default_expression];

Name Resolution Rules

3 The expected type for the default_expression, if any, of a formal object is the type of the formal object.

4 For a generic formal object of mode **in**, the expected type for the actual is the type of the formal.

5 For a generic formal object of mode **in out**, the type of the actual shall resolve to the type of the formal.

Legality Rules

6 If a generic formal object has a default_expression, then the mode shall be **in** (either explicitly or by default); otherwise, its mode shall be either **in** or **in out**.

7 For a generic formal object of mode **in**, the actual shall be an expression. For a generic formal object of mode **in out**, the actual shall be a name that denotes a variable for which renaming is allowed (see 8.5.1).

8 The type of a generic formal object of mode **in** shall be nonlimited.

Static Semantics

9 A formal_object_declaration declares a generic formal object. The default mode is **in**. For a formal object of mode **in**, the nominal subtype is the one denoted by the subtype_mark in the declaration of the formal.

For a formal object of mode **in out**, its type is determined by the subtype_mark in the declaration; its nominal subtype is nonstatic, even if the subtype_mark denotes a static subtype.

In an instance, a formal_object_declaration of mode **in** declares a new stand-alone constant object whose initialization expression is the actual, whereas a formal_object_declaration of mode **in out** declares a view whose properties are identical to those of the actual.

10

Dynamic Semantics

For the evaluation of a generic_association for a formal object of mode **in**, a constant object is created, the value of the actual parameter is converted to the nominal subtype of the formal object, and assigned to the object, including any value adjustment — see 7.6.

11

NOTES
6 The constraints that apply to a generic formal object of mode **in out** are those of the corresponding generic actual parameter (not those implied by the subtype_mark that appears in the formal_object_declaration). Therefore, to avoid confusion, it is recommended that the name of a first subtype be used for the declaration of such a formal object.

12

12.5 Formal Types

A generic formal subtype can be used to pass to a generic unit a subtype whose type is in a certain class of types.

1

Syntax

formal_type_declaration ::=
    type defining_identifier[discriminant_part] **is** formal_type_definition;

2

formal_type_definition ::=
     formal_private_type_definition
    | formal_derived_type_definition
    | formal_discrete_type_definition
    | formal_signed_integer_type_definition
    | formal_modular_type_definition
    | formal_floating_point_definition
    | formal_ordinary_fixed_point_definition
    | formal_decimal_fixed_point_definition
    | formal_array_type_definition
    | formal_access_type_definition

3

Legality Rules

For a generic formal subtype, the actual shall be a subtype_mark; it denotes the *(generic) actual subtype*.

4

Static Semantics

A formal_type_declaration declares a *(generic) formal type*, and its first subtype, the *(generic) formal subtype*.

5

The form of a formal_type_definition *determines a class* to which the formal type belongs. For a formal_private_type_definition the reserved words **tagged** and **limited** indicate the class (see 12.5.1). For a formal_derived_type_definition the class is the derivation class rooted at the ancestor type. For other formal types, the name of the syntactic category indicates the class; a formal_discrete_type_definition defines a discrete type, and so on.

6

7   The actual type shall be in the class determined for the formal.

8/1   The formal type also belongs to each class that contains the determined class. The primitive subprograms of the type are as for any type in the determined class. For a formal type other than a formal derived type, these are the predefined operators of the type. For an elementary formal type, the predefined operators are implicitly declared immediately after the declaration of the formal type. For a composite formal type, the predefined operators are implicitly declared either immediately after the declaration of the formal type, or later in its immediate scope according to the rules of 7.3.1. In an instance, the copy of such an implicit declaration declares a view of the predefined operator of the actual type, even if this operator has been overridden for the actual type. The rules specific to formal derived types are given in 12.5.1.

NOTES

9   7 Generic formal types, like all types, are not named. Instead, a name can denote a generic formal subtype. Within a generic unit, a generic formal type is considered as being distinct from all other (formal or nonformal) types.

10   8 A discriminant_part is allowed only for certain kinds of types, and therefore only for certain kinds of generic formal types. See 3.7.

Examples

11   *Examples of generic formal types:*

12
```
type Item is private;
type Buffer(Length : Natural) is limited private;
```

13
```
type Enum  is (<>);
type Int   is range <>;
type Angle is delta <>;
type Mass  is digits <>;
```

14
```
type Table is array (Enum) of Item;
```

15   *Example of a generic formal part declaring a formal integer type:*

16
```
generic
    type Rank is range <>;
    First  : Rank := Rank'First;
    Second : Rank := First + 1;   -- the operator "+" of the type Rank
```

12.5.1 Formal Private and Derived Types

1   The class determined for a formal private type can be either limited or nonlimited, and either tagged or untagged; no more specific class is known for such a type. The class determined for a formal derived type is the derivation class rooted at the ancestor type.

2   formal_private_type_definition ::= [[**abstract**] **tagged**] [**limited**] **private**

3   formal_derived_type_definition ::= [**abstract**] **new** subtype_mark [**with private**]

4   If a generic formal type declaration has a known_discriminant_part, then it shall not include a default_expression for a discriminant.

5   The *ancestor subtype* of a formal derived type is the subtype denoted by the subtype_mark of the formal_derived_type_definition. For a formal derived type declaration, the reserved words **with private** shall appear if and only if the ancestor type is a tagged type; in this case the formal derived type is a private

extension of the ancestor type and the ancestor shall not be a class-wide type. Similarly, the optional reserved word **abstract** shall appear only if the ancestor type is a tagged type.

If the formal subtype is definite, then the actual subtype shall also be definite.   6

For a generic formal derived type with no discriminant_part: 7

- If the ancestor subtype is constrained, the actual subtype shall be constrained, and shall be statically compatible with the ancestor;   8

- If the ancestor subtype is an unconstrained access or composite subtype, the actual subtype shall be unconstrained.   9

- If the ancestor subtype is an unconstrained discriminated subtype, then the actual shall have the same number of discriminants, and each discriminant of the actual shall correspond to a discriminant of the ancestor, in the sense of 3.7.   10

The declaration of a formal derived type shall not have a known_discriminant_part. For a generic formal private type with a known_discriminant_part: 11

- The actual type shall be a type with the same number of discriminants.   12

- The actual subtype shall be unconstrained.   13

- The subtype of each discriminant of the actual type shall statically match the subtype of the corresponding discriminant of the formal type.   14

For a generic formal type with an unknown_discriminant_part, the actual may, but need not, have discriminants, and may be definite or indefinite.   15

Static Semantics

The class determined for a formal private type is as follows: 16

Type Definition	*Determined Class*	17
limited private	the class of all types	
private	the class of all nonlimited types	
tagged limited private	the class of all tagged types	
tagged private	the class of all nonlimited tagged types	

The presence of the reserved word **abstract** determines whether the actual type may be abstract.   18

A formal private or derived type is a private or derived type, respectively. A formal derived tagged type is a private extension. A formal private or derived type is abstract if the reserved word **abstract** appears in its declaration.   19

If the ancestor type is a composite type that is not an array type, the formal type inherits components from the ancestor type (including discriminants if a new discriminant_part is not specified), as for a derived type defined by a derived_type_definition (see 3.4).   20

For a formal derived type, the predefined operators and inherited user-defined subprograms are determined by the ancestor type, and are implicitly declared at the earliest place, if any, within the immediate scope of the formal type, where the corresponding primitive subprogram of the ancestor is visible (see 7.3.1). In an instance, the copy of such an implicit declaration declares a view of the corresponding primitive subprogram of the ancestor of the formal derived type, even if this primitive has been overridden for the actual type. When the ancestor of the formal derived type is itself a formal type, the copy of the implicit declaration declares a view of the corresponding copied operation of the ancestor. In the case of a formal private extension, however, the tag of the formal type is that of the actual type, so if the tag in a call is   21/1

Formal Private and Derived Types **12.5.1**

statically determined to be that of the formal type, the body executed will be that corresponding to the actual type.

22/1　For a prefix S that denotes a formal indefinite subtype, the following attribute is defined:

23　S'Definite　　　S'Definite yields True if the actual subtype corresponding to S is definite; otherwise it yields False. The value of this attribute is of the predefined type Boolean.

NOTES

24　9 In accordance with the general rule that the actual type shall belong to the class determined for the formal (see 12.5, "Formal Types"):

25　　• If the formal type is nonlimited, then so shall be the actual;

26　　• For a formal derived type, the actual shall be in the class rooted at the ancestor subtype.

27　10 The actual type can be abstract only if the formal type is abstract (see 3.9.3).

28　11 If the formal has a discriminant_part, the actual can be either definite or indefinite. Otherwise, the actual has to be definite.

12.5.2 Formal Scalar Types

1　A *formal scalar type* is one defined by any of the formal_type_definitions in this subclause. The class determined for a formal scalar type is discrete, signed integer, modular, floating point, ordinary fixed point, or decimal.

Syntax

2　formal_discrete_type_definition ::= (<>)

3　formal_signed_integer_type_definition ::= **range** <>

4　formal_modular_type_definition ::= **mod** <>

5　formal_floating_point_definition ::= **digits** <>

6　formal_ordinary_fixed_point_definition ::= **delta** <>

7　formal_decimal_fixed_point_definition ::= **delta** <> **digits** <>

Legality Rules

8　The actual type for a formal scalar type shall not be a nonstandard numeric type.

NOTES

9　12 The actual type shall be in the class of types implied by the syntactic category of the formal type definition (see 12.5, "Formal Types"). For example, the actual for a formal_modular_type_definition shall be a modular type.

12.5.3 Formal Array Types

1　The class determined for a formal array type is the class of all array types.

Syntax

2　formal_array_type_definition ::= array_type_definition

Legality Rules

3　The only form of discrete_subtype_definition that is allowed within the declaration of a generic formal (constrained) array subtype is a subtype_mark.

4　For a formal array subtype, the actual subtype shall satisfy the following conditions:

- The formal array type and the actual array type shall have the same dimensionality; the formal subtype and the actual subtype shall be either both constrained or both unconstrained. 5

- For each index position, the index types shall be the same, and the index subtypes (if unconstrained), or the index ranges (if constrained), shall statically match (see 4.9.1). 6

- The component subtypes of the formal and actual array types shall statically match. 7

- If the formal type has aliased components, then so shall the actual. 8

Examples

Example of formal array types: 9

```
-- given the generic package                                              10
generic                                                                   11
    type Item    is private;
    type Index   is (<>);
    type Vector is array (Index range <>) of Item;
    type Table  is array (Index) of Item;
package P is
    ...
end P;
-- and the types                                                          12
type Mix     is array (Color range <>) of Boolean;                        13
type Option is array (Color) of Boolean;
-- then Mix can match Vector and Option can match Table                    14
package R is new P(Item    => Boolean, Index => Color,                     15
               Vector => Mix,      Table => Option);
-- Note that Mix cannot match Table and Option cannot match Vector         16
```

12.5.4 Formal Access Types

The class determined for a formal access type is the class of all access types. 1

Syntax

formal_access_type_definition ::= access_type_definition 2

Legality Rules

For a formal access-to-object type, the designated subtypes of the formal and actual types shall statically match. 3

If and only if the general_access_modifier **constant** applies to the formal, the actual shall be an access-to-constant type. If the general_access_modifier **all** applies to the formal, then the actual shall be a general access-to-variable type (see 3.10). 4

For a formal access-to-subprogram subtype, the designated profiles of the formal and the actual shall be mode-conformant, and the calling convention of the actual shall be *protected* if and only if that of the formal is *protected*. 5

Examples

Example of formal access types: 6

```
-- the formal types of the generic package                                7
```

8

```
generic
    type Node is private;
    type Link is access Node;
package P is
    . . .
end P;
```

9

-- *can be matched by the actual types*

10

```
type Car;
type Car_Name is access Car;
```

11

```
type Car is
    record
        Pred, Succ  : Car_Name;
        Number      : License_Number;
        Owner       : Person;
    end record;
```

12

-- *in the following generic instantiation*

13

```
package R is new P(Node => Car, Link => Car_Name);
```

12.6 Formal Subprograms

1

Formal subprograms can be used to pass callable entities to a generic unit.

Syntax

2

formal_subprogram_declaration ::= **with** subprogram_specification [**is** subprogram_default];

3

subprogram_default ::= default_name | <>

4

default_name ::= name

Name Resolution Rules

5

The expected profile for the default_name, if any, is that of the formal subprogram.

6

For a generic formal subprogram, the expected profile for the actual is that of the formal subprogram.

Legality Rules

7

The profiles of the formal and any named default shall be mode-conformant.

8

The profiles of the formal and actual shall be mode-conformant.

Static Semantics

9

A formal_subprogram_declaration declares a generic formal subprogram. The types of the formal parameters and result, if any, of the formal subprogram are those determined by the subtype_marks given in the formal_subprogram_declaration; however, independent of the particular subtypes that are denoted by the subtype_marks, the nominal subtypes of the formal parameters and result, if any, are defined to be nonstatic, and unconstrained if of an array type (no applicable index constraint is provided in a call on a formal subprogram). In an instance, a formal_subprogram_declaration declares a view of the actual. The profile of this view takes its subtypes and calling convention from the original profile of the actual entity, while taking the formal parameter names and default_expressions from the profile given in the formal_-subprogram_declaration. The view is a function or procedure, never an entry.

10

If a generic unit has a subprogram_default specified by a box, and the corresponding actual parameter is omitted, then it is equivalent to an explicit actual parameter that is a usage name identical to the defining name of the formal.

NOTES

13 The matching rules for formal subprograms state requirements that are similar to those applying to subprogram_renaming_declarations (see 8.5.4). In particular, the name of a parameter of the formal subprogram need not be the same as that of the corresponding parameter of the actual subprogram; similarly, for these parameters, default_expressions need not correspond.   11

14 The constraints that apply to a parameter of a formal subprogram are those of the corresponding formal parameter of the matching actual subprogram (not those implied by the corresponding subtype_mark in the _specification of the formal subprogram). A similar remark applies to the result of a function. Therefore, to avoid confusion, it is recommended that the name of a first subtype be used in any declaration of a formal subprogram.   12

15 The subtype specified for a formal parameter of a generic formal subprogram can be any visible subtype, including a generic formal subtype of the same generic_formal_part.   13

16 A formal subprogram is matched by an attribute of a type if the attribute is a function with a matching specification. An enumeration literal of a given type matches a parameterless formal function whose result type is the given type.   14

17 A default_name denotes an entity that is visible or directly visible at the place of the generic_declaration; a box used as a default is equivalent to a name that denotes an entity that is directly visible at the place of the _instantiation.   15

18 The actual subprogram cannot be abstract (see 3.9.3).   16

Examples

Examples of generic formal subprograms: 17

```
with function "+"(X, Y : Item) return Item is <>;
with function Image(X : Enum) return String is Enum'Image;
with procedure Update is Default_Update;
```
      18

```
-- given the generic procedure declaration
```
      19

```
generic
   with procedure Action (X : in Item);
procedure Iterate(Seq : in Item_Sequence);
```
      20

```
-- and the procedure
```
      21

```
procedure Put_Item(X : in Item);
```
      22

```
-- the following instantiation is possible
```
      23

```
procedure Put_List is new Iterate(Action => Put_Item);
```
      24

12.7 Formal Packages

Formal packages can be used to pass packages to a generic unit. The formal_package_declaration declares that the formal package is an instance of a given generic package. Upon instantiation, the actual package has to be an instance of that generic package.   1

Syntax

formal_package_declaration ::=   2
  with package defining_identifier **is new** *generic_package*_name formal_package_actual_part;

formal_package_actual_part ::=   3
  (<>) | [generic_actual_part]

Legality Rules

The *generic_package*_name shall denote a generic package (the *template* for the formal package); the formal package is an instance of the template.   4

The actual shall be an instance of the template. If the formal_package_actual_part is (<>), then the actual may be any instance of the template; otherwise, each actual parameter of the actual instance shall match the   5 corresponding actual parameter of the formal package (whether the actual parameter is given explicitly or by default), as follows:

6   • For a formal object of mode **in** the actuals match if they are static expressions with the same value, or if they statically denote the same constant, or if they are both the literal **null**.

7   • For a formal subtype, the actuals match if they denote statically matching subtypes.

8   • For other kinds of formals, the actuals match if they statically denote the same entity.

8.1/1   For the purposes of matching, any actual parameter that is the name of a formal object of mode **in** is replaced by the formal object's actual expression (recursively).

Static Semantics

9   A formal_package_declaration declares a generic formal package.

10   The visible part of a formal package includes the first list of basic_declarative_items of the package_-specification. In addition, if the formal_package_actual_part is (<>), it also includes the generic_-formal_part of the template for the formal package.

12.8 Example of a Generic Package

1   The following example provides a possible formulation of stacks by means of a generic package. The size of each stack and the type of the stack elements are provided as generic formal parameters.

Examples

2/1   *This paragraph was deleted.*

3
```
generic
    Size : Positive;
    type Item is private;
package Stack is
    procedure Push(E : in  Item);
    procedure Pop (E : out Item);
    Overflow, Underflow : exception;
end Stack;
```

4
```
package body Stack is
```

5
```
    type Table is array (Positive range <>) of Item;
    Space : Table(1 .. Size);
    Index : Natural := 0;
```

6
```
    procedure Push(E : in Item) is
    begin
        if Index >= Size then
            raise Overflow;
        end if;
        Index := Index + 1;
        Space(Index) := E;
    end Push;
```

7
```
    procedure Pop(E : out Item) is
    begin
        if Index = 0 then
            raise Underflow;
        end if;
        E := Space(Index);
        Index := Index - 1;
    end Pop;
```

8
```
end Stack;
```

Instances of this generic package can be obtained as follows:

9

```
package Stack_Int  is new Stack(Size => 200, Item => Integer);
package Stack_Bool is new Stack(100, Boolean);
```

10

Thereafter, the procedures of the instantiated packages can be called as follows:

11

```
Stack_Int.Push(N);
Stack_Bool.Push(True);
```

12

Alternatively, a generic formulation of the type Stack can be given as follows (package body omitted):

13

```
generic
   type Item is private;
package On_Stacks is
   type Stack(Size : Positive) is limited private;
   procedure Push(S : in out Stack; E : in  Item);
   procedure Pop (S : in out Stack; E : out Item);
   Overflow, Underflow : exception;
private
   type Table is array (Positive range <>) of Item;
   type Stack(Size : Positive) is
      record
         Space : Table(1 .. Size);
         Index : Natural := 0;
      end record;
end On_Stacks;
```

14

In order to use such a package, an instance has to be created and thereafter stacks of the corresponding type can be declared:

15

```
declare
   package Stack_Real is new On_Stacks(Real); use Stack_Real;
   S : Stack(100);
begin
   ...
   Push(S, 2.54);
   ...
end;
```

16

Example of a Generic Package **12.8**

Section 13: Representation Issues

This section describes features for querying and controlling certain aspects of entities and for interfacing to hardware.   1/1

13.1 Operational and Representation Items

Representation and operational items can be used to specify aspects of entities. Two kinds of aspects of entities can be specified: aspects of representation and operational aspects. Representation items specify how the types and other entities of the language are to be mapped onto the underlying machine. Operational items specify other properties of entities.   0.1/1

There are six kinds of *representation items*: attribute_definition_clauses for representation attributes, enumeration_representation_clauses, record_representation_clauses, at_clauses, component_clauses, and *representation pragmas*. They can be provided to give more efficient representation or to interface with features that are outside the domain of the language (for example, peripheral hardware).   1/1

An *operational item* is an attribute_definition_clause for an operational attribute.   1.1/1

An operational item or a representation item applies to an entity identified by a local_name, which denotes an entity declared local to the current declarative region, or a library unit declared immediately preceding a representation pragma in a compilation.   1.2/1

Syntax

aspect_clause ::= attribute_definition_clause   2/1
   | enumeration_representation_clause
   | record_representation_clause
   | at_clause

local_name ::= direct_name   3
   | direct_name'attribute_designator
   | *library_unit*_name

A representation pragma is allowed only at places where an aspect_clause or compilation_unit is allowed.   4/1

Name Resolution Rules

In an operational item or representation item, if the local_name is a direct_name, then it shall resolve to denote a declaration (or, in the case of a pragma, one or more declarations) that occurs immediately within the same declarative_region as the item. If the local_name has an attribute_designator, then it shall resolve to denote an implementation-defined component (see 13.5.1) or a class-wide type implicitly declared immediately within the same declarative_region as the item. A local_name that is a *library_unit*_name (only permitted in a representation pragma) shall resolve to denote the library_item that immediately precedes (except for other pragmas) the representation pragma.   5/1

Legality Rules

The local_name of a aspect_clause or representation pragma shall statically denote an entity (or, in the case of a pragma, one or more entities) declared immediately preceding it in a compilation, or within the same declarative_part, package_specification, task_definition, protected_definition, or record_definition as the representation or operational item. If a local_name denotes a local callable entity, it may do so   6/1 through a local subprogram_renaming_declaration (as a way to resolve ambiguity in the presence of overloading); otherwise, the local_name shall not denote a renaming_declaration.

7   The *representation* of an object consists of a certain number of bits (the *size* of the object). These are the bits that are normally read or updated by the machine code when loading, storing, or operating-on the value of the object. This includes some padding bits, when the size of the object is greater than the size of its subtype. Such padding bits are considered to be part of the representation of the object, rather than being gaps between objects, if these bits are normally read and updated.

8   A representation item *directly specifies* an *aspect of representation* of the entity denoted by the local_name, except in the case of a type-related representation item, whose local_name shall denote a first subtype, and which directly specifies an aspect of the subtype's type. A representation item that names a subtype is either *subtype-specific* (Size and Alignment clauses) or *type-related* (all others). Subtype-specific aspects may differ for different subtypes of the same type.

8.1/1   An operational item *directly specifies* an *operational aspect* of the type of the subtype denoted by the local_name. The local_name of an operational item shall denote a first subtype. An operational item that names a subtype is type-related.

9   A representation item that directly specifies an aspect of a subtype or type shall appear after the type is completely defined (see 3.11.1), and before the subtype or type is frozen (see 13.14). If a representation item is given that directly specifies an aspect of an entity, then it is illegal to give another representation item that directly specifies the same aspect of the entity.

9.1/1   An operational item that directly specifies an aspect of a type shall appear before the type is frozen (see 13.14). If an operational item is given that directly specifies an aspect of a type, then it is illegal to give another operational item that directly specifies the same aspect of the type.

10   For an untagged derived type, no type-related representation items are allowed if the parent type is a by-reference type, or has any user-defined primitive subprograms.

11/1   Operational and representation aspects of a generic formal parameter are the same as those of the actual. Operational and representation aspects of a partial view are the same as those of the full view. A type-related representation item is not allowed for a descendant of a generic formal untagged type.

12   A representation item that specifies the Size for a given subtype, or the size or storage place for an object (including a component) of a given subtype, shall allow for enough storage space to accommodate any value of the subtype.

13/1   A representation or operational item that is not supported by the implementation is illegal, or raises an exception at run time.

Static Semantics

14   If two subtypes statically match, then their subtype-specific aspects (Size and Alignment) are the same.

15/1   A derived type inherits each type-related aspect of representation of its parent type that was directly specified before the declaration of the derived type, or (in the case where the parent is derived) that was inherited by the parent type from the grandparent type. A derived subtype inherits each subtype-specific aspect of representation of its parent subtype that was directly specified before the declaration of the derived type, or (in the case where the parent is derived) that was inherited by the parent subtype from the grandparent subtype, but only if the parent subtype statically matches the first subtype of the parent type. An inherited aspect of representation is overridden by a subsequent representation item that specifies the same aspect of the type or subtype.

In contrast, whether operational aspects are inherited by a derived type depends on each specific aspect. When operational aspects are inherited by a derived type, aspects that were directly specified before the declaration of the derived type, or (in the case where the parent is derived) that were inherited by the parent type from the grandparent type are inherited. An inherited operational aspect is overridden by a subsequent operational item that specifies the same aspect of the type.   15.1/1

Each aspect of representation of an entity is as follows: 16

- If the aspect is *specified* for the entity, meaning that it is either directly specified or inherited, then that aspect of the entity is as specified, except in the case of Storage_Size, which specifies a minimum.   17

- If an aspect of representation of an entity is not specified, it is chosen by default in an unspecified manner.   18

If an operational aspect is *specified* for an entity (meaning that it is either directly specified or inherited), then that aspect of the entity is as specified. Otherwise, the aspect of the entity has the default value for that aspect.   18.1/1

Dynamic Semantics

For the elaboration of a aspect_clause, any evaluable constructs within it are evaluated.   19/1

Implementation Permissions

An implementation may interpret aspects of representation in an implementation-defined manner. An implementation may place implementation-defined restrictions on representation items. A *recommended level of support* is specified for representation items and related features in each subclause. These recommendations are changed to requirements for implementations that support the Systems Programming Annex (see C.2, "Required Representation Support").   20

Implementation Advice

The recommended level of support for all representation items is qualified as follows: 21

- An implementation need not support representation items containing nonstatic expressions, except that an implementation should support a representation item for a given entity if each nonstatic expression in the representation item is a name that statically denotes a constant declared before the entity.   22

- An implementation need not support a specification for the Size for a given composite subtype, nor the size or storage place for an object (including a component) of a given composite subtype, unless the constraints on the subtype and its composite subcomponents (if any) are all static constraints.   23

- An aliased component, or a component whose type is by-reference, should always be allocated at an addressable location.   24

13.2 Pragma Pack

A pragma Pack specifies that storage minimization should be the main criterion when selecting the representation of a composite type.   1

Syntax

The form of a pragma Pack is as follows: 2

pragma Pack(*first_subtype*_local_name);   3

Legality Rules

4 The *first_subtype*_local_name of a pragma Pack shall denote a composite subtype.

Static Semantics

5 A pragma Pack specifies the *packing* aspect of representation; the type (or the extension part) is said to be *packed*. For a type extension, the parent part is packed as for the parent type, and a pragma Pack causes packing only of the extension part.

Implementation Advice

6 If a type is packed, then the implementation should try to minimize storage allocated to objects of the type, possibly at the expense of speed of accessing components, subject to reasonable complexity in addressing calculations.

7 The recommended level of support for pragma Pack is:

8 • For a packed record type, the components should be packed as tightly as possible subject to the Sizes of the component subtypes, and subject to any record_representation_clause that applies to the type; the implementation may, but need not, reorder components or cross aligned word boundaries to improve the packing. A component whose Size is greater than the word size may be allocated an integral number of words.

9 • For a packed array type, if the component subtype's Size is less than or equal to the word size, and Component_Size is not specified for the type, Component_Size should be less than or equal to the Size of the component subtype, rounded up to the nearest factor of the word size.

13.3 Operational and Representation Attributes

1/1 The values of certain implementation-dependent characteristics can be obtained by interrogating appropriate operational or representation attributes. Some of these attributes are specifiable via an attribute_definition_clause.

Syntax

2 attribute_definition_clause ::=
    for local_name'attribute_designator **use** expression;
    | **for** local_name'attribute_designator **use** name;

Name Resolution Rules

3 For an attribute_definition_clause that specifies an attribute that denotes a value, the form with an expression shall be used. Otherwise, the form with a name shall be used.

4 For an attribute_definition_clause that specifies an attribute that denotes a value or an object, the expected type for the expression or name is that of the attribute. For an attribute_definition_clause that specifies an attribute that denotes a subprogram, the expected profile for the name is the profile required for the attribute. For an attribute_definition_clause that specifies an attribute that denotes some other kind of entity, the name shall resolve to denote an entity of the appropriate kind.

Legality Rules

5/1 An attribute_designator is allowed in an attribute_definition_clause only if this International Standard explicitly allows it, or for an implementation-defined attribute if the implementation allows it. Each specifiable attribute constitutes an operational aspect or aspect of representation.

For an attribute_definition_clause that specifies an attribute that denotes a subprogram, the profile shall be mode conformant with the one required for the attribute, and the convention shall be Ada. Additional requirements are defined for particular attributes. 6

Static Semantics

A *Size clause* is an attribute_definition_clause whose attribute_designator is Size. Similar definitions apply to the other specifiable attributes. 7

A *storage element* is an addressable element of storage in the machine. A *word* is the largest amount of storage that can be conveniently and efficiently manipulated by the hardware, given the implementation's run-time model. A word consists of an integral number of storage elements. 8

The following representation attributes are defined: Address, Alignment, Size, Storage_Size, and Component_Size. 9/1

For a prefix X that denotes an object, program unit, or label: 10/1

X'Address   Denotes the address of the first of the storage elements allocated to X. For a program unit or label, this value refers to the machine code associated with the corresponding body or statement. The value of this attribute is of type System.Address. 11

Address may be specified for stand-alone objects and for program units via an attribute_definition_clause. 12

Erroneous Execution

If an Address is specified, it is the programmer's responsibility to ensure that the address is valid; otherwise, program execution is erroneous. 13

Implementation Advice

For an array X, X'Address should point at the first component of the array, and not at the array bounds. 14

The recommended level of support for the Address attribute is: 15

- X'Address should produce a useful result if X is an object that is aliased or of a by-reference type, or is an entity whose Address has been specified. 16

- An implementation should support Address clauses for imported subprograms. 17

- Objects (including subcomponents) that are aliased or of a by-reference type should be allocated on storage element boundaries. 18

- If the Address of an object is specified, or it is imported or exported, then the implementation should not perform optimizations based on assumptions of no aliases. 19

NOTES
1 The specification of a link name in a pragma Export (see B.1) for a subprogram or object is an alternative to explicit specification of its link-time address, allowing a link-time directive to place the subprogram or object within memory. 20

2 The rules for the Size attribute imply, for an aliased object X, that if X'Size = Storage_Unit, then X'Address points at a storage element containing all of the bits of X, and only the bits of X. 21

Static Semantics

For a prefix X that denotes a subtype or object: 22/1

X'Alignment   The Address of an object that is allocated under control of the implementation is an integral multiple of the Alignment of the object (that is, the Address modulo the Alignment is zero). The offset of a record component is a multiple of the Alignment of the component. For an object that is not allocated under control of the implementation (that is, one that is 23 imported, that is allocated by a user-defined allocator, whose Address has been specified, or is designated by an access value returned by an instance of Unchecked_Conversion), the implementation may assume that the Address is an integral multiple of its Alignment. The implementation shall not assume a stricter alignment.

24 The value of this attribute is of type *universal_integer*, and nonnegative; zero means that the object is not necessarily aligned on a storage element boundary.

25 Alignment may be specified for first subtypes and stand-alone objects via an attribute_definition_clause; the expression of such a clause shall be static, and its value nonnegative. If the Alignment of a subtype is specified, then the Alignment of an object of the subtype is at least as strict, unless the object's Alignment is also specified. The Alignment of an object created by an allocator is that of the designated subtype.

26 If an Alignment is specified for a composite subtype or object, this Alignment shall be equal to the least common multiple of any specified Alignments of the subcomponent subtypes, or an integer multiple thereof.

Erroneous Execution

27 Program execution is erroneous if an Address clause is given that conflicts with the Alignment.

28 If the Alignment is specified for an object that is not allocated under control of the implementation, execution is erroneous if the object is not aligned according to the Alignment.

Implementation Advice

29 The recommended level of support for the Alignment attribute for subtypes is:

30 • An implementation should support specified Alignments that are factors and multiples of the number of storage elements per word, subject to the following:

31 • An implementation need not support specified Alignments for combinations of Sizes and Alignments that cannot be easily loaded and stored by available machine instructions.

32 • An implementation need not support specified Alignments that are greater than the maximum Alignment the implementation ever returns by default.

33 The recommended level of support for the Alignment attribute for objects is:

34 • Same as above, for subtypes, but in addition:

35 • For stand-alone library-level objects of statically constrained subtypes, the implementation should support all Alignments supported by the target linker. For example, page alignment is likely to be supported for such objects, but not for subtypes.

NOTES
36 3 Alignment is a subtype-specific attribute.

37 4 The Alignment of a composite object is always equal to the least common multiple of the Alignments of its components, or a multiple thereof.

38 5 A component_clause, Component_Size clause, or a pragma Pack can override a specified Alignment.

Static Semantics

39/1 For a prefix X that denotes an object:

40 X'Size Denotes the size in bits of the representation of the object. The value of this attribute is of the type *universal_integer*.

41 Size may be specified for stand-alone objects via an attribute_definition_clause; the expression of such a clause shall be static and its value nonnegative.

Implementation Advice

The recommended level of support for the Size attribute of objects is: 42

- A Size clause should be supported for an object if the specified Size is at least as large as its subtype's Size, and corresponds to a size in storage elements that is a multiple of the object's Alignment (if the Alignment is nonzero). 43

Static Semantics

For every subtype S: 44

S'Size   If S is definite, denotes the size (in bits) that the implementation would choose for the following objects of subtype S: 45

        - A record component of subtype S when the record type is packed. 46

        - The formal parameter of an instance of Unchecked_Conversion that converts from subtype S to some other subtype. 47

        If S is indefinite, the meaning is implementation defined. The value of this attribute is of the type *universal_integer*. The Size of an object is at least as large as that of its subtype, unless the object's Size is determined by a Size clause, a component_clause, or a Component_Size clause. Size may be specified for first subtypes via an attribute_definition_clause; the expression of such a clause shall be static and its value nonnegative. 48

Implementation Requirements

In an implementation, Boolean'Size shall be 1. 49

Implementation Advice

If the Size of a subtype is specified, and allows for efficient independent addressability (see 9.10) on the target architecture, then the Size of the following objects of the subtype should equal the Size of the subtype: 50

- Aliased objects (including components). 51

- Unaliased components, unless the Size of the component is determined by a component_clause or Component_Size clause. 52

A Size clause on a composite subtype should not affect the internal layout of components. 53

The recommended level of support for the Size attribute of subtypes is: 54

- The Size (if not specified) of a static discrete or fixed point subtype should be the number of bits needed to represent each value belonging to the subtype using an unbiased representation, leaving space for a sign bit only if the subtype contains negative values. If such a subtype is a first subtype, then an implementation should support a specified Size for it that reflects this representation. 55

- For a subtype implemented with levels of indirection, the Size should include the size of the pointers, but not the size of what they point at. 56

NOTES

6 Size is a subtype-specific attribute. 57

7 A component_clause or Component_Size clause can override a specified Size. A pragma Pack cannot. 58

Static Semantics

For a prefix T that denotes a task object (after any implicit dereference): 59/1

60   T'Storage_Size

> Denotes the number of storage elements reserved for the task. The value of this attribute is of the type *universal_integer*. The Storage_Size includes the size of the task's stack, if any. The language does not specify whether or not it includes other storage associated with the task (such as the "task control block" used by some implementations.) If a pragma Storage_Size is given, the value of the Storage_Size attribute is at least the value specified in the pragma.

61   A pragma Storage_Size specifies the amount of storage to be reserved for the execution of a task.

Syntax

62   The form of a pragma Storage_Size is as follows:

63   **pragma** Storage_Size(expression);

64   A pragma Storage_Size is allowed only immediately within a task_definition.

Name Resolution Rules

65   The expression of a pragma Storage_Size is expected to be of any integer type.

Dynamic Semantics

66   A pragma Storage_Size is elaborated when an object of the type defined by the immediately enclosing task_definition is created. For the elaboration of a pragma Storage_Size, the expression is evaluated; the Storage_Size attribute of the newly created task object is at least the value of the expression.

67   At the point of task object creation, or upon task activation, Storage_Error is raised if there is insufficient free storage to accommodate the requested Storage_Size.

Static Semantics

68/1   For a prefix X that denotes an array subtype or array object (after any implicit dereference):

69   X'Component_Size

> Denotes the size in bits of components of the type of X. The value of this attribute is of type *universal_integer*.

70   > Component_Size may be specified for array types via an attribute_definition_clause; the expression of such a clause shall be static, and its value nonnegative.

Implementation Advice

71   The recommended level of support for the Component_Size attribute is:

72   • An implementation need not support specified Component_Sizes that are less than the Size of the component subtype.

73   • An implementation should support specified Component_Sizes that are factors and multiples of the word size. For such Component_Sizes, the array should contain no gaps between components. For other Component_Sizes (if supported), the array should contain no gaps between components when packing is also specified; the implementation should forbid this combination in cases where it cannot support a no-gaps representation.

Static Semantics

73.1/1   The following operational attribute is defined: External_Tag.

74/1   For every subtype S of a tagged type *T* (specific or class-wide):

S'External_Tag   75/1

S'External_Tag denotes an external string representation for S'Tag; it is of the predefined
type String. External_Tag may be specified for a specific tagged type via an
attribute_definition_clause; the expression of such a clause shall be static. The default
external tag representation is implementation defined. See 3.9.2 and 13.13.2. The value of
External_Tag is never inherited; the default value is always used unless a new value is
directly specified for a type.

Implementation Requirements

In an implementation, the default external tag for each specific tagged type declared in a partition shall be   76
distinct, so long as the type is declared outside an instance of a generic body. If the compilation unit in
which a given tagged type is declared, and all compilation units on which it semantically depends, are the
same in two different partitions, then the external tag for the type shall be the same in the two partitions.
What it means for a compilation unit to be the same in two different partitions is implementation defined.
At a minimum, if the compilation unit is not recompiled between building the two different partitions that
include it, the compilation unit is considered the same in the two partitions.

NOTES
8 The following language-defined attributes are specifiable, at least for some of the kinds of entities to which they apply: 77
Address, Size, Component_Size, Alignment, External_Tag, Small, Bit_Order, Storage_Pool, Storage_Size, Write,
Output, Read, Input, and Machine_Radix.

9 It follows from the general rules in 13.1 that if one writes ''**for** X'Size **use** Y;'' then the X'Size attribute_reference will   78
return Y (assuming the implementation allows the Size clause). The same is true for all of the specifiable attributes
except Storage_Size.

Examples

Examples of attribute definition clauses: 79

```
Byte : constant := 8;                                                                                    80
Page : constant := 2**12;
```

```
type Medium is range 0 .. 65_000;                                                                        81
for Medium'Size use 2*Byte;
for Medium'Alignment use 2;
Device_Register : Medium;
for Device_Register'Size use Medium'Size;
for Device_Register'Address use
System.Storage_Elements.To_Address(16#FFFF_0020#);
```

```
type Short is delta 0.01 range -100.0 .. 100.0;                                                          82
for Short'Size use 15;
```

```
for Car_Name'Storage_Size use -- specify access type's storage pool size                                83
       2000*((Car'Size/System.Storage_Unit) +1); -- approximately 2000 cars
```

```
function My_Read(Stream : access Ada.Streams.Root_Stream_Type'Class)                                    84
   return T;
for T'Read use My_Read; -- see 13.13.2
```

NOTES
10 *Notes on the examples:* In the Size clause for Short, fifteen bits is the minimum necessary, since the type definition   85
requires Short'Small <= 2**(–7).

13.4 Enumeration Representation Clauses

An enumeration_representation_clause specifies the internal codes for enumeration literals.   1

Syntax

2 enumeration_representation_clause ::=
    for *first_subtype*_local_name **use** enumeration_aggregate;

3 enumeration_aggregate ::= array_aggregate

Name Resolution Rules

4 The enumeration_aggregate shall be written as a one-dimensional array_aggregate, for which the index subtype is the unconstrained subtype of the enumeration type, and each component expression is expected to be of any integer type.

Legality Rules

5 The *first_subtype*_local_name of an enumeration_representation_clause shall denote an enumeration subtype.

6 The expressions given in the array_aggregate shall be static, and shall specify distinct integer codes for each value of the enumeration type; the associated integer codes shall satisfy the predefined ordering relation of the type.

Static Semantics

7 An enumeration_representation_clause specifies the *coding* aspect of representation. The coding consists of the *internal code* for each enumeration literal, that is, the integral value used internally to represent each literal.

Implementation Requirements

8 For nonboolean enumeration types, if the coding is not specified for the type, then for each value of the type, the internal code shall be equal to its position number.

Implementation Advice

9 The recommended level of support for enumeration_representation_clauses is:

10 • An implementation should support at least the internal codes in the range System.Min_Int..System.Max_Int. An implementation need not support enumeration_-representation_clauses for boolean types.

NOTES

11/1 11 Unchecked_Conversion may be used to query the internal codes used for an enumeration type. The attributes of the type, such as Succ, Pred, and Pos, are unaffected by the enumeration_representation_clause. For example, Pos always returns the position number, *not* the internal integer code that might have been specified in a enumeration_representation_clause.

Examples

12 *Example of an enumeration representation clause:*

13   **type** Mix_Code **is** (ADD, SUB, MUL, LDA, STA, STZ);

14   **for** Mix_Code **use**
        (ADD => 1, SUB => 2, MUL => 3, LDA => 8, STA => 24, STZ =>33);

13.5 Record Layout

1 The *(record) layout* aspect of representation consists of the *storage places* for some or all components, that is, storage place attributes of the components. The layout can be specified with a record_representation_-clause.

13.5.1 Record Representation Clauses

A record_representation_clause specifies the storage representation of records and record extensions,   1
that is, the order, position, and size of components (including discriminants, if any).

Syntax

record_representation_clause ::=   2
    for *first_subtype*_local_name **use**
      record [mod_clause]
        {component_clause}
      end record;

component_clause ::=   3
    *component*_local_name **at** position **range** first_bit .. last_bit;

position ::= *static*_expression   4

first_bit ::= *static*_simple_expression   5

last_bit ::= *static*_simple_expression   6

Name Resolution Rules

Each position, first_bit, and last_bit is expected to be of any integer type.   7

Legality Rules

The *first_subtype*_local_name of a record_representation_clause shall denote a specific nonlimited   8
record or record extension subtype.

If the *component*_local_name is a direct_name, the local_name shall denote a component of the type. For   9
a record extension, the component shall not be inherited, and shall not be a discriminant that corresponds
to a discriminant of the parent type. If the *component*_local_name has an attribute_designator, the
direct_name of the local_name shall denote either the declaration of the type or a component of the type,
and the attribute_designator shall denote an implementation-defined implicit component of the type.

The position, first_bit, and last_bit shall be static expressions. The value of position and first_bit shall be   10
nonnegative. The value of last_bit shall be no less than first_bit − 1.

At most one component_clause is allowed for each component of the type, including for each   11
discriminant (component_clauses may be given for some, all, or none of the components). Storage places
within a component_list shall not overlap, unless they are for components in distinct variants of the same
variant_part.

A name that denotes a component of a type is not allowed within a record_representation_clause for the   12
type, except as the *component*_local_name of a component_clause.

Static Semantics

A record_representation_clause (without the mod_clause) specifies the layout. The storage place   13
attributes (see 13.5.2) are taken from the values of the position, first_bit, and last_bit expressions after
normalizing those values so that first_bit is less than Storage_Unit.

A record_representation_clause for a record extension does not override the layout of the parent part; if   14
the layout was specified for the parent type, it is inherited by the record extension.

Implementation Permissions

15 An implementation may generate implementation-defined components (for example, one containing the offset of another component). An implementation may generate names that denote such implementation-defined components; such names shall be implementation-defined attribute_references. An implementation may allow such implementation-defined names to be used in record_representation_clauses. An implementation can restrict such component_clauses in any manner it sees fit.

16 If a record_representation_clause is given for an untagged derived type, the storage place attributes for all of the components of the derived type may differ from those of the corresponding components of the parent type, even for components whose storage place is not specified explicitly in the record_-representation_clause.

Implementation Advice

17 The recommended level of support for record_representation_clauses is:

18 • An implementation should support storage places that can be extracted with a load, mask, shift sequence of machine code, and set with a load, shift, mask, store sequence, given the available machine instructions and run-time model.

19 • A storage place should be supported if its size is equal to the Size of the component subtype, and it starts and ends on a boundary that obeys the Alignment of the component subtype.

20 • If the default bit ordering applies to the declaration of a given type, then for a component whose subtype's Size is less than the word size, any storage place that does not cross an aligned word boundary should be supported.

21 • An implementation may reserve a storage place for the tag field of a tagged type, and disallow other components from overlapping that place.

22 • An implementation need not support a component_clause for a component of an extension part if the storage place is not after the storage places of all components of the parent type, whether or not those storage places had been specified.

NOTES

23 12 If no component_clause is given for a component, then the choice of the storage place for the component is left to the implementation. If component_clauses are given for all components, the record_representation_clause completely specifies the representation of the type and will be obeyed exactly by the implementation.

Examples

24 *Example of specifying the layout of a record type:*

25 ```
Word : constant := 4;   -- storage element is byte, 4 bytes per word
```

26 ```
type State          is (A,M,W,P);
type Mode           is (Fix, Dec, Exp, Signif);
```

27 ```
type Byte_Mask   is array (0..7) of Boolean;
type State_Mask   is array (State) of Boolean;
type Mode_Mask   is array (Mode) of Boolean;
```

28 ```
type Program_Status_Word is
  record
        System_Mask        : Byte_Mask;
        Protection_Key     : Integer range 0 .. 3;
        Machine_State      : State_Mask;
        Interrupt_Cause    : Interruption_Code;
        Ilc                : Integer range 0 .. 3;
        Cc                 : Integer range 0 .. 3;
        Program_Mask       : Mode_Mask;
        Inst_Address       : Address;
  end record;
```

```
for Program_Status_Word use                                          29
  record
      System_Mask        at 0*Word range 0   .. 7;
      Protection_Key     at 0*Word range 10  .. 11;  -- bits 8,9 unused
      Machine_State      at 0*Word range 12  .. 15;
      Interrupt_Cause    at 0*Word range 16  .. 31;
      Ilc                at 1*Word range 0   .. 1;   -- second word
      Cc                 at 1*Word range 2   .. 3;
      Program_Mask       at 1*Word range 4   .. 7;
      Inst_Address       at 1*Word range 8   .. 31;
  end record;
for Program_Status_Word'Size use 8*System.Storage_Unit;              30
for Program_Status_Word'Alignment use 8;
```

NOTES

13 *Note on the example:* The record_representation_clause defines the record layout. The Size clause guarantees that   31
(at least) eight storage elements are used for objects of the type. The Alignment clause guarantees that aliased, imported,
or exported objects of the type will have addresses divisible by eight.

13.5.2 Storage Place Attributes

Static Semantics

For a component C of a composite, non-array object R, the *storage place attributes* are defined: 1

R.C'Position   Denotes the same value as R.C'Address – R'Address. The value of this attribute is of the   2
                type *universal_integer*.

R.C'First_Bit   3
                Denotes the offset, from the start of the first of the storage elements occupied by C, of the
                first bit occupied by C. This offset is measured in bits. The first bit of a storage element is
                numbered zero. The value of this attribute is of the type *universal_integer*.

R.C'Last_Bit   4
                Denotes the offset, from the start of the first of the storage elements occupied by C, of the
                last bit occupied by C. This offset is measured in bits. The value of this attribute is of the
                type *universal_integer*.

Implementation Advice

If a component is represented using some form of pointer (such as an offset) to the actual data of the   5
component, and this data is contiguous with the rest of the object, then the storage place attributes should
reflect the place of the actual data, not the pointer. If a component is allocated discontiguously from the
rest of the object, then a warning should be generated upon reference to one of its storage place attributes.

13.5.3 Bit Ordering

The Bit_Order attribute specifies the interpretation of the storage place attributes.   1

Static Semantics

A bit ordering is a method of interpreting the meaning of the storage place attributes. High_Order_First   2
(known in the vernacular as ''big endian'') means that the first bit of a storage element (bit 0) is the most
significant bit (interpreting the sequence of bits that represent a component as an unsigned integer value).
Low_Order_First (known in the vernacular as ''little endian'') means the opposite: the first bit is the least
significant.

For every specific record subtype S, the following attribute is defined: 3

Record Representation Clauses **13.5.1**

4   S'Bit_Order   Denotes the bit ordering for the type of S. The value of this attribute is of type System.Bit_Order. Bit_Order may be specified for specific record types via an attribute_definition_clause; the expression of such a clause shall be static.

5   If Word_Size = Storage_Unit, the default bit ordering is implementation defined. If Word_Size > Storage_Unit, the default bit ordering is the same as the ordering of storage elements in a word, when interpreted as an integer.

6   The storage place attributes of a component of a type are interpreted according to the bit ordering of the type.

Implementation Advice

7   The recommended level of support for the nondefault bit ordering is:

8   • If Word_Size = Storage_Unit, then the implementation should support the nondefault bit ordering in addition to the default bit ordering.

13.6 Change of Representation

1   A type_conversion (see 4.6) can be used to convert between two different representations of the same array or record. To convert an array from one representation to another, two array types need to be declared with matching component subtypes, and convertible index types. If one type has packing specified and the other does not, then explicit conversion can be used to pack or unpack an array.

2   To convert a record from one representation to another, two record types with a common ancestor type need to be declared, with no inherited subprograms. Distinct representations can then be specified for the record types, and explicit conversion between the types can be used to effect a change in representation.

Examples

3   *Example of change of representation:*

4   *-- Packed_Descriptor and Descriptor are two different types*
    -- with identical characteristics, apart from their
    -- representation

5   ```
type Descriptor is
     record
         -- components of a descriptor
     end record;
```

6    ```
type Packed_Descriptor is new Descriptor;
```

7   ```
for Packed_Descriptor use
     record
         -- component clauses for some or for all components
     end record;
```

8    *-- Change of representation can now be accomplished by explicit type conversions:*

9    ```
D : Descriptor;
P : Packed_Descriptor;
```

10   ```
P := Packed_Descriptor(D);   -- pack D
D := Descriptor(P);   -- unpack P
```

## 13.7 The Package System

1    For each implementation there is a library package called System which includes the definitions of certain configuration-dependent characteristics.
```

Static Semantics

The following language-defined library package exists: 2

3

```ada
package System is
    pragma Preelaborate(System);

    type Name is implementation-defined-enumeration-type;
    System_Name : constant Name := implementation-defined;

    -- System-Dependent Named Numbers:

    Min_Int               : constant := root_integer'First;
    Max_Int               : constant := root_integer'Last;

    Max_Binary_Modulus    : constant := implementation-defined;
    Max_Nonbinary_Modulus : constant := implementation-defined;

    Max_Base_Digits       : constant := root_real'Digits;
    Max_Digits            : constant := implementation-defined;

    Max_Mantissa          : constant := implementation-defined;
    Fine_Delta            : constant := implementation-defined;

    Tick                  : constant := implementation-defined;

    -- Storage-related Declarations:

    type Address is implementation-defined;
    Null_Address : constant Address;

    Storage_Unit : constant := implementation-defined;
    Word_Size    : constant := implementation-defined * Storage_Unit;
    Memory_Size  : constant := implementation-defined;

    -- Address Comparison:
    function "<" (Left, Right : Address) return Boolean;
    function "<="(Left, Right : Address) return Boolean;
    function ">" (Left, Right : Address) return Boolean;
    function ">="(Left, Right : Address) return Boolean;
    function "=" (Left, Right : Address) return Boolean;
--  function "/=" (Left, Right : Address) return Boolean;
    -- "/=" is implicitly defined
    pragma Convention(Intrinsic, "<");
    ... -- and so on for all language-defined subprograms in this package

    -- Other System-Dependent Declarations:
    type Bit_Order is (High_Order_First, Low_Order_First);
    Default_Bit_Order : constant Bit_Order;

    -- Priority-related declarations (see D.1):
    subtype Any_Priority is Integer range implementation-defined;
    subtype Priority is Any_Priority range Any_Priority'First ..
            implementation-defined;
    subtype Interrupt_Priority is Any_Priority range Priority'Last+1 ..
            Any_Priority'Last;

    Default_Priority : constant Priority :=
            (Priority'First + Priority'Last)/2;

private
    ... -- not specified by the language
end System;
```

4

5

6

7

8

9

10

11

12

13

14

15

16

17

18

Name is an enumeration subtype. Values of type Name are the names of alternative machine configurations 19
handled by the implementation. System_Name represents the current machine configuration.

The named numbers Fine_Delta and Tick are of the type *universal_real*; the others are of the type 20
universal_integer.

The meanings of the named numbers are: 21

22 Min_Int   The smallest (most negative) value allowed for the expressions of a signed_integer_type_-definition.

23 Max_Int   The largest (most positive) value allowed for the expressions of a signed_integer_type_-definition.

24 Max_Binary_Modulus
            A power of two such that it, and all lesser positive powers of two, are allowed as the modulus of a modular_type_definition.

25 Max_Nonbinary_Modulus
            A value such that it, and all lesser positive integers, are allowed as the modulus of a modular_type_definition.

26 Max_Base_Digits
            The largest value allowed for the requested decimal precision in a floating_point_definition.

27 Max_Digits   The largest value allowed for the requested decimal precision in a floating_point_definition that has no real_range_specification. Max_Digits is less than or equal to Max_Base_Digits.

28 Max_Mantissa
            The largest possible number of binary digits in the mantissa of machine numbers of a user-defined ordinary fixed point type. (The mantissa is defined in Annex G.)

29 Fine_Delta   The smallest delta allowed in an ordinary_fixed_point_definition that has the real_range_-specification **range** −1.0 .. 1.0.

30 Tick   A period in seconds approximating the real time interval during which the value of Calendar.Clock remains constant.

31 Storage_Unit
            The number of bits per storage element.

32 Word_Size   The number of bits per word.

33 Memory_Size An implementation-defined value that is intended to reflect the memory size of the configuration in storage elements.

34 Address is of a definite, nonlimited type. Address represents machine addresses capable of addressing individual storage elements. Null_Address is an address that is distinct from the address of any object or program unit.

35 See 13.5.3 for an explanation of Bit_Order and Default_Bit_Order.

Implementation Permissions

36 An implementation may add additional implementation-defined declarations to package System and its children. However, it is usually better for the implementation to provide additional functionality via implementation-defined children of System. Package System may be declared pure.

Implementation Advice

37 Address should be a private type.

NOTES
38 14 There are also some language-defined child packages of System defined elsewhere.

13.7.1 The Package System.Storage_Elements

Static Semantics

The following language-defined library package exists: 1

```ada
package System.Storage_Elements is                                    2
   pragma Preelaborate(System.Storage_Elements);

   type Storage_Offset is range implementation-defined;               3

   subtype Storage_Count is Storage_Offset range 0..Storage_Offset'Last;  4

   type Storage_Element is mod implementation-defined;                5
   for Storage_Element'Size use Storage_Unit;
   type Storage_Array is array
      (Storage_Offset range <>) of aliased Storage_Element;
   for Storage_Array'Component_Size use Storage_Unit;

   -- Address Arithmetic:                                             6

   function "+"(Left : Address; Right : Storage_Offset)              7
      return Address;
   function "+"(Left : Storage_Offset; Right : Address)
      return Address;
   function "-"(Left : Address; Right : Storage_Offset)
      return Address;
   function "-"(Left, Right : Address)
      return Storage_Offset;

   function "mod"(Left : Address; Right : Storage_Offset)           8
      return Storage_Offset;

   -- Conversion to/from integers:                                   9

   type Integer_Address is implementation-defined;                   10
   function To_Address(Value : Integer_Address) return Address;
   function To_Integer(Value : Address) return Integer_Address;

   pragma Convention(Intrinsic, "+");                                11
      -- ...and so on for all language-defined subprograms declared in this package.
end System.Storage_Elements;
```

Storage_Element represents a storage element. Storage_Offset represents an offset in storage elements.   12
Storage_Count represents a number of storage elements. Storage_Array represents a contiguous sequence
of storage elements.

Integer_Address is a (signed or modular) integer subtype. To_Address and To_Integer convert back and   13
forth between this type and Address.

Implementation Requirements

Storage_Offset'Last shall be greater than or equal to Integer'Last or the largest possible storage offset,   14
whichever is smaller. Storage_Offset'First shall be <= (–Storage_Offset'Last).

Implementation Permissions

Package System.Storage_Elements may be declared pure.   15

Implementation Advice

Operations in System and its children should reflect the target environment semantics as closely as is   16
reasonable. For example, on most machines, it makes sense for address arithmetic to "wrap around."
Operations that do not make sense should raise Program_Error.

13.7.2 The Package System.Address_To_Access_Conversions

Static Semantics

1   The following language-defined generic library package exists:

2
```
generic
    type Object(<>) is limited private;
package System.Address_To_Access_Conversions is
    pragma Preelaborate(Address_To_Access_Conversions);
```

3
```
    type Object_Pointer is access all Object;
    function To_Pointer(Value : Address) return Object_Pointer;
    function To_Address(Value : Object_Pointer) return Address;
```

4
```
    pragma Convention(Intrinsic, To_Pointer);
    pragma Convention(Intrinsic, To_Address);
end System.Address_To_Access_Conversions;
```

5   The To_Pointer and To_Address subprograms convert back and forth between values of types
Object_Pointer and Address. To_Pointer(X'Address) is equal to X'Unchecked_Access for any X that
allows Unchecked_Access. To_Pointer(Null_Address) returns **null**. For other addresses, the behavior is
unspecified. To_Address(**null**) returns Null_Address (for **null** of the appropriate type). To_Address(Y),
where Y /= **null**, returns Y.**all**'Address.

Implementation Permissions

6   An implementation may place restrictions on instantiations of Address_To_Access_Conversions.

13.8 Machine Code Insertions

1   A machine code insertion can be achieved by a call to a subprogram whose sequence_of_statements
contains code_statements.

Syntax

2   code_statement ::= qualified_expression;

3   A code_statement is only allowed in the handled_sequence_of_statements of a subprogram_-
body. If a subprogram_body contains any code_statements, then within this subprogram_body the
only allowed form of statement is a code_statement (labeled or not), the only allowed declarative_-
items are use_clauses, and no exception_handler is allowed (comments and pragmas are allowed as
usual).

Name Resolution Rules

4   The qualified_expression is expected to be of any type.

Legality Rules

5   The qualified_expression shall be of a type declared in package System.Machine_Code.

6   A code_statement shall appear only within the scope of a with_clause that mentions package
System.Machine_Code.

Static Semantics

7   The contents of the library package System.Machine_Code (if provided) are implementation defined. The
meaning of code_statements is implementation defined. Typically, each qualified_expression represents a
machine instruction or assembly directive.

Implementation Permissions

An implementation may place restrictions on code_statements. An implementation is not required to provide package System.Machine_Code. 8

NOTES

15 An implementation may provide implementation-defined pragmas specifying register conventions and calling conventions. 9

16 Machine code functions are exempt from the rule that a return_statement is required. In fact, return_statements are forbidden, since only code_statements are allowed. 10

17 Intrinsic subprograms (see 6.3.1, ''Conformance Rules'') can also be used to achieve machine code insertions. Interface to assembly language can be achieved using the features in Annex B, ''Interface to Other Languages''. 11

Examples

Example of a code statement: 12

```
M : Mask;
procedure Set_Mask; pragma Inline(Set_Mask);
```
13

```
procedure Set_Mask is
   use System.Machine_Code;  -- assume "with System.Machine_Code;" appears somewhere above
begin
   SI_Format'(Code => SSM, B => M'Base_Reg, D => M'Disp);
   -- Base_Reg and Disp are implementation-defined attributes
end Set_Mask;
```
14

13.9 Unchecked Type Conversions

An unchecked type conversion can be achieved by a call to an instance of the generic function Unchecked_Conversion. 1

Static Semantics

The following language-defined generic library function exists: 2

```
generic
   type Source(<>) is limited private;
   type Target(<>) is limited private;
function Ada.Unchecked_Conversion(S : Source) return Target;
pragma Convention(Intrinsic, Ada.Unchecked_Conversion);
pragma Pure(Ada.Unchecked_Conversion);
```
3

Dynamic Semantics

The size of the formal parameter S in an instance of Unchecked_Conversion is that of its subtype. This is the actual subtype passed to Source, except when the actual is an unconstrained composite subtype, in which case the subtype is constrained by the bounds or discriminants of the value of the actual expression passed to S. 4

If all of the following are true, the effect of an unchecked conversion is to return the value of an object of the target subtype whose representation is the same as that of the source object S: 5

- S'Size = Target'Size. 6

- S'Alignment = Target'Alignment. 7

- The target subtype is not an unconstrained composite subtype. 8

- S and the target subtype both have a contiguous representation. 9

- The representation of S is a representation of an object of the target subtype. 10

11   Otherwise, the effect is implementation defined; in particular, the result can be abnormal (see 13.9.1).

Implementation Permissions

12   An implementation may return the result of an unchecked conversion by reference, if the Source type is not a by-copy type. In this case, the result of the unchecked conversion represents simply a different (read-only) view of the operand of the conversion.

13   An implementation may place restrictions on Unchecked_Conversion.

Implementation Advice

14   The Size of an array object should not include its bounds; hence, the bounds should not be part of the converted data.

15   The implementation should not generate unnecessary run-time checks to ensure that the representation of S is a representation of the target type. It should take advantage of the permission to return by reference when possible. Restrictions on unchecked conversions should be avoided unless required by the target environment.

16   The recommended level of support for unchecked conversions is:

17   • Unchecked conversions should be supported and should be reversible in the cases where this clause defines the result. To enable meaningful use of unchecked conversion, a contiguous representation should be used for elementary subtypes, for statically constrained array subtypes whose component subtype is one of the subtypes described in this paragraph, and for record subtypes without discriminants whose component subtypes are described in this paragraph.

13.9.1 Data Validity

1   Certain actions that can potentially lead to erroneous execution are not directly erroneous, but instead can cause objects to become *abnormal*. Subsequent uses of abnormal objects can be erroneous.

2   A scalar object can have an *invalid representation*, which means that the object's representation does not represent any value of the object's subtype. The primary cause of invalid representations is uninitialized variables.

3   Abnormal objects and invalid representations are explained in this subclause.

Dynamic Semantics

4   When an object is first created, and any explicit or default initializations have been performed, the object and all of its parts are in the *normal* state. Subsequent operations generally leave them normal. However, an object or part of an object can become *abnormal* in the following ways:

5   • An assignment to the object is disrupted due to an abort (see 9.8) or due to the failure of a language-defined check (see 11.6).

6   • The object is not scalar, and is passed to an **in out** or **out** parameter of an imported procedure or language-defined input procedure, if after return from the procedure the representation of the parameter does not represent a value of the parameter's subtype.

7   Whether or not an object actually becomes abnormal in these cases is not specified. An abnormal object becomes normal again upon successful completion of an assignment to the object as a whole.

Erroneous Execution

It is erroneous to evaluate a primary that is a name denoting an abnormal object, or to evaluate a prefix that denotes an abnormal object.　8

Bounded (Run-Time) Errors

If the representation of a scalar object does not represent a value of the object's subtype (perhaps because the object was not initialized), the object is said to have an *invalid representation*. It is a bounded error to evaluate the value of such an object. If the error is detected, either Constraint_Error or Program_Error is raised. Otherwise, execution continues using the invalid representation. The rules of the language outside this subclause assume that all objects have valid representations. The semantics of operations on invalid representations are as follows:　9

- If the representation of the object represents a value of the object's type, the value of the type is used.　10

- If the representation of the object does not represent a value of the object's type, the semantics of operations on such representations is implementation-defined, but does not by itself lead to erroneous or unpredictable execution, or to other objects becoming abnormal.　11

Erroneous Execution

A call to an imported function or an instance of Unchecked_Conversion is erroneous if the result is scalar, and the result object has an invalid representation.　12

The dereference of an access value is erroneous if it does not designate an object of an appropriate type or a subprogram with an appropriate profile, if it designates a nonexistent object, or if it is an access-to-variable value that designates a constant object. Such an access value can exist, for example, because of Unchecked_Deallocation, Unchecked_Access, or Unchecked_Conversion.　13

NOTES
18 Objects can become abnormal due to other kinds of actions that directly update the object's representation; such actions are generally considered directly erroneous, however.　14

13.9.2 The Valid Attribute

The Valid attribute can be used to check the validity of data produced by unchecked conversion, input, interface to foreign languages, and the like.　1

Static Semantics

For a prefix X that denotes a scalar object (after any implicit dereference), the following attribute is defined:　2

X'Valid　　　Yields True if and only if the object denoted by X is normal and has a valid representation. The value of this attribute is of the predefined type Boolean.　3

NOTES
19 Invalid data can be created in the following cases (not counting erroneous or unpredictable execution):　4

- an uninitialized scalar object,　5
- the result of an unchecked conversion,　6
- input,　7
- interface to another language (including machine code),　8
- aborting an assignment,　9
- disrupting an assignment due to the failure of a language-defined check (see 11.6), and　10
- use of an object whose Address has been specified.　11

12 20 X'Valid is not considered to be a read of X; hence, it is not an error to check the validity of invalid data.

13.10 Unchecked Access Value Creation

1   The attribute Unchecked_Access is used to create access values in an unsafe manner — the programmer is responsible for preventing "dangling references."

Static Semantics

2   The following attribute is defined for a prefix X that denotes an aliased view of an object:

3   X'Unchecked_Access
> All rules and semantics that apply to X'Access (see 3.10.2) apply also to X'Unchecked_Access, except that, for the purposes of accessibility rules and checks, it is as if X were declared immediately within a library package.

NOTES

4   21 This attribute is provided to support the situation where a local object is to be inserted into a global linked data structure, when the programmer knows that it will always be removed from the data structure prior to exiting the object's scope. The Access attribute would be illegal in this case (see 3.10.2, "Operations of Access Types").

5   22 There is no Unchecked_Access attribute for subprograms.

13.11 Storage Management

1   Each access-to-object type has an associated storage pool. The storage allocated by an allocator comes from the pool; instances of Unchecked_Deallocation return storage to the pool. Several access types can share the same pool.

2   A storage pool is a variable of a type in the class rooted at Root_Storage_Pool, which is an abstract limited controlled type. By default, the implementation chooses a *standard storage pool* for each access type. The user may define new pool types, and may override the choice of pool for an access type by specifying Storage_Pool for the type.

Legality Rules

3   If Storage_Pool is specified for a given access type, Storage_Size shall not be specified for it.

Static Semantics

4   The following language-defined library package exists:

5
```
with Ada.Finalization;
with System.Storage_Elements;
package System.Storage_Pools is
    pragma Preelaborate(System.Storage_Pools);
```

6
```
    type Root_Storage_Pool is
        abstract new Ada.Finalization.Limited_Controlled with private;
```

7
```
    procedure Allocate(
        Pool : in out Root_Storage_Pool;
        Storage_Address : out Address;
        Size_In_Storage_Elements : in Storage_Elements.Storage_Count;
        Alignment : in Storage_Elements.Storage_Count) is abstract;
```

8
```
    procedure Deallocate(
        Pool : in out Root_Storage_Pool;
        Storage_Address : in Address;
        Size_In_Storage_Elements : in Storage_Elements.Storage_Count;
        Alignment : in Storage_Elements.Storage_Count) is abstract;
```

```
   function Storage_Size(Pool : Root_Storage_Pool)                          9
       return Storage_Elements.Storage_Count is abstract;

   private                                                                   10
       ... -- not specified by the language
   end System.Storage_Pools;
```

A *storage pool type* (or *pool type*) is a descendant of Root_Storage_Pool. The *elements* of a storage pool   11
are the objects allocated in the pool by allocators.

For every access subtype S, the following representation attributes are defined: 12/1

S'Storage_Pool   13

             Denotes the storage pool of the type of S. The type of this attribute is Root_Storage_-
             Pool'Class.

S'Storage_Size   14

             Yields the result of calling Storage_Size(S'Storage_Pool), which is intended to be a
             measure of the number of storage elements reserved for the pool. The type of this attribute
             is *universal_integer*.

Storage_Size or Storage_Pool may be specified for a non-derived access-to-object type via an attribute_-   15
definition_clause; the name in a Storage_Pool clause shall denote a variable.

An allocator of type T allocates storage from T's storage pool. If the storage pool is a user-defined object,   16
then the storage is allocated by calling Allocate, passing T'Storage_Pool as the Pool parameter. The
Size_In_Storage_Elements parameter indicates the number of storage elements to be allocated, and is no
more than D'Max_Size_In_Storage_Elements, where D is the designated subtype. The Alignment
parameter is D'Alignment. The result returned in the Storage_Address parameter is used by the allocator as
the address of the allocated storage, which is a contiguous block of memory of Size_In_Storage_Elements
storage elements. Any exception propagated by Allocate is propagated by the allocator.

If Storage_Pool is not specified for a type defined by an access_to_object_definition, then the   17
implementation chooses a standard storage pool for it in an implementation-defined manner. In this case,
the exception Storage_Error is raised by an allocator if there is not enough storage. It is implementation
defined whether or not the implementation provides user-accessible names for the standard pool type(s).

If Storage_Size is specified for an access type, then the Storage_Size of this pool is at least that requested, 18
and the storage for the pool is reclaimed when the master containing the declaration of the access type is
left. If the implementation cannot satisfy the request, Storage_Error is raised at the point of the attribute_-
definition_clause. If neither Storage_Pool nor Storage_Size are specified, then the meaning of
Storage_Size is implementation defined.

If Storage_Pool is specified for an access type, then the specified pool is used.   19

The effect of calling Allocate and Deallocate for a standard storage pool directly (rather than implicitly via   20
an allocator or an instance of Unchecked_Deallocation) is unspecified.

Erroneous Execution

If Storage_Pool is specified for an access type, then if Allocate can satisfy the request, it should allocate a   21
contiguous block of memory, and return the address of the first storage element in Storage_Address. The
block should contain Size_In_Storage_Elements storage elements, and should be aligned according to
Alignment. The allocated storage should not be used for any other purpose while the pool element remains
in existence. If the request cannot be satisfied, then Allocate should propagate an exception (such as
Storage_Error). If Allocate behaves in any other manner, then the program execution is erroneous.

Documentation Requirements

22 An implementation shall document the set of values that a user-defined Allocate procedure needs to accept for the Alignment parameter. An implementation shall document how the standard storage pool is chosen, and how storage is allocated by standard storage pools.

Implementation Advice

23 An implementation should document any cases in which it dynamically allocates heap storage for a purpose other than the evaluation of an allocator.

24 A default (implementation-provided) storage pool for an access-to-constant type should not have overhead to support deallocation of individual objects.

25 A storage pool for an anonymous access type should be created at the point of an allocator for the type, and be reclaimed when the designated object becomes inaccessible.

NOTES

26 23 A user-defined storage pool type can be obtained by extending the Root_Storage_Pool type, and overriding the primitive subprograms Allocate, Deallocate, and Storage_Size. A user-defined storage pool can then be obtained by declaring an object of the type extension. The user can override Initialize and Finalize if there is any need for non-trivial initialization and finalization for a user-defined pool type. For example, Finalize might reclaim blocks of storage that are allocated separately from the pool object itself.

27 24 The writer of the user-defined allocation and deallocation procedures, and users of allocators for the associated access type, are responsible for dealing with any interactions with tasking. In particular:

28 • If the allocators are used in different tasks, they require mutual exclusion.

29 • If they are used inside protected objects, they cannot block.

30 • If they are used by interrupt handlers (see C.3, ''Interrupt Support''), the mutual exclusion mechanism has to work properly in that context.

31 25 The primitives Allocate, Deallocate, and Storage_Size are declared as abstract (see 3.9.3), and therefore they have to be overridden when a new (non-abstract) storage pool type is declared.

Examples

32 To associate an access type with a storage pool object, the user first declares a pool object of some type derived from Root_Storage_Pool. Then, the user defines its Storage_Pool attribute, as follows:

33
```
Pool_Object : Some_Storage_Pool_Type;
```

34
```
type T is access Designated;
for T'Storage_Pool use Pool_Object;
```

35 Another access type may be added to an existing storage pool, via:

36
```
for T2'Storage_Pool use T'Storage_Pool;
```

37 The semantics of this is implementation defined for a standard storage pool.

38 As usual, a derivative of Root_Storage_Pool may define additional operations. For example, presuming that Mark_Release_Pool_Type has two additional operations, Mark and Release, the following is a possible use:

39/1
```
type Mark_Release_Pool_Type
    (Pool_Size : Storage_Elements.Storage_Count;
     Block_Size : Storage_Elements.Storage_Count)
        is new Root_Storage_Pool with private;
```

40
```
...
```

41
```
MR_Pool : Mark_Release_Pool_Type (Pool_Size => 2000,
                                  Block_Size => 100);
```

```
type Acc is access ...;                                                      42
for Acc'Storage_Pool use MR_Pool;
...
Mark(MR_Pool);                                                               43
... -- Allocate objects using ''new Designated(...)''.
Release(MR_Pool); -- Reclaim the storage.
```

13.11.1 The Max_Size_In_Storage_Elements Attribute

The Max_Size_In_Storage_Elements attribute is useful in writing user-defined pool types.   1

Static Semantics

For every subtype S, the following attribute is defined: 2

S'Max_Size_In_Storage_Elements   3
>   Denotes the maximum value for Size_In_Storage_Elements that will be requested via
>   Allocate for an access type whose designated subtype is S. The value of this attribute is of
>   type *universal_integer*.

13.11.2 Unchecked Storage Deallocation

Unchecked storage deallocation of an object designated by a value of an access type is achieved by a call   1
to an instance of the generic procedure Unchecked_Deallocation.

Static Semantics

The following language-defined generic library procedure exists: 2

```
generic                                                                      3
   type Object(<>) is limited private;
   type Name    is access  Object;
procedure Ada.Unchecked_Deallocation(X : in out Name);
pragma Convention(Intrinsic, Ada.Unchecked_Deallocation);
pragma Preelaborate(Ada.Unchecked_Deallocation);
```

Dynamic Semantics

Given an instance of Unchecked_Deallocation declared as follows: 4

```
procedure Free is                                                            5
   new Ada.Unchecked_Deallocation(
        object_subtype_name, access_to_variable_subtype_name);
```

Procedure Free has the following effect: 6

1. After executing Free(X), the value of X is **null**.   7

2. Free(X), when X is already equal to **null**, has no effect.   8

3. Free(X), when X is not equal to **null** first performs finalization, as described in 7.6. It then   9
   deallocates the storage occupied by the object designated by X. If the storage pool is a user-
   defined object, then the storage is deallocated by calling Deallocate, passing *access_to_-
   variable_subtype_name*'Storage_Pool as the Pool parameter. Storage_Address is the value
   returned in the Storage_Address parameter of the corresponding Allocate call. Size_In_-
   Storage_Elements and Alignment are the same values passed to the corresponding Allocate call.
   There is one exception: if the object being freed contains tasks, the object might not be
   deallocated.

After Free(X), the object designated by X, and any subcomponents thereof, no longer exist; their storage   10
can be reused for other purposes.

Bounded (Run-Time) Errors

11 It is a bounded error to free a discriminated, unterminated task object. The possible consequences are:

12 • No exception is raised.

13 • Program_Error or Tasking_Error is raised at the point of the deallocation.

14 • Program_Error or Tasking_Error is raised in the task the next time it references any of the discriminants.

15 In the first two cases, the storage for the discriminants (and for any enclosing object if it is designated by an access discriminant of the task) is not reclaimed prior to task termination.

Erroneous Execution

16 Evaluating a name that denotes a nonexistent object is erroneous. The execution of a call to an instance of Unchecked_Deallocation is erroneous if the object was created other than by an allocator for an access type whose pool is Name'Storage_Pool.

Implementation Advice

17 For a standard storage pool, Free should actually reclaim the storage.

NOTES
18 26 The rules here that refer to Free apply to any instance of Unchecked_Deallocation.

19 27 Unchecked_Deallocation cannot be instantiated for an access-to-constant type. This is implied by the rules of 12.5.4.

13.11.3 Pragma Controlled

1 Pragma Controlled is used to prevent any automatic reclamation of storage (garbage collection) for the objects created by allocators of a given access type.

Syntax

2 The form of a pragma Controlled is as follows:

3 **pragma** Controlled(*first_subtype*_local_name);

Legality Rules

4 The *first_subtype*_local_name of a pragma Controlled shall denote a non-derived access subtype.

Static Semantics

5 A pragma Controlled is a representation pragma that specifies the *controlled* aspect of representation.

6 *Garbage collection* is a process that automatically reclaims storage, or moves objects to a different address, while the objects still exist.

7 If a pragma Controlled is specified for an access type with a standard storage pool, then garbage collection is not performed for objects in that pool.

Implementation Permissions

8 An implementation need not support garbage collection, in which case, a pragma Controlled has no effect.

13.12 Pragma Restrictions

A pragma Restrictions expresses the user's intent to abide by certain restrictions. This may facilitate the construction of simpler run-time environments.   1

The form of a pragma Restrictions is as follows: 2

pragma Restrictions(restriction{, restriction});   3

restriction ::= *restriction*_identifier   4
 | *restriction_parameter*_identifier => expression

Unless otherwise specified for a particular restriction, the expression is expected to be of any integer type.   5

Unless otherwise specified for a particular restriction, the expression shall be static, and its value shall be nonnegative.   6

The set of restrictions is implementation defined.   7

A pragma Restrictions is a configuration pragma; unless otherwise specified for a particular restriction, a partition shall obey the restriction if a pragma Restrictions applies to any compilation unit included in the partition.   8

For the purpose of checking whether a partition contains constructs that violate any restriction (unless specified otherwise for a particular restriction):   8.1/1

- Generic instances are logically expanded at the point of instantiation;   8.2/1
- If an object of a type is declared or allocated and not explicitly initialized, then all expressions appearing in the definition for the type and any of its ancestors are presumed to be used;   8.3/1
- A default_expression for a formal parameter or a generic formal object is considered to be used if and only if the corresponding actual parameter is not provided in a given call or instantiation.   8.4/1

An implementation may place limitations on the values of the expression that are supported, and limitations on the supported combinations of restrictions. The consequences of violating such limitations are implementation defined.   9

An implementation is permitted to omit restriction checks for code that is recognized at compile time to be unreachable and for which no code is generated.   9.1/1

Whenever enforcement of a restriction is not required prior to execution, an implementation may nevertheless enforce the restriction prior to execution of a partition to which the restriction applies, provided that every execution of the partition would violate the restriction.   9.2/1

NOTES
28 Restrictions intended to facilitate the construction of efficient tasking run-time systems are defined in D.7. Safety- and security-related restrictions are defined in H.4.   10

11   29 An implementation has to enforce the restrictions in cases where enforcement is required, even if it chooses not to take advantage of the restrictions in terms of efficiency.

13.13 Streams

1   A *stream* is a sequence of elements comprising values from possibly different types and allowing sequential access to these values. A *stream type* is a type in the class whose root type is Streams.Root_Stream_Type. A stream type may be implemented in various ways, such as an external sequential file, an internal buffer, or a network channel.

13.13.1 The Package Streams

Static Semantics

1   The abstract type Root_Stream_Type is the root type of the class of stream types. The types in this class represent different kinds of streams. A new stream type is defined by extending the root type (or some other stream type), overriding the Read and Write operations, and optionally defining additional primitive subprograms, according to the requirements of the particular kind of stream. The predefined stream-oriented attributes like T'Read and T'Write make dispatching calls on the Read and Write procedures of the Root_Stream_Type. (User-defined T'Read and T'Write attributes can also make such calls, or can call the Read and Write attributes of other types.)

2
```
package Ada.Streams is
    pragma Pure(Streams);
```

3
```
    type Root_Stream_Type is abstract tagged limited private;
```

4/1
```
    type Stream_Element is mod implementation-defined;
    type Stream_Element_Offset is range implementation-defined;
    subtype Stream_Element_Count is
        Stream_Element_Offset range 0..Stream_Element_Offset'Last;
    type Stream_Element_Array is
        array(Stream_Element_Offset range <>) of aliased Stream_Element;
```

5
```
    procedure Read(
        Stream : in out Root_Stream_Type;
        Item   : out Stream_Element_Array;
        Last   : out Stream_Element_Offset) is abstract;
```

6
```
    procedure Write(
        Stream : in out Root_Stream_Type;
        Item   : in Stream_Element_Array) is abstract;
```

7
```
private
    ... -- not specified by the language
end Ada.Streams;
```

8   The Read operation transfers Item'Length stream elements from the specified stream to fill the array Item. The index of the last stream element transferred is returned in Last. Last is less than Item'Last only if the end of the stream is reached.

9   The Write operation appends Item to the specified stream.

Implementation Permissions

9.1/1   If Stream_Element'Size is not a multiple of System.Storage_Unit, then the components of Stream_-Element_Array need not be aliased.

NOTES
10   30 See A.12.1, "The Package Streams.Stream_IO" for an example of extending type Root_Stream_Type.

13.13.2 Stream-Oriented Attributes

The operational attributes Write, Read, Output, and Input convert values to a stream of elements and reconstruct values from a stream.   1/1

Static Semantics

For every subtype S of a specific type *T*, the following attributes are defined.   2

S'Write   S'Write denotes a procedure with the following specification: 3

```
procedure S'Write(
    Stream : access Ada.Streams.Root_Stream_Type'Class;
    Item : in T)
```
4

   S'Write writes the value of *Item* to *Stream*.   5

S'Read   S'Read denotes a procedure with the following specification: 6

```
procedure S'Read(
    Stream : access Ada.Streams.Root_Stream_Type'Class;
    Item : out T)
```
7

   S'Read reads the value of *Item* from *Stream*.   8

For untagged derived types, the Write and Read attributes of the parent type are inherited as specified in 13.1; otherwise, the default implementations of these attributes are used. The default implementations of Write and Read attributes execute as follows: 8.1/1

For elementary types, the representation in terms of stream elements is implementation defined. For composite types, the Write or Read attribute for each component is called in canonical order, which is last dimension varying fastest for an array, and positional aggregate order for a record. Bounds are not included in the stream if *T* is an array type. If *T* is a discriminated type, discriminants are included only if they have defaults. If *T* is a tagged type, the tag is not included. For type extensions, the Write or Read attribute for the parent type is called, followed by the Write or Read attribute of each component of the extension part, in canonical order. For a limited type extension, if the attribute of any ancestor type of *T* has been directly specified and the attribute of any ancestor type of the type of any of the extension components which are of a limited type has not been specified, the attribute of *T* shall be directly specified.   9/1

For every subtype S'Class of a class-wide type *T*'Class: 10

S'Class'Write   11

   S'Class'Write denotes a procedure with the following specification:

```
procedure S'Class'Write(
    Stream : access Ada.Streams.Root_Stream_Type'Class;
    Item   : in T'Class)
```
12

   Dispatches to the subprogram denoted by the Write attribute of the specific type identified by the tag of Item.   13

S'Class'Read   S'Class'Read denotes a procedure with the following specification: 14

```
procedure S'Class'Read(
    Stream : access Ada.Streams.Root_Stream_Type'Class;
    Item : out T'Class)
```
15

   Dispatches to the subprogram denoted by the Read attribute of the specific type identified by the tag of Item.   16

Implementation Advice

17   If a stream element is the same size as a storage element, then the normal in-memory representation should be used by Read and Write for scalar objects. Otherwise, Read and Write should use the smallest number of stream elements needed to represent all values in the base range of the scalar type.

Static Semantics

18   For every subtype S of a specific type *T*, the following attributes are defined.

19   S'Output   S'Output denotes a procedure with the following specification:

20
```
procedure S'Output(
    Stream : access Ada.Streams.Root_Stream_Type'Class;
    Item : in T)
```

21   S'Output writes the value of *Item* to *Stream*, including any bounds or discriminants.

22   S'Input   S'Input denotes a function with the following specification:

23
```
function S'Input(
    Stream : access Ada.Streams.Root_Stream_Type'Class)
    return T
```

24   S'Input reads and returns one value from *Stream*, using any bounds or discriminants written by a corresponding S'Output to determine how much to read.

25/1   For untagged derived types, the Output and Input attributes of the parent type are inherited as specified in 13.1; otherwise, the default implementations of these attributes are used. The default implementations of Output and Input attributes execute as follows:

26   • If *T* is an array type, S'Output first writes the bounds, and S'Input first reads the bounds. If *T* has discriminants without defaults, S'Output first writes the discriminants (using S'Write for each), and S'Input first reads the discriminants (using S'Read for each).

27   • S'Output then calls S'Write to write the value of *Item* to the stream. S'Input then creates an object (with the bounds or discriminants, if any, taken from the stream), initializes it with S'Read, and returns the value of the object.

28   For every subtype S'Class of a class-wide type *T*'Class:

29   S'Class'Output
                S'Class'Output denotes a procedure with the following specification:

30
```
procedure S'Class'Output(
    Stream : access Ada.Streams.Root_Stream_Type'Class;
    Item   : in T'Class)
```

31   First writes the external tag of *Item* to *Stream* (by calling String'Output(Tags.-External_Tag(*Item*'Tag) — see 3.9) and then dispatches to the subprogram denoted by the Output attribute of the specific type identified by the tag.

32   S'Class'Input
                S'Class'Input denotes a function with the following specification:

33
```
function S'Class'Input(
    Stream : access Ada.Streams.Root_Stream_Type'Class)
    return T'Class
```

34   First reads the external tag from *Stream* and determines the corresponding internal tag (by calling Tags.Internal_Tag(String'Input(*Stream*)) — see 3.9) and then dispatches to the subprogram denoted by the Input attribute of the specific type identified by the internal tag; returns that result.

35   In the default implementation of Read and Input for a composite type, for each scalar component that is a discriminant or whose component_declaration includes a default_expression, a check is made that the

value returned by Read for the component belongs to its subtype. Constraint_Error is raised if this check fails. For other scalar components, no check is made. For each component that is of an access type, if the implementation can detect that the value returned by Read for the component is not a value of its subtype, Constraint_Error is raised. If the value is not a value of its subtype and this error is not detected, the component has an abnormal value, and erroneous execution can result (see 13.9.1).

In the default implementation of Read and Input for a type, End_Error is raised if the end of the stream is reached before the reading of a value of the type is completed.   35.1/1

The stream-oriented attributes may be specified for any type via an attribute_definition_clause. All nonlimited types have default implementations for these operations. An attribute_reference for one of these attributes is illegal if the type is limited, unless the attribute has been specified by an attribute_-definition_clause or (for a type extension) the attribute has been specified for an ancestor type. For an attribute_definition_clause specifying one of these attributes, the subtype of the Item parameter shall be the base subtype if scalar, and the first subtype otherwise. The same rule applies to the result of the Input function.   36/1

Implementation Requirements

For every subtype S of a language-defined nonlimited specific type T, the output generated by S'Output or S'Write shall be readable by S'Input or S'Read, respectively. This rule applies across partitions if the implementation conforms to the Distributed Systems Annex.   36.1/1

NOTES
31 For a definite subtype S of a type T, only T'Write and T'Read are needed to pass an arbitrary value of the subtype through a stream. For an indefinite subtype S of a type T, T'Output and T'Input will normally be needed, since T'Write and T'Read do not pass bounds, discriminants, or tags.   37

32 User-specified attributes of S'Class are not inherited by other class-wide types descended from S.   38

Examples

Example of user-defined Write attribute: 39

```
procedure My_Write(
   Stream : access Ada.Streams.Root_Stream_Type'Class; Item :
My_Integer'Base);
for My_Integer'Write use My_Write;
```
40

13.14 Freezing Rules

This clause defines a place in the program text where each declared entity becomes "frozen." A use of an entity, such as a reference to it by name, or (for a type) an expression of the type, causes freezing of the entity in some contexts, as described below. The Legality Rules forbid certain kinds of uses of an entity in the region of text where it is frozen.   1

The *freezing* of an entity occurs at one or more places (*freezing points*) in the program text where the representation for the entity has to be fully determined. Each entity is frozen from its first freezing point to the end of the program text (given the ordering of compilation units defined in 10.1.4).   2

The end of a declarative_part, protected_body, or a declaration of a library package or generic library package, causes *freezing* of each entity declared within it, except for incomplete types. A noninstance body other than a renames-as-body causes freezing of each entity declared before it within the same declarative_part.   3/1

4/1 A construct that (explicitly or implicitly) references an entity can cause the *freezing* of the entity, as defined by subsequent paragraphs. At the place where a construct causes freezing, each name, expression, implicit_dereference, or range within the construct causes freezing:

5 • The occurrence of a generic_instantiation causes freezing; also, if a parameter of the instantiation is defaulted, the default_expression or default_name for that parameter causes freezing.

6 • The occurrence of an object_declaration that has no corresponding completion causes freezing.

7 • The declaration of a record extension causes freezing of the parent subtype.

8/1 A static expression causes freezing where it occurs. An object name or nonstatic expression causes freezing where it occurs, unless the name or expression is part of a default_expression, a default_name, or a per-object expression of a component's constraint, in which case, the freezing occurs later as part of another construct.

8.1/1 An implicit call freezes the same entities that would be frozen by an explicit call. This is true even if the implicit call is removed via implementation permissions.

8.2/1 If an expression is implicitly converted to a type or subtype T, then at the place where the expression causes freezing, T is frozen.

9 The following rules define which entities are frozen at the place where a construct causes freezing:

10 • At the place where an expression causes freezing, the type of the expression is frozen, unless the expression is an enumeration literal used as a discrete_choice of the array_aggregate of an enumeration_representation_clause.

11 • At the place where a name causes freezing, the entity denoted by the name is frozen, unless the name is a prefix of an expanded name; at the place where an object name causes freezing, the nominal subtype associated with the name is frozen.

11.1/1 • At the place where an implicit_dereference causes freezing, the nominal subtype associated with the implicit_dereference is frozen.

12 • At the place where a range causes freezing, the type of the range is frozen.

13 • At the place where an allocator causes freezing, the designated subtype of its type is frozen. If the type of the allocator is a derived type, then all ancestor types are also frozen.

14 • At the place where a callable entity is frozen, each subtype of its profile is frozen. If the callable entity is a member of an entry family, the index subtype of the family is frozen. At the place where a function call causes freezing, if a parameter of the call is defaulted, the default_-expression for that parameter causes freezing.

15 • At the place where a subtype is frozen, its type is frozen. At the place where a type is frozen, any expressions or names within the full type definition cause freezing; the first subtype, and any component subtypes, index subtypes, and parent subtype of the type are frozen as well. For a specific tagged type, the corresponding class-wide type is frozen as well. For a class-wide type, the corresponding specific type is frozen as well.

Legality Rules

16 The explicit declaration of a primitive subprogram of a tagged type shall occur before the type is frozen (see 3.9.2).

17 A type shall be completely defined before it is frozen (see 3.11.1 and 7.3).

18 The completion of a deferred constant declaration shall occur before the constant is frozen (see 7.4).

19/1 An operational or representation item that directly specifies an aspect of an entity shall appear before the entity is frozen (see 13.1).

Annex A
(normative)
Predefined Language Environment

This Annex contains the specifications of library units that shall be provided by every implementation. 1
There are three root library units: Ada, Interfaces, and System; other library units are children of these:

2/1

S. Tucker Taft et al. (Eds.): Consolidated Ada Reference Manual, LNCS 2219, pp. 259– 345, 2001.

Implementation Requirements

3   The implementation shall ensure that each language defined subprogram is reentrant in the sense that concurrent calls on the same subprogram perform as specified, so long as all parameters that could be passed by reference denote nonoverlapping objects.

Implementation Permissions

4   The implementation may restrict the replacement of language-defined compilation units. The implementation may restrict children of language-defined library units (other than Standard).

A.1 The Package Standard

1   This clause outlines the specification of the package Standard containing all predefined identifiers in the language. The corresponding package body is not specified by the language.

2   The operators that are predefined for the types declared in the package Standard are given in comments since they are implicitly declared. Italics are used for pseudo-names of anonymous types (such as *root_real*) and for undefined information (such as *implementation-defined*).

Static Semantics

3   The library package Standard has the following declaration:

4
```
package Standard is
   pragma Pure(Standard);
```

5
```
   type Boolean is (False, True);
```

6
```
   -- The predefined relational operators for this type are as follows:
```

7/1
```
   -- function "="  (Left, Right : Boolean'Base) return Boolean;
   -- function "/=" (Left, Right : Boolean'Base) return Boolean;
   -- function "<"  (Left, Right : Boolean'Base) return Boolean;
   -- function "<=" (Left, Right : Boolean'Base) return Boolean;
   -- function ">"  (Left, Right : Boolean'Base) return Boolean;
   -- function ">=" (Left, Right : Boolean'Base) return Boolean;
```

8
```
   -- The predefined logical operators and the predefined logical
   -- negation operator are as follows:
```

9/1
```
   -- function "and" (Left, Right : Boolean'Base) return Boolean;
   -- function "or"  (Left, Right : Boolean'Base) return Boolean;
   -- function "xor" (Left, Right : Boolean'Base) return Boolean;
```

10/1
```
   -- function "not" (Right : Boolean'Base) return Boolean;
```

11
```
   -- The integer type root_integer is predefined.
   -- The corresponding universal type is universal_integer.
```

12
```
   type Integer is range implementation-defined;
```

13
```
   subtype Natural  is Integer range 0 .. Integer'Last;
   subtype Positive is Integer range 1 .. Integer'Last;
```

14
```
   -- The predefined operators for type Integer are as follows:
```

15
```
   -- function "="  (Left, Right : Integer'Base) return Boolean;
   -- function "/=" (Left, Right : Integer'Base) return Boolean;
   -- function "<"  (Left, Right : Integer'Base) return Boolean;
   -- function "<=" (Left, Right : Integer'Base) return Boolean;
   -- function ">"  (Left, Right : Integer'Base) return Boolean;
   -- function ">=" (Left, Right : Integer'Base) return Boolean;
```

16
```
   -- function "+"   (Right : Integer'Base) return Integer'Base;
   -- function "-"   (Right : Integer'Base) return Integer'Base;
   -- function "abs" (Right : Integer'Base) return Integer'Base;
```

```
--  function "+"   (Left, Right : Integer'Base) return Integer'Base;         17
--  function "-"   (Left, Right : Integer'Base) return Integer'Base;
--  function "*"   (Left, Right : Integer'Base) return Integer'Base;
--  function "/"   (Left, Right : Integer'Base) return Integer'Base;
--  function "rem" (Left, Right : Integer'Base) return Integer'Base;
--  function "mod" (Left, Right : Integer'Base) return Integer'Base;

--  function "**"  (Left : Integer'Base; Right : Natural)                     18
--                 return Integer'Base;
```

-- *The specification of each operator for the type*   19
-- *root_integer, or for any additional predefined integer*
-- *type, is obtained by replacing Integer by the name of the type*
-- *in the specification of the corresponding operator of the type*
-- *Integer. The right operand of the exponentiation operator*
-- *remains as subtype Natural.*

-- *The floating point type root_real is predefined.*   20
-- *The corresponding universal type is universal_real.*

type Float **is digits** *implementation-defined*;   21

-- *The predefined operators for this type are as follows:*   22

```
--  function "="   (Left, Right : Float) return Boolean;                      23
--  function "/="  (Left, Right : Float) return Boolean;
--  function "<"   (Left, Right : Float) return Boolean;
--  function "<="  (Left, Right : Float) return Boolean;
--  function ">"   (Left, Right : Float) return Boolean;
--  function ">="  (Left, Right : Float) return Boolean;

--  function "+"   (Right : Float) return Float;                              24
--  function "-"   (Right : Float) return Float;
--  function "abs" (Right : Float) return Float;

--  function "+"   (Left, Right : Float) return Float;                        25
--  function "-"   (Left, Right : Float) return Float;
--  function "*"   (Left, Right : Float) return Float;
--  function "/"   (Left, Right : Float) return Float;

--  function "**"  (Left : Float; Right : Integer'Base) return Float;         26
```

-- *The specification of each operator for the type root_real, or for*   27
-- *any additional predefined floating point type, is obtained by*
-- *replacing Float by the name of the type in the specification of the*
-- *corresponding operator of the type Float.*

-- *In addition, the following operators are predefined for the root*   28
-- *numeric types:*

```
function "*" (Left : root_integer; Right : root_real)                        29
   return root_real;

function "*" (Left : root_real;    Right : root_integer)                     30
   return root_real;

function "/" (Left : root_real;    Right : root_integer)                     31
   return root_real;
```

-- *The type universal_fixed is predefined.*   32
-- *The only multiplying operators defined between*
-- *fixed point types are*

```
function "*" (Left : universal_fixed; Right : universal_fixed)               33
   return universal_fixed;

function "/" (Left : universal_fixed; Right : universal_fixed)               34
   return universal_fixed;
```

35

    -- The declaration of type Character is based on the standard ISO 8859-1 character set.

    -- There are no character literals corresponding to the positions for control characters.
    -- They are indicated in italics in this definition. See 3.5.2.

```
type Character is
(nul,    soh,    stx,    etx,      eot,    enq,    ack,    bel,    --0 (16#00#) .. 7 (16#07#)
 bs,     ht,     lf,     vt,       ff,     cr,     so,     si,     --8 (16#08#) .. 15 (16#0F#)

 dle,    dc1,    dc2,    dc3,      dc4,    nak,    syn,    etb,    --16 (16#10#) .. 23 (16#17#)
 can,    em,     sub,    esc,      fs,     gs,     rs,     us,     --24 (16#18#) .. 31 (16#1F#)

 ' ',    '!',    '"',    '#',      '$',    '%',    '&',    ''',    --32 (16#20#) .. 39 (16#27#)
 '(',    ')',    '*',    '+',      ',',    '-',    '.',    '/',    --40 (16#28#) .. 47 (16#2F#)

 '0',    '1',    '2',    '3',      '4',    '5',    '6',    '7',    --48 (16#30#) .. 55 (16#37#)
 '8',    '9',    ':',    ';',      '<',    '=',    '>',    '?',    --56 (16#38#) .. 63 (16#3F#)

 '@',    'A',    'B',    'C',      'D',    'E',    'F',    'G',    --64 (16#40#) .. 71 (16#47#)
 'H',    'I',    'J',    'K',      'L',    'M',    'N',    'O',    --72 (16#48#) .. 79 (16#4F#)

 'P',    'Q',    'R',    'S',      'T',    'U',    'V',    'W',    --80 (16#50#) .. 87 (16#57#)
 'X',    'Y',    'Z',    '[',      '\',    ']',    '^',    '_',    --88 (16#58#) .. 95 (16#5F#)

 '`',    'a',    'b',    'c',      'd',    'e',    'f',    'g',    --96 (16#60#) .. 103 (16#67#)
 'h',    'i',    'j',    'k',      'l',    'm',    'n',    'o',    --104 (16#68#) .. 111 (16#6F#)

 'p',    'q',    'r',    's',      't',    'u',    'v',    'w',    --112 (16#70#) .. 119 (16#77#)
 'x',    'y',    'z',    '{',      '|',    '}',    '~',    del,    --120 (16#78#) .. 127 (16#7F#)

 reserved_128,   reserved_129,    bph,    nbh,                    --128 (16#80#) .. 131 (16#83#)
 reserved_132,   nel,    ssa,     esa,                            --132 (16#84#) .. 135 (16#87#)
 hts,    htj,    vts,    pld,      plu,    ri,     ss2,    ss3,    --136 (16#88#) .. 143 (16#8F#)

 dcs,    pu1,    pu2,    sts,      cch,    mw,     spa,    epa,    --144 (16#90#) .. 151 (16#97#)
 sos,    reserved_153,   sci,     csi,                            --152 (16#98#) .. 155 (16#9B#)
 st,     osc,    pm,     apc,                                     --156 (16#9C#) .. 159 (16#9F#)

 ' ',    '¡',    '¢',    '£',      '¤',    '¥',    '¦',    '§',    --160 (16#A0#) .. 167 (16#A7#)
 '¨',    '©',    'ª',    '«',      '¬',    '-',    '®',    '¯',    --168 (16#A8#) .. 175 (16#AF#)

 '°',    '±',    '²',    '³',      '´',    'µ',    '¶',    '·',    --176 (16#B0#) .. 183 (16#B7#)
 '¸',    '¹',    'º',    '»',      '¼',    '½',    '¾',    '¿',    --184 (16#B8#) .. 191 (16#BF#)

 'À',    'Á',    'Â',    'Ã',      'Ä',    'Å',    'Æ',    'Ç',    --192 (16#C0#) .. 199 (16#C7#)
 'È',    'É',    'Ê',    'Ë',      'Ì',    'Í',    'Î',    'Ï',    --200 (16#C8#) .. 207 (16#CF#)

 'Ð',    'Ñ',    'Ò',    'Ó',      'Ô',    'Õ',    'Ö',    '×',    --208 (16#D0#) .. 215 (16#D7#)
 'Ø',    'Ù',    'Ú',    'Û',      'Ü',    'Ý',    'Þ',    'ß',    --216 (16#D8#) .. 223 (16#DF#)

 'à',    'á',    'â',    'ã',      'ä',    'å',    'æ',    'ç',    --224 (16#E0#) .. 231 (16#E7#)
 'è',    'é',    'ê',    'ë',      'ì',    'í',    'î',    'ï',    --232 (16#E8#) .. 239 (16#EF#)

 'ð',    'ñ',    'ò',    'ó',      'ô',    'õ',    'ö',    '÷',    --240 (16#F0#) .. 247 (16#F7#)
 'ø',    'ù',    'ú',    'û',      'ü',    'ý',    'þ',    'ÿ',    --248 (16#F8#) .. 255 (16#FF#)
```

36

    -- The predefined operators for the type Character are the same as for
    -- any enumeration type.

    -- The declaration of type Wide_Character is based on the standard ISO 10646 BMP character set.
    -- The first 256 positions have the same contents as type Character. See 3.5.2.

```
type Wide_Character is (nul, soh ... FFFE, FFFF);

package ASCII is ... end ASCII;   --Obsolescent; see J.5
```

-- Predefined string types: 37

```
type String is array(Positive range <>) of Character;
pragma Pack(String);
```
-- The predefined operators for this type are as follows: 38

```
--      function "="  (Left, Right: String) return Boolean;    39
--      function "/=" (Left, Right: String) return Boolean;
--      function "<"  (Left, Right: String) return Boolean;
--      function "<=" (Left, Right: String) return Boolean;
--      function ">"  (Left, Right: String) return Boolean;
--      function ">=" (Left, Right: String) return Boolean;

--      function "&" (Left: String;    Right: String)    return String;    40
--      function "&" (Left: Character; Right: String)    return String;
--      function "&" (Left: String;    Right: Character) return String;
--      function "&" (Left: Character; Right: Character) return String;
```

```
type Wide_String is array(Positive range <>) of Wide_Character;    41
pragma Pack(Wide_String);
```
-- The predefined operators for this type correspond to those for String   42

```
type Duration is delta implementation-defined range implementation-defined;    43
```
  -- The predefined operators for the type Duration are the same as for   44
  -- any fixed point type.

-- The predefined exceptions: 45

```
Constraint_Error: exception;    46
Program_Error   : exception;
Storage_Error   : exception;
Tasking_Error   : exception;
```

```
end Standard;    47
```

Standard has no private part.   48

In each of the types Character and Wide_Character, the character literals for the space character (position   49
32) and the non-breaking space character (position 160) correspond to different values. Unless indicated
otherwise, each occurrence of the character literal ' ' in this International Standard refers to the space
character. Similarly, the character literals for hyphen (position 45) and soft hyphen (position 173)
correspond to different values. Unless indicated otherwise, each occurrence of the character literal '-' in this
International Standard refers to the hyphen character.

Dynamic Semantics

Elaboration of the body of Standard has no effect.   50

Implementation Permissions

An implementation may provide additional predefined integer types and additional predefined floating   51
point types. Not all of these types need have names.

Implementation Advice

If an implementation provides additional named predefined integer types, then the names should end with   52
''Integer'' as in ''Long_Integer''. If an implementation provides additional named predefined floating
point types, then the names should end with ''Float'' as in ''Long_Float''.

NOTES
1 Certain aspects of the predefined entities cannot be completely described in the language itself. For example, although   53
the enumeration type Boolean can be written showing the two enumeration literals False and True, the short-circuit
control forms cannot be expressed in the language.

54   2 As explained in 8.1, "Declarative Region" and 10.1.4, "The Compilation Process", the declarative region of the package Standard encloses every library unit and consequently the main subprogram; the declaration of every library unit is assumed to occur within this declarative region. Library_items are assumed to be ordered in such a way that there are no forward semantic dependences. However, as explained in 8.3, "Visibility", the only library units that are visible within a given compilation unit are the library units named by all with_clauses that apply to the given unit, and moreover, within the declarative region of a given library unit, that library unit itself.

55   3 If all block_statements of a program are named, then the name of each program unit can always be written as an expanded name starting with Standard (unless Standard is itself hidden). The name of a library unit cannot be a homograph of a name (such as Integer) that is already declared in Standard.

56   4 The exception Standard.Numeric_Error is defined in J.6.

A.2 The Package Ada

Static Semantics

1   The following language-defined library package exists:

2
```
package Ada is
    pragma Pure(Ada);
end Ada;
```

3   Ada serves as the parent of most of the other language-defined library units; its declaration is empty (except for the pragma Pure).

Legality Rules

4   In the standard mode, it is illegal to compile a child of package Ada.

A.3 Character Handling

1   This clause presents the packages related to character processing: an empty pure package Characters and child packages Characters.Handling and Characters.Latin_1. The package Characters.Handling provides classification and conversion functions for Character data, and some simple functions for dealing with Wide_Character data. The child package Characters.Latin_1 declares a set of constants initialized to values of type Character.

A.3.1 The Package Characters

Static Semantics

1   The library package Characters has the following declaration:

2
```
package Ada.Characters is
  pragma Pure(Characters);
end Ada.Characters;
```

A.3.2 The Package Characters.Handling

Static Semantics

1   The library package Characters.Handling has the following declaration:

2
```
package Ada.Characters.Handling is
  pragma Preelaborate(Handling);
```

--Character classification functions   3

```
function Is_Control           (Item : in Character) return Boolean;
function Is_Graphic           (Item : in Character) return Boolean;
function Is_Letter            (Item : in Character) return Boolean;
function Is_Lower             (Item : in Character) return Boolean;
function Is_Upper             (Item : in Character) return Boolean;
function Is_Basic             (Item : in Character) return Boolean;
function Is_Digit             (Item : in Character) return Boolean;
function Is_Decimal_Digit     (Item : in Character) return Boolean
                    renames Is_Digit;
function Is_Hexadecimal_Digit (Item : in Character) return Boolean;
function Is_Alphanumeric      (Item : in Character) return Boolean;
function Is_Special           (Item : in Character) return Boolean;
```
4

--Conversion functions for Character and String   5

```
function To_Lower (Item : in Character) return Character;
function To_Upper (Item : in Character) return Character;
function To_Basic (Item : in Character) return Character;
```
6

```
function To_Lower (Item : in String) return String;
function To_Upper (Item : in String) return String;
function To_Basic (Item : in String) return String;
```
7

--Classifications of and conversions between Character and ISO 646   8

```
subtype ISO_646 is
   Character range Character'Val(0) .. Character'Val(127);
```
9

```
function Is_ISO_646 (Item : in Character) return Boolean;
function Is_ISO_646 (Item : in String)    return Boolean;
```
10

```
function To_ISO_646 (Item        : in Character;
                     Substitute : in ISO_646 := ' ')
   return ISO_646;
```
11

```
function To_ISO_646 (Item        : in String;
                     Substitute : in ISO_646 := ' ')
   return String;
```
12

--Classifications of and conversions between Wide_Character and Character.   13

```
function Is_Character (Item : in Wide_Character) return Boolean;
function Is_String    (Item : in Wide_String)    return Boolean;
```
14

```
function To_Character (Item        : in Wide_Character;
                       Substitute : in Character := ' ')
   return Character;
```
15

```
function To_String    (Item        : in Wide_String;
                       Substitute : in Character := ' ')
   return String;
```
16

```
function To_Wide_Character (Item : in Character) return Wide_Character;
```
17

```
function To_Wide_String    (Item : in String)    return Wide_String;
```
18

```
end Ada.Characters.Handling;
```
19

In the description below for each function that returns a Boolean result, the effect is described in terms of the conditions under which the value True is returned. If these conditions are not met, then the function returns False.   20

Each of the following classification functions has a formal Character parameter, Item, and returns a Boolean result.   21

Is_Control   True if Item is a control character. A *control character* is a character whose position is in one of the ranges 0..31 or 127..159.   22

Is_Graphic   True if Item is a graphic character. A *graphic character* is a character whose position is in one of the ranges 32..126 or 160..255.   23

24   Is_Letter   True if Item is a letter. A *letter* is a character that is in one of the ranges 'A'..'Z' or 'a'..'z', or whose position is in one of the ranges 192..214, 216..246, or 248..255.

25   Is_Lower   True if Item is a lower-case letter. A *lower-case letter* is a character that is in the range 'a'..'z', or whose position is in one of the ranges 223..246 or 248..255.

26   Is_Upper   True if Item is an upper-case letter. An *upper-case letter* is a character that is in the range 'A'..'Z' or whose position is in one of the ranges 192..214 or 216.. 222.

27   Is_Basic   True if Item is a basic letter. A *basic letter* is a character that is in one of the ranges 'A'..'Z' and 'a'..'z', or that is one of the following: 'Æ', 'æ', 'Ð', 'ð', 'Þ', 'þ', or 'ß'.

28   Is_Digit   True if Item is a decimal digit. A *decimal digit* is a character in the range '0'..'9'.

29   Is_Decimal_Digit
           A renaming of Is_Digit.

30   Is_Hexadecimal_Digit
           True if Item is a hexadecimal digit. A *hexadecimal digit* is a character that is either a decimal digit or that is in one of the ranges 'A' .. 'F' or 'a' .. 'f'.

31   Is_Alphanumeric
           True if Item is an alphanumeric character. An *alphanumeric character* is a character that is either a letter or a decimal digit.

32   Is_Special   True if Item is a special graphic character. A *special graphic character* is a graphic character that is not alphanumeric.

33   Each of the names To_Lower, To_Upper, and To_Basic refers to two functions: one that converts from Character to Character, and the other that converts from String to String. The result of each Character-to-Character function is described below, in terms of the conversion applied to Item, its formal Character parameter. The result of each String-to-String conversion is obtained by applying to each element of the function's String parameter the corresponding Character-to-Character conversion; the result is the null String if the value of the formal parameter is the null String. The lower bound of the result String is 1.

34   To_Lower   Returns the corresponding lower-case value for Item if Is_Upper(Item), and returns Item otherwise.

35   To_Upper   Returns the corresponding upper-case value for Item if Is_Lower(Item) and Item has an upper-case form, and returns Item otherwise. The lower case letters 'ß' and 'ÿ' do not have upper case forms.

36   To_Basic   Returns the letter corresponding to Item but with no diacritical mark, if Item is a letter but not a basic letter; returns Item otherwise.

37   The following set of functions test for membership in the ISO 646 character range, or convert between ISO 646 and Character.

38   Is_ISO_646   The function whose formal parameter, Item, is of type Character returns True if Item is in the subtype ISO_646.

39   Is_ISO_646   The function whose formal parameter, Item, is of type String returns True if Is_ISO_646(Item(I)) is True for each I in Item'Range.

40   To_ISO_646
           The function whose first formal parameter, Item, is of type Character returns Item if Is_ISO_646(Item), and returns the Substitute ISO_646 character otherwise.

To_ISO_646   41

> The function whose first formal parameter, Item, is of type String returns the String whose Range is 1..Item'Length and each of whose elements is given by To_ISO_646 of the corresponding element in Item.

The following set of functions test Wide_Character values for membership in Character, or convert   42
between corresponding characters of Wide_Character and Character.

Is_Character   Returns True if Wide_Character'Pos(Item) <= Character'Pos(Character'Last).   43

Is_String   Returns True if Is_Character(Item(I)) is True for each I in Item'Range.   44

To_Character   Returns the Character corresponding to Item if Is_Character(Item), and returns the   45
                Substitute Character otherwise.

To_String   Returns the String whose range is 1..Item'Length and each of whose elements is given by   46
                To_Character of the corresponding element in Item.

To_Wide_Character   47

> Returns the Wide_Character X such that Character'Pos(Item) = Wide_Character'Pos(X).

To_Wide_String   48

> Returns the Wide_String whose range is 1..Item'Length and each of whose elements is given by To_Wide_Character of the corresponding element in Item.

Implementation Advice

If an implementation provides a localized definition of Character or Wide_Character, then the effects of   49
the subprograms in Characters.Handling should reflect the localizations. See also 3.5.2.

NOTES

5 A basic letter is a letter without a diacritical mark.   50

6 Except for the hexadecimal digits, basic letters, and ISO_646 characters, the categories identified in the classification   51
functions form a strict hierarchy:

    — Control characters   52

    — Graphic characters   53

      — Alphanumeric characters   54

        — Letters   55

          — Upper-case letters   56

          — Lower-case letters   57

        — Decimal digits   58

      — Special graphic characters   59

A.3.3 The Package Characters.Latin_1

The package Characters.Latin_1 declares constants for characters in ISO 8859-1.   1

Static Semantics

The library package Characters.Latin_1 has the following declaration: 2

```
package Ada.Characters.Latin_1 is
    pragma Pure(Latin_1);
```
3

4   *-- Control characters:*

```
5          NUL                      : constant Character := Character'Val(0);
           SOH                      : constant Character := Character'Val(1);
           STX                      : constant Character := Character'Val(2);
           ETX                      : constant Character := Character'Val(3);
           EOT                      : constant Character := Character'Val(4);
           ENQ                      : constant Character := Character'Val(5);
           ACK                      : constant Character := Character'Val(6);
           BEL                      : constant Character := Character'Val(7);
           BS                       : constant Character := Character'Val(8);
           HT                       : constant Character := Character'Val(9);
           LF                       : constant Character := Character'Val(10);
           VT                       : constant Character := Character'Val(11);
           FF                       : constant Character := Character'Val(12);
           CR                       : constant Character := Character'Val(13);
           SO                       : constant Character := Character'Val(14);
           SI                       : constant Character := Character'Val(15);

6          DLE                      : constant Character := Character'Val(16);
           DC1                      : constant Character := Character'Val(17);
           DC2                      : constant Character := Character'Val(18);
           DC3                      : constant Character := Character'Val(19);
           DC4                      : constant Character := Character'Val(20);
           NAK                      : constant Character := Character'Val(21);
           SYN                      : constant Character := Character'Val(22);
           ETB                      : constant Character := Character'Val(23);
           CAN                      : constant Character := Character'Val(24);
           EM                       : constant Character := Character'Val(25);
           SUB                      : constant Character := Character'Val(26);
           ESC                      : constant Character := Character'Val(27);
           FS                       : constant Character := Character'Val(28);
           GS                       : constant Character := Character'Val(29);
           RS                       : constant Character := Character'Val(30);
           US                       : constant Character := Character'Val(31);
```

7   *-- ISO 646 graphic characters:*

```
8          Space                    : constant Character := ' ';     -- Character'Val(32)
           Exclamation              : constant Character := '!';     -- Character'Val(33)
           Quotation                : constant Character := '"';     -- Character'Val(34)
           Number_Sign              : constant Character := '#';     -- Character'Val(35)
           Dollar_Sign              : constant Character := '$';     -- Character'Val(36)
           Percent_Sign             : constant Character := '%';     -- Character'Val(37)
           Ampersand                : constant Character := '&';     -- Character'Val(38)
           Apostrophe               : constant Character := ''';     -- Character'Val(39)
           Left_Parenthesis         : constant Character := '(';     -- Character'Val(40)
           Right_Parenthesis        : constant Character := ')';     -- Character'Val(41)
           Asterisk                 : constant Character := '*';     -- Character'Val(42)
           Plus_Sign                : constant Character := '+';     -- Character'Val(43)
           Comma                    : constant Character := ',';     -- Character'Val(44)
           Hyphen                   : constant Character := '-';     -- Character'Val(45)
           Minus_Sign               : Character renames Hyphen;
           Full_Stop                : constant Character := '.';     -- Character'Val(46)
           Solidus                  : constant Character := '/';     -- Character'Val(47)
```

9   *-- Decimal digits '0' though '9' are at positions 48 through 57*

```
10         Colon                    : constant Character := ':';     -- Character'Val(58)
           Semicolon                : constant Character := ';';     -- Character'Val(59)
           Less_Than_Sign           : constant Character := '<';     -- Character'Val(60)
           Equals_Sign              : constant Character := '=';     -- Character'Val(61)
           Greater_Than_Sign        : constant Character := '>';     -- Character'Val(62)
           Question                 : constant Character := '?';     -- Character'Val(63)
           Commercial_At            : constant Character := '@';     -- Character'Val(64)
```

```
-- Letters 'A' through 'Z' are at positions 65 through 90                              11

Left_Square_Bracket   : constant Character := '[';   -- Character'Val(91)             12
Reverse_Solidus       : constant Character := '\';   -- Character'Val(92)
Right_Square_Bracket  : constant Character := ']';   -- Character'Val(93)
Circumflex            : constant Character := '^';   -- Character'Val(94)
Low_Line              : constant Character := '_';   -- Character'Val(95)

Grave                 : constant Character := '`';   -- Character'Val(96)             13
LC_A                  : constant Character := 'a';   -- Character'Val(97)
LC_B                  : constant Character := 'b';   -- Character'Val(98)
LC_C                  : constant Character := 'c';   -- Character'Val(99)
LC_D                  : constant Character := 'd';   -- Character'Val(100)
LC_E                  : constant Character := 'e';   -- Character'Val(101)
LC_F                  : constant Character := 'f';   -- Character'Val(102)
LC_G                  : constant Character := 'g';   -- Character'Val(103)
LC_H                  : constant Character := 'h';   -- Character'Val(104)
LC_I                  : constant Character := 'i';   -- Character'Val(105)
LC_J                  : constant Character := 'j';   -- Character'Val(106)
LC_K                  : constant Character := 'k';   -- Character'Val(107)
LC_L                  : constant Character := 'l';   -- Character'Val(108)
LC_M                  : constant Character := 'm';   -- Character'Val(109)
LC_N                  : constant Character := 'n';   -- Character'Val(110)
LC_O                  : constant Character := 'o';   -- Character'Val(111)

LC_P                  : constant Character := 'p';   -- Character'Val(112)             14
LC_Q                  : constant Character := 'q';   -- Character'Val(113)
LC_R                  : constant Character := 'r';   -- Character'Val(114)
LC_S                  : constant Character := 's';   -- Character'Val(115)
LC_T                  : constant Character := 't';   -- Character'Val(116)
LC_U                  : constant Character := 'u';   -- Character'Val(117)
LC_V                  : constant Character := 'v';   -- Character'Val(118)
LC_W                  : constant Character := 'w';   -- Character'Val(119)
LC_X                  : constant Character := 'x';   -- Character'Val(120)
LC_Y                  : constant Character := 'y';   -- Character'Val(121)
LC_Z                  : constant Character := 'z';   -- Character'Val(122)
Left_Curly_Bracket    : constant Character := '{';   -- Character'Val(123)
Vertical_Line         : constant Character := '|';   -- Character'Val(124)
Right_Curly_Bracket   : constant Character := '}';   -- Character'Val(125)
Tilde                 : constant Character := '~';   -- Character'Val(126)
DEL                   : constant Character := Character'Val(127);

-- ISO 6429 control characters:                                                        15

IS4                   : Character renames FS;                                          16
IS3                   : Character renames GS;
IS2                   : Character renames RS;
IS1                   : Character renames US;

Reserved_128          : constant Character := Character'Val(128);                      17
Reserved_129          : constant Character := Character'Val(129);
BPH                   : constant Character := Character'Val(130);
NBH                   : constant Character := Character'Val(131);
Reserved_132          : constant Character := Character'Val(132);
NEL                   : constant Character := Character'Val(133);
SSA                   : constant Character := Character'Val(134);
ESA                   : constant Character := Character'Val(135);
HTS                   : constant Character := Character'Val(136);
HTJ                   : constant Character := Character'Val(137);
VTS                   : constant Character := Character'Val(138);
PLD                   : constant Character := Character'Val(139);
PLU                   : constant Character := Character'Val(140);
RI                    : constant Character := Character'Val(141);
SS2                   : constant Character := Character'Val(142);
SS3                   : constant Character := Character'Val(143);
```

18

```
DCS                             : constant Character := Character'Val(144);
PU1                             : constant Character := Character'Val(145);
PU2                             : constant Character := Character'Val(146);
STS                             : constant Character := Character'Val(147);
CCH                             : constant Character := Character'Val(148);
MW                              : constant Character := Character'Val(149);
SPA                             : constant Character := Character'Val(150);
EPA                             : constant Character := Character'Val(151);
```

19

```
SOS                             : constant Character := Character'Val(152);
Reserved_153                    : constant Character := Character'Val(153);
SCI                             : constant Character := Character'Val(154);
CSI                             : constant Character := Character'Val(155);
ST                              : constant Character := Character'Val(156);
OSC                             : constant Character := Character'Val(157);
PM                              : constant Character := Character'Val(158);
APC                             : constant Character := Character'Val(159);
```

20   -- *Other graphic characters:*

21   -- *Character positions 160 (16#A0#) .. 175 (16#AF#):*
```
No_Break_Space                   : constant Character := ' ';    --Character'Val(160)
NBSP                             : Character renames No_Break_Space;
Inverted_Exclamation             : constant Character := '¡';    --Character'Val(161)
Cent_Sign                        : constant Character := '¢';    --Character'Val(162)
Pound_Sign                       : constant Character := '£';    --Character'Val(163)
Currency_Sign                    : constant Character := '¤';    --Character'Val(164)
Yen_Sign                         : constant Character := '¥';    --Character'Val(165)
Broken_Bar                       : constant Character := '¦';    --Character'Val(166)
Section_Sign                     : constant Character := '§';    --Character'Val(167)
Diaeresis                        : constant Character := '¨';    --Character'Val(168)
Copyright_Sign                   : constant Character := '©';    --Character'Val(169)
Feminine_Ordinal_Indicator       : constant Character := 'ª';    --Character'Val(170)
Left_Angle_Quotation             : constant Character := '«';    --Character'Val(171)
Not_Sign                         : constant Character := '¬';    --Character'Val(172)
Soft_Hyphen                      : constant Character := '';    --Character'Val(173)
Registered_Trade_Mark_Sign       : constant Character := '®';    --Character'Val(174)
Macron                           : constant Character := '¯';    --Character'Val(175)
```

22   -- *Character positions 176 (16#B0#) .. 191 (16#BF#):*
```
Degree_Sign                      : constant Character := '°';    --Character'Val(176)
Ring_Above                       : Character renames Degree_Sign;
Plus_Minus_Sign                  : constant Character := '±';    --Character'Val(177)
Superscript_Two                  : constant Character := '²';    --Character'Val(178)
Superscript_Three                : constant Character := '³';    --Character'Val(179)
Acute                            : constant Character := '´';    --Character'Val(180)
Micro_Sign                       : constant Character := 'µ';    --Character'Val(181)
Pilcrow_Sign                     : constant Character := '¶';    --Character'Val(182)
Paragraph_Sign                   : Character renames Pilcrow_Sign;
Middle_Dot                       : constant Character := '·';    --Character'Val(183)
Cedilla                          : constant Character := '¸';    --Character'Val(184)
Superscript_One                  : constant Character := '¹';    --Character'Val(185)
Masculine_Ordinal_Indicator      : constant Character := 'º';    --Character'Val(186)
Right_Angle_Quotation            : constant Character := '»';    --Character'Val(187)
Fraction_One_Quarter             : constant Character := '¼';    --Character'Val(188)
Fraction_One_Half                : constant Character := '½';    --Character'Val(189)
Fraction_Three_Quarters          : constant Character := '¾';    --Character'Val(190)
Inverted_Question                : constant Character := '¿';    --Character'Val(191)
```

```
-- Character positions 192 (16#C0#) .. 207 (16#CF#):                                23
    UC_A_Grave            :  constant Character  :=  'À';    --Character'Val(192)
    UC_A_Acute            :  constant Character  :=  'Á';    --Character'Val(193)
    UC_A_Circumflex       :  constant Character  :=  'Â';    --Character'Val(194)
    UC_A_Tilde            :  constant Character  :=  'Ã';    --Character'Val(195)
    UC_A_Diaeresis        :  constant Character  :=  'Ä';    --Character'Val(196)
    UC_A_Ring             :  constant Character  :=  'Å';    --Character'Val(197)
    UC_AE_Diphthong       :  constant Character  :=  'Æ';    --Character'Val(198)
    UC_C_Cedilla          :  constant Character  :=  'Ç';    --Character'Val(199)
    UC_E_Grave            :  constant Character  :=  'È';    --Character'Val(200)
    UC_E_Acute            :  constant Character  :=  'É';    --Character'Val(201)
    UC_E_Circumflex       :  constant Character  :=  'Ê';    --Character'Val(202)
    UC_E_Diaeresis        :  constant Character  :=  'Ë';    --Character'Val(203)
    UC_I_Grave            :  constant Character  :=  'Ì';    --Character'Val(204)
    UC_I_Acute            :  constant Character  :=  'Í';    --Character'Val(205)
    UC_I_Circumflex       :  constant Character  :=  'Î';    --Character'Val(206)
    UC_I_Diaeresis        :  constant Character  :=  'Ï';    --Character'Val(207)

-- Character positions 208 (16#D0#) .. 223 (16#DF#):                                24
    UC_Icelandic_Eth      :  constant Character  :=  'Ð';    --Character'Val(208)
    UC_N_Tilde            :  constant Character  :=  'Ñ';    --Character'Val(209)
    UC_O_Grave            :  constant Character  :=  'Ò';    --Character'Val(210)
    UC_O_Acute            :  constant Character  :=  'Ó';    --Character'Val(211)
    UC_O_Circumflex       :  constant Character  :=  'Ô';    --Character'Val(212)
    UC_O_Tilde            :  constant Character  :=  'Õ';    --Character'Val(213)
    UC_O_Diaeresis        :  constant Character  :=  'Ö';    --Character'Val(214)
    Multiplication_Sign   :  constant Character  :=  '×';    --Character'Val(215)
    UC_O_Oblique_Stroke   :  constant Character  :=  'Ø';    --Character'Val(216)
    UC_U_Grave            :  constant Character  :=  'Ù';    --Character'Val(217)
    UC_U_Acute            :  constant Character  :=  'Ú';    --Character'Val(218)
    UC_U_Circumflex       :  constant Character  :=  'Û';    --Character'Val(219)
    UC_U_Diaeresis        :  constant Character  :=  'Ü';    --Character'Val(220)
    UC_Y_Acute            :  constant Character  :=  'Ý';    --Character'Val(221)
    UC_Icelandic_Thorn    :  constant Character  :=  'Þ';    --Character'Val(222)
    LC_German_Sharp_S     :  constant Character  :=  'ß';    --Character'Val(223)

-- Character positions 224 (16#E0#) .. 239 (16#EF#):                                25
    LC_A_Grave            :  constant Character  :=  'à';    --Character'Val(224)
    LC_A_Acute            :  constant Character  :=  'á';    --Character'Val(225)
    LC_A_Circumflex       :  constant Character  :=  'â';    --Character'Val(226)
    LC_A_Tilde            :  constant Character  :=  'ã';    --Character'Val(227)
    LC_A_Diaeresis        :  constant Character  :=  'ä';    --Character'Val(228)
    LC_A_Ring             :  constant Character  :=  'å';    --Character'Val(229)
    LC_AE_Diphthong       :  constant Character  :=  'æ';    --Character'Val(230)
    LC_C_Cedilla          :  constant Character  :=  'ç';    --Character'Val(231)
    LC_E_Grave            :  constant Character  :=  'è';    --Character'Val(232)
    LC_E_Acute            :  constant Character  :=  'é';    --Character'Val(233)
    LC_E_Circumflex       :  constant Character  :=  'ê';    --Character'Val(234)
    LC_E_Diaeresis        :  constant Character  :=  'ë';    --Character'Val(235)
    LC_I_Grave            :  constant Character  :=  'ì';    --Character'Val(236)
    LC_I_Acute            :  constant Character  :=  'í';    --Character'Val(237)
    LC_I_Circumflex       :  constant Character  :=  'î';    --Character'Val(238)
    LC_I_Diaeresis        :  constant Character  :=  'ï';    --Character'Val(239)
```

26 *-- Character positions 240 (16#F0#) .. 255 (16#FF#):*

```
         LC_Icelandic_Eth        : constant Character := 'ð';   --Character'Val(240)
         LC_N_Tilde              : constant Character := 'ñ';   --Character'Val(241)
         LC_O_Grave              : constant Character := 'ò';   --Character'Val(242)
         LC_O_Acute              : constant Character := 'ó';   --Character'Val(243)
         LC_O_Circumflex         : constant Character := 'ô';   --Character'Val(244)
         LC_O_Tilde              : constant Character := 'õ';   --Character'Val(245)
         LC_O_Diaeresis          : constant Character := 'ö';   --Character'Val(246)
         Division_Sign           : constant Character := '÷';   --Character'Val(247)
         LC_O_Oblique_Stroke     : constant Character := 'ø';   --Character'Val(248)
         LC_U_Grave              : constant Character := 'ù';   --Character'Val(249)
         LC_U_Acute              : constant Character := 'ú';   --Character'Val(250)
         LC_U_Circumflex         : constant Character := 'û';   --Character'Val(251)
         LC_U_Diaeresis          : constant Character := 'ü';   --Character'Val(252)
         LC_Y_Acute              : constant Character := 'ý';   --Character'Val(253)
         LC_Icelandic_Thorn      : constant Character := 'þ';   --Character'Val(254)
         LC_Y_Diaeresis          : constant Character := 'ÿ';   --Character'Val(255)
      end Ada.Characters.Latin_1;
```

Implementation Permissions

27 An implementation may provide additional packages as children of Ada.Characters, to declare names for the symbols of the local character set or other character sets.

A.4 String Handling

1 This clause presents the specifications of the package Strings and several child packages, which provide facilities for dealing with string data. Fixed-length, bounded-length, and unbounded-length strings are supported, for both String and Wide_String. The string-handling subprograms include searches for pattern strings and for characters in program-specified sets, translation (via a character-to-character mapping), and transformation (replacing, inserting, overwriting, and deleting of substrings).

A.4.1 The Package Strings

1 The package Strings provides declarations common to the string handling packages.

Static Semantics

2 The library package Strings has the following declaration:

3
```
package Ada.Strings is
   pragma Pure(Strings);
```

4
```
   Space      : constant Character      := ' ';
   Wide_Space : constant Wide_Character := ' ';
```

5
```
   Length_Error, Pattern_Error, Index_Error, Translation_Error : exception;
```

6
```
   type Alignment  is (Left, Right, Center);
   type Truncation is (Left, Right, Error);
   type Membership is (Inside, Outside);
   type Direction  is (Forward, Backward);
   type Trim_End   is (Left, Right, Both);
end Ada.Strings;
```

A.4.2 The Package Strings.Maps

The package Strings.Maps defines the types, operations, and other entities needed for character sets and character-to-character mappings.   1

Static Semantics

The library package Strings.Maps has the following declaration: 2

```ada
package Ada.Strings.Maps is
   pragma Preelaborate(Maps);

   -- Representation for a set of character values:
   type Character_Set is private;

   Null_Set : constant Character_Set;

   type Character_Range is
     record
        Low  : Character;
        High : Character;
     end record;
   -- Represents Character range Low..High

   type Character_Ranges is array (Positive range <>) of Character_Range;

   function To_Set    (Ranges : in Character_Ranges) return Character_Set;

   function To_Set    (Span   : in Character_Range) return Character_Set;

   function To_Ranges (Set    : in Character_Set)  return Character_Ranges;

   function "="    (Left, Right : in Character_Set) return Boolean;

   function "not" (Right : in Character_Set)        return Character_Set;
   function "and" (Left, Right : in Character_Set) return Character_Set;
   function "or"  (Left, Right : in Character_Set) return Character_Set;
   function "xor" (Left, Right : in Character_Set) return Character_Set;
   function "-"   (Left, Right : in Character_Set) return Character_Set;

   function Is_In (Element : in Character;
                   Set     : in Character_Set)
      return Boolean;

   function Is_Subset (Elements : in Character_Set;
                       Set      : in Character_Set)
      return Boolean;

   function "<=" (Left  : in Character_Set;
                  Right : in Character_Set)
      return Boolean renames Is_Subset;

   -- Alternative representation for a set of character values:
   subtype Character_Sequence is String;

   function To_Set (Sequence  : in Character_Sequence) return Character_Set;

   function To_Set (Singleton : in Character)          return Character_Set;

   function To_Sequence (Set  : in Character_Set) return Character_Sequence;

   -- Representation for a character to character mapping:
   type Character_Mapping is private;

   function Value (Map     : in Character_Mapping;
                   Element : in Character)
      return Character;

   Identity : constant Character_Mapping;

   function To_Mapping (From, To : in Character_Sequence)
      return Character_Mapping;
```

The Package Strings.Maps **A.4.2**

Column markers: 3, 4, 5, 6, 7, 8, 9, 10, 11, 12, 13, 14, 15, 16, 17, 18, 19, 20, 21, 22, 23

24
```
function To_Domain (Map : in Character_Mapping)
    return Character_Sequence;
function To_Range  (Map : in Character_Mapping)
    return Character_Sequence;
```

25
```
type Character_Mapping_Function is
    access function (From : in Character) return Character;
```

26
```
private
    ... -- not specified by the language
end Ada.Strings.Maps;
```

27　An object of type Character_Set represents a set of characters.

28　Null_Set represents the set containing no characters.

29　An object Obj of type Character_Range represents the set of characters in the range Obj.Low .. Obj.High.

30　An object Obj of type Character_Ranges represents the union of the sets corresponding to Obj(I) for I in Obj'Range.

31
```
function To_Set (Ranges : in Character_Ranges) return Character_Set;
```

32　If Ranges'Length=0 then Null_Set is returned; otherwise the returned value represents the set corresponding to Ranges.

33
```
function To_Set (Span : in Character_Range) return Character_Set;
```

34　The returned value represents the set containing each character in Span.

35
```
function To_Ranges (Set : in Character_Set) return Character_Ranges;
```

36　If Set = Null_Set then an empty Character_Ranges array is returned; otherwise the shortest array of contiguous ranges of Character values in Set, in increasing order of Low, is returned.

37
```
function "=" (Left, Right : in Character_Set) return Boolean;
```

38　The function "=" returns True if Left and Right represent identical sets, and False otherwise.

39　Each of the logical operators "**not**", "**and**", "**or**", and "**xor**" returns a Character_Set value that represents the set obtained by applying the corresponding operation to the set(s) represented by the parameter(s) of the operator. "−"(Left, Right) is equivalent to "and"(Left, "not"(Right)).

40
```
function Is_In (Element : in Character;
                Set     : in Character_Set);
    return Boolean;
```

41　Is_In returns True if Element is in Set, and False otherwise.

42
```
function Is_Subset (Elements : in Character_Set;
                    Set      : in Character_Set)
    return Boolean;
```

43　Is_Subset returns True if Elements is a subset of Set, and False otherwise.

44
```
subtype Character_Sequence is String;
```

45　The Character_Sequence subtype is used to portray a set of character values and also to identify the domain and range of a character mapping.

```
function To_Set (Sequence  : in Character_Sequence) return Character_Set;     46

function To_Set (Singleton : in Character)           return Character_Set;
```
46

Sequence portrays the set of character values that it explicitly contains (ignoring duplicates). Singleton portrays the set comprising a single Character. Each of the To_Set functions returns a Character_Set value that represents the set portrayed by Sequence or Singleton.   47

```
function To_Sequence (Set : in Character_Set) return Character_Sequence;      48
```

The function To_Sequence returns a Character_Sequence value containing each of the characters in the set represented by Set, in ascending order with no duplicates.   49

```
type Character_Mapping is private;      50
```

An object of type Character_Mapping represents a Character-to-Character mapping.   51

```
function Value (Map      : in Character_Mapping;      52
                Element  : in Character)
   return Character;
```

The function Value returns the Character value to which Element maps with respect to the mapping represented by Map.   53

A character C *matches* a pattern character P with respect to a given Character_Mapping value Map if Value(Map, C) = P. A string S *matches* a pattern string P with respect to a given Character_Mapping if their lengths are the same and if each character in S matches its corresponding character in the pattern string P.   54

String handling subprograms that deal with character mappings have parameters whose type is Character_Mapping.   55

```
Identity : constant Character_Mapping;      56
```

Identity maps each Character to itself.   57

```
function To_Mapping (From, To : in Character_Sequence)      58
   return Character_Mapping;
```

To_Mapping produces a Character_Mapping such that each element of From maps to the corresponding element of To, and each other character maps to itself. If From'Length /= To'Length, or if some character is repeated in From, then Translation_Error is propagated.   59

```
function To_Domain (Map : in Character_Mapping) return Character_Sequence;      60
```

To_Domain returns the shortest Character_Sequence value D such that each character not in D maps to itself, and such that the characters in D are in ascending order. The lower bound of D is 1.   61

```
function To_Range  (Map : in Character_Mapping) return Character_Sequence;      62
```

To_Range returns the Character_Sequence value R, such that if D = To_Domain(Map), then R has the same bounds as D, and D(I) maps to R(I) for each I in D'Range.   63/1

An object F of type Character_Mapping_Function maps a Character value C to the Character value F.**all**(C), which is said to *match* C with respect to mapping function F.   64

NOTES
7 Character_Mapping and Character_Mapping_Function are used both for character equivalence mappings in the search subprograms (such as for case insensitivity) and as transformational mappings in the Translate subprograms.   65

66   8 To_Domain(Identity) and To_Range(Identity) each returns the null string.

67   To_Mapping("ABCD", "ZZAB") returns a Character_Mapping that maps 'A' and 'B' to 'Z', 'C' to 'A', 'D' to 'B', and each other Character to itself.

A.4.3 Fixed-Length String Handling

1   The language-defined package Strings.Fixed provides string-handling subprograms for fixed-length strings; that is, for values of type Standard.String. Several of these subprograms are procedures that modify the contents of a String that is passed as an **out** or an **in out** parameter; each has additional parameters to control the effect when the logical length of the result differs from the parameter's length.

2   For each function that returns a String, the lower bound of the returned value is 1.

3   The basic model embodied in the package is that a fixed-length string comprises significant characters and possibly padding (with space characters) on either or both ends. When a shorter string is copied to a longer string, padding is inserted, and when a longer string is copied to a shorter one, padding is stripped. The Move procedure in Strings.Fixed, which takes a String as an **out** parameter, allows the programmer to control these effects. Similar control is provided by the string transformation procedures.

4   The library package Strings.Fixed has the following declaration:

5
```
with Ada.Strings.Maps;
package Ada.Strings.Fixed is
   pragma Preelaborate(Fixed);
```

6
```
   -- "Copy" procedure for strings of possibly different lengths
```

7
```
   procedure Move (Source   : in  String;
                   Target   : out String;
                   Drop     : in  Truncation := Error;
                   Justify  : in  Alignment  := Left;
                   Pad      : in  Character   := Space);
```

8
```
   -- Search subprograms
```

9
```
   function Index (Source  : in String;
                   Pattern : in String;
                   Going   : in Direction := Forward;
                   Mapping : in Maps.Character_Mapping
                             := Maps.Identity)
      return Natural;
```

10
```
   function Index (Source  : in String;
                   Pattern : in String;
                   Going   : in Direction := Forward;
                   Mapping : in Maps.Character_Mapping_Function)
      return Natural;
```

11
```
   function Index (Source : in String;
                   Set    : in Maps.Character_Set;
                   Test   : in Membership := Inside;
                   Going  : in Direction  := Forward)
      return Natural;
```

12
```
   function Index_Non_Blank (Source : in String;
                             Going  : in Direction := Forward)
      return Natural;
```

```
function Count (Source  : in String;                                      13
                Pattern : in String;
                Mapping : in Maps.Character_Mapping
                            := Maps.Identity)
   return Natural;

function Count (Source  : in String;                                      14
                Pattern : in String;
                Mapping : in Maps.Character_Mapping_Function)
   return Natural;

function Count (Source  : in String;                                      15
                Set     : in Maps.Character_Set)
   return Natural;

procedure Find_Token (Source : in String;                                 16
                      Set    : in Maps.Character_Set;
                      Test   : in Membership;
                      First  : out Positive;
                      Last   : out Natural);
```

-- *String translation subprograms*   17

```
function Translate (Source  : in String;                                  18
                    Mapping : in Maps.Character_Mapping)
   return String;

procedure Translate (Source  : in out String;                             19
                     Mapping : in Maps.Character_Mapping);

function Translate (Source  : in String;                                  20
                    Mapping : in Maps.Character_Mapping_Function)
   return String;

procedure Translate (Source  : in out String;                            21
                     Mapping : in Maps.Character_Mapping_Function);
```

-- *String transformation subprograms*   22

```
function Replace_Slice (Source : in String;                              23
                        Low    : in Positive;
                        High   : in Natural;
                        By     : in String)
   return String;

procedure Replace_Slice (Source  : in out String;                        24
                         Low     : in Positive;
                         High    : in Natural;
                         By      : in String;
                         Drop    : in Truncation := Error;
                         Justify : in Alignment  := Left;
                         Pad     : in Character   := Space);

function Insert (Source   : in String;                                   25
                 Before   : in Positive;
                 New_Item : in String)
   return String;

procedure Insert (Source   : in out String;                              26
                  Before   : in Positive;
                  New_Item : in String;
                  Drop     : in Truncation := Error);

function Overwrite (Source   : in String;                                27
                    Position : in Positive;
                    New_Item : in String)
   return String;

procedure Overwrite (Source   : in out String;                           28
                     Position : in Positive;
                     New_Item : in String;
                     Drop     : in Truncation := Right);
```

29
```
      function Delete (Source  : in String;
                       From    : in Positive;
                       Through : in Natural)
         return String;
```

30
```
      procedure Delete (Source  : in out String;
                        From    : in Positive;
                        Through : in Natural;
                        Justify : in Alignment := Left;
                        Pad     : in Character := Space);
```

31   *--String selector subprograms*
```
      function Trim (Source : in String;
                    Side   : in Trim_End)
         return String;
```

32
```
      procedure Trim (Source  : in out String;
                      Side    : in Trim_End;
                      Justify : in Alignment := Left;
                      Pad     : in Character := Space);
```

33
```
      function Trim (Source : in String;
                    Left   : in Maps.Character_Set;
                    Right  : in Maps.Character_Set)
         return String;
```

34
```
      procedure Trim (Source  : in out String;
                      Left    : in Maps.Character_Set;
                      Right   : in Maps.Character_Set;
                      Justify : in Alignment := Strings.Left;
                      Pad     : in Character := Space);
```

35
```
      function Head (Source : in String;
                     Count  : in Natural;
                     Pad    : in Character := Space)
         return String;
```

36
```
      procedure Head (Source  : in out String;
                      Count   : in Natural;
                      Justify : in Alignment := Left;
                      Pad     : in Character := Space);
```

37
```
      function Tail (Source : in String;
                     Count  : in Natural;
                     Pad    : in Character := Space)
         return String;
```

38
```
      procedure Tail (Source  : in out String;
                      Count   : in Natural;
                      Justify : in Alignment := Left;
                      Pad     : in Character := Space);
```

39   *--String constructor functions*
40
```
      function "*" (Left  : in Natural;
                    Right : in Character) return String;
```

41
```
      function "*" (Left  : in Natural;
                    Right : in String) return String;
```

42   **end** Ada.Strings.Fixed;

43   The effects of the above subprograms are as follows.

44
```
      procedure Move (Source  : in  String;
                      Target  : out String;
                      Drop    : in  Truncation := Error;
                      Justify : in  Alignment  := Left;
                      Pad     : in  Character   := Space);
```

45   The Move procedure copies characters from Source to Target. If Source has the same length as Target, then the effect is to assign Source to Target. If Source is shorter than Target then:

46   • If Justify=Left, then Source is copied into the first Source'Length characters of Target.

- If Justify=Right, then Source is copied into the last Source'Length characters of Target. 47

- If Justify=Center, then Source is copied into the middle Source'Length characters of Target. In this case, if the difference in length between Target and Source is odd, then the extra Pad character is on the right. 48

- Pad is copied to each Target character not otherwise assigned. 49

If Source is longer than Target, then the effect is based on Drop. 50

- If Drop=Left, then the rightmost Target'Length characters of Source are copied into Target. 51

- If Drop=Right, then the leftmost Target'Length characters of Source are copied into Target. 52

- If Drop=Error, then the effect depends on the value of the Justify parameter and also on whether any characters in Source other than Pad would fail to be copied: 53

  - If Justify=Left, and if each of the rightmost Source'Length-Target'Length characters in Source is Pad, then the leftmost Target'Length characters of Source are copied to Target. 54

  - If Justify=Right, and if each of the leftmost Source'Length-Target'Length characters in Source is Pad, then the rightmost Target'Length characters of Source are copied to Target. 55

  - Otherwise, Length_Error is propagated. 56

```ada
function Index (Source  : in String;
                Pattern : in String;
                Going   : in Direction := Forward;
                Mapping : in Maps.Character_Mapping
                          := Maps.Identity)
   return Natural;

function Index (Source  : in String;
                Pattern : in String;
                Going   : in Direction := Forward;
                Mapping : in Maps.Character_Mapping_Function)
   return Natural;
```
57

Each Index function searches for a slice of Source, with length Pattern'Length, that matches Pattern with respect to Mapping; the parameter Going indicates the direction of the lookup. If Going = Forward, then Index returns the smallest index I such that the slice of Source starting at I matches Pattern. If Going = Backward, then Index returns the largest index I such that the slice of Source starting at I matches Pattern. If there is no such slice, then 0 is returned. If Pattern is the null string then Pattern_Error is propagated. 58

```ada
function Index (Source : in String;
                Set    : in Maps.Character_Set;
                Test   : in Membership := Inside;
                Going  : in Direction  := Forward)
   return Natural;
```
59

Index searches for the first or last occurrence of any of a set of characters (when Test=Inside), or any of the complement of a set of characters (when Test=Outside). It returns the smallest index I (if Going=Forward) or the largest index I (if Going=Backward) such that Source(I) satisfies the Test condition with respect to Set; it returns 0 if there is no such Character in Source. 60

61
```
function Index_Non_Blank (Source : in String;
                          Going  : in Direction := Forward)
       return Natural;
```

62   Returns Index(Source, Maps.To_Set(Space), Outside, Going)

63
```
function Count (Source  : in String;
                Pattern : in String;
                Mapping : in Maps.Character_Mapping
                        := Maps.Identity)
       return Natural;

function Count (Source  : in String;
                Pattern : in String;
                Mapping : in Maps.Character_Mapping_Function)
       return Natural;
```

64   Returns the maximum number of nonoverlapping slices of Source that match Pattern with respect to Mapping. If Pattern is the null string then Pattern_Error is propagated.

65
```
function Count (Source : in String;
                Set    : in Maps.Character_Set)
       return Natural;
```

66   Returns the number of occurrences in Source of characters that are in Set.

67
```
procedure Find_Token (Source : in String;
                      Set    : in Maps.Character_Set;
                      Test   : in Membership;
                      First  : out Positive;
                      Last   : out Natural);
```

68/1   Find_Token returns in First and Last the indices of the beginning and end of the first slice of Source all of whose elements satisfy the Test condition, and such that the elements (if any) immediately before and after the slice do not satisfy the Test condition. If no such slice exists, then the value returned for Last is zero, and the value returned for First is Source'First; however, if Source'First is not in Positive then Constraint_Error is raised.

69
```
function Translate (Source  : in String;
                    Mapping : in Maps.Character_Mapping)
       return String;

function Translate (Source  : in String;
                    Mapping : in Maps.Character_Mapping_Function)
       return String;
```

70   Returns the string S whose length is Source'Length and such that S(I) is the character to which Mapping maps the corresponding element of Source, for I in 1..Source'Length.

71
```
procedure Translate (Source  : in out String;
                     Mapping : in Maps.Character_Mapping);

procedure Translate (Source  : in out String;
                     Mapping : in Maps.Character_Mapping_Function);
```

72   Equivalent to Source := Translate(Source, Mapping).

73
```
function Replace_Slice (Source : in String;
                        Low    : in Positive;
                        High   : in Natural;
                        By     : in String)
       return String;
```

74/1   If Low > Source'Last+1, or High < Source'First−1, then Index_Error is propagated. Otherwise:

- If High >= Low, then the returned string comprises Source(Source'First..Low-1) & By & Source(High+1..Source'Last), but with lower bound 1. 74.1/1

- If High < Low, then the returned string is Insert(Source, Before=>Low, New_Item=>By). 74.2/1

```
procedure Replace_Slice (Source   : in out String;
                         Low      : in Positive;
                         High     : in Natural;
                         By       : in String;
                         Drop     : in Truncation := Error;
                         Justify  : in Alignment  := Left;
                         Pad      : in Character  := Space);
```
75

Equivalent to Move(Replace_Slice(Source, Low, High, By), Source, Drop, Justify, Pad). 76

```
function Insert (Source   : in String;
                Before   : in Positive;
                New_Item : in String)
   return String;
```
77

Propagates Index_Error if Before is not in Source'First .. Source'Last+1; otherwise returns Source(Source'First..Before-1) & New_Item & Source(Before..Source'Last), but with lower bound 1. 78

```
procedure Insert (Source   : in out String;
                  Before   : in Positive;
                  New_Item : in String;
                  Drop     : in Truncation := Error);
```
79

Equivalent to Move(Insert(Source, Before, New_Item), Source, Drop). 80

```
function Overwrite (Source   : in String;
                    Position : in Positive;
                    New_Item : in String)
   return String;
```
81

Propagates Index_Error if Position is not in Source'First .. Source'Last+1; otherwise returns the string obtained from Source by consecutively replacing characters starting at Position with corresponding characters from New_Item. If the end of Source is reached before the characters in New_Item are exhausted, the remaining characters from New_Item are appended to the string. 82

```
procedure Overwrite (Source   : in out String;
                     Position : in Positive;
                     New_Item : in String;
                     Drop     : in Truncation := Right);
```
83

Equivalent to Move(Overwrite(Source, Position, New_Item), Source, Drop). 84

```
function Delete (Source   : in String;
                 From     : in Positive;
                 Through  : in Natural)
   return String;
```
85

If From <= Through, the returned string is Replace_Slice(Source, From, Through, ""), otherwise it is Source with lower bound 1. 86/1

```
procedure Delete (Source   : in out String;
                  From     : in Positive;
                  Through  : in Natural;
                  Justify  : in Alignment := Left;
                  Pad      : in Character := Space);
```
87

Equivalent to Move(Delete(Source, From, Through), Source, Justify => Justify, Pad => Pad). 88

89
```
function Trim (Source : in String;
               Side   : in Trim_End)
    return String;
```

90
Returns the string obtained by removing from Source all leading Space characters (if Side = Left), all trailing Space characters (if Side = Right), or all leading and trailing Space characters (if Side = Both).

91
```
procedure Trim (Source  : in out String;
                Side    : in Trim_End;
                Justify : in Alignment := Left;
                Pad     : in Character := Space);
```

92
Equivalent to Move(Trim(Source, Side), Source, Justify=>Justify, Pad=>Pad).

93
```
function Trim (Source : in String;
               Left   : in Maps.Character_Set;
               Right  : in Maps.Character_Set)
    return String;
```

94
Returns the string obtained by removing from Source all leading characters in Left and all trailing characters in Right.

95
```
procedure Trim (Source  : in out String;
                Left    : in Maps.Character_Set;
                Right   : in Maps.Character_Set;
                Justify : in Alignment := Strings.Left;
                Pad     : in Character := Space);
```

96
Equivalent to Move(Trim(Source, Left, Right), Source, Justify => Justify, Pad=>Pad).

97
```
function Head (Source : in String;
               Count  : in Natural;
               Pad    : in Character := Space)
    return String;
```

98
Returns a string of length Count. If Count <= Source'Length, the string comprises the first Count characters of Source. Otherwise its contents are Source concatenated with Count–Source'Length Pad characters.

99
```
procedure Head (Source  : in out String;
                Count   : in Natural;
                Justify : in Alignment := Left;
                Pad     : in Character := Space);
```

100
Equivalent to Move(Head(Source, Count, Pad), Source, Drop=>Error, Justify=>Justify, Pad=>Pad).

101
```
function Tail (Source : in String;
               Count  : in Natural;
               Pad    : in Character := Space)
    return String;
```

102
Returns a string of length Count. If Count <= Source'Length, the string comprises the last Count characters of Source. Otherwise its contents are Count-Source'Length Pad characters concatenated with Source.

103
```
procedure Tail (Source  : in out String;
                Count   : in Natural;
                Justify : in Alignment := Left;
                Pad     : in Character := Space);
```

104
Equivalent to Move(Tail(Source, Count, Pad), Source, Drop=>Error, Justify=>Justify, Pad=>Pad).

A.4.3 Fixed-Length String Handling

```
function "*" (Left  : in Natural;
              Right : in Character) return String;
```
105

```
function "*" (Left  : in Natural;
              Right : in String) return String;
```

These functions replicate a character or string a specified number of times. The first function returns a string whose length is Left and each of whose elements is Right. The second function returns a string whose length is Left*Right'Length and whose value is the null string if Left = 0 and otherwise is (Left–1)*Right & Right with lower bound 1.

106/1

NOTES

9 In the Index and Count functions taking Pattern and Mapping parameters, the actual String parameter passed to Pattern should comprise characters occurring as target characters of the mapping. Otherwise the pattern will not match.

107

10 In the Insert subprograms, inserting at the end of a string is obtained by passing Source'Last+1 as the Before parameter.

108

11 If a null Character_Mapping_Function is passed to any of the string handling subprograms, Constraint_Error is propagated.

109

A.4.4 Bounded-Length String Handling

The language-defined package Strings.Bounded provides a generic package each of whose instances yields a private type Bounded_String and a set of operations. An object of a particular Bounded_String type represents a String whose low bound is 1 and whose length can vary conceptually between 0 and a maximum size established at the generic instantiation. The subprograms for fixed-length string handling are either overloaded directly for Bounded_String, or are modified as needed to reflect the variability in length. Additionally, since the Bounded_String type is private, appropriate constructor and selector operations are provided.

1

Static Semantics

The library package Strings.Bounded has the following declaration:

2

```
with Ada.Strings.Maps;
```
3
```
package Ada.Strings.Bounded is
   pragma Preelaborate(Bounded);

   generic
      Max  : Positive;      -- Maximum length of a Bounded_String
   package Generic_Bounded_Length is

      Max_Length : constant Positive := Max;

      type Bounded_String is private;

      Null_Bounded_String : constant Bounded_String;

      subtype Length_Range is Natural range 0 .. Max_Length;

      function Length (Source : in Bounded_String) return Length_Range;

      -- Conversion, Concatenation, and Selection functions

      function To_Bounded_String (Source : in String;
                                  Drop   : in Truncation := Error)
         return Bounded_String;

      function To_String (Source : in Bounded_String) return String;

      function Append (Left, Right : in Bounded_String;
                       Drop        : in Truncation  := Error)
         return Bounded_String;
```

4

5

6

7

8

9

10

11

12

13

Fixed-Length String Handling **A.4.3**

14
```
function Append (Left  : in Bounded_String;
                 Right : in String;
                 Drop  : in Truncation := Error)
    return Bounded_String;
```

15
```
function Append (Left  : in String;
                 Right : in Bounded_String;
                 Drop  : in Truncation := Error)
    return Bounded_String;
```

16
```
function Append (Left  : in Bounded_String;
                 Right : in Character;
                 Drop  : in Truncation := Error)
    return Bounded_String;
```

17
```
function Append (Left  : in Character;
                 Right : in Bounded_String;
                 Drop  : in Truncation := Error)
    return Bounded_String;
```

18
```
procedure Append (Source   : in out Bounded_String;
                  New_Item : in Bounded_String;
                  Drop     : in Truncation  := Error);
```

19
```
procedure Append (Source   : in out Bounded_String;
                  New_Item : in String;
                  Drop     : in Truncation  := Error);
```

20
```
procedure Append (Source   : in out Bounded_String;
                  New_Item : in Character;
                  Drop     : in Truncation  := Error);
```

21
```
function "&" (Left, Right : in Bounded_String)
    return Bounded_String;
```

22
```
function "&" (Left : in Bounded_String; Right : in String)
    return Bounded_String;
```

23
```
function "&" (Left : in String; Right : in Bounded_String)
    return Bounded_String;
```

24
```
function "&" (Left : in Bounded_String; Right : in Character)
    return Bounded_String;
```

25
```
function "&" (Left : in Character; Right : in Bounded_String)
    return Bounded_String;
```

26
```
function Element (Source : in Bounded_String;
                  Index  : in Positive)
    return Character;
```

27
```
procedure Replace_Element (Source : in out Bounded_String;
                           Index  : in Positive;
                           By     : in Character);
```

28
```
function Slice (Source : in Bounded_String;
                Low    : in Positive;
                High   : in Natural)
    return String;
```

29
```
function "=" (Left, Right : in Bounded_String) return Boolean;
function "=" (Left : in Bounded_String; Right : in String)
    return Boolean;
```

30
```
function "=" (Left : in String; Right : in Bounded_String)
    return Boolean;
```

31
```
function "<" (Left, Right : in Bounded_String) return Boolean;
```

32
```
function "<" (Left : in Bounded_String; Right : in String)
    return Boolean;
```

33
```
function "<" (Left : in String; Right : in Bounded_String)
    return Boolean;
```

34
```
function "<=" (Left, Right : in Bounded_String) return Boolean;
```

A.4.4 Bounded-Length String Handling

```
function "<=" (Left : in Bounded_String; Right : in String)                35
   return Boolean;
function "<=" (Left : in String; Right : in Bounded_String)                36
   return Boolean;
function ">" (Left, Right : in Bounded_String) return Boolean;              37
function ">" (Left : in Bounded_String; Right : in String)                 38
   return Boolean;
function ">" (Left : in String; Right : in Bounded_String)                 39
   return Boolean;
function ">=" (Left, Right : in Bounded_String) return Boolean;            40
function ">=" (Left : in Bounded_String; Right : in String)                41
   return Boolean;
function ">=" (Left : in String; Right : in Bounded_String)                42
   return Boolean;
```

-- *Search functions*   43

```
function Index (Source   : in Bounded_String;                              44
                Pattern  : in String;
                Going    : in Direction := Forward;
                Mapping  : in Maps.Character_Mapping
                          := Maps.Identity)
   return Natural;

function Index (Source   : in Bounded_String;                              45
                Pattern  : in String;
                Going    : in Direction := Forward;
                Mapping  : in Maps.Character_Mapping_Function)
   return Natural;

function Index (Source : in Bounded_String;                                46
                Set    : in Maps.Character_Set;
                Test   : in Membership := Inside;
                Going  : in Direction  := Forward)
   return Natural;

function Index_Non_Blank (Source : in Bounded_String;                      47
                          Going  : in Direction := Forward)
   return Natural;

function Count (Source   : in Bounded_String;                              48
                Pattern  : in String;
                Mapping  : in Maps.Character_Mapping
                          := Maps.Identity)
   return Natural;

function Count (Source   : in Bounded_String;                              49
                Pattern  : in String;
                Mapping  : in Maps.Character_Mapping_Function)
   return Natural;

function Count (Source   : in Bounded_String;                              50
                Set      : in Maps.Character_Set)
   return Natural;

procedure Find_Token (Source : in Bounded_String;                          51
                      Set    : in Maps.Character_Set;
                      Test   : in Membership;
                      First  : out Positive;
                      Last   : out Natural);
```

-- *String translation subprograms*   52

```
function Translate (Source  : in Bounded_String;                           53
                    Mapping : in Maps.Character_Mapping)
   return Bounded_String;

procedure Translate (Source  : in out Bounded_String;                      54
                     Mapping : in Maps.Character_Mapping);
```

55
```
function Translate (Source  : in Bounded_String;
                    Mapping : in Maps.Character_Mapping_Function)
   return Bounded_String;
```

56
```
procedure Translate (Source  : in out Bounded_String;
                     Mapping : in Maps.Character_Mapping_Function);
```

57
    -- *String transformation subprograms*

58
```
function Replace_Slice (Source  : in Bounded_String;
                        Low     : in Positive;
                        High    : in Natural;
                        By      : in String;
                        Drop    : in Truncation := Error)
   return Bounded_String;
```

59
```
procedure Replace_Slice (Source  : in out Bounded_String;
                         Low     : in Positive;
                         High    : in Natural;
                         By      : in String;
                         Drop    : in Truncation := Error);
```

60
```
function Insert (Source   : in Bounded_String;
                 Before   : in Positive;
                 New_Item : in String;
                 Drop     : in Truncation := Error)
   return Bounded_String;
```

61
```
procedure Insert (Source   : in out Bounded_String;
                  Before   : in Positive;
                  New_Item : in String;
                  Drop     : in Truncation := Error);
```

62
```
function Overwrite (Source   : in Bounded_String;
                    Position : in Positive;
                    New_Item : in String;
                    Drop     : in Truncation := Error)
   return Bounded_String;
```

63
```
procedure Overwrite (Source   : in out Bounded_String;
                     Position : in Positive;
                     New_Item : in String;
                     Drop     : in Truncation := Error);
```

64
```
function Delete (Source  : in Bounded_String;
                 From    : in Positive;
                 Through : in Natural)
   return Bounded_String;
```

65
```
procedure Delete (Source  : in out Bounded_String;
                  From    : in Positive;
                  Through : in Natural);
```

66
    --*String selector subprograms*

67
```
function Trim (Source : in Bounded_String;
               Side   : in Trim_End)
   return Bounded_String;
procedure Trim (Source : in out Bounded_String;
                Side   : in Trim_End);
```

68
```
function Trim (Source : in Bounded_String;
               Left   : in Maps.Character_Set;
               Right  : in Maps.Character_Set)
   return Bounded_String;
```

69
```
procedure Trim (Source : in out Bounded_String;
                Left   : in Maps.Character_Set;
                Right  : in Maps.Character_Set);
```

```
    function Head (Source : in Bounded_String;                    70
                   Count  : in Natural;
                   Pad    : in Character   := Space;
                   Drop   : in Truncation := Error)
       return Bounded_String;

    procedure Head (Source : in out Bounded_String;               71
                    Count  : in Natural;
                    Pad    : in Character   := Space;
                    Drop   : in Truncation := Error);

    function Tail (Source : in Bounded_String;                    72
                   Count  : in Natural;
                   Pad    : in Character   := Space;
                   Drop   : in Truncation := Error)
       return Bounded_String;

    procedure Tail (Source : in out Bounded_String;               73
                    Count  : in Natural;
                    Pad    : in Character   := Space;
                    Drop   : in Truncation := Error);
```

```
  --String constructor subprograms                               74

    function "*" (Left  : in Natural;                             75
                  Right : in Character)
       return Bounded_String;

    function "*" (Left  : in Natural;                             76
                  Right : in String)
       return Bounded_String;

    function "*" (Left  : in Natural;                             77
                  Right : in Bounded_String)
       return Bounded_String;

    function Replicate (Count : in Natural;                       78
                        Item  : in Character;
                        Drop  : in Truncation := Error)
       return Bounded_String;

    function Replicate (Count : in Natural;                       79
                        Item  : in String;
                        Drop  : in Truncation := Error)
       return Bounded_String;

    function Replicate (Count : in Natural;                       80
                        Item  : in Bounded_String;
                        Drop  : in Truncation := Error)
       return Bounded_String;

  private                                                         81
    ... -- not specified by the language
  end Generic_Bounded_Length;

end Ada.Strings.Bounded;                                          82
```

Null_Bounded_String represents the null string. If an object of type Bounded_String is not otherwise initialized, it will be initialized to the same value as Null_Bounded_String.   83

```
function Length (Source : in Bounded_String) return Length_Range;    84
```

The Length function returns the length of the string represented by Source.   85

```
function To_Bounded_String (Source : in String;                 86
                            Drop   : in Truncation := Error)
   return Bounded_String;
```

If Source'Length <= Max_Length then this function returns a Bounded_String that represents Source. Otherwise the effect depends on the value of Drop: 87

- If Drop=Left, then the result is a Bounded_String that represents the string comprising the rightmost Max_Length characters of Source.   88

89　　　　　　• If Drop=Right, then the result is a Bounded_String that represents the string comprising the leftmost Max_Length characters of Source.

90　　　　　　• If Drop=Error, then Strings.Length_Error is propagated.

91
```
function To_String (Source : in Bounded_String) return String;
```

92　　　　　To_String returns the String value with lower bound 1 represented by Source. If B is a Bounded_String, then B = To_Bounded_String(To_String(B)).

93　Each of the Append functions returns a Bounded_String obtained by concatenating the string or character given or represented by one of the parameters, with the string or character given or represented by the other parameter, and applying To_Bounded_String to the concatenation result string, with Drop as provided to the Append function.

94　Each of the procedures Append(Source, New_Item, Drop) has the same effect as the corresponding assignment Source := Append(Source, New_Item, Drop).

95　Each of the "&" functions has the same effect as the corresponding Append function, with Error as the Drop parameter.

96
```
function Element (Source : in Bounded_String;
                  Index  : in Positive)
   return Character;
```

97　　　　　Returns the character at position Index in the string represented by Source; propagates Index_Error if Index > Length(Source).

98
```
procedure Replace_Element (Source : in out Bounded_String;
                           Index  : in Positive;
                           By     : in Character);
```

99　　　　　Updates Source such that the character at position Index in the string represented by Source is By; propagates Index_Error if Index > Length(Source).

100
```
function Slice (Source : in Bounded_String;
                Low    : in Positive;
                High   : in Natural)
   return String;
```

101/1　　　Returns the slice at positions Low through High in the string represented by Source; propagates Index_Error if Low > Length(Source)+1 or High > Length(Source).

102　Each of the functions "=", "<", ">","<=", and ">=" returns the same result as the corresponding String operation applied to the String values given or represented by the two parameters.

103　Each of the search subprograms (Index, Index_Non_Blank, Count, Find_Token) has the same effect as the corresponding subprogram in Strings.Fixed applied to the string represented by the Bounded_String parameter.

104　Each of the Translate subprograms, when applied to a Bounded_String, has an analogous effect to the corresponding subprogram in Strings.Fixed. For the Translate function, the translation is applied to the string represented by the Bounded_String parameter, and the result is converted (via To_Bounded_String) to a Bounded_String. For the Translate procedure, the string represented by the Bounded_String parameter after the translation is given by the Translate function for fixed-length strings applied to the string represented by the original value of the parameter.

105/1　Each of the transformation subprograms (Replace_Slice, Insert, Overwrite, Delete), selector subprograms (Trim, Head, Tail), and constructor functions ("*") has an effect based on its corresponding subprogram in

Strings.Fixed, and Replicate is based on Fixed."*". In the case of a function, the corresponding fixed-length string subprogram is applied to the string represented by the Bounded_String parameter. To_Bounded_String is applied the result string, with Drop (or Error in the case of Generic_Bounded_Length."*") determining the effect when the string length exceeds Max_Length. In the case of a procedure, the corresponding function in Strings.Bounded.Generic_Bounded_Length is applied, with the result assigned into the Source parameter.

Implementation Advice

Bounded string objects should not be implemented by implicit pointers and dynamic allocation. 106

A.4.5 Unbounded-Length String Handling

The language-defined package Strings.Unbounded provides a private type Unbounded_String and a set of 1 operations. An object of type Unbounded_String represents a String whose low bound is 1 and whose length can vary conceptually between 0 and Natural'Last. The subprograms for fixed-length string handling are either overloaded directly for Unbounded_String, or are modified as needed to reflect the flexibility in length. Since the Unbounded_String type is private, relevant constructor and selector operations are provided.

Static Semantics

The library package Strings.Unbounded has the following declaration: 2

```
with Ada.Strings.Maps;                                           3
package Ada.Strings.Unbounded is
   pragma Preelaborate(Unbounded);

   type Unbounded_String is private;                             4

   Null_Unbounded_String : constant Unbounded_String;           5

   function Length (Source : in Unbounded_String) return Natural;   6

   type String_Access is access all String;                     7
   procedure Free (X : in out String_Access);

   -- Conversion, Concatenation, and Selection functions         8

   function To_Unbounded_String (Source : in String)            9
      return Unbounded_String;

   function To_Unbounded_String (Length : in Natural)           10
      return Unbounded_String;

   function To_String (Source : in Unbounded_String) return String;   11

   procedure Append (Source   : in out Unbounded_String;        12
                     New_Item : in Unbounded_String);

   procedure Append (Source   : in out Unbounded_String;        13
                     New_Item : in String);

   procedure Append (Source   : in out Unbounded_String;        14
                     New_Item : in Character);

   function "&" (Left, Right : in Unbounded_String)             15
      return Unbounded_String;

   function "&" (Left : in Unbounded_String; Right : in String) 16
      return Unbounded_String;

   function "&" (Left : in String; Right : in Unbounded_String) 17
      return Unbounded_String;

   function "&" (Left : in Unbounded_String; Right : in Character)   18
      return Unbounded_String;
```

Bounded-Length String Handling **A.4.4**

19   **function** "&" (Left : **in** Character; Right : **in** Unbounded_String)
        return Unbounded_String;

20   **function** Element (Source : **in** Unbounded_String;
                  Index : **in** Positive)
        return Character;

21   **procedure** Replace_Element (Source : **in out** Unbounded_String;
                        Index : **in** Positive;
                        By   : **in** Character);

22   **function** Slice (Source : **in** Unbounded_String;
              Low   : **in** Positive;
              High   : **in** Natural)
        return String;

23   **function** "=" (Left, Right : **in** Unbounded_String) **return** Boolean;

24   **function** "=" (Left : **in** Unbounded_String; Right : **in** String)
        return Boolean;

25   **function** "=" (Left : **in** String; Right : **in** Unbounded_String)
        return Boolean;

26   **function** "<" (Left, Right : **in** Unbounded_String) **return** Boolean;

27   **function** "<" (Left : **in** Unbounded_String; Right : **in** String)
        return Boolean;

28   **function** "<" (Left : **in** String; Right : **in** Unbounded_String)
        return Boolean;

29   **function** "<=" (Left, Right : **in** Unbounded_String) **return** Boolean;

30   **function** "<=" (Left : **in** Unbounded_String; Right : **in** String)
        return Boolean;

31   **function** "<=" (Left : **in** String; Right : **in** Unbounded_String)
        return Boolean;

32   **function** ">" (Left, Right : **in** Unbounded_String) **return** Boolean;

33   **function** ">" (Left : **in** Unbounded_String; Right : **in** String)
        return Boolean;

34   **function** ">" (Left : **in** String; Right : **in** Unbounded_String)
        return Boolean;

35   **function** ">=" (Left, Right : **in** Unbounded_String) **return** Boolean;

36   **function** ">=" (Left : **in** Unbounded_String; Right : **in** String)
        return Boolean;

37   **function** ">=" (Left : **in** String; Right : **in** Unbounded_String)
        return Boolean;

38   *-- Search subprograms*

39   **function** Index (Source : **in** Unbounded_String;
                  Pattern : **in** String;
                  Going   : **in** Direction := Forward;
                  Mapping : **in** Maps.Character_Mapping
                      := Maps.Identity)
        return Natural;

40   **function** Index (Source : **in** Unbounded_String;
                  Pattern : **in** String;
                  Going   : **in** Direction := Forward;
                  Mapping : **in** Maps.Character_Mapping_Function)
        return Natural;

41   **function** Index (Source : **in** Unbounded_String;
                  Set   : **in** Maps.Character_Set;
                  Test   : **in** Membership := Inside;
                  Going : **in** Direction := Forward) **return** Natural;

```
function Index_Non_Blank (Source : in Unbounded_String;          42
                          Going  : in Direction := Forward)
   return Natural;
function Count (Source  : in Unbounded_String;                   43
               Pattern : in String;
               Mapping : in Maps.Character_Mapping
                          := Maps.Identity)
   return Natural;
function Count (Source  : in Unbounded_String;                   44
               Pattern : in String;
               Mapping : in Maps.Character_Mapping_Function)
   return Natural;
function Count (Source  : in Unbounded_String;                   45
               Set     : in Maps.Character_Set)
   return Natural;
procedure Find_Token (Source : in Unbounded_String;              46
                      Set    : in Maps.Character_Set;
                      Test   : in Membership;
                      First  : out Positive;
                      Last   : out Natural);
```

-- *String translation subprograms*   47

```
function Translate (Source  : in Unbounded_String;               48
                    Mapping : in Maps.Character_Mapping)
   return Unbounded_String;
procedure Translate (Source  : in out Unbounded_String;          49
                     Mapping : in Maps.Character_Mapping);
function Translate (Source  : in Unbounded_String;               50
                    Mapping : in Maps.Character_Mapping_Function)
   return Unbounded_String;
procedure Translate (Source  : in out Unbounded_String;          51
                     Mapping : in Maps.Character_Mapping_Function);
```

-- *String transformation subprograms*   52

```
function Replace_Slice (Source : in Unbounded_String;            53
                        Low    : in Positive;
                        High   : in Natural;
                        By     : in String)
   return Unbounded_String;
procedure Replace_Slice (Source : in out Unbounded_String;       54
                         Low    : in Positive;
                         High   : in Natural;
                         By     : in String);
function Insert (Source   : in Unbounded_String;                 55
                Before   : in Positive;
                New_Item : in String)
   return Unbounded_String;
procedure Insert (Source   : in out Unbounded_String;            56
                  Before   : in Positive;
                  New_Item : in String);
function Overwrite (Source   : in Unbounded_String;              57
                    Position : in Positive;
                    New_Item : in String)
   return Unbounded_String;
procedure Overwrite (Source   : in out Unbounded_String;         58
                     Position : in Positive;
                     New_Item : in String);
```

59
```
function Delete (Source  : in Unbounded_String;
                 From    : in Positive;
                 Through : in Natural)
   return Unbounded_String;
```

60
```
procedure Delete (Source  : in out Unbounded_String;
                  From    : in Positive;
                  Through : in Natural);
```

61
```
function Trim (Source : in Unbounded_String;
               Side   : in Trim_End)
   return Unbounded_String;
```

62
```
procedure Trim (Source : in out Unbounded_String;
                Side   : in Trim_End);
```

63
```
function Trim (Source : in Unbounded_String;
               Left   : in Maps.Character_Set;
               Right  : in Maps.Character_Set)
   return Unbounded_String;
```

64
```
procedure Trim (Source : in out Unbounded_String;
                Left   : in Maps.Character_Set;
                Right  : in Maps.Character_Set);
```

65
```
function Head (Source : in Unbounded_String;
               Count  : in Natural;
               Pad    : in Character := Space)
   return Unbounded_String;
```

66
```
procedure Head (Source : in out Unbounded_String;
                Count  : in Natural;
                Pad    : in Character := Space);
```

67
```
function Tail (Source : in Unbounded_String;
               Count  : in Natural;
               Pad    : in Character := Space)
   return Unbounded_String;
```

68
```
procedure Tail (Source : in out Unbounded_String;
                Count  : in Natural;
                Pad    : in Character := Space);
```

69
```
function "*" (Left  : in Natural;
              Right : in Character)
   return Unbounded_String;
```

70
```
function "*" (Left  : in Natural;
              Right : in String)
   return Unbounded_String;
```

71
```
function "*" (Left  : in Natural;
              Right : in Unbounded_String)
   return Unbounded_String;
```

72
```
private
   ... -- not specified by the language
end Ada.Strings.Unbounded;
```

73 Null_Unbounded_String represents the null String. If an object of type Unbounded_String is not otherwise initialized, it will be initialized to the same value as Null_Unbounded_String.

74 The function Length returns the length of the String represented by Source.

75 The type String_Access provides a (non-private) access type for explicit processing of unbounded-length strings. The procedure Free performs an unchecked deallocation of an object of type String_Access.

76 The function To_Unbounded_String(Source : in String) returns an Unbounded_String that represents Source. The function To_Unbounded_String(Length : in Natural) returns an Unbounded_String that represents an uninitialized String whose length is Length.

The function To_String returns the String with lower bound 1 represented by Source. To_String and To_Unbounded_String are related as follows: 77

- If S is a String, then To_String(To_Unbounded_String(S)) = S.   78

- If U is an Unbounded_String, then To_Unbounded_String(To_String(U)) = U.   79

For each of the Append procedures, the resulting string represented by the Source parameter is given by   80
the concatenation of the original value of Source and the value of New_Item.

Each of the "&" functions returns an Unbounded_String obtained by concatenating the string or character 81
given or represented by one of the parameters, with the string or character given or represented by the
other parameter, and applying To_Unbounded_String to the concatenation result string.

The Element, Replace_Element, and Slice subprograms have the same effect as the corresponding   82
bounded-length string subprograms.

Each of the functions "=", "<", ">","<=", and ">=" returns the same result as the corresponding String   83
operation applied to the String values given or represented by Left and Right.

Each of the search subprograms (Index, Index_Non_Blank, Count, Find_Token) has the same effect as the   84
corresponding subprogram in Strings.Fixed applied to the string represented by the Unbounded_String
parameter.

The Translate function has an analogous effect to the corresponding subprogram in Strings.Fixed. The   85
translation is applied to the string represented by the Unbounded_String parameter, and the result is
converted (via To_Unbounded_String) to an Unbounded_String.

Each of the transformation functions (Replace_Slice, Insert, Overwrite, Delete), selector functions (Trim, 86
Head, Tail), and constructor functions ("*") is likewise analogous to its corresponding subprogram in
Strings.Fixed. For each of the subprograms, the corresponding fixed-length string subprogram is applied to
the string represented by the Unbounded_String parameter, and To_Unbounded_String is applied the
result string.

For each of the procedures Translate, Replace_Slice, Insert, Overwrite, Delete, Trim, Head, and Tail, the 87
resulting string represented by the Source parameter is given by the corresponding function for fixed-
length strings applied to the string represented by Source's original value.

Implementation Requirements

No storage associated with an Unbounded_String object shall be lost upon assignment or scope exit.   88

A.4.6 String-Handling Sets and Mappings

The language-defined package Strings.Maps.Constants declares Character_Set and Character_Mapping   1
constants corresponding to classification and conversion functions in package Characters.Handling.

Static Semantics

The library package Strings.Maps.Constants has the following declaration: 2

```
package Ada.Strings.Maps.Constants is
   pragma Preelaborate(Constants);
```
3

4

```
     Control_Set          : constant Character_Set;
     Graphic_Set          : constant Character_Set;
     Letter_Set           : constant Character_Set;
     Lower_Set            : constant Character_Set;
     Upper_Set            : constant Character_Set;
     Basic_Set            : constant Character_Set;
     Decimal_Digit_Set    : constant Character_Set;
     Hexadecimal_Digit_Set : constant Character_Set;
     Alphanumeric_Set     : constant Character_Set;
     Special_Set          : constant Character_Set;
     ISO_646_Set          : constant Character_Set;
```

5

```
     Lower_Case_Map       : constant Character_Mapping;
         --Maps to lower case for letters, else identity
     Upper_Case_Map           : constant Character_Mapping;
         --Maps to upper case for letters, else identity
     Basic_Map                : constant Character_Mapping;
         --Maps to basic letter for letters, else identity
```

6

```
  private
     ... -- not specified by the language
  end Ada.Strings.Maps.Constants;
```

7 Each of these constants represents a correspondingly named set of characters or character mapping in Characters.Handling (see A.3.2).

A.4.7 Wide_String Handling

1 Facilities for handling strings of Wide_Character elements are found in the packages Strings.Wide_Maps, Strings.Wide_Fixed, Strings.Wide_Bounded, Strings.Wide_Unbounded, and Strings.Wide_Maps.Wide_-Constants. They provide the same string-handling operations as the corresponding packages for strings of Character elements.

Static Semantics

2 The package Strings.Wide_Maps has the following declaration.

3

```
  package Ada.Strings.Wide_Maps is
     pragma Preelaborate(Wide_Maps);
```

4

```
     -- Representation for a set of Wide_Character values:
     type Wide_Character_Set is private;
```

5

```
  Null_Set : constant Wide_Character_Set;
```

6

```
     type Wide_Character_Range is
       record
           Low  : Wide_Character;
           High : Wide_Character;
       end record;
     -- Represents Wide_Character range Low..High
```

7

```
     type Wide_Character_Ranges is array (Positive range <>)
       of Wide_Character_Range;
```

8

```
     function To_Set     (Ranges : in Wide_Character_Ranges)
       return Wide_Character_Set;
```

9

```
     function To_Set     (Span   : in Wide_Character_Range)
       return Wide_Character_Set;
```

10

```
     function To_Ranges (Set    : in Wide_Character_Set)
       return Wide_Character_Ranges;
```

11

```
     function "="     (Left, Right : in Wide_Character_Set) return Boolean;
```

```
function "not" (Right : in Wide_Character_Set)
    return Wide_Character_Set;
function "and" (Left, Right : in Wide_Character_Set)
    return Wide_Character_Set;
function "or"  (Left, Right : in Wide_Character_Set)
    return Wide_Character_Set;
function "xor" (Left, Right : in Wide_Character_Set)
    return Wide_Character_Set;
function "-"   (Left, Right : in Wide_Character_Set)
    return Wide_Character_Set;
```
12

```
function Is_In (Element : in Wide_Character;
                Set     : in Wide_Character_Set)
    return Boolean;
```
13

```
function Is_Subset (Elements : in Wide_Character_Set;
                    Set      : in Wide_Character_Set)
    return Boolean;
```
14

```
function "<=" (Left  : in Wide_Character_Set;
               Right : in Wide_Character_Set)
    return Boolean renames Is_Subset;
```
15

```
-- Alternative representation for a set of Wide_Character values:
subtype Wide_Character_Sequence is Wide_String;
```
16

```
function To_Set (Sequence  : in Wide_Character_Sequence)
    return Wide_Character_Set;
```
17

```
function To_Set (Singleton : in Wide_Character)
    return Wide_Character_Set;
```
18

```
function To_Sequence (Set  : in Wide_Character_Set)
    return Wide_Character_Sequence;
```
19

```
-- Representation for a Wide_Character to Wide_Character mapping:
type Wide_Character_Mapping is private;
```
20

```
function Value (Map     : in Wide_Character_Mapping;
                Element : in Wide_Character)
    return Wide_Character;
```
21

```
Identity : constant Wide_Character_Mapping;
```
22

```
function To_Mapping (From, To : in Wide_Character_Sequence)
    return Wide_Character_Mapping;
```
23

```
function To_Domain (Map : in Wide_Character_Mapping)
    return Wide_Character_Sequence;
```
24

```
function To_Range  (Map : in Wide_Character_Mapping)
    return Wide_Character_Sequence;
```
25

```
type Wide_Character_Mapping_Function is
    access function (From : in Wide_Character) return Wide_Character;
```
26

```
private
    ... -- not specified by the language
end Ada.Strings.Wide_Maps;
```
27

The context clause for each of the packages Strings.Wide_Fixed, Strings.Wide_Bounded, and Strings.Wide_Unbounded identifies Strings.Wide_Maps instead of Strings.Maps. | 28

For each of the packages Strings.Fixed, Strings.Bounded, Strings.Unbounded, and Strings.Maps.Constants the corresponding wide string package has the same contents except that | 29

- Wide_Space replaces Space | 30

- Wide_Character replaces Character | 31

- Wide_String replaces String | 32

- Wide_Character_Set replaces Character_Set | 33

34   • Wide_Character_Mapping replaces Character_Mapping

35   • Wide_Character_Mapping_Function replaces Character_Mapping_Function

36   • Wide_Maps replaces Maps

37   • Bounded_Wide_String replaces Bounded_String

38   • Null_Bounded_Wide_String replaces Null_Bounded_String

39   • To_Bounded_Wide_String replaces To_Bounded_String

40   • To_Wide_String replaces To_String

41   • Unbounded_Wide_String replaces Unbounded_String

42   • Null_Unbounded_Wide_String replaces Null_Unbounded_String

43   • Wide_String_Access replaces String_Access

44   • To_Unbounded_Wide_String replaces To_Unbounded_String

45   The following additional declaration is present in Strings.Wide_Maps.Wide_Constants:

46
```
Character_Set : constant Wide_Maps.Wide_Character_Set;
  --Contains each Wide_Character value WC such that Characters.Is_Character(WC) is True
```

NOTES

47   12 If a null Wide_Character_Mapping_Function is passed to any of the Wide_String handling subprograms, Constraint_Error is propagated.

48   13 Each Wide_Character_Set constant in the package Strings.Wide_Maps.Wide_Constants contains no values outside the Character portion of Wide_Character. Similarly, each Wide_Character_Mapping constant in this package is the identity mapping when applied to any element outside the Character portion of Wide_Character.

A.5 The Numerics Packages

1   The library package Numerics is the parent of several child units that provide facilities for mathematical computation. One child, the generic package Generic_Elementary_Functions, is defined in A.5.1, together with nongeneric equivalents; two others, the package Float_Random and the generic package Discrete_Random, are defined in A.5.2. Additional (optional) children are defined in Annex G, ''Numerics''.

Static Semantics

2/1   *This paragraph was deleted.*

3
```
package Ada.Numerics is
   pragma Pure(Numerics);
   Argument_Error : exception;
   Pi : constant :=
         3.14159_26535_89793_23846_26433_83279_50288_41971_69399_37511;
   e  : constant :=
         2.71828_18284_59045_23536_02874_71352_66249_77572_47093_69996;
end Ada.Numerics;
```

4   The Argument_Error exception is raised by a subprogram in a child unit of Numerics to signal that one or more of the actual subprogram parameters are outside the domain of the corresponding mathematical function.

Implementation Permissions

5   The implementation may specify the values of Pi and e to a larger number of significant digits.

A.5.1 Elementary Functions

Implementation-defined approximations to the mathematical functions known as the "elementary functions" are provided by the subprograms in Numerics.Generic_Elementary_Functions. Nongeneric equivalents of this generic package for each of the predefined floating point types are also provided as children of Numerics.

1

Static Semantics

The generic library package Numerics.Generic_Elementary_Functions has the following declaration:

2

```
generic
   type Float_Type is digits <>;

package Ada.Numerics.Generic_Elementary_Functions is
   pragma Pure(Generic_Elementary_Functions);
   function Sqrt    (X              : Float_Type'Base) return Float_Type'Base;
   function Log     (X              : Float_Type'Base) return Float_Type'Base;
   function Log     (X, Base        : Float_Type'Base) return Float_Type'Base;
   function Exp     (X              : Float_Type'Base) return Float_Type'Base;
   function "**"    (Left, Right    : Float_Type'Base) return Float_Type'Base;

   function Sin     (X              : Float_Type'Base) return Float_Type'Base;
   function Sin     (X, Cycle       : Float_Type'Base) return Float_Type'Base;
   function Cos     (X              : Float_Type'Base) return Float_Type'Base;
   function Cos     (X, Cycle       : Float_Type'Base) return Float_Type'Base;
   function Tan     (X              : Float_Type'Base) return Float_Type'Base;
   function Tan     (X, Cycle       : Float_Type'Base) return Float_Type'Base;
   function Cot     (X              : Float_Type'Base) return Float_Type'Base;
   function Cot     (X, Cycle       : Float_Type'Base) return Float_Type'Base;

   function Arcsin  (X              : Float_Type'Base) return Float_Type'Base;
   function Arcsin  (X, Cycle       : Float_Type'Base) return Float_Type'Base;
   function Arccos  (X              : Float_Type'Base) return Float_Type'Base;
   function Arccos  (X, Cycle       : Float_Type'Base) return Float_Type'Base;
   function Arctan  (Y              : Float_Type'Base;
                     X              : Float_Type'Base := 1.0)
                                                        return Float_Type'Base;
   function Arctan  (Y              : Float_Type'Base;
                     X              : Float_Type'Base := 1.0;
                     Cycle          : Float_Type'Base) return Float_Type'Base;
   function Arccot  (X              : Float_Type'Base;
                     Y              : Float_Type'Base := 1.0)
                                                        return Float_Type'Base;
   function Arccot  (X              : Float_Type'Base;
                     Y              : Float_Type'Base := 1.0;
                     Cycle          : Float_Type'Base) return Float_Type'Base;

   function Sinh    (X              : Float_Type'Base) return Float_Type'Base;
   function Cosh    (X              : Float_Type'Base) return Float_Type'Base;
   function Tanh    (X              : Float_Type'Base) return Float_Type'Base;
   function Coth    (X              : Float_Type'Base) return Float_Type'Base;
   function Arcsinh (X              : Float_Type'Base) return Float_Type'Base;
   function Arccosh (X              : Float_Type'Base) return Float_Type'Base;
   function Arctanh (X              : Float_Type'Base) return Float_Type'Base;
   function Arccoth (X              : Float_Type'Base) return Float_Type'Base;
end Ada.Numerics.Generic_Elementary_Functions;
```

3

4

5

6

7

8

The library package Numerics.Elementary_Functions is declared pure and defines the same subprograms as Numerics.Generic_Elementary_Functions, except that the predefined type Float is systematically substituted for Float_Type'Base throughout. Nongeneric equivalents of Numerics.Generic_Elementary_Functions for each of the other predefined floating point types are defined similarly, with the names Numerics.Short_Elementary_Functions, Numerics.Long_Elementary_Functions, etc.

9/1

10 The functions have their usual mathematical meanings. When the Base parameter is specified, the Log function computes the logarithm to the given base; otherwise, it computes the natural logarithm. When the Cycle parameter is specified, the parameter X of the forward trigonometric functions (Sin, Cos, Tan, and Cot) and the results of the inverse trigonometric functions (Arcsin, Arccos, Arctan, and Arccot) are measured in units such that a full cycle of revolution has the given value; otherwise, they are measured in radians.

11 The computed results of the mathematically multivalued functions are rendered single-valued by the following conventions, which are meant to imply the principal branch:

12 • The results of the Sqrt and Arccosh functions and that of the exponentiation operator are nonnegative.

13 • The result of the Arcsin function is in the quadrant containing the point (1.0, x), where x is the value of the parameter X. This quadrant is I or IV; thus, the range of the Arcsin function is approximately -π/2.0 to π/2.0 (-Cycle/4.0 to Cycle/4.0, if the parameter Cycle is specified).

14 • The result of the Arccos function is in the quadrant containing the point (x, 1.0), where x is the value of the parameter X. This quadrant is I or II; thus, the Arccos function ranges from 0.0 to approximately π (Cycle/2.0, if the parameter Cycle is specified).

15 • The results of the Arctan and Arccot functions are in the quadrant containing the point (x, y), where x and y are the values of the parameters X and Y, respectively. This may be any quadrant (I through IV) when the parameter X (resp., Y) of Arctan (resp., Arccot) is specified, but it is restricted to quadrants I and IV (resp., I and II) when that parameter is omitted. Thus, the range when that parameter is specified is approximately -π to π (-Cycle/2.0 to Cycle/2.0, if the parameter Cycle is specified); when omitted, the range of Arctan (resp., Arccot) is that of Arcsin (resp., Arccos), as given above. When the point (x, y) lies on the negative x-axis, the result approximates

16   • π (resp., -π) when the sign of the parameter Y is positive (resp., negative), if Float_Type'Signed_Zeros is True;

17   • π, if Float_Type'Signed_Zeros is False.

18 (In the case of the inverse trigonometric functions, in which a result lying on or near one of the axes may not be exactly representable, the approximation inherent in computing the result may place it in an adjacent quadrant, close to but on the wrong side of the axis.)

Dynamic Semantics

19 The exception Numerics.Argument_Error is raised, signaling a parameter value outside the domain of the corresponding mathematical function, in the following cases:

20 • by any forward or inverse trigonometric function with specified cycle, when the value of the parameter Cycle is zero or negative;

21 • by the Log function with specified base, when the value of the parameter Base is zero, one, or negative;

22 • by the Sqrt and Log functions, when the value of the parameter X is negative;

23 • by the exponentiation operator, when the value of the left operand is negative or when both operands have the value zero;

24 • by the Arcsin, Arccos, and Arctanh functions, when the absolute value of the parameter X exceeds one;

25 • by the Arctan and Arccot functions, when the parameters X and Y both have the value zero;

26 • by the Arccosh function, when the value of the parameter X is less than one; and

A.5.1 Elementary Functions

- by the Arccoth function, when the absolute value of the parameter X is less than one. 27

The exception Constraint_Error is raised, signaling a pole of the mathematical function (analogous to 28 dividing by zero), in the following cases, provided that Float_Type'Machine_Overflows is True:

- by the Log, Cot, and Coth functions, when the value of the parameter X is zero; 29

- by the exponentiation operator, when the value of the left operand is zero and the value of the 30 exponent is negative;

- by the Tan function with specified cycle, when the value of the parameter X is an odd multiple of 31 the quarter cycle;

- by the Cot function with specified cycle, when the value of the parameter X is zero or a multiple 32 of the half cycle; and

- by the Arctanh and Arccoth functions, when the absolute value of the parameter X is one. 33

Constraint_Error can also be raised when a finite result overflows (see G.2.4); this may occur for 34 parameter values sufficiently *near* poles, and, in the case of some of the functions, for parameter values with sufficiently large magnitudes. When Float_Type'Machine_Overflows is False, the result at poles is unspecified.

When one parameter of a function with multiple parameters represents a pole and another is outside the 35 function's domain, the latter takes precedence (i.e., Numerics.Argument_Error is raised).

Implementation Requirements

In the implementation of Numerics.Generic_Elementary_Functions, the range of intermediate values 36 allowed during the calculation of a final result shall not be affected by any range constraint of the subtype Float_Type.

In the following cases, evaluation of an elementary function shall yield the *prescribed result*, provided that 37 the preceding rules do not call for an exception to be raised:

- When the parameter X has the value zero, the Sqrt, Sin, Arcsin, Tan, Sinh, Arcsinh, Tanh, and 38 Arctanh functions yield a result of zero, and the Exp, Cos, and Cosh functions yield a result of one.

- When the parameter X has the value one, the Sqrt function yields a result of one, and the Log, 39 Arccos, and Arccosh functions yield a result of zero.

- When the parameter Y has the value zero and the parameter X has a positive value, the Arctan 40 and Arccot functions yield a result of zero.

- The results of the Sin, Cos, Tan, and Cot functions with specified cycle are exact when the 41 mathematical result is zero; those of the first two are also exact when the mathematical result is ± 1.0.

- Exponentiation by a zero exponent yields the value one. Exponentiation by a unit exponent 42 yields the value of the left operand. Exponentiation of the value one yields the value one. Exponentiation of the value zero yields the value zero.

Other accuracy requirements for the elementary functions, which apply only in implementations 43 conforming to the Numerics Annex, and then only in the "strict" mode defined there (see G.2), are given in G.2.4.

When Float_Type'Signed_Zeros is True, the sign of a zero result shall be as follows: 44

45 • A prescribed zero result delivered *at the origin* by one of the odd functions (Sin, Arcsin, Sinh, Arcsinh, Tan, Arctan or Arccot as a function of Y when X is fixed and positive, Tanh, and Arctanh) has the sign of the parameter X (Y, in the case of Arctan or Arccot).

46 • A prescribed zero result delivered by one of the odd functions *away from the origin*, or by some other elementary function, has an implementation-defined sign.

47 • A zero result that is not a prescribed result (i.e., one that results from rounding or underflow) has the correct mathematical sign.

Implementation Permissions

48 The nongeneric equivalent packages may, but need not, be actual instantiations of the generic package for the appropriate predefined type.

A.5.2 Random Number Generation

1 Facilities for the generation of pseudo-random floating point numbers are provided in the package Numerics.Float_Random; the generic package Numerics.Discrete_Random provides similar facilities for the generation of pseudo-random integers and pseudo-random values of enumeration types. For brevity, pseudo-random values of any of these types are called *random numbers*.

2 Some of the facilities provided are basic to all applications of random numbers. These include a limited private type each of whose objects serves as the generator of a (possibly distinct) sequence of random numbers; a function to obtain the "next" random number from a given sequence of random numbers (that is, from its generator); and subprograms to initialize or reinitialize a given generator to a time-dependent state or a state denoted by a single integer.

3 Other facilities are provided specifically for advanced applications. These include subprograms to save and restore the state of a given generator; a private type whose objects can be used to hold the saved state of a generator; and subprograms to obtain a string representation of a given generator state, or, given such a string representation, the corresponding state.

Static Semantics

4 The library package Numerics.Float_Random has the following declaration:

```
package Ada.Numerics.Float_Random is

   -- Basic facilities

   type Generator is limited private;

   subtype Uniformly_Distributed is Float range 0.0 .. 1.0;
   function Random (Gen : Generator) return Uniformly_Distributed;

   procedure Reset (Gen       : in Generator;
                    Initiator : in Integer);
   procedure Reset (Gen       : in Generator);

   -- Advanced facilities

   type State is private;

   procedure Save (Gen      : in  Generator;
                   To_State : out State);
   procedure Reset (Gen       : in Generator;
                    From_State : in State);

   Max_Image_Width : constant := implementation-defined integer value;

   function Image (Of_State    : State)  return String;
   function Value (Coded_State : String) return State;
```

```
private
    ... -- not specified by the language
end Ada.Numerics.Float_Random;
```
15

The generic library package Numerics.Discrete_Random has the following declaration:
16

17

```
generic
    type Result_Subtype is (<>);
package Ada.Numerics.Discrete_Random is

    -- Basic facilities

    type Generator is limited private;

    function Random (Gen : Generator) return Result_Subtype;

    procedure Reset (Gen       : in Generator;
                     Initiator : in Integer);
    procedure Reset (Gen       : in Generator);

    -- Advanced facilities

    type State is private;

    procedure Save (Gen      : in  Generator;
                    To_State : out State);
    procedure Reset (Gen        : in  Generator;
                     From_State : in  State);

    Max_Image_Width : constant := implementation-defined integer value;

    function Image (Of_State   : State)  return String;
    function Value (Coded_State : String) return State;

private
    ... -- not specified by the language
end Ada.Numerics.Discrete_Random;
```
18
19
20
21
22
23
24
25
26
27

An object of the limited private type Generator is associated with a sequence of random numbers. Each generator has a hidden (internal) state, which the operations on generators use to determine the position in the associated sequence. All generators are implicitly initialized to an unspecified state that does not vary from one program execution to another; they may also be explicitly initialized, or reinitialized, to a time-dependent state, to a previously saved state, or to a state uniquely denoted by an integer value.
28

An object of the private type State can be used to hold the internal state of a generator. Such objects are only needed if the application is designed to save and restore generator states or to examine or manufacture them.
29

The operations on generators affect the state and therefore the future values of the associated sequence. The semantics of the operations on generators and states are defined below.
30

```
function Random (Gen : Generator) return Uniformly_Distributed;
function Random (Gen : Generator) return Result_Subtype;
```
31

Obtains the "next" random number from the given generator, relative to its current state, according to an implementation-defined algorithm. The result of the function in Numerics.Float_Random is delivered as a value of the subtype Uniformly_Distributed, which is a subtype of the predefined type Float having a range of 0.0 .. 1.0. The result of the function in an instantiation of Numerics.Discrete_Random is delivered as a value of the generic formal subtype Result_Subtype.
32

```
procedure Reset (Gen       : in Generator;
                 Initiator : in Integer);
procedure Reset (Gen       : in Generator);
```
33

34   Sets the state of the specified generator to one that is an unspecified function of the value of the parameter Initiator (or to a time-dependent state, if only a generator parameter is specified). The latter form of the procedure is known as the *time-dependent Reset procedure*.

35
```
procedure Save  (Gen        : in  Generator;
                 To_State   : out State);
procedure Reset (Gen        : in  Generator;
                 From_State : in  State);
```

36   Save obtains the current state of a generator. Reset gives a generator the specified state. A generator that is reset to a state previously obtained by invoking Save is restored to the state it had when Save was invoked.

37
```
function Image (Of_State    : State)  return String;
function Value (Coded_State : String) return State;
```

38   Image provides a representation of a state coded (in an implementation-defined way) as a string whose length is bounded by the value of Max_Image_Width. Value is the inverse of Image: Value(Image(S)) = S for each state S that can be obtained from a generator by invoking Save.

Dynamic Semantics

39   Instantiation of Numerics.Discrete_Random with a subtype having a null range raises Constraint_Error.

40/1   *This paragraph was deleted.*

Bounded (Run-Time) Errors

40.1/1   It is a bounded error to invoke Value with a string that is not the image of any generator state. If the error is detected, Constraint_Error or Program_Error is raised. Otherwise, a call to Reset with the resulting state will produce a generator such that calls to Random with this generator will produce a sequence of values of the appropriate subtype, but which might not be random in character. That is, the sequence of values might not fulfill the implementation requirements of this subclause.

Implementation Requirements

41   A sufficiently long sequence of random numbers obtained by successive calls to Random is approximately uniformly distributed over the range of the result subtype.

42   The Random function in an instantiation of Numerics.Discrete_Random is guaranteed to yield each value in its result subtype in a finite number of calls, provided that the number of such values does not exceed 2[15].

43   Other performance requirements for the random number generator, which apply only in implementations conforming to the Numerics Annex, and then only in the "strict" mode defined there (see G.2), are given in G.2.5.

Documentation Requirements

44   No one algorithm for random number generation is best for all applications. To enable the user to determine the suitability of the random number generators for the intended application, the implementation shall describe the algorithm used and shall give its period, if known exactly, or a lower bound on the period, if the exact period is unknown. Periods that are so long that the periodicity is unobservable in practice can be described in such terms, without giving a numerical bound.

The implementation also shall document the minimum time interval between calls to the time-dependent Reset procedure that are guaranteed to initiate different sequences, and it shall document the nature of the strings that Value will accept without raising Constraint_Error. `45`

Implementation Advice

Any storage associated with an object of type Generator should be reclaimed on exit from the scope of the object. `46`

If the generator period is sufficiently long in relation to the number of distinct initiator values, then each possible value of Initiator passed to Reset should initiate a sequence of random numbers that does not, in a practical sense, overlap the sequence initiated by any other value. If this is not possible, then the mapping between initiator values and generator states should be a rapidly varying function of the initiator value. `47`

NOTES

14 If two or more tasks are to share the same generator, then the tasks have to synchronize their access to the generator as for any shared variable (see 9.10). `48`

15 Within a given implementation, a repeatable random number sequence can be obtained by relying on the implicit initialization of generators or by explicitly initializing a generator with a repeatable initiator value. Different sequences of random numbers can be obtained from a given generator in different program executions by explicitly initializing the generator to a time-dependent state. `49`

16 A given implementation of the Random function in Numerics.Float_Random may or may not be capable of delivering the values 0.0 or 1.0. Portable applications should assume that these values, or values sufficiently close to them to behave indistinguishably from them, can occur. If a sequence of random integers from some fixed range is needed, the application should use the Random function in an appropriate instantiation of Numerics.Discrete_Random, rather than transforming the result of the Random function in Numerics.Float_Random. However, some applications with unusual requirements, such as for a sequence of random integers each drawn from a different range, will find it more convenient to transform the result of the floating point Random function. For $M \geq 1$, the expression `50`

```
Integer(Float(M) * Random(G)) mod M
```
`51`

transforms the result of Random(G) to an integer uniformly distributed over the range 0 .. M-1; it is valid even if Random delivers 0.0 or 1.0. Each value of the result range is possible, provided that M is not too large. Exponentially distributed (floating point) random numbers with mean and standard deviation 1.0 can be obtained by the transformation `52`

```
-Log(Random(G) + Float'Model_Small))
```
`53`

where Log comes from Numerics.Elementary_Functions (see A.5.1); in this expression, the addition of Float'Model_Small avoids the exception that would be raised were Log to be given the value zero, without affecting the result (in most implementations) when Random returns a nonzero value. `54`

Examples

Example of a program that plays a simulated dice game: `55`

```
with Ada.Numerics.Discrete_Random;
procedure Dice_Game is
    subtype Die is Integer range 1 .. 6;
    subtype Dice is Integer range 2*Die'First .. 2*Die'Last;
    package Random_Die is new Ada.Numerics.Discrete_Random (Die);
    use Random_Die;
    G : Generator;
    D : Dice;
begin
    Reset (G);   -- Start the generator in a unique state in each run
    loop
        -- Roll a pair of dice; sum and process the results
        D := Random(G) + Random(G);
        ...
    end loop;
end Dice_Game;
```
`56`

Random Number Generation   **A.5.2**

57   *Example of a program that simulates coin tosses:*

58
```
with Ada.Numerics.Discrete_Random;
procedure Flip_A_Coin is
    type Coin is (Heads, Tails);
    package Random_Coin is new Ada.Numerics.Discrete_Random (Coin);
    use Random_Coin;
    G : Generator;
begin
    Reset (G);   -- Start the generator in a unique state in each run
    loop
        -- Toss a coin and process the result
        case Random(G) is
            when Heads =>
                ...
            when Tails =>
                ...
        end case;
    ...
    end loop;
end Flip_A_Coin;
```

59   *Example of a parallel simulation of a physical system, with a separate generator of event probabilities in each task:*

60
```
with Ada.Numerics.Float_Random;
procedure Parallel_Simulation is
    use Ada.Numerics.Float_Random;
    task type Worker is
        entry Initialize_Generator (Initiator : in Integer);
        ...
    end Worker;
    W : array (1 .. 10) of Worker;
    task body Worker is
        G : Generator;
        Probability_Of_Event : Uniformly_Distributed;
    begin
        accept Initialize_Generator (Initiator : in Integer) do
            Reset (G, Initiator);
        end Initialize_Generator;
        loop
            ...
            Probability_Of_Event := Random(G);
            ...
        end loop;
    end Worker;
begin
    -- Initialize the generators in the Worker tasks to different states
    for I in W'Range loop
        W(I).Initialize_Generator (I);
    end loop;
    ... -- Wait for the Worker tasks to terminate
end Parallel_Simulation;
```

NOTES

61   17 *Notes on the last example:* Although each Worker task initializes its generator to a different state, those states will be the same in every execution of the program. The generator states can be initialized uniquely in each program execution by instantiating Ada.Numerics.Discrete_Random for the type Integer in the main procedure, resetting the generator obtained from that instance to a time-dependent state, and then using random integers obtained from that generator to initialize the generators in each Worker task.

A.5.3 Attributes of Floating Point Types

Static Semantics

The following *representation-oriented attributes* are defined for every subtype S of a floating point type *T*.   1

S'Machine_Radix   2

> Yields the radix of the hardware representation of the type *T*. The value of this attribute is of the type *universal_integer*.

The values of other representation-oriented attributes of a floating point subtype, and of the "primitive   3
function" attributes of a floating point subtype described later, are defined in terms of a particular
representation of nonzero values called the *canonical form*. The canonical form (for the type *T*) is the form

$$\pm\, mantissa \cdot T\text{Machine\_Radix}^{exponent}$$

where

- *mantissa* is a fraction in the number base *T*Machine_Radix, the first digit of which is nonzero,   4
  and

- *exponent* is an integer.   5

S'Machine_Mantissa   6

> Yields the largest value of p such that every value expressible in the canonical form (for the
> type *T*), having a p-digit *mantissa* and an *exponent* between *T*Machine_Emin and
> *T*Machine_Emax, is a machine number (see 3.5.7) of the type *T*. This attribute yields a
> value of the type *universal_integer*.

S'Machine_Emin   7

> Yields the smallest (most negative) value of *exponent* such that every value expressible in
> the canonical form (for the type *T*), having a *mantissa* of *T*Machine_Mantissa digits, is a
> machine number (see 3.5.7) of the type *T*. This attribute yields a value of the type
> *universal_integer*.

S'Machine_Emax   8

> Yields the largest (most positive) value of *exponent* such that every value expressible in the
> canonical form (for the type *T*), having a *mantissa* of *T*Machine_Mantissa digits, is a
> machine number (see 3.5.7) of the type *T*. This attribute yields a value of the type
> *universal_integer*.

S'Denorm   Yields the value True if every value expressible in the form   9

$$\pm\, mantissa \cdot T\text{Machine\_Radix}^{T\text{Machine\_Emin}}$$

> where *mantissa* is a nonzero *T*Machine_Mantissa-digit fraction in the number base
> *T*Machine_Radix, the first digit of which is zero, is a machine number (see 3.5.7) of the
> type *T*; yields the value False otherwise. The value of this attribute is of the predefined type
> Boolean.

The values described by the formula in the definition of S'Denorm are called *denormalized numbers*. A   10
nonzero machine number that is not a denormalized number is a *normalized number*. A normalized
number x of a given type *T* is said to be *represented in canonical form* when it is expressed in the
canonical form (for the type *T*) with a *mantissa* having *T*Machine_Mantissa digits; the resulting form is
the *canonical-form representation* of x.

S'Machine_Rounds   11

> Yields the value True if rounding is performed on inexact results of every predefined
> operation that yields a result of the type *T*; yields the value False otherwise. The value of
> this attribute is of the predefined type Boolean.

12 S'Machine_Overflows

Yields the value True if overflow and divide-by-zero are detected and reported by raising Constraint_Error for every predefined operation that yields a result of the type T; yields the value False otherwise. The value of this attribute is of the predefined type Boolean.

13 S'Signed_Zeros

Yields the value True if the hardware representation for the type T has the capability of representing both positively and negatively signed zeros, these being generated and used by the predefined operations of the type T as specified in IEC 559:1989; yields the value False otherwise. The value of this attribute is of the predefined type Boolean.

14 For every value x of a floating point type T, the *normalized exponent* of x is defined as follows:

15 • the normalized exponent of zero is (by convention) zero;

16 • for nonzero x, the normalized exponent of x is the unique integer k such that TMachine_Radix^{k-1} $\leq |x| < T$Machine_Radix^k.

17 The following *primitive function attributes* are defined for any subtype S of a floating point type T.

18 S'Exponent   S'Exponent denotes a function with the following specification:

19
```
function S'Exponent (X : T)
   return universal_integer
```

20 The function yields the normalized exponent of X.

21 S'Fraction   S'Fraction denotes a function with the following specification:

22
```
function S'Fraction (X : T)
   return T
```

23 The function yields the value $X \cdot T$Machine_Radix^{-k}, where k is the normalized exponent of X. A zero result, which can only occur when X is zero, has the sign of X.

24 S'Compose   S'Compose denotes a function with the following specification:

25
```
function S'Compose (Fraction : T;
                    Exponent : universal_integer)
   return T
```

26 Let v be the value *Fraction* $\cdot T$Machine_Radix$^{Exponent-k}$, where k is the normalized exponent of *Fraction*. If v is a machine number of the type T, or if $|v| \geq T$Model_Small, the function yields v; otherwise, it yields either one of the machine numbers of the type T adjacent to v. Constraint_Error is optionally raised if v is outside the base range of S. A zero result has the sign of *Fraction* when S'Signed_Zeros is True.

27 S'Scaling   S'Scaling denotes a function with the following specification:

28
```
function S'Scaling (X : T;
                    Adjustment : universal_integer)
   return T
```

29 Let v be the value $X \cdot T$Machine_Radix^{Adjustment}. If v is a machine number of the type T, or if $|v| \geq T$Model_Small, the function yields v; otherwise, it yields either one of the machine numbers of the type T adjacent to v. Constraint_Error is optionally raised if v is outside the base range of S. A zero result has the sign of X when S'Signed_Zeros is True.

30 S'Floor   S'Floor denotes a function with the following specification:

31
```
function S'Floor (X : T)
   return T
```

32 The function yields the value $\lfloor X \rfloor$, i.e., the largest (most positive) integral value less than or equal to X. When X is zero, the result has the sign of X; a zero result otherwise has a positive sign.

S'Ceiling S'Ceiling denotes a function with the following specification: 33

> **function** S'Ceiling (*X* : *T*) 34
> **return** *T*

The function yields the value $\lceil X \rceil$, i.e., the smallest (most negative) integral value greater 35
than or equal to *X*. When *X* is zero, the result has the sign of *X*; a zero result otherwise has a
negative sign when S'Signed_Zeros is True.

S'Rounding S'Rounding denotes a function with the following specification: 36

> **function** S'Rounding (*X* : *T*) 37
> **return** *T*

The function yields the integral value nearest to *X*, rounding away from zero if *X* lies 38
exactly halfway between two integers. A zero result has the sign of *X* when S'Signed_Zeros
is True.

S'Unbiased_Rounding 39
> S'Unbiased_Rounding denotes a function with the following specification:

> **function** S'Unbiased_Rounding (*X* : *T*) 40
> **return** *T*

The function yields the integral value nearest to *X*, rounding toward the even integer if *X* 41
lies exactly halfway between two integers. A zero result has the sign of *X* when
S'Signed_Zeros is True.

S'Truncation S'Truncation denotes a function with the following specification: 42

> **function** S'Truncation (*X* : *T*) 43
> **return** *T*

The function yields the value $\lceil X \rceil$ when *X* is negative, and $\lfloor X \rfloor$ otherwise. A zero result has 44
the sign of *X* when S'Signed_Zeros is True.

S'Remainder S'Remainder denotes a function with the following specification: 45

> **function** S'Remainder (*X*, *Y* : *T*) 46
> **return** *T*

For nonzero *Y*, let *v* be the value $X - n \cdot Y$, where *n* is the integer nearest to the exact value 47
of *X*/*Y*; if $|n - X/Y| = 1/2$, then *n* is chosen to be even. If *v* is a machine number of the type
T, the function yields *v*; otherwise, it yields zero. Constraint_Error is raised if *Y* is zero. A
zero result has the sign of *X* when S'Signed_Zeros is True.

S'Adjacent S'Adjacent denotes a function with the following specification: 48

> **function** S'Adjacent (*X*, *Towards* : *T*) 49
> **return** *T*

If *Towards* = *X*, the function yields *X*; otherwise, it yields the machine number of the type 50
T adjacent to *X* in the direction of *Towards*, if that machine number exists. If the result
would be outside the base range of S, Constraint_Error is raised. When *T*'Signed_Zeros is
True, a zero result has the sign of *X*. When *Towards* is zero, its sign has no bearing on the
result.

S'Copy_Sign S'Copy_Sign denotes a function with the following specification: 51

> **function** S'Copy_Sign (*Value*, *Sign* : *T*) 52
> **return** *T*

If the value of *Value* is nonzero, the function yields a result whose magnitude is that of 53
Value and whose sign is that of *Sign*; otherwise, it yields the value zero. Constraint_Error is
optionally raised if the result is outside the base range of S. A zero result has the sign of
Sign when S'Signed_Zeros is True.

S'Leading_Part 54
> S'Leading_Part denotes a function with the following specification:

55
```
function S'Leading_Part (X : T;
                    Radix_Digits : universal_integer)
    return T
```

56 Let v be the value T'Machine_Radix$^{k-Radix\_Digits}$, where k is the normalized exponent of X. The function yields the value

57 • $\lfloor X/v \rfloor \cdot v$, when X is nonnegative and *Radix_Digits* is positive;

58 • $\lceil X/v \rceil \cdot v$, when X is negative and *Radix_Digits* is positive.

59 Constraint_Error is raised when *Radix_Digits* is zero or negative. A zero result, which can only occur when X is zero, has the sign of X.

60 S'Machine S'Machine denotes a function with the following specification:

61
```
function S'Machine (X : T)
    return T
```

62 If X is a machine number of the type T, the function yields X; otherwise, it yields the value obtained by rounding or truncating X to either one of the adjacent machine numbers of the type T. Constraint_Error is raised if rounding or truncating X to the precision of the machine numbers results in a value outside the base range of S. A zero result has the sign of X when S'Signed_Zeros is True.

63 The following *model-oriented attributes* are defined for any subtype S of a floating point type T.

64 S'Model_Mantissa
If the Numerics Annex is not supported, this attribute yields an implementation defined value that is greater than or equal to $\lceil d \cdot \log(10) / \log(T\text{'Machine\_Radix}) \rceil + 1$, where d is the requested decimal precision of T, and less than or equal to the value of T'Machine_Mantissa. See G.2.2 for further requirements that apply to implementations supporting the Numerics Annex. The value of this attribute is of the type *universal_integer*.

65 S'Model_Emin
If the Numerics Annex is not supported, this attribute yields an implementation defined value that is greater than or equal to the value of T'Machine_Emin. See G.2.2 for further requirements that apply to implementations supporting the Numerics Annex. The value of this attribute is of the type *universal_integer*.

66 S'Model_Epsilon
Yields the value T'Machine_Radix$^{1 - T\text{'Model\_Mantissa}}$. The value of this attribute is of the type *universal_real*.

67 S'Model_Small
Yields the value T'Machine_Radix$^{T\text{'Model\_Emin} - 1}$. The value of this attribute is of the type *universal_real*.

68 S'Model S'Model denotes a function with the following specification:

69
```
function S'Model (X : T)
    return T
```

70 If the Numerics Annex is not supported, the meaning of this attribute is implementation defined; see G.2.2 for the definition that applies to implementations supporting the Numerics Annex.

71 S'Safe_First
Yields the lower bound of the safe range (see 3.5.7) of the type T. If the Numerics Annex is not supported, the value of this attribute is implementation defined; see G.2.2 for the definition that applies to implementations supporting the Numerics Annex. The value of this attribute is of the type *universal_real*.

S'Safe_Last Yields the upper bound of the safe range (see 3.5.7) of the type *T*. If the Numerics Annex is not supported, the value of this attribute is implementation defined; see G.2.2 for the definition that applies to implementations supporting the Numerics Annex. The value of this attribute is of the type *universal_real*.   72

A.5.4 Attributes of Fixed Point Types

Static Semantics

The following *representation-oriented* attributes are defined for every subtype S of a fixed point type *T*.   1

S'Machine_Radix   2
> Yields the radix of the hardware representation of the type *T*. The value of this attribute is of the type *universal_integer*.

S'Machine_Rounds   3
> Yields the value True if rounding is performed on inexact results of every predefined operation that yields a result of the type *T*; yields the value False otherwise. The value of this attribute is of the predefined type Boolean.

S'Machine_Overflows   4
> Yields the value True if overflow and divide-by-zero are detected and reported by raising Constraint_Error for every predefined operation that yields a result of the type *T*; yields the value False otherwise. The value of this attribute is of the predefined type Boolean.

A.6 Input-Output

Input-output is provided through language-defined packages, each of which is a child of the root package Ada. The generic packages Sequential_IO and Direct_IO define input-output operations applicable to files containing elements of a given type. The generic package Storage_IO supports reading from and writing to an in-memory buffer. Additional operations for text input-output are supplied in the packages Text_IO and Wide_Text_IO. Heterogeneous input-output is provided through the child packages Streams.Stream_IO and Text_IO.Text_Streams (see also 13.13). The package IO_Exceptions defines the exceptions needed by the predefined input-output packages.   1

A.7 External Files and File Objects

Static Semantics

Values input from the external environment of the program, or output to the external environment, are considered to occupy *external files*. An external file can be anything external to the program that can produce a value to be read or receive a value to be written. An external file is identified by a string (the *name*). A second string (the *form*) gives further system-dependent characteristics that may be associated with the file, such as the physical organization or access rights. The conventions governing the interpretation of such strings shall be documented.   1

Input and output operations are expressed as operations on objects of some *file type*, rather than directly in terms of the external files. In the remainder of this section, the term *file* is always used to refer to a file object; the term *external file* is used otherwise.   2

Input-output for sequential files of values of a single element type is defined by means of the generic package Sequential_IO. In order to define sequential input-output for a given element type, an instantiation of this generic unit, with the given type as actual parameter, has to be declared. The resulting package   3 contains the declaration of a file type (called File_Type) for files of such elements, as well as the operations applicable to these files, such as the Open, Read, and Write procedures.

4 Input-output for direct access files is likewise defined by a generic package called Direct_IO. Input-output in human-readable form is defined by the (nongeneric) packages Text_IO for Character and String data, and Wide_Text_IO for Wide_Character and Wide_String data. Input-output for files containing streams of elements representing values of possibly different types is defined by means of the (nongeneric) package Streams.Stream_IO.

5 Before input or output operations can be performed on a file, the file first has to be associated with an external file. While such an association is in effect, the file is said to be *open*, and otherwise the file is said to be *closed*.

6 The language does not define what happens to external files after the completion of the main program and all the library tasks (in particular, if corresponding files have not been closed). The effect of input-output for access types is unspecified.

7 An open file has a *current mode*, which is a value of one of the following enumeration types:

8   **type** File_Mode **is** (In_File, Inout_File, Out_File);   *-- for Direct_IO*

9   These values correspond respectively to the cases where only reading, both reading and writing, or only writing are to be performed.

10   **type** File_Mode **is** (In_File, Out_File, Append_File);
       -- for Sequential_IO, Text_IO, Wide_Text_IO, and Stream_IO

11   These values correspond respectively to the cases where only reading, only writing, or only appending are to be performed.

12   The mode of a file can be changed.

13 Several file management operations are common to Sequential_IO, Direct_IO, Text_IO, and Wide_Text_IO. These operations are described in subclause A.8.2 for sequential and direct files. Any additional effects concerning text input-output are described in subclause A.10.2.

14 The exceptions that can be propagated by the execution of an input-output subprogram are defined in the package IO_Exceptions; the situations in which they can be propagated are described following the description of the subprogram (and in clause A.13). The exceptions Storage_Error and Program_Error may be propagated. (Program_Error can only be propagated due to errors made by the caller of the subprogram.) Finally, exceptions can be propagated in certain implementation-defined situations.

NOTES

15 18 Each instantiation of the generic packages Sequential_IO and Direct_IO declares a different type File_Type. In the case of Text_IO, Wide_Text_IO, and Streams.Stream_IO, the corresponding type File_Type is unique.

16 19 A bidirectional device can often be modeled as two sequential files associated with the device, one of mode In_File, and one of mode Out_File. An implementation may restrict the number of files that may be associated with a given external file.

A.8 Sequential and Direct Files

Static Semantics

Two kinds of access to external files are defined in this subclause: *sequential access* and *direct access*. The corresponding file types and the associated operations are provided by the generic packages Sequential_IO and Direct_IO. A file object to be used for sequential access is called a *sequential file*, and one to be used for direct access is called a *direct file*. Access to stream files is described in A.12.1.

1

For sequential access, the file is viewed as a sequence of values that are transferred in the order of their appearance (as produced by the program or by the external environment). When the file is opened with mode In_File or Out_File, transfer starts respectively from or to the beginning of the file. When the file is opened with mode Append_File, transfer to the file starts after the last element of the file.

2

For direct access, the file is viewed as a set of elements occupying consecutive positions in linear order; a value can be transferred to or from an element of the file at any selected position. The position of an element is specified by its *index*, which is a number, greater than zero, of the implementation-defined integer type Count. The first element, if any, has index one; the index of the last element, if any, is called the *current size*; the current size is zero if there are no elements. The current size is a property of the external file.

3

An open direct file has a *current index*, which is the index that will be used by the next read or write operation. When a direct file is opened, the current index is set to one. The current index of a direct file is a property of a file object, not of an external file.

4

A.8.1 The Generic Package Sequential_IO

Static Semantics

The generic library package Sequential_IO has the following declaration:

1

```ada
with Ada.IO_Exceptions;                                                    2
generic
   type Element_Type(<>) is private;
package Ada.Sequential_IO is

   type File_Type is limited private;                                      3

   type File_Mode is (In_File, Out_File, Append_File);                     4

   -- File management                                                      5

   procedure Create(File : in out File_Type;                               6
                    Mode : in File_Mode := Out_File;
                    Name : in String := "";
                    Form : in String := "");

   procedure Open   (File : in out File_Type;                              7
                    Mode : in File_Mode;
                    Name : in String;
                    Form : in String := "");

   procedure Close (File : in out File_Type);                              8
   procedure Delete(File : in out File_Type);
   procedure Reset (File : in out File_Type; Mode : in File_Mode);
   procedure Reset (File : in out File_Type);

   function Mode    (File : in File_Type) return File_Mode;                9
   function Name    (File : in File_Type) return String;
   function Form    (File : in File_Type) return String;

   function Is_Open(File : in File_Type) return Boolean;                   10
```

11   *-- Input and output operations*

12
```
procedure Read  (File : in File_Type; Item : out Element_Type);
procedure Write (File : in File_Type; Item : in Element_Type);
```

13
```
function End_Of_File(File : in File_Type) return Boolean;
```

14   *-- Exceptions*

15
```
Status_Error : exception renames IO_Exceptions.Status_Error;
Mode_Error   : exception renames IO_Exceptions.Mode_Error;
Name_Error   : exception renames IO_Exceptions.Name_Error;
Use_Error    : exception renames IO_Exceptions.Use_Error;
Device_Error : exception renames IO_Exceptions.Device_Error;
End_Error    : exception renames IO_Exceptions.End_Error;
Data_Error   : exception renames IO_Exceptions.Data_Error;
```

16
```
private
    ... -- not specified by the language
end Ada.Sequential_IO;
```

A.8.2 File Management

Static Semantics

1   The procedures and functions described in this subclause provide for the control of external files; their declarations are repeated in each of the packages for sequential, direct, text, and stream input-output. For text input-output, the procedures Create, Open, and Reset have additional effects described in subclause A.10.2.

2
```
procedure Create(File : in out File_Type;
                 Mode : in File_Mode := default_mode;
                 Name : in String := "";
                 Form : in String := "");
```

3   Establishes a new external file, with the given name and form, and associates this external file with the given file. The given file is left open. The current mode of the given file is set to the given access mode. The default access mode is the mode Out_File for sequential and text input-output; it is the mode Inout_File for direct input-output. For direct access, the size of the created file is implementation defined.

4   A null string for Name specifies an external file that is not accessible after the completion of the main program (a temporary file). A null string for Form specifies the use of the default options of the implementation for the external file.

5   The exception Status_Error is propagated if the given file is already open. The exception Name_Error is propagated if the string given as Name does not allow the identification of an external file. The exception Use_Error is propagated if, for the specified mode, the external environment does not support creation of an external file with the given name (in the absence of Name_Error) and form.

6
```
procedure Open(File : in out File_Type;
               Mode : in File_Mode;
               Name : in String;
               Form : in String := "");
```

7   Associates the given file with an existing external file having the given name and form, and sets the current mode of the given file to the given mode. The given file is left open.

8   The exception Status_Error is propagated if the given file is already open. The exception Name_Error is propagated if the string given as Name does not allow the identification of an external file; in particular, this exception is propagated if no external file with the given name

exists. The exception Use_Error is propagated if, for the specified mode, the external environment does not support opening for an external file with the given name (in the absence of Name_Error) and form.

procedure Close(File : **in out** File_Type);   9

Severs the association between the given file and its associated external file. The given file is left   10
closed. In addition, for sequential files, if the file being closed has mode Out_File or
Append_File, then the last element written since the most recent open or reset is the last element
that can be read from the file. If no elements have been written and the file mode is Out_File,
then the closed file is empty. If no elements have been written and the file mode is Append_File,
then the closed file is unchanged.

The exception Status_Error is propagated if the given file is not open.   11

procedure Delete(File : **in out** File_Type);   12

Deletes the external file associated with the given file. The given file is closed, and the external   13
file ceases to exist.

The exception Status_Error is propagated if the given file is not open. The exception Use_Error   14
is propagated if deletion of the external file is not supported by the external environment.

procedure Reset(File : **in out** File_Type; Mode : **in** File_Mode);   15
procedure Reset(File : **in out** File_Type);

Resets the given file so that reading from its elements can be restarted from the beginning of the   16
file (for modes In_File and Inout_File), and so that writing to its elements can be restarted at the
beginning of the file (for modes Out_File and Inout_File) or after the last element of the file (for
mode Append_File). In particular, for direct access this means that the current index is set to
one. If a Mode parameter is supplied, the current mode of the given file is set to the given mode.
In addition, for sequential files, if the given file has mode Out_File or Append_File when Reset
is called, the last element written since the most recent open or reset is the last element that can
be read from the file. If no elements have been written and the file mode is Out_File, the reset
file is empty. If no elements have been written and the file mode is Append_File, then the reset
file is unchanged.

The exception Status_Error is propagated if the file is not open. The exception Use_Error is   17
propagated if the external environment does not support resetting for the external file and, also,
if the external environment does not support resetting to the specified mode for the external file.

function Mode(File : **in** File_Type) **return** File_Mode;   18

Returns the current mode of the given file.   19

The exception Status_Error is propagated if the file is not open.   20

function Name(File : **in** File_Type) **return** String;   21

Returns a string which uniquely identifies the external file currently associated with the given   22
file (and may thus be used in an Open operation). If an external environment allows alternative
specifications of the name (for example, abbreviations), the string returned by the function
should correspond to a full specification of the name.

23   The exception Status_Error is propagated if the given file is not open. The exception Use_Error is propagated if the associated external file is a temporary file that cannot be opened by any name.

24   **function** Form(File : **in** File_Type) **return** String;

25   Returns the form string for the external file currently associated with the given file. If an external environment allows alternative specifications of the form (for example, abbreviations using default options), the string returned by the function should correspond to a full specification (that is, it should indicate explicitly all options selected, including default options).

26   The exception Status_Error is propagated if the given file is not open.

27   **function** Is_Open(File : **in** File_Type) **return** Boolean;

28   Returns True if the file is open (that is, if it is associated with an external file), otherwise returns False.

Implementation Permissions

29   An implementation may propagate Name_Error or Use_Error if an attempt is made to use an I/O feature that cannot be supported by the implementation due to limitations in the external environment. Any such restriction should be documented.

A.8.3 Sequential Input-Output Operations

Static Semantics

1   The operations available for sequential input and output are described in this subclause. The exception Status_Error is propagated if any of these operations is attempted for a file that is not open.

2   **procedure** Read(File : **in** File_Type; Item : **out** Element_Type);

3   Operates on a file of mode In_File. Reads an element from the given file, and returns the value of this element in the Item parameter.

4   The exception Mode_Error is propagated if the mode is not In_File. The exception End_Error is propagated if no more elements can be read from the given file. The exception Data_Error can be propagated if the element read cannot be interpreted as a value of the subtype Element_Type (see A.13, "Exceptions in Input-Output").

5   **procedure** Write(File : **in** File_Type; Item : **in** Element_Type);

6   Operates on a file of mode Out_File or Append_File. Writes the value of Item to the given file.

7   The exception Mode_Error is propagated if the mode is not Out_File or Append_File. The exception Use_Error is propagated if the capacity of the external file is exceeded.

8   **function** End_Of_File(File : **in** File_Type) **return** Boolean;

9   Operates on a file of mode In_File. Returns True if no more elements can be read from the given file; otherwise returns False.

10   The exception Mode_Error is propagated if the mode is not In_File.

A.8.4 The Generic Package Direct_IO

Static Semantics

The generic library package Direct_IO has the following declaration: 1

```ada
with Ada.IO_Exceptions;                                                                 2
generic
   type Element_Type is private;
package Ada.Direct_IO is

   type File_Type is limited private;                                                   3

   type File_Mode is (In_File, Inout_File, Out_File);                                   4
   type Count       is range 0 .. implementation-defined;
   subtype Positive_Count is Count range 1 .. Count'Last;

   -- File management                                                                    5

   procedure Create(File : in out File_Type;                                            6
                    Mode : in File_Mode := Inout_File;
                    Name : in String := "";
                    Form : in String := "");

   procedure Open  (File : in out File_Type;                                            7
                    Mode : in File_Mode;
                    Name : in String;
                    Form : in String := "");

   procedure Close (File : in out File_Type);                                           8
   procedure Delete(File : in out File_Type);
   procedure Reset (File : in out File_Type; Mode : in File_Mode);
   procedure Reset (File : in out File_Type);

   function Mode   (File : in File_Type) return File_Mode;                              9
   function Name   (File : in File_Type) return String;
   function Form   (File : in File_Type) return String;

   function Is_Open(File : in File_Type) return Boolean;                                10

   -- Input and output operations                                                       11

   procedure Read (File : in File_Type; Item : out Element_Type;                        12
                                        From : in Positive_Count);
   procedure Read (File : in File_Type; Item : out Element_Type);

   procedure Write(File : in File_Type; Item : in  Element_Type;                        13
                                        To   : in Positive_Count);
   procedure Write(File : in File_Type; Item : in Element_Type);

   procedure Set_Index(File : in File_Type; To : in Positive_Count);                    14

   function Index(File : in File_Type) return Positive_Count;                           15
   function Size (File : in File_Type) return Count;

   function End_Of_File(File : in File_Type) return Boolean;                            16

   -- Exceptions                                                                         17

   Status_Error : exception renames IO_Exceptions.Status_Error;                         18
   Mode_Error   : exception renames IO_Exceptions.Mode_Error;
   Name_Error   : exception renames IO_Exceptions.Name_Error;
   Use_Error    : exception renames IO_Exceptions.Use_Error;
   Device_Error : exception renames IO_Exceptions.Device_Error;
   End_Error    : exception renames IO_Exceptions.End_Error;
   Data_Error   : exception renames IO_Exceptions.Data_Error;

private                                                                                 19
   ... -- not specified by the language
end Ada.Direct_IO;
```

A.8.5 Direct Input-Output Operations

Static Semantics

1   The operations available for direct input and output are described in this subclause. The exception Status_Error is propagated if any of these operations is attempted for a file that is not open.

2   ```
procedure Read(File : in File_Type; Item : out Element_Type;
                                    From : in Positive_Count);
procedure Read(File : in File_Type; Item : out Element_Type);
```

3   Operates on a file of mode In_File or Inout_File. In the case of the first form, sets the current index of the given file to the index value given by the parameter From. Then (for both forms) returns, in the parameter Item, the value of the element whose position in the given file is specified by the current index of the file; finally, increases the current index by one.

4   The exception Mode_Error is propagated if the mode of the given file is Out_File. The exception End_Error is propagated if the index to be used exceeds the size of the external file. The exception Data_Error can be propagated if the element read cannot be interpreted as a value of the subtype Element_Type (see A.13).

5   ```
procedure Write(File : in File_Type; Item : in Element_Type;
                                     To   : in Positive_Count);
procedure Write(File : in File_Type; Item : in Element_Type);
```

6   Operates on a file of mode Inout_File or Out_File. In the case of the first form, sets the index of the given file to the index value given by the parameter To. Then (for both forms) gives the value of the parameter Item to the element whose position in the given file is specified by the current index of the file; finally, increases the current index by one.

7   The exception Mode_Error is propagated if the mode of the given file is In_File. The exception Use_Error is propagated if the capacity of the external file is exceeded.

8   ```
procedure Set_Index(File : in File_Type; To : in Positive_Count);
```

9   Operates on a file of any mode. Sets the current index of the given file to the given index value (which may exceed the current size of the file).

10   ```
function Index(File : in File_Type) return Positive_Count;
```

11   Operates on a file of any mode. Returns the current index of the given file.

12   ```
function Size(File : in File_Type) return Count;
```

13   Operates on a file of any mode. Returns the current size of the external file that is associated with the given file.

14   ```
function End_Of_File(File : in File_Type) return Boolean;
```

15   Operates on a file of mode In_File or Inout_File. Returns True if the current index exceeds the size of the external file; otherwise returns False.

16   The exception Mode_Error is propagated if the mode of the given file is Out_File.

NOTES

17   20 Append_File mode is not supported for the generic package Direct_IO.

A.9 The Generic Package Storage_IO

The generic package Storage_IO provides for reading from and writing to an in-memory buffer. This generic package supports the construction of user-defined input-output packages. — 1

Static Semantics

The generic library package Storage_IO has the following declaration: — 2

```
with Ada.IO_Exceptions;                                                          3
with System.Storage_Elements;
generic
   type Element_Type is private;
package Ada.Storage_IO is
   pragma Preelaborate(Storage_IO);

   Buffer_Size : constant System.Storage_Elements.Storage_Count :=           4
      implementation-defined;
   subtype Buffer_Type is
      System.Storage_Elements.Storage_Array(1..Buffer_Size);

   -- Input and output operations                                              5

   procedure Read (Buffer : in  Buffer_Type; Item : out Element_Type);         6

   procedure Write(Buffer : out Buffer_Type; Item : in  Element_Type);         7

   -- Exceptions                                                               8

   Data_Error   : exception renames IO_Exceptions.Data_Error;                  9
end Ada.Storage_IO;
```

In each instance, the constant Buffer_Size has a value that is the size (in storage elements) of the buffer required to represent the content of an object of subtype Element_Type, including any implicit levels of indirection used by the implementation. The Read and Write procedures of Storage_IO correspond to the Read and Write procedures of Direct_IO (see A.8.4), but with the content of the Item parameter being read from or written into the specified Buffer, rather than an external file. — 10

NOTES
21 A buffer used for Storage_IO holds only one element at a time; an external file used for Direct_IO holds a sequence of elements. — 11

A.10 Text Input-Output

Static Semantics

This clause describes the package Text_IO, which provides facilities for input and output in human-readable form. Each file is read or written sequentially, as a sequence of characters grouped into lines, and as a sequence of lines grouped into pages. The specification of the package is given below in subclause A.10.1. — 1

The facilities for file management given above, in subclauses A.8.2 and A.8.3, are available for text input-output. In place of Read and Write, however, there are procedures Get and Put that input values of suitable types from text files, and output values to them. These values are provided to the Put procedures, and returned by the Get procedures, in a parameter Item. Several overloaded procedures of these names exist, for different types of Item. These Get procedures analyze the input sequences of characters based on lexical elements (see Section 2) and return the corresponding values; the Put procedures output the given values as appropriate lexical elements. Procedures Get and Put are also available that input and output individual characters treated as character values rather than as lexical elements. Related to character input — 2 are procedures to look ahead at the next character without reading it, and to read a character ''immediately'' without waiting for an end-of-line to signal availability.

3   In addition to the procedures Get and Put for numeric and enumeration types of Item that operate on text files, analogous procedures are provided that read from and write to a parameter of type String. These procedures perform the same analysis and composition of character sequences as their counterparts which have a file parameter.

4   For all Get and Put procedures that operate on text files, and for many other subprograms, there are forms with and without a file parameter. Each such Get procedure operates on an input file, and each such Put procedure operates on an output file. If no file is specified, a default input file or a default output file is used.

5   At the beginning of program execution the default input and output files are the so-called standard input file and standard output file. These files are open, have respectively the current modes In_File and Out_File, and are associated with two implementation-defined external files. Procedures are provided to change the current default input file and the current default output file.

6   At the beginning of program execution a default file for program-dependent error-related text output is the so-called standard error file. This file is open, has the current mode Out_File, and is associated with an implementation-defined external file. A procedure is provided to change the current default error file.

7   From a logical point of view, a text file is a sequence of pages, a page is a sequence of lines, and a line is a sequence of characters; the end of a line is marked by a *line terminator*; the end of a page is marked by the combination of a line terminator immediately followed by a *page terminator*; and the end of a file is marked by the combination of a line terminator immediately followed by a page terminator and then a *file terminator*. Terminators are generated during output; either by calls of procedures provided expressly for that purpose; or implicitly as part of other operations, for example, when a bounded line length, a bounded page length, or both, have been specified for a file.

8   The actual nature of terminators is not defined by the language and hence depends on the implementation. Although terminators are recognized or generated by certain of the procedures that follow, they are not necessarily implemented as characters or as sequences of characters. Whether they are characters (and if so which ones) in any particular implementation need not concern a user who neither explicitly outputs nor explicitly inputs control characters. The effect of input (Get) or output (Put) of control characters (other than horizontal tabulation) is not specified by the language.

9   The characters of a line are numbered, starting from one; the number of a character is called its *column number*. For a line terminator, a column number is also defined: it is one more than the number of characters in the line. The lines of a page, and the pages of a file, are similarly numbered. The current column number is the column number of the next character or line terminator to be transferred. The current line number is the number of the current line. The current page number is the number of the current page. These numbers are values of the subtype Positive_Count of the type Count (by convention, the value zero of the type Count is used to indicate special conditions).

10
```
type Count is range 0 .. implementation-defined;
subtype Positive_Count is Count range 1 .. Count'Last;
```

11 For an output file or an append file, a *maximum line length* can be specified and a *maximum page length* can be specified. If a value to be output cannot fit on the current line, for a specified maximum line length, then a new line is automatically started before the value is output; if, further, this new line cannot fit on the current page, for a specified maximum page length, then a new page is automatically started before the value is output. Functions are provided to determine the maximum line length and the maximum page

ength. When a file is opened with mode Out_File or Append_File, both values are zero: by convention, his means that the line lengths and page lengths are unbounded. (Consequently, output consists of a single ine if the subprograms for explicit control of line and page structure are not used.) The constant Unbounded is provided for this purpose.

A.10.1 The Package Text_IO

Static Semantics

The library package Text_IO has the following declaration: 1

```ada
with Ada.IO_Exceptions;                                                2
package Ada.Text_IO is

   type File_Type is limited private;                                  3

   type File_Mode is (In_File, Out_File, Append_File);                 4

   type Count is range 0 .. implementation-defined;                    5
   subtype Positive_Count is Count range 1 .. Count'Last;
   Unbounded : constant Count := 0;  -- line and page length

   subtype Field       is Integer range 0 .. implementation-defined;   6
   subtype Number_Base is Integer range 2 .. 16;

   type Type_Set is (Lower_Case, Upper_Case);                          7

   -- File Management                                                   8

   procedure Create (File : in out File_Type;                          9
                     Mode : in File_Mode := Out_File;
                     Name : in String    := "";
                     Form : in String    := "");

   procedure Open   (File : in out File_Type;                          10
                     Mode : in File_Mode;
                     Name : in String;
                     Form : in String := "");

   procedure Close  (File : in out File_Type);                         11
   procedure Delete (File : in out File_Type);
   procedure Reset  (File : in out File_Type; Mode : in File_Mode);
   procedure Reset  (File : in out File_Type);

   function Mode    (File : in File_Type) return File_Mode;            12
   function Name    (File : in File_Type) return String;
   function Form    (File : in File_Type) return String;

   function Is_Open(File : in File_Type) return Boolean;               13

   -- Control of default input and output files                        14

   procedure Set_Input (File : in File_Type);                          15
   procedure Set_Output(File : in File_Type);
   procedure Set_Error (File : in File_Type);

   function Standard_Input  return File_Type;                          16
   function Standard_Output return File_Type;
   function Standard_Error  return File_Type;

   function Current_Input   return File_Type;                          17
   function Current_Output  return File_Type;
   function Current_Error   return File_Type;

   type File_Access is access constant File_Type;                      18

   function Standard_Input  return File_Access;                        19
   function Standard_Output return File_Access;
   function Standard_Error  return File_Access;

   function Current_Input   return File_Access;                        20
   function Current_Output  return File_Access;
   function Current_Error   return File_Access;
```

21/1   *--Buffer control*
```
   procedure Flush (File : in File_Type);
   procedure Flush;
```

22   *-- Specification of line and page lengths*

23
```
   procedure Set_Line_Length(File : in File_Type; To : in Count);
   procedure Set_Line_Length(To   : in Count);
```

24
```
   procedure Set_Page_Length(File : in File_Type; To : in Count);
   procedure Set_Page_Length(To   : in Count);
```

25
```
   function Line_Length(File : in File_Type) return Count;
   function Line_Length return Count;
```

26
```
   function Page_Length(File : in File_Type) return Count;
   function Page_Length return Count;
```

27   *-- Column, Line, and Page Control*

28
```
   procedure New_Line   (File    : in File_Type;
                         Spacing : in Positive_Count := 1);
   procedure New_Line   (Spacing : in Positive_Count := 1);
```

29
```
   procedure Skip_Line  (File    : in File_Type;
                         Spacing : in Positive_Count := 1);
   procedure Skip_Line  (Spacing : in Positive_Count := 1);
```

30
```
   function End_Of_Line(File : in File_Type) return Boolean;
   function End_Of_Line return Boolean;
```

31
```
   procedure New_Page   (File : in File_Type);
   procedure New_Page;
```

32
```
   procedure Skip_Page  (File : in File_Type);
   procedure Skip_Page;
```

33
```
   function End_Of_Page(File : in File_Type) return Boolean;
   function End_Of_Page return Boolean;
```

34
```
   function End_Of_File(File : in File_Type) return Boolean;
   function End_Of_File return Boolean;
```

35
```
   procedure Set_Col (File : in File_Type; To : in Positive_Count);
   procedure Set_Col (To   : in Positive_Count);
```

36
```
   procedure Set_Line(File : in File_Type; To : in Positive_Count);
   procedure Set_Line(To   : in Positive_Count);
```

37
```
   function Col (File : in File_Type) return Positive_Count;
   function Col  return Positive_Count;
```

38
```
   function Line(File : in File_Type) return Positive_Count;
   function Line return Positive_Count;
```

39
```
   function Page(File : in File_Type) return Positive_Count;
   function Page return Positive_Count;
```

40   *-- Character Input-Output*

41
```
   procedure Get(File : in  File_Type; Item : out Character);
   procedure Get(Item : out Character);
```

42
```
   procedure Put(File : in  File_Type; Item : in Character);
   procedure Put(Item : in  Character);
```

43
```
   procedure Look_Ahead (File       : in  File_Type;
                         Item       : out Character;
                         End_Of_Line : out Boolean);
   procedure Look_Ahead (Item       : out Character;
                         End_Of_Line : out Boolean);
```

44
```
   procedure Get_Immediate(File       : in  File_Type;
                           Item       : out Character);
   procedure Get_Immediate(Item       : out Character);
```

```
procedure Get_Immediate(File     : in  File_Type;                45
                        Item     : out Character;
                        Available : out Boolean);
procedure Get_Immediate(Item     : out Character;
                        Available : out Boolean);
```

-- String Input-Output   46

```
procedure Get(File : in  File_Type; Item : out String);          47
procedure Get(Item : out String);

procedure Put(File : in  File_Type; Item : in String);           48
procedure Put(Item : in  String);

procedure Get_Line(File : in  File_Type;                         49
                   Item : out String;
                   Last : out Natural);
procedure Get_Line(Item : out String; Last : out Natural);

procedure Put_Line(File : in  File_Type; Item : in String);      50
procedure Put_Line(Item : in  String);
```

-- Generic packages for Input-Output of Integer Types   51

```
generic                                                          52
   type Num is range <>;
package Integer_IO is

   Default_Width : Field := Num'Width;                           53
   Default_Base  : Number_Base := 10;

   procedure Get(File  : in  File_Type;                          54
                 Item  : out Num;
                 Width : in Field := 0);
   procedure Get(Item  : out Num;
                 Width : in  Field := 0);

   procedure Put(File  : in File_Type;                           55
                 Item  : in Num;
                 Width : in Field := Default_Width;
                 Base  : in Number_Base := Default_Base);
   procedure Put(Item  : in Num;
                 Width : in Field := Default_Width;
                 Base  : in Number_Base := Default_Base);
   procedure Get(From : in  String;
                 Item : out Num;
                 Last : out Positive);
   procedure Put(To   : out String;
                 Item : in Num;
                 Base : in Number_Base := Default_Base);

end Integer_IO;                                                  56

generic                                                          57
   type Num is mod <>;
package Modular_IO is

   Default_Width : Field := Num'Width;                           58
   Default_Base  : Number_Base := 10;

   procedure Get(File  : in  File_Type;                          59
                 Item  : out Num;
                 Width : in Field := 0);
   procedure Get(Item  : out Num;
                 Width : in  Field := 0);
```

60
```
         procedure Put(File  : in File_Type;
                       Item  : in Num;
                       Width : in Field := Default_Width;
                       Base  : in Number_Base := Default_Base);
         procedure Put(Item  : in Num;
                       Width : in Field := Default_Width;
                       Base  : in Number_Base := Default_Base);
         procedure Get(From : in  String;
                       Item : out Num;
                       Last : out Positive);
         procedure Put(To   : out String;
                       Item : in Num;
                       Base : in Number_Base := Default_Base);
```

61
```
     end Modular_IO;
```

62
```
     -- Generic packages for Input-Output of Real Types
```

63
```
     generic
        type Num is digits <>;
     package Float_IO is
```

64
```
        Default_Fore : Field := 2;
        Default_Aft  : Field := Num'Digits-1;
        Default_Exp  : Field := 3;
```

65
```
        procedure Get(File  : in  File_Type;
                      Item  : out Num;
                      Width : in  Field := 0);
        procedure Get(Item  : out Num;
                      Width : in  Field := 0);
```

66
```
        procedure Put(File : in File_Type;
                      Item : in Num;
                      Fore : in Field := Default_Fore;
                      Aft  : in Field := Default_Aft;
                      Exp  : in Field := Default_Exp);
        procedure Put(Item : in Num;
                      Fore : in Field := Default_Fore;
                      Aft  : in Field := Default_Aft;
                      Exp  : in Field := Default_Exp);
```

67
```
        procedure Get(From : in String;
                      Item : out Num;
                      Last : out Positive);
        procedure Put(To   : out String;
                      Item : in Num;
                      Aft  : in Field := Default_Aft;
                      Exp  : in Field := Default_Exp);
     end Float_IO;
```

68
```
     generic
        type Num is delta <>;
     package Fixed_IO is
```

69
```
        Default_Fore : Field := Num'Fore;
        Default_Aft  : Field := Num'Aft;
        Default_Exp  : Field := 0;
```

70
```
        procedure Get(File  : in  File_Type;
                      Item  : out Num;
                      Width : in  Field := 0);
        procedure Get(Item  : out Num;
                      Width : in  Field := 0);
```

```
   procedure Put(File : in File_Type;                                    71
                 Item : in Num;
                 Fore : in Field := Default_Fore;
                 Aft  : in Field := Default_Aft;
                 Exp  : in Field := Default_Exp);
   procedure Put(Item : in Num;
                 Fore : in Field := Default_Fore;
                 Aft  : in Field := Default_Aft;
                 Exp  : in Field := Default_Exp);

   procedure Get(From : in  String;                                      72
                 Item : out Num;
                 Last : out Positive);
   procedure Put(To   : out String;
                 Item : in Num;
                 Aft  : in Field := Default_Aft;
                 Exp  : in Field := Default_Exp);
end Fixed_IO;

generic                                                                  73
   type Num is delta <> digits <>;
package Decimal_IO is

   Default_Fore : Field := Num'Fore;                                     74
   Default_Aft  : Field := Num'Aft;
   Default_Exp  : Field := 0;

   procedure Get(File  : in  File_Type;                                  75
                 Item  : out Num;
                 Width : in  Field := 0);
   procedure Get(Item  : out Num;
                 Width : in  Field := 0);

   procedure Put(File : in File_Type;                                    76
                 Item : in Num;
                 Fore : in Field := Default_Fore;
                 Aft  : in Field := Default_Aft;
                 Exp  : in Field := Default_Exp);
   procedure Put(Item : in Num;
                 Fore : in Field := Default_Fore;
                 Aft  : in Field := Default_Aft;
                 Exp  : in Field := Default_Exp);

   procedure Get(From : in  String;                                      77
                 Item : out Num;
                 Last : out Positive);
   procedure Put(To   : out String;
                 Item : in Num;
                 Aft  : in Field := Default_Aft;
                 Exp  : in Field := Default_Exp);
end Decimal_IO;
```

-- *Generic package for Input-Output of Enumeration Types*   78

```
generic                                                                  79
   type Enum is (<>);
package Enumeration_IO is

   Default_Width   : Field := 0;                                         80
   Default_Setting : Type_Set := Upper_Case;

   procedure Get(File : in  File_Type;                                   81
                 Item : out Enum);
   procedure Get(Item : out Enum);

   procedure Put(File  : in File_Type;                                   82
                 Item  : in Enum;
                 Width : in Field    := Default_Width;
                 Set   : in Type_Set := Default_Setting);
   procedure Put(Item  : in Enum;
                 Width : in Field    := Default_Width;
                 Set   : in Type_Set := Default_Setting);
```

The Package Text_IO **A.10.1**

```
83                  procedure Get(From :  in  String;
                                 Item :  out Enum;
                                 Last :  out Positive);
                    procedure Put(To   :  out String;
                                 Item :  in  Enum;
                                 Set  :  in  Type_Set := Default_Setting);
                    end Enumeration_IO;

84          -- Exceptions

85             Status_Error : exception renames IO_Exceptions.Status_Error;
               Mode_Error   : exception renames IO_Exceptions.Mode_Error;
               Name_Error   : exception renames IO_Exceptions.Name_Error;
               Use_Error    : exception renames IO_Exceptions.Use_Error;
               Device_Error : exception renames IO_Exceptions.Device_Error;
               End_Error    : exception renames IO_Exceptions.End_Error;
               Data_Error   : exception renames IO_Exceptions.Data_Error;
               Layout_Error : exception renames IO_Exceptions.Layout_Error;
            private
               ...  -- not specified by the language
            end Ada.Text_IO;
```

A.10.2 Text File Management

Static Semantics

1   The only allowed file modes for text files are the modes In_File, Out_File, and Append_File. The subprograms given in subclause A.8.2 for the control of external files, and the function End_Of_File given in subclause A.8.3 for sequential input-output, are also available for text files. There is also a version of End_Of_File that refers to the current default input file. For text files, the procedures have the following additional effects:

2   • For the procedures Create and Open: After a file with mode Out_File or Append_File is opened, the page length and line length are unbounded (both have the conventional value zero). After a file (of any mode) is opened, the current column, current line, and current page numbers are set to one. If the mode is Append_File, it is implementation defined whether a page terminator will separate preexisting text in the file from the new text to be written.

3   • For the procedure Close: If the file has the current mode Out_File or Append_File, has the effect of calling New_Page, unless the current page is already terminated; then outputs a file terminator.

4   • For the procedure Reset: If the file has the current mode Out_File or Append_File, has the effect of calling New_Page, unless the current page is already terminated; then outputs a file terminator. The current column, line, and page numbers are set to one, and the line and page lengths to Unbounded. If the new mode is Append_File, it is implementation defined whether a page terminator will separate preexisting text in the file from the new text to be written.

5   The exception Mode_Error is propagated by the procedure Reset upon an attempt to change the mode of a file that is the current default input file, the current default output file, or the current default error file.

NOTES

6   22 An implementation can define the Form parameter of Create and Open to control effects including the following:

7   • the interpretation of line and column numbers for an interactive file, and

8   • the interpretation of text formats in a file created by a foreign program.

A.10.3 Default Input, Output, and Error Files

Static Semantics

The following subprograms provide for the control of the particular default files that are used when a file parameter is omitted from a Get, Put, or other operation of text input-output described below, or when application-dependent error-related text is to be output.   1

```
procedure Set_Input(File : in File_Type);
```
2

Operates on a file of mode In_File. Sets the current default input file to File.   3

The exception Status_Error is propagated if the given file is not open. The exception Mode_Error is propagated if the mode of the given file is not In_File.   4

```
procedure Set_Output(File : in File_Type);
procedure Set_Error (File : in File_Type);
```
5

Each operates on a file of mode Out_File or Append_File. Set_Output sets the current default output file to File. Set_Error sets the current default error file to File. The exception Status_Error is propagated if the given file is not open. The exception Mode_Error is propagated if the mode of the given file is not Out_File or Append_File.   6

```
function Standard_Input return File_Type;
function Standard_Input return File_Access;
```
7

Returns the standard input file (see A.10), or an access value designating the standard input file, respectively.   8

```
function Standard_Output return File_Type;
function Standard_Output return File_Access;
```
9

Returns the standard output file (see A.10) or an access value designating the standard output file, respectively.   10

```
function Standard_Error return File_Type;
function Standard_Error return File_Access;
```
11

Returns the standard error file (see A.10), or an access value designating the standard error file, respectively.   12/1

The Form strings implicitly associated with the opening of Standard_Input, Standard_Output, and Standard_Error at the start of program execution are implementation defined.   13

```
function Current_Input return File_Type;
function Current_Input return File_Access;
```
14

Returns the current default input file, or an access value designating the current default input file, respectively.   15

```
function Current_Output return File_Type;
function Current_Output return File_Access;
```
16

Returns the current default output file, or an access value designating the current default output file, respectively.   17

18
```
function Current_Error return File_Type;
function Current_Error return File_Access;
```

19   Returns the current default error file, or an access value designating the current default error file, respectively.

20/1
```
procedure Flush (File : in File_Type);
procedure Flush;
```

21   The effect of Flush is the same as the corresponding subprogram in Streams.Stream_IO (see A.12.1). If File is not explicitly specified, Current_Output is used.

Erroneous Execution

22/1 The execution of a program is erroneous if it invokes an operation on a current default input, default output, or default error file, and if the corresponding file object is closed or no longer exists.

23/1 *This paragraph was deleted.*

NOTES
24   23 The standard input, standard output, and standard error files cannot be opened, closed, reset, or deleted, because the parameter File of the corresponding procedures has the mode **in out**.

25   24 The standard input, standard output, and standard error files are different file objects, but not necessarily different external files.

A.10.4 Specification of Line and Page Lengths

Static Semantics

1   The subprograms described in this subclause are concerned with the line and page structure of a file of mode Out_File or Append_File. They operate either on the file given as the first parameter, or, in the absence of such a file parameter, on the current default output file. They provide for output of text with a specified maximum line length or page length. In these cases, line and page terminators are output implicitly and automatically when needed. When line and page lengths are unbounded (that is, when they have the conventional value zero), as in the case of a newly opened file, new lines and new pages are only started when explicitly called for.

2   In all cases, the exception Status_Error is propagated if the file to be used is not open; the exception Mode_Error is propagated if the mode of the file is not Out_File or Append_File.

3
```
procedure Set_Line_Length(File : in File_Type; To : in Count);
procedure Set_Line_Length(To   : in Count);
```

4   Sets the maximum line length of the specified output or append file to the number of characters specified by To. The value zero for To specifies an unbounded line length.

5   The exception Use_Error is propagated if the specified line length is inappropriate for the associated external file.

6
```
procedure Set_Page_Length(File : in File_Type; To : in Count);
procedure Set_Page_Length(To   : in Count);
```

7   Sets the maximum page length of the specified output or append file to the number of lines specified by To. The value zero for To specifies an unbounded page length.

8   The exception Use_Error is propagated if the specified page length is inappropriate for the associated external file.

```
function Line_Length(File : in File_Type) return Count;
function Line_Length return Count;
```
9

Returns the maximum line length currently set for the specified output or append file, or zero if the line length is unbounded.
10

```
function Page_Length(File : in File_Type) return Count;
function Page_Length return Count;
```
11

Returns the maximum page length currently set for the specified output or append file, or zero if the page length is unbounded.
12

A.10.5 Operations on Columns, Lines, and Pages

Static Semantics

The subprograms described in this subclause provide for explicit control of line and page structure; they operate either on the file given as the first parameter, or, in the absence of such a file parameter, on the appropriate (input or output) current default file. The exception Status_Error is propagated by any of these subprograms if the file to be used is not open.
1

```
procedure New_Line(File : in File_Type; Spacing : in Positive_Count := 1);
procedure New_Line(Spacing : in Positive_Count := 1);
```
2

Operates on a file of mode Out_File or Append_File.
3

For a Spacing of one: Outputs a line terminator and sets the current column number to one. Then increments the current line number by one, except in the case that the current line number is already greater than or equal to the maximum page length, for a bounded page length; in that case a page terminator is output, the current page number is incremented by one, and the current line number is set to one.
4

For a Spacing greater than one, the above actions are performed Spacing times.
5

The exception Mode_Error is propagated if the mode is not Out_File or Append_File.
6

```
procedure Skip_Line(File  : in File_Type; Spacing : in Positive_Count := 1);
procedure Skip_Line(Spacing : in Positive_Count := 1);
```
7

Operates on a file of mode In_File.
8

For a Spacing of one: Reads and discards all characters until a line terminator has been read, and then sets the current column number to one. If the line terminator is not immediately followed by a page terminator, the current line number is incremented by one. Otherwise, if the line terminator is immediately followed by a page terminator, then the page terminator is skipped, the current page number is incremented by one, and the current line number is set to one.
9

For a Spacing greater than one, the above actions are performed Spacing times.
10

The exception Mode_Error is propagated if the mode is not In_File. The exception End_Error is propagated if an attempt is made to read a file terminator.
11

```
function End_Of_Line(File : in File_Type) return Boolean;
function End_Of_Line return Boolean;
```
12

Operates on a file of mode In_File. Returns True if a line terminator or a file terminator is next; otherwise returns False.
13

The exception Mode_Error is propagated if the mode is not In_File.
14

Specification of Line and Page Lengths **A.10.4**

15
```
procedure New_Page(File : in File_Type);
procedure New_Page;
```

16   Operates on a file of mode Out_File or Append_File. Outputs a line terminator if the current line is not terminated, or if the current page is empty (that is, if the current column and line numbers are both equal to one). Then outputs a page terminator, which terminates the current page. Adds one to the current page number and sets the current column and line numbers to one.

17   The exception Mode_Error is propagated if the mode is not Out_File or Append_File.

18
```
procedure Skip_Page(File : in File_Type);
procedure Skip_Page;
```

19   Operates on a file of mode In_File. Reads and discards all characters and line terminators until a page terminator has been read. Then adds one to the current page number, and sets the current column and line numbers to one.

20   The exception Mode_Error is propagated if the mode is not In_File. The exception End_Error is propagated if an attempt is made to read a file terminator.

21
```
function End_Of_Page(File : in File_Type) return Boolean;
function End_Of_Page return Boolean;
```

22   Operates on a file of mode In_File. Returns True if the combination of a line terminator and a page terminator is next, or if a file terminator is next; otherwise returns False.

23   The exception Mode_Error is propagated if the mode is not In_File.

24
```
function End_Of_File(File : in File_Type) return Boolean;
function End_Of_File return Boolean;
```

25   Operates on a file of mode In_File. Returns True if a file terminator is next, or if the combination of a line, a page, and a file terminator is next; otherwise returns False.

26   The exception Mode_Error is propagated if the mode is not In_File.

27   The following subprograms provide for the control of the current position of reading or writing in a file. In all cases, the default file is the current output file.

28
```
procedure Set_Col(File : in File_Type; To : in Positive_Count);
procedure Set_Col(To   : in Positive_Count);
```

29   If the file mode is Out_File or Append_File:

30   • If the value specified by To is greater than the current column number, outputs spaces, adding one to the current column number after each space, until the current column number equals the specified value. If the value specified by To is equal to the current column number, there is no effect. If the value specified by To is less than the current column number, has the effect of calling New_Line (with a spacing of one), then outputs (To − 1) spaces, and sets the current column number to the specified value.

31   • The exception Layout_Error is propagated if the value specified by To exceeds Line_Length when the line length is bounded (that is, when it does not have the conventional value zero).

32   If the file mode is In_File:

33   • Reads (and discards) individual characters, line terminators, and page terminators, until the next character to be read has a column number that equals the value specified by To; there is no effect if the current column number already equals this value. Each transfer of a character or terminator maintains the current column, line, and page

numbers in the same way as a Get procedure (see A.10.6). (Short lines will be skipped until a line is reached that has a character at the specified column position.)

- The exception End_Error is propagated if an attempt is made to read a file terminator. 34

```
procedure Set_Line(File : in File_Type; To : in Positive_Count);
procedure Set_Line(To   : in Positive_Count);
```
35

If the file mode is Out_File or Append_File: 36

- If the value specified by To is greater than the current line number, has the effect of repeatedly calling New_Line (with a spacing of one), until the current line number equals the specified value. If the value specified by To is equal to the current line number, there is no effect. If the value specified by To is less than the current line number, has the effect of calling New_Page followed by a call of New_Line with a spacing equal to (To − 1). 37

- The exception Layout_Error is propagated if the value specified by To exceeds Page_Length when the page length is bounded (that is, when it does not have the conventional value zero). 38

If the mode is In_File: 39

- Has the effect of repeatedly calling Skip_Line (with a spacing of one), until the current line number equals the value specified by To; there is no effect if the current line number already equals this value. (Short pages will be skipped until a page is reached that has a line at the specified line position.) 40

- The exception End_Error is propagated if an attempt is made to read a file terminator. 41

```
function Col(File : in File_Type) return Positive_Count;
function Col return Positive_Count;
```
42

Returns the current column number. 43

The exception Layout_Error is propagated if this number exceeds Count'Last. 44

```
function Line(File : in File_Type) return Positive_Count;
function Line return Positive_Count;
```
45

Returns the current line number. 46

The exception Layout_Error is propagated if this number exceeds Count'Last. 47

```
function Page(File : in File_Type) return Positive_Count;
function Page return Positive_Count;
```
48

Returns the current page number. 49

The exception Layout_Error is propagated if this number exceeds Count'Last. 50

The column number, line number, or page number are allowed to exceed Count'Last (as a consequence of the input or output of sufficiently many characters, lines, or pages). These events do not cause any exception to be propagated. However, a call of Col, Line, or Page propagates the exception Layout_Error if the corresponding number exceeds Count'Last. 51

NOTES

25 A page terminator is always skipped whenever the preceding line terminator is skipped. An implementation may represent the combination of these terminators by a single character, provided that it is properly recognized on input. 52

Operations on Columns, Lines, and Pages **A.10.5**

A.10.6 Get and Put Procedures

Static Semantics

1   The procedures Get and Put for items of the type Character, String, numeric types, and enumeration types are described in subsequent subclauses. Features of these procedures that are common to most of these types are described in this subclause. The Get and Put procedures for items of type Character and String deal with individual character values; the Get and Put procedures for numeric and enumeration types treat the items as lexical elements.

2   All procedures Get and Put have forms with a file parameter, written first. Where this parameter is omitted, the appropriate (input or output) current default file is understood to be specified. Each procedure Get operates on a file of mode In_File. Each procedure Put operates on a file of mode Out_File or Append_File.

3   All procedures Get and Put maintain the current column, line, and page numbers of the specified file: the effect of each of these procedures upon these numbers is the result of the effects of individual transfers of characters and of individual output or skipping of terminators. Each transfer of a character adds one to the current column number. Each output of a line terminator sets the current column number to one and adds one to the current line number. Each output of a page terminator sets the current column and line numbers to one and adds one to the current page number. For input, each skipping of a line terminator sets the current column number to one and adds one to the current line number; each skipping of a page terminator sets the current column and line numbers to one and adds one to the current page number. Similar considerations apply to the procedures Get_Line, Put_Line, and Set_Col.

4   Several Get and Put procedures, for numeric and enumeration types, have *format* parameters which specify field lengths; these parameters are of the nonnegative subtype Field of the type Integer.

5   Input-output of enumeration values uses the syntax of the corresponding lexical elements. Any Get procedure for an enumeration type begins by skipping any leading blanks, or line or page terminators. Get procedures for numeric or enumeration types start by skipping leading blanks, where a *blank* is defined as a space or a horizontal tabulation character. Next, characters are input only so long as the sequence input is an initial sequence of an identifier or of a character literal (in particular, input ceases when a line terminator is encountered). The character or line terminator that causes input to cease remains available for subsequent input.

6   For a numeric type, the Get procedures have a format parameter called Width. If the value given for this parameter is zero, the Get procedure proceeds in the same manner as for enumeration types, but using the syntax of numeric literals instead of that of enumeration literals. If a nonzero value is given, then exactly Width characters are input, or the characters up to a line terminator, whichever comes first; any skipped leading blanks are included in the count. The syntax used for numeric literals is an extended syntax that allows a leading sign (but no intervening blanks, or line or page terminators) and that also allows (for real types) an integer literal as well as forms that have digits only before the point or only after the point.

7   Any Put procedure, for an item of a numeric or an enumeration type, outputs the value of the item as a numeric literal, identifier, or character literal, as appropriate. This is preceded by leading spaces if required by the format parameters Width or Fore (as described in later subclauses), and then a minus sign for a negative value; for an enumeration type, the spaces follow instead of leading. The format given for a Put procedure is overridden if it is insufficiently wide, by using the minimum needed width.

8   Two further cases arise for Put procedures for numeric and enumeration types, if the line length of the specified output file is bounded (that is, if it does not have the conventional value zero). If the number of

haracters to be output does not exceed the maximum line length, but is such that they cannot fit on the urrent line, starting from the current column, then (in effect) New_Line is called (with a spacing of one) efore output of the item. Otherwise, if the number of characters exceeds the maximum line length, then he exception Layout_Error is propagated and nothing is output.

The exception Status_Error is propagated by any of the procedures Get, Get_Line, Put, and Put_Line if the ile to be used is not open. The exception Mode_Error is propagated by the procedures Get and Get_Line f the mode of the file to be used is not In_File; and by the procedures Put and Put_Line, if the mode is not Out_File or Append_File.   9

The exception End_Error is propagated by a Get procedure if an attempt is made to skip a file terminator. The exception Data_Error is propagated by a Get procedure if the sequence finally input is not a lexical element corresponding to the type, in particular if no characters were input; for this test, leading blanks are ignored; for an item of a numeric type, when a sign is input, this rule applies to the succeeding numeric literal. The exception Layout_Error is propagated by a Put procedure that outputs to a parameter of type String, if the length of the actual string is insufficient for the output of the item.   10

Examples

In the examples, here and in subclauses A.10.8 and A.10.9, the string quotes and the lower case letter b are not transferred: they are shown only to reveal the layout and spaces.   11

```
N : Integer;                                                              12
    ...
Get(N);
```
    13
	Characters at input	*Sequence input*	*Value of N*
--			
--	*bb–12535b*	*–12535*	*–12535*
--	*bb12_535e1b*	*12_535e1*	*125350*
--	*bb12_535e;*	*12_535e*	*(none) Data_Error raised*

Example of overridden width parameter: 14

```
Put(Item => -23, Width => 2);   -- "–23"                                  15
```

A.10.7 Input-Output of Characters and Strings

Static Semantics

For an item of type Character the following procedures are provided: 1

```
procedure Get(File : in File_Type; Item : out Character);                 2
procedure Get(Item : out Character);
```

After skipping any line terminators and any page terminators, reads the next character from the specified input file and returns the value of this character in the out parameter Item.   3

The exception End_Error is propagated if an attempt is made to skip a file terminator.   4

```
procedure Put(File : in File_Type; Item : in Character);                  5
procedure Put(Item : in Character);
```

If the line length of the specified output file is bounded (that is, does not have the conventional value zero), and the current column number exceeds it, has the effect of calling New_Line with a spacing of one. Then, or otherwise, outputs the given character to the file.   6

7
```
procedure Look_Ahead (File       : in  File_Type;
                      Item       : out Character;
                      End_Of_Line : out Boolean);
procedure Look_Ahead (Item       : out Character;
                      End_Of_Line : out Boolean);
```

8/1
Mode_Error is propagated if the mode of the file is not In_File. Sets End_Of_Line to True if at end of line, including if at end of page or at end of file; in each of these cases the value of Item is not specified. Otherwise End_Of_Line is set to False and Item is set to the next character (without consuming it) from the file.

9
```
procedure Get_Immediate(File : in  File_Type;
                        Item : out Character);
procedure Get_Immediate(Item : out Character);
```

10
Reads the next character, either control or graphic, from the specified File or the default input file. Mode_Error is propagated if the mode of the file is not In_File. End_Error is propagated if at the end of the file. The current column, line and page numbers for the file are not affected.

11
```
procedure Get_Immediate(File       : in  File_Type;
                        Item       : out Character;
                        Available  : out Boolean);
procedure Get_Immediate(Item       : out Character;
                        Available  : out Boolean);
```

12
If a character, either control or graphic, is available from the specified File or the default input file, then the character is read; Available is True and Item contains the value of this character. If a character is not available, then Available is False and the value of Item is not specified. Mode_Error is propagated if the mode of the file is not In_File. End_Error is propagated if at the end of the file. The current column, line and page numbers for the file are not affected.

13
For an item of type String the following procedures are provided:

14
```
procedure Get(File : in File_Type; Item : out String);
procedure Get(Item : out String);
```

15
Determines the length of the given string and attempts that number of Get operations for successive characters of the string (in particular, no operation is performed if the string is null).

16
```
procedure Put(File : in File_Type; Item : in String);
procedure Put(Item : in String);
```

17
Determines the length of the given string and attempts that number of Put operations for successive characters of the string (in particular, no operation is performed if the string is null).

18
```
procedure Get_Line(File : in File_Type;
                   Item : out String;
                   Last : out Natural);
procedure Get_Line(Item : out String;   Last : out Natural);
```

19
Reads successive characters from the specified input file and assigns them to successive characters of the specified string. Reading stops if the end of the string is met. Reading also stops if the end of the line is met before meeting the end of the string; in this case Skip_Line is (in effect) called with a spacing of 1. The values of characters not assigned are not specified.

20
If characters are read, returns in Last the index value such that Item(Last) is the last character assigned (the index of the first character assigned is Item'First). If no characters are read, returns in Last an index value that is one less than Item'First. The exception End_Error is propagated if an attempt is made to skip a file terminator.

```
procedure Put_Line(File : in File_Type; Item : in String);          21
procedure Put_Line(Item : in String);
```

Calls the procedure Put for the given string, and then the procedure New_Line with a spacing of   22
one.

Implementation Advice

The Get_Immediate procedures should be implemented with unbuffered input. For a device such as a   23
keyboard, input should be "available" if a key has already been typed, whereas for a disk file, input
should always be available except at end of file. For a file associated with a keyboard-like device, any line-
editing features of the underlying operating system should be disabled during the execution of
Get_Immediate.

NOTES
26 Get_Immediate can be used to read a single key from the keyboard "immediately"; that is, without waiting for an   24
end of line. In a call of Get_Immediate without the parameter Available, the caller will wait until a character is available.

27 In a literal string parameter of Put, the enclosing string bracket characters are not output. Each doubled string bracket   25
character in the enclosed string is output as a single string bracket character, as a consequence of the rule for string
literals (see 2.6).

28 A string read by Get or written by Put can extend over several lines. An implementation is allowed to assume that   26
certain external files do not contain page terminators, in which case Get_Line and Skip_Line can return as soon as a line
terminator is read.

A.10.8 Input-Output for Integer Types

Static Semantics

The following procedures are defined in the generic packages Integer_IO and Modular_IO, which have to   1
be instantiated for the appropriate signed integer or modular type respectively (indicated by Num in the
specifications).

Values are output as decimal or based literals, without low line characters or exponent, and, for   2
Integer_IO, preceded by a minus sign if negative. The format (which includes any leading spaces and
minus sign) can be specified by an optional field width parameter. Values of widths of fields in output
formats are of the nonnegative integer subtype Field. Values of bases are of the integer subtype
Number_Base.

```
subtype Number_Base is Integer range 2 .. 16;                        3
```

The default field width and base to be used by output procedures are defined by the following variables   4
that are declared in the generic packages Integer_IO and Modular_IO:

```
Default_Width : Field      := Num'Width;                             5
Default_Base  : Number_Base := 10;
```

The following procedures are provided: 6

```
procedure Get(File : in File_Type; Item : out Num; Width : in Field := 0);   7
procedure Get(Item : out Num; Width : in Field := 0);
```

If the value of the parameter Width is zero, skips any leading blanks, line terminators, or page   8
terminators, then reads a plus sign if present or (for a signed type only) a minus sign if present,
then reads the longest possible sequence of characters matching the syntax of a numeric literal
without a point. If a nonzero value of Width is supplied, then exactly Width characters are input,
or the characters (possibly none) up to a line terminator, whichever comes first; any skipped
leading blanks are included in the count.

Input-Output of Characters and Strings **A.10.7**

9   Returns, in the parameter Item, the value of type Num that corresponds to the sequence input.

10   The exception Data_Error is propagated if the sequence of characters read does not form a legal integer literal or if the value obtained is not of the subtype Num (for Integer_IO) or is not in the base range of Num (for Modular_IO).

11
```
procedure Put(File  : in File_Type;
              Item  : in Num;
              Width : in Field := Default_Width;
              Base  : in Number_Base := Default_Base);

procedure Put(Item  : in Num;
              Width : in Field := Default_Width;
              Base  : in Number_Base := Default_Base);
```

12   Outputs the value of the parameter Item as an integer literal, with no low lines, no exponent, and no leading zeros (but a single zero for the value zero), and a preceding minus sign for a negative value.

13   If the resulting sequence of characters to be output has fewer than Width characters, then leading spaces are first output to make up the difference.

14   Uses the syntax for decimal literal if the parameter Base has the value ten (either explicitly or through Default_Base); otherwise, uses the syntax for based literal, with any letters in upper case.

15
```
procedure Get(From : in String; Item : out Num; Last : out Positive);
```

16   Reads an integer value from the beginning of the given string, following the same rules as the Get procedure that reads an integer value from a file, but treating the end of the string as a file terminator. Returns, in the parameter Item, the value of type Num that corresponds to the sequence input. Returns in Last the index value such that From(Last) is the last character read.

17   The exception Data_Error is propagated if the sequence input does not have the required syntax or if the value obtained is not of the subtype Num.

18
```
procedure Put(To   : out String;
              Item : in Num;
              Base : in Number_Base := Default_Base);
```

19   Outputs the value of the parameter Item to the given string, following the same rule as for output to a file, using the length of the given string as the value for Width.

20   Integer_Text_IO is a library package that is a nongeneric equivalent to Text_IO.Integer_IO for the predefined type Integer:

21
```
with Ada.Text_IO;
package Ada.Integer_Text_IO is new Ada.Text_IO.Integer_IO(Integer);
```

22   For each predefined signed integer type, a nongeneric equivalent to Text_IO.Integer_IO is provided, with names such as Ada.Long_Integer_Text_IO.

Implementation Permissions

23   The nongeneric equivalent packages may, but need not, be actual instantiations of the generic package for the appropriate predefined type.

NOTES

24   29 For Modular_IO, execution of Get propagates Data_Error if the sequence of characters read forms an integer literal outside the range 0..Num'Last.

Examples

This paragraph was deleted. 25/1

package Int_IO **is new** Integer_IO(Small_Int); **use** Int_IO; 26
-- default format used at instantiation,
-- Default_Width = 4, Default_Base = 10

```
Put(126);                        -- "b126"                    27
Put(-126, 7);                    -- "bbb-126"
Put(126, Width => 13, Base => 2);  -- "bbb2#1111110#"
```

A.10.9 Input-Output for Real Types

Static Semantics

The following procedures are defined in the generic packages Float_IO, Fixed_IO, and Decimal_IO, which 1
have to be instantiated for the appropriate floating point, ordinary fixed point, or decimal fixed point type
respectively (indicated by Num in the specifications).

Values are output as decimal literals without low line characters. The format of each value output consists 2
of a Fore field, a decimal point, an Aft field, and (if a nonzero Exp parameter is supplied) the letter E and
an Exp field. The two possible formats thus correspond to:

```
Fore  .  Aft                                                3
```

and to: 4

```
Fore  .  Aft  E  Exp                                        5
```

without any spaces between these fields. The Fore field may include leading spaces, and a minus sign for 6
negative values. The Aft field includes only decimal digits (possibly with trailing zeros). The Exp field
includes the sign (plus or minus) and the exponent (possibly with leading zeros).

For floating point types, the default lengths of these fields are defined by the following variables that are 7
declared in the generic package Float_IO:

```
Default_Fore : Field := 2;                                  8
Default_Aft  : Field := Num'Digits-1;
Default_Exp  : Field := 3;
```

For ordinary or decimal fixed point types, the default lengths of these fields are defined by the following 9
variables that are declared in the generic packages Fixed_IO and Decimal_IO, respectively:

```
Default_Fore : Field := Num'Fore;                           10
Default_Aft  : Field := Num'Aft;
Default_Exp  : Field := 0;
```

The following procedures are provided: 11

```
procedure Get(File : in File_Type; Item : out Num; Width : in Field := 0);   12
procedure Get(Item : out Num; Width : in Field := 0);
```

If the value of the parameter Width is zero, skips any leading blanks, line terminators, or page 13
terminators, then reads the longest possible sequence of characters matching the syntax of any of
the following (see 2.4):

- [+|–]numeric_literal 14

- [+|–]numeral.[exponent] 15

- [+|–].numeral[exponent] 16

- [+|–]base#based_numeral.#[exponent] 17

- [+|–]base#.based_numeral#[exponent] 18

19   If a nonzero value of Width is supplied, then exactly Width characters are input, or the characters (possibly none) up to a line terminator, whichever comes first; any skipped leading blanks are included in the count.

20   Returns in the parameter Item the value of type Num that corresponds to the sequence input, preserving the sign (positive if none has been specified) of a zero value if Num is a floating point type and Num'Signed_Zeros is True.

21   The exception Data_Error is propagated if the sequence input does not have the required syntax or if the value obtained is not of the subtype Num.

22
```
procedure Put(File : in File_Type;
              Item : in Num;
              Fore : in Field := Default_Fore;
              Aft  : in Field := Default_Aft;
              Exp  : in Field := Default_Exp);

procedure Put(Item : in Num;
              Fore : in Field := Default_Fore;
              Aft  : in Field := Default_Aft;
              Exp  : in Field := Default_Exp);
```

23   Outputs the value of the parameter Item as a decimal literal with the format defined by Fore, Aft and Exp. If the value is negative, or if Num is a floating point type where Num'Signed_Zeros is True and the value is a negatively signed zero, then a minus sign is included in the integer part. If Exp has the value zero, then the integer part to be output has as many digits as are needed to represent the integer part of the value of Item, overriding Fore if necessary, or consists of the digit zero if the value of Item has no integer part.

24   If Exp has a value greater than zero, then the integer part to be output has a single digit, which is nonzero except for the value 0.0 of Item.

25   In both cases, however, if the integer part to be output has fewer than Fore characters, including any minus sign, then leading spaces are first output to make up the difference. The number of digits of the fractional part is given by Aft, or is one if Aft equals zero. The value is rounded; a value of exactly one half in the last place is rounded away from zero.

26   If Exp has the value zero, there is no exponent part. If Exp has a value greater than zero, then the exponent part to be output has as many digits as are needed to represent the exponent part of the value of Item (for which a single digit integer part is used), and includes an initial sign (plus or minus). If the exponent part to be output has fewer than Exp characters, including the sign, then leading zeros precede the digits, to make up the difference. For the value 0.0 of Item, the exponent has the value zero.

27
```
procedure Get(From : in String; Item : out Num; Last : out Positive);
```

28   Reads a real value from the beginning of the given string, following the same rule as the Get procedure that reads a real value from a file, but treating the end of the string as a file terminator. Returns, in the parameter Item, the value of type Num that corresponds to the sequence input. Returns in Last the index value such that From(Last) is the last character read.

29   The exception Data_Error is propagated if the sequence input does not have the required syntax, or if the value obtained is not of the subtype Num.

```
procedure Put(To   : out String;
              Item : in Num;
              Aft  : in Field := Default_Aft;
              Exp  : in Field := Default_Exp);
```
30

Outputs the value of the parameter Item to the given string, following the same rule as for output to a file, using a value for Fore such that the sequence of characters output exactly fills the string, including any leading spaces.
31

Float_Text_IO is a library package that is a nongeneric equivalent to Text_IO.Float_IO for the predefined type Float:
32

```
with Ada.Text_IO;
package Ada.Float_Text_IO is new Ada.Text_IO.Float_IO(Float);
```
33

For each predefined floating point type, a nongeneric equivalent to Text_IO.Float_IO is provided, with names such as Ada.Long_Float_Text_IO.
34

Implementation Permissions

An implementation may extend Get and Put for floating point types to support special values such as infinities and NaNs.
35

The implementation of Put need not produce an output value with greater accuracy than is supported for the base subtype. The additional accuracy, if any, of the value produced by Put when the number of requested digits in the integer and fractional parts exceeds the required accuracy is implementation defined.
36

The nongeneric equivalent packages may, but need not, be actual instantiations of the generic package for the appropriate predefined type.
37

NOTES

30 For an item with a positive value, if output to a string exactly fills the string without leading spaces, then output of the corresponding negative value will propagate Layout_Error.
38

31 The rules for the Value attribute (see 3.5) and the rules for Get are based on the same set of formats.
39

Examples

```
This paragraph was deleted.
```
40/1

```
package Real_IO is new Float_IO(Real); use Real_IO;
-- default format used at instantiation, Default_Exp = 3
```
41

```
X : Real := -123.4567;   -- digits 8   (see 3.5.7)
```
42

```
Put(X);    -- default format              "-1.2345670E+02"
Put(X, Fore => 5, Aft => 3, Exp => 2);    -- "bbb-1.235E+2"
Put(X, 5, 3, 0);                          -- "b-123.457"
```
43

A.10.10 Input-Output for Enumeration Types

Static Semantics

The following procedures are defined in the generic package Enumeration_IO, which has to be instantiated for the appropriate enumeration type (indicated by Enum in the specification).
1

Values are output using either upper or lower case letters for identifiers. This is specified by the parameter Set, which is of the enumeration type Type_Set.
2

```
type Type_Set is (Lower_Case, Upper_Case);
```
3

4   The format (which includes any trailing spaces) can be specified by an optional field width parameter. The default field width and letter case are defined by the following variables that are declared in the generic package Enumeration_IO:

5
```
Default_Width   : Field := 0;
Default_Setting : Type_Set := Upper_Case;
```

6   The following procedures are provided:

7
```
procedure Get(File : in File_Type; Item : out Enum);
procedure Get(Item : out Enum);
```

8   After skipping any leading blanks, line terminators, or page terminators, reads an identifier according to the syntax of this lexical element (lower and upper case being considered equivalent), or a character literal according to the syntax of this lexical element (including the apostrophes). Returns, in the parameter Item, the value of type Enum that corresponds to the sequence input.

9   The exception Data_Error is propagated if the sequence input does not have the required syntax, or if the identifier or character literal does not correspond to a value of the subtype Enum.

10
```
procedure Put(File  : in File_Type;
              Item  : in Enum;
              Width : in Field := Default_Width;
              Set   : in Type_Set := Default_Setting);

procedure Put(Item  : in Enum;
              Width : in Field := Default_Width;
              Set   : in Type_Set := Default_Setting);
```

11   Outputs the value of the parameter Item as an enumeration literal (either an identifier or a character literal). The optional parameter Set indicates whether lower case or upper case is used for identifiers; it has no effect for character literals. If the sequence of characters produced has fewer than Width characters, then trailing spaces are finally output to make up the difference. If Enum is a character type, the sequence of characters produced is as for Enum'Image(Item), as modified by the Width and Set parameters.

12
```
procedure Get(From : in String; Item : out Enum; Last : out Positive);
```

13   Reads an enumeration value from the beginning of the given string, following the same rule as the Get procedure that reads an enumeration value from a file, but treating the end of the string as a file terminator. Returns, in the parameter Item, the value of type Enum that corresponds to the sequence input. Returns in Last the index value such that From(Last) is the last character read.

14   The exception Data_Error is propagated if the sequence input does not have the required syntax, or if the identifier or character literal does not correspond to a value of the subtype Enum.

15
```
procedure Put(To   : out String;
              Item : in Enum;
              Set  : in Type_Set := Default_Setting);
```

16   Outputs the value of the parameter Item to the given string, following the same rule as for output to a file, using the length of the given string as the value for Width.

17/1   Although the specification of the generic package Enumeration_IO would allow instantiation for an integer type, this is not the intended purpose of this generic package, and the effect of such instantiations is not defined by the language.

NOTES

32 There is a difference between Put defined for characters, and for enumeration values. Thus   18

```
Ada.Text_IO.Put('A');   -- outputs the character A
```
19

```
package Char_IO is new Ada.Text_IO.Enumeration_IO(Character);
Char_IO.Put('A');   -- outputs the character 'A', between apostrophes
```
20

33 The type Boolean is an enumeration type, hence Enumeration_IO can be instantiated for this type.   21

A.11 Wide Text Input-Output

The package Wide_Text_IO provides facilities for input and output in human-readable form. Each file is   1
read or written sequentially, as a sequence of wide characters grouped into lines, and as a sequence of lines
grouped into pages.

Static Semantics

The specification of package Wide_Text_IO is the same as that for Text_IO, except that in each Get,   2
Look_Ahead, Get_Immediate, Get_Line, Put, and Put_Line procedure, any occurrence of Character is
replaced by Wide_Character, and any occurrence of String is replaced by Wide_String.

Nongeneric equivalents of Wide_Text_IO.Integer_IO and Wide_Text_IO.Float_IO are provided (as for   3
Text_IO) for each predefined numeric type, with names such as Ada.Integer_Wide_Text_IO, Ada.Long_-
Integer_Wide_Text_IO, Ada.Float_Wide_Text_IO, Ada.Long_Float_Wide_Text_IO.

A.12 Stream Input-Output

The packages Streams.Stream_IO, Text_IO.Text_Streams, and Wide_Text_IO.Text_Streams provide   1
stream-oriented operations on files.

A.12.1 The Package Streams.Stream_IO

The subprograms in the child package Streams.Stream_IO provide control over stream files. Access to a   1
stream file is either sequential, via a call on Read or Write to transfer an array of stream elements, or
positional (if supported by the implementation for the given file), by specifying a relative index for an
element. Since a stream file can be converted to a Stream_Access value, calling stream-oriented attribute
subprograms of different element types with the same Stream_Access value provides heterogeneous input-
output. See 13.13 for a general discussion of streams.

Static Semantics

The elements of a stream file are stream elements. If positioning is supported for the specified external file,   1.1/1
a current index and current size are maintained for the file as described in A.8. If positioning is not
supported, a current index is not maintained, and the current size is implementation defined.

The library package Streams.Stream_IO has the following declaration: 2

```
with Ada.IO_Exceptions;
package Ada.Streams.Stream_IO is
```
3

```
    type Stream_Access is access all Root_Stream_Type'Class;
```
4

```
    type File_Type is limited private;
```
5

```
    type File_Mode is (In_File, Out_File, Append_File);
```
6

```
7          type    Count              is range 0 .. implementation-defined;
           subtype Positive_Count is Count range 1 .. Count'Last;
              -- Index into file, in stream elements.

8          procedure Create (File : in out File_Type;
                             Mode : in File_Mode := Out_File;
                             Name : in String    := "";
                             Form : in String    := "");

9          procedure Open (File : in out File_Type;
                           Mode : in File_Mode;
                           Name : in String;
                           Form : in String := "");

10         procedure Close  (File : in out File_Type);
           procedure Delete (File : in out File_Type);
           procedure Reset  (File : in out File_Type; Mode : in File_Mode);
           procedure Reset  (File : in out File_Type);

11         function Mode (File : in File_Type) return File_Mode;
           function Name (File : in File_Type) return String;
           function Form (File : in File_Type) return String;

12         function Is_Open     (File : in File_Type) return Boolean;
           function End_Of_File (File : in File_Type) return Boolean;

13         function Stream (File : in File_Type) return Stream_Access;
              -- Return stream access for use with T'Input and T'Output
```

14/1   *This paragraph was deleted.*

```
15            -- Read array of stream elements from file
           procedure Read (File : in  File_Type;
                          Item : out Stream_Element_Array;
                          Last : out Stream_Element_Offset;
                          From : in  Positive_Count);

16         procedure Read (File : in  File_Type;
                          Item : out Stream_Element_Array;
                          Last : out Stream_Element_Offset);
```

17/1   *This paragraph was deleted.*

```
18            -- Write array of stream elements into file
           procedure Write (File : in File_Type;
                           Item : in Stream_Element_Array;
                           To   : in Positive_Count);

19         procedure Write (File : in File_Type;
                           Item : in Stream_Element_Array);
```

20/1   *This paragraph was deleted.*

```
21            -- Operations on position within file

22         procedure Set_Index(File : in File_Type; To : in Positive_Count);

23         function Index(File : in File_Type) return Positive_Count;
           function Size (File : in File_Type) return Count;

24         procedure Set_Mode(File : in out File_Type; Mode : in File_Mode);

25/1       procedure Flush(File : in File_Type);

26            -- exceptions
           Status_Error : exception renames IO_Exceptions.Status_Error;
           Mode_Error   : exception renames IO_Exceptions.Mode_Error;
           Name_Error   : exception renames IO_Exceptions.Name_Error;
           Use_Error    : exception renames IO_Exceptions.Use_Error;
           Device_Error : exception renames IO_Exceptions.Device_Error;
           End_Error    : exception renames IO_Exceptions.End_Error;
           Data_Error   : exception renames IO_Exceptions.Data_Error;

27      private
           ... -- not specified by the language
        end Ada.Streams.Stream_IO;
```

The subprograms Create, Open, Close, Delete, Reset, Mode, Name, Form, Is_Open, and End_of_File have the same effect as the corresponding subprograms in Sequential_IO (see A.8.2).   28

The Set_Mode procedure changes the mode of the file. If the new mode is Append_File, the file is positioned to its end; otherwise, the position in the file is unchanged.   28.1/1

The Flush procedure synchronizes the external file with the internal file (by flushing any internal buffers) without closing the file or changing the position. Mode_Error is propagated if the mode of the file is In_File.   28.2/1

The Stream function returns a Stream_Access result from a File_Type object, thus allowing the stream-oriented attributes Read, Write, Input, and Output to be used on the same file for multiple types. Stream propagates Status_Error if File is not open.   29/1

The procedures Read and Write are equivalent to the corresponding operations in the package Streams. Read propagates Mode_Error if the mode of File is not In_File. Write propagates Mode_Error if the mode of File is not Out_File or Append_File. The Read procedure with a Positive_Count parameter starts reading at the specified index. The Write procedure with a Positive_Count parameter starts writing at the specified index.   30

The Size function returns the current size of the file.   30.1/1

The Index function returns the current index.   31/1

The Set_Index procedure sets the current index to the specified value.   32

If positioning is supported for the external file, the current index is maintained as follows: 32.1/1

- For Open and Create, if the Mode parameter is Append_File, the current index is set to the current size of the file plus one; otherwise, the current index is set to one.   32.2/1

- For Reset, if the Mode parameter is Append_File, or no Mode parameter is given and the current mode is Append_File, the current index is set to the current size of the file plus one; otherwise, the current index is set to one.   32.3/1

- For Set_Mode, if the new mode is Append_File, the current index is set to current size plus one; otherwise, the current index is unchanged.   32.4/1

- For Read and Write without a Positive_Count parameter, the current index is incremented by the number of stream elements read or written.   32.5/1

- For Read and Write with a Positive_Count parameter, the value of the current index is set to the value of the Positive_Count parameter plus the number of stream elements read or written.   32.6/1

If positioning is not supported for the given file, then a call of Index or Set_Index propagates Use_Error. Similarly, a call of Read or Write with a Positive_Count parameter propagates Use_Error.   33

This paragraph was deleted.   34/1

This paragraph was deleted.   35/1

This paragraph was deleted.   36/1

Erroneous Execution

If the File_Type object passed to the Stream function is later closed or finalized, and the stream-oriented attributes are subsequently called (explicitly or implicitly) on the Stream_Access value returned by Stream, execution is erroneous. This rule applies even if the File_Type object was opened again after it had been closed.   36.1/1

A.12.2 The Package Text_IO.Text_Streams

1   The package Text_IO.Text_Streams provides a function for treating a text file as a stream.

Static Semantics

2   The library package Text_IO.Text_Streams has the following declaration:

3
```
with Ada.Streams;
package Ada.Text_IO.Text_Streams is
   type Stream_Access is access all Streams.Root_Stream_Type'Class;
```

4
```
   function Stream (File : in File_Type) return Stream_Access;
end Ada.Text_IO.Text_Streams;
```

5   The Stream function has the same effect as the corresponding function in Streams.Stream_IO.

NOTES

6   34 The ability to obtain a stream for a text file allows Current_Input, Current_Output, and Current_Error to be processed with the functionality of streams, including the mixing of text and binary input-output, and the mixing of binary input-output for different types.

7   35 Performing operations on the stream associated with a text file does not affect the column, line, or page counts.

A.12.3 The Package Wide_Text_IO.Text_Streams

1   The package Wide_Text_IO.Text_Streams provides a function for treating a wide text file as a stream.

Static Semantics

2   The library package Wide_Text_IO.Text_Streams has the following declaration:

3
```
with Ada.Streams;
package Ada.Wide_Text_IO.Text_Streams is
   type Stream_Access is access all Streams.Root_Stream_Type'Class;
```

4
```
   function Stream (File : in File_Type) return Stream_Access;
end Ada.Wide_Text_IO.Text_Streams;
```

5   The Stream function has the same effect as the corresponding function in Streams.Stream_IO.

A.13 Exceptions in Input-Output

1   The package IO_Exceptions defines the exceptions needed by the predefined input-output packages.

Static Semantics

2   The library package IO_Exceptions has the following declaration:

3
```
package Ada.IO_Exceptions is
   pragma Pure(IO_Exceptions);
```

4
```
   Status_Error : exception;
   Mode_Error   : exception;
   Name_Error   : exception;
   Use_Error    : exception;
   Device_Error : exception;
   End_Error    : exception;
   Data_Error   : exception;
   Layout_Error : exception;
```

5
```
end Ada.IO_Exceptions;
```

If more than one error condition exists, the corresponding exception that appears earliest in the following list is the one that is propagated. 6

The exception Status_Error is propagated by an attempt to operate upon a file that is not open, and by an attempt to open a file that is already open. 7

The exception Mode_Error is propagated by an attempt to read from, or test for the end of, a file whose current mode is Out_File or Append_File, and also by an attempt to write to a file whose current mode is In_File. In the case of Text_IO, the exception Mode_Error is also propagated by specifying a file whose current mode is Out_File or Append_File in a call of Set_Input, Skip_Line, End_Of_Line, Skip_Page, or End_Of_Page; and by specifying a file whose current mode is In_File in a call of Set_Output, Set_Line_Length, Set_Page_Length, Line_Length, Page_Length, New_Line, or New_Page. 8

The exception Name_Error is propagated by a call of Create or Open if the string given for the parameter Name does not allow the identification of an external file. For example, this exception is propagated if the string is improper, or, alternatively, if either none or more than one external file corresponds to the string. 9

The exception Use_Error is propagated if an operation is attempted that is not possible for reasons that depend on characteristics of the external file. For example, this exception is propagated by the procedure Create, among other circumstances, if the given mode is Out_File but the form specifies an input only device, if the parameter Form specifies invalid access rights, or if an external file with the given name already exists and overwriting is not allowed. 10

The exception Device_Error is propagated if an input-output operation cannot be completed because of a malfunction of the underlying system. 11

The exception End_Error is propagated by an attempt to skip (read past) the end of a file. 12

The exception Data_Error can be propagated by the procedure Read (or by the Read attribute) if the element read cannot be interpreted as a value of the required subtype. This exception is also propagated by a procedure Get (defined in the package Text_IO) if the input character sequence fails to satisfy the required syntax, or if the value input does not belong to the range of the required subtype. 13

The exception Layout_Error is propagated (in text input-output) by Col, Line, or Page if the value returned exceeds Count'Last. The exception Layout_Error is also propagated on output by an attempt to set column or line numbers in excess of specified maximum line or page lengths, respectively (excluding the unbounded cases). It is also propagated by an attempt to Put too many characters to a string. 14

Documentation Requirements

The implementation shall document the conditions under which Name_Error, Use_Error and Device_Error are propagated. 15

Implementation Permissions

If the associated check is too complex, an implementation need not propagate Data_Error as part of a procedure Read (or the Read attribute) if the value read cannot be interpreted as a value of the required subtype. 16

Erroneous Execution

If the element read by the procedure Read (or by the Read attribute) cannot be interpreted as a value of the required subtype, but this is not detected and Data_Error is not propagated, then the resulting value can be abnormal, and subsequent references to the value can lead to erroneous execution, as explained in 13.9.1. 17

A.14 File Sharing

Dynamic Semantics

1   It is not specified by the language whether the same external file can be associated with more than one file object. If such sharing is supported by the implementation, the following effects are defined:

2   • Operations on one text file object do not affect the column, line, and page numbers of any other file object.

3/1   • *This paragraph was deleted.*

4   • For direct and stream files, the current index is a property of each file object; an operation on one file object does not affect the current index of any other file object.

5   • For direct and stream files, the current size of the file is a property of the external file.

6   All other effects are identical.

A.15 The Package Command_Line

1   The package Command_Line allows a program to obtain the values of its arguments and to set the exit status code to be returned on normal termination.

Static Semantics

2   The library package Ada.Command_Line has the following declaration:

3
```
package Ada.Command_Line is
   pragma Preelaborate(Command_Line);
```

4
```
   function Argument_Count return Natural;
```

5
```
   function Argument (Number : in Positive) return String;
```

6
```
   function Command_Name return String;
```

7
```
   type Exit_Status is implementation-defined integer type;
```

8
```
   Success : constant Exit_Status;
   Failure : constant Exit_Status;
```

9
```
   procedure Set_Exit_Status (Code : in Exit_Status);
```

10
```
private
   ... -- not specified by the language
end Ada.Command_Line;
```

11
```
   function Argument_Count return Natural;
```

12   If the external execution environment supports passing arguments to a program, then Argument_Count returns the number of arguments passed to the program invoking the function. Otherwise it returns 0. The meaning of "number of arguments" is implementation defined.

13
```
   function Argument (Number : in Positive) return String;
```

14   If the external execution environment supports passing arguments to a program, then Argument returns an implementation-defined value corresponding to the argument at relative position Number. If Number is outside the range 1..Argument_Count, then Constraint_Error is propagated.

function Command_Name **return** String;   15

If the external execution environment supports passing arguments to a program, then   16
Command_Name returns an implementation-defined value corresponding to the name of the
command invoking the program; otherwise Command_Name returns the null string.

type Exit_Status **is** *implementation-defined integer type;*   16.1/1

The type Exit_Status represents the range of exit status values supported by the external   17
execution environment. The constants Success and Failure correspond to success and failure,
respectively.

procedure Set_Exit_Status (Code : **in** Exit_Status);   18

If the external execution environment supports returning an exit status from a program, then   19
Set_Exit_Status sets Code as the status. Normal termination of a program returns as the exit
status the value most recently set by Set_Exit_Status, or, if no such value has been set, then the
value Success. If a program terminates abnormally, the status set by Set_Exit_Status is ignored,
and an implementation-defined exit status value is set.

If the external execution environment does not support returning an exit value from a program,   20
then Set_Exit_Status does nothing.

Implementation Permissions

An alternative declaration is allowed for package Command_Line if different functionality is appropriate   21
for the external execution environment.

NOTES
36 Argument_Count, Argument, and Command_Name correspond to the C language's argc, argv[n] (for n>0) and   22
argv[0], respectively.

Annex B
(normative)
Interface to Other Languages

This Annex describes features for writing mixed-language programs. General interface support is presented first; then specific support for C, COBOL, and Fortran is defined, in terms of language interface packages for each of these languages.   1

B.1 Interfacing Pragmas

A pragma Import is used to import an entity defined in a foreign language into an Ada program, thus allowing a foreign-language subprogram to be called from Ada, or a foreign-language variable to be accessed from Ada. In contrast, a pragma Export is used to export an Ada entity to a foreign language, thus allowing an Ada subprogram to be called from a foreign language, or an Ada object to be accessed from a foreign language. The pragmas Import and Export are intended primarily for objects and subprograms, although implementations are allowed to support other entities.   1

A pragma Convention is used to specify that an Ada entity should use the conventions of another language. It is intended primarily for types and "callback" subprograms. For example, "**pragma** Convention(Fortran, Matrix);" implies that Matrix should be represented according to the conventions of the supported Fortran implementation, namely column-major order.   2

A pragma Linker_Options is used to specify the system linker parameters needed when a given compilation unit is included in a partition.   3

Syntax

An *interfacing pragma* is a representation pragma that is one of the pragmas Import, Export, or Convention. Their forms, together with that of the related pragma Linker_Options, are as follows: 4

   pragma Import(5
     [Convention =>] *convention*_identifier, [Entity =>] local_name
   [, [External_Name =>] *string*_expression] [, [Link_Name =>] *string*_expression]);

   pragma Export(6
     [Convention =>] *convention*_identifier, [Entity =>] local_name
   [, [External_Name =>] *string*_expression] [, [Link_Name =>] *string*_expression]);

   pragma Convention([Convention =>] *convention*_identifier,[Entity =>] local_name);   7

   pragma Linker_Options(*string*_expression);   8

A pragma Linker_Options is allowed only at the place of a declarative_item.   9

For pragmas Import and Export, the argument for Link_Name shall not be given without the pragma_argument_identifier unless the argument for External_Name is given.   9.1/1

Name Resolution Rules

The expected type for a *string*_expression in an interfacing pragma or in pragma Linker_Options is String.   10

Legality Rules

The *convention*_identifier of an interfacing pragma shall be the name of a *convention*. The convention names are implementation defined, except for certain language-defined ones, such as Ada and Intrinsic, as explained in 6.3.1, "Conformance Rules". Additional convention names generally represent the calling   11

S. Tucker Taft et al. (Eds.): Consolidated Ada Reference Manual, LNCS 2219, pp. 347–370, 2001.

conventions of foreign languages, language implementations, or specific run-time models. The convention of a callable entity is its *calling convention*.

12 If *L* is a *convention*_identifier for a language, then a type T is said to be *compatible with convention L*, (alternatively, is said to be an *L-compatible type*) if any of the following conditions are met:

13 • T is declared in a language interface package corresponding to *L* and is defined to be *L*-compatible (see B.3, B.3.1, B.3.2, B.4, B.5),

14 • Convention *L* has been specified for T in a pragma Convention, and T is *eligible for convention L*; that is:

15   • T is an array type with either an unconstrained or statically-constrained first subtype, and its component type is *L*-compatible,

16   • T is a record type that has no discriminants and that only has components with statically-constrained subtypes, and each component type is *L*-compatible,

17   • T is an access-to-object type, and its designated type is *L*-compatible,

18   • T is an access-to-subprogram type, and its designated profile's parameter and result types are all *L*-compatible.

19 • T is derived from an *L*-compatible type,

20 • The implementation permits T as an *L*-compatible type.

21 If pragma Convention applies to a type, then the type shall either be compatible with or eligible for the convention specified in the pragma.

22 A pragma Import shall be the completion of a declaration. Notwithstanding any rule to the contrary, a pragma Import may serve as the completion of any kind of (explicit) declaration if supported by an implementation for that kind of declaration. If a completion is a pragma Import, then it shall appear in the same declarative_part, package_specification, task_definition or protected_definition as the declaration. For a library unit, it shall appear in the same compilation, before any subsequent compilation_units other than pragmas. If the local_name denotes more than one entity, then the pragma Import is the completion of all of them.

23 An entity specified as the Entity argument to a pragma Import (or pragma Export) is said to be *imported* (respectively, *exported*).

24 The declaration of an imported object shall not include an explicit initialization expression. Default initializations are not performed.

25 The type of an imported or exported object shall be compatible with the convention specified in the corresponding pragma.

26 For an imported or exported subprogram, the result and parameter types shall each be compatible with the convention specified in the corresponding pragma.

27 The external name and link name *string*_expressions of a pragma Import or Export, and the *string*_expression of a pragma Linker_Options, shall be static.

Static Semantics

28 Import, Export, and Convention pragmas are representation pragmas that specify the *convention* aspect of representation. In addition, Import and Export pragmas specify the *imported* and *exported* aspects of representation, respectively.

An interfacing pragma is a program unit pragma when applied to a program unit (see 10.1.5). 29

An interfacing pragma defines the convention of the entity denoted by the local_name. The convention 30
represents the calling convention or representation convention of the entity. For an access-to-subprogram
type, it represents the calling convention of designated subprograms. In addition:

- A pragma Import specifies that the entity is defined externally (that is, outside the Ada 31
  program).

- A pragma Export specifies that the entity is used externally. 32

- A pragma Import or Export optionally specifies an entity's external name, link name, or both. 33

An *external name* is a string value for the name used by a foreign language program either for an entity 34
that an Ada program imports, or for referring to an entity that an Ada program exports.

A *link name* is a string value for the name of an exported or imported entity, based on the conventions of 35
the foreign language's compiler in interfacing with the system's linker tool.

The meaning of link names is implementation defined. If neither a link name nor the Address attribute of 36
an imported or exported entity is specified, then a link name is chosen in an implementation-defined
manner, based on the external name if one is specified.

Pragma Linker_Options has the effect of passing its string argument as a parameter to the system linker (if 37
one exists), if the immediately enclosing compilation unit is included in the partition being linked. The
interpretation of the string argument, and the way in which the string arguments from multiple
Linker_Options pragmas are combined, is implementation defined.

Dynamic Semantics

Notwithstanding what this International Standard says elsewhere, the elaboration of a declaration denoted 38
by the local_name of a pragma Import does not create the entity. Such an elaboration has no other effect
than to allow the defining name to denote the external entity.

Implementation Advice

If an implementation supports pragma Export to a given language, then it should also allow the main 39
subprogram to be written in that language. It should support some mechanism for invoking the elaboration
of the Ada library units included in the system, and for invoking the finalization of the environment task.
On typical systems, the recommended mechanism is to provide two subprograms whose link names are
"adainit" and "adafinal". Adainit should contain the elaboration code for library units. Adafinal should
contain the finalization code. These subprograms should have no effect the second and subsequent time
they are called.

Automatic elaboration of preelaborated packages should be provided when pragma Export is supported. 40

For each supported convention *L* other than Intrinsic, an implementation should support Import and 41
Export pragmas for objects of *L*-compatible types and for subprograms, and pragma Convention for *L*-
eligible types and for subprograms, presuming the other language has corresponding features. Pragma
Convention need not be supported for scalar types.

NOTES
1 Implementations may place restrictions on interfacing pragmas; for example, requiring each exported entity to be 42
declared at the library level.

2 A pragma Import specifies the conventions for accessing external entities. It is possible that the actual entity is written 43
in assembly language, but reflects the conventions of a particular language. For example, **pragma** Import(Ada, ...) can be
used to interface to an assembly language routine that obeys the Ada compiler's calling conventions.

44   3 To obtain "call-back" to an Ada subprogram from a foreign language environment, **pragma** Convention should be specified both for the access-to-subprogram type and the specific subprogram(s) to which 'Access is applied.

45   4 It is illegal to specify more than one of Import, Export, or Convention for a given entity.

46   5 The local_name in an interfacing pragma can denote more than one entity in the case of overloading. Such a pragma applies to all of the denoted entities.

47   6 See also 13.8, "Machine Code Insertions".

48   7 If both External_Name and Link_Name are specified for an Import or Export pragma, then the External_Name is ignored.

49   8 An interfacing pragma might result in an effect that violates Ada semantics.

Examples

50   *Example of interfacing pragmas:*

51
```
package Fortran_Library is
   function Sqrt (X : Float) return Float;
   function Exp  (X : Float) return Float;
private
   pragma Import(Fortran, Sqrt);
   pragma Import(Fortran, Exp);
end Fortran_Library;
```

B.2 The Package Interfaces

1   Package Interfaces is the parent of several library packages that declare types and other entities useful for interfacing to foreign languages. It also contains some implementation-defined types that are useful across more than one language (in particular for interfacing to assembly language).

Static Semantics

2   The library package Interfaces has the following skeletal declaration:

3
```
package Interfaces is
   pragma Pure(Interfaces);
```

4
```
   type Integer_n is range -2**(n-1) .. 2**(n-1) - 1;   --2's complement
```

5
```
   type Unsigned_n is mod 2**n;
```

6
```
   function Shift_Left  (Value : Unsigned_n; Amount : Natural)
      return Unsigned_n;
   function Shift_Right (Value : Unsigned_n; Amount : Natural)
      return Unsigned_n;
   function Shift_Right_Arithmetic (Value : Unsigned_n; Amount : Natural)
      return Unsigned_n;
   function Rotate_Left  (Value : Unsigned_n; Amount : Natural)
      return Unsigned_n;
   function Rotate_Right (Value : Unsigned_n; Amount : Natural)
      return Unsigned_n;
   ...
end Interfaces;
```

Implementation Requirements

7   An implementation shall provide the following declarations in the visible part of package Interfaces:

8   • Signed and modular integer types of n bits, if supported by the target architecture, for each n that is at least the size of a storage element and that is a factor of the word size. The names of these types are of the form Integer_n for the signed types, and Unsigned_n for the modular types;

- For each such modular type in Interfaces, shifting and rotating subprograms as specified in the declaration of Interfaces above. These subprograms are Intrinsic. They operate on a bit-by-bit basis, using the binary representation of the value of the operands to yield a binary representation for the result. The Amount parameter gives the number of bits by which to shift or rotate. For shifting, zero bits are shifted in, except in the case of Shift_Right_Arithmetic, where one bits are shifted in if Value is at least half the modulus.   9

- Floating point types corresponding to each floating point format fully supported by the hardware.   10

Implementation Permissions

An implementation may provide implementation-defined library units that are children of Interfaces, and may add declarations to the visible part of Interfaces in addition to the ones defined above.   11

Implementation Advice

For each implementation-defined convention identifier, there should be a child package of package Interfaces with the corresponding name. This package should contain any declarations that would be useful for interfacing to the language (implementation) represented by the convention. Any declarations useful for interfacing to any language on the given hardware architecture should be provided directly in Interfaces.   12

An implementation supporting an interface to C, COBOL, or Fortran should provide the corresponding package or packages described in the following clauses.   13

B.3 Interfacing with C

The facilities relevant to interfacing with the C language are the package Interfaces.C and its children; support for the Import, Export, and Convention pragmas with *convention*_identifier C; and support for the Convention pragma with *convention*_identifier C_Pass_By_Copy.   1/1

The package Interfaces.C contains the basic types, constants and subprograms that allow an Ada program to pass scalars and strings to C functions.   2

Static Semantics

The library package Interfaces.C has the following declaration: 3

```
package Interfaces.C is
   pragma Pure(C);

   -- Declarations based on C's <limits.h>

   CHAR_BIT  : constant := implementation-defined;   -- typically 8
   SCHAR_MIN : constant := implementation-defined;   -- typically -128
   SCHAR_MAX : constant := implementation-defined;   -- typically 127
   UCHAR_MAX : constant := implementation-defined;   -- typically 255

   -- Signed and Unsigned Integers
   type int   is range implementation-defined;
   type short is range implementation-defined;
   type long  is range implementation-defined;

   type signed_char is range SCHAR_MIN .. SCHAR_MAX;
   for signed_char'Size use CHAR_BIT;

   type unsigned       is mod implementation-defined;
   type unsigned_short is mod implementation-defined;
   type unsigned_long  is mod implementation-defined;

   type unsigned_char is mod (UCHAR_MAX+1);
   for unsigned_char'Size use CHAR_BIT;
```

   4

   5

   6

   7

   8

   9

   10

11   **subtype** plain_char **is** *implementation-defined*;

12   **type** ptrdiff_t **is range** *implementation-defined*;

13   **type** size_t **is mod** *implementation-defined*;

14   *-- Floating Point*

15   **type** C_float   **is digits** *implementation-defined*;

16   **type** double   **is digits** *implementation-defined*;

17   **type** long_double **is digits** *implementation-defined*;

18   *-- Characters and Strings*

19   **type** char **is** *<implementation-defined character type>*;

20/1   nul : **constant** char := *implementation-defined*;

21   **function** To_C   (Item : **in** Character) **return** char;

22   **function** To_Ada (Item : **in** char) **return** Character;

23   **type** char_array **is array** (size_t **range** <>) **of aliased** char;
           pragma Pack(char_array);
           for char_array'Component_Size **use** CHAR_BIT;

24   **function** Is_Nul_Terminated (Item : **in** char_array) **return** Boolean;

25   **function** To_C   (Item   : **in** String;
                         Append_Nul : **in** Boolean := True)
        return char_array;

26   **function** To_Ada (Item   : **in** char_array;
                      Trim_Nul : **in** Boolean := True)
        return String;

27   **procedure** To_C (Item   : **in** String;
                   Target   : **out** char_array;
                   Count   : **out** size_t;
                   Append_Nul : **in** Boolean := True);

28   **procedure** To_Ada (Item   : **in** char_array;
                     Target   : **out** String;
                     Count   : **out** Natural;
                     Trim_Nul : **in** Boolean := True);

29   *-- Wide Character and Wide String*

30/1   **type** wchar_t **is** *<implementation-defined character type>*;

31/1   wide_nul : **constant** wchar_t := *implementation-defined*;

32   **function** To_C   (Item : **in** Wide_Character) **return** wchar_t;
        function To_Ada (Item : **in** wchar_t   ) **return** Wide_Character;

33   **type** wchar_array **is array** (size_t **range** <>) **of aliased** wchar_t;

34   **pragma** Pack(wchar_array);

35   **function** Is_Nul_Terminated (Item : **in** wchar_array) **return** Boolean;

36   **function** To_C   (Item   : **in** Wide_String;
                         Append_Nul : **in** Boolean := True)
        return wchar_array;

37   **function** To_Ada (Item   : **in** wchar_array;
                      Trim_Nul : **in** Boolean := True)
        return Wide_String;

38   **procedure** To_C (Item   : **in** Wide_String;
                   Target   : **out** wchar_array;
                   Count   : **out** size_t;
                   Append_Nul : **in** Boolean := True);

39   **procedure** To_Ada (Item   : **in** wchar_array;
                     Target   : **out** Wide_String;
                     Count   : **out** Natural;
                     Trim_Nul : **in** Boolean := True);

```
      Terminator_Error : exception;                                              40
   end Interfaces.C;                                                             41
```

Each of the types declared in Interfaces.C is C-compatible.   42

The types int, short, long, unsigned, ptrdiff_t, size_t, double, char, and wchar_t correspond respectively to   43
the C types having the same names. The types signed_char, unsigned_short, unsigned_long, unsigned_-
char, C_float, and long_double correspond respectively to the C types signed char, unsigned short,
unsigned long, unsigned char, float, and long double.

The type of the subtype plain_char is either signed_char or unsigned_char, depending on the C   44
implementation.

```
   function To_C   (Item : in Character) return char;                           45
   function To_Ada (Item : in char      ) return Character;
```

The functions To_C and To_Ada map between the Ada type Character and the C type char.   46

```
   function Is_Nul_Terminated (Item : in char_array) return Boolean;            47
```

The result of Is_Nul_Terminated is True if Item contains nul, and is False otherwise.   48

```
   function To_C   (Item : in String;    Append_Nul : in Boolean := True)       49
      return char_array;

   function To_Ada (Item : in char_array; Trim_Nul   : in Boolean := True)
      return String;
```

The result of To_C is a char_array value of length Item'Length (if Append_Nul is False) or   50
Item'Length+1 (if Append_Nul is True). The lower bound is 0. For each component Item(I), the
corresponding component in the result is To_C applied to Item(I). The value nul is appended if
Append_Nul is True.

The result of To_Ada is a String whose length is Item'Length (if Trim_Nul is False) or the length   51
of the slice of Item preceding the first nul (if Trim_Nul is True). The lower bound of the result is
1. If Trim_Nul is False, then for each component Item(I) the corresponding component in the
result is To_Ada applied to Item(I). If Trim_Nul is True, then for each component Item(I) before
the first nul the corresponding component in the result is To_Ada applied to Item(I). The
function propagates Terminator_Error if Trim_Nul is True and Item does not contain nul.

```
   procedure To_C (Item        : in String;                                     52
                   Target    , : out char_array;
                   Count       : out size_t;
                   Append_Nul  : in Boolean := True);

   procedure To_Ada (Item      : in char_array;
                     Target    : out String;
                     Count     : out Natural;
                     Trim_Nul  : in Boolean := True);
```

For procedure To_C, each element of Item is converted (via the To_C function) to a char, which   53
is assigned to the corresponding element of Target. If Append_Nul is True, nul is then assigned
to the next element of Target. In either case, Count is set to the number of Target elements
assigned. If Target is not long enough, Constraint_Error is propagated.

For procedure To_Ada, each element of Item (if Trim_Nul is False) or each element of Item   54
preceding the first nul (if Trim_Nul is True) is converted (via the To_Ada function) to a
Character, which is assigned to the corresponding element of Target. Count is set to the number

of Target elements assigned. If Target is not long enough, Constraint_Error is propagated. If Trim_Nul is True and Item does not contain nul, then Terminator_Error is propagated.

55 **function** Is_Nul_Terminated (Item : **in** wchar_array) **return** Boolean;

56 The result of Is_Nul_Terminated is True if Item contains wide_nul, and is False otherwise.

57 **function** To_C   (Item : **in** Wide_Character) **return** wchar_t;
    function To_Ada (Item : **in** wchar_t   ) **return** Wide_Character;

58 To_C and To_Ada provide the mappings between the Ada and C wide character types.

59 **function** To_C   (Item   : **in** Wide_String;
                           Append_Nul : **in** Boolean := True)
        return wchar_array;

    function To_Ada (Item   : **in** wchar_array;
                          Trim_Nul : **in** Boolean := True)
        return Wide_String;

    procedure To_C (Item   : **in** Wide_String;
                         Target   : **out** wchar_array;
                         Count   : **out** size_t;
                         Append_Nul : **in** Boolean := True);

    procedure To_Ada (Item   : **in** wchar_array;
                           Target   : **out** Wide_String;
                           Count   : **out** Natural;
                           Trim_Nul : **in** Boolean := True);

60 The To_C and To_Ada subprograms that convert between Wide_String and wchar_array have analogous effects to the To_C and To_Ada subprograms that convert between String and char_array, except that wide_nul is used instead of nul.

60.1/1 A Convention pragma with *convention*_identifier C_Pass_By_Copy shall only be applied to a type.

60.2/1 The eligibility rules in B.1 do not apply to convention C_Pass_By_Copy. Instead, a type T is eligible for convention C_Pass_By_Copy if T is a record type that has no discriminants and that only has components with statically constrained subtypes, and each component is C-compatible.

60.3/1 If a type is C_Pass_By_Copy-compatible then it is also C-compatible.

Implementation Requirements

61/1 An implementation shall support pragma Convention with a C *convention*_identifier for a C-eligible type (see B.1). An implementation shall support pragma Convention with a C_Pass_By_Copy *convention*_identifier for a C_Pass_By_Copy-eligible type.

Implementation Permissions

62 An implementation may provide additional declarations in the C interface packages.

Implementation Advice

62.1/1 The constants nul and wide_nul should have a representation of zero.

63 An implementation should support the following interface correspondences between Ada and C.

64 • An Ada procedure corresponds to a void-returning C function.

65 • An Ada function corresponds to a non-void C function.

66 • An Ada **in** scalar parameter is passed as a scalar argument to a C function.

- An Ada **in** parameter of an access-to-object type with designated type T is passed as a t*   67
argument to a C function, where t is the C type corresponding to the Ada type T.

- An Ada **access** T parameter, or an Ada **out** or **in out** parameter of an elementary type T, is passed   68
as a t* argument to a C function, where t is the C type corresponding to the Ada type T. In the
case of an elementary **out** or **in out** parameter, a pointer to a temporary copy is used to preserve
by-copy semantics.

- An Ada parameter of a C_Pass_By_Copy-compatible (record) type T, of mode **in**, is passed as a t   68.1/1
argument to a C function, where t is the C struct corresponding to the Ada type T.

- An Ada parameter of a record type T, of any mode, other than an **in** parameter of a   69/1
C_Pass_By_Copy-compatible type, is passed as a t* argument to a C function, where t is the C
struct corresponding to the Ada type T.

- An Ada parameter of an array type with component type T, of any mode, is passed as a t*   70
argument to a C function, where t is the C type corresponding to the Ada type T.

- An Ada parameter of an access-to-subprogram type is passed as a pointer to a C function whose   71
prototype corresponds to the designated subprogram's specification.

NOTES
9 Values of type char_array are not implicitly terminated with nul. If a char_array is to be passed as a parameter to an   72
imported C function requiring nul termination, it is the programmer's responsibility to obtain this effect.

10 To obtain the effect of C's sizeof(item_type), where Item_Type is the corresponding Ada type, evaluate the   73
expression: size_t(Item_Type'Size/CHAR_BIT).

11 There is no explicit support for C's union types. Unchecked conversions can be used to obtain the effect of C unions.   74

12 A C function that takes a variable number of arguments can correspond to several Ada subprograms, taking various   75
specific numbers and types of parameters.

Examples

Example of using the Interfaces.C package: 76

```
--Calling the C Library Function strcpy                                          77
with Interfaces.C;
procedure Test is
    package C renames Interfaces.C;
    use type C.char_array;
    -- Call <string.h>strcpy:
    -- C definition of strcpy: char *strcpy(char *s1, const char *s2);
    --   This function copies the string pointed to by s2 (including the terminating null character)
    --   into the array pointed to by s1. If copying takes place between objects that overlap,
    --   the behavior is undefined. The strcpy function returns the value of s1.

    -- Note: since the C function's return value is of no interest, the Ada interface is a procedure    78
    procedure Strcpy (Target : out C.char_array;
                      Source : in  C.char_array);

    pragma Import(C, Strcpy, "strcpy");                                          79

    Chars1 :  C.char_array(1..20);                                              80
    Chars2 :  C.char_array(1..20);
begin                                                                          81
    Chars2(1..6) := "qwert" & C.nul;

    Strcpy(Chars1, Chars2);                                                     82

-- Now Chars1(1..6) = "qwert" & C.Nul                                           83

end Test;                                                                      84
```

B.3.1 The Package Interfaces.C.Strings

1   The package Interfaces.C.Strings declares types and subprograms allowing an Ada program to allocate, reference, update, and free C-style strings. In particular, the private type chars_ptr corresponds to a common use of "char *" in C programs, and an object of this type can be passed to a subprogram to which pragma Import(C,...) has been applied, and for which "char *" is the type of the argument of the C function.

Static Semantics

2   The library package Interfaces.C.Strings has the following declaration:

3   ```
package Interfaces.C.Strings is
    pragma Preelaborate(Strings);
```

4   ```
    type char_array_access is access all char_array;
```

5   ```
    type chars_ptr is private;
```

6   ```
    type chars_ptr_array is array (size_t range <>) of chars_ptr;
```

7   ```
    Null_Ptr : constant chars_ptr;
```

8   ```
    function To_Chars_Ptr (Item      : in char_array_access;
                           Nul_Check : in Boolean := False)
        return chars_ptr;
```

9   ```
    function New_Char_Array (Chars   : in char_array) return chars_ptr;
```

10  ```
    function New_String (Str : in String) return chars_ptr;
```

11 ```
    procedure Free (Item : in out chars_ptr);
```

12  ```
    Dereference_Error : exception;
```

13 ```
    function Value (Item : in chars_ptr) return char_array;
```

14  ```
    function Value (Item : in chars_ptr; Length : in size_t)
        return char_array;
```

15 ```
    function Value (Item : in chars_ptr) return String;
```

16  ```
    function Value (Item : in chars_ptr; Length : in size_t)
        return String;
```

17 ```
    function Strlen (Item : in chars_ptr) return size_t;
```

18  ```
    procedure Update (Item   : in chars_ptr;
                      Offset : in size_t;
                      Chars  : in char_array;
                      Check  : in Boolean := True);
```

19 ```
    procedure Update (Item   : in chars_ptr;
                      Offset : in size_t;
                      Str   : in String;
                      Check : in Boolean := True);
```

20  ```
    Update_Error : exception;
```

21 ```
private
    ... -- not specified by the language
end Interfaces.C.Strings;
```

22  The type chars_ptr is C-compatible and corresponds to the use of C's "char *" for a pointer to the first char in a char array terminated by nul. When an object of type chars_ptr is declared, its value is by default set to Null_Ptr, unless the object is imported (see B.1).
```

```
function To_Chars_Ptr (Item      : in char_array_access;                    23
                       Nul_Check : in Boolean := False)
   return chars_ptr;
```

If Item is **null**, then To_Chars_Ptr returns Null_Ptr. If Item is not **null**,Nul_Check is True, and   24/1
Item.**all** does not contain nul, then the function propagates Terminator_Error; otherwise
To_Chars_Ptr performs a pointer conversion with no allocation of memory.

```
function New_Char_Array (Chars   : in char_array) return chars_ptr;          25
```

This function returns a pointer to an allocated object initialized to Chars(Chars'First .. Index) &   26
nul, where

- Index = Chars'Last if Chars does not contain nul, or   27

- Index is the smallest size_t value I such that Chars(I+1) = nul.   28

Storage_Error is propagated if the allocation fails.   28.1

```
function New_String (Str : in String) return chars_ptr;                      29
```

This function is equivalent to New_Char_Array(To_C(Str)).   30

```
procedure Free (Item : in out chars_ptr);                                    31
```

If Item is Null_Ptr, then Free has no effect. Otherwise, Free releases the storage occupied by   32
Value(Item), and resets Item to Null_Ptr.

```
function Value (Item : in chars_ptr) return char_array;                      33
```

If Item = Null_Ptr then Value propagates Dereference_Error. Otherwise Value returns the prefix   34
of the array of chars pointed to by Item, up to and including the first nul. The lower bound of the
result is 0. If Item does not point to a nul-terminated string, then execution of Value is
erroneous.

```
function Value (Item : in chars_ptr; Length : in size_t)                     35
   return char_array;
```

If Item = Null_Ptr then Value propagates Dereference_Error. Otherwise Value returns the   36/1
shorter of two arrays, either the first Length chars pointed to by Item, or Value(Item). The lower
bound of the result is 0. If Length is 0, then Value propagates Constraint_Error.

```
function Value (Item : in chars_ptr) return String;                          37
```

Equivalent to To_Ada(Value(Item), Trim_Nul=>True).   38

```
function Value (Item : in chars_ptr; Length : in size_t)                     39
   return String;
```

Equivalent to To_Ada(Value(Item, Length) & nul, Trim_Nul=>True).   40/1

```
function Strlen (Item : in chars_ptr) return size_t;                         41
```

Returns *Val*'Length–1 where *Val* = Value(Item); propagates Dereference_Error if Item =   42
Null_Ptr.

```
procedure Update (Item   : in chars_ptr;                                     43
                  Offset : in size_t;
                  Chars  : in char_array;
                  Check  : Boolean := True);
```

If Item = Null_Ptr, then Update propagates Dereference_Error. Otherwise, this procedure   44/1
updates the value pointed to by Item, starting at position Offset, using Chars as the data to be

copied into the array. Overwriting the nul terminator, and skipping with the Offset past the nul terminator, are both prevented if Check is True, as follows:

45   • Let N = Strlen(Item). If Check is True, then:

46   • If Offset+Chars'Length>N, propagate Update_Error.

47   • Otherwise, overwrite the data in the array pointed to by Item, starting at the char at position Offset, with the data in Chars.

48   • If Check is False, then processing is as above, but with no check that Offset+Chars'Length>N.

49
```
procedure Update (Item   : in chars_ptr;
                  Offset : in size_t;
                  Str    : in String;
                  Check  : in Boolean := True);
```

50   Equivalent to Update(Item, Offset, To_C(Str), Check).

Erroneous Execution

51   Execution of any of the following is erroneous if the Item parameter is not null_ptr and Item does not point to a nul-terminated array of chars.

52   • a Value function not taking a Length parameter,

53   • the Free procedure,

54   • the Strlen function.

55   Execution of Free(X) is also erroneous if the chars_ptr X was not returned by New_Char_Array or New_String.

56   Reading or updating a freed char_array is erroneous.

57   Execution of Update is erroneous if Check is False and a call with Check equal to True would have propagated Update_Error.

NOTES
58   13 New_Char_Array and New_String might be implemented either through the allocation function from the C environment (''malloc'') or through Ada dynamic memory allocation (''new''). The key points are

59   • the returned value (a chars_ptr) is represented as a C ''char *'' so that it may be passed to C functions;
60   • the allocated object should be freed by the programmer via a call of Free, not by a called C function.

B.3.2 The Generic Package Interfaces.C.Pointers

1   The generic package Interfaces.C.Pointers allows the Ada programmer to perform C-style operations on pointers. It includes an access type Pointer, Value functions that dereference a Pointer and deliver the designated array, several pointer arithmetic operations, and ''copy'' procedures that copy the contents of a source pointer into the array designated by a destination pointer. As in C, it treats an object Ptr of type Pointer as a pointer to the first element of an array, so that for example, adding 1 to Ptr yields a pointer to the second element of the array.

2   The generic allows two styles of usage: one in which the array is terminated by a special terminator element; and another in which the programmer needs to keep track of the length.

Static Semantics

3   The generic library package Interfaces.C.Pointers has the following declaration:

```ada
generic                                                                    4
   type Index is (<>);
   type Element is private;
   type Element_Array is array (Index range <>) of aliased Element;
   Default_Terminator : Element;
package Interfaces.C.Pointers is
   pragma Preelaborate(Pointers);

   type Pointer is access all Element;                                     5

   function Value(Ref        : in Pointer;                                 6
                  Terminator : in Element := Default_Terminator)
      return Element_Array;

   function Value(Ref    : in Pointer;                                     7
                  Length : in ptrdiff_t)
      return Element_Array;

   Pointer_Error : exception;                                             8

   -- C-style Pointer arithmetic                                          9

   function "+" (Left : in Pointer;    Right : in ptrdiff_t) return Pointer;   10
   function "+" (Left : in ptrdiff_t; Right : in Pointer)    return Pointer;
   function "-" (Left : in Pointer;    Right : in ptrdiff_t) return Pointer;
   function "-" (Left : in Pointer;    Right : in Pointer) return ptrdiff_t;

   procedure Increment (Ref : in out Pointer);                            11
   procedure Decrement (Ref : in out Pointer);

   pragma Convention (Intrinsic, "+");                                    12
   pragma Convention (Intrinsic, "-");
   pragma Convention (Intrinsic, Increment);
   pragma Convention (Intrinsic, Decrement);

   function Virtual_Length (Ref        : in Pointer;                      13
                            Terminator : in Element := Default_Terminator)
      return ptrdiff_t;

   procedure Copy_Terminated_Array                                        14
     (Source     : in Pointer;
      Target     : in Pointer;
      Limit      : in ptrdiff_t := ptrdiff_t'Last;
      Terminator : in Element :=  Default_Terminator);

   procedure Copy_Array (Source : in Pointer;                             15
                         Target : in Pointer;
                         Length : in ptrdiff_t);

end Interfaces.C.Pointers;                                                16
```

The type Pointer is C-compatible and corresponds to one use of C's "Element *". An object of type   17
Pointer is interpreted as a pointer to the initial Element in an Element_Array. Two styles are supported:

- Explicit termination of an array value with Default_Terminator (a special terminator value);   18

- Programmer-managed length, with Default_Terminator treated simply as a data element.   19

```ada
function Value(Ref        : in Pointer;                                   20
              Terminator : in Element := Default_Terminator)
   return Element_Array;
```

This function returns an Element_Array whose value is the array pointed to by Ref, up to and   21
including the first Terminator; the lower bound of the array is Index'First.
Interfaces.C.Strings.Dereference_Error is propagated if Ref is **null**.

```ada
function Value(Ref    : in Pointer;                                       22
              Length : in ptrdiff_t)
   return Element_Array;
```

This function returns an Element_Array comprising the first Length elements pointed to by Ref.   23
The exception Interfaces.C.Strings.Dereference_Error is propagated if Ref is **null**.

24　The "+" and "−" functions perform arithmetic on Pointer values, based on the Size of the array elements. In each of these functions, Pointer_Error is propagated if a Pointer parameter is **null**.

25
```
procedure Increment (Ref : in out Pointer);
```

26　Equivalent to Ref := Ref+1.

27
```
procedure Decrement (Ref : in out Pointer);
```

28　Equivalent to Ref := Ref−1.

29
```
function Virtual_Length (Ref        : in Pointer;
                         Terminator : in Element := Default_Terminator)
   return ptrdiff_t;
```

30　Returns the number of Elements, up to the one just before the first Terminator, in Value(Ref, Terminator).

31
```
procedure Copy_Terminated_Array
   (Source     : in Pointer;
    Target     : in Pointer;
    Limit      : in ptrdiff_t := ptrdiff_t'Last;
    Terminator : in Element := Default_Terminator);
```

32　This procedure copies Value(Source, Terminator) into the array pointed to by Target; it stops either after Terminator has been copied, or the number of elements copied is Limit, whichever occurs first. Dereference_Error is propagated if either Source or Target is **null**.

33
```
procedure Copy_Array (Source : in Pointer;
                      Target : in Pointer;
                      Length : in ptrdiff_t);
```

34　This procedure copies the first Length elements from the array pointed to by Source, into the array pointed to by Target. Dereference_Error is propagated if either Source or Target is **null**.

Erroneous Execution

35　It is erroneous to dereference a Pointer that does not designate an aliased Element.

36　Execution of Value(Ref, Terminator) is erroneous if Ref does not designate an aliased Element in an Element_Array terminated by Terminator.

37　Execution of Value(Ref, Length) is erroneous if Ref does not designate an aliased Element in an Element_Array containing at least Length Elements between the designated Element and the end of the array, inclusive.

38　Execution of Virtual_Length(Ref, Terminator) is erroneous if Ref does not designate an aliased Element in an Element_Array terminated by Terminator.

39　Execution of Copy_Terminated_Array(Source, Target, Limit, Terminator) is erroneous in either of the following situations:

40　● Execution of both Value(Source,Terminator) and Value(Source,Limit) are erroneous, or

41　● Copying writes past the end of the array containing the Element designated by Target.

42　Execution of Copy_Array(Source, Target, Length) is erroneous if either Value(Source, Length) is erroneous, or copying writes past the end of the array containing the Element designated by Target.

NOTES

43　14 To compose a Pointer from an Element_Array, use 'Access on the first element. For example (assuming appropriate instantiations):

```
Some_Array   : Element_Array(0..5) ;                                      44
Some_Pointer : Pointer := Some_Array(0)'Access;
```

Examples

Example of Interfaces.C.Pointers: 45

```
with Interfaces.C.Pointers;                                               46
with Interfaces.C.Strings;
procedure Test_Pointers is
   package C renames Interfaces.C;
   package Char_Ptrs is
      new C.Pointers (Index               => C.size_t,
                      Element             => C.char,
                      Element_Array       => C.char_array,
                      Default_Terminator => C.nul);

   use type Char_Ptrs.Pointer;                                           47
   subtype Char_Star is Char_Ptrs.Pointer;

   procedure Strcpy (Target_Ptr, Source_Ptr : Char_Star) is              48
      Target_Temp_Ptr : Char_Star := Target_Ptr;
      Source_Temp_Ptr : Char_Star := Source_Ptr;
      Element : C.char;
   begin
      if Target_Temp_Ptr = null or Source_Temp_Ptr = null then
         raise C.Strings.Dereference_Error;
      end if;

      loop                                                               49/1
         Element             := Source_Temp_Ptr.all;
         Target_Temp_Ptr.all := Element;
         exit when C."="(Element, C.nul);
         Char_Ptrs.Increment(Target_Temp_Ptr);
         Char_Ptrs.Increment(Source_Temp_Ptr);
      end loop;
   end Strcpy;
begin
   ...
end Test_Pointers;
```

B.4 Interfacing with COBOL

The facilities relevant to interfacing with the COBOL language are the package Interfaces.COBOL and   1
support for the Import, Export and Convention pragmas with *convention*_identifier COBOL.

The COBOL interface package supplies several sets of facilities: 2

- A set of types corresponding to the native COBOL types of the supported COBOL   3
  implementation (so-called "internal COBOL representations"), allowing Ada data to be passed
  as parameters to COBOL programs

- A set of types and constants reflecting external data representations such as might be found in   4
  files or databases, allowing COBOL-generated data to be read by an Ada program, and Ada-
  generated data to be read by COBOL programs

- A generic package for converting between an Ada decimal type value and either an internal or   5
  external COBOL representation

Static Semantics

The library package Interfaces.COBOL has the following declaration: 6

```
package Interfaces.COBOL is                                               7
   pragma Preelaborate(COBOL);
```

-- Types and operations for internal data representations   8

9
```
type Floating      is digits implementation-defined;
type Long_Floating is digits implementation-defined;
```

10
```
type Binary      is range implementation-defined;
type Long_Binary is range implementation-defined;
```

11
```
Max_Digits_Binary      : constant := implementation-defined;
Max_Digits_Long_Binary : constant := implementation-defined;
```

12
```
type Decimal_Element  is mod implementation-defined;
type Packed_Decimal is array (Positive range <>) of Decimal_Element;
pragma Pack(Packed_Decimal);
```

13
```
type COBOL_Character is implementation-defined character type;
```

14
```
Ada_To_COBOL : array (Character) of COBOL_Character := implementation-defined;
```

15
```
COBOL_To_Ada : array (COBOL_Character) of Character := implementation-defined;
```

16
```
type Alphanumeric is array (Positive range <>) of COBOL_Character;
pragma Pack(Alphanumeric);
```

17
```
function To_COBOL (Item : in String) return Alphanumeric;
function To_Ada   (Item : in Alphanumeric) return String;
```

18
```
procedure To_COBOL (Item   : in String;
                    Target : out Alphanumeric;
                    Last   : out Natural);
```

19
```
procedure To_Ada (Item   : in Alphanumeric;
                  Target : out String;
                  Last   : out Natural);
```

20
```
type Numeric is array (Positive range <>) of COBOL_Character;
pragma Pack(Numeric);
```

21
```
-- Formats for COBOL data representations
```

22
```
type Display_Format is private;
```

23
```
Unsigned             : constant Display_Format;
Leading_Separate     : constant Display_Format;
Trailing_Separate    : constant Display_Format;
Leading_Nonseparate  : constant Display_Format;
Trailing_Nonseparate : constant Display_Format;
```

24
```
type Binary_Format is private;
```

25
```
High_Order_First : constant Binary_Format;
Low_Order_First  : constant Binary_Format;
Native_Binary    : constant Binary_Format;
```

26
```
type Packed_Format is private;
```

27
```
Packed_Unsigned : constant Packed_Format;
Packed_Signed   : constant Packed_Format;
```

28
```
-- Types for external representation of COBOL binary data
```

29
```
type Byte is mod 2**COBOL_Character'Size;
type Byte_Array is array (Positive range <>) of Byte;
pragma Pack (Byte_Array);
```

30
```
Conversion_Error : exception;
```

31
```
generic
   type Num is delta <> digits <>;
package Decimal_Conversions is
```

32
```
   -- Display Formats: data values are represented as Numeric
```

33
```
   function Valid (Item   : in Numeric;
                   Format : in Display_Format) return Boolean;
```

34
```
   function Length (Format : in Display_Format) return Natural;
```

35
```
   function To_Decimal (Item   : in Numeric;
                        Format : in Display_Format) return Num;
```

```
      function To_Display (Item   : in Num;                          36
                          Format : in Display_Format) return Numeric;
      -- Packed Formats: data values are represented as Packed_Decimal    37
      function Valid (Item   : in Packed_Decimal;                     38
                     Format : in Packed_Format) return Boolean;
      function Length (Format : in Packed_Format) return Natural;     39
      function To_Decimal (Item   : in Packed_Decimal;                40
                          Format : in Packed_Format) return Num;
      function To_Packed (Item   : in Num;                            41
                         Format : in Packed_Format) return Packed_Decimal;
      -- Binary Formats: external data values are represented as Byte_Array  42
      function Valid (Item   : in Byte_Array;                         43
                     Format : in Binary_Format) return Boolean;
      function Length (Format : in Binary_Format) return Natural;     44
      function To_Decimal (Item   : in Byte_Array;
                          Format : in Binary_Format) return Num;
      function To_Binary (Item   : in Num;                            45
                         Format : in Binary_Format) return Byte_Array;
      -- Internal Binary formats: data values are of type Binary or Long_Binary  46
      function To_Decimal (Item : in Binary)       return Num;        47
      function To_Decimal (Item : in Long_Binary)  return Num;
      function To_Binary      (Item : in Num)  return Binary;         48
      function To_Long_Binary (Item : in Num)  return Long_Binary;
   end Decimal_Conversions;                                           49
private                                                               50
   ... -- not specified by the language
end Interfaces.COBOL;
```

Each of the types in Interfaces.COBOL is COBOL-compatible.   51

The types Floating and Long_Floating correspond to the native types in COBOL for data items with   52
computational usage implemented by floating point. The types Binary and Long_Binary correspond to the
native types in COBOL for data items with binary usage, or with computational usage implemented by
binary.

Max_Digits_Binary is the largest number of decimal digits in a numeric value that is represented as   53
Binary. Max_Digits_Long_Binary is the largest number of decimal digits in a numeric value that is
represented as Long_Binary.

The type Packed_Decimal corresponds to COBOL's packed-decimal usage.   54

The type COBOL_Character defines the run-time character set used in the COBOL implementation.   55
Ada_To_COBOL and COBOL_To_Ada are the mappings between the Ada and COBOL run-time
character sets.

Type Alphanumeric corresponds to COBOL's alphanumeric data category.   56

Each of the functions To_COBOL and To_Ada converts its parameter based on the mappings   57
Ada_To_COBOL and COBOL_To_Ada, respectively. The length of the result for each is the length of the
parameter, and the lower bound of the result is 1. Each component of the result is obtained by applying the
relevant mapping to the corresponding component of the parameter.

Each of the procedures To_COBOL and To_Ada copies converted elements from Item to Target, using the   58
appropriate mapping (Ada_To_COBOL or COBOL_To_Ada, respectively). The index in Target of the last

element assigned is returned in Last (0 if Item is a null array). If Item'Length exceeds Target'Length, Constraint_Error is propagated.

59　　Type Numeric corresponds to COBOL's numeric data category with display usage.

60　　The types Display_Format, Binary_Format, and Packed_Format are used in conversions between Ada decimal type values and COBOL internal or external data representations. The value of the constant Native_Binary is either High_Order_First or Low_Order_First, depending on the implementation.

61
```
function Valid (Item   : in Numeric;
                Format : in Display_Format) return Boolean;
```

62　　The function Valid checks that the Item parameter has a value consistent with the value of Format. If the value of Format is other than Unsigned, Leading_Separate, and Trailing_Separate, the effect is implementation defined. If Format does have one of these values, the following rules apply:

63/1　　　• Format=Unsigned: if Item comprises one or more decimal digit characters then Valid returns True, else it returns False.

64/1　　　• Format=Leading_Separate: if Item comprises a single occurrence of the plus or minus sign character, and then one or more decimal digit characters, then Valid returns True, else it returns False.

65/1　　　• Format=Trailing_Separate: if Item comprises one or more decimal digit characters and finally a plus or minus sign character, then Valid returns True, else it returns False.

66
```
function Length (Format : in Display_Format) return Natural;
```

67　　The Length function returns the minimal length of a Numeric value sufficient to hold any value of type Num when represented as Format.

68
```
function To_Decimal (Item   : in Numeric;
                     Format : in Display_Format) return Num;
```

69　　Produces a value of type Num corresponding to Item as represented by Format. The number of digits after the assumed radix point in Item is Num'Scale. Conversion_Error is propagated if the value represented by Item is outside the range of Num.

70
```
function To_Display (Item   : in Num;
                     Format : in Display_Format) return Numeric;
```

71/1　　This function returns the Numeric value for Item, represented in accordance with Format. The length of the returned value is Length(Format), and the lower bound is 1. Conversion_Error is propagated if Num is negative and Format is Unsigned.

72
```
function Valid (Item   : in Packed_Decimal;
                Format : in Packed_Format) return Boolean;
```

73　　This function returns True if Item has a value consistent with Format, and False otherwise. The rules for the formation of Packed_Decimal values are implementation defined.

74
```
function Length (Format : in Packed_Format) return Natural;
```

75　　This function returns the minimal length of a Packed_Decimal value sufficient to hold any value of type Num when represented as Format.

```
function To_Decimal (Item   : in Packed_Decimal;                          76
                     Format : in Packed_Format) return Num;
```

Produces a value of type Num corresponding to Item as represented by Format. Num'Scale is the   77
number of digits after the assumed radix point in Item. Conversion_Error is propagated if the
value represented by Item is outside the range of Num.

```
function To_Packed (Item   : in Num;                                      78
                    Format : in Packed_Format) return Packed_Decimal;
```

This function returns the Packed_Decimal value for Item, represented in accordance with   79/1
Format. The length of the returned value is Length(Format), and the lower bound is 1.
Conversion_Error is propagated if Num is negative and Format is Packed_Unsigned.

```
function Valid (Item   : in Byte_Array;                                   80
                Format : in Binary_Format) return Boolean;
```

This function returns True if Item has a value consistent with Format, and False otherwise.   81

```
function Length (Format : in Binary_Format) return Natural;               82
```

This function returns the minimal length of a Byte_Array value sufficient to hold any value of   83
type Num when represented as Format.

```
function To_Decimal (Item   : in Byte_Array;                              84
                     Format : in Binary_Format) return Num;
```

Produces a value of type Num corresponding to Item as represented by Format. Num'Scale is the   85
number of digits after the assumed radix point in Item. Conversion_Error is propagated if the
value represented by Item is outside the range of Num.

```
function To_Binary (Item   : in Num;                                      86
                    Format : in Binary_Format) return Byte_Array;
```

This function returns the Byte_Array value for Item, represented in accordance with Format. The   87/1
length of the returned value is Length(Format), and the lower bound is 1.

```
function To_Decimal (Item : in Binary)      return Num;                   88

function To_Decimal (Item : in Long_Binary) return Num;
```

These functions convert from COBOL binary format to a corresponding value of the decimal   89
type Num. Conversion_Error is propagated if Item is too large for Num.

```
function To_Binary      (Item : in Num)  return Binary;                   90

function To_Long_Binary (Item : in Num)  return Long_Binary;
```

These functions convert from Ada decimal to COBOL binary format. Conversion_Error is   91
propagated if the value of Item is too large to be represented in the result type.

Implementation Requirements

An implementation shall support pragma Convention with a COBOL *convention*_identifier for a COBOL-   92
eligible type (see B.1).

Implementation Permissions

An implementation may provide additional constants of the private types Display_Format, Binary_Format,   93
or Packed_Format.

94 An implementation may provide further floating point and integer types in Interfaces.COBOL to match additional native COBOL types, and may also supply corresponding conversion functions in the generic package Decimal_Conversions.

Implementation Advice

95 An Ada implementation should support the following interface correspondences between Ada and COBOL.

96 • An Ada **access** T parameter is passed as a ''BY REFERENCE'' data item of the COBOL type corresponding to T.

97 • An Ada **in** scalar parameter is passed as a ''BY CONTENT'' data item of the corresponding COBOL type.

98 • Any other Ada parameter is passed as a ''BY REFERENCE'' data item of the COBOL type corresponding to the Ada parameter type; for scalars, a local copy is used if necessary to ensure by-copy semantics.

NOTES

99 15 An implementation is not required to support pragma Convention for access types, nor is it required to support pragma Import, Export or Convention for functions.

100 16 If an Ada subprogram is exported to COBOL, then a call from COBOL call may specify either ''BY CONTENT'' or ''BY REFERENCE''.

Examples

101 *Examples of Interfaces.COBOL:*

102
```
with Interfaces.COBOL;
procedure Test_Call is
```

103
```
   -- Calling a foreign COBOL program
   -- Assume that a COBOL program PROG has the following declaration
   -- in its LINKAGE section:
   -- 01 Parameter-Area
   --    05 NAME  PIC X(20).
   --    05 SSN   PIC X(9).
   --    05 SALARY PIC 99999V99 USAGE COMP.
   -- The effect of PROG is to update SALARY based on some algorithm
```

104
```
   package COBOL renames Interfaces.COBOL;
```

105
```
   type Salary_Type is delta 0.01 digits 7;
```

106
```
   type COBOL_Record is
       record
           Name   : COBOL.Numeric(1..20);
           SSN    : COBOL.Numeric(1..9);
           Salary : COBOL.Binary;   -- Assume Binary = 32 bits
       end record;
   pragma Convention (COBOL, COBOL_Record);
```

107
```
   procedure Prog (Item : in out COBOL_Record);
   pragma Import (COBOL, Prog, "PROG");
```

108
```
   package Salary_Conversions is
       new COBOL.Decimal_Conversions(Salary_Type);
```

109
```
   Some_Salary : Salary_Type := 12_345.67;
   Some_Record : COBOL_Record :=
       (Name   => "Johnson, John        ",
        SSN    => "111223333",
        Salary => Salary_Conversions.To_Binary(Some_Salary));
```

```
begin                                                                          110
    Prog (Some_Record);
    ...
end Test_Call;

with Interfaces.COBOL;                                                         111
with COBOL_Sequential_IO; -- Assumed to be supplied by implementation
procedure Test_External_Formats is

    -- Using data created by a COBOL program                                    112
    -- Assume that a COBOL program has created a sequential file with
    -- the following record structure, and that we need to
    -- process the records in an Ada program
    -- 01 EMPLOYEE-RECORD
    --    05 NAME    PIC X(20).
    --    05 SSN     PIC X(9).
    --    05 SALARY  PIC 99999V99 USAGE COMP.
    --    05 ADJUST  PIC S999V999 SIGN LEADING SEPARATE.
    -- The COMP data is binary (32 bits), high-order byte first

    package COBOL renames Interfaces.COBOL;                                     113

    type Salary_Type        is delta 0.01  digits 7;                           114
    type Adjustments_Type is delta 0.001 digits 6;

    type COBOL_Employee_Record_Type is   -- External representation            115
        record
            Name    : COBOL.Alphanumeric(1..20);
            SSN     : COBOL.Alphanumeric(1..9);
            Salary  : COBOL.Byte_Array(1..4);
            Adjust  : COBOL.Numeric(1..7);   -- Sign and 6 digits
        end record;
    pragma Convention (COBOL, COBOL_Employee_Record_Type);

    package COBOL_Employee_IO is                                               116
        new COBOL_Sequential_IO(COBOL_Employee_Record_Type);
    use COBOL_Employee_IO;

    COBOL_File : File_Type;                                                    117

    type Ada_Employee_Record_Type is   -- Internal representation              118
        record
            Name    : String(1..20);
            SSN     : String(1..9);
            Salary  : Salary_Type;
            Adjust  : Adjustments_Type;
        end record;

    COBOL_Record : COBOL_Employee_Record_Type;                                 119
    Ada_Record   : Ada_Employee_Record_Type;

    package Salary_Conversions is                                             120
        new COBOL.Decimal_Conversions(Salary_Type);
    use Salary_Conversions;

    package Adjustments_Conversions is                                        121
        new COBOL.Decimal_Conversions(Adjustments_Type);
    use Adjustments_Conversions;
begin                                                                          122
    Open (COBOL_File, Name => "Some_File");

    loop                                                                       123
        Read (COBOL_File, COBOL_Record);
```

Interfacing with COBOL **B.4**

124
```
          Ada_Record.Name := To_Ada(COBOL_Record.Name);
          Ada_Record.SSN  := To_Ada(COBOL_Record.SSN);
          Ada_Record.Salary :=
             To_Decimal(COBOL_Record.Salary, COBOL.High_Order_First);
          Ada_Record.Adjust :=
             To_Decimal(COBOL_Record.Adjust, COBOL.Leading_Separate);
          ... -- Process Ada_Record
       end loop;
   exception
      when End_Error => ...
   end Test_External_Formats;
```

B.5 Interfacing with Fortran

1 The facilities relevant to interfacing with the Fortran language are the package Interfaces.Fortran and support for the Import, Export and Convention pragmas with *convention*_identifier Fortran.

2 The package Interfaces.Fortran defines Ada types whose representations are identical to the default representations of the Fortran intrinsic types Integer, Real, Double Precision, Complex, Logical, and Character in a supported Fortran implementation. These Ada types can therefore be used to pass objects between Ada and Fortran programs.

Static Semantics

3 The library package Interfaces.Fortran has the following declaration:

4
```
   with Ada.Numerics.Generic_Complex_Types;   -- see G.1.1
   pragma Elaborate_All(Ada.Numerics.Generic_Complex_Types);
   package Interfaces.Fortran is
      pragma Pure(Fortran);
```

5
```
      type Fortran_Integer is range implementation-defined;
```

6
```
      type Real             is digits implementation-defined;
      type Double_Precision is digits implementation-defined;
```

7
```
      type Logical is new Boolean;
```

8
```
      package Single_Precision_Complex_Types is
         new Ada.Numerics.Generic_Complex_Types (Real);
```

9
```
      type Complex is new Single_Precision_Complex_Types.Complex;
```

10
```
      subtype Imaginary is Single_Precision_Complex_Types.Imaginary;
      i : Imaginary renames Single_Precision_Complex_Types.i;
      j : Imaginary renames Single_Precision_Complex_Types.j;
```

11
```
      type Character_Set is implementation-defined character type;
```

12
```
      type Fortran_Character is array (Positive range <>) of Character_Set;
      pragma Pack (Fortran_Character);
```

13
```
      function To_Fortran (Item : in Character) return Character_Set;
      function To_Ada (Item : in Character_Set) return Character;
```

14
```
      function To_Fortran (Item : in String) return Fortran_Character;
      function To_Ada      (Item : in Fortran_Character) return String;
```

15
```
      procedure To_Fortran (Item         : in String;
                            Target       : out Fortran_Character;
                            Last         : out Natural);
```

16
```
      procedure To_Ada (Item     : in Fortran_Character;
                        Target   : out String;
                        Last     : out Natural);
```

17
```
   end Interfaces.Fortran;
```

18 The types Fortran_Integer, Real, Double_Precision, Logical, Complex, and Fortran_Character are Fortran-compatible.

The To_Fortran and To_Ada functions map between the Ada type Character and the Fortran type Character_Set, and also between the Ada type String and the Fortran type Fortran_Character. The To_Fortran and To_Ada procedures have analogous effects to the string conversion subprograms found in Interfaces.COBOL. | 19

Implementation Requirements

An implementation shall support pragma Convention with a Fortran *convention*_identifier for a Fortran-eligible type (see B.1). | 20

Implementation Permissions

An implementation may add additional declarations to the Fortran interface packages. For example, the Fortran interface package for an implementation of Fortran 77 (ANSI X3.9-1978) that defines types like Integer*n, Real*n, Logical*n, and Complex*n may contain the declarations of types named Integer_Star_n, Real_Star_n, Logical_Star_n, and Complex_Star_n. (This convention should not apply to Character*n, for which the Ada analog is the constrained array subtype Fortran_Character (1..n).) Similarly, the Fortran interface package for an implementation of Fortran 90 that provides multiple *kinds* of intrinsic types, e.g. Integer (Kind=n), Real (Kind=n), Logical (Kind=n), Complex (Kind=n), and Character (Kind=n), may contain the declarations of types with the recommended names Integer_Kind_n, Real_Kind_n, Logical_Kind_n, Complex_Kind_n, and Character_Kind_n. | 21

Implementation Advice

An Ada implementation should support the following interface correspondences between Ada and Fortran: | 22

- An Ada procedure corresponds to a Fortran subroutine. | 23

- An Ada function corresponds to a Fortran function. | 24

- An Ada parameter of an elementary, array, or record type T is passed as a T_F argument to a Fortran procedure, where T_F is the Fortran type corresponding to the Ada type T, and where the INTENT attribute of the corresponding dummy argument matches the Ada formal parameter mode; the Fortran implementation's parameter passing conventions are used. For elementary types, a local copy is used if necessary to ensure by-copy semantics. | 25

- An Ada parameter of an access-to-subprogram type is passed as a reference to a Fortran procedure whose interface corresponds to the designated subprogram's specification. | 26

NOTES
17 An object of a Fortran-compatible record type, declared in a library package or subprogram, can correspond to a Fortran common block; the type also corresponds to a Fortran "derived type". | 27

Examples

Example of Interfaces.Fortran: | 28

```
with Interfaces.Fortran;                                               | 29
use Interfaces.Fortran;
procedure Ada_Application is

    type Fortran_Matrix is array (Integer range <>,                    | 30
                                  Integer range <>) of Double_Precision;
    pragma Convention (Fortran, Fortran_Matrix);    -- stored in Fortran's
                                                    -- column-major order
    procedure Invert (Rank : in Fortran_Integer; X : in out Fortran_Matrix);
    pragma Import (Fortran, Invert);                -- a Fortran subroutine

    Rank      : constant Fortran_Integer := 100;                       | 31
    My_Matrix : Fortran_Matrix (1 .. Rank, 1 .. Rank);

begin                                                                  | 32
```

33
```
        ...
        My_Matrix := ...;
        ...
        Invert (Rank, My_Matrix);
        ...
```

34
```
    end Ada_Application;
```

Annex C
(normative)
Systems Programming

The Systems Programming Annex specifies additional capabilities provided for low-level programming.   1
These capabilities are also required in many real-time, embedded, distributed, and information systems.

C.1 Access to Machine Operations

This clause specifies rules regarding access to machine instructions from within an Ada program.   1

Implementation Requirements

The implementation shall support machine code insertions (see 13.8) or intrinsic subprograms (see 6.3.1)   2
(or both). Implementation-defined attributes shall be provided to allow the use of Ada entities as operands.

Implementation Advice

The machine code or intrinsics support should allow access to all operations normally available to   3
assembly language programmers for the target environment, including privileged instructions, if any.

The interfacing pragmas (see Annex B) should support interface to assembler; the default assembler should   4
be associated with the convention identifier Assembler.

If an entity is exported to assembly language, then the implementation should allocate it at an addressable   5
location, and should ensure that it is retained by the linking process, even if not otherwise referenced from
the Ada code. The implementation should assume that any call to a machine code or assembler subprogram
is allowed to read or update every object that is specified as exported.

Documentation Requirements

The implementation shall document the overhead associated with calling machine-code or intrinsic   6
subprograms, as compared to a fully-inlined call, and to a regular out-of-line call.

The implementation shall document the types of the package System.Machine_Code usable for machine   7
code insertions, and the attributes to be used in machine code insertions for references to Ada entities.

The implementation shall document the subprogram calling conventions associated with the convention   8
identifiers available for use with the interfacing pragmas (Ada and Assembler, at a minimum), including
register saving, exception propagation, parameter passing, and function value returning.

For exported and imported subprograms, the implementation shall document the mapping between the   9
Link_Name string, if specified, or the Ada designator, if not, and the external link name used for such a
subprogram.

Implementation Advice

The implementation should ensure that little or no overhead is associated with calling intrinsic and   10
machine-code subprograms.

It is recommended that intrinsic subprograms be provided for convenient access to any machine operations   11
that provide special capabilities or efficiency and that are not otherwise available through the language
constructs. Examples of such instructions include:

S. Tucker Taft et al. (Eds.): Consolidated Ada Reference Manual, LNCS 2219, pp. 371–385, 2001.

12   • Atomic read-modify-write operations — e.g., test and set, compare and swap, decrement and test, enqueue/dequeue.

13   • Standard numeric functions — e.g., *sin*, *log*.

14   • String manipulation operations — e.g., translate and test.

15   • Vector operations — e.g., compare vector against thresholds.

16   • Direct operations on I/O ports.

C.2 Required Representation Support

1   This clause specifies minimal requirements on the implementation's support for representation items and related features.

Implementation Requirements

2   The implementation shall support at least the functionality defined by the recommended levels of support in Section 13.

C.3 Interrupt Support

1   This clause specifies the language-defined model for hardware interrupts in addition to mechanisms for handling interrupts.

Dynamic Semantics

2   An *interrupt* represents a class of events that are detected by the hardware or the system software. Interrupts are said to occur. An *occurrence* of an interrupt is separable into generation and delivery. *Generation* of an interrupt is the event in the underlying hardware or system that makes the interrupt available to the program. *Delivery* is the action that invokes part of the program as response to the interrupt occurrence. Between generation and delivery, the interrupt occurrence (or interrupt) is *pending*. Some or all interrupts may be *blocked*. When an interrupt is blocked, all occurrences of that interrupt are prevented from being delivered. Certain interrupts are *reserved*. The set of reserved interrupts is implementation defined. A reserved interrupt is either an interrupt for which user-defined handlers are not supported, or one which already has an attached handler by some other implementation-defined means. Program units can be connected to non-reserved interrupts. While connected, the program unit is said to be *attached* to that interrupt. The execution of that program unit, the *interrupt handler*, is invoked upon delivery of the interrupt occurrence.

3   While a handler is attached to an interrupt, it is called once for each delivered occurrence of that interrupt. While the handler executes, the corresponding interrupt is blocked.

4   While an interrupt is blocked, all occurrences of that interrupt are prevented from being delivered. Whether such occurrences remain pending or are lost is implementation defined.

5   Each interrupt has a *default treatment* which determines the system's response to an occurrence of that interrupt when no user-defined handler is attached. The set of possible default treatments is implementation defined, as is the method (if one exists) for configuring the default treatments for interrupts.

6   An interrupt is delivered to the handler (or default treatment) that is in effect for that interrupt at the time of delivery.

An exception propagated from a handler that is invoked by an interrupt has no effect. 7

If the Ceiling_Locking policy (see D.3) is in effect, the interrupt handler executes with the active priority that is the ceiling priority of the corresponding protected object. 8

Implementation Requirements

The implementation shall provide a mechanism to determine the minimum stack space that is needed for each interrupt handler and to reserve that space for the execution of the handler. This space should accommodate nested invocations of the handler where the system permits this. 9

If the hardware or the underlying system holds pending interrupt occurrences, the implementation shall provide for later delivery of these occurrences to the program. 10

If the Ceiling_Locking policy is not in effect, the implementation shall provide means for the application to specify whether interrupts are to be blocked during protected actions. 11

Documentation Requirements

The implementation shall document the following items: 12

1. For each interrupt, which interrupts are blocked from delivery when a handler attached to that interrupt executes (either as a result of an interrupt delivery or of an ordinary call on a procedure of the corresponding protected object). 13

2. Any interrupts that cannot be blocked, and the effect of attaching handlers to such interrupts, if this is permitted. 14

3. Which run-time stack an interrupt handler uses when it executes as a result of an interrupt delivery; if this is configurable, what is the mechanism to do so; how to specify how much space to reserve on that stack. 15

4. Any implementation- or hardware-specific activity that happens before a user-defined interrupt handler gets control (e.g., reading device registers, acknowledging devices). 16

5. Any timing or other limitations imposed on the execution of interrupt handlers. 17

6. The state (blocked/unblocked) of the non-reserved interrupts when the program starts; if some interrupts are unblocked, what is the mechanism a program can use to protect itself before it can attach the corresponding handlers. 18

7. Whether the interrupted task is allowed to resume execution before the interrupt handler returns. 19

8. The treatment of interrupt occurrences that are generated while the interrupt is blocked; i.e., whether one or more occurrences are held for later delivery, or all are lost. 20

9. Whether predefined or implementation-defined exceptions are raised as a result of the occurrence of any interrupt, and the mapping between the machine interrupts (or traps) and the predefined exceptions. 21

10. 22
    On a multi-processor, the rules governing the delivery of an interrupt to a particular processor.

Implementation Permissions

If the underlying system or hardware does not allow interrupts to be blocked, then no blocking is required as part of the execution of subprograms of a protected object whose one of its subprograms is an interrupt handler. 23

24   In a multi-processor with more than one interrupt subsystem, it is implementation defined whether (and how) interrupt sources from separate subsystems share the same Interrupt_ID type (see C.3.2). In particular, the meaning of a blocked or pending interrupt may then be applicable to one processor only.

25   Implementations are allowed to impose timing or other limitations on the execution of interrupt handlers.

26   Other forms of handlers are allowed to be supported, in which case, the rules of this subclause should be adhered to.

27   The active priority of the execution of an interrupt handler is allowed to vary from one occurrence of the same interrupt to another.

Implementation Advice

28   If the Ceiling_Locking policy is not in effect, the implementation should provide means for the application to specify which interrupts are to be blocked during protected actions, if the underlying system allows for a finer-grain control of interrupt blocking.

NOTES

29   1 The default treatment for an interrupt can be to keep the interrupt pending or to deliver it to an implementation-defined handler. Examples of actions that an implementation-defined handler is allowed to perform include aborting the partition, ignoring (i.e., discarding occurrences of) the interrupt, or queuing one or more occurrences of the interrupt for possible later delivery when a user-defined handler is attached to that interrupt.

30   2 It is a bounded error to call Task_Identification.Current_Task (see C.7.1) from an interrupt handler.

31   3 The rule that an exception propagated from an interrupt handler has no effect is modeled after the rule about exceptions propagated out of task bodies.

C.3.1 Protected Procedure Handlers

Syntax

1   The form of a pragma Interrupt_Handler is as follows:

2   **pragma** Interrupt_Handler(*handler_*name);

3   The form of a pragma Attach_Handler is as follows:

4   **pragma** Attach_Handler(*handler_*name, expression);

Name Resolution Rules

5   For the Interrupt_Handler and Attach_Handler pragmas, the *handler_*name shall resolve to denote a protected procedure with a parameterless profile.

6   For the Attach_Handler pragma, the expected type for the expression is Interrupts.Interrupt_ID (see C.3.2).

Legality Rules

7   The Attach_Handler pragma is only allowed immediately within the protected_definition where the corresponding subprogram is declared. The corresponding protected_type_declaration or single_-protected_declaration shall be a library level declaration.

8   The Interrupt_Handler pragma is only allowed immediately within a protected_definition. The corresponding protected_type_declaration shall be a library level declaration. In addition, any object_-declaration of such a type shall be a library level declaration.

Dynamic Semantics

f the pragma Interrupt_Handler appears in a protected_definition, then the corresponding procedure can be attached dynamically, as a handler, to interrupts (see C.3.2). Such procedures are allowed to be attached o multiple interrupts. 9

The expression in the Attach_Handler pragma as evaluated at object creation time specifies an interrupt. As part of the initialization of that object, if the Attach_Handler pragma is specified, the *handler* procedure s attached to the specified interrupt. A check is made that the corresponding interrupt is not reserved. Program_Error is raised if the check fails, and the existing treatment for the interrupt is not affected. 10

If the Ceiling_Locking policy (see D.3) is in effect then upon the initialization of a protected object that either an Attach_Handler or Interrupt_Handler pragma applies to one of its procedures, a check is made that the ceiling priority defined in the protected_definition is in the range of System.Interrupt_Priority. If the check fails, Program_Error is raised. 11

When a protected object is finalized, for any of its procedures that are attached to interrupts, the handler is detached. If the handler was attached by a procedure in the Interrupts package or if no user handler was previously attached to the interrupt, the default treatment is restored. If an Attach_Handler pragma was used and the most recently attached handler for the same interrupt is the same as the one that was attached at the time the protected object was initialized, the previous handler is restored. 12/1

When a handler is attached to an interrupt, the interrupt is blocked (subject to the Implementation Permission in C.3) during the execution of every protected action on the protected object containing the handler. 13

Erroneous Execution

If the Ceiling_Locking policy (see D.3) is in effect and an interrupt is delivered to a handler, and the interrupt hardware priority is higher than the ceiling priority of the corresponding protected object, the execution of the program is erroneous. 14

If the handlers for a given interrupt attached via pragma Attach_Handler are not attached and detached in a stack-like (LIFO) order, program execution is erroneous. In particular, when a protected object is finalized, the execution is erroneous if any of the procedures of the protected object are attached to interrupts via pragma Attach_Handler and the most recently attached handler for the same interrupt is not the same as the one that was attached at the time the protected object was initialized. 14.1/1

Metrics

The following metric shall be documented by the implementation: 15

1. The worst case overhead for an interrupt handler that is a parameterless protected procedure, in clock cycles. This is the execution time not directly attributable to the handler procedure or the interrupted execution. It is estimated as $C - (A+B)$, where A is how long it takes to complete a given sequence of instructions without any interrupt, B is how long it takes to complete a normal call to a given protected procedure, and C is how long it takes to complete the same sequence of instructions when it is interrupted by one execution of the same procedure called via an interrupt. 16

Implementation Permissions

When the pragmas Attach_Handler or Interrupt_Handler apply to a protected procedure, the implementation is allowed to impose implementation-defined restrictions on the corresponding protected_type_declaration and protected_body. 17

18   An implementation may use a different mechanism for invoking a protected procedure in response to a hardware interrupt than is used for a call to that protected procedure from a task.

19   Notwithstanding what this subclause says elsewhere, the Attach_Handler and Interrupt_Handler pragmas are allowed to be used for other, implementation defined, forms of interrupt handlers.

Implementation Advice

20   Whenever possible, the implementation should allow interrupt handlers to be called directly by the hardware.

21   Whenever practical, the implementation should detect violations of any implementation-defined restrictions before run time.

NOTES

22   4 The Attach_Handler pragma can provide static attachment of handlers to interrupts if the implementation supports preelaboration of protected objects. (See C.4.)

23   5 The ceiling priority of a protected object that one of its procedures is attached to an interrupt should be at least as high as the highest processor priority at which that interrupt will ever be delivered.

24   6 Protected procedures can also be attached dynamically to interrupts via operations declared in the predefined package Interrupts.

25   7 An example of a possible implementation-defined restriction is disallowing the use of the standard storage pools within the body of a protected procedure that is an interrupt handler.

C.3.2 The Package Interrupts

Static Semantics

1   The following language-defined packages exist:

2
```
with System;
package Ada.Interrupts is
    type Interrupt_ID is implementation-defined;
    type Parameterless_Handler is
        access protected procedure;
```

3/1   *This paragraph was deleted.*

4
```
    function Is_Reserved (Interrupt : Interrupt_ID)
        return Boolean;
```

5
```
    function Is_Attached (Interrupt : Interrupt_ID)
        return Boolean;
```

6
```
    function Current_Handler (Interrupt : Interrupt_ID)
        return Parameterless_Handler;
```

7
```
    procedure Attach_Handler
        (New_Handler : in Parameterless_Handler;
         Interrupt   : in Interrupt_ID);
```

8
```
    procedure Exchange_Handler
        (Old_Handler : out Parameterless_Handler;
         New_Handler : in Parameterless_Handler;
         Interrupt   : in Interrupt_ID);
```

9
```
    procedure Detach_Handler
        (Interrupt : in Interrupt_ID);
```

10
```
    function Reference(Interrupt : Interrupt_ID)
        return System.Address;
```

11
```
private
    ... -- not specified by the language
end Ada.Interrupts;
```

```
package Ada.Interrupts.Names is
    implementation-defined : constant Interrupt_ID :=
        implementation-defined;
        . . .
    implementation-defined : constant Interrupt_ID :=
        implementation-defined;
end Ada.Interrupts.Names;
```
12

Dynamic Semantics

The Interrupt_ID type is an implementation-defined discrete type used to identify interrupts.   13

The Is_Reserved function returns True if and only if the specified interrupt is reserved.   14

The Is_Attached function returns True if and only if a user-specified interrupt handler is attached to the   15
interrupt.

The Current_Handler function returns a value that represents the attached handler of the interrupt. If no   16/1
user-defined handler is attached to the interrupt, Current_Handler returns **null**.

The Attach_Handler procedure attaches the specified handler to the interrupt, overriding any existing   17
treatment (including a user handler) in effect for that interrupt. If New_Handler is **null**, the default
treatment is restored. If New_Handler designates a protected procedure to which the pragma Interrupt_-
Handler does not apply, Program_Error is raised. In this case, the operation does not modify the existing
interrupt treatment.

The Exchange_Handler procedure operates in the same manner as Attach_Handler with the addition that   18/1
the value returned in Old_Handler designates the previous treatment for the specified interrupt. If the
previous treatment is not a user-defined handler, **null** is returned.

The Detach_Handler procedure restores the default treatment for the specified interrupt.   19

For all operations defined in this package that take a parameter of type Interrupt_ID, with the exception of   20
Is_Reserved and Reference, a check is made that the specified interrupt is not reserved. Program_Error is
raised if this check fails.

If, by using the Attach_Handler, Detach_Handler, or Exchange_Handler procedures, an attempt is made to   21
detach a handler that was attached statically (using the pragma Attach_Handler), the handler is not
detached and Program_Error is raised.

The Reference function returns a value of type System.Address that can be used to attach a task entry, via   22
an address clause (see J.7.1) to the interrupt specified by Interrupt. This function raises Program_Error if
attaching task entries to interrupts (or to this particular interrupt) is not supported.

Implementation Requirements

At no time during attachment or exchange of handlers shall the current handler of the corresponding   23
interrupt be undefined.

Documentation Requirements

If the Ceiling_Locking policy (see D.3) is in effect the implementation shall document the default ceiling   24
priority assigned to a protected object that contains either the Attach_Handler or Interrupt_Handler
pragmas, but not the Interrupt_Priority pragma. This default need not be the same for all interrupts.

Implementation Advice

If implementation-defined forms of interrupt handler procedures are supported, such as protected   25
procedures with parameters, then for each such form of a handler, a type analogous to Parameterless_-

Handler should be specified in a child package of Interrupts, with the same operations as in the predefined package Interrupts.

NOTES

26   8 The package Interrupts.Names contains implementation-defined names (and constant values) for the interrupts that are supported by the implementation.

Examples

27   *Example of interrupt handlers:*

28
```
Device_Priority : constant
   array (1..5) of System.Interrupt_Priority := ( ... );
protected type Device_Interface
   (Int_ID : Ada.Interrupts.Interrupt_ID) is
   procedure Handler;
   pragma Attach_Handler(Handler, Int_ID);
   ...
   pragma Interrupt_Priority(Device_Priority(Int_ID));
end Device_Interface;
   ...
Device_1_Driver : Device_Interface(1);
   ...
Device_5_Driver : Device_Interface(5);
   ...
```

C.4 Preelaboration Requirements

1   This clause specifies additional implementation and documentation requirements for the Preelaborate pragma (see 10.2.1).

Implementation Requirements

2   The implementation shall not incur any run-time overhead for the elaboration checks of subprograms and protected_bodies declared in preelaborated library units.

3   The implementation shall not execute any memory write operations after load time for the elaboration of constant objects declared immediately within the declarative region of a preelaborated library package, so long as the subtype and initial expression (or default initial expressions if initialized by default) of the object_declaration satisfy the following restrictions. The meaning of *load time* is implementation defined.

4   • Any subtype_mark denotes a statically constrained subtype, with statically constrained subcomponents, if any;

5   • any constraint is a static constraint;

6   • any allocator is for an access-to-constant type;

7   • any uses of predefined operators appear only within static expressions;

8   • any primaries that are names, other than attribute_references for the Access or Address attributes, appear only within static expressions;

9   • any name that is not part of a static expression is an expanded name or direct_name that statically denotes some entity;

10   • any discrete_choice of an array_aggregate is static;

11   • no language-defined check associated with the elaboration of the object_declaration can fail.

Documentation Requirements

The implementation shall document any circumstances under which the elaboration of a preelaborated package causes code to be executed at run time. 12

The implementation shall document whether the method used for initialization of preelaborated variables allows a partition to be restarted without reloading. 13

Implementation Advice

It is recommended that preelaborated packages be implemented in such a way that there should be little or no code executed at run time for the elaboration of entities not already covered by the Implementation Requirements. 14

C.5 Pragma Discard_Names

A pragma Discard_Names may be used to request a reduction in storage used for the names of certain entities. 1

Syntax

The form of a pragma Discard_Names is as follows: 2

pragma Discard_Names[([On =>] local_name)]; 3

A pragma Discard_Names is allowed only immediately within a declarative_part, immediately within a package_specification, or as a configuration pragma. 4

Legality Rules

The local_name (if present) shall denote a non-derived enumeration first subtype, a tagged first subtype, or an exception. The pragma applies to the type or exception. Without a local_name, the pragma applies to all such entities declared after the pragma, within the same declarative region. Alternatively, the pragma can be used as a configuration pragma. If the pragma applies to a type, then it applies also to all descendants of the type. 5

Static Semantics

If a local_name is given, then a pragma Discard_Names is a representation pragma. 6

If the pragma applies to an enumeration type, then the semantics of the Wide_Image and Wide_Value attributes are implementation defined for that type; the semantics of Image and Value are still defined in terms of Wide_Image and Wide_Value. In addition, the semantics of Text_IO.Enumeration_IO are implementation defined. If the pragma applies to a tagged type, then the semantics of the Tags.Expanded_-Name function are implementation defined for that type. If the pragma applies to an exception, then the semantics of the Exceptions.Exception_Name function are implementation defined for that exception. 7

Implementation Advice

If the pragma applies to an entity, then the implementation should reduce the amount of storage used for storing names associated with that entity. 8

C.6 Shared Variable Control

1   This clause specifies representation pragmas that control the use of shared variables.

Syntax

2   The form for pragmas Atomic, Volatile, Atomic_Components, and Volatile_Components is as follows:

3   **pragma** Atomic(local_name);

4   **pragma** Volatile(local_name);

5   **pragma** Atomic_Components(*array*_local_name);

6   **pragma** Volatile_Components(*array*_local_name);

7   An *atomic* type is one to which a pragma Atomic applies. An *atomic* object (including a component) is one to which a pragma Atomic applies, or a component of an array to which a pragma Atomic_Components applies, or any object of an atomic type.

8   A *volatile* type is one to which a pragma Volatile applies. A *volatile* object (including a component) is one to which a pragma Volatile applies, or a component of an array to which a pragma Volatile_Components applies, or any object of a volatile type. In addition, every atomic type or object is also defined to be volatile. Finally, if an object is volatile, then so are all of its subcomponents (the same does not apply to atomic).

Name Resolution Rules

9   The local_name in an Atomic or Volatile pragma shall resolve to denote either an object_declaration, a non-inherited component_declaration, or a full_type_declaration. The *array*_local_name in an Atomic_- Components or Volatile_Components pragma shall resolve to denote the declaration of an array type or an array object of an anonymous type.

Legality Rules

10   It is illegal to apply either an Atomic or Atomic_Components pragma to an object or type if the implementation cannot support the indivisible reads and updates required by the pragma (see below).

11   It is illegal to specify the Size attribute of an atomic object, the Component_Size attribute for an array type with atomic components, or the layout attributes of an atomic component, in a way that prevents the implementation from performing the required indivisible reads and updates.

12   If an atomic object is passed as a parameter, then the type of the formal parameter shall either be atomic or allow pass by copy (that is, not be a nonatomic by-reference type). If an atomic object is used as an actual for a generic formal object of mode **in out**, then the type of the generic formal object shall be atomic. If the prefix of an attribute_reference for an Access attribute denotes an atomic object (including a component), then the designated type of the resulting access type shall be atomic. If an atomic type is used as an actual for a generic formal derived type, then the ancestor of the formal type shall be atomic or allow pass by copy. Corresponding rules apply to volatile objects and types.

13   If a pragma Volatile, Volatile_Components, Atomic, or Atomic_Components applies to a stand-alone constant object, then a pragma Import shall also apply to it.

Static Semantics

14   These pragmas are representation pragmas (see 13.1).

Dynamic Semantics

For an atomic object (including an atomic component) all reads and updates of the object as a whole are indivisible. 15

For a volatile object all reads and updates of the object as a whole are performed directly to memory. 16

Two actions are sequential (see 9.10) if each is the read or update of the same atomic object. 17

If a type is atomic or volatile and it is not a by-copy type, then the type is defined to be a by-reference type. If any subcomponent of a type is atomic or volatile, then the type is defined to be a by-reference type. 18

If an actual parameter is atomic or volatile, and the corresponding formal parameter is not, then the parameter is passed by copy. 19

Implementation Requirements

The external effect of a program (see 1.1.3) is defined to include each read and update of a volatile or atomic object. The implementation shall not generate any memory reads or updates of atomic or volatile objects other than those specified by the program. 20

If a pragma Pack applies to a type any of whose subcomponents are atomic, the implementation shall not pack the atomic subcomponents more tightly than that for which it can support indivisible reads and updates. 21

NOTES
9 An imported volatile or atomic constant behaves as a constant (i.e. read-only) with respect to other parts of the Ada program, but can still be modified by an "external source." 22

C.7 Task Identification and Attributes

This clause describes operations and attributes that can be used to obtain the identity of a task. In addition, a package that associates user-defined information with a task is defined. 1

C.7.1 The Package Task_Identification

Static Semantics

The following language-defined library package exists: 1

```
package Ada.Task_Identification is                              2
    type Task_ID is private;
    Null_Task_ID : constant Task_ID;
    function   "=" (Left, Right : Task_ID) return Boolean;

    function   Image        (T : Task_ID) return String;       3/1
    function   Current_Task return Task_ID;
    procedure  Abort_Task   (T : in Task_ID);

    function   Is_Terminated(T : Task_ID) return Boolean;      4
    function   Is_Callable  (T : Task_ID) return Boolean;
private
    ... -- not specified by the language
end Ada.Task_Identification;
```

Dynamic Semantics

A value of the type Task_ID identifies an existent task. The constant Null_Task_ID does not identify any task. Each object of the type Task_ID is default initialized to the value of Null_Task_ID. 5

6   The function "=" returns True if and only if Left and Right identify the same task or both have the value Null_Task_ID.

7   The function Image returns an implementation-defined string that identifies T. If T equals Null_Task_ID, Image returns an empty string.

8   The function Current_Task returns a value that identifies the calling task.

9   The effect of Abort_Task is the same as the abort_statement for the task identified by T. In addition, if T identifies the environment task, the entire partition is aborted, See E.1.

10   The functions Is_Terminated and Is_Callable return the value of the corresponding attribute of the task identified by T.

11   For a prefix T that is of a task type (after any implicit dereference), the following attribute is defined:

12   T'Identity   Yields a value of the type Task_ID that identifies the task denoted by T.

13   For a prefix E that denotes an entry_declaration, the following attribute is defined:

14   E'Caller   Yields a value of the type Task_ID that identifies the task whose call is now being serviced. Use of this attribute is allowed only inside an entry_body or accept_statement corresponding to the entry_declaration denoted by E.

15   Program_Error is raised if a value of Null_Task_ID is passed as a parameter to Abort_Task, Is_Terminated, and Is_Callable.

16   Abort_Task is a potentially blocking operation (see 9.5.1).

Bounded (Run-Time) Errors

17   It is a bounded error to call the Current_Task function from an entry body or an interrupt handler. Program_Error is raised, or an implementation-defined value of the type Task_ID is returned.

Erroneous Execution

18   If a value of Task_ID is passed as a parameter to any of the operations declared in this package (or any language-defined child of this package), and the corresponding task object no longer exists, the execution of the program is erroneous.

Documentation Requirements

19   The implementation shall document the effect of calling Current_Task from an entry body or interrupt handler.

NOTES

20   10 This package is intended for use in writing user-defined task scheduling packages and constructing server tasks. Current_Task can be used in conjunction with other operations requiring a task as an argument such as Set_Priority (see D.5).

21   11 The function Current_Task and the attribute Caller can return a Task_ID value that identifies the environment task.

C.7.2 The Package Task_Attributes

Static Semantics

The following language-defined generic library package exists: 1

```
with Ada.Task_Identification; use Ada.Task_Identification;
generic
   type Attribute is private;
   Initial_Value : in Attribute;
package Ada.Task_Attributes is

   type Attribute_Handle is access all Attribute;

   function Value(T : Task_ID := Current_Task)
     return Attribute;

   function Reference(T : Task_ID := Current_Task)
     return Attribute_Handle;

   procedure Set_Value(Val : in Attribute;
                       T : in Task_ID := Current_Task);
   procedure Reinitialize(T : in Task_ID := Current_Task);

end Ada.Task_Attributes;
```

2

3

4

5

6

7

Dynamic Semantics

When an instance of Task_Attributes is elaborated in a given active partition, an object of the actual type   8
corresponding to the formal type Attribute is implicitly created for each task (of that partition) that exists
and is not yet terminated. This object acts as a user-defined attribute of the task. A task created previously
in the partition and not yet terminated has this attribute from that point on. Each task subsequently created
in the partition will have this attribute when created. In all these cases, the initial value of the given
attribute is Initial_Value.

The Value operation returns the value of the corresponding attribute of T.   9

The Reference operation returns an access value that designates the corresponding attribute of T.   10

The Set_Value operation performs any finalization on the old value of the attribute of T and assigns Val to   11
that attribute (see 5.2 and 7.6).

The effect of the Reinitialize operation is the same as Set_Value where the Val parameter is replaced with   12
Initial_Value.

For all the operations declared in this package, Tasking_Error is raised if the task identified by T is   13
terminated. Program_Error is raised if the value of T is Null_Task_ID.

Bounded (Run-Time) Errors

If the package Ada.Task_Attributes is instantiated with a controlled type and the controlled type has user-   13.1/1
defined Adjust or Finalize operations that in turn access task attributes by any of the above operations,
then a call of Set_Value of the instantiated package constitutes a bounded error. The call may perform as
expected or may result in forever blocking the calling task and subsequently some or all tasks of the
partition.

Erroneous Execution

It is erroneous to dereference the access value returned by a given call on Reference after a subsequent call   14
on Reinitialize for the same task attribute, or after the associated task terminates.

15   If a value of Task_ID is passed as a parameter to any of the operations declared in this package and the corresponding task object no longer exists, the execution of the program is erroneous.

15.1/1   Accesses to task attributes via a value of type Attribute_Handle are erroneous if executed concurrently with each other or with calls of any of the operations declared in package Task_Attributes.

Implementation Requirements

16/1   For a given attribute of a given task, the implementation shall perform the operations declared in this package atomically with respect to any of these operations of the same attribute of the same task. The granularity of any locking mechanism necessary to achieve such atomicity is implementation defined.

17   When a task terminates, the implementation shall finalize all attributes of the task, and reclaim any other storage associated with the attributes.

Documentation Requirements

18   The implementation shall document the limit on the number of attributes per task, if any, and the limit on the total storage for attribute values per task, if such a limit exists.

19   In addition, if these limits can be configured, the implementation shall document how to configure them.

Metrics

20   The implementation shall document the following metrics: A task calling the following subprograms shall execute in a sufficiently high priority as to not be preempted during the measurement period. This period shall start just before issuing the call and end just after the call completes. If the attributes of task T are accessed by the measurement tests, no other task shall access attributes of that task during the measurement period. For all measurements described here, the Attribute type shall be a scalar whose size is equal to the size of the predefined integer size. For each measurement, two cases shall be documented: one where the accessed attributes are of the calling task (that is, the default value for the T parameter is used), and the other, where T identifies another, non-terminated, task.

21   The following calls (to subprograms in the Task_Attributes package) shall be measured:

22   • a call to Value, where the return value is Initial_Value;

23   • a call to Value, where the return value is not equal to Initial_Value;

24   • a call to Reference, where the return value designates a value equal to Initial_Value;

25   • a call to Reference, where the return value designates a value not equal to Initial_Value;

26   • a call to Set_Value where the Val parameter is not equal to Initial_Value and the old attribute value is equal to Initial_Value.

27   • a call to Set_Value where the Val parameter is not equal to Initial_Value and the old attribute value is not equal to Initial_Value.

Implementation Permissions

28   An implementation need not actually create the object corresponding to a task attribute until its value is set to something other than that of Initial_Value, or until Reference is called for the task attribute. Similarly, when the value of the attribute is to be reinitialized to that of Initial_Value, the object may instead be finalized and its storage reclaimed, to be recreated when needed later. While the object does not exist, the function Value may simply return Initial_Value, rather than implicitly creating the object.

29   An implementation is allowed to place restrictions on the maximum number of attributes a task may have, the maximum size of each attribute, and the total storage size allocated for all the attributes of a task.

Implementation Advice

Some implementations are targeted to domains in which memory use at run time must be completely deterministic. For such implementations, it is recommended that the storage for task attributes will be pre-allocated statically and not from the heap. This can be accomplished by either placing restrictions on the number and the size of the task's attributes, or by using the pre-allocated storage for the first N attribute objects, and the heap for the others. In the latter case, N should be documented.   30

NOTES

12 An attribute always exists (after instantiation), and has the initial value. It need not occupy memory until the first   31
operation that potentially changes the attribute value. The same holds true after Reinitialize.

13 The result of the Reference function should be used with care; it is always safe to use that result in the task body   32
whose attribute is being accessed. However, when the result is being used by another task, the programmer must make
sure that the task whose attribute is being accessed is not yet terminated. Failing to do so could make the program
execution erroneous.

14 As specified in C.7.1, if the parameter T (in a call on a subprogram of an instance of this package) identifies a   33
nonexistent task, the execution of the program is erroneous.

Annex D
(normative)
Real-Time Systems

This Annex specifies additional characteristics of Ada implementations intended for real-time systems software. To conform to this Annex, an implementation shall also conform to the Systems Programming Annex.   1

Metrics

The metrics are documentation requirements; an implementation shall document the values of the language-defined metrics for at least one configuration of hardware or an underlying system supported by the implementation, and shall document the details of that configuration.   2

The metrics do not necessarily yield a simple number. For some, a range is more suitable, for others a formula dependent on some parameter is appropriate, and for others, it may be more suitable to break the metric into several cases. Unless specified otherwise, the metrics in this annex are expressed in processor clock cycles. For metrics that require documentation of an upper bound, if there is no upper bound, the implementation shall report that the metric is unbounded.   3

NOTES

1 The specification of the metrics makes a distinction between upper bounds and simple execution times. Where   4
something is just specified as "the execution time of" a piece of code, this leaves one the freedom to choose a
nonpathological case. This kind of metric is of the form "there exists a program such that the value of the metric is V".
Conversely, the meaning of upper bounds is "there is no program such that the value of the metric is greater than V".
This kind of metric can only be partially tested, by finding the value of V for one or more test programs.

2 The metrics do not cover the whole language; they are limited to features that are specified in Annex C, "Systems   5
Programming" and in this Annex. The metrics are intended to provide guidance to potential users as to whether a
particular implementation of such a feature is going to be adequate for a particular real-time application. As such, the
metrics are aimed at known implementation choices that can result in significant performance differences.

3 The purpose of the metrics is not necessarily to provide fine-grained quantitative results or to serve as a comparison   6
between different implementations on the same or different platforms. Instead, their goal is rather qualitative; to define a
standard set of approximate values that can be measured and used to estimate the general suitability of an
implementation, or to evaluate the comparative utility of certain features of an implementation for a particular real-time
application.

D.1 Task Priorities

This clause specifies the priority model for real-time systems. In addition, the methods for specifying   1
priorities are defined.

Syntax

The form of a pragma Priority is as follows: 2

  pragma Priority(expression);   3

The form of a pragma Interrupt_Priority is as follows: 4

  pragma Interrupt_Priority[(expression)];   5

Name Resolution Rules

The expected type for the expression in a Priority or Interrupt_Priority pragma is Integer.   6

S. Tucker Taft et al. (Eds.): Consolidated Ada Reference Manual, LNCS 2219, pp. 387–405, 2001.

Legality Rules

7   A Priority pragma is allowed only immediately within a task_definition, a protected_definition, or the declarative_part of a subprogram_body. An Interrupt_Priority pragma is allowed only immediately within a task_definition or a protected_definition. At most one such pragma shall appear within a given construct.

8   For a Priority pragma that appears in the declarative_part of a subprogram_body, the expression shall be static, and its value shall be in the range of System.Priority.

Static Semantics

9   The following declarations exist in package System:

10
```
      subtype Any_Priority is Integer range implementation-defined;
      subtype Priority is Any_Priority
          range Any_Priority'First .. implementation-defined;
      subtype Interrupt_Priority is Any_Priority
          range Priority'Last+1 .. Any_Priority'Last;
```

11
```
      Default_Priority : constant Priority := (Priority'First + Priority'Last)/2;
```

12   The full range of priority values supported by an implementation is specified by the subtype Any_Priority. The subrange of priority values that are high enough to require the blocking of one or more interrupts is specified by the subtype Interrupt_Priority. The subrange of priority values below System.Interrupt_Priority'First is specified by the subtype System.Priority.

13   The priority specified by a Priority or Interrupt_Priority pragma is the value of the expression in the pragma, if any. If there is no expression in an Interrupt_Priority pragma, the priority value is Interrupt_Priority'Last.

Dynamic Semantics

14   A Priority pragma has no effect if it occurs in the declarative_part of the subprogram_body of a subprogram other than the main subprogram.

15   A *task priority* is an integer value that indicates a degree of urgency and is the basis for resolving competing demands of tasks for resources. Unless otherwise specified, whenever tasks compete for processors or other implementation-defined resources, the resources are allocated to the task with the highest priority value. The *base priority* of a task is the priority with which it was created, or to which it was later set by Dynamic_Priorities.Set_Priority (see D.5). At all times, a task also has an *active priority*, which generally reflects its base priority as well as any priority it inherits from other sources. *Priority inheritance* is the process by which the priority of a task or other entity (e.g. a protected object; see D.3) is used in the evaluation of another task's active priority.

16   The effect of specifying such a pragma in a protected_definition is discussed in D.3.

17   The expression in a Priority or Interrupt_Priority pragma that appears in a task_definition is evaluated for each task object (see 9.1). For a Priority pragma, the value of the expression is converted to the subtype Priority; for an Interrupt_Priority pragma, this value is converted to the subtype Any_Priority. The priority value is then associated with the task object whose task_definition contains the pragma.

18   Likewise, the priority value is associated with the environment task if the pragma appears in the declarative_part of the main subprogram.

19   The initial value of a task's base priority is specified by default or by means of a Priority or Interrupt_Priority pragma. After a task is created, its base priority can be changed only by a call to Dynamic_Priorities.Set_Priority (see D.5). The initial base priority of a task in the absence of a pragma is the base priority of the task that creates it at the time of creation (see 9.1). If a pragma Priority does not

pply to the main subprogram, the initial base priority of the environment task is System.Default_Priority.
The task's active priority is used when the task competes for processors. Similarly, the task's active priority
s used to determine the task's position in any queue when Priority_Queuing is specified (see D.4).

At any time, the active priority of a task is the maximum of all the priorities the task is inheriting at that   20
instant. For a task that is not held (see D.11), its base priority is always a source of priority inheritance.
Other sources of priority inheritance are specified under the following conditions:

- During activation, a task being activated inherits the active priority that its activator (see 9.2) had   21/1
  at the time the activation was initiated.

- During rendezvous, the task accepting the entry call inherits the priority of the entry call (see   22/1
  9.5.3 and D.4).

- During a protected action on a protected object, a task inherits the ceiling priority of the   23
  protected object (see 9.5 and D.3).

In all of these cases, the priority ceases to be inherited as soon as the condition calling for the inheritance   24
no longer exists.

Implementation Requirements

The range of System.Interrupt_Priority shall include at least one value.   25

The range of System.Priority shall include at least 30 values.   26

NOTES
4 The priority expression can include references to discriminants of the enclosing type.   27

5 It is a consequence of the active priority rules that at the point when a task stops inheriting a priority from another   28
source, its active priority is re-evaluated. This is in addition to other instances described in this Annex for such re-
evaluation.

6 An implementation may provide a non-standard mode in which tasks inherit priorities under conditions other than   29
those specified above.

D.2 Priority Scheduling

This clause describes the rules that determine which task is selected for execution when more than one task   1
is ready (see 9.2). The rules have two parts: the task dispatching model (see D.2.1), and a specific task
dispatching policy (see D.2.2).

D.2.1 The Task Dispatching Model

The task dispatching model specifies preemptive scheduling, based on conceptual priority-ordered ready   1
queues.

Dynamic Semantics

A task runs (that is, it becomes a *running task*) only when it is ready (see 9.2) and the execution resources   2
required by that task are available. Processors are allocated to tasks based on each task's active priority.

It is implementation defined whether, on a multiprocessor, a task that is waiting for access to a protected   3
object keeps its processor busy.

Task dispatching is the process by which one ready task is selected for execution on a processor. This   4
selection is done at certain points during the execution of a task called *task dispatching points*. A task
reaches a task dispatching point whenever it becomes blocked, and whenever it becomes ready. In

addition, the completion of an accept_statement (see 9.5.2), and task termination are task dispatching points for the executing task. Other task dispatching points are defined throughout this Annex.

5   *Task dispatching policies* are specified in terms of conceptual *ready queues*, task states, and task preemption. A ready queue is an ordered list of ready tasks. The first position in a queue is called the *head of the queue*, and the last position is called the *tail of the queue*. A task is *ready* if it is in a ready queue, or if it is running. Each processor has one ready queue for each priority value. At any instant, each ready queue of a processor contains exactly the set of tasks of that priority that are ready for execution on that processor, but are not running on any processor; that is, those tasks that are ready, are not running on any processor, and can be executed using that processor and other available resources. A task can be on the ready queues of more than one processor.

6   Each processor also has one *running task*, which is the task currently being executed by that processor. Whenever a task running on a processor reaches a task dispatching point, one task is selected to run on that processor. The task selected is the one at the head of the highest priority nonempty ready queue; this task is then removed from all ready queues to which it belongs.

7   A preemptible resource is a resource that while allocated to one task can be allocated (temporarily) to another instead. Processors are preemptible resources. Access to a protected object (see 9.5.1) is a nonpreemptible resource. When a higher-priority task is dispatched to the processor, and the previously running task is placed on the appropriate ready queue, the latter task is said to be *preempted*.

8   A new running task is also selected whenever there is a nonempty ready queue with a higher priority than the priority of the running task, or when the task dispatching policy requires a running task to go back to a ready queue. These are also task dispatching points.

Implementation Permissions

9   An implementation is allowed to define additional resources as execution resources, and to define the corresponding allocation policies for them. Such resources may have an implementation defined effect on task dispatching (see D.2.2).

10   An implementation may place implementation-defined restrictions on tasks whose active priority is in the Interrupt_Priority range.

NOTES

11   7 Section 9 specifies under which circumstances a task becomes ready. The ready state is affected by the rules for task activation and termination, delay statements, and entry calls. When a task is not ready, it is said to be blocked.

12   8 An example of a possible implementation-defined execution resource is a page of physical memory, which needs to be loaded with a particular page of virtual memory before a task can continue execution.

13   9 The ready queues are purely conceptual; there is no requirement that such lists physically exist in an implementation.

14   10 While a task is running, it is not on any ready queue. Any time the task that is running on a processor is added to a ready queue, a new running task is selected for that processor.

15   11 In a multiprocessor system, a task can be on the ready queues of more than one processor. At the extreme, if several processors share the same set of ready tasks, the contents of their ready queues is identical, and so they can be viewed as sharing one ready queue, and can be implemented that way. Thus, the dispatching model covers multiprocessors where dispatching is implemented using a single ready queue, as well as those with separate dispatching domains.

16   12 The priority of a task is determined by rules specified in this subclause, and under D.1, "Task Priorities", D.3, "Priority Ceiling Locking", and D.5, "Dynamic Priorities".

D.2.2 The Standard Task Dispatching Policy

Syntax

The form of a pragma Task_Dispatching_Policy is as follows: 1

pragma Task_Dispatching_Policy(*policy*_identifier); 2

Legality Rules

The *policy*_identifier shall either be FIFO_Within_Priorities or an implementation-defined identifier. 3

Post-Compilation Rules

A Task_Dispatching_Policy pragma is a configuration pragma. 4

If the FIFO_Within_Priorities policy is specified for a partition, then the Ceiling_Locking policy (see D.3) 5
shall also be specified for the partition.

Dynamic Semantics

A *task dispatching policy* specifies the details of task dispatching that are not covered by the basic task 6
dispatching model. These rules govern when tasks are inserted into and deleted from the ready queues, and
whether a task is inserted at the head or the tail of the queue for its active priority. The task dispatching
policy is specified by a Task_Dispatching_Policy configuration pragma. If no such pragma appears in any
of the program units comprising a partition, the task dispatching policy for that partition is unspecified.

The language defines only one task dispatching policy, FIFO_Within_Priorities; when this policy is in 7
effect, modifications to the ready queues occur only as follows:

- When a blocked task becomes ready, it is added at the tail of the ready queue for its active 8
  priority.

- When the active priority of a ready task that is not running changes, or the setting of its base 9
  priority takes effect, the task is removed from the ready queue for its old active priority and is
  added at the tail of the ready queue for its new active priority, except in the case where the active
  priority is lowered due to the loss of inherited priority, in which case the task is added at the
  head of the ready queue for its new active priority.

- When the setting of the base priority of a running task takes effect, the task is added to the tail of 10
  the ready queue for its active priority.

- When a task executes a delay_statement that does not result in blocking, it is added to the tail of 11
  the ready queue for its active priority.

Each of the events specified above is a task dispatching point (see D.2.1). 12

In addition, when a task is preempted, it is added at the head of the ready queue for its active priority. 13

Documentation Requirements

Priority inversion is the duration for which a task remains at the head of the highest priority ready queue 14
while the processor executes a lower priority task. The implementation shall document:

- The maximum priority inversion a user task can experience due to activity of the implementation 15
  (on behalf of lower priority tasks), and

- whether execution of a task can be preempted by the implementation processing of delay 16
  expirations for lower priority tasks, and if so, for how long.

The Standard Task Dispatching Policy **D.2.2**

Implementation Permissions

17 Implementations are allowed to define other task dispatching policies, but need not support more than one such policy per partition.

18 For optimization purposes, an implementation may alter the points at which task dispatching occurs, in an implementation defined manner. However, a delay_statement always corresponds to at least one task dispatching point.

NOTES

19 13 If the active priority of a running task is lowered due to loss of inherited priority (as it is on completion of a protected operation) and there is a ready task of the same active priority that is not running, the running task continues to run (provided that there is no higher priority task).

20 14 The setting of a task's base priority as a result of a call to Set_Priority does not always take effect immediately when Set_Priority is called. The effect of setting the task's base priority is deferred while the affected task performs a protected action.

21 15 Setting the base priority of a ready task causes the task to move to the end of the queue for its active priority, regardless of whether the active priority of the task actually changes.

D.3 Priority Ceiling Locking

1 This clause specifies the interactions between priority task scheduling and protected object ceilings. This interaction is based on the concept of the *ceiling priority* of a protected object.

Syntax

2 The form of a pragma Locking_Policy is as follows:

3   **pragma** Locking_Policy(*policy*_identifier);

Legality Rules

4 The *policy*_identifier shall either be Ceiling_Locking or an implementation-defined identifier.

Post-Compilation Rules

5 A Locking_Policy pragma is a configuration pragma.

Dynamic Semantics

6/1 A locking policy specifies the details of protected object locking. These rules specify whether or not protected objects have priorities, and the relationships between these priorities and task priorities. In addition, the policy specifies the state of a task when it executes a protected action, and how its active priority is affected by the locking. The *locking policy* is specified by a Locking_Policy pragma. For implementation-defined locking policies, the effect of a Priority or Interrupt_Priority pragma on a protected object is implementation defined. If no Locking_Policy pragma applies to any of the program units comprising a partition, the locking policy for that partition, as well as the effect of specifying either a Priority or Interrupt_Priority pragma for a protected object, are implementation defined.

7 There is one predefined locking policy, Ceiling_Locking; this policy is defined as follows:

8 • Every protected object has a *ceiling priority*, which is determined by either a Priority or Interrupt_Priority pragma as defined in D.1. The ceiling priority of a protected object (or ceiling, for short) is an upper bound on the active priority a task can have when it calls protected operations of that protected object.

9 • The expression of a Priority or Interrupt_Priority pragma is evaluated as part of the creation of the corresponding protected object and converted to the subtype System.Any_Priority or

System.Interrupt_Priority, respectively. The value of the expression is the ceiling priority of the corresponding protected object.

- If an Interrupt_Handler or Attach_Handler pragma (see C.3.1) appears in a protected_definition 10
  without an Interrupt_Priority pragma, the ceiling priority of protected objects of that type is
  implementation defined, but in the range of the subtype System.Interrupt_Priority.

- If no pragma Priority, Interrupt_Priority, Interrupt_Handler, or Attach_Handler is specified in 11
  the protected_definition, then the ceiling priority of the corresponding protected object is
  System.Priority'Last.

- While a task executes a protected action, it inherits the ceiling priority of the corresponding 12
  protected object.

- When a task calls a protected operation, a check is made that its active priority is not higher than 13
  the ceiling of the corresponding protected object; Program_Error is raised if this check fails.

Implementation Permissions

The implementation is allowed to round all ceilings in a certain subrange of System.Priority or 14
System.Interrupt_Priority up to the top of that subrange, uniformly.

Implementations are allowed to define other locking policies, but need not support more than one such 15
policy per partition.

Since implementations are allowed to place restrictions on code that runs at an interrupt-level active 16
priority (see C.3.1 and D.2.1), the implementation may implement a language feature in terms of a
protected object with an implementation-defined ceiling, but the ceiling shall be no less than Priority'Last.

Implementation Advice

The implementation should use names that end with ''_Locking'' for implementation-defined locking 17
policies.

NOTES
16 While a task executes in a protected action, it can be preempted only by tasks whose active priorities are higher than 18
the ceiling priority of the protected object.

17 If a protected object has a ceiling priority in the range of Interrupt_Priority, certain interrupts are blocked while 19
protected actions of that object execute. In the extreme, if the ceiling is Interrupt_Priority'Last, all blockable interrupts
are blocked during that time.

18 The ceiling priority of a protected object has to be in the Interrupt_Priority range if one of its procedures is to be used 20
as an interrupt handler (see C.3).

19 When specifying the ceiling of a protected object, one should choose a value that is at least as high as the highest 21
active priority at which tasks can be executing when they call protected operations of that object. In determining this
value the following factors, which can affect active priority, should be considered: the effect of Set_Priority, nested
protected operations, entry calls, task activation, and other implementation-defined factors.

20 Attaching a protected procedure whose ceiling is below the interrupt hardware priority to an interrupt causes the 22
execution of the program to be erroneous (see C.3.1).

21 On a single processor implementation, the ceiling priority rules guarantee that there is no possibility of deadlock 23
involving only protected subprograms (excluding the case where a protected operation calls another protected operation
on the same protected object).

D.4 Entry Queuing Policies

1/1 This clause specifies a mechanism for a user to choose an entry *queuing policy*. It also defines two such policies. Other policies are implementation defined.

Syntax

2 The form of a pragma Queuing_Policy is as follows:

3 **pragma** Queuing_Policy(*policy*_identifier);

Legality Rules

4 The *policy*_identifier shall be either FIFO_Queuing, Priority_Queuing or an implementation-defined identifier.

Post-Compilation Rules

5 A Queuing_Policy pragma is a configuration pragma.

Dynamic Semantics

6 A *queuing policy* governs the order in which tasks are queued for entry service, and the order in which different entry queues are considered for service. The queuing policy is specified by a Queuing_Policy pragma.

7 Two queuing policies, FIFO_Queuing and Priority_Queuing, are language defined. If no Queuing_Policy pragma appears in any of the program units comprising the partition, the queuing policy for that partition is FIFO_Queuing. The rules for this policy are specified in 9.5.3 and 9.7.1.

8 The Priority_Queuing policy is defined as follows:

9 • The calls to an entry (including a member of an entry family) are queued in an order consistent with the priorities of the calls. The *priority of an entry call* is initialized from the active priority of the calling task at the time the call is made, but can change later. Within the same priority, the order is consistent with the calling (or requeuing, or priority setting) time (that is, a FIFO order).

10/1 • After a call is first queued, changes to the active priority of a task do not affect the priority of the call, unless the base priority of the task is set while the task is blocked on an entry call.

11 • When the base priority of a task is set (see D.5), if the task is blocked on an entry call, and the call is queued, the priority of the call is updated to the new active priority of the calling task. This causes the call to be removed from and then reinserted in the queue at the new active priority.

12 • When more than one condition of an entry_barrier of a protected object becomes True, and more than one of the respective queues is nonempty, the call with the highest priority is selected. If more than one such call has the same priority, the call that is queued on the entry whose declaration is first in textual order in the protected_definition is selected. For members of the same entry family, the one with the lower family index is selected.

13 • If the expiration time of two or more open delay_alternatives is the same and no other accept_alternatives are open, the sequence_of_statements of the delay_alternative that is first in textual order in the selective_accept is executed.

14 • When more than one alternative of a selective_accept is open and has queued calls, an alternative whose queue has the highest-priority call at its head is selected. If two or more open alternatives have equal-priority queued calls, then a call on the entry in the accept_alternative that is first in textual order in the selective_accept is selected.

Implementation Permissions

Implementations are allowed to define other queuing policies, but need not support more than one such policy per partition.

15

Implementation Advice

The implementation should use names that end with "_Queuing" for implementation-defined queuing policies.

16

D.5 Dynamic Priorities

This clause specifies how the base priority of a task can be modified or queried at run time.

1

Static Semantics

The following language-defined library package exists:

2

```ada
with System;
with Ada.Task_Identification; -- See C.7.1
package Ada.Dynamic_Priorities is
    procedure Set_Priority(Priority : in System.Any_Priority;
                           T : in Ada.Task_Identification.Task_ID :=
                           Ada.Task_Identification.Current_Task);
    function Get_Priority (T : Ada.Task_Identification.Task_ID :=
                           Ada.Task_Identification.Current_Task)
                           return System.Any_Priority;
end Ada.Dynamic_Priorities;
```

3

4

5

6

Dynamic Semantics

The procedure Set_Priority sets the base priority of the specified task to the specified Priority value. Set_Priority has no effect if the task is terminated.

7

The function Get_Priority returns T's current base priority. Tasking_Error is raised if the task is terminated.

8

Program_Error is raised by Set_Priority and Get_Priority if T is equal to Null_Task_ID.

9

Setting the task's base priority to the new value takes place as soon as is practical but not while the task is performing a protected action. This setting occurs no later then the next abort completion point of the task T (see 9.8).

10

Bounded (Run-Time) Errors

If a task is blocked on a protected entry call, and the call is queued, it is a bounded error to raise its base priority above the ceiling priority of the corresponding protected object. When an entry call is cancelled, it is a bounded error if the priority of the calling task is higher than the ceiling priority of the corresponding protected object. In either of these cases, either Program_Error is raised in the task that called the entry, or its priority is temporarily lowered, or both, or neither.

11

Erroneous Execution

If any subprogram in this package is called with a parameter T that specifies a task object that no longer exists, the execution of the program is erroneous.

12

Metrics

The implementation shall document the following metric:

13

14   • The execution time of a call to Set_Priority, for the nonpreempting case, in processor clock cycles. This is measured for a call that modifies the priority of a ready task that is not running (which cannot be the calling one), where the new base priority of the affected task is lower than the active priority of the calling task, and the affected task is not on any entry queue and is not executing a protected operation.

NOTES

15   22 Setting a task's base priority affects task dispatching. First, it can change the task's active priority. Second, under the standard task dispatching policy it always causes the task to move to the tail of the ready queue corresponding to its active priority, even if the new base priority is unchanged.

16   23 Under the priority queuing policy, setting a task's base priority has an effect on a queued entry call if the task is blocked waiting for the call. That is, setting the base priority of a task causes the priority of a queued entry call from that task to be updated and the call to be removed and then reinserted in the entry queue at the new priority (see D.4), unless the call originated from the triggering_statement of an asynchronous_select.

17   24 The effect of two or more Set_Priority calls executed in parallel on the same task is defined as executing these calls in some serial order.

18   25 The rule for when Tasking_Error is raised for Set_Priority or Get_Priority is different from the rule for when Tasking_Error is raised on an entry call (see 9.5.3). In particular, setting or querying the priority of a completed or an abnormal task is allowed, so long as the task is not yet terminated.

19   26 Changing the priorities of a set of tasks can be performed by a series of calls to Set_Priority for each task separately. For this to work reliably, it should be done within a protected operation that has high enough ceiling priority to guarantee that the operation completes without being preempted by any of the affected tasks.

D.6 Preemptive Abort

1   This clause specifies requirements on the immediacy with which an aborted construct is completed.

Dynamic Semantics

2   On a system with a single processor, an aborted construct is completed immediately at the first point that is outside the execution of an abort-deferred operation.

Documentation Requirements

3   On a multiprocessor, the implementation shall document any conditions that cause the completion of an aborted construct to be delayed later than what is specified for a single processor.

Metrics

4   The implementation shall document the following metrics:

5   • The execution time, in processor clock cycles, that it takes for an abort_statement to cause the completion of the aborted task. This is measured in a situation where a task T2 preempts task T1 and aborts T1. T1 does not have any finalization code. T2 shall verify that T1 has terminated, by means of the Terminated attribute.

6   • On a multiprocessor, an upper bound in seconds, on the time that the completion of an aborted task can be delayed beyond the point that it is required for a single processor.

7   • An upper bound on the execution time of an asynchronous_select, in processor clock cycles. This is measured between a point immediately before a task T1 executes a protected operation Pr.Set that makes the condition of an entry_barrier Pr.Wait true, and the point where task T2 resumes execution immediately after an entry call to Pr.Wait in an asynchronous_select. T1 preempts T2 while T2 is executing the abortable part, and then blocks itself so that T2 can execute. The execution time of T1 is measured separately, and subtracted.

- An upper bound on the execution time of an asynchronous_select, in the case that no asynchronous transfer of control takes place. This is measured between a point immediately before a task executes the asynchronous_select with a nonnull abortable part, and the point where the task continues execution immediately after it. The execution time of the abortable part is subtracted.   8

Implementation Advice

Even though the abort_statement is included in the list of potentially blocking operations (see 9.5.1), it is recommended that this statement be implemented in a way that never requires the task executing the abort_statement to block.   9

On a multi-processor, the delay associated with aborting a task on another processor should be bounded; the implementation should use periodic polling, if necessary, to achieve this.   10

NOTES

27 Abortion does not change the active or base priority of the aborted task.   11

28 Abortion cannot be more immediate than is allowed by the rules for deferral of abortion during finalization and in protected actions.   12

D.7 Tasking Restrictions

This clause defines restrictions that can be used with a pragma Restrictions (see 13.12) to facilitate the construction of highly efficient tasking run-time systems.   1

Static Semantics

The following *restriction*_identifiers are language defined: 2

No_Task_Hierarchy   3
> All (nonenvironment) tasks depend directly on the environment task of the partition.

No_Nested_Finalization   4/1
> Objects with controlled, protected, or task parts and access types that designate such objects, shall be declared only at library level.

No_Abort_Statements   5
> There are no abort_statements, and there are no calls on Task_Identification.Abort_Task.

No_Terminate_Alternatives   6
> There are no selective_accepts with terminate_alternatives.

No_Task_Allocators   7
> There are no allocators for task types or types containing task subcomponents.

No_Implicit_Heap_Allocations   8
> There are no operations that implicitly require heap storage allocation to be performed by the implementation. The operations that implicitly require heap storage allocation are implementation defined.

No_Dynamic_Priorities   9
> There are no semantic dependences on the package Dynamic_Priorities.

No_Asynchronous_Control   10
> There are no semantic dependences on the package Asynchronous_Task_Control.

The following *restriction_parameter*_identifiers are language defined: 11

Max_Select_Alternatives   12
> Specifies the maximum number of alternatives in a selective_accept.

13   Max_Task_Entries

Specifies the maximum number of entries per task. The bounds of every entry family of a task unit shall be static, or shall be defined by a discriminant of a subtype whose corresponding bound is static. A value of zero indicates that no rendezvous are possible.

14   Max_Protected_Entries

Specifies the maximum number of entries per protected type. The bounds of every entry family of a protected unit shall be static, or shall be defined by a discriminant of a subtype whose corresponding bound is static.

Dynamic Semantics

15/1 *This paragraph was deleted.*

16   The following *restriction_parameter_*identifiers are language defined:

17/1 Max_Storage_At_Blocking

Specifies the maximum portion (in storage elements) of a task's Storage_Size that can be retained by a blocked task. If an implementation chooses to detect a violation of this restriction, Storage_Error should be raised; otherwise, the behavior is implementation defined.

18/1 Max_Asynchronous_Select_Nesting

Specifies the maximum dynamic nesting level of asynchronous_selects. A value of zero prevents the use of any asynchronous_select and, if a program contains an asynchronous_select, it is illegal. If an implementation chooses to detect a violation of this restriction for values other than zero, Storage_Error should be raised; otherwise, the behavior is implementation defined.

19/1 Max_Tasks   Specifies the maximum number of task creations that may be executed over the lifetime of a partition, not counting the creation of the environment task. A value of zero prevents any task creation and, if a program contains a task creation, it is illegal. If an implementation chooses to detect a violation of this restriction, Storage_Error should be raised; otherwise, the behavior is implementation defined.

20   It is implementation defined whether the use of pragma Restrictions results in a reduction in executable program size, storage requirements, or execution time. If possible, the implementation should provide quantitative descriptions of such effects for each restriction.

Implementation Advice

21   When feasible, the implementation should take advantage of the specified restrictions to produce a more efficient implementation.

NOTES

22   29 The above Storage_Checks can be suppressed with pragma Suppress.

D.8 Monotonic Time

1   This clause specifies a high-resolution, monotonic clock package.

Static Semantics

2   The following language-defined library package exists:

3   ```
package Ada.Real_Time is
```
```

```
   type Time is private;                                                          4
   Time_First : constant Time;
   Time_Last : constant Time;
   Time_Unit : constant := implementation-defined-real-number;

   type Time_Span is private;                                                     5
   Time_Span_First : constant Time_Span;
   Time_Span_Last : constant Time_Span;
   Time_Span_Zero : constant Time_Span;
   Time_Span_Unit : constant Time_Span;

   Tick : constant Time_Span;                                                     6
   function Clock return Time;

   function "+" (Left : Time; Right : Time_Span) return Time;                     7
   function "+" (Left : Time_Span; Right : Time) return Time;
   function "-" (Left : Time; Right : Time_Span) return Time;
   function "-" (Left : Time; Right : Time) return Time_Span;

   function "<" (Left, Right : Time) return Boolean;                              8
   function "<="(Left, Right : Time) return Boolean;
   function ">" (Left, Right : Time) return Boolean;
   function ">="(Left, Right : Time) return Boolean;

   function "+" (Left, Right : Time_Span) return Time_Span;                       9
   function "-" (Left, Right : Time_Span) return Time_Span;
   function "-" (Right : Time_Span) return Time_Span;
   function "*" (Left : Time_Span; Right : Integer) return Time_Span;
   function "*" (Left : Integer; Right : Time_Span) return Time_Span;
   function "/" (Left, Right : Time_Span) return Integer;
   function "/" (Left : Time_Span; Right : Integer) return Time_Span;

   function "abs"(Right : Time_Span) return Time_Span;                            10
```

This paragraph was deleted.   11/1

```
   function "<" (Left, Right : Time_Span) return Boolean;                         12
   function "<="(Left, Right : Time_Span) return Boolean;
   function ">" (Left, Right : Time_Span) return Boolean;
   function ">="(Left, Right : Time_Span) return Boolean;

   function To_Duration (TS : Time_Span) return Duration;                         13
   function To_Time_Span (D : Duration) return Time_Span;

   function Nanoseconds  (NS : Integer) return Time_Span;                         14
   function Microseconds (US : Integer) return Time_Span;
   function Milliseconds (MS : Integer) return Time_Span;

   type Seconds_Count is range implementation-defined;                           15

   procedure Split(T : in Time; SC : out Seconds_Count; TS : out Time_Span);      16
   function Time_Of(SC : Seconds_Count; TS : Time_Span) return Time;

private                                                                          17
   ... -- not specified by the language
end Ada.Real_Time;
```

In this Annex, *real time* is defined to be the physical time as observed in the external environment. The   18
type Time is a *time type* as defined by 9.6; values of this type may be used in a delay_until_statement.
Values of this type represent segments of an ideal time line. The set of values of the type Time corresponds
one-to-one with an implementation-defined range of mathematical integers.

The Time value I represents the half-open real time interval that starts with E+I*Time_Unit and is limited   19
by E+(I+1)*Time_Unit, where Time_Unit is an implementation-defined real number and E is an
unspecified origin point, the *epoch*, that is the same for all values of the type Time. It is not specified by
the language whether the time values are synchronized with any standard time reference. For example, E
can correspond to the time of system initialization or it can correspond to the epoch of some time standard.

20   Values of the type Time_Span represent length of real time duration. The set of values of this type corresponds one-to-one with an implementation-defined range of mathematical integers. The Time_Span value corresponding to the integer I represents the real-time duration I*Time_Unit.

21   Time_First and Time_Last are the smallest and largest values of the Time type, respectively. Similarly, Time_Span_First and Time_Span_Last are the smallest and largest values of the Time_Span type, respectively.

22   A value of type Seconds_Count represents an elapsed time, measured in seconds, since the epoch.

Dynamic Semantics

23   Time_Unit is the smallest amount of real time representable by the Time type; it is expressed in seconds. Time_Span_Unit is the difference between two successive values of the Time type. It is also the smallest positive value of type Time_Span. Time_Unit and Time_Span_Unit represent the same real time duration. A *clock tick* is a real time interval during which the clock value (as observed by calling the Clock function) remains constant. Tick is the average length of such intervals.

24   The function To_Duration converts the value TS to a value of type Duration. Similarly, the function To_Time_Span converts the value D to a value of type Time_Span. For both operations, the result is rounded to the nearest exactly representable value (away from zero if exactly halfway between two exactly representable values).

25   To_Duration(Time_Span_Zero) returns 0.0, and To_Time_Span(0.0) returns Time_Span_Zero.

26   The functions Nanoseconds, Microseconds, and Milliseconds convert the input parameter to a value of the type Time_Span. NS, US, and MS are interpreted as a number of nanoseconds, microseconds, and milliseconds respectively. The result is rounded to the nearest exactly representable value (away from zero if exactly halfway between two exactly representable values).

27   The effects of the operators on Time and Time_Span are as for the operators defined for integer types.

28   The function Clock returns the amount of time since the epoch.

29   The effects of the Split and Time_Of operations are defined as follows, treating values of type Time, Time_Span, and Seconds_Count as mathematical integers. The effect of Split(T,SC,TS) is to set SC and TS to values such that T*Time_Unit = SC*1.0 + TS*Time_Unit, and 0.0 <= TS*Time_Unit < 1.0. The value returned by Time_Of(SC,TS) is the value T such that T*Time_Unit = SC*1.0 + TS*Time_Unit.

Implementation Requirements

30   The range of Time values shall be sufficient to uniquely represent the range of real times from program start-up to 50 years later. Tick shall be no greater than 1 millisecond. Time_Unit shall be less than or equal to 20 microseconds.

31   Time_Span_First shall be no greater than −3600 seconds, and Time_Span_Last shall be no less than 3600 seconds.

32   A *clock jump* is the difference between two successive distinct values of the clock (as observed by calling the Clock function). There shall be no backward clock jumps.

Documentation Requirements

33   The implementation shall document the values of Time_First, Time_Last, Time_Span_First, Time_Span_Last, Time_Span_Unit, and Tick.

The implementation shall document the properties of the underlying time base used for the clock and for type Time, such as the range of values supported and any relevant aspects of the underlying hardware or operating system facilities used. 34

The implementation shall document whether or not there is any synchronization with external time references, and if such synchronization exists, the sources of synchronization information, the frequency of synchronization, and the synchronization method applied. 35

The implementation shall document any aspects of the external environment that could interfere with the clock behavior as defined in this clause. 36/1

Metrics

For the purpose of the metrics defined in this clause, real time is defined to be the International Atomic Time (TAI). 37

The implementation shall document the following metrics: 38

- An upper bound on the real-time duration of a clock tick. This is a value D such that if t1 and t2 are any real times such that t1 < t2 and $Clock_{t1}$ = $Clock_{t2}$ then t2 – t1 <= D. 39

- An upper bound on the size of a clock jump. 40

- An upper bound on the *drift rate* of Clock with respect to real time. This is a real number D such that 41

$$E*(1\text{-}D) <= (Clock_{t+E} - Clock_t) <= E*(1+D)$$ 42
$$\text{provided that: } Clock_t + E*(1+D) <= Time\_Last.$$

- where $Clock_t$ is the value of Clock at time t, and E is a real time duration not less than 24 hours. The value of E used for this metric shall be reported. 43

- An upper bound on the execution time of a call to the Clock function, in processor clock cycles. 44

- Upper bounds on the execution times of the operators of the types Time and Time_Span, in processor clock cycles. 45

Implementation Permissions

Implementations targeted to machines with word size smaller than 32 bits need not support the full range and granularity of the Time and Time_Span types. 46

Implementation Advice

When appropriate, implementations should provide configuration mechanisms to change the value of Tick. 47

It is recommended that Calendar.Clock and Real_Time.Clock be implemented as transformations of the same time base. 48

It is recommended that the "best" time base which exists in the underlying system be available to the application through Clock. "Best" may mean highest accuracy or largest range. 49

NOTES
30 The rules in this clause do not imply that the implementation can protect the user from operator or installation errors which could result in the clock being set incorrectly. 50

31 Time_Unit is the granularity of the Time type. In contrast, Tick represents the granularity of Real_Time.Clock. There is no requirement that these be the same. 51

D.9 Delay Accuracy

1   This clause specifies performance requirements for the delay_statement. The rules apply both to delay_-relative_statement and to delay_until_statement. Similarly, they apply equally to a simple delay_-statement and to one which appears in a delay_alternative.

Dynamic Semantics

2   The effect of the delay_statement for Real_Time.Time is defined in terms of Real_Time.Clock:

3   • If C_1 is a value of Clock read before a task executes a delay_relative_statement with duration D, and C_2 is a value of Clock read after the task resumes execution following that delay_statement, then $C_2 - C_1 >= D$.

4   • If C is a value of Clock read after a task resumes execution following a delay_until_statement with Real_Time.Time value T, then $C >= T$.

5   A simple delay_statement with a negative or zero value for the expiration time does not cause the calling task to be blocked; it is nevertheless a potentially blocking operation (see 9.5.1).

6   When a delay_statement appears in a delay_alternative of a timed_entry_call the selection of the entry call is attempted, regardless of the specified expiration time. When a delay_statement appears in a selective_accept_alternative, and a call is queued on one of the open entries, the selection of that entry call proceeds, regardless of the value of the delay expression.

Documentation Requirements

7   The implementation shall document the minimum value of the delay expression of a delay_relative_statement that causes the task to actually be blocked.

8   The implementation shall document the minimum difference between the value of the delay expression of a delay_until_statement and the value of Real_Time.Clock, that causes the task to actually be blocked.

Metrics

9   The implementation shall document the following metrics:

10   • An upper bound on the execution time, in processor clock cycles, of a delay_relative_statement whose requested value of the delay expression is less than or equal to zero.

11   • An upper bound on the execution time, in processor clock cycles, of a delay_until_statement whose requested value of the delay expression is less than or equal to the value of Real_Time.Clock at the time of executing the statement. Similarly, for Calendar.Clock.

12   • An upper bound on the *lateness* of a delay_relative_statement, for a positive value of the delay expression, in a situation where the task has sufficient priority to preempt the processor as soon as it becomes ready, and does not need to wait for any other execution resources. The upper bound is expressed as a function of the value of the delay expression. The lateness is obtained by subtracting the value of the delay expression from the *actual duration*. The actual duration is measured from a point immediately before a task executes the delay_statement to a point immediately after the task resumes execution following this statement.

13   • An upper bound on the lateness of a delay_until_statement, in a situation where the value of the requested expiration time is after the time the task begins executing the statement, the task has sufficient priority to preempt the processor as soon as it becomes ready, and it does not need to wait for any other execution resources. The upper bound is expressed as a function of the difference between the requested expiration time and the clock value at the time the statement begins execution. The lateness of a delay_until_statement is obtained by subtracting the

requested expiration time from the real time that the task resumes execution following this statement.

NOTES

32 The execution time of a delay_statement that does not cause the task to be blocked (e.g. "**delay** 0.0;") is of interest   14
in situations where delays are used to achieve voluntary round-robin task dispatching among equal-priority tasks.

D.10 Synchronous Task Control

This clause describes a language-defined private semaphore (suspension object), which can be used for   1
two-stage suspend operations and as a simple building block for implementing higher-level queues.

Static Semantics

The following language-defined package exists: 2

```
package Ada.Synchronous_Task_Control is                                       3

  type Suspension_Object is limited private;                                  4
  procedure Set_True(S : in out Suspension_Object);
  procedure Set_False(S : in out Suspension_Object);
  function Current_State(S : Suspension_Object) return Boolean;
  procedure Suspend_Until_True(S : in out Suspension_Object);
private
    ... -- not specified by the language
end Ada.Synchronous_Task_Control;
```

The type Suspension_Object is a by-reference type.   5

Dynamic Semantics

An object of the type Suspension_Object has two visible states: true and false. Upon initialization, its   6
value is set to false.

The operations Set_True and Set_False are atomic with respect to each other and with respect to   7
Suspend_Until_True; they set the state to true and false respectively.

Current_State returns the current state of the object.   8

The procedure Suspend_Until_True blocks the calling task until the state of the object S is true; at that   9
point the task becomes ready and the state of the object becomes false.

Program_Error is raised upon calling Suspend_Until_True if another task is already waiting on that   10
suspension object. Suspend_Until_True is a potentially blocking operation (see 9.5.1).

Implementation Requirements

The implementation is required to allow the calling of Set_False and Set_True during any protected action,   11
even one that has its ceiling priority in the Interrupt_Priority range.

D.11 Asynchronous Task Control

This clause introduces a language-defined package to do asynchronous suspend/resume on tasks. It uses a   1
conceptual *held priority* value to represent the task's *held* state.

Static Semantics

The following language-defined library package exists: 2

3
```
with Ada.Task_Identification;
package Ada.Asynchronous_Task_Control is
   procedure Hold(T : in Ada.Task_Identification.Task_ID);
   procedure Continue(T : in Ada.Task_Identification.Task_ID);
   function Is_Held(T : Ada.Task_Identification.Task_ID)
      return Boolean;
end Ada.Asynchronous_Task_Control;
```

Dynamic Semantics

4 After the Hold operation has been applied to a task, the task becomes *held*. For each processor there is a conceptual *idle task*, which is always ready. The base priority of the idle task is below System.Any_-Priority'First. The *held priority* is a constant of the type integer whose value is below the base priority of the idle task.

5 The Hold operation sets the state of T to held. For a held task: the task's own base priority does not constitute an inheritance source (see D.1), and the value of the held priority is defined to be such a source instead.

6 The Continue operation resets the state of T to not-held; T's active priority is then reevaluated as described in D.1. This time, T's base priority is taken into account.

7 The Is_Held function returns True if and only if T is in the held state.

8 As part of these operations, a check is made that the task identified by T is not terminated. Tasking_Error is raised if the check fails. Program_Error is raised if the value of T is Null_Task_ID.

Erroneous Execution

9 If any operation in this package is called with a parameter T that specifies a task object that no longer exists, the execution of the program is erroneous.

Implementation Permissions

10 An implementation need not support Asynchronous_Task_Control if it is infeasible to support it in the target environment.

NOTES

11 33 It is a consequence of the priority rules that held tasks cannot be dispatched on any processor in a partition (unless they are inheriting priorities) since their priorities are defined to be below the priority of any idle task.

12 34 The effect of calling Get_Priority and Set_Priority on a Held task is the same as on any other task.

13 35 Calling Hold on a held task or Continue on a non-held task has no effect.

14 36 The rules affecting queuing are derived from the above rules, in addition to the normal priority rules:

15 • When a held task is on the ready queue, its priority is so low as to never reach the top of the queue as long as there are other tasks on that queue.

16 • If a task is executing in a protected action, inside a rendezvous, or is inheriting priorities from other sources (e.g. when activated), it continues to execute until it is no longer executing the corresponding construct.

17 • If a task becomes held while waiting (as a caller) for a rendezvous to complete, the active priority of the accepting task is not affected.

18/1 • If a task becomes held while waiting in a selective_accept, and an entry call is issued to one of the open entries, the corresponding accept_alternative executes. When the rendezvous completes, the active priority of the accepting task is lowered to the held priority (unless it is still inheriting from other sources), and the task does not execute until another Continue.

19 • The same holds if the held task is the only task on a protected entry queue whose barrier becomes open. The corresponding entry body executes.

D.12 Other Optimizations and Determinism Rules

This clause describes various requirements for improving the response and determinism in a real-time system. 1

Implementation Requirements

If the implementation blocks interrupts (see C.3) not as a result of direct user action (e.g. an execution of a protected action) there shall be an upper bound on the duration of this blocking. 2

The implementation shall recognize entry-less protected types. The overhead of acquiring the execution resource of an object of such a type (see 9.5.1) shall be minimized. In particular, there should not be any overhead due to evaluating entry_barrier conditions. 3

Unchecked_Deallocation shall be supported for terminated tasks that are designated by access types, and shall have the effect of releasing all the storage associated with the task. This includes any run-time system or heap storage that has been implicitly allocated for the task by the implementation. 4

Documentation Requirements

The implementation shall document the upper bound on the duration of interrupt blocking caused by the implementation. If this is different for different interrupts or interrupt priority levels, it should be documented for each case. 5

Metrics

The implementation shall document the following metric: 6

- The overhead associated with obtaining a mutual-exclusive access to an entry-less protected object. This shall be measured in the following way: 7

  For a protected object of the form: 8

```
protected Lock is
   procedure Set;
   function Read return Boolean;
private
   Flag : Boolean := False;
end Lock;
```
9

```
protected body Lock is
   procedure Set is
   begin
      Flag := True;
   end Set;
   function Read return Boolean
   Begin
      return Flag;
   end Read;
end Lock;
```
10

  The execution time, in processor clock cycles, of a call to Set. This shall be measured between the point just before issuing the call, and the point just after the call completes. The function Read shall be called later to verify that Set was indeed called (and not optimized away). The calling task shall have sufficiently high priority as to not be preempted during the measurement period. The protected object shall have sufficiently high ceiling priority to allow the task to call Set. 11

  For a multiprocessor, if supported, the metric shall be reported for the case where no contention (on the execution resource) exists from tasks executing on other processors. 12

Annex E
(normative)
Distributed Systems

This Annex defines facilities for supporting the implementation of distributed systems using multiple partitions working cooperatively as part of a single Ada program.　　1

Post-Compilation Rules

A *distributed system* is an interconnection of one or more *processing nodes* (a system resource that has both computational and storage capabilities), and zero or more *storage nodes* (a system resource that has only storage capabilities, with the storage addressable by one or more processing nodes).　　2

A *distributed program* comprises one or more partitions that execute independently (except when they communicate) in a distributed system.　　3

The process of mapping the partitions of a program to the nodes in a distributed system is called *configuring the partitions of the program*.　　4

Implementation Requirements

The implementation shall provide means for explicitly assigning library units to a partition and for the configuring and execution of a program consisting of multiple partitions on a distributed system; the means are implementation defined.　　5

Implementation Permissions

An implementation may require that the set of processing nodes of a distributed system be homogeneous.　　6

NOTES
1 The partitions comprising a program may be executed on differently configured distributed systems or on a non-distributed system without requiring recompilation. A distributed program may be partitioned differently from the same set of library units without recompilation. The resulting execution is semantically equivalent.　　7

2 A distributed program retains the same type safety as the equivalent single partition program.　　8

E.1 Partitions

The partitions of a distributed program are classified as either active or passive.　　1

Post-Compilation Rules

An *active partition* is a partition as defined in 10.2. A *passive partition* is a partition that has no thread of control of its own, whose library units are all preelaborated, and whose data and subprograms are accessible to one or more active partitions.　　2

A passive partition shall include only library_items that either are declared pure or are shared passive (see 10.2.1 and E.2.1).　　3

An active partition shall be configured on a processing node. A passive partition shall be configured either on a storage node or on a processing node.　　4

The configuration of the partitions of a program onto a distributed system shall be consistent with the possibility for data references or calls between the partitions implied by their semantic dependences. Any reference to data or call of a subprogram across partitions is called a *remote access*.　　5

S. Tucker Taft et al. (Eds.): Consolidated Ada Reference Manual, LNCS 2219, pp. 407– 419, 2001.

Dynamic Semantics

6   A library_item is elaborated as part of the elaboration of each partition that includes it. If a normal library unit (see E.2) has state, then a separate copy of the state exists in each active partition that elaborates it. The state evolves independently in each such partition.

7   An active partition *terminates* when its environment task terminates. A partition becomes *inaccessible* if it terminates or if it is *aborted*. An active partition is aborted when its environment task is aborted. In addition, if a partition fails during its elaboration, it becomes inaccessible to other partitions. Other implementation-defined events can also result in a partition becoming inaccessible.

8/1 For a prefix D that denotes a library-level declaration, excepting a declaration of or within a declared-pure library unit, the following attribute is defined:

9   D'Partition_ID
               Denotes a value of the type *universal_integer* that identifies the partition in which D was elaborated. If D denotes the declaration of a remote call interface library unit (see E.2.3) the given partition is the one where the body of D was elaborated.

Bounded (Run-Time) Errors

10   It is a bounded error for there to be cyclic elaboration dependences between the active partitions of a single distributed program. The possible effects are deadlock during elaboration, or the raising of Program_Error in one or all of the active partitions involved.

Implementation Permissions

11   An implementation may allow multiple active or passive partitions to be configured on a single processing node, and multiple passive partitions to be configured on a single storage node. In these cases, the scheduling policies, treatment of priorities, and management of shared resources between these partitions are implementation defined.

12   An implementation may allow separate copies of an active partition to be configured on different processing nodes, and to provide appropriate interactions between the copies to present a consistent state of the partition to other active partitions.

13   In an implementation, the partitions of a distributed program need not be loaded and elaborated all at the same time; they may be loaded and elaborated one at a time over an extended period of time. An implementation may provide facilities to abort and reload a partition during the execution of a distributed program.

14   An implementation may allow the state of some of the partitions of a distributed program to persist while other partitions of the program terminate and are later reinvoked.

     NOTES
15   3 Library units are grouped into partitions after compile time, but before run time. At compile time, only the relevant library unit properties are identified using categorization pragmas.

16   4 The value returned by the Partition_ID attribute can be used as a parameter to implementation-provided subprograms in order to query information about the partition.

E.2 Categorization of Library Units

1   Library units can be categorized according to the role they play in a distributed program. Certain restrictions are associated with each category to ensure that the semantics of a distributed program remain close to the semantics for a nondistributed program.

categorization pragma is a library unit pragma (see 10.1.5) that restricts the declarations, child units, or 2
semantic dependences of the library unit to which it applies. A *categorized library unit* is a library unit to
which a categorization pragma applies.

The pragmas Shared_Passive, Remote_Types, and Remote_Call_Interface are categorization pragmas. In 3
addition, for the purposes of this Annex, the pragma Pure (see 10.2.1) is considered a categorization
pragma.

A library package or generic library package is called a *shared passive* library unit if a Shared_Passive 4/1
pragma applies to it. A library package or generic library package is called a *remote types* library unit if a
Remote_Types pragma applies to it. A library unit is called a *remote call interface* if a
Remote_Call_Interface pragma applies to it. A *normal library unit* is one to which no categorization
pragma applies.

The various categories of library units and the associated restrictions are described in this clause and its 5
subclauses. The categories are related hierarchically in that the library units of one category can depend
semantically only on library units of that category or an earlier one, except that the body of a remote types
or remote call interface library unit is unrestricted.

The overall hierarchy (including declared pure) is as follows: 6

Declared Pure 7
       Can depend only on other declared pure library units;

Shared Passive 8
       Can depend only on other shared passive or declared pure library units;

Remote Types 9
       The declaration of the library unit can depend only on other remote types library units, or
       one of the above; the body of the library unit is unrestricted;

Remote Call Interface 10
       The declaration of the library unit can depend only on other remote call interfaces, or one of
       the above; the body of the library unit is unrestricted;

Normal   Unrestricted. 11

Declared pure and shared passive library units are preelaborated. The declaration of a remote types or 12
remote call interface library unit is required to be preelaborable.

Implementation Requirements

This paragraph was deleted. 13/1

Implementation Permissions

Implementations are allowed to define other categorization pragmas. 14

E.2.1 Shared Passive Library Units

A shared passive library unit is used for managing global data shared between active partitions. The 1
restrictions on shared passive library units prevent the data or tasks of one active partition from being
accessible to another active partition through references implicit in objects declared in the shared passive
library unit.

Syntax

The form of a pragma Shared_Passive is as follows: 2

3   **pragma** Shared_Passive[(*library_unit_*name)];

Legality Rules

4   A *shared passive library unit* is a library unit to which a Shared_Passive pragma applies. The following restrictions apply to such a library unit:

5   • it shall be preelaborable (see 10.2.1);

6   • it shall depend semantically only upon declared pure or shared passive library units;

7/1   • it shall not contain a library-level declaration of an access type that designates a class-wide type, task type, or protected type with entry_declarations.

8   Notwithstanding the definition of accessibility given in 3.10.2, the declaration of a library unit P1 is not accessible from within the declarative region of a shared passive library unit P2, unless the shared passive library unit P2 depends semantically on P1.

Static Semantics

9   A shared passive library unit is preelaborated.

Post-Compilation Rules

10   A shared passive library unit shall be assigned to at most one partition within a given program.

11   Notwithstanding the rule given in 10.2, a compilation unit in a given partition does not *need* (in the sense of 10.2) the shared passive library units on which it depends semantically to be included in that same partition; they will typically reside in separate passive partitions.

E.2.2 Remote Types Library Units

1   A remote types library unit supports the definition of types intended for use in communication between active partitions.

Syntax

2   The form of a pragma Remote_Types is as follows:

3   **pragma** Remote_Types[(*library_unit_*name)];

Legality Rules

4   A *remote types library unit* is a library unit to which the pragma Remote_Types applies. The following restrictions apply to the declaration of such a library unit:

5   • it shall be preelaborable;

6   • it shall depend semantically only on declared pure, shared passive, or other remote types library units;

7   • it shall not contain the declaration of any variable within the visible part of the library unit;

8   • if the full view of a type declared in the visible part of the library unit has a part that is of a non-remote access type, then that access type, or the type of some part that includes the access type subcomponent, shall have user-specified Read and Write attributes.

9/1   An access type declared in the visible part of a remote types or remote call interface library unit is called a *remote access type*. Such a type shall be:

9.1/1 • an access-to-subprogram type, or

- a general access type that designates a class-wide limited private type or a class-wide private type   9.2/1
extension all of whose ancestors are either private type extensions or limited private types.

A type that is derived from a remote access type is also a remote access type.   9.3/1

The following restrictions apply to the use of a remote access-to-subprogram type: 10

- A value of a remote access-to-subprogram type shall be converted only to another (subtype-   11
conformant) remote access-to-subprogram type;

- The prefix of an Access attribute_reference that yields a value of a remote access-to-subprogram   12
type shall statically denote a (subtype-conformant) remote subprogram.

The following restrictions apply to the use of a remote access-to-class-wide type: 13

- The primitive subprograms of the corresponding specific limited private type shall only have   14/1
access parameters if they are controlling formal parameters; each non-controlling formal
parameter shall have either a nonlimited type or a type with Read and Write attributes specified
via an attribute_definition_clause;

- A value of a remote access-to-class-wide type shall be explicitly converted only to another   15
remote access-to-class-wide type;

- A value of a remote access-to-class-wide type shall be dereferenced (or implicitly converted to   16/1
an anonymous access type) only as part of a dispatching call where the value designates a
controlling operand of the call (see E.4, "Remote Subprogram Calls").

- The Storage_Pool and Storage_Size attributes are not defined for remote access-to-class-wide   17/1
types; the expected type for an allocator shall not be a remote access-to-class-wide type; a
remote access-to-class-wide type shall not be an actual parameter for a generic formal access
type.

NOTES
5 A remote types library unit need not be pure, and the types it defines may include levels of indirection implemented   18
by using access types. User-specified Read and Write attributes (see 13.13.2) provide for sending values of such a type
between active partitions, with Write marshalling the representation, and Read unmarshalling any levels of indirection.

E.2.3 Remote Call Interface Library Units

A remote call interface library unit can be used as an interface for remote procedure calls (RPCs) (or   1
remote function calls) between active partitions.

Syntax

The form of a pragma Remote_Call_Interface is as follows: 2

   pragma Remote_Call_Interface[(*library_unit_*name)];   3

The form of a pragma All_Calls_Remote is as follows: 4

   pragma All_Calls_Remote[(*library_unit_*name)];   5

A pragma All_Calls_Remote is a library unit pragma.   6

Legality Rules

A *remote call interface (RCI)* is a library unit to which the pragma Remote_Call_Interface applies. A   7/1
subprogram declared in the visible part of such a library unit, or declared by such a library unit, is called a
remote subprogram.

The declaration of an RCI library unit shall be preelaborable (see 10.2.1), and shall depend semantically   8
only upon declared pure, shared passive, remote types, or other remote call interface library units.

9/1 In addition, the following restrictions apply to an RCI library unit:

10/1 • its visible part shall not contain the declaration of a variable;

11/1 • its visible part shall not contain the declaration of a limited type;

12/1 • its visible part shall not contain a nested generic_declaration;

13/1 • it shall not be, nor shall its visible part contain, the declaration of a subprogram to which a pragma Inline applies;

14/1 • it shall not be, nor shall its visible part contain, a subprogram (or access-to-subprogram) declaration whose profile has an access parameter, or a formal parameter of a limited type unless that limited type has user-specified Read and Write attributes;

15 • any public child of the library unit shall be a remote call interface library unit.

16 If a pragma All_Calls_Remote applies to a library unit, the library unit shall be a remote call interface.

Post-Compilation Rules

17 A remote call interface library unit shall be assigned to at most one partition of a given program. A remote call interface library unit whose parent is also an RCI library unit shall be assigned only to the same partition as its parent.

18 Notwithstanding the rule given in 10.2, a compilation unit in a given partition that semantically depends on the declaration of an RCI library unit, *needs* (in the sense of 10.2) only the declaration of the RCI library unit, not the body, to be included in that same partition. Therefore, the body of an RCI library unit is included only in the partition to which the RCI library unit is explicitly assigned.

Implementation Requirements

19/1 If a pragma All_Calls_Remote applies to a given RCI library unit, then the implementation shall route any call to a subprogram of the RCI unit from outside the declarative region of the unit through the Partition Communication Subsystem (PCS); see E.5. Calls to such subprograms from within the declarative region of the unit are defined to be local and shall not go through the PCS.

Implementation Permissions

20 An implementation need not support the Remote_Call_Interface pragma nor the All_Calls_Remote pragma. Explicit message-based communication between active partitions can be supported as an alternative to RPC.

E.3 Consistency of a Distributed System

1 This clause defines attributes and rules associated with verifying the consistency of a distributed program.

Static Semantics

2/1 For a prefix P that statically denotes a program unit, the following attributes are defined:

3 P'Version   Yields a value of the predefined type String that identifies the version of the compilation unit that contains the declaration of the program unit.

4 P'Body_Version

Yields a value of the predefined type String that identifies the version of the compilation unit that contains the body (but not any subunits) of the program unit.

The *version* of a compilation unit changes whenever the compilation unit changes in a semantically significant way. This International Standard does not define the exact meaning of "semantically significant". It is unspecified whether there are other events (such as recompilation) that result in the version of a compilation unit changing. 5/1

f P is not a library unit, and P has no completion, then P'Body_Version returns the Body_Version of the innermost program unit enclosing the declaration of P. If P is a library unit, and P has no completion, then P'Body_Version returns a value that is different from Body_Version of any version of P that has a completion. 5.1/1

Bounded (Run-Time) Errors

In a distributed program, a library unit is *consistent* if the same version of its declaration is used throughout. It is a bounded error to elaborate a partition of a distributed program that contains a compilation unit that depends on a different version of the declaration of a shared passive or RCI library unit than that included in the partition to which the shared passive or RCI library unit was assigned. As a result of this error, Program_Error can be raised in one or both partitions during elaboration; in any case, the partitions become inaccessible to one another. 6

E.4 Remote Subprogram Calls

A *remote subprogram call* is a subprogram call that invokes the execution of a subprogram in another partition. The partition that originates the remote subprogram call is the *calling partition*, and the partition that executes the corresponding subprogram body is the *called partition*. Some remote procedure calls are allowed to return prior to the completion of subprogram execution. These are called *asynchronous remote procedure calls*. 1

There are three different ways of performing a remote subprogram call: 2

- As a direct call on a (remote) subprogram explicitly declared in a remote call interface; 3
- As an indirect call through a value of a remote access-to-subprogram type; 4
- As a dispatching call with a controlling operand designated by a value of a remote access-to-class-wide type. 5

The first way of calling corresponds to a *static* binding between the calling and the called partition. The latter two ways correspond to a *dynamic* binding between the calling and the called partition. 6

A remote call interface library unit (see E.2.3) defines the remote subprograms or remote access types used for remote subprogram calls. 7

Legality Rules

In a dispatching call with two or more controlling operands, if one controlling operand is designated by a value of a remote access-to-class-wide type, then all shall be. 8

Dynamic Semantics

For the execution of a remote subprogram call, subprogram parameters (and later the results, if any) are passed using a stream-oriented representation (see 13.13.1) which is suitable for transmission between partitions. This action is called *marshalling*. *Unmarshalling* is the reverse action of reconstructing the parameters or results from the stream-oriented representation. Marshalling is performed initially as part of the remote subprogram call in the calling partition; unmarshalling is done in the called partition. After the 9 remote subprogram completes, marshalling is performed in the called partition, and finally unmarshalling is done in the calling partition.

10   A *calling stub* is the sequence of code that replaces the subprogram body of a remotely called subprogram in the calling partition. A *receiving stub* is the sequence of code (the "wrapper") that receives a remote subprogram call on the called partition and invokes the appropriate subprogram body.

11   Remote subprogram calls are executed at most once, that is, if the subprogram call returns normally, then the called subprogram's body was executed exactly once.

12   The task executing a remote subprogram call blocks until the subprogram in the called partition returns, unless the call is asynchronous. For an asynchronous remote procedure call, the calling task can become ready before the procedure in the called partition returns.

13   If a construct containing a remote call is aborted, the remote subprogram call is *cancelled*. Whether the execution of the remote subprogram is immediately aborted as a result of the cancellation is implementation defined.

14   If a remote subprogram call is received by a called partition before the partition has completed its elaboration, the call is kept pending until the called partition completes its elaboration (unless the call is cancelled by the calling partition prior to that).

15   If an exception is propagated by a remotely called subprogram, and the call is not an asynchronous call, the corresponding exception is reraised at the point of the remote subprogram call. For an asynchronous call, if the remote procedure call returns prior to the completion of the remotely called subprogram, any exception is lost.

16   The exception Communication_Error (see E.5) is raised if a remote call cannot be completed due to difficulties in communicating with the called partition.

17   All forms of remote subprogram calls are potentially blocking operations (see 9.5.1).

18/1   In a remote subprogram call with a formal parameter of a class-wide type, a check is made that the tag of the actual parameter identifies a tagged type declared in a declared-pure or shared passive library unit, or in the visible part of a remote types or remote call interface library unit. Program_Error is raised if this check fails. In a remote function call which returns a class-wide type, the same check is made on the function result.

19   In a dispatching call with two or more controlling operands that are designated by values of a remote access-to-class-wide type, a check is made (in addition to the normal Tag_Check — see 11.5) that all the remote access-to-class-wide values originated from Access attribute_references that were evaluated by tasks of the same active partition. Constraint_Error is raised if this check fails.

Implementation Requirements

20   The implementation of remote subprogram calls shall conform to the PCS interface as defined by the specification of the language-defined package System.RPC (see E.5). The calling stub shall use the Do_RPC procedure unless the remote procedure call is asynchronous in which case Do_APC shall be used. On the receiving side, the corresponding receiving stub shall be invoked by the RPC-receiver.

20.1/1 With respect to shared variables in shared passive library units, the execution of the corresponding subprogram body of a synchronous remote procedure call is considered to be part of the execution of the calling task. The execution of the corresponding subprogram body of an asynchronous remote procedure all proceeds in parallel with the calling task and does not signal the next action of the calling task (see .10).

NOTES

6 A given active partition can both make and receive remote subprogram calls. Thus, an active partition can act as both a client and a server.   21

7 If a given exception is propagated by a remote subprogram call, but the exception does not exist in the calling partition, the exception can be handled by an **others** choice or be propagated to and handled by a third partition.   22

E.4.1 Pragma Asynchronous

This subclause introduces the pragma Asynchronous which allows a remote subprogram call to return prior to completion of the execution of the corresponding remote subprogram body.   1

Syntax

The form of a pragma Asynchronous is as follows: 2

  pragma Asynchronous(local_name);   3

Legality Rules

The local_name of a pragma Asynchronous shall denote either: 4

- One or more remote procedures; the formal parameters of the procedure(s) shall all be of mode **in**;   5

- The first subtype of a remote access-to-procedure type; the formal parameters of the designated profile of the type shall all be of mode **in**;   6

- The first subtype of a remote access-to-class-wide type.   7

Static Semantics

A pragma Asynchronous is a representation pragma. When applied to a type, it specifies the type-related *asynchronous* aspect of the type.   8

Dynamic Semantics

A remote call is *asynchronous* if it is a call to a procedure, or a call through a value of an access-to-procedure type, to which a pragma Asynchronous applies. In addition, if a pragma Asynchronous applies to a remote access-to-class-wide type, then a dispatching call on a procedure with a controlling operand designated by a value of the type is asynchronous if the formal parameters of the procedure are all of mode **in**.   9

Implementation Requirements

Asynchronous remote procedure calls shall be implemented such that the corresponding body executes at most once as a result of the call.   10

E.4.2 Example of Use of a Remote Access-to-Class-Wide Type

Examples

Example of using a remote access-to-class-wide type to achieve dynamic binding across active partitions: 1

2
```
package Tapes is
    pragma Pure(Tapes);
    type Tape is abstract tagged limited private;
    -- Primitive dispatching operations where
    -- Tape is controlling operand
    procedure Copy (From, To : access Tape; Num_Recs : in Natural) is
abstract;
    procedure Rewind (T : access Tape) is abstract;
    -- More operations
private
    type Tape is ...
end Tapes;
```

3
```
with Tapes;
package Name_Server is
    pragma Remote_Call_Interface;
    -- Dynamic binding to remote operations is achieved
    -- using the access-to-limited-class-wide type Tape_Ptr
    type Tape_Ptr is access all Tapes.Tape'Class;
    -- The following statically bound remote operations
    -- allow for a name-server capability in this example
    function  Find     (Name : String) return Tape_Ptr;
    procedure Register (Name : in String; T : in Tape_Ptr);
    procedure Remove   (T : in Tape_Ptr);
    -- More operations
end Name_Server;
```

4
```
package Tape_Driver is
    -- Declarations are not shown, they are irrelevant here
end Tape_Driver;
```

5
```
with Tapes, Name_Server;
package body Tape_Driver is
    type New_Tape is new Tapes.Tape with ...
    procedure Copy
      (From, To : access New_Tape; Num_Recs: in Natural) is
    begin
        . . .
    end Copy;
    procedure Rewind (T : access New_Tape) is
    begin
        . . .
    end Rewind;
    -- Objects remotely accessible through use
    -- of Name_Server operations
    Tape1, Tape2 : aliased New_Tape;
begin
    Name_Server.Register ("NINE-TRACK",  Tape1'Access);
    Name_Server.Register ("SEVEN-TRACK", Tape2'Access);
end Tape_Driver;
```

6
```
with Tapes, Name_Server;
-- Tape_Driver is not needed and thus not mentioned in the with_clause
procedure Tape_Client is
    T1, T2 : Name_Server.Tape_Ptr;
begin
    T1 := Name_Server.Find ("NINE-TRACK");
    T2 := Name_Server.Find ("SEVEN-TRACK");
    Tapes.Rewind (T1);
    Tapes.Rewind (T2);
    Tapes.Copy (T1, T2, 3);
end Tape_Client;
```

7 *Notes on the example*:

8/1 *This paragraph was deleted.*

9 • The package Tapes provides the necessary declarations of the type and its primitive operations.

- Name_Server is a remote call interface package and is elaborated in a separate active partition to provide the necessary naming services (such as Register and Find) to the entire distributed program through remote subprogram calls.   10

- Tape_Driver is a normal package that is elaborated in a partition configured on the processing node that is connected to the tape device(s). The abstract operations are overridden to support the locally declared tape devices (Tape1, Tape2). The package is not visible to its clients, but it exports the tape devices (as remote objects) through the services of the Name_Server. This allows for tape devices to be dynamically added, removed or replaced without requiring the modification of the clients' code.   11

- The Tape_Client procedure references only declarations in the Tapes and Name_Server packages. Before using a tape for the first time, it needs to query the Name_Server for a system-wide identity for that tape. From then on, it can use that identity to access the tape device.   12

- Values of remote access type Tape_Ptr include the necessary information to complete the remote dispatching operations that result from dereferencing the controlling operands T1 and T2.   13

E.5 Partition Communication Subsystem

The *Partition Communication Subsystem* (PCS) provides facilities for supporting communication between the active partitions of a distributed program. The package System.RPC is a language-defined interface to the PCS. An implementation conforming to this Annex shall use the RPC interface to implement remote subprogram calls.   1

Static Semantics

The following language-defined library package exists: 2

```
with Ada.Streams; -- see 13.13.1                                               3
package System.RPC is

   type Partition_ID is range 0 .. implementation-defined;                     4

   Communication_Error : exception;                                            5

   type Params_Stream_Type (                                                   6
       Initial_Size : Ada.Streams.Stream_Element_Count) is new
       Ada.Streams.Root_Stream_Type with private;

   procedure Read(                                                             7
       Stream : in out Params_Stream_Type;
       Item : out Ada.Streams.Stream_Element_Array;
       Last : out Ada.Streams.Stream_Element_Offset);

   procedure Write(                                                            8
       Stream : in out Params_Stream_Type;
       Item : in Ada.Streams.Stream_Element_Array);

   -- Synchronous call                                                         9
   procedure Do_RPC(
       Partition  : in Partition_ID;
       Params     : access Params_Stream_Type;
       Result     : access Params_Stream_Type);

   -- Asynchronous call                                                        10
   procedure Do_APC(
       Partition  : in Partition_ID;
       Params     : access Params_Stream_Type);

   -- The handler for incoming RPCs                                            11
   type RPC_Receiver is access procedure(
       Params     : access Params_Stream_Type;
       Result     : access Params_Stream_Type);
```

12
```
        procedure Establish_RPC_Receiver(
            Partition : in Partition_ID;
            Receiver  : in RPC_Receiver);
```

13
```
    private
        ... -- not specified by the language
    end System.RPC;
```

14 A value of the type Partition_ID is used to identify a partition.

15 An object of the type Params_Stream_Type is used for identifying the particular remote subprogram that is being called, as well as marshalling and unmarshalling the parameters or result of a remote subprogram call, as part of sending them between partitions.

16 The Read and Write procedures override the corresponding abstract operations for the type Params_Stream_Type.

Dynamic Semantics

17 The Do_RPC and Do_APC procedures send a message to the active partition identified by the Partition parameter.

18 After sending the message, Do_RPC blocks the calling task until a reply message comes back from the called partition or some error is detected by the underlying communication system in which case Communication_Error is raised at the point of the call to Do_RPC.

19 Do_APC operates in the same way as Do_RPC except that it is allowed to return immediately after sending the message.

20 Upon normal return, the stream designated by the Result parameter of Do_RPC contains the reply message.

21 The procedure System.RPC.Establish_RPC_Receiver is called once, immediately after elaborating the library units of an active partition (that is, right after the *elaboration of the partition*) if the partition includes an RCI library unit, but prior to invoking the main subprogram, if any. The Partition parameter is the Partition_ID of the active partition being elaborated. The Receiver parameter designates an implementation-provided procedure called the *RPC-receiver* which will handle all RPCs received by the partition from the PCS. Establish_RPC_Receiver saves a reference to the RPC-receiver; when a message is received at the called partition, the RPC-receiver is called with the Params stream containing the message. When the RPC-receiver returns, the contents of the stream designated by Result is placed in a message and sent back to the calling partition.

22 If a call on Do_RPC is aborted, a cancellation message is sent to the called partition, to request that the execution of the remotely called subprogram be aborted.

23 The subprograms declared in System.RPC are potentially blocking operations.

Implementation Requirements

24 The implementation of the RPC-receiver shall be reentrant, thereby allowing concurrent calls on it from the PCS to service concurrent remote subprogram calls into the partition.

24.1/1 An implementation shall not restrict the replacement of the body of System.RPC. An implementation shall not restrict children of System.RPC. The related implementation permissions in the introduction to Annex A do not apply.

24.2/1 If the implementation of System.RPC is provided by the user, an implementation shall support remote subprogram calls as specified.

Documentation Requirements

The implementation of the PCS shall document whether the RPC-receiver is invoked from concurrent tasks. If there is an upper limit on the number of such tasks, this limit shall be documented as well, together with the mechanisms to configure it (if this is supported).   25

Implementation Permissions

The PCS is allowed to contain implementation-defined interfaces for explicit message passing, broadcasting, etc. Similarly, it is allowed to provide additional interfaces to query the state of some remote partition (given its partition ID) or of the PCS itself, to set timeouts and retry parameters, to get more detailed error status, etc. These additional interfaces should be provided in child packages of System.RPC.   26

A body for the package System.RPC need not be supplied by the implementation.   27

Implementation Advice

Whenever possible, the PCS on the called partition should allow for multiple tasks to call the RPC-receiver with different messages and should allow them to block until the corresponding subprogram body returns.   28

The Write operation on a stream of type Params_Stream_Type should raise Storage_Error if it runs out of space trying to write the Item into the stream.   29

NOTES
8 The package System.RPC is not designed for direct calls by user programs. It is instead designed for use in the implementation of remote subprograms calls, being called by the calling stubs generated for a remote call interface library unit to initiate a remote call, and in turn calling back to an RPC-receiver that dispatches to the receiving stubs generated for the body of a remote call interface, to handle a remote call received from elsewhere.   30

Annex F
(normative)
Information Systems

This Annex provides a set of facilities relevant to Information Systems programming. These fall into several categories: 1

- an attribute definition clause specifying Machine_Radix for a decimal subtype;   2

- the package Decimal, which declares a set of constants defining the implementation's capacity for decimal types, and a generic procedure for decimal division; and   3

- the child packages Text_IO.Editing and Wide_Text_IO.Editing, which support formatted and localized output of decimal data, based on ''picture String'' values.   4

See also: 3.5.9, ''Fixed Point Types''; 3.5.10, ''Operations of Fixed Point Types''; 4.6, ''Type Conversions''; 13.3, ''Operational and Representation Attributes''; A.10.9, ''Input-Output for Real Types''; B.4, ''Interfacing with COBOL''; B.3, ''Interfacing with C''; Annex G, ''Numerics''.   5

The character and string handling packages in Annex A, ''Predefined Language Environment'' are also relevant for Information Systems.   6

Implementation Advice

If COBOL (respectively, C) is widely supported in the target environment, implementations supporting the Information Systems Annex should provide the child package Interfaces.COBOL (respectively, Interfaces.C) specified in Annex B and should support a *convention*_identifier of COBOL (respectively, C) in the interfacing pragmas (see Annex B), thus allowing Ada programs to interface with programs written in that language.   7

F.1 Machine_Radix Attribute Definition Clause

Static Semantics

Machine_Radix may be specified for a decimal first subtype (see 3.5.9) via an attribute_definition_clause; the expression of such a clause shall be static, and its value shall be 2 or 10. A value of 2 implies a binary base range; a value of 10 implies a decimal base range.   1

Implementation Advice

Packed decimal should be used as the internal representation for objects of subtype S when S'Machine_Radix = 10.   2

Examples

Example of Machine_Radix attribute definition clause: 3

```
type Money is delta 0.01 digits 15;
for Money'Machine_Radix use 10;
```
   4

S. Tucker Taft et al. (Eds.): Consolidated Ada Reference Manual, LNCS 2219, pp. 421–435, 2001.

F.2 The Package Decimal

Static Semantics

1   The library package Decimal has the following declaration:

2
```
package Ada.Decimal is
   pragma Pure(Decimal);
```

3
```
   Max_Scale : constant := implementation-defined;
   Min_Scale : constant := implementation-defined;
```

4
```
   Min_Delta : constant := 10.0**(-Max_Scale);
   Max_Delta : constant := 10.0**(-Min_Scale);
```

5
```
   Max_Decimal_Digits : constant := implementation-defined;
```

6
```
   generic
      type Dividend_Type  is delta <> digits <>;
      type Divisor_Type   is delta <> digits <>;
      type Quotient_Type  is delta <> digits <>;
      type Remainder_Type is delta <> digits <>;
   procedure Divide (Dividend  : in Dividend_Type;
                     Divisor   : in Divisor_Type;
                     Quotient  : out Quotient_Type;
                     Remainder : out Remainder_Type);
   pragma Convention(Intrinsic, Divide);
```

7
```
end Ada.Decimal;
```

8   Max_Scale is the largest N such that 10.0**(-N) is allowed as a decimal type's delta. Its type is *universal_integer*.

9   Min_Scale is the smallest N such that 10.0**(-N) is allowed as a decimal type's delta. Its type is *universal_integer*.

10   Min_Delta is the smallest value allowed for *delta* in a decimal_fixed_point_definition. Its type is *universal_real*.

11   Max_Delta is the largest value allowed for *delta* in a decimal_fixed_point_definition. Its type is *universal_real*.

12   Max_Decimal_Digits is the largest value allowed for *digits* in a decimal_fixed_point_definition. Its type is *universal_integer*.

Static Semantics

13   The effect of Divide is as follows. The value of Quotient is Quotient_Type(Dividend/Divisor). The value of Remainder is Remainder_Type(Intermediate), where Intermediate is the difference between Dividend and the product of Divisor and Quotient; this result is computed exactly.

Implementation Requirements

14   Decimal.Max_Decimal_Digits shall be at least 18.

15   Decimal.Max_Scale shall be at least 18.

16   Decimal.Min_Scale shall be at most 0.

NOTES

17   1 The effect of division yielding a quotient with control over rounding versus truncation is obtained by applying either the function attribute Quotient_Type'Round or the conversion Quotient_Type to the expression Dividend/Divisor.

F.3 Edited Output for Decimal Types

The child packages Text_IO.Editing and Wide_Text_IO.Editing provide localizable formatted text output, known as *edited output* , for decimal types. An edited output string is a function of a numeric value, program-specifiable locale elements, and a format control value. The numeric value is of some decimal type. The locale elements are: 1

- the currency string;   2
- the digits group separator character;   3
- the radix mark character; and   4
- the fill character that replaces leading zeros of the numeric value.   5

For Text_IO.Editing the edited output and currency strings are of type String, and the locale characters are of type Character. For Wide_Text_IO.Editing their types are Wide_String and Wide_Character, respectively.   6

Each of the locale elements has a default value that can be replaced or explicitly overridden.   7

A format-control value is of the private type Picture; it determines the composition of the edited output string and controls the form and placement of the sign, the position of the locale elements and the decimal digits, the presence or absence of a radix mark, suppression of leading zeros, and insertion of particular character values.   8

A Picture object is composed from a String value, known as a *picture String*, that serves as a template for the edited output string, and a Boolean value that controls whether a string of all space characters is produced when the number's value is zero. A picture String comprises a sequence of one- or two-Character symbols, each serving as a placeholder for a character or string at a corresponding position in the edited output string. The picture String symbols fall into several categories based on their effect on the edited output string: 9

Decimal Digit:	'9'					
Radix Control:	'.'	'V'				
Sign Control:	'+'	'-'	'<'	'>'	"CR"	"DB"
Currency Control:	'$'	'#'				
Zero Suppression:	'Z'	'*'				
Simple Insertion:	'_'	'B'	'0'	'/'		

10

The entries are not case-sensitive. Mixed- or lower-case forms for "CR" and "DB", and lower-case forms for 'V', 'Z', and 'B', have the same effect as the upper-case symbols shown.   11

An occurrence of a '9' Character in the picture String represents a decimal digit position in the edited output string.   12

A radix control Character in the picture String indicates the position of the radix mark in the edited output string: an actual character position for '.', or an assumed position for 'V'.   13

A sign control Character in the picture String affects the form of the sign in the edited output string. The '<' and '>' Character values indicate parentheses for negative values. A Character '+', '-', or '<' appears either singly, signifying a fixed-position sign in the edited output, or repeated, signifying a floating-position sign that is preceded by zero or more space characters and that replaces a leading 0.   14

A currency control Character in the picture String indicates an occurrence of the currency string in the edited output string. The '$' Character represents the complete currency string; the '#' Character represents   15 one character of the currency string. A '$' Character appears either singly, indicating a fixed-position currency string in the edited output, or repeated, indicating a floating-position currency string that occurs in place of a leading 0. A sequence of '#' Character values indicates either a fixed- or floating-position currency string, depending on context.

16 A zero suppression Character in the picture String allows a leading zero to be replaced by either the space character (for 'Z') or the fill character (for '*').

17 A simple insertion Character in the picture String represents, in general, either itself (if '/' or '0'), the space character (if 'B'), or the digits group separator character (if '_'). In some contexts it is treated as part of a floating sign, floating currency, or zero suppression string.

18 An example of a picture String is "<###Z_ZZ9.99>". If the currency string is "FF", the separator character is ',', and the radix mark is '.' then the edited output string values for the decimal values 32.10 and − 5432.10 are "bbFFbbb32.10b" and "(bFF5,432.10)", respectively, where 'b' indicates the space character.

19 The generic packages Text_IO.Decimal_IO and Wide_Text_IO.Decimal_IO (see A.10.9, ''Input-Output for Real Types'') provide text input and non-edited text output for decimal types.

NOTES
20 2 A picture String is of type Standard.String, both for Text_IO.Editing and Wide_Text_IO.Editing.

F.3.1 Picture String Formation

1 A *well-formed picture String*, or simply *picture String*, is a String value that conforms to the syntactic rules, composition constraints, and character replication conventions specified in this clause.

Dynamic Semantics

2/1 *This paragraph was deleted.*

3
```
picture_string ::=
    fixed_$_picture_string
  | fixed_#_picture_string
  | floating_currency_picture_string
  | non_currency_picture_string
```

4
```
fixed_$_picture_string ::=
    [fixed_LHS_sign] fixed_$_char {direct_insertion} [zero_suppression]
      number [RHS_sign]

  | [fixed_LHS_sign {direct_insertion}] [zero_suppression]
      number fixed_$_char {direct_insertion} [RHS_sign]

  | floating_LHS_sign number fixed_$_char {direct_insertion} [RHS_sign]

  | [fixed_LHS_sign] fixed_$_char {direct_insertion}
      all_zero_suppression_number {direct_insertion}  [RHS_sign]

  | [fixed_LHS_sign {direct_insertion}] all_zero_suppression_number {direct_insertion}
      fixed_$_char {direct_insertion} [RHS_sign]

  | all_sign_number {direct_insertion} fixed_$_char {direct_insertion} [RHS_sign]
```

fixed_#_picture_string ::=   5
   [fixed_LHS_sign] single_#_currency {direct_insertion}
   [zero_suppression] number [RHS_sign]

| [fixed_LHS_sign] multiple_#_currency {direct_insertion}
   zero_suppression number [RHS_sign]

| [fixed_LHS_sign {direct_insertion}] [zero_suppression]
   number fixed_#_currency {direct_insertion} [RHS_sign]

| floating_LHS_sign number fixed_#_currency {direct_insertion} [RHS_sign]

| [fixed_LHS_sign] single_#_currency {direct_insertion}
   all_zero_suppression_number {direct_insertion} [RHS_sign]

| [fixed_LHS_sign] multiple_#_currency {direct_insertion}
   all_zero_suppression_number {direct_insertion} [RHS_sign]

| [fixed_LHS_sign {direct_insertion}] all_zero_suppression_number {direct_insertion}
   fixed_#_currency {direct_insertion} [RHS_sign]

| all_sign_number {direct_insertion} fixed_#_currency {direct_insertion} [RHS_sign]

floating_currency_picture_string ::=   6
   [fixed_LHS_sign] {direct_insertion} floating_$_currency number [RHS_sign]
   | [fixed_LHS_sign] {direct_insertion} floating_#_currency number [RHS_sign]
   | [fixed_LHS_sign] {direct_insertion} all_currency_number {direct_insertion} [RHS_sign]

non_currency_picture_string ::=   7
   [fixed_LHS_sign {direct_insertion}] zero_suppression number [RHS_sign]
   | [floating_LHS_sign] number [RHS_sign]
   | [fixed_LHS_sign {direct_insertion}] all_zero_suppression_number {direct_insertion}
     [RHS_sign]
   | all_sign_number {direct_insertion}
   | fixed_LHS_sign direct_insertion {direct_insertion} number [RHS_sign]

fixed_LHS_sign ::= LHS_Sign   8

LHS_Sign ::= + | – | <   9

fixed_$_char ::= $ 10

direct_insertion ::= simple_insertion   11

simple_insertion ::= _ | B | 0 | /   12

zero_suppression ::= Z {Z | context_sensitive_insertion} | fill_string   13

context_sensitive_insertion ::= simple_insertion   14

fill_string ::= * {* | context_sensitive_insertion}   15

16   number ::=
      fore_digits [radix [aft_digits] {direct_insertion}]
      | radix aft_digits {direct_insertion}

17   fore_digits ::= 9 {9 | direct_insertion}

18   aft_digits ::= {9 | direct_insertion} 9

19   radix ::= . | V

20   RHS_sign ::= + | – | > | CR | DB

21   floating_LHS_sign ::=
      LHS_Sign {context_sensitive_insertion} LHS_Sign {LHS_Sign | context_sensitive_insertion}

22   single_#_currency ::= #

23   multiple_#_currency ::= ## {#}

24   fixed_#_currency ::= single_#_currency | multiple_#_currency

25   floating_$_currency ::=
      $ {context_sensitive_insertion} $ {$ | context_sensitive_insertion}

26   floating_#_currency ::=
      # {context_sensitive_insertion} # {# | context_sensitive_insertion}

27   all_sign_number ::= all_sign_fore [radix [all_sign_aft]] [>]

28   all_sign_fore ::=
      sign_char {context_sensitive_insertion} sign_char {sign_char | context_sensitive_insertion}

29   all_sign_aft ::= {all_sign_aft_char} sign_char

     all_sign_aft_char ::= sign_char | context_sensitive_insertion

30   sign_char ::= + | - | <

31   all_currency_number ::= all_currency_fore [radix [all_currency_aft]]

32   all_currency_fore ::=
      currency_char {context_sensitive_insertion}
       currency_char {currency_char | context_sensitive_insertion}

33   all_currency_aft ::= {all_currency_aft_char} currency_char

     all_currency_aft_char ::= currency_char | context_sensitive_insertion

34   currency_char ::= $ | #

35   all_zero_suppression_number ::= all_zero_suppression_fore [radix [all_zero_suppression_aft]]

36   all_zero_suppression_fore ::=
      zero_suppression_char {zero_suppression_char | context_sensitive_insertion}

F.3.1 Picture String Formation

all_zero_suppression_aft ::= {all_zero_suppression_aft_char} zero_suppression_char   37

all_zero_suppression_aft_char ::= zero_suppression_char I context_sensitive_insertion

zero_suppression_char ::= Z I *   38

The following composition constraints apply to a picture String: 39

- A floating_LHS_sign does not have occurrences of different LHS_Sign Character values.   40

- If a picture String has '<' as fixed_LHS_sign, then it has '>' as RHS_sign.   41

- If a picture String has '<' in a floating_LHS_sign or in an all_sign_number, then it has an occurrence of '>'.   42

- If a picture String has '+' or '-' as fixed_LHS_sign, in a floating_LHS_sign, or in an all_sign_number, then it has no RHS_sign or '>' character.   43/1

- An instance of all_sign_number does not have occurrences of different sign_char Character values.   44

- An instance of all_currency_number does not have occurrences of different currency_char Character values.   45

- An instance of all_zero_suppression_number does not have occurrences of different zero_suppression_char Character values, except for possible case differences between 'Z' and 'z'.   46

A *replicable Character* is a Character that, by the above rules, can occur in two consecutive positions in a picture String.   47

A *Character replication* is a String   48

     char & ' (' & *spaces* & *count_string* & ') '   49

where *char* is a replicable Character, *spaces* is a String (possibly empty) comprising only space Character values, and *count_string* is a String of one or more decimal digit Character values. A Character replication in a picture String has the same effect as (and is said to be *equivalent to*) a String comprising n consecutive occurrences of *char*, where n=Integer'Value(*count_string*).   50

An *expanded picture String* is a picture String containing no Character replications.   51

NOTES
3 Although a sign to the left of the number can float, a sign to the right of the number is in a fixed position.   52

F.3.2 Edited Output Generation

Dynamic Semantics

The contents of an edited output string are based on: 1

- A value, Item, of some decimal type Num,   2

- An expanded picture String Pic_String,   3

- A Boolean value, Blank_When_Zero,   4

- A Currency string,   5

- A Fill character,   6

- A Separator character, and   7

- A Radix_Mark character.   8

9 The combination of a True value for Blank_When_Zero and a '*' character in Pic_String is inconsistent; no edited output string is defined.

10 A layout error is identified in the rules below if leading non-zero digits of Item, character values of the Currency string, or a negative sign would be truncated; in such cases no edited output string is defined.

11 The edited output string has lower bound 1 and upper bound N where N = Pic_String'Length + Currency_Length_Adjustment - Radix_Adjustment, and

12 • Currency_Length_Adjustment = Currency'Length – 1 if there is some occurrence of '$' in Pic_String, and 0 otherwise.

13 • Radix_Adjustment = 1 if there is an occurrence of 'V' or 'v' in Pic_Str, and 0 otherwise.

14 Let the magnitude of Item be expressed as a base-10 number $I_p \cdots I_1.F_1 \cdots F_q$, called the *displayed magnitude* of Item, where:

15 • q = Min(Max(Num'Scale, 0), n) where n is 0 if Pic_String has no radix and is otherwise the number of digit positions following radix in Pic_String, where a digit position corresponds to an occurrence of '9', a zero_suppression_char (for an all_zero_suppression_number), a currency_char (for an all_currency_number), or a sign_char (for an all_sign_number).

16 • $I_p \ne 0$ if p>0.

17 If n < Num'Scale, then the above number is the result of rounding (away from 0 if exactly midway between values).

18 If Blank_When_Zero = True and the displayed magnitude of Item is zero, then the edited output string comprises all space character values. Otherwise, the picture String is treated as a sequence of instances of syntactic categories based on the rules in F.3.1, and the edited output string is the concatenation of string values derived from these categories according to the following mapping rules.

19 Table F-1 shows the mapping from a sign control symbol to a corresponding character or string in the edited output. In the columns showing the edited output, a lower-case 'b' represents the space character. If there is no sign control symbol but the value of Item is negative, a layout error occurs and no edited output string is produced.

Table F-1: Edited Output for Sign Control Symbols		
Sign Control Symbol	Edited Output for Non-Negative Number	Edited Output for Negative Number
'+'	'+'	'_'
'_'	'b'	'_'
'<'	'b'	'('
'>'	'b'	')'
"CR"	"bb"	"CR"
"DB"	"bb"	"DB"

20 An instance of fixed_LHS_sign maps to a character as shown in Table F-1.

21 An instance of fixed_$_char maps to Currency.

An instance of direct_insertion maps to Separator if direct_insertion = '_', and to the direct_insertion Character otherwise. 22

An instance of number maps to a string *integer_part* & *radix_part* & *fraction_part* where: 23

- The string for *integer_part* is obtained as follows: 24

 1. Occurrences of '9' in fore_digits of number are replaced from right to left with the decimal digit character values for $I_1, ..., I_p$, respectively. 25

 2. Each occurrence of '9' in fore_digits to the left of the leftmost '9' replaced according to rule 1 is replaced with '0'. 26

 3. If p exceeds the number of occurrences of '9' in fore_digits of number, then the excess leftmost digits are eligible for use in the mapping of an instance of zero_suppression, floating_LHS_sign, floating_$_currency, or floating_#_currency to the left of number; if there is no such instance, then a layout error occurs and no edited output string is produced. 27

- The *radix_part* is: 28

 - "" if number does not include a radix, if radix = 'V', or if radix = 'v' 29

 - Radix_Mark if number includes '.' as radix 30

- The string for *fraction_part* is obtained as follows: 31

 1. Occurrences of '9' in aft_digits of number are replaced from left to right with the decimal digit character values for $F_1, ... F_q$. 32

 2. Each occurrence of '9' in aft_digits to the right of the rightmost '9' replaced according to rule 1 is replaced by '0'. 33

An instance of zero_suppression maps to the string obtained as follows: 34

1. The rightmost 'Z', 'z', or '*' Character values are replaced with the excess digits (if any) from the *integer_part* of the mapping of the number to the right of the zero_suppression instance, 35

2. A context_sensitive_insertion Character is replaced as though it were a direct_insertion Character, if it occurs to the right of some 'Z', 'z', or '*' in zero_suppression that has been mapped to an excess digit, 36

3. Each Character to the left of the leftmost Character replaced according to rule 1 above is replaced by: 37

 - the space character if the zero suppression Character is 'Z' or 'z', or 38

 - the Fill character if the zero suppression Character is '*'. 39

4. A layout error occurs if some excess digits remain after all 'Z', 'z', and '*' Character values in zero_suppression have been replaced via rule 1; no edited output string is produced. 40

An instance of RHS_sign maps to a character or string as shown in Table F-1. 41

An instance of floating_LHS_sign maps to the string obtained as follows. 42

1. Up to all but one of the rightmost LHS_Sign Character values are replaced by the excess digits (if any) from the *integer_part* of the mapping of the number to the right of the floating_LHS_sign instance. 43

2. The next Character to the left is replaced with the character given by the entry in Table F-1 corresponding to the LHS_Sign Character. 44

3. A context_sensitive_insertion Character is replaced as though it were a direct_insertion Character, if it occurs to the right of the leftmost LHS_Sign character replaced according to rule 1. 45

Edited Output Generation **F.3.2**

46   4. Any other Character is replaced by the space character..

47   5. A layout error occurs if some excess digits remain after replacement via rule 1; no edited output string is produced.

48   An instance of fixed_#_currency maps to the Currency string with n space character values concatenated on the left (if the instance does not follow a radix) or on the right (if the instance does follow a radix), where n is the difference between the length of the fixed_#_currency instance and Currency'Length. A layout error occurs if Currency'Length exceeds the length of the fixed_#_currency instance; no edited output string is produced.

49   An instance of floating_$_currency maps to the string obtained as follows:

50   1. Up to all but one of the rightmost '$' Character values are replaced with the excess digits (if any) from the *integer_part* of the mapping of the number to the right of the floating_$_currency instance.

51   2. The next Character to the left is replaced by the Currency string.

52   3. A context_sensitive_insertion Character is replaced as though it were a direct_insertion Character, if it occurs to the right of the leftmost '$' Character replaced via rule 1.

53   4. Each other Character is replaced by the space character.

54   5. A layout error occurs if some excess digits remain after replacement by rule 1; no edited output string is produced.

55   An instance of floating_#_currency maps to the string obtained as follows:

56   1. Up to all but one of the rightmost '#' Character values are replaced with the excess digits (if any) from the *integer_part* of the mapping of the number to the right of the floating_#_currency instance.

57   2. The substring whose last Character occurs at the position immediately preceding the leftmost Character replaced via rule 1, and whose length is Currency'Length, is replaced by the Currency string.

58   3. A context_sensitive_insertion Character is replaced as though it were a direct_insertion Character, if it occurs to the right of the leftmost '#' replaced via rule 1.

59   4. Any other Character is replaced by the space character.

60   5. A layout error occurs if some excess digits remain after replacement rule 1, or if there is no substring with the required length for replacement rule 2; no edited output string is produced.

61   An instance of all_zero_suppression_number maps to:

62   • a string of all spaces if the displayed magnitude of Item is zero, the zero_suppression_char is 'Z' or 'z', and the instance of all_zero_suppression_number does not have a radix at its last character position;

63   • a string containing the Fill character in each position except for the character (if any) corresponding to radix, if zero_suppression_char = '*' and the displayed magnitude of Item is zero;

64   • otherwise, the same result as if each zero_suppression_char in all_zero_suppression_aft were '9', interpreting the instance of all_zero_suppression_number as either zero_suppression number (if a radix and all_zero_suppression_aft are present), or as zero_suppression otherwise.

65   An instance of all_sign_number maps to:

- a string of all spaces if the displayed magnitude of Item is zero and the instance of all_sign_number does not have a radix at its last character position;   66

- otherwise, the same result as if each sign_char in all_sign_number_aft were '9', interpreting the instance of all_sign_number as either floating_LHS_sign number (if a radix and all_sign_number_aft are present), or as floating_LHS_sign otherwise.   67

An instance of all_currency_number maps to: 68

- a string of all spaces if the displayed magnitude of Item is zero and the instance of all_currency_number does not have a radix at its last character position;   69

- otherwise, the same result as if each currency_char in all_currency_number_aft were '9', interpreting the instance of all_currency_number as floating_$_currency number or floating_#_currency number (if a radix and all_currency_number_aft are present), or as floating_$_currency or floating_#_currency otherwise.   70

Examples

In the result string values shown below, 'b' represents the space character.   71

```
Item:              Picture and Result Strings:                              72
123456.78          Picture:  "-###**_***_**9.99"                           73
                             "bbb$***123,456.78"
                             "bbFF***123.456,78" (currency = "FF",
                                                  separator = '.',
                                                  radix mark = ',')
123456.78          Picture:  "-$**_***_**9.99"                           74/1
                   Result:    "b$***123,456.78"
                             "bFF***123.456,78" (currency = "FF",
                                                  separator = '.',
                                                  radix mark = ',')
0.0                Picture:  "-$$$$$.$$"                                    75
                   Result:   "bbbbbbbbbb"
0.20               Picture:  "-$$$$$.$$"                                    76
                   Result:   "bbbbbb$.20"
-1234.565          Picture:  "<<<<_<<<.<<###>"                             77
                   Result:   "bb(1,234.57DMb)"  (currency = "DM")
12345.67           Picture:  "###_###_##9.99"                              78
                   Result:   "bbCHF12,345.67"  (currency = "CHF")
```

F.3.3 The Package Text_IO.Editing

The package Text_IO.Editing provides a private type Picture with associated operations, and a generic package Decimal_Output. An object of type Picture is composed from a well-formed picture String (see F.3.1) and a Boolean item indicating whether a zero numeric value will result in an edited output string of all space characters. The package Decimal_Output contains edited output subprograms implementing the effects defined in F.3.2.   1

Static Semantics

The library package Text_IO.Editing has the following declaration: 2

```
package Ada.Text_IO.Editing is                                            3

    type Picture is private;                                              4

    function Valid (Pic_String      : in String;                          5
                    Blank_When_Zero : in Boolean := False) return Boolean;
```

6
```
   function To_Picture (Pic_String      : in String;
                        Blank_When_Zero : in Boolean := False)
      return Picture;
```

7
```
   function Pic_String      (Pic : in Picture) return String;
   function Blank_When_Zero (Pic : in Picture) return Boolean;
```

8
```
   Max_Picture_Length  : constant := implementation_defined;
```

9
```
   Picture_Error       : exception;
```

10
```
   Default_Currency    : constant String    := "$";
   Default_Fill        : constant Character := '*';
   Default_Separator   : constant Character := ',';
   Default_Radix_Mark  : constant Character := '.';
```

11
```
   generic
      type Num is delta <> digits <>;
      Default_Currency   : in String    := Text_IO.Editing.Default_Currency;
      Default_Fill       : in Character := Text_IO.Editing.Default_Fill;
      Default_Separator  : in Character :=
                              Text_IO.Editing.Default_Separator;
      Default_Radix_Mark : in Character :=
                              Text_IO.Editing.Default_Radix_Mark;
   package Decimal_Output is
      function Length (Pic      : in Picture;
                       Currency : in String := Default_Currency)
         return Natural;
```

12
```
      function Valid (Item     : in Num;
                      Pic      : in Picture;
                      Currency : in String := Default_Currency)
         return Boolean;
```

13
```
      function Image (Item      : in Num;
                      Pic       : in Picture;
                      Currency  : in String    := Default_Currency;
                      Fill      : in Character := Default_Fill;
                      Separator : in Character := Default_Separator;
                      Radix_Mark : in Character := Default_Radix_Mark)
         return String;
```

14
```
      procedure Put (File      : in File_Type;
                     Item      : in Num;
                     Pic       : in Picture;
                     Currency  : in String    := Default_Currency;
                     Fill      : in Character := Default_Fill;
                     Separator : in Character := Default_Separator;
                     Radix_Mark : in Character := Default_Radix_Mark);
```

15
```
      procedure Put (Item      : in Num;
                     Pic       : in Picture;
                     Currency  : in String    := Default_Currency;
                     Fill      : in Character := Default_Fill;
                     Separator : in Character := Default_Separator;
                     Radix_Mark : in Character := Default_Radix_Mark);
```

16
```
      procedure Put (To        : out String;
                     Item      : in Num;
                     Pic       : in Picture;
                     Currency  : in String    := Default_Currency;
                     Fill      : in Character := Default_Fill;
                     Separator : in Character := Default_Separator;
                     Radix_Mark : in Character := Default_Radix_Mark);
   end Decimal_Output;
private
   ... -- not specified by the language
end Ada.Text_IO.Editing;
```

17 The exception Constraint_Error is raised if the Image function or any of the Put procedures is invoked with a null string for Currency.

```
function Valid (Pic_String      : in String;
                Blank_When_Zero : in Boolean := False) return Boolean;
```
18

Valid returns True if Pic_String is a well-formed picture String (see F.3.1) the length of whose expansion does not exceed Max_Picture_Length, and if either Blank_When_Zero is False or Pic_String contains no '*'.
19

```
function To_Picture (Pic_String      : in String;
                     Blank_When_Zero : in Boolean := False)
   return Picture;
```
20

To_Picture returns a result Picture such that the application of the function Pic_String to this result yields an expanded picture String equivalent to Pic_String, and such that Blank_When_Zero applied to the result Picture is the same value as the parameter Blank_When_Zero. Picture_Error is raised if not Valid(Pic_String, Blank_When_Zero).
21

```
function Pic_String      (Pic : in Picture) return String;
```
22

```
function Blank_When_Zero (Pic : in Picture) return Boolean;
```

If Pic is To_Picture(String_Item, Boolean_Item) for some String_Item and Boolean_Item, then:
23

- Pic_String(Pic) returns an expanded picture String equivalent to String_Item and with any lower-case letter replaced with its corresponding upper-case form, and
24

- Blank_When_Zero(Pic) returns Boolean_Item.
25

If Pic_1 and Pic_2 are objects of type Picture, then "="(Pic_1, Pic_2) is True when
26

- Pic_String(Pic_1) = Pic_String(Pic_2), and
27

- Blank_When_Zero(Pic_1) = Blank_When_Zero(Pic_2).
28

```
function Length (Pic      : in Picture;
                 Currency : in String := Default_Currency)
   return Natural;
```
29

Length returns Pic_String(Pic)'Length + Currency_Length_Adjustment - Radix_Adjustment where
30

- Currency_Length_Adjustment =
31

  - Currency'Length – 1 if there is some occurrence of '$' in Pic_String(Pic), and
32

  - 0 otherwise.
33

- Radix_Adjustment =
34

  - 1 if there is an occurrence of 'V' or 'v' in Pic_Str(Pic), and
35

  - 0 otherwise.
36

```
function Valid (Item     : in Num;
                Pic      : in Picture;
                Currency : in String := Default_Currency)
   return Boolean;
```
37

Valid returns True if Image(Item, Pic, Currency) does not raise Layout_Error, and returns False otherwise.
38

The Package Text_IO.Editing   **F.3.3**

39
```
function Image (Item       : in Num;
                Pic        : in Picture;
                Currency   : in String    := Default_Currency;
                Fill       : in Character := Default_Fill;
                Separator  : in Character := Default_Separator;
                Radix_Mark : in Character := Default_Radix_Mark)
       return String;
```

40   Image returns the edited output String as defined in F.3.2 for Item, Pic_String(Pic), Blank_When_Zero(Pic), Currency, Fill, Separator, and Radix_Mark. If these rules identify a layout error, then Image raises the exception Layout_Error.

41
```
procedure Put (File       : in File_Type;
               Item       : in Num;
               Pic        : in Picture;
               Currency   : in String    := Default_Currency;
               Fill       : in Character := Default_Fill;
               Separator  : in Character := Default_Separator;
               Radix_Mark : in Character := Default_Radix_Mark);

procedure Put (Item       : in Num;
               Pic        : in Picture;
               Currency   : in String    := Default_Currency;
               Fill       : in Character := Default_Fill;
               Separator  : in Character := Default_Separator;
               Radix_Mark : in Character := Default_Radix_Mark);
```

42   Each of these Put procedures outputs Image(Item, Pic, Currency, Fill, Separator, Radix_Mark) consistent with the conventions for Put for other real types in case of bounded line length (see A.10.6, "Get and Put Procedures").

43
```
procedure Put (To         : out String;
               Item       : in Num;
               Pic        : in Picture;
               Currency   : in String    := Default_Currency;
               Fill       : in Character := Default_Fill;
               Separator  : in Character := Default_Separator;
               Radix_Mark : in Character := Default_Radix_Mark);
```

44   Put copies Image(Item, Pic, Currency, Fill, Separator, Radix_Mark) to the given string, right justified. Otherwise unassigned Character values in To are assigned the space character. If To'Length is less than the length of the string resulting from Image, then Layout_Error is raised.

Implementation Requirements

45   Max_Picture_Length shall be at least 30. The implementation shall support currency strings of length up to at least 10, both for Default_Currency in an instantiation of Decimal_Output, and for Currency in an invocation of Image or any of the Put procedures.

NOTES

46   4 The rules for edited output are based on COBOL (ANSI X3.23:1985, endorsed by ISO as ISO 1989-1985), with the following differences:

47   • The COBOL provisions for picture string localization and for 'P' format are absent from Ada.

48   • The following Ada facilities are not in COBOL:

49   • currency symbol placement after the number,

50   • localization of edited output string for multi-character currency string values, including support for both length-preserving and length-expanding currency symbols in picture strings

51   • localization of the radix mark, digits separator, and fill character, and

52   • parenthesization of negative values.

52.1   The value of 30 for Max_Picture_Length is the same limit as in COBOL.

F.3.4 The Package Wide_Text_IO.Editing

Static Semantics

The child package Wide_Text_IO.Editing has the same contents as Text_IO.Editing, except that: 1

- each occurrence of Character is replaced by Wide_Character,   2

- each occurrence of Text_IO is replaced by Wide_Text_IO,   3

- the subtype of Default_Currency is Wide_String rather than String, and   4

- each occurrence of String in the generic package Decimal_Output is replaced by Wide_String.   5

NOTES
5 Each of the functions Wide_Text_IO.Editing.Valid, To_Picture, and Pic_String has String (versus Wide_String) as its   6
parameter or result subtype, since a picture String is not localizable.

Annex G
(normative)
Numerics

The Numerics Annex specifies   1

- features for complex arithmetic, including complex I/O;   2

- a mode ("strict mode"), in which the predefined arithmetic operations of floating point and   3
  fixed point types and the functions and operations of various predefined packages have to
  provide guaranteed accuracy or conform to other numeric performance requirements, which the
  Numerics Annex also specifies;

- a mode ("relaxed mode"), in which no accuracy or other numeric performance requirements   4
  need be satisfied, as for implementations not conforming to the Numerics Annex;

- models of floating point and fixed point arithmetic on which the accuracy requirements of strict 5
  mode are based; and

- the definitions of the model-oriented attributes of floating point types that apply in the strict 6
  mode.

Implementation Advice

If Fortran (respectively, C) is widely supported in the target environment, implementations supporting the   7
Numerics Annex should provide the child package Interfaces.Fortran (respectively, Interfaces.C) specified
in Annex B and should support a *convention*_identifier of Fortran (respectively, C) in the interfacing
pragmas (see Annex B), thus allowing Ada programs to interface with programs written in that language.

G.1 Complex Arithmetic

Types and arithmetic operations for complex arithmetic are provided in Generic_Complex_Types, which is   1
defined in G.1.1. Implementation-defined approximations to the complex analogs of the mathematical
functions known as the "elementary functions" are provided by the subprograms in Generic_Complex_-
Elementary_Functions, which is defined in G.1.2. Both of these library units are generic children of the
predefined package Numerics (see A.5). Nongeneric equivalents of these generic packages for each of the
predefined floating point types are also provided as children of Numerics.

G.1.1 Complex Types

Static Semantics

The generic library package Numerics.Generic_Complex_Types has the following declaration: 1

```
generic                                                                                          2/1
   type Real is digits <>;
package Ada.Numerics.Generic_Complex_Types is
   pragma Pure(Generic_Complex_Types);

   type Complex is                                                                                3
      record
         Re, Im : Real'Base;
      end record;

   type Imaginary is private;                                                                     4
```

S. Tucker Taft et al. (Eds.): Consolidated Ada Reference Manual, LNCS 2219, pp. 437–457, 2001.

5
```
    i : constant Imaginary;
    j : constant Imaginary;
```

6
```
    function Re (X : Complex)    return Real'Base;
    function Im (X : Complex)    return Real'Base;
    function Im (X : Imaginary) return Real'Base;
```

7
```
    procedure Set_Re (X  : in out Complex;
                      Re : in     Real'Base);
    procedure Set_Im (X  : in out Complex;
                      Im : in     Real'Base);
    procedure Set_Im (X  :    out Imaginary;
                      Im : in     Real'Base);
```

8
```
    function Compose_From_Cartesian (Re, Im : Real'Base) return Complex;
    function Compose_From_Cartesian (Re     : Real'Base) return Complex;
    function Compose_From_Cartesian (Im     : Imaginary) return Complex;
```

9
```
    function Modulus (X     : Complex) return Real'Base;
    function "abs"   (Right : Complex) return Real'Base renames Modulus;
```

10
```
    function Argument (X     : Complex)          return Real'Base;
    function Argument (X     : Complex;
                       Cycle : Real'Base) return Real'Base;
```

11
```
    function Compose_From_Polar (Modulus, Argument        : Real'Base)
        return Complex;
    function Compose_From_Polar (Modulus, Argument, Cycle : Real'Base)
        return Complex;
```

12
```
    function "+"       (Right : Complex) return Complex;
    function "-"       (Right : Complex) return Complex;
    function Conjugate (X     : Complex) return Complex;
```

13
```
    function "+" (Left, Right : Complex) return Complex;
    function "-" (Left, Right : Complex) return Complex;
    function "*" (Left, Right : Complex) return Complex;
    function "/" (Left, Right : Complex) return Complex;
```

14
```
    function "**" (Left : Complex; Right : Integer) return Complex;
```

15
```
    function "+"       (Right : Imaginary) return Imaginary;
    function "-"       (Right : Imaginary) return Imaginary;
    function Conjugate (X     : Imaginary) return Imaginary renames "-";
    function "abs"     (Right : Imaginary) return Real'Base;
```

16
```
    function "+" (Left, Right : Imaginary) return Imaginary;
    function "-" (Left, Right : Imaginary) return Imaginary;
    function "*" (Left, Right : Imaginary) return Real'Base;
    function "/" (Left, Right : Imaginary) return Real'Base;
```

17
```
    function "**" (Left : Imaginary; Right : Integer) return Complex;
```

18
```
    function "<"  (Left, Right : Imaginary) return Boolean;
    function "<=" (Left, Right : Imaginary) return Boolean;
    function ">"  (Left, Right : Imaginary) return Boolean;
    function ">=" (Left, Right : Imaginary) return Boolean;
```

19
```
    function "+" (Left : Complex;   Right : Real'Base) return Complex;
    function "+" (Left : Real'Base; Right : Complex)   return Complex;
    function "-" (Left : Complex;   Right : Real'Base) return Complex;
    function "-" (Left : Real'Base; Right : Complex)   return Complex;
    function "*" (Left : Complex;   Right : Real'Base) return Complex;
    function "*" (Left : Real'Base; Right : Complex)   return Complex;
    function "/" (Left : Complex;   Right : Real'Base) return Complex;
    function "/" (Left : Real'Base; Right : Complex)   return Complex;
```

```
function "+" (Left : Complex;   Right : Imaginary) return Complex;      20
function "+" (Left : Imaginary; Right : Complex)   return Complex;
function "-" (Left : Complex;   Right : Imaginary) return Complex;
function "-" (Left : Imaginary; Right : Complex)   return Complex;
function "*" (Left : Complex;   Right : Imaginary) return Complex;
function "*" (Left : Imaginary; Right : Complex)   return Complex;
function "/" (Left : Complex;   Right : Imaginary) return Complex;
function "/" (Left : Imaginary; Right : Complex)   return Complex;

function "+" (Left : Imaginary; Right : Real'Base) return Complex;      21
function "+" (Left : Real'Base; Right : Imaginary) return Complex;
function "-" (Left : Imaginary; Right : Real'Base) return Complex;
function "-" (Left : Real'Base; Right : Imaginary) return Complex;
function "*" (Left : Imaginary; Right : Real'Base) return Imaginary;
function "*" (Left : Real'Base; Right : Imaginary) return Imaginary;
function "/" (Left : Imaginary; Right : Real'Base) return Imaginary;
function "/" (Left : Real'Base; Right : Imaginary) return Imaginary;

private                                                                 22

  type Imaginary is new Real'Base;                                      23
  i : constant Imaginary := 1.0;
  j : constant Imaginary := 1.0;

end Ada.Numerics.Generic_Complex_Types;                                24
```

The library package Numerics.Complex_Types is declared pure and defines the same types, constants, and subprograms as Numerics.Generic_Complex_Types, except that the predefined type Float is systematically substituted for Real'Base throughout. Nongeneric equivalents of Numerics.Generic_Complex_Types for each of the other predefined floating point types are defined similarly, with the names Numerics.Short_-Complex_Types, Numerics.Long_Complex_Types, etc.   25/1

Complex is a visible type with cartesian components.   26

Imaginary is a private type; its full type is derived from Real'Base.   27

The arithmetic operations and the Re, Im, Modulus, Argument, and Conjugate functions have their usual mathematical meanings. When applied to a parameter of pure-imaginary type, the ''imaginary-part'' function Im yields the value of its parameter, as the corresponding real value. The remaining subprograms have the following meanings: 28

- The Set_Re and Set_Im procedures replace the designated component of a complex parameter with the given real value; applied to a parameter of pure-imaginary type, the Set_Im procedure replaces the value of that parameter with the imaginary value corresponding to the given real value.   29

- The Compose_From_Cartesian function constructs a complex value from the given real and imaginary components. If only one component is given, the other component is implicitly zero.   30

- The Compose_From_Polar function constructs a complex value from the given modulus (radius) and argument (angle). When the value of the parameter Modulus is positive (resp., negative), the result is the complex value represented by the point in the complex plane lying at a distance from the origin given by the absolute value of Modulus and forming an angle measured counterclockwise from the positive (resp., negative) real axis given by the value of the parameter Argument.   31

When the Cycle parameter is specified, the result of the Argument function and the parameter Argument of the Compose_From_Polar function are measured in units such that a full cycle of revolution has the given value; otherwise, they are measured in radians.   32

The computed results of the mathematically multivalued functions are rendered single-valued by the following conventions, which are meant to imply the principal branch: 33

Complex Types   **G.1.1**

34   •   The result of the Modulus function is nonnegative.

35   •   The result of the Argument function is in the quadrant containing the point in the complex plane represented by the parameter X. This may be any quadrant (I through IV); thus, the range of the Argument function is approximately -π to π (-Cycle/2.0 to Cycle/2.0, if the parameter Cycle is specified). When the point represented by the parameter X lies on the negative real axis, the result approximates

36   •   π (resp., -π) when the sign of the imaginary component of X is positive (resp., negative), if Real'Signed_Zeros is True;

37   •   π, if Real'Signed_Zeros is False.

38   •   Because a result lying on or near one of the axes may not be exactly representable, the approximation inherent in computing the result may place it in an adjacent quadrant, close to but on the wrong side of the axis.

Dynamic Semantics

39   The exception Numerics.Argument_Error is raised by the Argument and Compose_From_Polar functions with specified cycle, signaling a parameter value outside the domain of the corresponding mathematical function, when the value of the parameter Cycle is zero or negative.

40   The exception Constraint_Error is raised by the division operator when the value of the right operand is zero, and by the exponentiation operator when the value of the left operand is zero and the value of the exponent is negative, provided that Real'Machine_Overflows is True; when Real'Machine_Overflows is False, the result is unspecified. Constraint_Error can also be raised when a finite result overflows (see G.2.6).

Implementation Requirements

41   In the implementation of Numerics.Generic_Complex_Types, the range of intermediate values allowed during the calculation of a final result shall not be affected by any range constraint of the subtype Real.

42   In the following cases, evaluation of a complex arithmetic operation shall yield the *prescribed result*, provided that the preceding rules do not call for an exception to be raised:

43   •   The results of the Re, Im, and Compose_From_Cartesian functions are exact.

44   •   The real (resp., imaginary) component of the result of a binary addition operator that yields a result of complex type is exact when either of its operands is of pure-imaginary (resp., real) type.

45   •   The real (resp., imaginary) component of the result of a binary subtraction operator that yields a result of complex type is exact when its right operand is of pure-imaginary (resp., real) type.

46   •   The real component of the result of the Conjugate function for the complex type is exact.

47   •   When the point in the complex plane represented by the parameter X lies on the nonnegative real axis, the Argument function yields a result of zero.

48   •   When the value of the parameter Modulus is zero, the Compose_From_Polar function yields a result of zero.

49   •   When the value of the parameter Argument is equal to a multiple of the quarter cycle, the result of the Compose_From_Polar function with specified cycle lies on one of the axes. In this case, one of its components is zero, and the other has the magnitude of the parameter Modulus.

50   •   Exponentiation by a zero exponent yields the value one. Exponentiation by a unit exponent yields the value of the left operand. Exponentiation of the value one yields the value one. Exponentiation of the value zero yields the value zero, provided that the exponent is nonzero.

When the left operand is of pure-imaginary type, one component of the result of the exponentiation operator is zero.

When the result, or a result component, of any operator of Numerics.Generic_Complex_Types has a mathematical definition in terms of a single arithmetic or relational operation, that result or result component exhibits the accuracy of the corresponding operation of the type Real.   51

Other accuracy requirements for the Modulus, Argument, and Compose_From_Polar functions, and accuracy requirements for the multiplication of a pair of complex operands or for division by a complex operand, all of which apply only in the strict mode, are given in G.2.6.   52

The sign of a zero result or zero result component yielded by a complex arithmetic operation or function is implementation defined when Real'Signed_Zeros is True.   53

Implementation Permissions

The nongeneric equivalent packages may, but need not, be actual instantiations of the generic package for the appropriate predefined type.   54

Implementations may obtain the result of exponentiation of a complex or pure-imaginary operand by repeated complex multiplication, with arbitrary association of the factors and with a possible final complex reciprocation (when the exponent is negative). Implementations are also permitted to obtain the result of exponentiation of a complex operand, but not of a pure-imaginary operand, by converting the left operand to a polar representation; exponentiating the modulus by the given exponent; multiplying the argument by the given exponent; and reconverting to a cartesian representation. Because of this implementation freedom, no accuracy requirement is imposed on complex exponentiation (except for the prescribed results given above, which apply regardless of the implementation method chosen).   55/1

Implementation Advice

Because the usual mathematical meaning of multiplication of a complex operand and a real operand is that of the scaling of both components of the former by the latter, an implementation should not perform this operation by first promoting the real operand to complex type and then performing a full complex multiplication. In systems that, in the future, support an Ada binding to IEC 559:1989, the latter technique will not generate the required result when one of the components of the complex operand is infinite. (Explicit multiplication of the infinite component by the zero component obtained during promotion yields a NaN that propagates into the final result.) Analogous advice applies in the case of multiplication of a complex operand and a pure-imaginary operand, and in the case of division of a complex operand by a real or pure-imaginary operand.   56

Likewise, because the usual mathematical meaning of addition of a complex operand and a real operand is that the imaginary operand remains unchanged, an implementation should not perform this operation by first promoting the real operand to complex type and then performing a full complex addition. In implementations in which the Signed_Zeros attribute of the component type is True (and which therefore conform to IEC 559:1989 in regard to the handling of the sign of zero in predefined arithmetic operations), the latter technique will not generate the required result when the imaginary component of the complex operand is a negatively signed zero. (Explicit addition of the negative zero to the zero obtained during promotion yields a positive zero.) Analogous advice applies in the case of addition of a complex operand and a pure-imaginary operand, and in the case of subtraction of a complex operand and a real or pure-imaginary operand.   57

Implementations in which Real'Signed_Zeros is True should attempt to provide a rational treatment of the signs of zero results and result components. As one example, the result of the Argument function should   58

Complex Types   **G.1.1**

have the sign of the imaginary component of the parameter X when the point represented by that parameter lies on the positive real axis; as another, the sign of the imaginary component of the Compose_From_Polar function should be the same as (resp., the opposite of) that of the Argument parameter when that parameter has a value of zero and the Modulus parameter has a nonnegative (resp., negative) value.

G.1.2 Complex Elementary Functions

Static Semantics

1   The generic library package Numerics.Generic_Complex_Elementary_Functions has the following declaration:

2
```
with Ada.Numerics.Generic_Complex_Types;
generic
   with package Complex_Types is
      new Ada.Numerics.Generic_Complex_Types (<>);
   use Complex_Types;
package Ada.Numerics.Generic_Complex_Elementary_Functions is
   pragma Pure(Generic_Complex_Elementary_Functions);
```

3
```
   function Sqrt (X : Complex)    return Complex;
   function Log  (X : Complex)    return Complex;
   function Exp  (X : Complex)    return Complex;
   function Exp  (X : Imaginary) return Complex;
   function "**" (Left : Complex;    Right : Complex)    return Complex;
   function "**" (Left : Complex;    Right : Real'Base) return Complex;
   function "**" (Left : Real'Base; Right : Complex)    return Complex;
```

4
```
   function Sin (X : Complex) return Complex;
   function Cos (X : Complex) return Complex;
   function Tan (X : Complex) return Complex;
   function Cot (X : Complex) return Complex;
```

5
```
   function Arcsin (X : Complex) return Complex;
   function Arccos (X : Complex) return Complex;
   function Arctan (X : Complex) return Complex;
   function Arccot (X : Complex) return Complex;
```

6
```
   function Sinh (X : Complex) return Complex;
   function Cosh (X : Complex) return Complex;
   function Tanh (X : Complex) return Complex;
   function Coth (X : Complex) return Complex;
```

7
```
   function Arcsinh (X : Complex) return Complex;
   function Arccosh (X : Complex) return Complex;
   function Arctanh (X : Complex) return Complex;
   function Arccoth (X : Complex) return Complex;
```

8
```
end Ada.Numerics.Generic_Complex_Elementary_Functions;
```

9/1   The library package Numerics.Complex_Elementary_Functions is declared pure and defines the same subprograms as Numerics.Generic_Complex_Elementary_Functions, except that the predefined type Float is systematically substituted for Real'Base, and the Complex and Imaginary types exported by Numerics.-Complex_Types are systematically substituted for Complex and Imaginary, throughout. Nongeneric equivalents of Numerics.Generic_Complex_Elementary_Functions corresponding to each of the other predefined floating point types are defined similarly, with the names Numerics.Short_Complex_-Elementary_Functions, Numerics.Long_Complex_Elementary_Functions, etc.

10   The overloading of the Exp function for the pure-imaginary type is provided to give the user an alternate way to compose a complex value from a given modulus and argument. In addition to Compose_From_-Polar(Rho, Theta) (see G.1.1), the programmer may write Rho * Exp(i * Theta).

The imaginary (resp., real) component of the parameter X of the forward hyperbolic (resp., trigonometric) functions and of the Exp function (and the parameter X, itself, in the case of the overloading of the Exp function for the pure-imaginary type) represents an angle measured in radians, as does the imaginary (resp., real) component of the result of the Log and inverse hyperbolic (resp., trigonometric) functions.   11

The functions have their usual mathematical meanings. However, the arbitrariness inherent in the placement of branch cuts, across which some of the complex elementary functions exhibit discontinuities, is eliminated by the following conventions: 12

- The imaginary component of the result of the Sqrt and Log functions is discontinuous as the parameter X crosses the negative real axis.   13

- The result of the exponentiation operator when the left operand is of complex type is discontinuous as that operand crosses the negative real axis.   14

- The real (resp., imaginary) component of the result of the Arcsin and Arccos (resp., Arctanh) functions is discontinuous as the parameter X crosses the real axis to the left of -1.0 or the right of 1.0.   15

- The real (resp., imaginary) component of the result of the Arctan (resp., Arcsinh) function is discontinuous as the parameter X crosses the imaginary axis below $-i$ or above i.   16

- The real component of the result of the Arccot function is discontinuous as the parameter X crosses the imaginary axis between $-i$ and i.   17

- The imaginary component of the Arccosh function is discontinuous as the parameter X crosses the real axis to the left of 1.0.   18

- The imaginary component of the result of the Arccoth function is discontinuous as the parameter X crosses the real axis between -1.0 and 1.0.   19

The computed results of the mathematically multivalued functions are rendered single-valued by the following conventions, which are meant to imply the principal branch: 20

- The real component of the result of the Sqrt and Arccosh functions is nonnegative.   21

- The same convention applies to the imaginary component of the result of the Log function as applies to the result of the natural-cycle version of the Argument function of Numerics.Generic_Complex_Types (see G.1.1).   22

- The range of the real (resp., imaginary) component of the result of the Arcsin and Arctan (resp., Arcsinh and Arctanh) functions is approximately $-\pi/2.0$ to $\pi/2.0$.   23

- The real (resp., imaginary) component of the result of the Arccos and Arccot (resp., Arccoth) functions ranges from 0.0 to approximately π.   24

- The range of the imaginary component of the result of the Arccosh function is approximately $-\pi$ to π.   25

In addition, the exponentiation operator inherits the single-valuedness of the Log function.   26

Dynamic Semantics

The exception Numerics.Argument_Error is raised by the exponentiation operator, signaling a parameter value outside the domain of the corresponding mathematical function, when the value of the left operand is zero and the real component of the exponent (or the exponent itself, when it is of real type) is zero.   27

The exception Constraint_Error is raised, signaling a pole of the mathematical function (analogous to dividing by zero), in the following cases, provided that Complex_Types.Real'Machine_Overflows is True: 28

- by the Log, Cot, and Coth functions, when the value of the parameter X is zero;   29

Complex Elementary Functions   **G.1.2**

30   • by the exponentiation operator, when the value of the left operand is zero and the real component of the exponent (or the exponent itself, when it is of real type) is negative;

31   • by the Arctan and Arccot functions, when the value of the parameter X is ± *i*;

32   • by the Arctanh and Arccoth functions, when the value of the parameter X is ± 1.0.

33   Constraint_Error can also be raised when a finite result overflows (see G.2.6); this may occur for parameter values sufficiently *near* poles, and, in the case of some of the functions, for parameter values having components of sufficiently large magnitude. When Complex_Types.Real'Machine_Overflows is False, the result at poles is unspecified.

Implementation Requirements

34   In the implementation of Numerics.Generic_Complex_Elementary_Functions, the range of intermediate values allowed during the calculation of a final result shall not be affected by any range constraint of the subtype Complex_Types.Real.

35   In the following cases, evaluation of a complex elementary function shall yield the *prescribed result* (or a result having the prescribed component), provided that the preceding rules do not call for an exception to be raised:

36   • When the parameter X has the value zero, the Sqrt, Sin, Arcsin, Tan, Arctan, Sinh, Arcsinh, Tanh, and Arctanh functions yield a result of zero; the Exp, Cos, and Cosh functions yield a result of one; the Arccos and Arccot functions yield a real result; and the Arccoth function yields an imaginary result.

37   • When the parameter X has the value one, the Sqrt function yields a result of one; the Log, Arccos, and Arccosh functions yield a result of zero; and the Arcsin function yields a real result.

38   • When the parameter X has the value -1.0, the Sqrt function yields the result

39   • *i* (resp., -*i*), when the sign of the imaginary component of X is positive (resp., negative), if Complex_Types.Real'Signed_Zeros is True;

40   • *i*, if Complex_Types.Real'Signed_Zeros is False;

41   • the Log function yields an imaginary result; and the Arcsin and Arccos functions yield a real result.

42   • When the parameter X has the value ± *i*, the Log function yields an imaginary result.

43   • Exponentiation by a zero exponent yields the value one. Exponentiation by a unit exponent yields the value of the left operand (as a complex value). Exponentiation of the value one yields the value one. Exponentiation of the value zero yields the value zero.

44   Other accuracy requirements for the complex elementary functions, which apply only in the strict mode, are given in G.2.6.

45   The sign of a zero result or zero result component yielded by a complex elementary function is implementation defined when Complex_Types.Real'Signed_Zeros is True.

Implementation Permissions

46   The nongeneric equivalent packages may, but need not, be actual instantiations of the generic package with the appropriate predefined nongeneric equivalent of Numerics.Generic_Complex_Types; if they are, then the latter shall have been obtained by actual instantiation of Numerics.Generic_Complex_Types.

The exponentiation operator may be implemented in terms of the Exp and Log functions. Because this implementation yields poor accuracy in some parts of the domain, no accuracy requirement is imposed on complex exponentiation.   47

The implementation of the Exp function of a complex parameter X is allowed to raise the exception Constraint_Error, signaling overflow, when the real component of X exceeds an unspecified threshold that is approximately log(Complex_Types.Real'Safe_Last). This permission recognizes the impracticality of avoiding overflow in the marginal case that the exponential of the real component of X exceeds the safe range of Complex_Types.Real but both components of the final result do not. Similarly, the Sin and Cos (resp., Sinh and Cosh) functions are allowed to raise the exception Constraint_Error, signaling overflow, when the absolute value of the imaginary (resp., real) component of the parameter X exceeds an unspecified threshold that is approximately log(Complex_Types.Real'Safe_Last) + log(2.0). This permission recognizes the impracticality of avoiding overflow in the marginal case that the hyperbolic sine or cosine of the imaginary (resp., real) component of X exceeds the safe range of Complex_Types.Real but both components of the final result do not.   48

Implementation Advice

Implementations in which Complex_Types.Real'Signed_Zeros is True should attempt to provide a rational treatment of the signs of zero results and result components. For example, many of the complex elementary functions have components that are odd functions of one of the parameter components; in these cases, the result component should have the sign of the parameter component at the origin. Other complex elementary functions have zero components whose sign is opposite that of a parameter component at the origin, or is always positive or always negative.   49

G.1.3 Complex Input-Output

The generic package Text_IO.Complex_IO defines procedures for the formatted input and output of complex values. The generic actual parameter in an instantiation of Text_IO.Complex_IO is an instance of Numerics.Generic_Complex_Types for some floating point subtype. Exceptional conditions are reported by raising the appropriate exception defined in Text_IO.   1

Static Semantics

The generic library package Text_IO.Complex_IO has the following declaration: 2

```
with Ada.Numerics.Generic_Complex_Types;                              3
generic
   with package Complex_Types is
         new Ada.Numerics.Generic_Complex_Types (<>);
package Ada.Text_IO.Complex_IO is

   use Complex_Types;                                                 4

   Default_Fore : Field := 2;                                        5
   Default_Aft  : Field := Real'Digits - 1;
   Default_Exp  : Field := 3;

   procedure Get (File  : in  File_Type;                             6
                  Item  : out Complex;
                  Width : in  Field := 0);
   procedure Get (Item  : out Complex;
                  Width : in  Field := 0);
```

```
7              procedure Put (File : in File_Type;
                              Item : in Complex;
                              Fore : in Field := Default_Fore;
                              Aft  : in Field := Default_Aft;
                              Exp  : in Field := Default_Exp);
               procedure Put (Item : in Complex;
                              Fore : in Field := Default_Fore;
                              Aft  : in Field := Default_Aft;
                              Exp  : in Field := Default_Exp);

8              procedure Get (From : in  String;
                              Item : out Complex;
                              Last : out Positive);
               procedure Put (To   : out String;
                              Item : in  Complex;
                              Aft  : in  Field := Default_Aft;
                              Exp  : in  Field := Default_Exp);

9        end Ada.Text_IO.Complex_IO;
```

10   The semantics of the Get and Put procedures are as follows:

```
11       procedure Get (File  : in  File_Type;
                        Item  : out Complex;
                        Width : in  Field := 0);
         procedure Get (Item  : out Complex;
                        Width : in  Field := 0);
```

12/1   The input sequence is a pair of optionally signed real literals representing the real and imaginary components of a complex value These components have the format defined for the corresponding Get procedure of an instance of Text_IO.Float_IO (see A.10.9) for the base subtype of Complex_Types.Real. The pair of components may be separated by a comma or surrounded by a pair of parentheses or both. Blanks are freely allowed before each of the components and before the parentheses and comma, if either is used. If the value of the parameter Width is zero, then

13   • line and page terminators are also allowed in these places;

14   • the components shall be separated by at least one blank or line terminator if the comma is omitted; and

15   • reading stops when the right parenthesis has been read, if the input sequence includes a left parenthesis, or when the imaginary component has been read, otherwise.

15.1   If a nonzero value of Width is supplied, then

16   • the components shall be separated by at least one blank if the comma is omitted; and

17   • exactly Width characters are read, or the characters (possibly none) up to a line terminator, whichever comes first (blanks are included in the count).

18   Returns, in the parameter Item, the value of type Complex that corresponds to the input sequence.

19   The exception Text_IO.Data_Error is raised if the input sequence does not have the required syntax or if the components of the complex value obtained are not of the base subtype of Complex_Types.Real.

```
procedure Put (File : in File_Type;                                    20
               Item : in Complex;
               Fore : in Field := Default_Fore;
               Aft  : in Field := Default_Aft;
               Exp  : in Field := Default_Exp);
procedure Put (Item : in Complex;
               Fore : in Field := Default_Fore;
               Aft  : in Field := Default_Aft;
               Exp  : in Field := Default_Exp);
```

Outputs the value of the parameter Item as a pair of decimal literals representing the real and   21
imaginary components of the complex value, using the syntax of an aggregate. More specifically,

- outputs a left parenthesis;   22

- outputs the value of the real component of the parameter Item with the format defined   23
  by the corresponding Put procedure of an instance of Text_IO.Float_IO for the base
  subtype of Complex_Types.Real, using the given values of Fore, Aft, and Exp;

- outputs a comma;   24

- outputs the value of the imaginary component of the parameter Item with the format   25
  defined by the corresponding Put procedure of an instance of Text_IO.Float_IO for the
  base subtype of Complex_Types.Real, using the given values of Fore, Aft, and Exp;

- outputs a right parenthesis.   26

```
procedure Get (From : in  String;                                      27
               Item : out Complex;
               Last : out Positive);
```

Reads a complex value from the beginning of the given string, following the same rule as the Get   28
procedure that reads a complex value from a file, but treating the end of the string as a line
terminator. Returns, in the parameter Item, the value of type Complex that corresponds to the
input sequence. Returns in Last the index value such that From(Last) is the last character read.

The exception Text_IO.Data_Error is raised if the input sequence does not have the required   29
syntax or if the components of the complex value obtained are not of the base subtype of
Complex_Types.Real.

```
procedure Put (To   : out String;                                      30
               Item : in  Complex;
               Aft  : in  Field := Default_Aft;
               Exp  : in  Field := Default_Exp);
```

Outputs the value of the parameter Item to the given string as a pair of decimal literals   31
representing the real and imaginary components of the complex value, using the syntax of an
aggregate. More specifically,

- a left parenthesis, the real component, and a comma are left justified in the given   32
  string, with the real component having the format defined by the Put procedure (for
  output to a file) of an instance of Text_IO.Float_IO for the base subtype of
  Complex_Types.Real, using a value of zero for Fore and the given values of Aft and
  Exp;

- the imaginary component and a right parenthesis are right justified in the given string,   33
  with the imaginary component having the format defined by the Put procedure (for
  output to a file) of an instance of Text_IO.Float_IO for the base subtype of
  Complex_Types.Real, using a value for Fore that completely fills the remainder of the
  string, together with the given values of Aft and Exp.

34   The exception Text_IO.Layout_Error is raised if the given string is too short to hold the formatted output.

Implementation Permissions

35   Other exceptions declared (by renaming) in Text_IO may be raised by the preceding procedures in the appropriate circumstances, as for the corresponding procedures of Text_IO.Float_IO.

G.1.4 The Package Wide_Text_IO.Complex_IO

Static Semantics

1   Implementations shall also provide the generic library package Wide_Text_IO.Complex_IO. Its declaration is obtained from that of Text_IO.Complex_IO by systematically replacing Text_IO by Wide_Text_IO and String by Wide_String; the description of its behavior is obtained by additionally replacing references to particular characters (commas, parentheses, etc.) by those for the corresponding wide characters.

G.2 Numeric Performance Requirements

Implementation Requirements

1   Implementations shall provide a user-selectable mode in which the accuracy and other numeric performance requirements detailed in the following subclauses are observed. This mode, referred to as the *strict mode*, may or may not be the default mode; it directly affects the results of the predefined arithmetic operations of real types and the results of the subprograms in children of the Numerics package, and indirectly affects the operations in other language defined packages. Implementations shall also provide the opposing mode, which is known as the *relaxed mode*.

Implementation Permissions

2   Either mode may be the default mode.

3   The two modes need not actually be different.

G.2.1 Model of Floating Point Arithmetic

1   In the strict mode, the predefined operations of a floating point type shall satisfy the accuracy requirements specified here and shall avoid or signal overflow in the situations described. This behavior is presented in terms of a model of floating point arithmetic that builds on the concept of the canonical form (see A.5.3).

Static Semantics

2   Associated with each floating point type is an infinite set of model numbers. The model numbers of a type are used to define the accuracy requirements that have to be satisfied by certain predefined operations of the type; through certain attributes of the model numbers, they are also used to explain the meaning of a user-declared floating point type declaration. The model numbers of a derived type are those of the parent type; the model numbers of a subtype are those of its type.

3   The *model numbers* of a floating point type T are zero and all the values expressible in the canonical form (for the type T), in which *mantissa* has T'Model_Mantissa digits and *exponent* has a value greater than or equal to T'Model_Emin. (These attributes are defined in G.2.2.)

A *model interval* of a floating point type is any interval whose bounds are model numbers of the type. The *model interval* of a type T *associated with a value v* is the smallest model interval of T that includes *v*. The model interval associated with a model number of a type consists of that number only.) 4

Implementation Requirements

The accuracy requirements for the evaluation of certain predefined operations of floating point types are as follows. 5

An *operand interval* is the model interval, of the type specified for the operand of an operation, associated with the value of the operand. 6

For any predefined arithmetic operation that yields a result of a floating point type T, the required bounds on the result are given by a model interval of T (called the *result interval*) defined in terms of the operand values as follows: 7

- The result interval is the smallest model interval of T that includes the minimum and the maximum of all the values obtained by applying the (exact) mathematical operation to values arbitrarily selected from the respective operand intervals. 8

The result interval of an exponentiation is obtained by applying the above rule to the sequence of multiplications defined by the exponent, assuming arbitrary association of the factors, and to the final division in the case of a negative exponent. 9

The result interval of a conversion of a numeric value to a floating point type T is the model interval of T associated with the operand value, except when the source expression is of a fixed point type with a *small* that is not a power of T'Machine_Radix or is a fixed point multiplication or division either of whose operands has a *small* that is not a power of T'Machine_Radix; in these cases, the result interval is implementation defined. 10

For any of the foregoing operations, the implementation shall deliver a value that belongs to the result interval when both bounds of the result interval are in the safe range of the result type T, as determined by the values of T'Safe_First and T'Safe_Last; otherwise, 11

- if T'Machine_Overflows is True, the implementation shall either deliver a value that belongs to the result interval or raise Constraint_Error; 12

- if T'Machine_Overflows is False, the result is implementation defined. 13

For any predefined relation on operands of a floating point type T, the implementation may deliver any value (i.e., either True or False) obtained by applying the (exact) mathematical comparison to values arbitrarily chosen from the respective operand intervals. 14

The result of a membership test is defined in terms of comparisons of the operand value with the lower and upper bounds of the given range or type mark (the usual rules apply to these comparisons). 15

Implementation Permissions

If the underlying floating point hardware implements division as multiplication by a reciprocal, the result interval for division (and exponentiation by a negative exponent) is implementation defined. 16

G.2.2 Model-Oriented Attributes of Floating Point Types

In implementations that support the Numerics Annex, the model-oriented attributes of floating point types shall yield the values defined here, in both the strict and the relaxed modes. These definitions add conditions to those in A.5.3. 1

Static Semantics

2   For every subtype S of a floating point type *T*:

3   S'Model_Mantissa

Yields the number of digits in the mantissa of the canonical form of the model numbers of *T* (see A.5.3). The value of this attribute shall be greater than or equal to $\lceil d \cdot \log(10) / \log(T\text{'Machine\_Radix}) \rceil + 1$, where *d* is the requested decimal precision of *T*. In addition, it shall be less than or equal to the value of *T*'Machine_Mantissa. This attribute yields a value of the type *universal_integer*.

4   S'Model_Emin

Yields the minimum exponent of the canonical form of the model numbers of *T* (see A.5.3). The value of this attribute shall be greater than or equal to the value of *T*'Machine_Emin. This attribute yields a value of the type *universal_integer*.

5   S'Safe_First

Yields the lower bound of the safe range of *T*. The value of this attribute shall be a model number of *T* and greater than or equal to the lower bound of the base range of *T*. In addition, if *T* is declared by a floating_point_definition or is derived from such a type, and the floating_point_definition includes a real_range_specification specifying a lower bound of *lb*, then the value of this attribute shall be less than or equal to *lb*; otherwise, it shall be less than or equal to $-10.0^{4 \cdot d}$, where *d* is the requested decimal precision of *T*. This attribute yields a value of the type *universal_real*.

6   S'Safe_Last

Yields the upper bound of the safe range of *T*. The value of this attribute shall be a model number of *T* and less than or equal to the upper bound of the base range of *T*. In addition, if *T* is declared by a floating_point_definition or is derived from such a type, and the floating_point_definition includes a real_range_specification specifying an upper bound of *ub*, then the value of this attribute shall be greater than or equal to *ub*; otherwise, it shall be greater than or equal to $10.0^{4 \cdot d}$, where d is the requested decimal precision of *T*. This attribute yields a value of the type *universal_real*.

7   S'Model

Denotes a function (of a parameter *X*) whose specification is given in A.5.3. If *X* is a model number of *T*, the function yields *X*; otherwise, it yields the value obtained by rounding or truncating *X* to either one of the adjacent model numbers of *T*. Constraint_Error is raised if the resulting model number is outside the safe range of S. A zero result has the sign of *X* when S'Signed_Zeros is True.

8   Subject to the constraints given above, the values of S'Model_Mantissa and S'Safe_Last are to be maximized, and the values of S'Model_Emin and S'Safe_First minimized, by the implementation as follows:

9   • First, S'Model_Mantissa is set to the largest value for which values of S'Model_Emin, S'Safe_First, and S'Safe_Last can be chosen so that the implementation satisfies the strict-mode requirements of G.2.1 in terms of the model numbers and safe range induced by these attributes.

10 • Next, S'Model_Emin is set to the smallest value for which values of S'Safe_First and S'Safe_Last can be chosen so that the implementation satisfies the strict-mode requirements of G.2.1 in terms of the model numbers and safe range induced by these attributes and the previously determined value of S'Model_Mantissa.

11 • Finally, S'Safe_First and S'Safe_last are set (in either order) to the smallest and largest values, respectively, for which the implementation satisfies the strict-mode requirements of G.2.1 in terms of the model numbers and safe range induced by these attributes and the previously determined values of S'Model_Mantissa and S'Model_Emin.

G.2.3 Model of Fixed Point Arithmetic

In the strict mode, the predefined arithmetic operations of a fixed point type shall satisfy the accuracy requirements specified here and shall avoid or signal overflow in the situations described.

Implementation Requirements

The accuracy requirements for the predefined fixed point arithmetic operations and conversions, and the results of relations on fixed point operands, are given below.

The operands of the fixed point adding operators, absolute value, and comparisons have the same type. These operations are required to yield exact results, unless they overflow.

Multiplications and divisions are allowed between operands of any two fixed point types; the result has to be (implicitly or explicitly) converted to some other numeric type. For purposes of defining the accuracy rules, the multiplication or division and the conversion are treated as a single operation whose accuracy depends on three types (those of the operands and the result). For decimal fixed point types, the attribute T'Round may be used to imply explicit conversion with rounding (see 3.5.10).

When the result type is a floating point type, the accuracy is as given in G.2.1. For some combinations of the operand and result types in the remaining cases, the result is required to belong to a small set of values called the *perfect result set*; for other combinations, it is required merely to belong to a generally larger and implementation-defined set of values called the *close result set*. When the result type is a decimal fixed point type, the perfect result set contains a single value; thus, operations on decimal types are always fully specified.

When one operand of a fixed-fixed multiplication or division is of type *universal_real*, that operand is not implicitly converted in the usual sense, since the context does not determine a unique target type, but the accuracy of the result of the multiplication or division (i.e., whether the result has to belong to the perfect result set or merely the close result set) depends on the value of the operand of type *universal_real* and on the types of the other operand and of the result.

For a fixed point multiplication or division whose (exact) mathematical result is v, and for the conversion of a value v to a fixed point type, the perfect result set and close result set are defined as follows:

- If the result type is an ordinary fixed point type with a *small* of s,
  - if v is an integer multiple of s, then the perfect result set contains only the value v;
  - otherwise, it contains the integer multiple of s just below v and the integer multiple of s just above v.

  The close result set is an implementation-defined set of consecutive integer multiples of s containing the perfect result set as a subset.

- If the result type is a decimal type with a *small* of s,
  - if v is an integer multiple of s, then the perfect result set contains only the value v;
  - otherwise, if truncation applies then it contains only the integer multiple of s in the direction toward zero, whereas if rounding applies then it contains only the nearest integer multiple of s (with ties broken by rounding away from zero).

  The close result set is an implementation-defined set of consecutive integer multiples of s containing the perfect result set as a subset.

16 • If the result type is an integer type,

17   • if v is an integer, then the perfect result set contains only the value v;

18   • otherwise, it contains the integer nearest to the value v (if v lies equally distant from two consecutive integers, the perfect result set contains the one that is further from zero).

19   The close result set is an implementation-defined set of consecutive integers containing the perfect result set as a subset.

20 The result of a fixed point multiplication or division shall belong either to the perfect result set or to the close result set, as described below, if overflow does not occur. In the following cases, if the result type is a fixed point type, let s be its *small*; otherwise, i.e. when the result type is an integer type, let s be 1.0.

21 • For a multiplication or division neither of whose operands is of type *universal_real*, let l and r be the *smalls* of the left and right operands. For a multiplication, if $(l \cdot r) / s$ is an integer or the reciprocal of an integer (the *smalls* are said to be "compatible" in this case), the result shall belong to the perfect result set; otherwise, it belongs to the close result set. For a division, if $l / (r \cdot s)$ is an integer or the reciprocal of an integer (i.e., the *smalls* are compatible), the result shall belong to the perfect result set; otherwise, it belongs to the close result set.

22 • For a multiplication or division having one *universal_real* operand with a value of v, note that it is always possible to factor v as an integer multiple of a "compatible" *small*, but the integer multiple may be "too big." If there exists a factorization in which that multiple is less than some implementation-defined limit, the result shall belong to the perfect result set; otherwise, it belongs to the close result set.

23 A multiplication P * Q of an operand of a fixed point type F by an operand of an integer type I, or vice-versa, and a division P / Q of an operand of a fixed point type F by an operand of an integer type I, are also allowed. In these cases, the result has a type of F; explicit conversion of the result is never required. The accuracy required in these cases is the same as that required for a multiplication F(P * Q) or a division F(P / Q) obtained by interpreting the operand of the integer type to have a fixed point type with a *small* of 1.0.

24 The accuracy of the result of a conversion from an integer or fixed point type to a fixed point type, or from a fixed point type to an integer type, is the same as that of a fixed point multiplication of the source value by a fixed point operand having a *small* of 1.0 and a value of 1.0, as given by the foregoing rules. The result of a conversion from a floating point type to a fixed point type shall belong to the close result set. The result of a conversion of a *universal_real* operand to a fixed point type shall belong to the perfect result set.

25 The possibility of overflow in the result of a predefined arithmetic operation or conversion yielding a result of a fixed point type T is analogous to that for floating point types, except for being related to the base range instead of the safe range. If all of the permitted results belong to the base range of T, then the implementation shall deliver one of the permitted results; otherwise,

26 • if T'Machine_Overflows is True, the implementation shall either deliver one of the permitted results or raise Constraint_Error;

27 • if T'Machine_Overflows is False, the result is implementation defined.

G.2.4 Accuracy Requirements for the Elementary Functions

In the strict mode, the performance of Numerics.Generic_Elementary_Functions shall be as specified here.   1

Implementation Requirements

When an exception is not raised, the result of evaluating a function in an instance *EF* of   2
Numerics.Generic_Elementary_Functions belongs to a *result interval*, defined as the smallest model
interval of *EF*.Float_Type that contains all the values of the form $f \cdot (1.0 + d)$, where f is the exact value of
the corresponding mathematical function at the given parameter values, d is a real number, and $|d|$ is less
than or equal to the function's *maximum relative error*. The function delivers a value that belongs to the
result interval when both of its bounds belong to the safe range of *EF*.Float_Type; otherwise,

- if *EF*.Float_Type'Machine_Overflows is True, the function either delivers a value that belongs to   3
  the result interval or raises Constraint_Error, signaling overflow;

- if *EF*.Float_Type'Machine_Overflows is False, the result is implementation defined.   4

The maximum relative error exhibited by each function is as follows: 5

- $2.0 \cdot$ *EF*.Float_Type'Model_Epsilon, in the case of the Sqrt, Sin, and Cos functions;   6

- $4.0 \cdot$ *EF*.Float_Type'Model_Epsilon, in the case of the Log, Exp, Tan, Cot, and inverse   7
  trigonometric functions; and

- $8.0 \cdot$ *EF*.Float_Type'Model_Epsilon, in the case of the forward and inverse hyperbolic functions.   8

The maximum relative error exhibited by the exponentiation operator, which depends on the values of the   9
operands, is $(4.0 + |Right \cdot log(Left)| / 32.0) \cdot$ *EF*.Float_Type'Model_Epsilon.

The maximum relative error given above applies throughout the domain of the forward trigonometric   10
functions when the Cycle parameter is specified. When the Cycle parameter is omitted, the maximum
relative error given above applies only when the absolute value of the angle parameter X is less than or
equal to some implementation-defined *angle threshold*, which shall be at least *EF*.Float_Type'Machine_-
Radix $^{\lfloor EF.Float\_Type'Machine\_Mantissa/2 \rfloor}$. Beyond the angle threshold, the accuracy of the forward trigonometric
functions is implementation defined.

The prescribed results specified in A.5.1 for certain functions at particular parameter values take   11
precedence over the maximum relative error bounds; effectively, they narrow to a single value the result
interval allowed by the maximum relative error bounds. Additional rules with a similar effect are given by
the table below for the inverse trigonometric functions, at particular parameter values for which the
mathematical result is possibly not a model number of *EF*.Float_Type (or is, indeed, even transcendental).
In each table entry, the values of the parameters are such that the result lies on the axis between two
quadrants; the corresponding accuracy rule, which takes precedence over the maximum relative error
bounds, is that the result interval is the model interval of *EF*.Float_Type associated with the exact
mathematical result given in the table.

This paragraph was deleted.   12/1

The last line of the table is meant to apply when *EF*.Float_Type'Signed_Zeros is False; the two lines just   13
above it, when *EF*.Float_Type'Signed_Zeros is True and the parameter Y has a zero value with the
indicated sign.

The amount by which the result of an inverse trigonometric function is allowed to spill over into a   14
quadrant adjacent to the one corresponding to the principal branch, as given in A.5.1, is limited. The rule

Accuracy Requirements for the Elementary Functions   **G.2.4** is that the result belongs to the smallest model interval of *EF*.Float_Type that contains both boundaries of the quadrant corresponding to the principal branch. This rule also takes precedence over the maximum relative error bounds, effectively narrowing the result interval allowed by them.

Tightly Approximated Elementary Function Results				
Function	**Value of X**	**Value of Y**	**Exact Result when Cycle Specified**	**Exact Result when Cycle Omitted**
Arcsin	1.0	n.a.	Cycle/4.0	$\pi/2.0$
Arcsin	-1.0	n.a.	-Cycle/4.0	$-\pi/2.0$
Arccos	0.0	n.a.	Cycle/4.0	$\pi/2.0$
Arccos	-1.0	n.a.	Cycle/2.0	π
Arctan and Arccot	0.0	positive	Cycle/4.0	$\pi/2.0$
Arctan and Arccot	0.0	negative	-Cycle/4.0	$-\pi/2.0$
Arctan and Arccot	negative	+0.0	Cycle/2.0	π
Arctan and Arccot	negative	-0.0	-Cycle/2.0	$-\pi$
Arctan and Arccot	negative	0.0	Cycle/2.0	π

15   Finally, the following specifications also take precedence over the maximum relative error bounds:

16   • The absolute value of the result of the Sin, Cos, and Tanh functions never exceeds one.

17   • The absolute value of the result of the Coth function is never less than one.

18   • The result of the Cosh function is never less than one.

Implementation Advice

19   The versions of the forward trigonometric functions without a Cycle parameter should not be implemented by calling the corresponding version with a Cycle parameter of 2.0*Numerics.Pi, since this will not provide the required accuracy in some portions of the domain. For the same reason, the version of Log without a Base parameter should not be implemented by calling the corresponding version with a Base parameter of Numerics.e.

G.2.5 Performance Requirements for Random Number Generation

1   In the strict mode, the performance of Numerics.Float_Random and Numerics.Discrete_Random shall be as specified here.

Implementation Requirements

2   Two different calls to the time-dependent Reset procedure shall reset the generator to different states, provided that the calls are separated in time by at least one second and not more than fifty years.

3   The implementation's representations of generator states and its algorithms for generating random numbers shall yield a period of at least $2^{31}-2$; much longer periods are desirable but not required.

4   The implementations of Numerics.Float_Random.Random and Numerics.Discrete_Random.Random shall pass at least 85% of the individual trials in a suite of statistical tests. For Numerics.Float_Random, the

ests are applied directly to the floating point values generated (i.e., they are not converted to integers first), while for Numerics.Discrete_Random they are applied to the generated values of various discrete types. Each test suite performs 6 different tests, with each test repeated 10 times, yielding a total of 60 individual trials. An individual trial is deemed to pass if the chi-square value (or other statistic) calculated for the observed counts or distribution falls within the range of values corresponding to the 2.5 and 97.5 percentage points for the relevant degrees of freedom (i.e., it shall be neither too high nor too low). For the purpose of determining the degrees of freedom, measurement categories are combined whenever the expected counts are fewer than 5.

G.2.6 Accuracy Requirements for Complex Arithmetic

In the strict mode, the performance of Numerics.Generic_Complex_Types and Numerics.Generic_-Complex_Elementary_Functions shall be as specified here.   1

Implementation Requirements

When an exception is not raised, the result of evaluating a real function of an instance *CT* of Numerics.Generic_Complex_Types (i.e., a function that yields a value of subtype *CT*.Real'Base or *CT*.Imaginary) belongs to a result interval defined as for a real elementary function (see G.2.4).   2

When an exception is not raised, each component of the result of evaluating a complex function of such an instance, or of an instance of Numerics.Generic_Complex_Elementary_Functions obtained by instantiating the latter with *CT* (i.e., a function that yields a value of subtype *CT*.Complex), also belongs to a *result interval*. The result intervals for the components of the result are either defined by a *maximum relative error* bound or by a *maximum box error* bound. When the result interval for the real (resp., imaginary) component is defined by maximum relative error, it is defined as for that of a real function, relative to the exact value of the real (resp., imaginary) part of the result of the corresponding mathematical function. When defined by maximum box error, the result interval for a component of the result is the smallest model interval of *CT*.Real that contains all the values of the corresponding part of $f \cdot (1.0 + d)$, where f is the exact complex value of the corresponding mathematical function at the given parameter values, d is complex, and $|d|$ is less than or equal to the given maximum box error. The function delivers a value that belongs to the result interval (or a value both of whose components belong to their respective result intervals) when both bounds of the result interval(s) belong to the safe range of *CT*.Real; otherwise,   3

- if *CT*.Real'Machine_Overflows is True, the function either delivers a value that belongs to the result interval (or a value both of whose components belong to their respective result intervals) or raises Constraint_Error, signaling overflow;   4

- if *CT*.Real'Machine_Overflows is False, the result is implementation defined.   5

The error bounds for particular complex functions are tabulated below. In the table, the error bound is given as the coefficient of *CT*.Real'Model_Epsilon.   6

This paragraph was deleted.   7/1

The maximum relative error given above applies throughout the domain of the Compose_From_Polar function when the Cycle parameter is specified. When the Cycle parameter is omitted, the maximum relative error applies only when the absolute value of the parameter Argument is less than or equal to the angle threshold (see G.2.4). For the Exp function, and for the forward hyperbolic (resp., trigonometric) functions, the maximum relative error given above likewise applies only when the absolute value of the imaginary (resp., real) component of the parameter X (or the absolute value of the parameter itself, in the case of the Exp function with a parameter of pure-imaginary type) is less than or equal to the angle threshold. For larger angles, the accuracy is implementation defined.   8

Error Bounds for Particular Complex Functions			
Function or Operator	**Nature of Result**	**Nature of Bound**	**Error Bound**
Modulus	real	max. rel. error	3.0
Argument	real	max. rel. error	4.0
Compose_From_Polar	complex	max. rel. error	3.0
"*" (both operands complex)	complex	max. box error	5.0
"/" (right operand complex)	complex	max. box error	13.0
Sqrt	complex	max. rel. error	6.0
Log	complex	max. box error	13.0
Exp (complex parameter)	complex	max. rel. error	7.0
Exp (imaginary parameter)	complex	max. rel. error	2.0
Sin, Cos, Sinh, and Cosh	complex	max. rel. error	11.0
Tan, Cot, Tanh, and Coth	complex	max. rel. error	35.0
inverse trigonometric	complex	max. rel. error	14.0
inverse hyperbolic	complex	max. rel. error	14.0

9 The prescribed results specified in G.1.2 for certain functions at particular parameter values take precedence over the error bounds; effectively, they narrow to a single value the result interval allowed by the error bounds for a component of the result. Additional rules with a similar effect are given below for certain inverse trigonometric and inverse hyperbolic functions, at particular parameter values for which a component of the mathematical result is transcendental. In each case, the accuracy rule, which takes precedence over the error bounds, is that the result interval for the stated result component is the model interval of CT.Real associated with the component's exact mathematical value. The cases in question are as follows:

10 • When the parameter X has the value zero, the real (resp., imaginary) component of the result of the Arccot (resp., Arccoth) function is in the model interval of CT.Real associated with the value $\pi/2.0$.

11 • When the parameter X has the value one, the real component of the result of the Arcsin function is in the model interval of CT.Real associated with the value $\pi/2.0$.

12 • When the parameter X has the value -1.0, the real component of the result of the Arcsin (resp., Arccos) function is in the model interval of CT.Real associated with the value $-\pi/2.0$ (resp., π).

13 The amount by which a component of the result of an inverse trigonometric or inverse hyperbolic function is allowed to spill over into a quadrant adjacent to the one corresponding to the principal branch, as given in G.1.2, is limited. The rule is that the result belongs to the smallest model interval of CT.Real that contains both boundaries of the quadrant corresponding to the principal branch. This rule also takes precedence to the maximum error bounds, effectively narrowing the result interval allowed by them.

14 Finally, the results allowed by the error bounds are narrowed by one further rule: The absolute value of each component of the result of the Exp function, for a pure-imaginary parameter, never exceeds one.

Implementation Advice

The version of the Compose_From_Polar function without a Cycle parameter should not be implemented by calling the corresponding version with a Cycle parameter of 2.0*Numerics.Pi, since this will not provide the required accuracy in some portions of the domain.   15

Annex H
(normative)
Safety and Security

This Annex addresses requirements for systems that are safety critical or have security constraints. It provides facilities and specifies documentation requirements that relate to several needs: 1

- Understanding program execution;   2

- Reviewing object code;   3

- Restricting language constructs whose usage might complicate the demonstration of program correctness   4

Execution understandability is supported by pragma Normalize_Scalars, and also by requirements for the implementation to document the effect of a program in the presence of a bounded error or where the language rules leave the effect unspecified.   4.1

The pragmas Reviewable and Restrictions relate to the other requirements addressed by this Annex.   5

NOTES
1 The Valid attribute (see 13.9.2) is also useful in addressing these needs, to avoid problems that could otherwise arise from scalars that have values outside their declared range constraints.   6

H.1 Pragma Normalize_Scalars

This pragma ensures that an otherwise uninitialized scalar object is set to a predictable value, but out of range if possible.   1

Syntax

The form of a pragma Normalize_Scalars is as follows: 2

pragma Normalize_Scalars;   3

Post-Compilation Rules

Pragma Normalize_Scalars is a configuration pragma. It applies to all compilation_units included in a partition.   4

Documentation Requirements

If a pragma Normalize_Scalars applies, the implementation shall document the implicit initial value for scalar subtypes, and shall identify each case in which such a value is used and is not an invalid representation.   5

Implementation Advice

Whenever possible, the implicit initial value for a scalar subtype should be an invalid representation (see 13.9.1).   6

NOTES
2 The initialization requirement applies to uninitialized scalar objects that are subcomponents of composite objects, to allocated objects, and to stand-alone objects. It also applies to scalar **out** parameters. Scalar subcomponents of composite **out** parameters are initialized to the corresponding part of the actual, by virtue of 6.4.1.   7

3 The initialization requirement does not apply to a scalar for which pragma Import has been specified, since initialization of an imported object is performed solely by the foreign language environment (see B.1).   8

S. Tucker Taft et al. (Eds.): Consolidated Ada Reference Manual, LNCS 2219, pp. 459–463, 2001.

9   4 The use of pragma Normalize_Scalars in conjunction with Pragma Restrictions(No_Exceptions) may result in erroneous execution (see H.4).

H.2 Documentation of Implementation Decisions

Documentation Requirements

1   The implementation shall document the range of effects for each situation that the language rules identify as either a bounded error or as having an unspecified effect. If the implementation can constrain the effects of erroneous execution for a given construct, then it shall document such constraints. The documentation might be provided either independently of any compilation unit or partition, or as part of an annotated listing for a given unit or partition. See also 1.1.3, and 1.1.2.

NOTES

2   5 Among the situations to be documented are the conventions chosen for parameter passing, the methods used for the management of run-time storage, and the method used to evaluate numeric expressions if this involves extended range or extra precision.

H.3 Reviewable Object Code

1   Object code review and validation are supported by pragmas Reviewable and Inspection_Point.

H.3.1 Pragma Reviewable

1   This pragma directs the implementation to provide information to facilitate analysis and review of a program's object code, in particular to allow determination of execution time and storage usage and to identify the correspondence between the source and object programs.

Syntax

2   The form of a pragma Reviewable is as follows:

3   **pragma** Reviewable;

Post-Compilation Rules

4   Pragma Reviewable is a configuration pragma. It applies to all compilation_units included in a partition.

Implementation Requirements

5   The implementation shall provide the following information for any compilation unit to which such a pragma applies:

6   • Where compiler-generated run-time checks remain;

7   • An identification of any construct with a language-defined check that is recognized prior to run time as certain to fail if executed (even if the generation of run-time checks has been suppressed);

8   • For each reference to a scalar object, an identification of the reference as either "known to be initialized," or "possibly uninitialized," independent of whether pragma Normalize_Scalars applies;

9   • Where run-time support routines are implicitly invoked;

10   • An object code listing, including:

11   • Machine instructions, with relative offsets;

- Where each data object is stored during its lifetime; 12

- Correspondence with the source program, including an identification of the code produced per declaration and per statement. 13

- An identification of each construct for which the implementation detects the possibility of erroneous execution; 14

- For each subprogram, block, task, or other construct implemented by reserving and subsequently freeing an area on a run-time stack, an identification of the length of the fixed-size portion of the area and an indication of whether the non-fixed size portion is reserved on the stack or in a dynamically-managed storage region. 15

The implementation shall provide the following information for any partition to which the pragma applies: 16

- An object code listing of the entire partition, including initialization and finalization code as well as run-time system components, and with an identification of those instructions and data that will be relocated at load time; 17

- A description of the run-time model relevant to the partition. 18

The implementation shall provide control- and data-flow information, both within each compilation unit and across the compilation units of the partition. 18.1

Implementation Advice

The implementation should provide the above information in both a human-readable and machine-readable form, and should document the latter so as to ease further processing by automated tools. 19

Object code listings should be provided both in a symbolic format and also in an appropriate numeric format (such as hexadecimal or octal). 20

NOTES
6 The order of elaboration of library units will be documented even in the absence of pragma Reviewable (see 10.2). 21

H.3.2 Pragma Inspection_Point

An occurrence of a pragma Inspection_Point identifies a set of objects each of whose values is to be available at the point(s) during program execution corresponding to the position of the pragma in the compilation unit. The purpose of such a pragma is to facilitate code validation. 1

Syntax

The form of a pragma Inspection_Point is as follows: 2

pragma Inspection_Point[(*object*_name {, *object*_name})]; 3

Legality Rules

A pragma Inspection_Point is allowed wherever a declarative_item or statement is allowed. Each *object*_name shall statically denote the declaration of an object. 4

Static Semantics

An *inspection point* is a point in the object code corresponding to the occurrence of a pragma Inspection_- Point in the compilation unit. An object is *inspectable* at an inspection point if the corresponding pragma Inspection_Point either has an argument denoting that object, or has no arguments and the object is visible at the inspection point. 5/1

Dynamic Semantics

6 Execution of a pragma Inspection_Point has no effect.

Implementation Requirements

7 Reaching an inspection point is an external interaction with respect to the values of the inspectable objects at that point (see 1.1.3).

Documentation Requirements

8 For each inspection point, the implementation shall identify a mapping between each inspectable object and the machine resources (such as memory locations or registers) from which the object's value can be obtained.

NOTES

9 7 The implementation is not allowed to perform "dead store elimination" on the last assignment to a variable prior to a point where the variable is inspectable. Thus an inspection point has the effect of an implicit reference to each of its inspectable objects.

10 8 Inspection points are useful in maintaining a correspondence between the state of the program in source code terms, and the machine state during the program's execution. Assertions about the values of program objects can be tested in machine terms at inspection points. Object code between inspection points can be processed by automated tools to verify programs mechanically.

11 9 The identification of the mapping from source program objects to machine resources is allowed to be in the form of an annotated object listing, in human-readable or tool-processable form.

H.4 Safety and Security Restrictions

1 This clause defines restrictions that can be used with pragma Restrictions (see 13.12); these facilitate the demonstration of program correctness by allowing tailored versions of the run-time system.

Static Semantics

2 The following restrictions, the same as in D.7, apply in this Annex: No_Task_Hierarchy, No_Abort_-Statement, No_Implicit_Heap_Allocation, Max_Task_Entries is 0, Max_Asynchronous_Select_Nesting is 0, and Max_Tasks is 0. The last three restrictions are checked prior to program execution.

3 The following additional restrictions apply in this Annex.

4 **Tasking-related restriction:**

5 No_Protected_Types
    There are no declarations of protected types or protected objects.

6 **Memory-management related restrictions:**

7 No_Allocators
    There are no occurrences of an allocator.

8/1 No_Local_Allocators
    Allocators are prohibited in subprograms, generic subprograms, tasks, and entry bodies.

9 No_Unchecked_Deallocation
    Semantic dependence on Unchecked_Deallocation is not allowed.

10 Immediate_Reclamation
    Except for storage occupied by objects created by allocators and not deallocated via unchecked deallocation, any storage reserved at run time for an object is immediately reclaimed when the object no longer exists.

Exception-related restriction: 11

No_Exceptions 12
> Raise_statements and exception_handlers are not allowed. No language-defined run-time checks are generated; however, a run-time check performed automatically by the hardware is permitted.

Other restrictions: 13

No_Floating_Point 14
> Uses of predefined floating point types and operations, and declarations of new floating point types, are not allowed.

No_Fixed_Point 15
> Uses of predefined fixed point types and operations, and declarations of new fixed point types, are not allowed.

No_Unchecked_Conversion 16
> Semantic dependence on the predefined generic Unchecked_Conversion is not allowed.

No_Access_Subprograms 17
> The declaration of access-to-subprogram types is not allowed.

No_Unchecked_Access 18
> The Unchecked_Access attribute is not allowed.

No_Dispatch   Occurrences of T'Class are not allowed, for any (tagged) subtype T. 19

No_IO   Semantic dependence on any of the library units Sequential_IO, Direct_IO, Text_IO, Wide_Text_IO, or Stream_IO is not allowed. 20

No_Delay   Delay_Statements and semantic dependence on package Calendar are not allowed. 21

No_Recursion 22
> As part of the execution of a subprogram, the same subprogram is not invoked.

No_Reentrancy 23
> During the execution of a subprogram by a task, no other task invokes the same subprogram.

Implementation Requirements

If an implementation supports pragma Restrictions for a particular argument, then except for the restrictions No_Unchecked_Deallocation, No_Unchecked_Conversion, No_Access_Subprograms, and No_Unchecked_Access, the associated restriction applies to the run-time system. 24

Documentation Requirements

If a pragma Restrictions(No_Exceptions) is specified, the implementation shall document the effects of all constructs where language-defined checks are still performed automatically (for example, an overflow check performed by the processor). 25

Erroneous Execution

Program execution is erroneous if pragma Restrictions(No_Exceptions) has been specified and the conditions arise under which a generated language-defined run-time check would fail. 26

Program execution is erroneous if pragma Restrictions(No_Recursion) has been specified and a subprogram is invoked as part of its own execution, or if pragma Restrictions(No_Reentrancy) has been specified and during the execution of a subprogram by a task, another task invokes the same subprogram. 27

Safety and Security Restrictions **H.4**

Annex J
(normative)
Obsolescent Features

This Annex contains descriptions of features of the language whose functionality is largely redundant with other features defined by this International Standard. Use of these features is not recommended in newly written programs.   1

J.1 Renamings of Ada 83 Library Units

Static Semantics

The following library_unit_renaming_declarations exist: 1

```
with Ada.Unchecked_Conversion;                                                    2
generic function Unchecked_Conversion renames Ada.Unchecked_Conversion;

with Ada.Unchecked_Deallocation;                                                  3
generic procedure Unchecked_Deallocation renames Ada.Unchecked_Deallocation;

with Ada.Sequential_IO;                                                           4
generic package Sequential_IO renames Ada.Sequential_IO;

with Ada.Direct_IO;                                                               5
generic package Direct_IO renames Ada.Direct_IO;

with Ada.Text_IO;                                                                 6
package Text_IO renames Ada.Text_IO;

with Ada.IO_Exceptions;                                                           7
package IO_Exceptions renames Ada.IO_Exceptions;

with Ada.Calendar;                                                                8
package Calendar renames Ada.Calendar;

with System.Machine_Code;                                                         9
package Machine_Code renames System.Machine_Code;  -- If supported.
```

Implementation Requirements

The implementation shall allow the user to replace these renamings.   10

J.2 Allowed Replacements of Characters

Syntax

The following replacements are allowed for the vertical line, number sign, and quotation mark characters: 1

- A vertical line character (|) can be replaced by an exclamation mark (!) where used as a delimiter.   2

- The number sign characters (#) of a based_literal can be replaced by colons (:) provided that the replacement is done for both occurrences.   3

- The quotation marks (") used as string brackets at both ends of a string literal can be replaced by percent signs (%) provided that the enclosed sequence of characters contains no quotation mark, and provided that both string brackets are replaced. Any percent sign within the sequence of characters shall then be doubled and each such doubled percent sign is interpreted as a single percent sign character value.   4

S. Tucker Taft et al. (Eds.): Consolidated Ada Reference Manual, LNCS 2219, pp. 465–470, 2001.

5   These replacements do not change the meaning of the program.

J.3 Reduced Accuracy Subtypes

1   A digits_constraint may be used to define a floating point subtype with a new value for its requested decimal precision, as reflected by its Digits attribute. Similarly, a delta_constraint may be used to define an ordinary fixed point subtype with a new value for its *delta*, as reflected by its Delta attribute.

2   delta_constraint ::= **delta** *static*_expression [range_constraint]

3   The expression of a delta_constraint is expected to be of any real type.

4   The expression of a delta_constraint shall be static.

5   For a subtype_indication with a delta_constraint, the subtype_mark shall denote an ordinary fixed point subtype.

6   For a subtype_indication with a digits_constraint, the subtype_mark shall denote either a decimal fixed point subtype or a floating point subtype (notwithstanding the rule given in 3.5.9 that only allows a decimal fixed point subtype).

7   A subtype_indication with a subtype_mark that denotes an ordinary fixed point subtype and a delta_constraint defines an ordinary fixed point subtype with a *delta* given by the value of the expression of the delta_constraint. If the delta_constraint includes a range_constraint, then the ordinary fixed point subtype is constrained by the range_constraint.

8   A subtype_indication with a subtype_mark that denotes a floating point subtype and a digits_constraint defines a floating point subtype with a requested decimal precision (as reflected by its Digits attribute) given by the value of the expression of the digits_constraint. If the digits_constraint includes a range_-constraint, then the floating point subtype is constrained by the range_constraint.

9   A delta_constraint is *compatible* with an ordinary fixed point subtype if the value of the expression is no less than the *delta* of the subtype, and the range_constraint, if any, is compatible with the subtype.

10   A digits_constraint is *compatible* with a floating point subtype if the value of the expression is no greater than the requested decimal precision of the subtype, and the range_constraint, if any, is compatible with the subtype.

11   The elaboration of a delta_constraint consists of the elaboration of the range_constraint, if any.

J.4 The Constrained Attribute

1   For every private subtype S, the following attribute is defined:

'Constrained 2

> Yields the value False if S denotes an unconstrained nonformal private subtype with discriminants; also yields the value False if S denotes a generic formal private subtype, and the associated actual subtype is either an unconstrained subtype with discriminants or an unconstrained array subtype; yields the value True otherwise. The value of this attribute is of the predefined subtype Boolean.

J.5 ASCII

Static Semantics

The following declaration exists in the declaration of package Standard: 1

```
package ASCII is                                                              2
    -- Control characters:                                                    3
    NUL   : constant Character := nul;    SOH   : constant Character := soh;   4
    STX   : constant Character := stx;    ETX   : constant Character := etx;
    EOT   : constant Character := eot;    ENQ   : constant Character := enq;
    ACK   : constant Character := ack;    BEL   : constant Character := bel;
    BS    : constant Character := bs;     HT    : constant Character := ht;
    LF    : constant Character := lf;     VT    : constant Character := vt;
    FF    : constant Character := ff;     CR    : constant Character := cr;
    SO    : constant Character := so;     SI    : constant Character := si;
    DLE   : constant Character := dle;    DC1   : constant Character := dc1;
    DC2   : constant Character := dc2;    DC3   : constant Character := dc3;
    DC4   : constant Character := dc4;    NAK   : constant Character := nak;
    SYN   : constant Character := syn;    ETB   : constant Character := etb;
    CAN   : constant Character := can;    EM    : constant Character := em;
    SUB   : constant Character := sub;    ESC   : constant Character := esc;
    FS    : constant Character := fs;     GS    : constant Character := gs;
    RS    : constant Character := rs;     US    : constant Character := us;
    DEL   : constant Character := del;

    -- Other characters:                                                      5
    Exclam    : constant Character:= '!';  Quotation : constant Character:= '"';  6
    Sharp     : constant Character:= '#';  Dollar    : constant Character:= '$';
    Percent   : constant Character:= '%';  Ampersand : constant Character:= '&';
    Colon     : constant Character:= ':';  Semicolon : constant Character:= ';';
    Query     : constant Character:= '?';  At_Sign   : constant Character:= '@';
    L_Bracket : constant Character:= '[';  Back_Slash: constant Character:= '\';
    R_Bracket : constant Character:= ']';  Circumflex: constant Character:= '^';
    Underline : constant Character:= '_';  Grave     : constant Character:= '`';
    L_Brace   : constant Character:= '{';  Bar       : constant Character:= '|';
    R_Brace   : constant Character:= '}';  Tilde     : constant Character:= '~';

    -- Lower case letters:                                                    7
    LC_A: constant Character:= 'a';                                           8
    ...
    LC_Z: constant Character:= 'z';
end ASCII;                                                                     9
```

J.6 Numeric_Error

Static Semantics

The following declaration exists in the declaration of package Standard: 1

```
Numeric_Error : exception renames Constraint_Error;                          2
```

J.7 At Clauses

Syntax

1   at_clause ::= **for** direct_name **use at** expression;

Static Semantics

2   An at_clause of the form ''for *x* use at *y*;'' is equivalent to an attribute_definition_clause of the form ''for *x*'Address use *y*;''.

J.7.1 Interrupt Entries

1   Implementations are permitted to allow the attachment of task entries to interrupts via the address clause. Such an entry is referred to as an *interrupt entry*.

2   The address of the task entry corresponds to a hardware interrupt in an implementation-defined manner. (See Ada.Interrupts.Reference in C.3.2.)

Static Semantics

3   The following attribute is defined:

4   For any task entry X:

5   X'Address   For a task entry whose address is specified (an *interrupt entry*), the value refers to the corresponding hardware interrupt. For such an entry, as for any other task entry, the meaning of this value is implementation defined. The value of this attribute is of the type of the subtype System.Address.

6   Address may be specified for single entries via an attribute_definition_clause.

Dynamic Semantics

7   As part of the initialization of a task object, the address clause for an interrupt entry is elaborated, which evaluates the **expression** of the address clause. A check is made that the address specified is associated with some interrupt to which a task entry may be attached. If this check fails, Program_Error is raised. Otherwise, the interrupt entry is attached to the interrupt associated with the specified address.

8   Upon finalization of the task object, the interrupt entry, if any, is detached from the corresponding interrupt and the default treatment is restored.

9   While an interrupt entry is attached to an interrupt, the interrupt is reserved (see C.3).

10   An interrupt delivered to a task entry acts as a call to the entry issued by a hardware task whose priority is in the System.Interrupt_Priority range. It is implementation defined whether the call is performed as an ordinary entry call, a timed entry call, or a conditional entry call; which kind of call is performed can depend on the specific interrupt.

Bounded (Run-Time) Errors

11   It is a bounded error to evaluate E'Caller (see C.7.1) in an accept_statement for an interrupt entry. The possible effects are the same as for calling Current_Task from an entry body.

Documentation Requirements

12   The implementation shall document to which interrupts a task entry may be attached.

The implementation shall document whether the invocation of an interrupt entry has the effect of an ordinary entry call, conditional call, or a timed call, and whether the effect varies in the presence of pending interrupts.   13

Implementation Permissions

The support for this subclause is optional.   14

Interrupts to which the implementation allows a task entry to be attached may be designated as reserved for the entire duration of program execution; that is, not just when they have an interrupt entry attached to them.   15

Interrupt entry calls may be implemented by having the hardware execute directly the appropriate accept_statement. Alternatively, the implementation is allowed to provide an internal interrupt handler to simulate the effect of a normal task calling the entry.   16/1

The implementation is allowed to impose restrictions on the specifications and bodies of tasks that have interrupt entries.   17

It is implementation defined whether direct calls (from the program) to interrupt entries are allowed.   18

If a select_statement contains both a terminate_alternative and an accept_alternative for an interrupt entry, then an implementation is allowed to impose further requirements for the selection of the terminate_alternative in addition to those given in 9.3.   19

NOTES

1 Queued interrupts correspond to ordinary entry calls. Interrupts that are lost if not immediately processed correspond to conditional entry calls. It is a consequence of the priority rules that an accept_statement executed in response to an interrupt can be executed with the active priority at which the hardware generates the interrupt, taking precedence over lower priority tasks, without a scheduling action.   20/1

2 Control information that is supplied upon an interrupt can be passed to an associated interrupt entry as one or more parameters of mode **in**.   21

Examples

Example of an interrupt entry: 22

```
task Interrupt_Handler is
   entry Done;
   for Done'Address use
Ada.Interrupts.Reference(Ada.Interrupts.Names.Device_Done);
   end Interrupt_Handler;
```
23

J.8 Mod Clauses

Syntax

mod_clause ::= **at mod** *static_*expression;   1

Static Semantics

A record_representation_clause of the form: 2

```
for r use
   record at mod a
      ...
   end record;
```
3

4   is equivalent to:

5
```
    for r'Alignment use a;
    for r use
        record
            ...
        end record;
```

J.9 The Storage_Size Attribute

Static Semantics

1   For any task subtype T, the following attribute is defined:

2   T'Storage_Size
> Denotes an implementation-defined value of type *universal_integer* representing the number of storage elements reserved for a task of the subtype T.

3   Storage_Size may be specified for a task first subtype via an attribute_definition_clause.

Annex K
(informative)
Language-Defined Attributes

This annex summarizes the definitions given elsewhere of the language-defined attributes.   1

P'Access   For a prefix P that denotes a subprogram: 2

P'Access yields an access value that designates the subprogram denoted by P. The type of   3
P'Access is an access-to-subprogram type (*S*), as determined by the expected type. See
3.10.2.

X'Access   For a prefix X that denotes an aliased view of an object: 4

X'Access yields an access value that designates the object denoted by X. The type of   5
X'Access is an access-to-object type, as determined by the expected type. The expected type
shall be a general access type. See 3.10.2.

X'Address   For a prefix X that denotes an object, program unit, or label: 6/1

Denotes the address of the first of the storage elements allocated to X. For a program unit or   7
label, this value refers to the machine code associated with the corresponding body or
statement. The value of this attribute is of type System.Address. See 13.3.

S'Adjacent For every subtype S of a floating point type *T*:   8

S'Adjacent denotes a function with the following specification: 9

```
function S'Adjacent (X, Towards : T)
   return T
```
                                                                                                            10

If *Towards = X*, the function yields *X*; otherwise, it yields the machine number of the type   11
T adjacent to *X* in the direction of *Towards*, if that machine number exists. If the result
would be outside the base range of S, Constraint_Error is raised. When *T*'Signed_Zeros is
True, a zero result has the sign of *X*. When *Towards* is zero, its sign has no bearing on the
result. See A.5.3.

S'Aft   For every fixed point subtype S: 12

S'Aft yields the number of decimal digits needed after the decimal point to accommodate   13
the *delta* of the subtype S, unless the *delta* of the subtype S is greater than 0.1, in which
case the attribute yields the value one. (S'Aft is the smallest positive integer N for which
$(10**N)*S'Delta$ is greater than or equal to one.) The value of this attribute is of the type
universal_integer. See 3.5.10.

X'Alignment For a prefix X that denotes a subtype or object: 14/1

The Address of an object that is allocated under control of the implementation is an integral   15
multiple of the Alignment of the object (that is, the Address modulo the Alignment is zero).
The offset of a record component is a multiple of the Alignment of the component. For an
object that is not allocated under control of the implementation (that is, one that is
imported, that is allocated by a user-defined allocator, whose Address has been specified, or
is designated by an access value returned by an instance of Unchecked_Conversion), the
implementation may assume that the Address is an integral multiple of its Alignment. The
implementation shall not assume a stricter alignment.

The value of this attribute is of type *universal_integer*, and nonnegative; zero means that   16
the object is not necessarily aligned on a storage element boundary. See 13.3.

S'Base   For every scalar subtype S: 17

18   S'Base denotes an unconstrained subtype of the type of S. This unconstrained subtype is called the *base subtype* of the type. See 3.5.

19   S'Bit_Order   For every specific record subtype S:

20   Denotes the bit ordering for the type of S. The value of this attribute is of type System.Bit_Order. See 13.5.3.

21/1   P'Body_Version

     For a prefix P that statically denotes a program unit:

22   Yields a value of the predefined type String that identifies the version of the compilation unit that contains the body (but not any subunits) of the program unit. See E.3.

23   T'Callable   For a prefix T that is of a task type (after any implicit dereference):

24   Yields the value True when the task denoted by T is *callable*, and False otherwise; See 9.9.

25   E'Caller   For a prefix E that denotes an entry_declaration:

26   Yields a value of the type Task_ID that identifies the task whose call is now being serviced. Use of this attribute is allowed only inside an entry_body or accept_statement corresponding to the entry_declaration denoted by E. See C.7.1.

27   S'Ceiling   For every subtype S of a floating point type *T*:

28   S'Ceiling denotes a function with the following specification:

29
```
function S'Ceiling (X : T)
   return T
```

30   The function yields the value $\lceil X \rceil$, i.e., the smallest (most negative) integral value greater than or equal to X. When X is zero, the result has the sign of X; a zero result otherwise has a negative sign when S'Signed_Zeros is True. See A.5.3.

31   S'Class   For every subtype S of an untagged private type whose full view is tagged:

32   Denotes the class-wide subtype corresponding to the full view of S. This attribute is allowed only from the beginning of the private part in which the full view is declared, until the declaration of the full view. After the full view, the Class attribute of the full view can be used. See 7.3.1.

33   S'Class   For every subtype S of a tagged type *T* (specific or class-wide):

34   S'Class denotes a subtype of the class-wide type (called *T*Class in this International Standard) for the class rooted at *T* (or if S already denotes a class-wide subtype, then S'Class is the same as S).

35   S'Class is unconstrained. However, if S is constrained, then the values of S'Class are only those that when converted to the type *T* belong to S. See 3.9.

36/1   X'Component_Size

     For a prefix X that denotes an array subtype or array object (after any implicit dereference):

37   Denotes the size in bits of components of the type of X. The value of this attribute is of type *universal_integer*. See 13.3.

38   S'Compose   For every subtype S of a floating point type *T*:

39   S'Compose denotes a function with the following specification:

40
```
function S'Compose (Fraction : T;
                    Exponent : universal_integer)
   return T
```

41   Let *v* be the value *Fraction* · *T*Machine_Radix$^{Exponent-k}$, where *k* is the normalized exponent of *Fraction*. If *v* is a machine number of the type *T*, or if |*v*| ≥ *T*Model_Small, the function

yields v; otherwise, it yields either one of the machine numbers of the type T adjacent to v. Constraint_Error is optionally raised if v is outside the base range of S. A zero result has the sign of *Fraction* when S'Signed_Zeros is True. See A.5.3.

A'Constrained   42

For a **prefix** A that is of a discriminated type (after any implicit dereference):

Yields the value True if A denotes a constant, a value, or a constrained variable, and False   43
otherwise. See 3.7.2.

S'Copy_Sign   For every subtype S of a floating point type T: 44

S'Copy_Sign denotes a function with the following specification: 45

```
function S'Copy_Sign (Value, Sign : T)
   return T
```
46

If the value of *Value* is nonzero, the function yields a result whose magnitude is that of   47
Value and whose sign is that of *Sign*; otherwise, it yields the value zero. Constraint_Error is
optionally raised if the result is outside the base range of S. A zero result has the sign of
Sign when S'Signed_Zeros is True. See A.5.3.

E'Count   For a **prefix** E that denotes an entry of a task or protected unit: 48

Yields the number of calls presently queued on the entry E of the current instance of the   49
unit. The value of this attribute is of the type *universal_integer*. See 9.9.

S'Definite   For a **prefix** S that denotes a formal indefinite subtype: 50/1

S'Definite yields True if the actual subtype corresponding to S is definite; otherwise it   51
yields False. The value of this attribute is of the predefined type Boolean. See 12.5.1.

S'Delta   For every fixed point subtype S: 52

S'Delta denotes the *delta* of the fixed point subtype S. The value of this attribute is of the   53
type *universal_real*. See 3.5.10.

S'Denorm   For every subtype S of a floating point type T: 54

Yields the value True if every value expressible in the form   55
$$\pm \; mantissa \cdot T\text{'Machine\_Radix}^{T\text{'Machine\_Emin}}$$
where *mantissa* is a nonzero T'Machine_Mantissa-digit fraction in the number base
T'Machine_Radix, the first digit of which is zero, is a machine number (see 3.5.7) of the
type T; yields the value False otherwise. The value of this attribute is of the predefined type
Boolean. See A.5.3.

S'Digits   For every decimal fixed point subtype S: 56

S'Digits denotes the *digits* of the decimal fixed point subtype S, which corresponds to the   57
number of decimal digits that are representable in objects of the subtype. The value of this
attribute is of the type *universal_integer*. See 3.5.10.

S'Digits   For every floating point subtype S: 58

S'Digits denotes the requested decimal precision for the subtype S. The value of this   59
attribute is of the type *universal_integer*. See 3.5.8.

S'Exponent   For every subtype S of a floating point type T: 60

S'Exponent denotes a function with the following specification: 61

```
function S'Exponent (X : T)
   return universal_integer
```
62

The function yields the normalized exponent of X. See A.5.3.   63

64   S'External_Tag

> For every subtype S of a tagged type *T* (specific or class-wide):

65

> S'External_Tag denotes an external string representation for S'Tag; it is of the predefined type String. External_Tag may be specified for a specific tagged type via an attribute_definition_clause; the expression of such a clause shall be static. The default external tag representation is implementation defined. See 3.9.2 and 13.13.2. See 13.3.

66/1   A'First

> For a **prefix** A that is of an array type (after any implicit dereference), or denotes a constrained array subtype:

67

> A'First denotes the lower bound of the first index range; its type is the corresponding index type. See 3.6.2.

68   S'First

> For every scalar subtype S:

69

> S'First denotes the lower bound of the range of S. The value of this attribute is of the type of S. See 3.5.

70/1   A'First(N)

> For a **prefix** A that is of an array type (after any implicit dereference), or denotes a constrained array subtype:

71

> A'First(N) denotes the lower bound of the N-th index range; its type is the corresponding index type. See 3.6.2.

72   R.C'First_Bit

> For a component C of a composite, non-array object R:

73

> Denotes the offset, from the start of the first of the storage elements occupied by C, of the first bit occupied by C. This offset is measured in bits. The first bit of a storage element is numbered zero. The value of this attribute is of the type *universal_integer*. See 13.5.2.

74   S'Floor

> For every subtype S of a floating point type *T*:

75

> S'Floor denotes a function with the following specification:

76

```
function S'Floor (X : T)
  return T
```

77

> The function yields the value $\lfloor X \rfloor$, i.e., the largest (most positive) integral value less than or equal to *X*. When *X* is zero, the result has the sign of *X*; a zero result otherwise has a positive sign. See A.5.3.

78   S'Fore

> For every fixed point subtype S:

79

> S'Fore yields the minimum number of characters needed before the decimal point for the decimal representation of any value of the subtype S, assuming that the representation does not include an exponent, but includes a one-character prefix that is either a minus sign or a space. (This minimum number does not include superfluous zeros or underlines, and is at least 2.) The value of this attribute is of the type *universal_integer*. See 3.5.10.

80   S'Fraction

> For every subtype S of a floating point type *T*:

81

> S'Fraction denotes a function with the following specification:

82

```
function S'Fraction (X : T)
  return T
```

83

> The function yields the value $X \cdot T\text{'Machine\_Radix}^{-k}$, where *k* is the normalized exponent of *X*. A zero result, which can only occur when *X* is zero, has the sign of *X*. See A.5.3.

84   T'Identity

> For a **prefix** T that is of a task type (after any implicit dereference):

85

> Yields a value of the type Task_ID that identifies the task denoted by T. See C.7.1.

86/1   E'Identity

> For a **prefix** E that denotes an exception:

E'Identity returns the unique identity of the exception. The type of this attribute is Exception_Id. See 11.4.1. | 87

S'Image | For every scalar subtype S: | 88

S'Image denotes a function with the following specification: | 89

```
function S'Image(Arg : S'Base)
  return String
```
| 90

The function returns an image of the value of *Arg* as a String. See 3.5. | 91

S'Class'Input | | 92

For every subtype S'Class of a class-wide type *T*'Class:

S'Class'Input denotes a function with the following specification: | 93

```
function S'Class'Input(
  Stream : access Ada.Streams.Root_Stream_Type'Class)
  return T'Class
```
| 94

First reads the external tag from *Stream* and determines the corresponding internal tag (by calling Tags.Internal_Tag(String'Input(*Stream*)) — see 3.9) and then dispatches to the subprogram denoted by the Input attribute of the specific type identified by the internal tag; returns that result. See 13.13.2. | 95

S'Input | For every subtype S of a specific type *T*: | 96

S'Input denotes a function with the following specification: | 97

```
function S'Input(
  Stream : access Ada.Streams.Root_Stream_Type'Class)
  return T
```
| 98

S'Input reads and returns one value from *Stream*, using any bounds or discriminants written by a corresponding S'Output to determine how much to read. See 13.13.2. | 99

A'Last | For a prefix A that is of an array type (after any implicit dereference), or denotes a constrained array subtype: | 100/1

A'Last denotes the upper bound of the first index range; its type is the corresponding index type. See 3.6.2. | 101

S'Last | For every scalar subtype S: | 102

S'Last denotes the upper bound of the range of S. The value of this attribute is of the type of S. See 3.5. | 103

A'Last(N) | For a prefix A that is of an array type (after any implicit dereference), or denotes a constrained array subtype: | 104/1

A'Last(N) denotes the upper bound of the N-th index range; its type is the corresponding index type. See 3.6.2. | 105

R.C'Last_Bit | | 106

For a component C of a composite, non-array object R:

Denotes the offset, from the start of the first of the storage elements occupied by C, of the last bit occupied by C. This offset is measured in bits. The value of this attribute is of the type *universal_integer*. See 13.5.2. | 107

S'Leading_Part | | 108

For every subtype S of a floating point type *T*:

S'Leading_Part denotes a function with the following specification: | 109

110
function S'Leading_Part $(X : T;$
$\qquad Radix\_Digits : universal\_integer)$
return T

111 Let v be the value T'Machine_Radix$^{k-Radix\_Digits}$, where k is the normalized exponent of X. The function yields the value

112 • $\lfloor X/v \rfloor \cdot v$, when X is nonnegative and *Radix_Digits* is positive;

113 • $\lceil X/v \rceil \cdot v$, when X is negative and *Radix_Digits* is positive.

114 Constraint_Error is raised when *Radix_Digits* is zero or negative. A zero result, which can only occur when X is zero, has the sign of X. See A.5.3.

115/1 A'Length For a **prefix** A that is of an array type (after any implicit dereference), or denotes a constrained array subtype:

116 A'Length denotes the number of values of the first index range (zero for a null range); its type is *universal_integer*. See 3.6.2.

117/1 A'Length(N) For a **prefix** A that is of an array type (after any implicit dereference), or denotes a constrained array subtype:

118 A'Length(N) denotes the number of values of the N-th index range (zero for a null range); its type is *universal_integer*. See 3.6.2.

119 S'Machine For every subtype S of a floating point type T:

120 S'Machine denotes a function with the following specification:

121
function S'Machine $(X : T)$
return T

122 If X is a machine number of the type T, the function yields X; otherwise, it yields the value obtained by rounding or truncating X to either one of the adjacent machine numbers of the type T. Constraint_Error is raised if rounding or truncating X to the precision of the machine numbers results in a value outside the base range of S. A zero result has the sign of X when S'Signed_Zeros is True. See A.5.3.

123 S'Machine_Emax For every subtype S of a floating point type T:

124 Yields the largest (most positive) value of *exponent* such that every value expressible in the canonical form (for the type T), having a *mantissa* of T'Machine_Mantissa digits, is a machine number (see 3.5.7) of the type T. This attribute yields a value of the type *universal_integer*. See A.5.3.

125 S'Machine_Emin For every subtype S of a floating point type T:

126 Yields the smallest (most negative) value of *exponent* such that every value expressible in the canonical form (for the type T), having a *mantissa* of T'Machine_Mantissa digits, is a machine number (see 3.5.7) of the type T. This attribute yields a value of the type *universal_integer*. See A.5.3.

127 S'Machine_Mantissa For every subtype S of a floating point type T:

128 Yields the largest value of p such that every value expressible in the canonical form (for the type T), having a p-digit *mantissa* and an *exponent* between T'Machine_Emin and T'Machine_Emax, is a machine number (see 3.5.7) of the type T. This attribute yields a value of the type *universal_integer*. See A.5.3.

S'Machine_Overflows 129

For every subtype S of a fixed point type *T*:

Yields the value True if overflow and divide-by-zero are detected and reported by raising 130
Constraint_Error for every predefined operation that yields a result of the type *T*; yields the
value False otherwise. The value of this attribute is of the predefined type Boolean. See
A.5.4.

S'Machine_Overflows 131

For every subtype S of a floating point type *T*:

Yields the value True if overflow and divide-by-zero are detected and reported by raising 132
Constraint_Error for every predefined operation that yields a result of the type *T*; yields the
value False otherwise. The value of this attribute is of the predefined type Boolean. See
A.5.3.

S'Machine_Radix 133

For every subtype S of a fixed point type *T*:

Yields the radix of the hardware representation of the type *T*. The value of this attribute is 134
of the type *universal_integer*. See A.5.4.

S'Machine_Radix 135

For every subtype S of a floating point type *T*:

Yields the radix of the hardware representation of the type *T*. The value of this attribute is 136
of the type *universal_integer*. See A.5.3.

S'Machine_Rounds 137

For every subtype S of a fixed point type *T*:

Yields the value True if rounding is performed on inexact results of every predefined 138
operation that yields a result of the type *T*; yields the value False otherwise. The value of
this attribute is of the predefined type Boolean. See A.5.4.

S'Machine_Rounds 139

For every subtype S of a floating point type *T*:

Yields the value True if rounding is performed on inexact results of every predefined 140
operation that yields a result of the type *T*; yields the value False otherwise. The value of
this attribute is of the predefined type Boolean. See A.5.3.

S'Max For every scalar subtype S: 141

S'Max denotes a function with the following specification: 142

```
function S'Max(Left, Right : S'Base)
   return S'Base
```
143

The function returns the greater of the values of the two parameters. See 3.5. 144

S'Max_Size_In_Storage_Elements 145
For every subtype S:

Denotes the maximum value for Size_In_Storage_Elements that will be requested via 146
Allocate for an access type whose designated subtype is S. The value of this attribute is of
type *universal_integer*. See 13.11.1.

S'Min For every scalar subtype S: 147

S'Min denotes a function with the following specification: 148

```
function S'Min(Left, Right : S'Base)
   return S'Base
```
149

150   The function returns the lesser of the values of the two parameters. See 3.5.

151   S'Model   For every subtype S of a floating point type T:

152   S'Model denotes a function with the following specification:

153
```
function S'Model (X : T)
   return T
```

154   If the Numerics Annex is not supported, the meaning of this attribute is implementation defined; see G.2.2 for the definition that applies to implementations supporting the Numerics Annex. See A.5.3.

155   S'Model_Emin
                 For every subtype S of a floating point type T:

156   If the Numerics Annex is not supported, this attribute yields an implementation defined value that is greater than or equal to the value of T'Machine_Emin. See G.2.2 for further requirements that apply to implementations supporting the Numerics Annex. The value of this attribute is of the type *universal_integer*. See A.5.3.

157   S'Model_Epsilon
                 For every subtype S of a floating point type T:

158   Yields the value T'Machine_Radix$^{1 - T\text{Model\_Mantissa}}$. The value of this attribute is of the type *universal_real*. See A.5.3.

159   S'Model_Mantissa
                 For every subtype S of a floating point type T:

160   If the Numerics Annex is not supported, this attribute yields an implementation defined value that is greater than or equal to $\lceil d \cdot \log(10) / \log(T\text{'Machine\_Radix}) \rceil + 1$, where d is the requested decimal precision of T, and less than or equal to the value of T'Machine_Mantissa. See G.2.2 for further requirements that apply to implementations supporting the Numerics Annex. The value of this attribute is of the type *universal_integer*. See A.5.3.

161   S'Model_Small
                 For every subtype S of a floating point type T:

162   Yields the value T'Machine_Radix$^{T\text{Model\_Emin} - 1}$. The value of this attribute is of the type *universal_real*. See A.5.3.

163   S'Modulus   For every modular subtype S:

164   S'Modulus yields the modulus of the type of S, as a value of the type *universal_integer*. See 3.5.4.

165   S'Class'Output
                 For every subtype S'Class of a class-wide type T'Class:

166   S'Class'Output denotes a procedure with the following specification:

167
```
procedure S'Class'Output(
   Stream : access Ada.Streams.Root_Stream_Type'Class;
   Item   : in T'Class)
```

168   First writes the external tag of *Item* to *Stream* (by calling String'Output(Tags.External_Tag(*Item*'Tag) — see 3.9) and then dispatches to the subprogram denoted by the Output attribute of the specific type identified by the tag. See 13.13.2.

169   S'Output   For every subtype S of a specific type T:

170   S'Output denotes a procedure with the following specification:

```
procedure S'Output(                                                   171
   Stream : access Ada.Streams.Root_Stream_Type'Class;
   Item : in T)
```

S'Output writes the value of *Item* to *Stream*, including any bounds or discriminants. See   172
13.13.2.

D'Partition_ID   173/1

For a prefix D that denotes a library-level declaration, excepting a declaration of or within a
declared-pure library unit:

Denotes a value of the type *universal_integer* that identifies the partition in which D was   174
elaborated. If D denotes the declaration of a remote call interface library unit (see E.2.3) the
given partition is the one where the body of D was elaborated. See E.1.

S'Pos   For every discrete subtype S: 175

S'Pos denotes a function with the following specification: 176

```
function S'Pos(Arg : S'Base)                                          177
   return universal_integer
```

This function returns the position number of the value of *Arg*, as a value of type   178
universal_integer. See 3.5.5.

R.C'Position   For a component C of a composite, non-array object R: 179

Denotes the same value as R.C'Address − R'Address. The value of this attribute is of the   180
type *universal_integer*. See 13.5.2.

S'Pred   For every scalar subtype S: 181

S'Pred denotes a function with the following specification: 182

```
function S'Pred(Arg : S'Base)                                        183
   return S'Base
```

For an enumeration type, the function returns the value whose position number is one less   184
than that of the value of *Arg*; Constraint_Error is raised if there is no such value of the type.
For an integer type, the function returns the result of subtracting one from the value of *Arg*.
For a fixed point type, the function returns the result of subtracting *small* from the value of
Arg. For a floating point type, the function returns the machine number (as defined in 3.5.7)
immediately below the value of *Arg*; Constraint_Error is raised if there is no such machine
number. See 3.5.

A'Range   For a prefix A that is of an array type (after any implicit dereference), or denotes a   185/1
constrained array subtype:

A'Range is equivalent to the range A'First .. A'Last, except that the prefix A is only   186
evaluated once. See 3.6.2.

S'Range   For every scalar subtype S: 187

S'Range is equivalent to the range S'First .. S'Last. See 3.5.   188

A'Range(N)   For a prefix A that is of an array type (after any implicit dereference), or denotes a   189/1
constrained array subtype:

A'Range(N) is equivalent to the range A'First(N) .. A'Last(N), except that the prefix A is   190
only evaluated once. See 3.6.2.

S'Class'Read   For every subtype S'Class of a class-wide type *T*'Class: 191

S'Class'Read denotes a procedure with the following specification: 192

Language-Defined Attributes   **K**

193
```
procedure S'Class'Read(
  Stream : access Ada.Streams.Root_Stream_Type'Class;
  Item : out T'Class)
```

194   Dispatches to the subprogram denoted by the Read attribute of the specific type identified by the tag of Item. See 13.13.2.

195   S'Read   For every subtype S of a specific type *T*:

196   S'Read denotes a procedure with the following specification:

197
```
procedure S'Read(
  Stream : access Ada.Streams.Root_Stream_Type'Class;
  Item : out T)
```

198   S'Read reads the value of *Item* from *Stream*. See 13.13.2.

199   S'Remainder   For every subtype S of a floating point type *T*:

200   S'Remainder denotes a function with the following specification:

201
```
function S'Remainder (X, Y : T)
  return T
```

202   For nonzero *Y*, let *v* be the value $X - n \cdot Y$, where *n* is the integer nearest to the exact value of *X/Y*; if |*n* - *X/Y*| = 1/2, then *n* is chosen to be even. If *v* is a machine number of the type *T*, the function yields *v*; otherwise, it yields zero. Constraint_Error is raised if *Y* is zero. A zero result has the sign of *X* when S'Signed_Zeros is True. See A.5.3.

203   S'Round   For every decimal fixed point subtype S:

204   S'Round denotes a function with the following specification:

205
```
function S'Round(X : universal_real)
  return S'Base
```

206   The function returns the value obtained by rounding X (away from 0, if X is midway between two values of the type of S). See 3.5.10.

207   S'Rounding   For every subtype S of a floating point type *T*:

208   S'Rounding denotes a function with the following specification:

209
```
function S'Rounding (X : T)
  return T
```

210   The function yields the integral value nearest to *X*, rounding away from zero if *X* lies exactly halfway between two integers. A zero result has the sign of *X* when S'Signed_Zeros is True. See A.5.3.

211   S'Safe_First

For every subtype S of a floating point type *T*:

212   Yields the lower bound of the safe range (see 3.5.7) of the type *T*. If the Numerics Annex is not supported, the value of this attribute is implementation defined; see G.2.2 for the definition that applies to implementations supporting the Numerics Annex. The value of this attribute is of the type *universal_real*. See A.5.3.

213   S'Safe_Last   For every subtype S of a floating point type *T*:

214   Yields the upper bound of the safe range (see 3.5.7) of the type *T*. If the Numerics Annex is not supported, the value of this attribute is implementation defined; see G.2.2 for the definition that applies to implementations supporting the Numerics Annex. The value of this attribute is of the type *universal_real*. See A.5.3.

215   S'Scale   For every decimal fixed point subtype S:

216   S'Scale denotes the *scale* of the subtype S, defined as the value N such that S'Delta = 10.0**(–N). The scale indicates the position of the point relative to the rightmost significant

digits of values of subtype S. The value of this attribute is of the type *universal_integer*. See 3.5.10.

S'Scaling   For every subtype S of a floating point type *T*:   217

S'Scaling denotes a function with the following specification: 218

```
function S'Scaling (X : T;    219
                    Adjustment : universal_integer)
       return T
```

Let *v* be the value $X \cdot T$Machine_Radix^{Adjustment}. If *v* is a machine number of the type *T*, or if   220
$|v| \geq T$Model_Small, the function yields *v*; otherwise, it yields either one of the machine numbers of the type *T* adjacent to *v*. Constraint_Error is optionally raised if *v* is outside the base range of S. A zero result has the sign of *X* when S'Signed_Zeros is True. See A.5.3.

S'Signed_Zeros   221
For every subtype S of a floating point type *T*:

Yields the value True if the hardware representation for the type *T* has the capability of   222
representing both positively and negatively signed zeros, these being generated and used by the predefined operations of the type *T* as specified in IEC 559:1989; yields the value False otherwise. The value of this attribute is of the predefined type Boolean. See A.5.3.

S'Size   For every subtype S: 223

If S is definite, denotes the size (in bits) that the implementation would choose for the   224
following objects of subtype S:

- • A record component of subtype S when the record type is packed.   225

- • The formal parameter of an instance of Unchecked_Conversion that converts   226
  from subtype S to some other subtype.

If S is indefinite, the meaning is implementation defined. The value of this attribute is of the   227
type *universal_integer*. See 13.3.

X'Size   For a prefix X that denotes an object: 228/1

Denotes the size in bits of the representation of the object. The value of this attribute is of   229
the type *universal_integer*. See 13.3.

S'Small   For every fixed point subtype S: 230

S'Small denotes the *small* of the type of S. The value of this attribute is of the type   231
universal_real. See 3.5.10.

S'Storage_Pool   232
For every access subtype S:

Denotes the storage pool of the type of S. The type of this attribute is Root_Storage_-   233
Pool'Class. See 13.11.

S'Storage_Size   234
For every access subtype S:

Yields the result of calling Storage_Size(S'Storage_Pool), which is intended to be a   235
measure of the number of storage elements reserved for the pool. The type of this attribute is *universal_integer*. See 13.11.

T'Storage_Size   236/1
For a prefix T that denotes a task object (after any implicit dereference):

Denotes the number of storage elements reserved for the task. The value of this attribute is   237
of the type *universal_integer*. The Storage_Size includes the size of the task's stack, if any.

The language does not specify whether or not it includes other storage associated with the task (such as the "task control block" used by some implementations.) See 13.3.

238   S'Succ   For every scalar subtype S:

239   S'Succ denotes a function with the following specification:

240
```
function S'Succ(Arg : S'Base)
   return S'Base
```

241   For an enumeration type, the function returns the value whose position number is one more than that of the value of *Arg*; Constraint_Error is raised if there is no such value of the type. For an integer type, the function returns the result of adding one to the value of *Arg*. For a fixed point type, the function returns the result of adding *small* to the value of *Arg*. For a floating point type, the function returns the machine number (as defined in 3.5.7) immediately above the value of *Arg*; Constraint_Error is raised if there is no such machine number. See 3.5.

242   X'Tag   For a **prefix** X that is of a class-wide tagged type (after any implicit dereference):

243   X'Tag denotes the tag of X. The value of this attribute is of type Tag. See 3.9.

244   S'Tag   For every subtype S of a tagged type *T* (specific or class-wide):

245   S'Tag denotes the tag of the type *T* (or if *T* is class-wide, the tag of the root type of the corresponding class). The value of this attribute is of type Tag. See 3.9.

246   T'Terminated   For a **prefix** T that is of a task type (after any implicit dereference):

247   Yields the value True if the task denoted by T is terminated, and False otherwise. The value of this attribute is of the predefined type Boolean. See 9.9.

248   S'Truncation   For every subtype S of a floating point type *T*:

249   S'Truncation denotes a function with the following specification:

250
```
function S'Truncation (X : T)
   return T
```

251   The function yields the value $\lceil X \rceil$ when X is negative, and $\lfloor X \rfloor$ otherwise. A zero result has the sign of X when S'Signed_Zeros is True. See A.5.3.

252   S'Unbiased_Rounding
           For every subtype S of a floating point type *T*:

253   S'Unbiased_Rounding denotes a function with the following specification:

254
```
function S'Unbiased_Rounding (X : T)
   return T
```

255   The function yields the integral value nearest to X, rounding toward the even integer if X lies exactly halfway between two integers. A zero result has the sign of X when S'Signed_Zeros is True. See A.5.3.

256   X'Unchecked_Access
           For a **prefix** X that denotes an aliased view of an object:

257   All rules and semantics that apply to X'Access (see 3.10.2) apply also to X'Unchecked_Access, except that, for the purposes of accessibility rules and checks, it is as if X were declared immediately within a library package. See 13.10.

258   S'Val   For every discrete subtype S:

259   S'Val denotes a function with the following specification:

260
```
function S'Val(Arg : universal_integer)
   return S'Base
```

This function returns a value of the type of S whose position number equals the value of *Arg*. See 3.5.5. 261

X'Valid For a **prefix** X that denotes a scalar object (after any implicit dereference): 262

Yields True if and only if the object denoted by X is normal and has a valid representation. The value of this attribute is of the predefined type Boolean. See 13.9.2. 263

S'Value For every scalar subtype S: 264

S'Value denotes a function with the following specification: 265

```
function S'Value(Arg : String)
   return S'Base
```
266

This function returns a value given an image of the value as a String, ignoring any leading or trailing spaces. See 3.5. 267

P'Version For a **prefix** P that statically denotes a program unit: 268/1

Yields a value of the predefined type String that identifies the version of the compilation unit that contains the declaration of the program unit. See E.3. 269

S'Wide_Image For every scalar subtype S: 270

S'Wide_Image denotes a function with the following specification: 271

```
function S'Wide_Image(Arg : S'Base)
   return Wide_String
```
272

The function returns an *image* of the value of *Arg*, that is, a sequence of characters representing the value in display form. See 3.5. 273

S'Wide_Value 274
For every scalar subtype S:

S'Wide_Value denotes a function with the following specification: 275

```
function S'Wide_Value(Arg : Wide_String)
   return S'Base
```
276

This function returns a value given an image of the value as a Wide_String, ignoring any leading or trailing spaces. See 3.5. 277

S'Wide_Width 278
For every scalar subtype S:

S'Wide_Width denotes the maximum length of a Wide_String returned by S'Wide_Image over all values of the subtype S. It denotes zero for a subtype that has a null range. Its type is *universal_integer*. See 3.5. 279

S'Width For every scalar subtype S: 280

S'Width denotes the maximum length of a String returned by S'Image over all values of the subtype S. It denotes zero for a subtype that has a null range. Its type is *universal_integer*. See 3.5. 281

S'Class'Write 282
For every subtype S'Class of a class-wide type *T*'Class:

S'Class'Write denotes a procedure with the following specification: 283

```
procedure S'Class'Write(
   Stream : access Ada.Streams.Root_Stream_Type'Class;
   Item   : in T'Class)
```
284

Dispatches to the subprogram denoted by the Write attribute of the specific type identified by the tag of Item. See 13.13.2. 285

286 S'Write   For every subtype S of a specific type *T*:

287   S'Write denotes a procedure with the following specification:

288
```
procedure S'Write(
    Stream : access Ada.Streams.Root_Stream_Type'Class;
    Item : in T)
```

289   S'Write writes the value of *Item* to *Stream*. See 13.13.2.

Annex L
(informative)
Language-Defined Pragmas

This Annex summarizes the definitions given elsewhere of the language-defined pragmas. 1

pragma All_Calls_Remote[(*library_unit*_name)]; — See E.2.3. 2

pragma Asynchronous(local_name); — See E.4.1. 3

pragma Atomic(local_name); — See C.6. 4

pragma Atomic_Components(*array*_local_name); — See C.6. 5

pragma Attach_Handler(*handler*_name, expression); — See C.3.1. 6

pragma Controlled(*first_subtype*_local_name); — See 13.11.3. 7

pragma Convention([Convention =>] *convention*_identifier,[Entity =>] local_name); — See B.1. 8

pragma Discard_Names[([On =>] local_name)]; — See C.5. 9

pragma Elaborate(*library_unit*_name{, *library_unit*_name}); — See 10.2.1. 10

pragma Elaborate_All(*library_unit*_name{, *library_unit*_name}); — See 10.2.1. 11

pragma Elaborate_Body[(*library_unit*_name)]; — See 10.2.1. 12

pragma Export(13
    [Convention =>] *convention*_identifier, [Entity =>] local_name
[, [External_Name =>] *string*_expression] [, [Link_Name =>] *string*_expression]); — See B.1.

pragma Import(14
    [Convention =>] *convention*_identifier, [Entity =>] local_name
[, [External_Name =>] *string*_expression] [, [Link_Name =>] *string*_expression]); — See B.1.

pragma Inline(name {, name}); — See 6.3.2. 15

pragma Inspection_Point[(*object*_name {, *object*_name})]; — See H.3.2. 16

pragma Interrupt_Handler(*handler*_name); — See C.3.1. 17

pragma Interrupt_Priority[(expression)]; — See D.1. 18

pragma Linker_Options(*string*_expression); — See B.1. 19

pragma List(identifier); — See 2.8. 20

pragma Locking_Policy(*policy*_identifier); — See D.3. 21

pragma Normalize_Scalars; — See H.1. 22

pragma Optimize(identifier); — See 2.8. 23

pragma Pack(*first_subtype*_local_name); — See 13.2. 24

pragma Page; — See 2.8. 25

S. Tucker Taft et al. (Eds.): Consolidated Ada Reference Manual, LNCS 2219, pp. 485– 486, 2001.

26   **pragma** Preelaborate[(*library_unit_*name)]; — See 10.2.1.

27   **pragma** Priority(expression); — See D.1.

28   **pragma** Pure[(*library_unit_*name)]; — See 10.2.1.

29   **pragma** Queuing_Policy(*policy_*identifier); — See D.4.

30   **pragma** Remote_Call_Interface[(*library_unit_*name)]; — See E.2.3.

31   **pragma** Remote_Types[(*library_unit_*name)]; — See E.2.2.

32   **pragma** Restrictions(restriction{, restriction}); — See 13.12.

33   **pragma** Reviewable; — See H.3.1.

34   **pragma** Shared_Passive[(*library_unit_*name)]; — See E.2.1.

35   **pragma** Storage_Size(expression); — See 13.3.

36   **pragma** Suppress(identifier [, [On =>] name]); — See 11.5.

37   **pragma** Task_Dispatching_Policy(*policy_*identifier); — See D.2.2.

38   **pragma** Volatile(local_name); — See C.6.

39   **pragma** Volatile_Components(*array_*local_name); — See C.6.

Annex M
(informative)
Implementation-Defined Characteristics

The Ada language allows for certain machine dependences in a controlled manner. Each Ada implementation must document all implementation-defined characteristics: 1

- Whether or not each recommendation given in Implementation Advice is followed. See 1.1.2(37).   2

- Capacity limitations of the implementation. See 1.1.3(3).   3

- Variations from the standard that are impractical to avoid given the implementation's execution environment. See 1.1.3(6).   4

- Which code_statements cause external interactions. See 1.1.3(10).   5

- The coded representation for the text of an Ada program. See 2.1(4).   6

- The control functions allowed in comments. See 2.1(14).   7

- The representation for an end of line. See 2.2(2).   8

- Maximum supported line length and lexical element length. See 2.2(14).   9

- Implementation-defined pragmas. See 2.8(14).   10

- Effect of pragma Optimize. See 2.8(27).   11

- The sequence of characters of the value returned by S'Image when some of the graphic characters of S'Wide_Image are not defined in Character. See 3.5(37).   12

- The predefined integer types declared in Standard. See 3.5.4(25).   13

- Any nonstandard integer types and the operators defined for them. See 3.5.4(26).   14

- Any nonstandard real types and the operators defined for them. See 3.5.6(8).   15

- What combinations of requested decimal precision and range are supported for floating point types. See 3.5.7(7).   16

- The predefined floating point types declared in Standard. See 3.5.7(16).   17

- The *small* of an ordinary fixed point type. See 3.5.9(8).   18

- What combinations of *small*, range, and *digits* are supported for fixed point types. See 3.5.9(10).   19

- The result of Tags.Expanded_Name for types declared within an unnamed block_statement. See 3.9(10).   20

- Implementation-defined attributes. See 4.1.4(12/1).   21

- Any implementation-defined time types. See 9.6(6).   22

- The time base associated with relative delays. See 9.6(20).   23

- The time base of the type Calendar.Time. See 9.6(23).   24

- The timezone used for package Calendar operations. See 9.6(24).   25

- Any limit on delay_until_statements of select_statements. See 9.6(29).   26

S. Tucker Taft et al. (Eds.): Consolidated Ada Reference Manual, LNCS 2219, pp. 487–491, 2001.

27 • Whether or not two nonoverlapping parts of a composite object are independently addressable, in the case where packing, record layout, or Component_Size is specified for the object. See 9.10(1).

28 • The representation for a compilation. See 10.1(2).

29 • Any restrictions on compilations that contain multiple compilation_units. See 10.1(4).

30 • The mechanisms for creating an environment and for adding and replacing compilation units. See 10.1.4(3).

31 • The implementation-defined means, if any, of specifying which compilation units are needed by a given compilation unit. See 10.2(2).

32 • The manner of explicitly assigning library units to a partition. See 10.2(2).

33 • The manner of designating the main subprogram of a partition. See 10.2(7).

34 • The order of elaboration of library_items. See 10.2(18).

35 • Parameter passing and function return for the main subprogram. See 10.2(21).

36 • The mechanisms for building and running partitions. See 10.2(24).

37 • The details of program execution, including program termination. See 10.2(25).

38 • The semantics of any nonactive partitions supported by the implementation. See 10.2(28).

39 • The information returned by Exception_Message. See 11.4.1(10).

40 • The result of Exceptions.Exception_Name for types declared within an unnamed block_statement. See 11.4.1(12).

41 • The information returned by Exception_Information. See 11.4.1(13).

42 • Implementation-defined check names. See 11.5(27).

43 • Any restrictions placed upon representation items. See 13.1(20).

44 • The interpretation of each aspect of representation. See 13.1(20).

45 • The meaning of Size for indefinite subtypes. See 13.3(48).

46 • The default external representation for a type tag. See 13.3(75/1).

47 • What determines whether a compilation unit is the same in two different partitions. See 13.3(76).

48 • Implementation-defined components. See 13.5.1(15).

49 • If Word_Size = Storage_Unit, the default bit ordering. See 13.5.3(5).

50 • The contents of the visible part of package System and its language-defined children. See 13.7(2).

51 • The contents of the visible part of package System.Machine_Code, and the meaning of code_statements. See 13.8(7).

52 • The effect of unchecked conversion. See 13.9(11).

53 • Whether or not the implementation provides user-accessible names for the standard pool type(s). See 13.11(17).

54 • The manner of choosing a storage pool for an access type when Storage_Pool is not specified for the type. See 13.11(17).

55 • The meaning of Storage_Size. See 13.11(18).

56 • Implementation-defined aspects of storage pools. See 13.11(22).

- The set of restrictions allowed in a pragma Restrictions. See 13.12(7). 57

- The consequences of violating limitations on Restrictions pragmas. See 13.12(9). 58

- The representation used by the Read and Write attributes of elementary types in terms of stream elements. See 13.13.2(9). 59

- The names and characteristics of the numeric subtypes declared in the visible part of package Standard. See A.1(3). 60

- The accuracy actually achieved by the elementary functions. See A.5.1(1). 61

- The sign of a zero result from some of the operators or functions in Numerics.Generic_Elementary_Functions, when Float_Type'Signed_Zeros is True. See A.5.1(46). 62

- The value of Numerics.Discrete_Random.Max_Image_Width. See A.5.2(27). 63

- The value of Numerics.Float_Random.Max_Image_Width. See A.5.2(27). 64

- The algorithms for random number generation. See A.5.2(32). 65

- The string representation of a random number generator's state. See A.5.2(38). 66

- The minimum time interval between calls to the time-dependent Reset procedure that are guaranteed to initiate different random number sequences. See A.5.2(45). 67

- The values of the Model_Mantissa, Model_Emin, Model_Epsilon, Model, Safe_First, and Safe_Last attributes, if the Numerics Annex is not supported. See A.5.3(72). 68

- Any implementation-defined characteristics of the input-output packages. See A.7(14). 69

- The value of Buffer_Size in Storage_IO. See A.9(10). 70

- external files for standard input, standard output, and standard error See A.10(5). 71

- The accuracy of the value produced by Put. See A.10.9(36). 72

- Current size for a stream file for which positioning is not supported. See A.12.1(1.1/1). 72.1/1

- The meaning of Argument_Count, Argument, and Command_Name. See A.15(1). 73

- Implementation-defined convention names. See B.1(11). 74

- The manner of choosing link names when neither the link name nor the address of an imported or exported entity is specified. See B.1(36). 75

- The meaning of link names. See B.1(36). 76

- The effect of pragma Linker_Options. See B.1(37). 77

- The contents of the visible part of package Interfaces and its language-defined descendants. See B.2(1). 78

- Implementation-defined children of package Interfaces. The contents of the visible part of package Interfaces. See B.2(11). 79

- The definitions of types and constants in Interfaces.C. See B.3(41). 79.1/1

- The types Floating, Long_Floating, Binary, Long_Binary, Decimal_Element, and COBOL_Character; and the initializations of the variables Ada_To_COBOL and COBOL_To_Ada, in Interfaces.COBOL. See B.4(50). 80/1

- The types Fortran_Integer, Real, Double_Precision, and Character_Set in Interfaces.Fortran. See B.5(17). 80.1/1

- Support for access to machine instructions. See C.1(1). 81

Implementation-Defined Characteristics **M**

82 • Implementation-defined aspects of access to machine operations. See C.1(9).

83 • Implementation-defined aspects of interrupts. See C.3(2).

84 • Implementation-defined aspects of preelaboration. See C.4(13).

85 • The semantics of pragma Discard_Names. See C.5(7).

86 • The result of the Task_Identification.Image attribute. See C.7.1(7).

87 • The value of Current_Task when in a protected entry or interrupt handler. See C.7.1(17).

88 • The effect of calling Current_Task from an entry body or interrupt handler. See C.7.1(19).

88.1/1 • Granularity of locking for Task_Attributes. See C.7.2(16/1).

89/1 • Limits on the number and size of task attributes, and how to configure them. See C.7.2(19).

90 • Values of all Metrics. See D(2).

91 • The declarations of Any_Priority and Priority. See D.1(11).

92 • Implementation-defined execution resources. See D.1(15).

93 • Whether, on a multiprocessor, a task that is waiting for access to a protected object keeps its processor busy. See D.2.1(3).

94 • The affect of implementation defined execution resources on task dispatching. See D.2.1(9).

95 • Implementation-defined *policy*_identifiers allowed in a pragma Task_Dispatching_Policy. See D.2.2(3).

96 • Implementation-defined aspects of priority inversion. See D.2.2(16).

97 • Implementation defined task dispatching. See D.2.2(18).

98 • Implementation-defined *policy*_identifiers allowed in a pragma Locking_Policy. See D.3(4).

99 • Default ceiling priorities. See D.3(10).

100 • The ceiling of any protected object used internally by the implementation. See D.3(16).

101 • Implementation-defined queuing policies. See D.4(1/1).

102 • On a multiprocessor, any conditions that cause the completion of an aborted construct to be delayed later than what is specified for a single processor. See D.6(3).

103 • Any operations that implicitly require heap storage allocation. See D.7(8).

104 • Implementation-defined aspects of pragma Restrictions. See D.7(20).

105 • Implementation-defined aspects of package Real_Time. See D.8(17).

106 • Implementation-defined aspects of delay_statements. See D.9(8).

107 • The upper bound on the duration of interrupt blocking caused by the implementation. See D.12(5).

108 • The means for creating and executing distributed programs. See E(5).

109 • Any events that can result in a partition becoming inaccessible. See E.1(7).

110 • The scheduling policies, treatment of priorities, and management of shared resources between partitions in certain cases. See E.1(11).

111/1 • *This paragraph was deleted.*

112 • Whether the execution of the remote subprogram is immediately aborted as a result of cancellation. See E.4(13).

- Implementation-defined aspects of the PCS. See E.5(25).   113

- Implementation-defined interfaces in the PCS. See E.5(26).   114

- The values of named numbers in the package Decimal. See F.2(7).   115

- The value of Max_Picture_Length in the package Text_IO.Editing See F.3.3(16).   116

- The value of Max_Picture_Length in the package Wide_Text_IO.Editing See F.3.4(5).   117

- The accuracy actually achieved by the complex elementary functions and by other complex   118
  arithmetic operations. See G.1(1).

- The sign of a zero result (or a component thereof) from any operator or function in   119
  Numerics.Generic_Complex_Types, when Real'Signed_Zeros is True. See G.1.1(53).

- The sign of a zero result (or a component thereof) from any operator or function in   120
  Numerics.Generic_Complex_Elementary_Functions, when Complex_Types.Real'Signed_Zeros
  is True. See G.1.2(45).

- Whether the strict mode or the relaxed mode is the default. See G.2(2).   121

- The result interval in certain cases of fixed-to-float conversion. See G.2.1(10).   122

- The result of a floating point arithmetic operation in overflow situations, when the   123
  Machine_Overflows attribute of the result type is False. See G.2.1(13).

- The result interval for division (or exponentiation by a negative exponent), when the floating   124
  point hardware implements division as multiplication by a reciprocal. See G.2.1(16).

- The definition of *close result set*, which determines the accuracy of certain fixed point   125
  multiplications and divisions. See G.2.3(5).

- Conditions on a *universal_real* operand of a fixed point multiplication or division for which the   126
  result shall be in the *perfect result set*. See G.2.3(22).

- The result of a fixed point arithmetic operation in overflow situations, when the   127
  Machine_Overflows attribute of the result type is False. See G.2.3(27).

- The result of an elementary function reference in overflow situations, when the   128
  Machine_Overflows attribute of the result type is False. See G.2.4(4).

- The accuracy of certain elementary functions for parameters beyond the angle threshold. See   129
  G.2.4(10).

- The value of the *angle threshold*, within which certain elementary functions, complex arithmetic   130
  operations, and complex elementary functions yield results conforming to a maximum relative
  error bound. See G.2.4(10).

- The result of a complex arithmetic operation or complex elementary function reference in   131
  overflow situations, when the Machine_Overflows attribute of the corresponding real type is
  False. See G.2.6(5).

- The accuracy of certain complex arithmetic operations and certain complex elementary functions   132
  for parameters (or components thereof) beyond the angle threshold. See G.2.6(8).

- Information regarding bounded errors and erroneous execution. See H.2(1).   133

- Implementation-defined aspects of pragma Inspection_Point. See H.3.2(8).   134

- Implementation-defined aspects of pragma Restrictions. See H.4(25).   135

- Any restrictions on pragma Restrictions. See H.4(27).   136

Annex N
(informative)
Glossary

This Annex contains informal descriptions of some terms used in this International Standard. To find more formal definitions, look the term up in the index.   1

Access type. An access type has values that designate aliased objects. Access types correspond to "pointer types" or "reference types" in some other languages.   2

Aliased. An aliased view of an object is one that can be designated by an access value. Objects allocated by allocators are aliased. Objects can also be explicitly declared as aliased with the reserved word **aliased**. The Access attribute can be used to create an access value designating an aliased object.   3

Array type. An array type is a composite type whose components are all of the same type. Components are selected by indexing.   4

Character type. A character type is an enumeration type whose values include characters.   5

Class. A class is a set of types that is closed under derivation, which means that if a given type is in the class, then all types derived from that type are also in the class. The set of types of a class share common properties, such as their primitive operations.   6

Compilation unit. The text of a program can be submitted to the compiler in one or more compilations. Each compilation is a succession of compilation_units. A compilation_unit contains either the declaration, the body, or a renaming of a program unit.   7

Composite type. A composite type has components.   8

Construct. A *construct* is a piece of text (explicit or implicit) that is an instance of a syntactic category defined under "Syntax."   9

Controlled type. A controlled type supports user-defined assignment and finalization. Objects are always finalized before being destroyed.   10

Declaration. A *declaration* is a language construct that associates a name with (a view of) an entity. A declaration may appear explicitly in the program text (an *explicit* declaration), or may be supposed to occur at a given place in the text as a consequence of the semantics of another construct (an *implicit* declaration).   11

Definition. All declarations contain a *definition* for a *view* of an entity. A view consists of an identification of the entity (the entity *of* the view), plus view-specific characteristics that affect the use of the entity through that view (such as mode of access to an object, formal parameter names and defaults for a subprogram, or visibility to components of a type). In most cases, a declaration also contains the definition for the entity itself (a renaming_declaration is an example of a declaration that does not define a new entity, but instead defines a view of an existing entity (see 8.5)).   12

Derived type. A derived type is a type defined in terms of another type, which is the parent type of the derived type. Each class containing the parent type also contains the derived type. The derived type inherits properties such as components and primitive operations from the parent. A type together with the types derived from it (directly or indirectly) form a derivation class.   13

Discrete type. A discrete type is either an integer type or an enumeration type. Discrete types may be used, for example, in case_statements and as array indices.   14

S. Tucker Taft et al. (Eds.): Consolidated Ada Reference Manual, LNCS 2219, pp. 493–495, 2001.

15   **Discriminant.** A discriminant is a parameter of a composite type. It can control, for example, the bounds of a component of the type if that type is an array type. A discriminant of a task type can be used to pass data to a task of the type upon creation.

16   **Elementary type.** An elementary type does not have components.

17   **Enumeration type.** An enumeration type is defined by an enumeration of its values, which may be named by identifiers or character literals.

18   **Exception.** An *exception* represents a kind of exceptional situation; an occurrence of such a situation (at run time) is called an *exception occurrence*. To *raise* an exception is to abandon normal program execution so as to draw attention to the fact that the corresponding situation has arisen. Performing some actions in response to the arising of an exception is called *handling* the exception.

19   **Execution.** The process by which a construct achieves its run-time effect is called *execution*. Execution of a declaration is also called *elaboration*. Execution of an expression is also called *evaluation*.

20   **Generic unit.** A generic unit is a template for a (nongeneric) program unit; the template can be parameterized by objects, types, subprograms, and packages. An instance of a generic unit is created by a generic_instantiation. The rules of the language are enforced when a generic unit is compiled, using a generic contract model; additional checks are performed upon instantiation to verify the contract is met. That is, the declaration of a generic unit represents a contract between the body of the generic and instances of the generic. Generic units can be used to perform the role that macros sometimes play in other languages.

21   **Integer type.** Integer types comprise the signed integer types and the modular types. A signed integer type has a base range that includes both positive and negative numbers, and has operations that may raise an exception when the result is outside the base range. A modular type has a base range whose lower bound is zero, and has operations with "wraparound" semantics. Modular types subsume what are called "unsigned types" in some other languages.

22   **Library unit.** A library unit is a separately compiled program unit, and is always a package, subprogram, or generic unit. Library units may have other (logically nested) library units as children, and may have other program units physically nested within them. A root library unit, together with its children and grandchildren and so on, form a *subsystem*.

23   **Limited type.** A limited type is (a view of) a type for which the assignment operation is not allowed. A nonlimited type is a (view of a) type for which the assignment operation is allowed.

24   **Object.** An object is either a constant or a variable. An object contains a value. An object is created by an object_declaration or by an allocator. A formal parameter is (a view of) an object. A subcomponent of an object is an object.

25   **Package.** Packages are program units that allow the specification of groups of logically related entities. Typically, a package contains the declaration of a type (often a private type or private extension) along with the declarations of primitive subprograms of the type, which can be called from outside the package, while their inner workings remain hidden from outside users.

26   **Partition.** A *partition* is a part of a program. Each partition consists of a set of library units. Each partition may run in a separate address space, possibly on a separate computer. A program may contain just one partition. A distributed program typically contains multiple partitions, which can execute concurrently.

Pragma. A pragma is a compiler directive. There are language-defined pragmas that give instructions for optimization, listing control, etc. An implementation may support additional (implementation-defined) pragmas. 27

Primitive operations. The primitive operations of a type are the operations (such as subprograms) declared together with the type declaration. They are inherited by other types in the same class of types. For a tagged type, the primitive subprograms are dispatching subprograms, providing run-time polymorphism. A dispatching subprogram may be called with statically tagged operands, in which case the subprogram body invoked is determined at compile time. Alternatively, a dispatching subprogram may be called using a dispatching call, in which case the subprogram body invoked is determined at run time. 28

Private extension. A private extension is like a record extension, except that the components of the extension part are hidden from its clients. 29

Private type. A private type is a partial view of a type whose full view is hidden from its clients. 30

Program. A *program* is a set of *partitions*, each of which may execute in a separate address space, possibly on a separate computer. A partition consists of a set of library units. 31

Program unit. A *program unit* is either a package, a task unit, a protected unit, a protected entry, a generic unit, or an explicitly declared subprogram other than an enumeration literal. Certain kinds of program units can be separately compiled. Alternatively, they can appear physically nested within other program units. 32

Protected type. A protected type is a composite type whose components are protected from concurrent access by multiple tasks. 33

Real type. A real type has values that are approximations of the real numbers. Floating point and fixed point types are real types. 34

Record extension. A record extension is a type that extends another type by adding additional components. 35

Record type. A record type is a composite type consisting of zero or more named components, possibly of different types. 36

Scalar type. A scalar type is either a discrete type or a real type. 37

Subtype. A subtype is a type together with a constraint, which constrains the values of the subtype to satisfy a certain condition. The values of a subtype are a subset of the values of its type. 38

Tagged type. The objects of a tagged type have a run-time type tag, which indicates the specific type with which the object was originally created. An operand of a class-wide tagged type can be used in a dispatching call; the tag indicates which subprogram body to invoke. Nondispatching calls, in which the subprogram body to invoke is determined at compile time, are also allowed. Tagged types may be extended with additional components. 39

Task type. A task type is a composite type whose values are tasks, which are active entities that may execute concurrently with other tasks. The top-level task of a partition is called the environment task. 40

Type. Each object has a type. A *type* has an associated set of values, and a set of *primitive operations* which implement the fundamental aspects of its semantics. Types are grouped into *classes*. The types of a given class share a set of primitive operations. Classes are closed under derivation; that is, if a type is in a class, then all of its derivatives are in that class. 41

View. (See **Definition**.) 42

Annex P
(informative)
Syntax Summary

This Annex summarizes the complete syntax of the language. See 1.1.4 for a description of the notation used.

2.1:
character::= graphic_character | format_effector | other_control_function

2.1:
graphic_character::= identifier_letter | digit | space_character | special_character

2.3:
identifier::=
  identifier_letter {[underline] letter_or_digit}

2.3:
letter_or_digit::= identifier_letter | digit

2.4:
numeric_literal::= decimal_literal | based_literal

2.4.1:
decimal_literal::= numeral [.numeral] [exponent]

2.4.1:
numeral::= digit {[underline] digit}

2.4.1:
exponent::= E [+] numeral | E – numeral

2.4.2:
based_literal::=
  base # based_numeral [.based_numeral] # [exponent]

2.4.2:
base::= numeral

2.4.2:
based_numeral::=
  extended_digit {[underline] extended_digit}

2.4.2:
extended_digit::= digit | A | B | C | D | E | F

2.5:
character_literal::= 'graphic_character'

2.6:
string_literal::= "{string_element}"

2.6:
string_element::= "" | *non_quotation_mark*_graphic_character

2.7:
comment::= --{*non_end_of_line*_character}

2.8:
pragma::=
  pragma identifier [(pragma_argument_association {, pragma_argument_association})];

2.8:
pragma_argument_association::=
    [*pragma_argument*_identifier =>] name
  | [*pragma_argument*_identifier =>] expression

S. Tucker Taft et al. (Eds.): Consolidated Ada Reference Manual, LNCS 2219, pp. 497–521, 2001.

3.1:
basic_declaration::=
    type_declaration | subtype_declaration
   | object_declaration | number_declaration
   | subprogram_declaration | abstract_subprogram_declaration
   | package_declaration | renaming_declaration
   | exception_declaration | generic_declaration
   | generic_instantiation

3.1:
defining_identifier::= identifier

3.2.1:
type_declaration::= full_type_declaration
   | incomplete_type_declaration
   | private_type_declaration
   | private_extension_declaration

3.2.1:
full_type_declaration::=
   type defining_identifier [known_discriminant_part] **is** type_definition;
   | task_type_declaration
   | protected_type_declaration

3.2.1:
type_definition::=
   enumeration_type_definition | integer_type_definition
   | real_type_definition | array_type_definition
   | record_type_definition | access_type_definition
   | derived_type_definition

3.2.2:
subtype_declaration::=
   subtype defining_identifier **is** subtype_indication;

3.2.2:
subtype_indication::= subtype_mark [constraint]

3.2.2:
subtype_mark::= *subtype*_name

3.2.2:
constraint::= scalar_constraint | composite_constraint

3.2.2:
scalar_constraint::=
   range_constraint | digits_constraint | delta_constraint

3.2.2:
composite_constraint::=
   index_constraint | discriminant_constraint

3.3.1:
object_declaration::=
   defining_identifier_list : [**aliased**] [**constant**] subtype_indication [:= expression];
   | defining_identifier_list : [**aliased**] [**constant**] array_type_definition [:= expression];
   | single_task_declaration
   | single_protected_declaration

3.3.1:
defining_identifier_list::=
 defining_identifier {, defining_identifier}

3.3.2:
number_declaration::=
   defining_identifier_list : **constant** := *static*_expression;

3.4:
derived_type_definition::= [**abstract**] **new** *parent*_subtype_indication [record_extension_part]

3.5:
range_constraint::= **range** range

3.5:
range::= range_attribute_reference
 | simple_expression .. simple_expression

3.5.1:
enumeration_type_definition::=
 (enumeration_literal_specification {, enumeration_literal_specification})

3.5.1:
enumeration_literal_specification::= defining_identifier | defining_character_literal

3.5.1:
defining_character_literal::= character_literal

3.5.4:
integer_type_definition::= signed_integer_type_definition | modular_type_definition

3.5.4:
signed_integer_type_definition::= **range** *static*_simple_expression .. *static*_simple_expression

3.5.4:
modular_type_definition::= **mod** *static*_expression

3.5.6:
real_type_definition::=
 floating_point_definition | fixed_point_definition

3.5.7:
floating_point_definition::=
 digits *static*_expression [real_range_specification]

3.5.7:
real_range_specification::=
 range *static*_simple_expression .. *static*_simple_expression

3.5.9:
fixed_point_definition::= ordinary_fixed_point_definition | decimal_fixed_point_definition

3.5.9:
ordinary_fixed_point_definition::=
 delta *static*_expression real_range_specification

3.5.9:
decimal_fixed_point_definition::=
 delta *static*_expression **digits** *static*_expression [real_range_specification]

3.5.9:
digits_constraint::=
 digits *static*_expression [range_constraint]

3.6:
array_type_definition::=
 unconstrained_array_definition | constrained_array_definition

3.6:
unconstrained_array_definition::=
 array(index_subtype_definition {, index_subtype_definition}) **of** component_definition

3.6:
index_subtype_definition::= subtype_mark **range** <>

3.6:
constrained_array_definition::=
 array (discrete_subtype_definition {, discrete_subtype_definition}) **of** component_definition

3.6:
discrete_subtype_definition::= *discrete*_subtype_indication | range

3.6:
component_definition::= [**aliased**] subtype_indication

3.6.1:
index_constraint::= (discrete_range {, discrete_range})

3.6.1:
discrete_range::= *discrete*_subtype_indication | range

3.7:
discriminant_part::= unknown_discriminant_part I known_discriminant_part

3.7:
unknown_discriminant_part::= (<>)

3.7:
known_discriminant_part::=
 (discriminant_specification {; discriminant_specification})

3.7:
discriminant_specification::=
 defining_identifier_list : subtype_mark [:= default_expression]
 I defining_identifier_list : access_definition [:= default_expression]

3.7:
default_expression::= expression

3.7.1:
discriminant_constraint::=
 (discriminant_association {, discriminant_association})

3.7.1:
discriminant_association::=
 [*discriminant*_selector_name {I *discriminant*_selector_name} =>] expression

3.8:
record_type_definition::= [[**abstract**] **tagged**] [**limited**] record_definition

3.8:
record_definition::=
  record
    component_list
  end record
 I **null record**

3.8:
component_list::=
   component_item {component_item}
 I {component_item} variant_part
 I **null**;

3.8:
component_item::= component_declaration I aspect_clause

3.8:
component_declaration::=
 defining_identifier_list : component_definition [:= default_expression];

3.8.1:
variant_part::=
  case *discriminant*_direct_name **is**
    variant
    {variant}
  end case;

3.8.1:
variant::=
  when discrete_choice_list =>
    component_list

3.8.1:
discrete_choice_list::= discrete_choice {I discrete_choice}

3.8.1:
discrete_choice::= expression I discrete_range I **others**

3.9.1:
record_extension_part::= **with** record_definition

3.10:
access_type_definition::=
   access_to_object_definition
   | access_to_subprogram_definition

3.10:
access_to_object_definition::=
   access [general_access_modifier] subtype_indication

3.10:
general_access_modifier::= **all** | **constant**

3.10:
access_to_subprogram_definition::=
   access [**protected**] **procedure** parameter_profile
   | **access** [**protected**] **function** parameter_and_result_profile

3.10:
access_definition::= **access** subtype_mark

3.10.1:
incomplete_type_declaration::= **type** defining_identifier [discriminant_part];

3.11:
declarative_part::= {declarative_item}

3.11:
declarative_item::=
   basic_declarative_item | body

3.11:
basic_declarative_item::=
   basic_declaration | aspect_clause | use_clause

3.11:
body::= proper_body | body_stub

3.11:
proper_body::=
   subprogram_body | package_body | task_body | protected_body

4.1:
name::=
   direct_name | explicit_dereference
   | indexed_component | slice
   | selected_component | attribute_reference
   | type_conversion | function_call
   | character_literal

4.1:
direct_name::= identifier | operator_symbol

4.1:
prefix::= name | implicit_dereference

4.1:
explicit_dereference::= name.**all**

4.1:
implicit_dereference::= name

4.1.1:
indexed_component::= prefix(expression {, expression})

4.1.2:
slice::= prefix(discrete_range)

4.1.3:
selected_component::= prefix . selector_name

4.1.3:
selector_name::= identifier | character_literal | operator_symbol

4.1.4:
attribute_reference::= prefix'attribute_designator

4.1.4:
attribute_designator::=
  identifier[(*static*_expression)]
  | Access | Delta | Digits

4.1.4:
range_attribute_reference::= prefix'range_attribute_designator

4.1.4:
range_attribute_designator::= Range[(*static*_expression)]

4.3:
aggregate::= record_aggregate | extension_aggregate | array_aggregate

4.3.1:
record_aggregate::= (record_component_association_list)

4.3.1:
record_component_association_list::=
  record_component_association {, record_component_association}
  | **null record**

4.3.1:
record_component_association::=
  [component_choice_list =>] expression

4.3.1:
component_choice_list::=
  *component*_selector_name {| *component*_selector_name}
  | **others**

4.3.2:
extension_aggregate::=
  (ancestor_part **with** record_component_association_list)

4.3.2:
ancestor_part::= expression | subtype_mark

4.3.3:
array_aggregate::=
  positional_array_aggregate | named_array_aggregate

4.3.3:
positional_array_aggregate::=
  (expression, expression {, expression})
  | (expression {, expression}, **others** => expression)

4.3.3:
named_array_aggregate::=
  (array_component_association {, array_component_association})

4.3.3:
array_component_association::=
  discrete_choice_list => expression

4.4:
expression::=
  relation {**and** relation} | relation {**and then** relation}
  | relation {**or** relation} | relation {**or else** relation}
  | relation {**xor** relation}

4.4:
relation::=
  simple_expression [relational_operator simple_expression]
  | simple_expression [**not**] **in** range
  | simple_expression [**not**] **in** subtype_mark

4.4:
simple_expression::= [unary_adding_operator] term {binary_adding_operator term}

4.4:
term::= factor {multiplying_operator factor}

4.4:
factor::= primary [** primary] | **abs** primary | **not** primary

4.4:
primary::=
  numeric_literal | **null** | string_literal | aggregate
  | name | qualified_expression | allocator | (expression)

4.5:
logical_operator::=   **and** | **or** | **xor**

4.5:
relational_operator::=   = | /= | < | <= | > | >=

4.5:
binary_adding_operator::=   + | – | &

4.5:
unary_adding_operator::=   + | –

4.5:
multiplying_operator::=   * | / | **mod** | **rem**

4.5:
highest_precedence_operator::=   ** | **abs** | **not**

4.6:
type_conversion::=
  subtype_mark(expression)
  | subtype_mark(name)

4.7:
qualified_expression::=
  subtype_mark'(expression) | subtype_mark'aggregate

4.8:
allocator::=
  new subtype_indication | **new** qualified_expression

5.1:
sequence_of_statements::= statement {statement}

5.1:
statement::=
  {label} simple_statement | {label} compound_statement

5.1:
simple_statement::= null_statement
  | assignment_statement | exit_statement
  | goto_statement | procedure_call_statement
  | return_statement | entry_call_statement
  | requeue_statement | delay_statement
  | abort_statement | raise_statement
  | code_statement

5.1:
compound_statement::=
    if_statement | case_statement
  | loop_statement | block_statement
  | accept_statement | select_statement

5.1:
null_statement::= **null**;

5.1:
label::= <<*label*_statement_identifier>>

5.1:
statement_identifier::= direct_name

5.2:
assignment_statement::=
  *variable*_name := expression;

5.3:
if_statement::=
  if condition **then**
    sequence_of_statements
  {**elsif** condition **then**
    sequence_of_statements}
  [**else**
    sequence_of_statements]
  end if;

5.3:
condition::= *boolean*_expression

5.4:
case_statement::=
  case expression **is**
    case_statement_alternative
    {case_statement_alternative}
  end case;

5.4:
case_statement_alternative::=
  when discrete_choice_list =>
    sequence_of_statements

5.5:
loop_statement::=
  [*loop*_statement_identifier:]
    [iteration_scheme] **loop**
      sequence_of_statements
    end loop [*loop*_identifier];

5.5:
iteration_scheme::= **while** condition
  | **for** loop_parameter_specification

5.5:
loop_parameter_specification::=
  defining_identifier **in** [**reverse**] discrete_subtype_definition

5.6:
block_statement::=
  [*block*_statement_identifier:]
    [**declare**
      declarative_part]
    begin
      handled_sequence_of_statements
    end [*block*_identifier];

5.7:
exit_statement::=
  exit [*loop*_name] [**when** condition];

5.8:
goto_statement::= **goto** *label*_name;

6.1:
subprogram_declaration::= subprogram_specification;

6.1:
abstract_subprogram_declaration::= subprogram_specification **is abstract**;

6.1:
subprogram_specification::=
  procedure defining_program_unit_name parameter_profile
  | **function** defining_designator parameter_and_result_profile

6.1:
designator::= [parent_unit_name .]identifier | operator_symbol

6.1:
defining_designator::= defining_program_unit_name | defining_operator_symbol

6.1:
defining_program_unit_name::= [parent_unit_name .]defining_identifier

6.1:
operator_symbol::= string_literal

6.1:
defining_operator_symbol::= operator_symbol

6.1:
parameter_profile::= [formal_part]

6.1:
parameter_and_result_profile::= [formal_part] **return** subtype_mark

6.1:
formal_part::=
   (parameter_specification {; parameter_specification})

6.1:
parameter_specification::=
   defining_identifier_list : mode subtype_mark [:= default_expression]
 | defining_identifier_list : access_definition [:= default_expression]

6.1:
mode::= [**in**] | **in out** | **out**

6.3:
subprogram_body::=
   subprogram_specification **is**
     declarative_part
   begin
     handled_sequence_of_statements
   end [designator];

6.4:
procedure_call_statement::=
   *procedure*_name;
 | *procedure*_prefix actual_parameter_part;

6.4:
function_call::=
   *function*_name
 | *function*_prefix actual_parameter_part

6.4:
actual_parameter_part::=
   (parameter_association {, parameter_association})

6.4:
parameter_association::=
   [*formal_parameter*_selector_name =>] explicit_actual_parameter

6.4:
explicit_actual_parameter::= expression | *variable*_name

6.5:
return_statement::= **return** [expression];

7.1:
package_declaration::= package_specification;

7.1:
package_specification::=
   package defining_program_unit_name **is**
     {basic_declarative_item}
   [**private**
     {basic_declarative_item}]
   end [[parent_unit_name.]identifier]

7.2:
package_body::=
   package body defining_program_unit_name **is**
     declarative_part
   [**begin**
      handled_sequence_of_statements]
   end [[parent_unit_name.]identifier];

7.3:
private_type_declaration::=
   type defining_identifier [discriminant_part] **is** [[**abstract**] **tagged**] [**limited**] **private**;

7.3:
private_extension_declaration::=
   type defining_identifier [discriminant_part] **is**
    [**abstract**] **new** *ancestor*_subtype_indication **with private**;

8.4:
use_clause::= use_package_clause I use_type_clause

8.4:
use_package_clause::= **use** *package*_name { , *package*_name };

8.4:
use_type_clause::= **use type** subtype_mark { , subtype_mark };

8.5:
renaming_declaration::=
    object_renaming_declaration
   I exception_renaming_declaration
   I package_renaming_declaration
   I subprogram_renaming_declaration
   I generic_renaming_declaration

8.5.1:
object_renaming_declaration::= defining_identifier : subtype_mark **renames** *object*_name;

8.5.2:
exception_renaming_declaration::= defining_identifier : **exception renames** *exception*_name;

8.5.3:
package_renaming_declaration::= **package** defining_program_unit_name **renames** *package*_name;

8.5.4:
subprogram_renaming_declaration::= subprogram_specification **renames** *callable_entity*_name;

8.5.5:
generic_renaming_declaration::=
   generic package   defining_program_unit_name **renames** *generic_package*_name;
   I **generic procedure** defining_program_unit_name **renames** *generic_procedure*_name;
   I **generic function**   defining_program_unit_name **renames** *generic_function*_name;

9.1:
task_type_declaration::=
   task type defining_identifier [known_discriminant_part] [**is** task_definition];

9.1:
single_task_declaration::=
   task defining_identifier [**is** task_definition];

9.1:
task_definition::=
   {task_item}
  [**private**
   {task_item}]
   end [*task*_identifier]

9.1:
task_item::= entry_declaration I aspect_clause

9.1:
task_body::=
  task body defining_identifier **is**
    declarative_part
  begin
    handled_sequence_of_statements
  end [*task_*identifier];

9.4:
protected_type_declaration::=
  protected type defining_identifier [known_discriminant_part] **is** protected_definition;

9.4:
single_protected_declaration::=
  protected defining_identifier **is** protected_definition;

9.4:
protected_definition::=
    { protected_operation_declaration }
  [**private**
    { protected_element_declaration }]
  end [*protected_*identifier]

9.4:
protected_operation_declaration::= subprogram_declaration
    | entry_declaration
    | aspect_clause

9.4:
protected_element_declaration::= protected_operation_declaration
    | component_declaration

9.4:
protected_body::=
  protected body defining_identifier **is**
    { protected_operation_item }
  end [*protected_*identifier];

9.4:
protected_operation_item::= subprogram_declaration
    | subprogram_body
    | entry_body
    | aspect_clause

9.5.2:
entry_declaration::=
  entry defining_identifier [(discrete_subtype_definition)] parameter_profile;

9.5.2:
accept_statement::=
  accept *entry_*direct_name [(entry_index)] parameter_profile [**do**
    handled_sequence_of_statements
  end [*entry_*identifier]];

9.5.2:
entry_index::= expression

9.5.2:
entry_body::=
  entry defining_identifier entry_body_formal_part entry_barrier **is**
    declarative_part
  begin
    handled_sequence_of_statements
  end [*entry_*identifier];

9.5.2:
entry_body_formal_part::= [(entry_index_specification)] parameter_profile

9.5.2:
entry_barrier::= **when** condition

9.5.2:
entry_index_specification::= **for** defining_identifier **in** discrete_subtype_definition

9.5.3:
entry_call_statement::= *entry*_name [actual_parameter_part];

9.5.4:
requeue_statement::= **requeue** *entry*_name [**with abort**];

9.6:
delay_statement::= delay_until_statement I delay_relative_statement

9.6:
delay_until_statement::= **delay until** *delay*_expression;

9.6:
delay_relative_statement::= **delay** *delay*_expression;

9.7:
select_statement::=
  selective_accept
  I timed_entry_call
  I conditional_entry_call
  I asynchronous_select

9.7.1:
selective_accept::=
 select
  [guard]
   select_alternative
 { **or**
  [guard]
   select_alternative }
 [**else**
  sequence_of_statements]
 end select;

9.7.1:
guard::= **when** condition =>

9.7.1:
select_alternative::=
  accept_alternative
  I delay_alternative
  I terminate_alternative

9.7.1:
accept_alternative::=
  accept_statement [sequence_of_statements]

9.7.1:
delay_alternative::=
  delay_statement [sequence_of_statements]

9.7.1:
terminate_alternative::= **terminate**;

9.7.2:
timed_entry_call::=
 select
  entry_call_alternative
 or
  delay_alternative
 end select;

9.7.2:
entry_call_alternative::=
  entry_call_statement [sequence_of_statements]

9.7.3:
conditional_entry_call::=
  select
   entry_call_alternative
  else
   sequence_of_statements
  end select;

9.7.4:
asynchronous_select::=
  select
   triggering_alternative
  then abort
   abortable_part
  end select;

9.7.4:
triggering_alternative::= triggering_statement [sequence_of_statements]

9.7.4:
triggering_statement::= entry_call_statement I delay_statement

9.7.4:
abortable_part::= sequence_of_statements

9.8:
abort_statement::= **abort** *task*_name {, *task*_name};

10.1.1:
compilation::= {compilation_unit}

10.1.1:
compilation_unit::=
   context_clause library_item
  I context_clause subunit

10.1.1:
library_item::= [**private**] library_unit_declaration
  I library_unit_body
  I [**private**] library_unit_renaming_declaration

10.1.1:
library_unit_declaration::=
   subprogram_declaration   I package_declaration
  I generic_declaration   I generic_instantiation

10.1.1:
library_unit_renaming_declaration::=
   package_renaming_declaration
  I generic_renaming_declaration
  I subprogram_renaming_declaration

10.1.1:
library_unit_body::= subprogram_body I package_body

10.1.1:
parent_unit_name::= name

10.1.2:
context_clause::= {context_item}

10.1.2:
context_item::= with_clause I use_clause

10.1.2:
with_clause::= **with** *library_unit*_name {, *library_unit*_name};

10.1.3:
body_stub::= subprogram_body_stub I package_body_stub I task_body_stub I protected_body_stub

10.1.3:
subprogram_body_stub::= subprogram_specification **is separate**;

10.1.3:
package_body_stub::= **package body** defining_identifier **is separate**;

10.1.3:
task_body_stub::= **task body** defining_identifier **is separate**;

10.1.3:
protected_body_stub::= **protected body** defining_identifier **is separate**;

10.1.3:
subunit::= **separate** (parent_unit_name) proper_body

11.1:
exception_declaration::= defining_identifier_list : **exception**;

11.2:
handled_sequence_of_statements::=
    sequence_of_statements
  [**exception**
    exception_handler
    {exception_handler}]

11.2:
exception_handler::=
  when [choice_parameter_specification:] exception_choice {| exception_choice} =>
    sequence_of_statements

11.2:
choice_parameter_specification::= defining_identifier

11.2:
exception_choice::= *exception*_name | **others**

11.3:
raise_statement::= **raise** [*exception*_name];

12.1:
generic_declaration::= generic_subprogram_declaration | generic_package_declaration

12.1:
generic_subprogram_declaration::=
    generic_formal_part subprogram_specification;

12.1:
generic_package_declaration::=
    generic_formal_part package_specification;

12.1:
generic_formal_part::= **generic** {generic_formal_parameter_declaration | use_clause}

12.1:
generic_formal_parameter_declaration::=
    formal_object_declaration
  | formal_type_declaration
  | formal_subprogram_declaration
  | formal_package_declaration

12.3:
generic_instantiation::=
    package defining_program_unit_name **is**
      new *generic_package_*name [generic_actual_part];
  | **procedure** defining_program_unit_name **is**
      new *generic_procedure_*name [generic_actual_part];
  | **function** defining_designator **is**
      new *generic_function_*name [generic_actual_part];

12.3:
generic_actual_part::=
  (generic_association {, generic_association})

12.3:
generic_association::=
  [*generic_formal_parameter_*selector_name =>] explicit_generic_actual_parameter

12.3:
explicit_generic_actual_parameter::= expression | *variable*_name
  | *subprogram*_name | *entry*_name | subtype_mark
  | *package_instance*_name

12.4:
formal_object_declaration::=
  defining_identifier_list : mode subtype_mark [:= default_expression];

12.5:
formal_type_declaration::=
  type defining_identifier[discriminant_part] **is** formal_type_definition;

12.5:
formal_type_definition::=
   formal_private_type_definition
  | formal_derived_type_definition
  | formal_discrete_type_definition
  | formal_signed_integer_type_definition
  | formal_modular_type_definition
  | formal_floating_point_definition
  | formal_ordinary_fixed_point_definition
  | formal_decimal_fixed_point_definition
  | formal_array_type_definition
  | formal_access_type_definition

12.5.1:
formal_private_type_definition::= [[**abstract**] **tagged**] [**limited**] **private**

12.5.1:
formal_derived_type_definition::= [**abstract**] **new** subtype_mark [**with private**]

12.5.2:
formal_discrete_type_definition::= (<>)

12.5.2:
formal_signed_integer_type_definition::= **range** <>

12.5.2:
formal_modular_type_definition::= **mod** <>

12.5.2:
formal_floating_point_definition::= **digits** <>

12.5.2:
formal_ordinary_fixed_point_definition::= **delta** <>

12.5.2:
formal_decimal_fixed_point_definition::= **delta** <> **digits** <>

12.5.3:
formal_array_type_definition::= array_type_definition

12.5.4:
formal_access_type_definition::= access_type_definition

12.6:
formal_subprogram_declaration::= **with** subprogram_specification [**is** subprogram_default];

12.6:
subprogram_default::= default_name | <>

12.6:
default_name::= name

12.7:
formal_package_declaration::=
  with package defining_identifier **is new** *generic_package*_name formal_package_actual_part;

12.7:
formal_package_actual_part::=
  (<>) | [generic_actual_part]

13.1:
aspect_clause::= attribute_definition_clause
   | enumeration_representation_clause
   | record_representation_clause
   | at_clause

13.1:
local_name::= direct_name
   | direct_name'attribute_designator
   | *library_unit*_name

13.3:
attribute_definition_clause::=
   for local_name'attribute_designator **use** expression;
   | **for** local_name'attribute_designator **use** name;

13.4:
enumeration_representation_clause::=
   for *first_subtype*_local_name **use** enumeration_aggregate;

13.4:
enumeration_aggregate::= array_aggregate

13.5.1:
record_representation_clause::=
   for *first_subtype*_local_name **use**
    record [mod_clause]
     {component_clause}
    end record;

13.5.1:
component_clause::=
   *component*_local_name **at** position **range** first_bit .. last_bit;

13.5.1:
position::= *static*_expression

13.5.1:
first_bit::= *static*_simple_expression

13.5.1:
last_bit::= *static*_simple_expression

13.8:
code_statement::= qualified_expression;

13.12:
restriction::= *restriction*_identifier
   | *restriction_parameter*_identifier => expression

J.3:
delta_constraint::= **delta** *static*_expression [range_constraint]

J.7:
at_clause::= **for** direct_name **use at** expression;

J.8:
mod_clause::= **at mod** *static*_expression;

Syntax Cross Reference

      Syntax Summary **P**

Index

Index entries are given by paragraph number. A list of all language-defined library units may be found under Language-Defined Library Units. A list of all language-defined types may be found under Language-Defined Types. A list of all language-defined subprograms may be found under Language-Defined Subprograms.

delay_statement 9.6(2)
  used 5.1(4), 9.7.1(6), 9.7.4(4), P
delay_until_statement 9.6(3)
  used 9.6(2), P
Delete
  in Ada.Direct_IO A.8.4(8)
  in Ada.Sequential_IO A.8.1(8)
  in Ada.Streams.Stream_IO A.12.1(10)
  in Ada.Strings.Bounded A.4.4(64),
    A.4.4(65)
  in Ada.Strings.Fixed A.4.3(29),
    A.4.3(30)
  in Ada.Strings.Unbounded A.4.5(59),
    A.4.5(60)
  in Ada.Text_IO A.10.1(11)
delimiter 2.2(8)
delivery
  of an interrupt C.3(2)
delta
  of a fixed point type 3.5.9(1)
Delta attribute 3.5.10(3)
delta_constraint J.3(2)
  used 3.2.2(6), P
Denorm attribute A.5.3(9)
denormalized number A.5.3(10)
denote 8.6(16)
  informal definition 3.1(8)
  name used as a pragma argument
    8.6(32)
depend on a discriminant
  for a component 3.7(20)
  for a constraint or
    component_definition 3.7(19)
dependence
  elaboration 10.2(9)
  of a task on a master 9.3(1)
  of a task on another task 9.3(4)
  semantic 10.1.1(26)
depth
  accessibility level 3.10.2(3)
dereference 4.1(8)
Dereference_Error
  in Interfaces.C.Strings B.3.1(12)
derivation class
  for a type 3.4.1(2)
derived from
  directly or indirectly 3.4.1(2)
derived type 3.4(1)
  [*partial*] 3.4(24)
derived_type_definition 3.4(2)
  used 3.2.1(4), P
descendant 10.1.1(11)
  of a type 3.4.1(10)
  relationship with scope 8.2(4)
designate 3.10(1)
designated profile
  of an access-to-subprogram type
    3.10(11)

designated subtype
  of a named access type 3.10(10)
  of an anonymous access type 3.10(12)
designated type
  of a named access type 3.10(10)
  of an anonymous access type 3.10(12)
designator 6.1(5)
  used 6.3(2), P
destructor
  See finalization 7.6(1)
  See finalization 7.6.1(1)
Detach_Handler
  in Ada.Interrupts C.3.2(9)
determined class for a formal type
  12.5(6)
determines
  a type by a subtype_mark 3.2.2(8)
Device_Error
  in Ada.Direct_IO A.8.4(18)
  in Ada.IO_Exceptions A.13(4)
  in Ada.Sequential_IO A.8.1(15)
  in Ada.Streams.Stream_IO A.12.1(26)
  in Ada.Text_IO A.10.1(85)
Diaeresis
  in Ada.Characters.Latin_1 A.3.3(21)
digit 2.1(10)
  used 2.1(3), 2.3(3), 2.4.1(3), 2.4.2(5),
    P
digits
  of a decimal fixed point subtype
    3.5.9(6), 3.5.10(7)
Digits attribute 3.5.8(2/1), 3.5.10(7)
digits_constraint 3.5.9(5)
  used 3.2.2(6), P
dimensionality
  of an array 3.6(12)
direct access A.8(3)
direct file A.8(1)
Direct_IO
  child of Ada A.8.4(2)
direct_name 4.1(3)
  used 3.8.1(2), 4.1(2), 5.1(8), 9.5.2(3),
    13.1(3), J.7(1), P
Direction
  in Ada.Strings A.4.1(6)
directly specified
  of an aspect of representation of an
    entity 13.1(8)
  of an operational aspect of an entity
    13.1(8.1/1)
directly visible 8.3(2), 8.3(21)
  within a pragma in a context_clause
    10.1.6(3)
  within a pragma that appears at the
    place of a compilation unit 10.1.6(5)
  within a use_clause in a
    context_clause 10.1.6(3)
  within a with_clause 10.1.6(2)
  within the parent_unit_name of a library
    unit 10.1.6(2)

within the parent_unit_name of a
  subunit 10.1.6(4)
discontiguous representation
  [*partial*] 13.5.2(5), 13.7.1(12),
    13.9(9), 13.9(17), 13.11(16)
discrete array type 4.5.2(1)
discrete type 3.2(3), 3.5(1)
Discrete_Random
  child of Ada.Numerics A.5.2(17)
discrete_choice 3.8.1(5)
  used 3.8.1(4), P
discrete_choice_list 3.8.1(4)
  used 3.8.1(3), 4.3.3(5), 5.4(3), P
discrete_range 3.6.1(3)
  used 3.6.1(2), 3.8.1(5), 4.1.2(2), P
discrete_subtype_definition 3.6(6)
  used 3.6(5), 5.5(4), 9.5.2(2), 9.5.2(8),
    P
discriminant 3.2(5), 3.7(1)
  of a variant_part 3.8.1(6)
discriminant_association 3.7.1(3)
  used 3.7.1(2), P
Discriminant_Check 11.5(12)
  [*partial*] 4.1.3(15), 4.3(6), 4.3.2(8),
    4.6(43), 4.6(45), 4.6(51), 4.6(52),
    4.7(4), 4.8(10/1)
discriminant_constraint 3.7.1(2)
  used 3.2.2(7), P
discriminant_part 3.7(2)
  used 3.10.1(2), 7.3(2), 7.3(3), 12.5(2),
    P
discriminant_specification 3.7(5)
  used 3.7(4), P
discriminants
  known 3.7(26)
  unknown 3.7(26)
discriminated type 3.7(8/1)
dispatching 3.9(3)
dispatching call
  on a dispatching operation 3.9.2(1)
dispatching operation 3.9.2(1), 3.9.2(2)
  [*partial*] 3.9(1)
dispatching point D.2.1(4)
  [*partial*] D.2.1(8), D.2.2(12)
dispatching policy for tasks
  [*partial*] D.2.1(5)
dispatching, task D.2.1(4)
Display_Format
  in Interfaces.COBOL B.4(22)
displayed magnitude (of a decimal
  value) F.3.2(14)
disruption of an assignment 9.8(21),
  13.9.1(5)
  [*partial*] 11.6(6)
distinct access paths 6.2(12)
distributed program E(3)
distributed system E(2)
distributed systems C(1)
divide 2.1(15)
  in Ada.Decimal F.2(6)

of Component_Size for array types
13.3(70)
of External_Tag for a tagged type
13.3(75/1), K(65)
of Input for a type 13.13.2(36/1)
of Machine_Radix for decimal first
subtypes F.1(1)
of Output for a type 13.13.2(36/1)
of Read for a type 13.13.2(36/1)
of Size for first subtypes 13.3(48)
of Size for stand-alone objects
13.3(41)
of Small for fixed point types
3.5.10(2/1)
of Storage_Pool for a non-derived
access-to-object type 13.11(15)
of Storage_Size for a non-derived
access-to-object type 13.11(15)
of Storage_Size for a task first subtype
J.9(3)
of Write for a type 13.13.2(36/1)
specifiable (of an attribute and for an
entity) 13.3(5/1)
specific type 3.4.1(3)
specified
of an aspect of representation of an
entity 13.1(17)
of an operational aspect of an entity
13.1(18.1/1)
specified (not!) 1.1.3(18)
specified discriminant 3.7(18)
Split
in Ada.Calendar 9.6(14)
in Ada.Real_Time D.8(16)
Sqrt
in Ada.Numerics.Generic_Complex_-
Elementary_Functions G.1.2(3)
in Ada.Numerics.Generic_Elementary_-
Functions A.5.1(4)
SS2
in Ada.Characters.Latin_1 A.3.3(17)
SS3
in Ada.Characters.Latin_1 A.3.3(17)
SSA
in Ada.Characters.Latin_1 A.3.3(17)
ST
in Ada.Characters.Latin_1 A.3.3(19)
stand-alone constant 3.3.1(23)
corresponding to a formal object of
mode in 12.4(10)
stand-alone object 3.3.1(1)
stand-alone variable 3.3.1(23)
Standard A.1(4)
standard error file A.10(6)
standard input file A.10(5)
standard mode 1.1.5(11)
standard output file A.10(5)
standard storage pool 13.11(17)

Standard_Error
in Ada.Text_IO A.10.1(16),
A.10.1(19)
Standard_Input
in Ada.Text_IO A.10.1(16),
A.10.1(19)
Standard_Output
in Ada.Text_IO A.10.1(16),
A.10.1(19)
State
in Ada.Numerics.Discrete_Random
A.5.2(23)
in Ada.Numerics.Float_Random
A.5.2(11)
statement 5.1(3)
used 5.1(2), P
statement_identifier 5.1(8)
used 5.1(7), 5.5(2), 5.6(2), P
static 4.9(1)
constant 4.9(24)
constraint 4.9(27)
delta constraint 4.9(29)
digits constraint 4.9(29)
discrete_range 4.9(25)
discriminant constraint 4.9(31)
expression 4.9(2)
function 4.9(18)
index constraint 4.9(30)
range 4.9(25)
range constraint 4.9(29)
scalar subtype 4.9(26)
string subtype 4.9(26)
subtype 4.9(26)
subtype 12.4(9)
static semantics 1.1.2(28)
statically
constrained 4.9(32)
denote 4.9(14)
statically compatible
for a constraint and a scalar subtype
4.9.1(4)
for a constraint and an access or
composite subtype 4.9.1(4)
for two subtypes 4.9.1(4)
statically deeper 3.10.2(4), 3.10.2(17)
statically determined tag 3.9.2(1)
[*partial*] 3.9.2(15), 3.9.2(19)
statically matching
effect on subtype-specific aspects
13.1(14)
for constraints 4.9.1(1)
for ranges 4.9.1(3)
for subtypes 4.9.1(2)
required 3.9.2(10/1), 3.10.2(27/1),
4.6(12/1), 4.6(16), 6.3.1(16),
6.3.1(17), 6.3.1(23), 7.3(13),
12.5.1(14), 12.5.3(6), 12.5.3(7),
12.5.4(3), 12.7(7)
statically tagged 3.9.2(4)

Status_Error
in Ada.Direct_IO A.8.4(18)
in Ada.IO_Exceptions A.13(4)
in Ada.Sequential_IO A.8.1(15)
in Ada.Streams.Stream_IO A.12.1(26)
in Ada.Text_IO A.10.1(85)
storage deallocation
unchecked 13.11.2(1)
storage element 13.3(8)
storage management
user-defined 13.11(1)
storage node E(2)
storage place
of a component 13.5(1)
storage place attributes
of a component 13.5.2(1)
storage pool 3.10(7/1)
storage pool element 13.11(11)
storage pool type 13.11(11)
Storage_Array
in System.Storage_Elements 13.7.1(5)
Storage_Check 11.5(23)
[*partial*] 11.1(6), 13.3(67), 13.11(17),
D.7(17/1), D.7(18/1), D.7(19/1)
Storage_Count
in System.Storage_Elements 13.7.1(4)
Storage_Element
in System.Storage_Elements 13.7.1(5)
Storage_Elements
child of System 13.7.1(2)
Storage_Error
raised by failure of run-time check
4.8(14), 8.5.4(8.1/1), 11.1(4), 11.1(6),
11.5(23), 13.3(67), 13.11(17),
13.11(18), A.7(14), D.7(17/1),
D.7(18/1), D.7(19/1)
in Standard A.1(46)
Storage_IO
child of Ada A.9(3)
Storage_Offset
in System.Storage_Elements 13.7.1(3)
Storage_Pool attribute 13.11(13)
Storage_Pool clause 13.3(7), 13.11(15)
Storage_Pools
child of System 13.11(5)
Storage_Size
in System.Storage_Pools 13.11(9)
Storage_Size attribute 13.3(60),
13.11(14)
Storage_Size clause 13.3(7), 13.11(15)
See also pragma Storage_Size
13.3(61)
Storage_Unit
in System 13.7(13)
stream 13.13(1)
in Ada.Streams.Stream_IO A.12.1(13)
in Ada.Text_IO.Text_Streams
A.12.2(4)
in Ada.Wide_Text_IO.Text_Streams
A.12.3(4)

within a pragma in a context_clause
10.1.6(3)
within a pragma that appears at the
place of a compilation unit 10.1.6(5)
within a with_clause 10.1.6(2)
within the parent_unit_name of a library
unit 10.1.6(2)
within the parent_unit_name of a
subunit 10.1.6(4)
visible part 8.2(5)
of a formal package 12.7(10)
of a generic unit 8.2(8)
of a package (other than a generic
formal package) 7.1(6)
of a protected unit 9.4(11)
of a task unit 9.1(9)
of a view of a callable entity 8.2(6)
of a view of a composite type 8.2(7)
volatile C.6(8)
VT
in Ada.Characters.Latin_1 A.3.3(5)
VTS
in Ada.Characters.Latin_1 A.3.3(17)

W

wchar_array
in Interfaces.C B.3(33)
wchar_t
in Interfaces.C B.3(30/1)
well-formed picture String
for edited output F.3.1(1)
Wide_Bounded
child of Ada.Strings A.4.7(1)
Wide_Constants
child of Ada.Strings.Wide_Maps
A.4.7(28)
Wide_Fixed
child of Ada.Strings A.4.7(1)
Wide_Text_IO
child of Ada A.11(2)
Wide_Unbounded
child of Ada.Strings A.4.7(1)
Wide_Character 3.5.2(3)
in Standard A.1(36)
Wide_Character_Mapping
in Ada.Strings.Wide_Maps A.4.7(20)
Wide_Character_Mapping_Function
in Ada.Strings.Wide_Maps A.4.7(26)
Wide_Character_Range
in Ada.Strings.Wide_Maps A.4.7(6)
Wide_Character_Ranges
in Ada.Strings.Wide_Maps A.4.7(7)
Wide_Character_Sequence
in Ada.Strings.Wide_Maps A.4.7(16)
Wide_Character_Set
in Ada.Strings.Wide_Maps A.4.7(4)
Wide_Image attribute 3.5(28)
Wide_Maps
child of Ada.Strings A.4.7(3)

wide_nul
in Interfaces.C B.3(31/1)
Wide_Space
in Ada.Strings A.4.1(4)
Wide_String
in Standard A.1(41)
Wide_Value attribute 3.5(40)
Wide_Width attribute 3.5(38)
Width attribute 3.5(39)
with_clause 10.1.2(4)
mentioned in 10.1.2(6)
used 10.1.2(3), P
within
immediately 8.1(13)
word 13.3(8)
Word_Size
in System 13.7(13)
Write
in Ada.Direct_IO A.8.4(13)
in Ada.Sequential_IO A.8.1(12)
in Ada.Storage_IO A.9(7)
in Ada.Streams 13.13.1(6)
in Ada.Streams.Stream_IO A.12.1(18),
A.12.1(19)
in System.RPC E.5(8)
Write attribute 13.13.2(3), 13.13.2(11)
Write clause 13.3(7), 13.13.2(36/1)

X

xor operator 4.4(1), 4.5.1(2)

Y

Year
in Ada.Calendar 9.6(13)
Year_Number
in Ada.Calendar 9.6(11)
Yen_Sign
in Ada.Characters.Latin_1 A.3.3(21)